PARASYTE
5

HITOSHI IWAAKI

TRANSLATED AND ADAPTED BY ANDREW CUNNINGHAM
LETTERED BY FOLTZ DESIGN

DEL
REY

BALLANTINE BOOKS · NEW YORK

Parasyte volume 5 is a work of fiction. Names,
characters, places, and incidents are the products of
the author's imagination or are used fictitiously. Any
resemblance to actual events, locales, or persons,
living or dead, is entirely coincidental.

A Del Rey Manga/Kodansha Trade Paperback Original

Parasyte volume 5 copyright © 2003 by Hitoshi Iwaaki
English translation copyright © 2008 by Hitoshi Iwaaki

Published in the United States by Del Rey,
an imprint of The Random House Publishing Group,
a division of Random House, Inc., New York.

DEL REY is a registered trademark and the Del Rey
colophon is a trademark of Random House, Inc.

Publication rights arranged through Kodansha Ltd.

First published in Japan in 2003 by Kodansha
Ltd., Tokyo

ISBN 978-0-345-50033-5

Printed in the United States of America

www.delreymanga.com

9 8 7 6 5 4 3 2 1

Translator/adapter: Andrew Cunningham
Lettering: Foltz Design

CONTENTS

HONORIFICS EXPLAINED

Throughout the Del Rey Manga books, you will find Japanese honorifics left intact in the translations. For those not familiar with how the Japanese use honorifics and, more important, how they differ from American honorifics, we present this brief overview.

Politeness has always been a critical facet of Japanese culture. Ever since the feudal era, when Japan was a highly stratified society, use of honorifics—which can be defined as polite speech that indicates relationship or status—has played an essential role in the Japanese language. When addressing someone in Japanese, an honorific usually takes the form of a suffix attached to one's name (example: "Asuna-san"), is used as a title at the end of one's name, or appears in place of the name itself (example: "Negi-sensei," or simply "Sensei!").

Honorifics can be expressions of respect or endearment. In the context of manga and anime, honorifics give insight into the nature of the relationship between characters. Many English translations leave out these important honorifics and therefore distort the feel of the original Japanese. Because Japanese honorifics contain nuances that English honorifics lack, it is our policy at Del Rey not to translate them. Here, instead, is a guide to some of the honorifics you may encounter in Del Rey Manga.

-san: This is the most common honorific and is equivalent to Mr., Miss, Ms., or Mrs. It is the all-purpose honorific and can be used in any situation where politeness is required.

-sama: This is one level higher than "-san" and is used to confer great respect.

-dono: This comes from the word "tono," which means "lord." It is an even higher level than "-sama" and confers utmost respect.

-kun: This suffix is used at the end of boys' names to express familiarity or endearment. It is also sometimes used by men among friends, or when addressing someone younger or of a lower station.

-chan: This is used to express endearment, mostly toward girls. It is also used for little boys, pets, and even among lovers. It gives a sense of childish cuteness.

Bozu: This is an informal way to refer to a boy, similar to the English terms "kid" and "squirt."

Sempai/
Senpai: This title suggests that the addressee is one's senior in a group or organization. It is most often used in a school setting, where underclassmen refer to their upperclassmen as "sempai." It can also be used in the workplace, such as when a newer employee addresses an employee who has seniority in the company.

Kohai: This is the opposite of "sempai" and is used toward underclassmen in school or newcomers in the workplace. It connotes that the addressee is of a lower station.

Sensei: Literally meaning "one who has come before," this title is used for teachers, doctors, or masters of any profession or art.

-[blank]: This is usually forgotten in these lists, but it is perhaps the most significant difference between Japanese and English. The lack of honorific means that the speaker has permission to address the person in a very intimate way. Usually, only family, spouses, or very close friends have this kind of permission. Known as *yobisute*, it can be gratifying when someone who has earned the intimacy starts to call one by one's name without an honorific. But when that intimacy hasn't been earned, it can be very insulting.

PARASYTE 5

HITOSHI IWAAKI

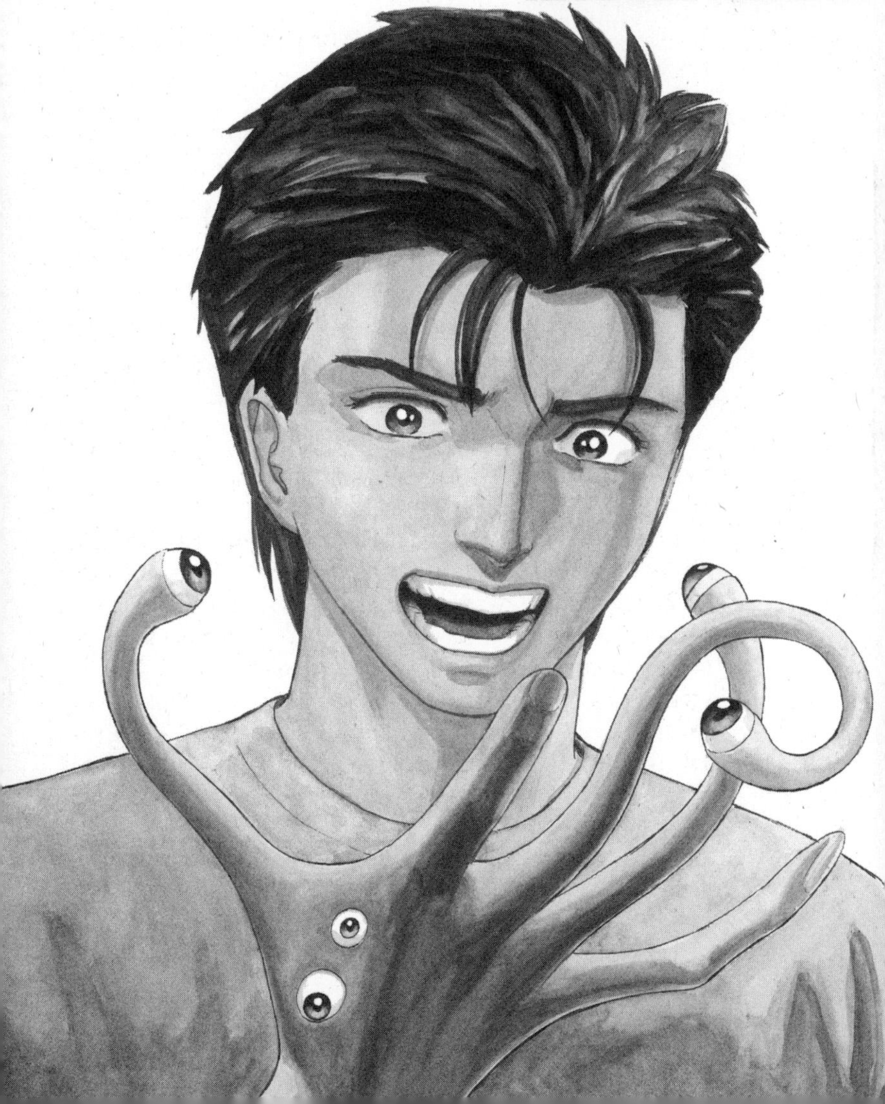

CONTENTS

CHAPTER 34: IRON AND GLASS

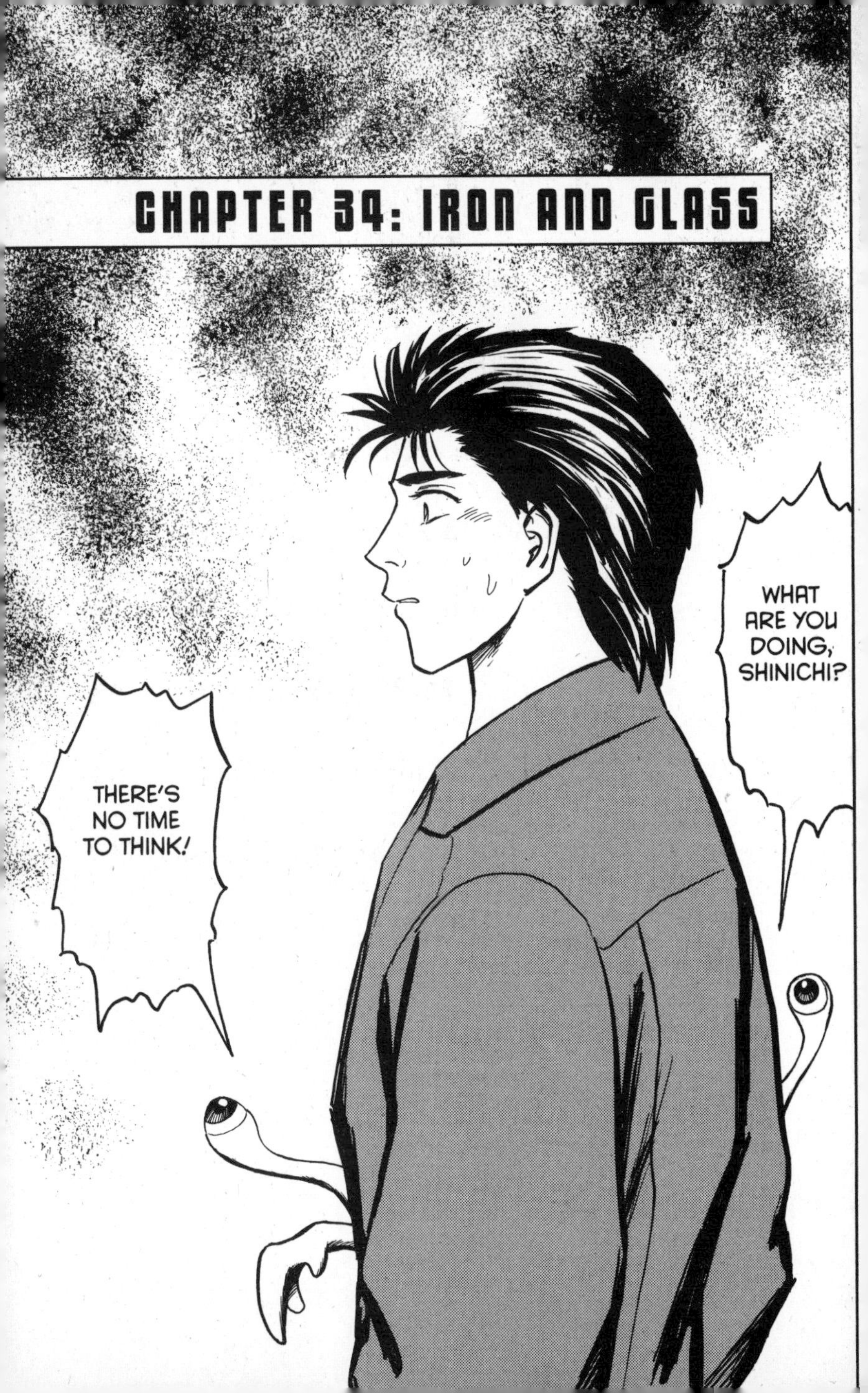
WHAT ARE YOU DOING, SHINICHI?
THERE'S NO TIME TO THINK!

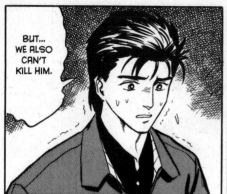

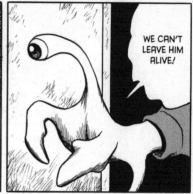

WE CAN'T LEAVE HIM ALIVE!
BUT... WE ALSO CAN'T KILL HIM.
OUR NECKS ARE ON THE LINE! HURRY!
グイイイ
VROOOO...
...OOOOOOOON
イイイイン
GRAB
!!
グンッ
YANK

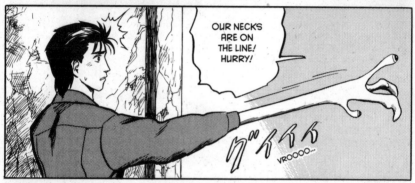

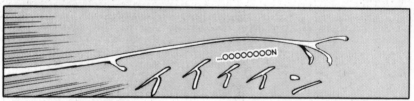

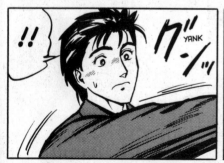

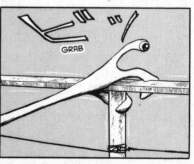

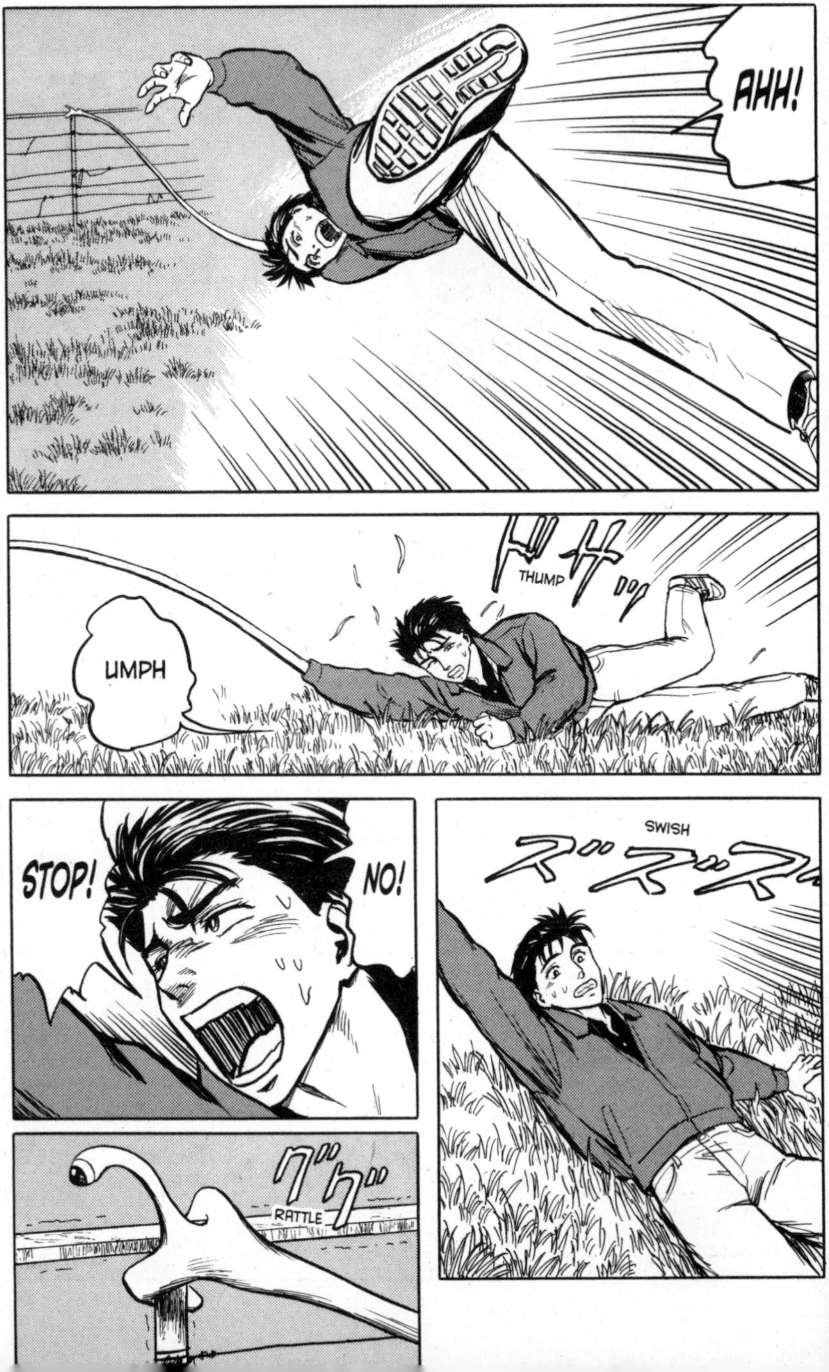
AHH!
THUMP
UMPH
SWISH
NO!
STOP!
RATTLE

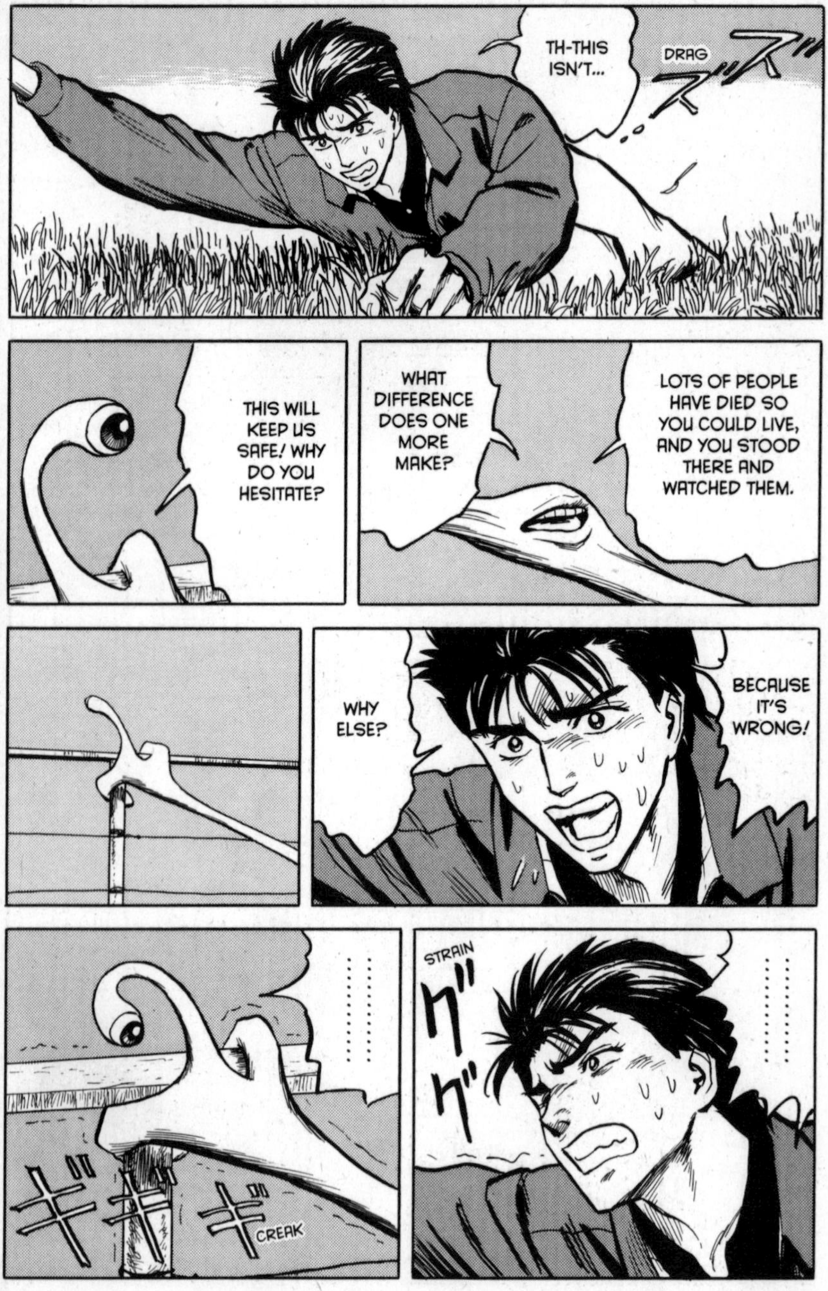

TH-THIS ISN'T...
DRAG
ズズ
LOTS OF PEOPLE HAVE DIED SO YOU COULD LIVE, AND YOU STOOD THERE AND WATCHED THEM.
WHAT DIFFERENCE DOES ONE MORE MAKE?
THIS WILL KEEP US SAFE! WHY DO YOU HESITATE?
BECAUSE IT'S WRONG!
WHY ELSE?
......
STRAIN
ググ
......
ギギギ
CREAK

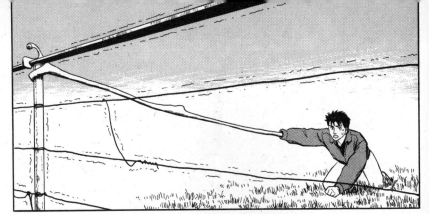

I'M TIRED.

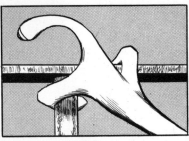

KILLING PEOPLE IS WRONG. NO MATTER WHAT THE REASON.

HE'S LONG GONE BY NOW.

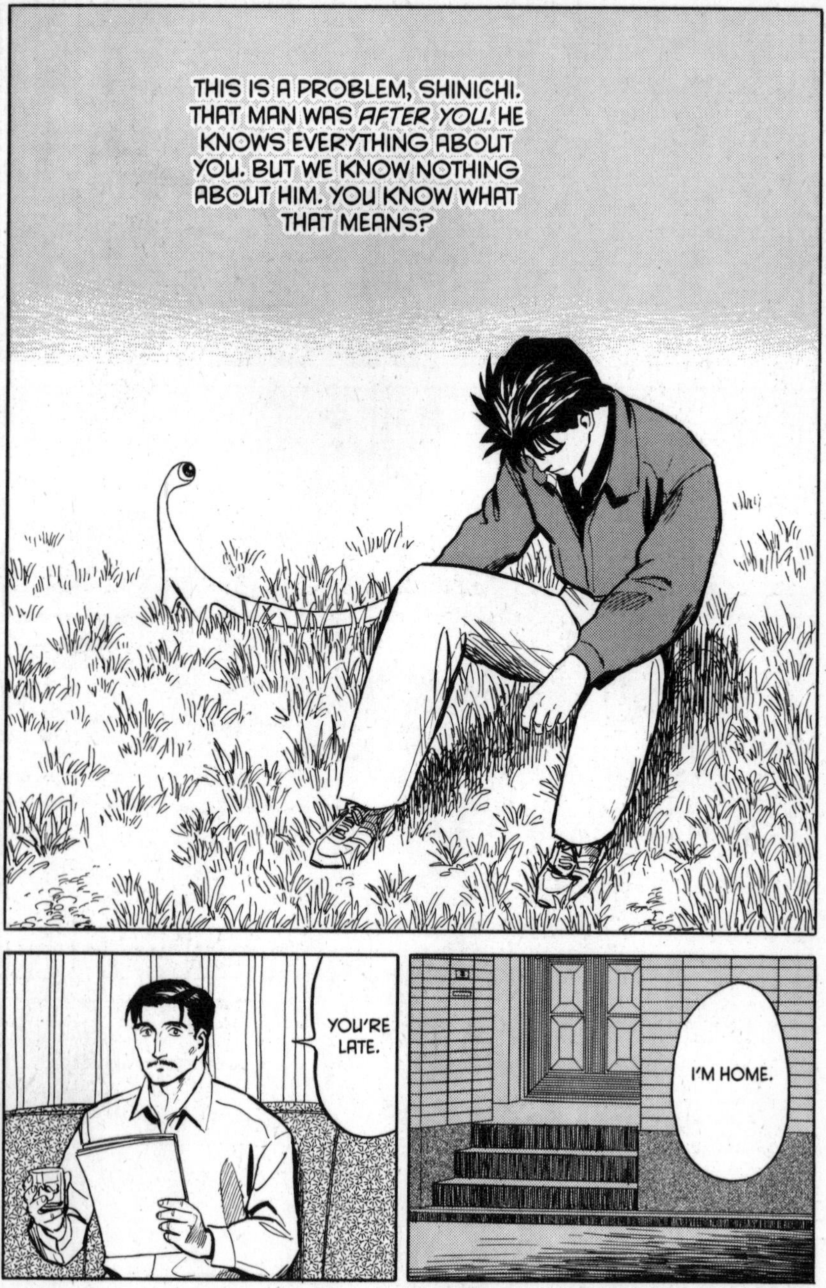
THIS IS A PROBLEM, SHINICHI. THAT MAN WAS *AFTER YOU*. HE KNOWS EVERYTHING ABOUT YOU. BUT WE KNOW NOTHING ABOUT HIM. YOU KNOW WHAT THAT MEANS?
I'M HOME.
YOU'RE LATE.

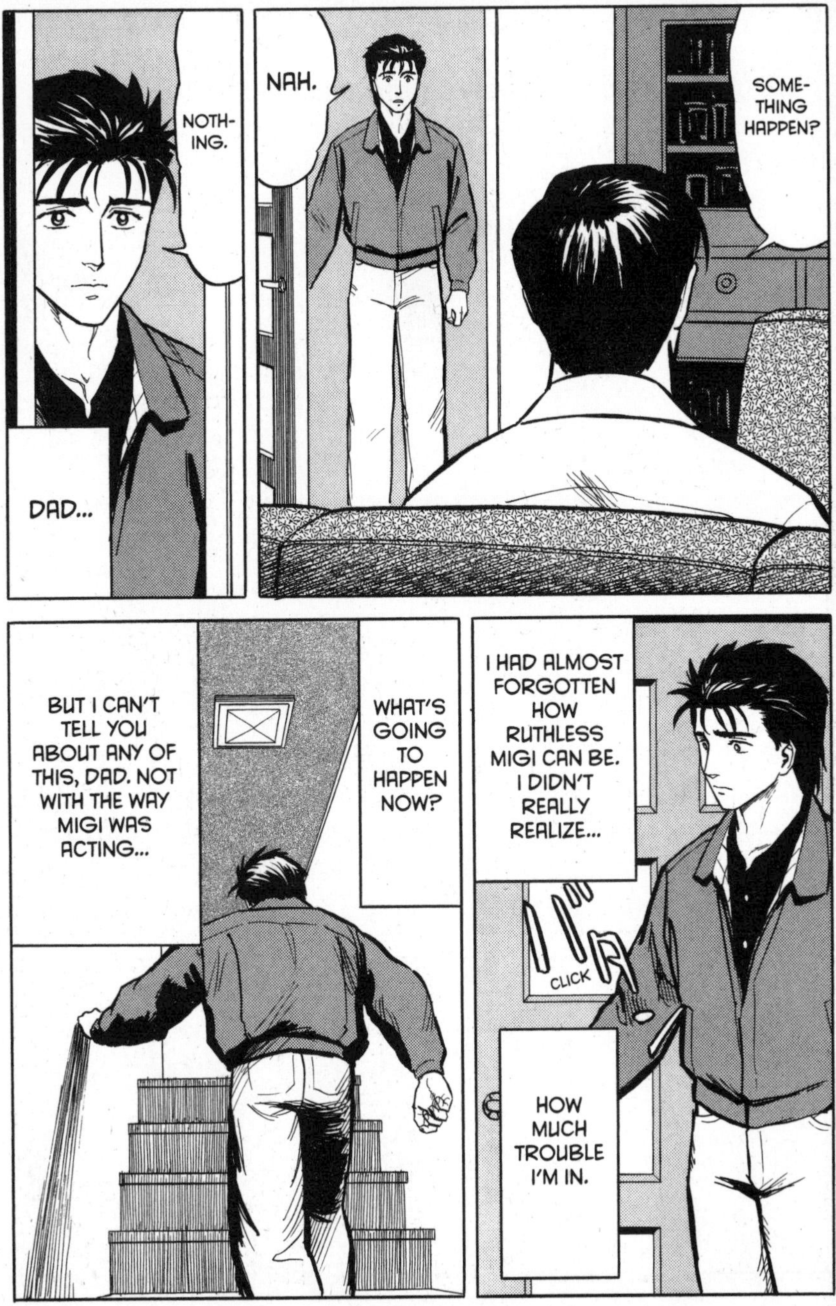
SOME-THING HAPPEN?
NAH.
NOTH-ING.
DAD...
I HAD ALMOST FORGOTTEN HOW RUTHLESS MIGI CAN BE. I DIDN'T REALLY REALIZE...
CLICK
HOW MUCH TROUBLE I'M IN.
WHAT'S GOING TO HAPPEN NOW?
BUT I CAN'T TELL YOU ABOUT ANY OF THIS, DAD. NOT WITH THE WAY MIGI WAS ACTING...

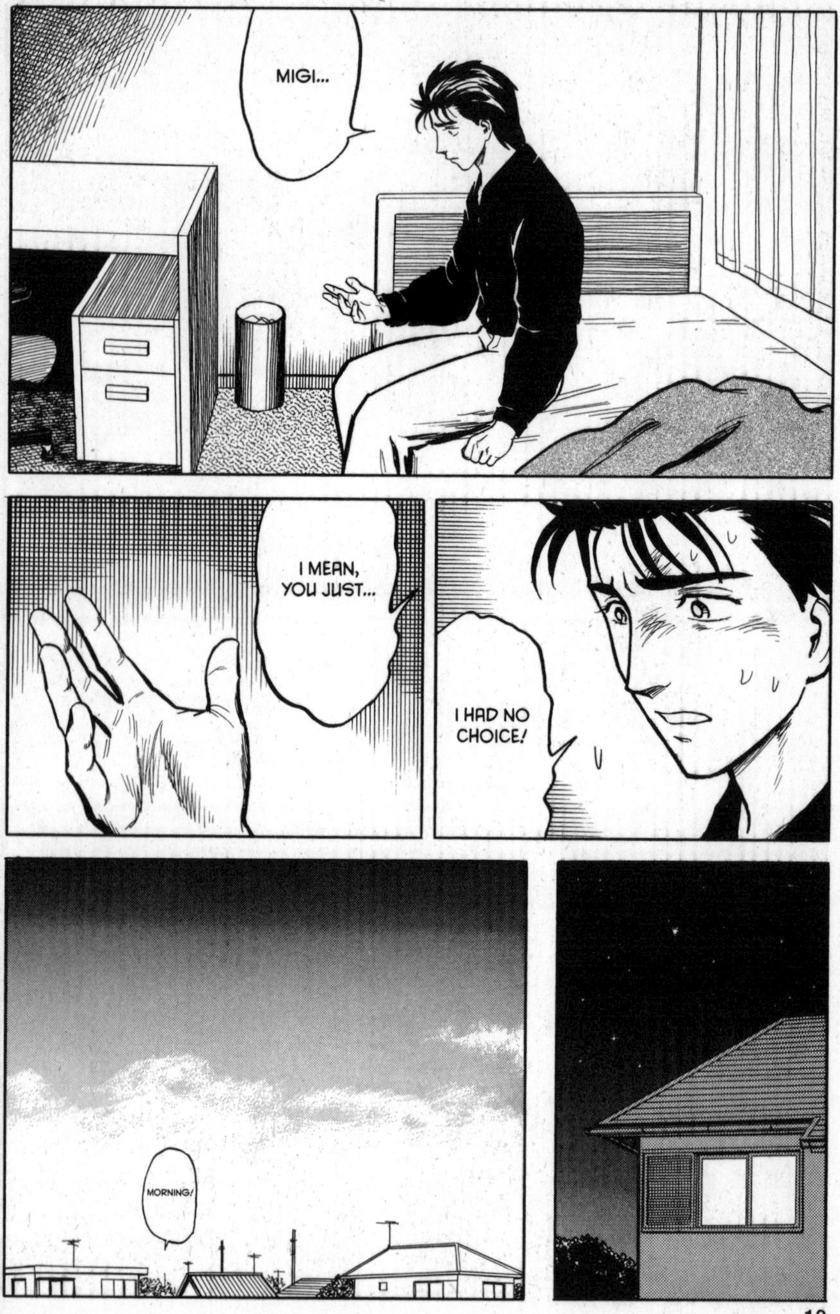
MIGI...
I HAD NO CHOICE!
I MEAN, YOU JUST...
MORNING!

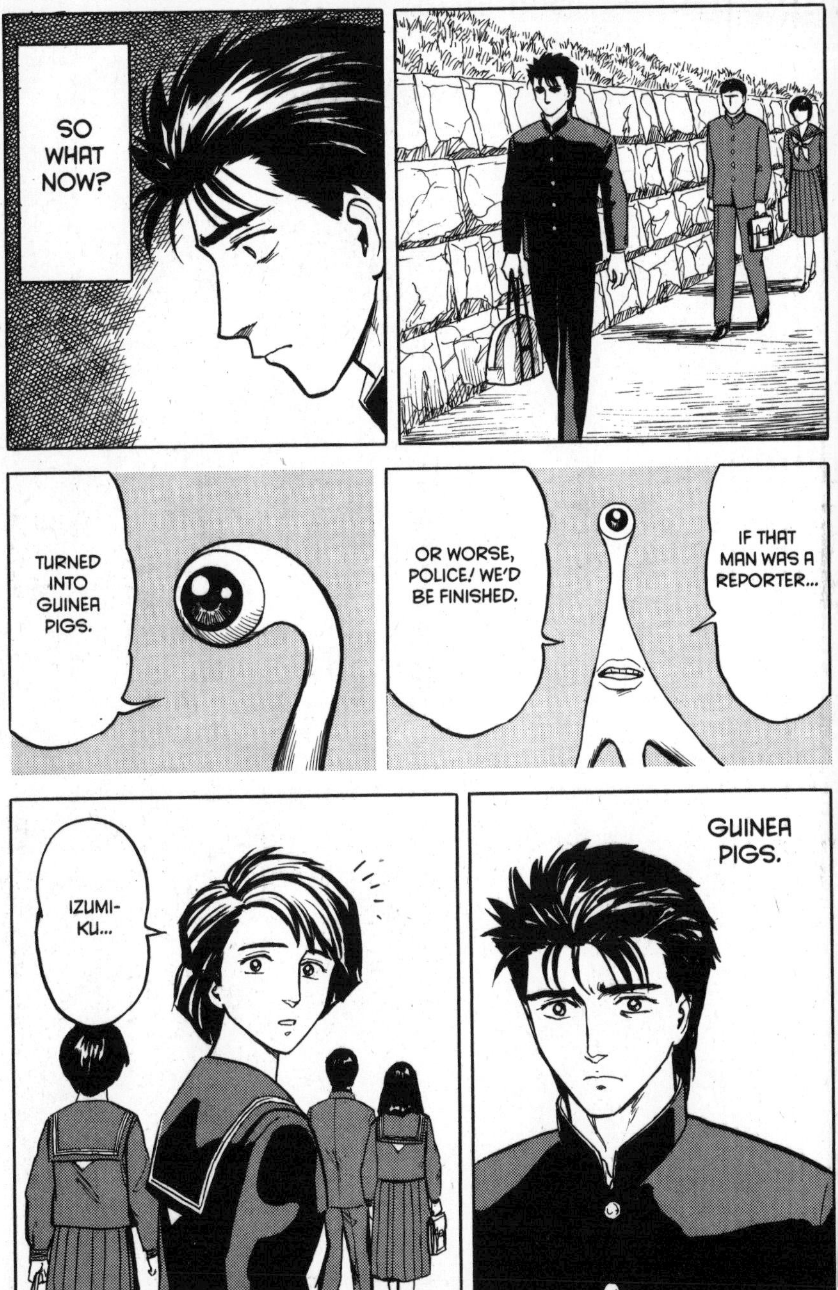
SO WHAT NOW?
IF THAT MAN WAS A REPORTER...
OR WORSE, POLICE! WE'D BE FINISHED.
TURNED INTO GUINEA PIGS.
GUINEA PIGS.
IZUMI-KU...

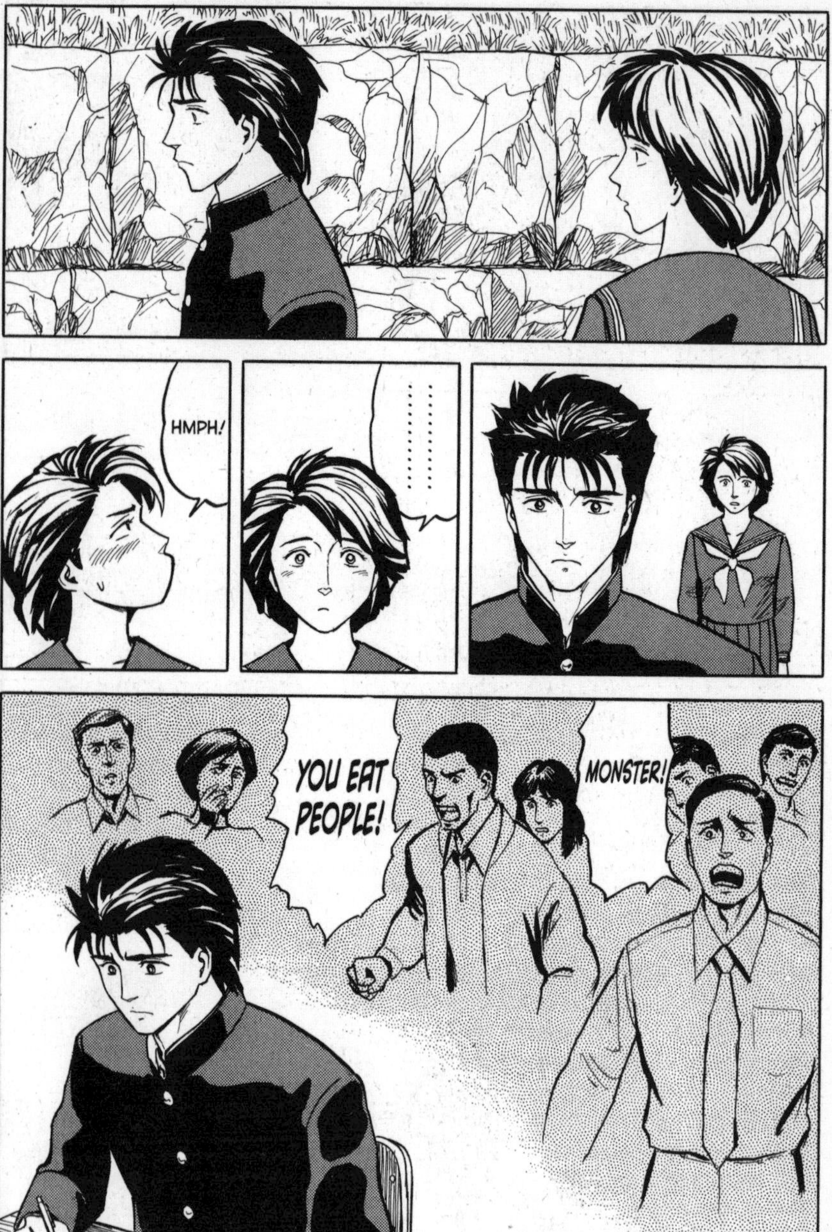
......
HMPH!
MONSTER!
YOU EAT PEOPLE!

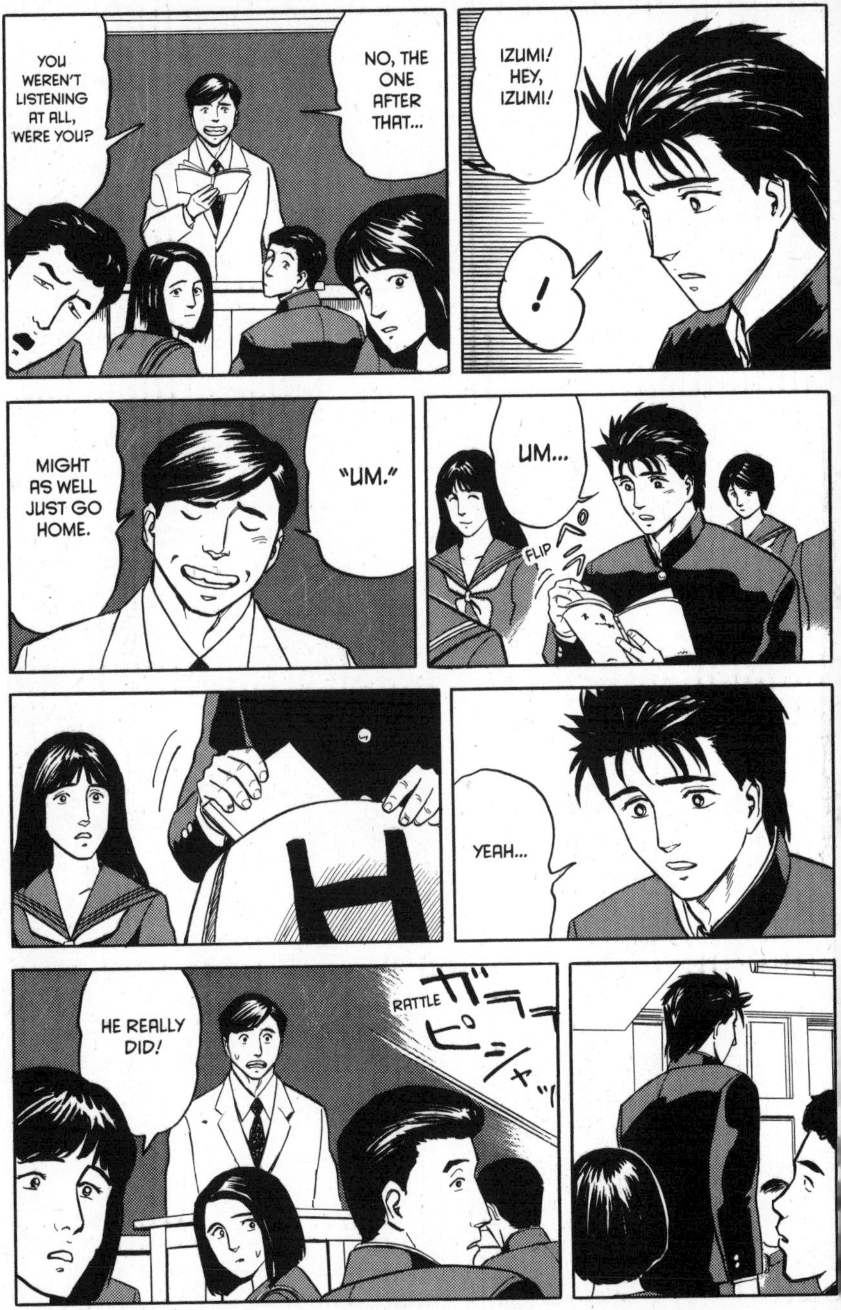
IZUMI! HEY, IZUMI!
!
NO, THE ONE AFTER THAT...
YOU WEREN'T LISTENING AT ALL, WERE YOU?
UM...
FLIP
"UM."
MIGHT AS WELL JUST GO HOME.
YEAH...
RATTLE
HE REALLY DID!

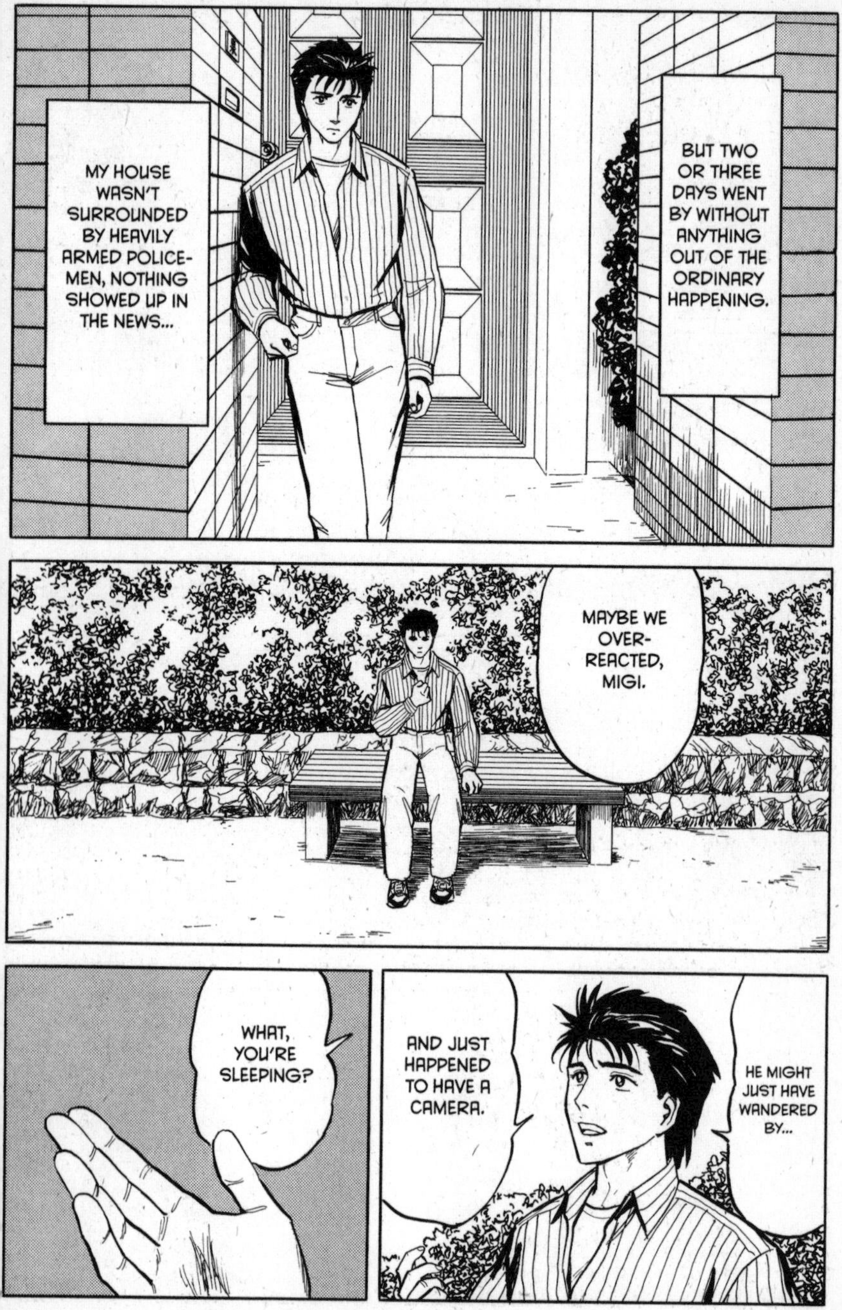
MY HOUSE WASN'T SURROUNDED BY HEAVILY ARMED POLICE-MEN, NOTHING SHOWED UP IN THE NEWS...
BUT TWO OR THREE DAYS WENT BY WITHOUT ANYTHING OUT OF THE ORDINARY HAPPENING.
MAYBE WE OVER-REACTED, MIGI.
HE MIGHT JUST HAVE WANDERED BY...
AND JUST HAPPENED TO HAVE A CAMERA.
WHAT, YOU'RE SLEEPING?

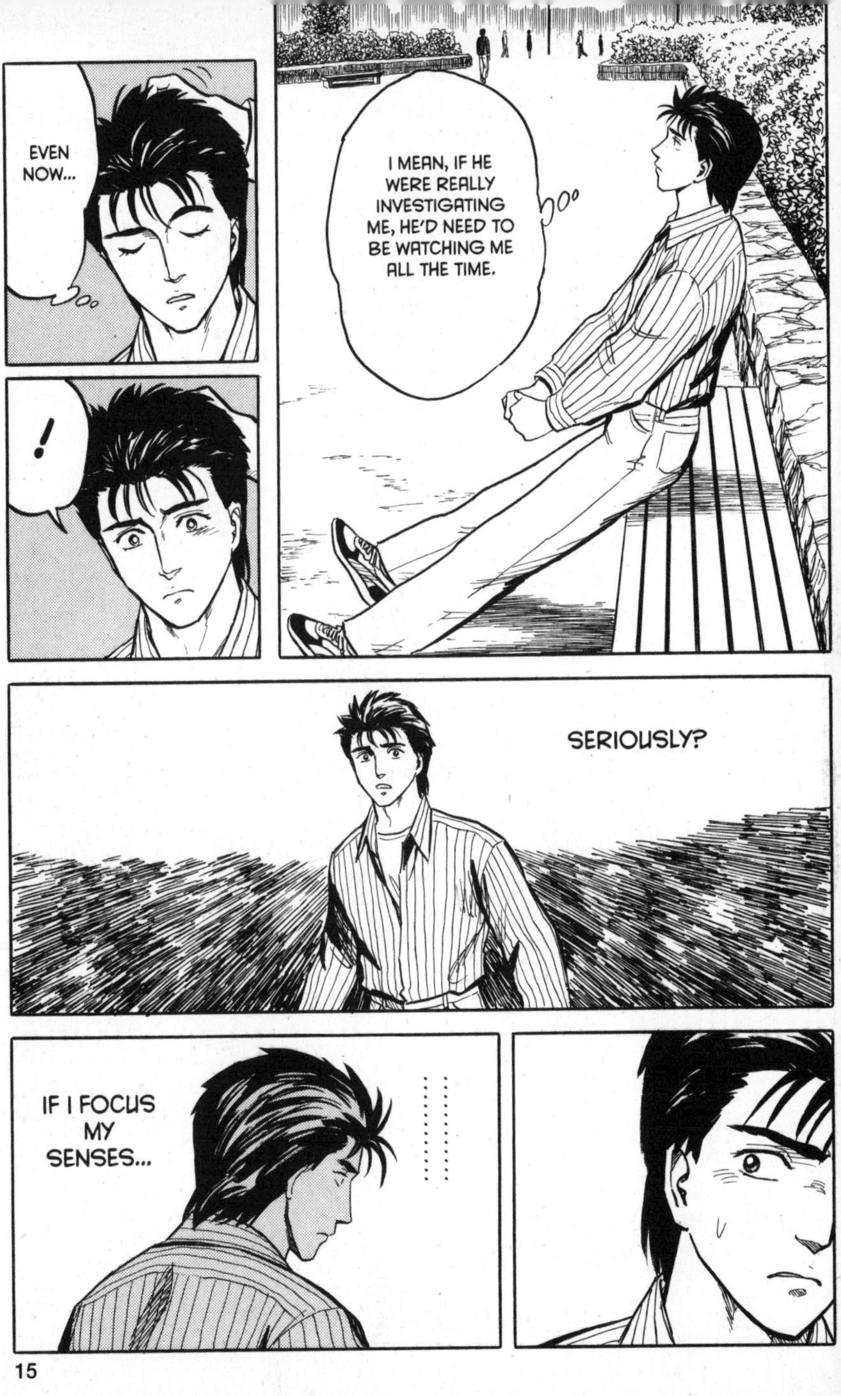
I MEAN, IF HE WERE REALLY INVESTIGATING ME, HE'D NEED TO BE WATCHING ME ALL THE TIME.
EVEN NOW...
!
SERIOUSLY?
IF I FOCUS MY SENSES...

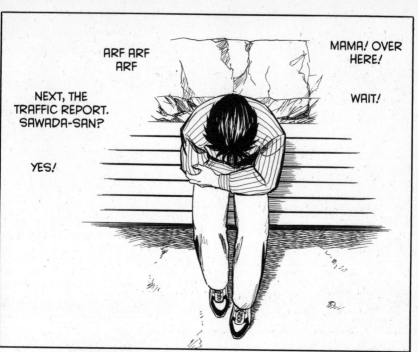

ARF ARF
ARF

MAMA! OVER
HERE!

NEXT, THE
TRAFFIC REPORT.
SAWADA-SAN?

WAIT!

YES!

HAHH
HAHH HAHH
HAHH

M-
MONSTER!!

HAHHHHHH...
HAHHHHHH...

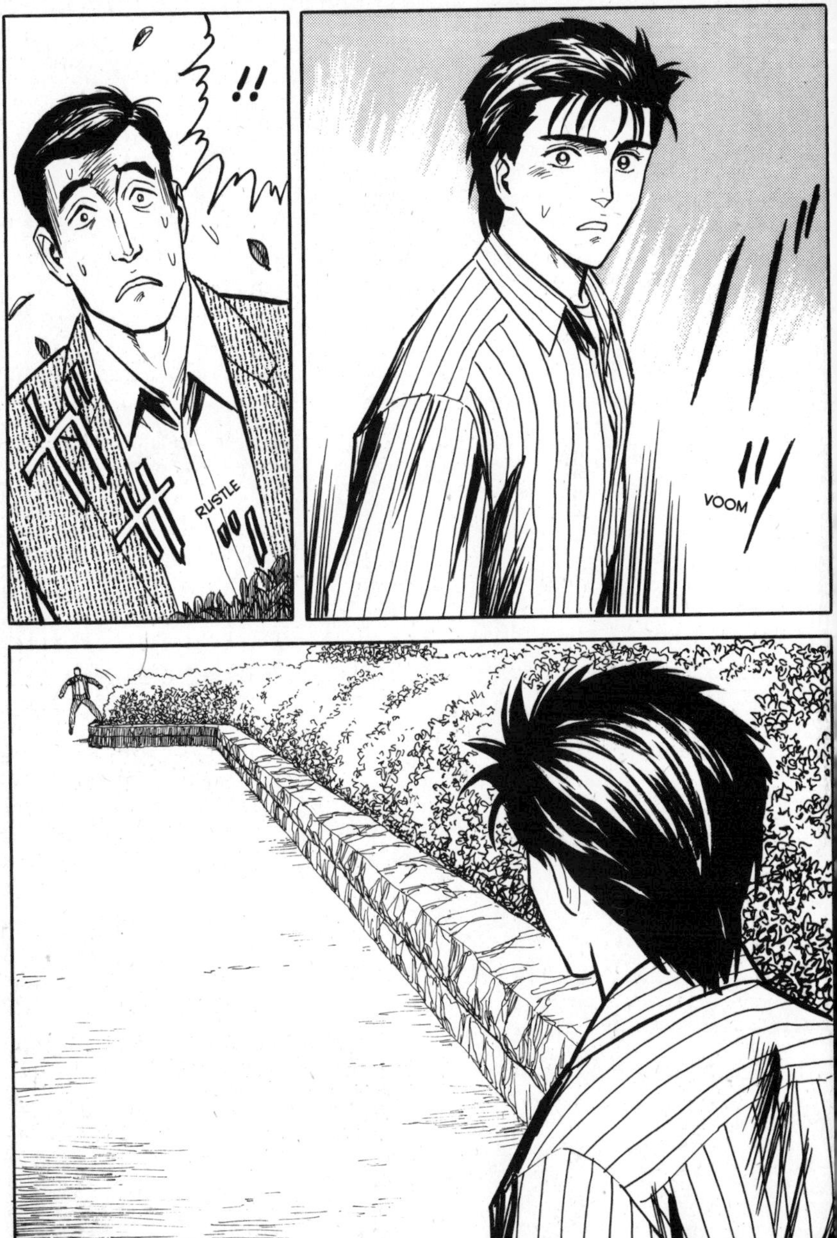
VOOM
!!
RUSTLE

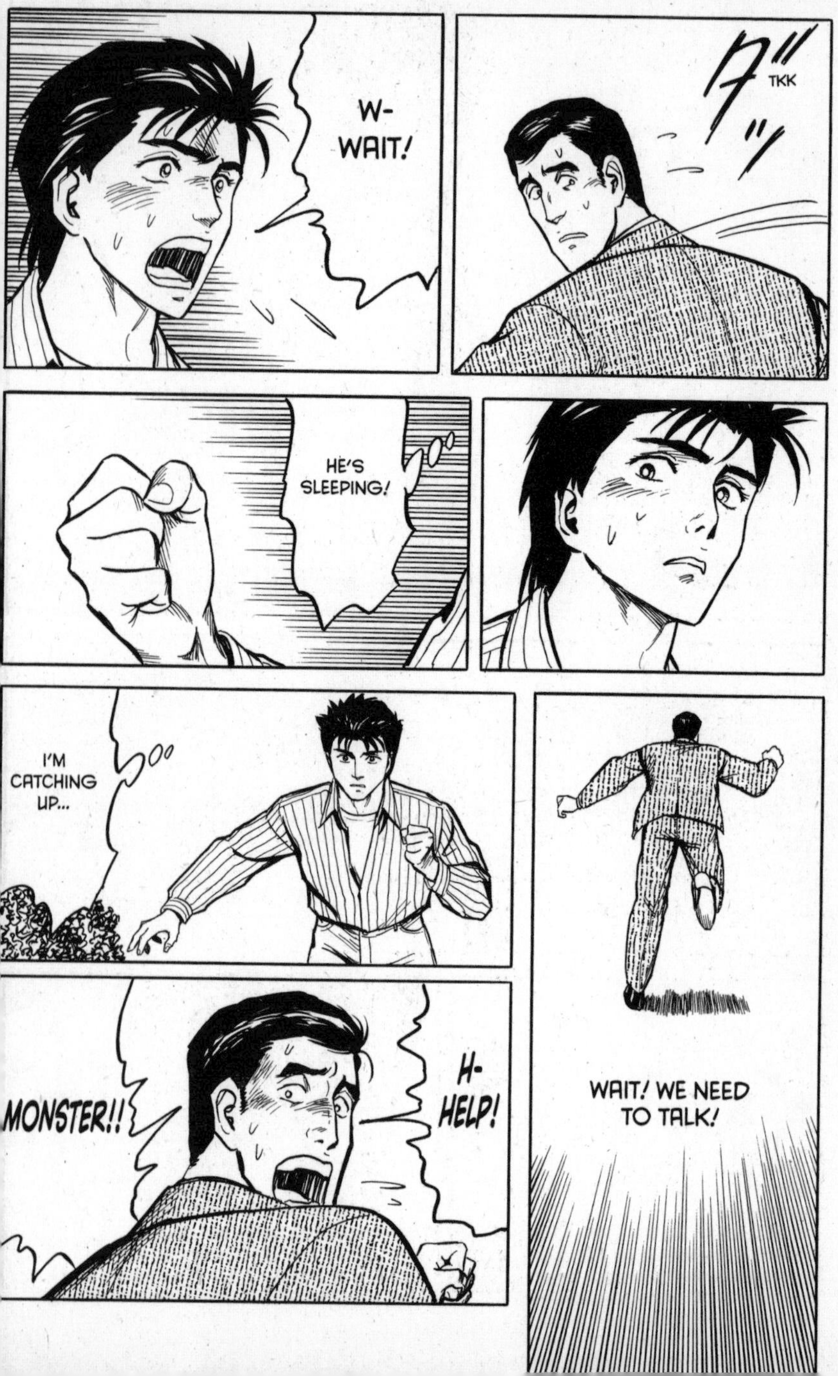
ダッ
TKK
W- WAIT!
HE'S SLEEPING!
WAIT! WE NEED TO TALK!
I'M CATCHING UP...
H- HELP!
MONSTER!!

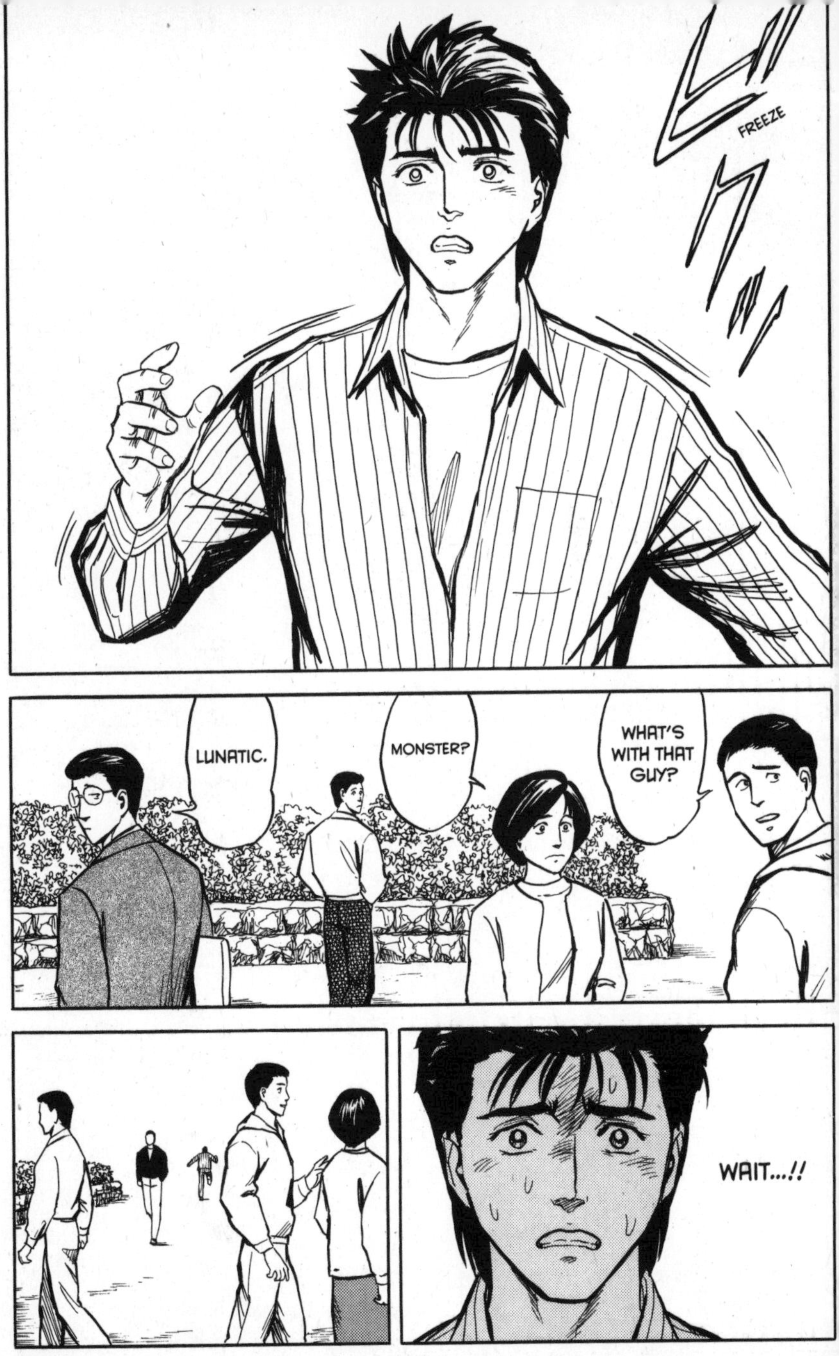
FREEZE
WHAT'S WITH THAT GUY?
MONSTER?
LUNATIC.
WAIT...!!

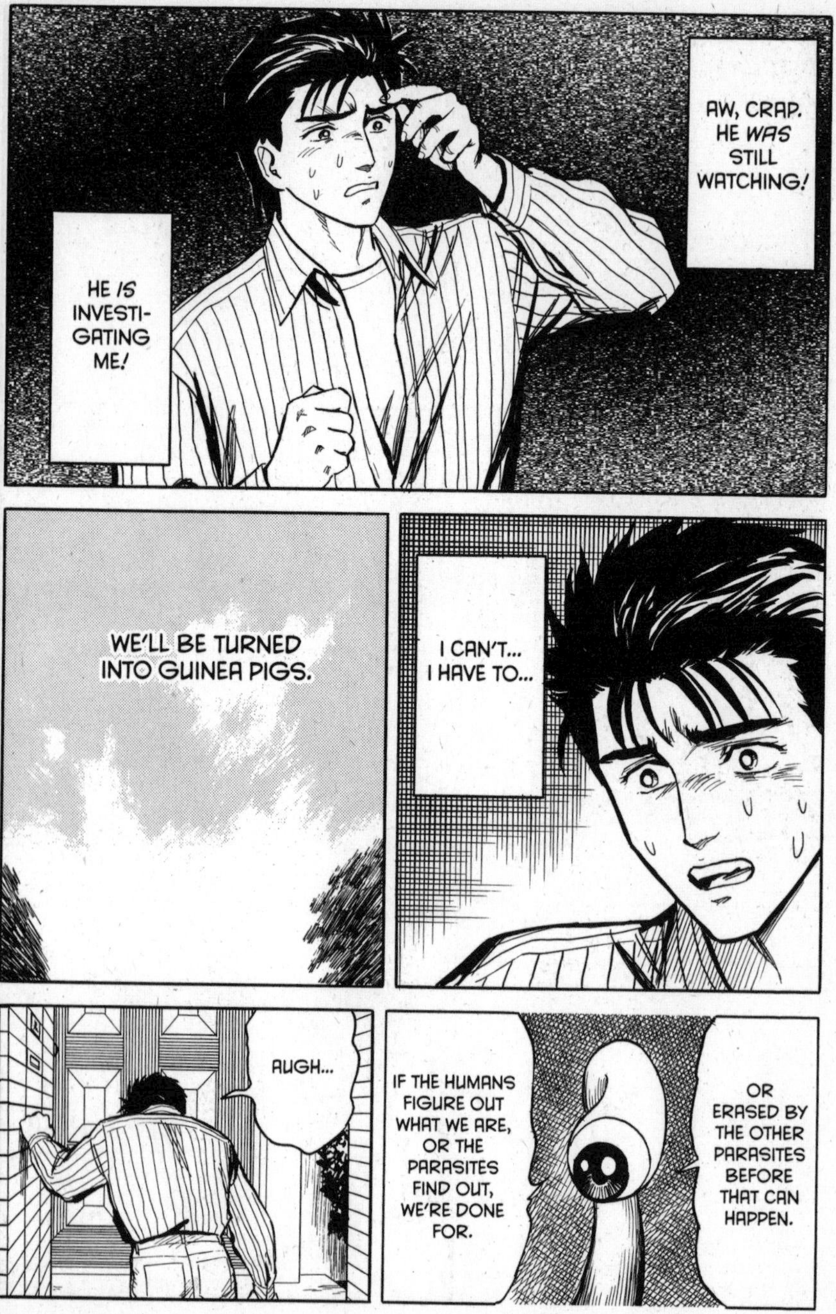
AW, CRAP. HE *WAS* STILL WATCHING!
HE *IS* INVESTIGATING ME!
I CAN'T... I HAVE TO...
WE'LL BE TURNED INTO GUINEA PIGS.
OR ERASED BY THE OTHER PARASITES BEFORE THAT CAN HAPPEN.
IF THE HUMANS FIGURE OUT WHAT WE ARE, OR THE PARASITES FIND OUT, WE'RE DONE FOR.
AUGH...

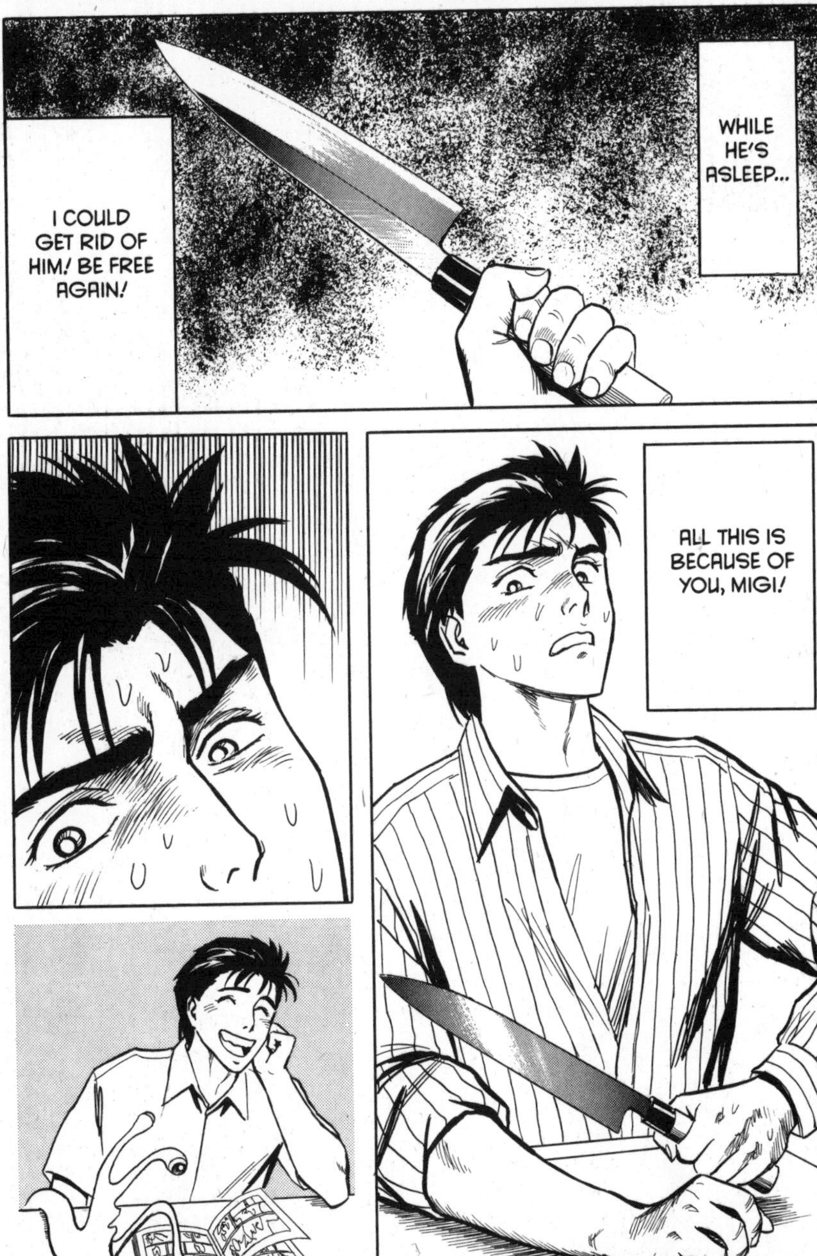
WHILE HE'S ASLEEP...
I COULD GET RID OF HIM! BE FREE AGAIN!
ALL THIS IS BECAUSE OF YOU, MIGI!

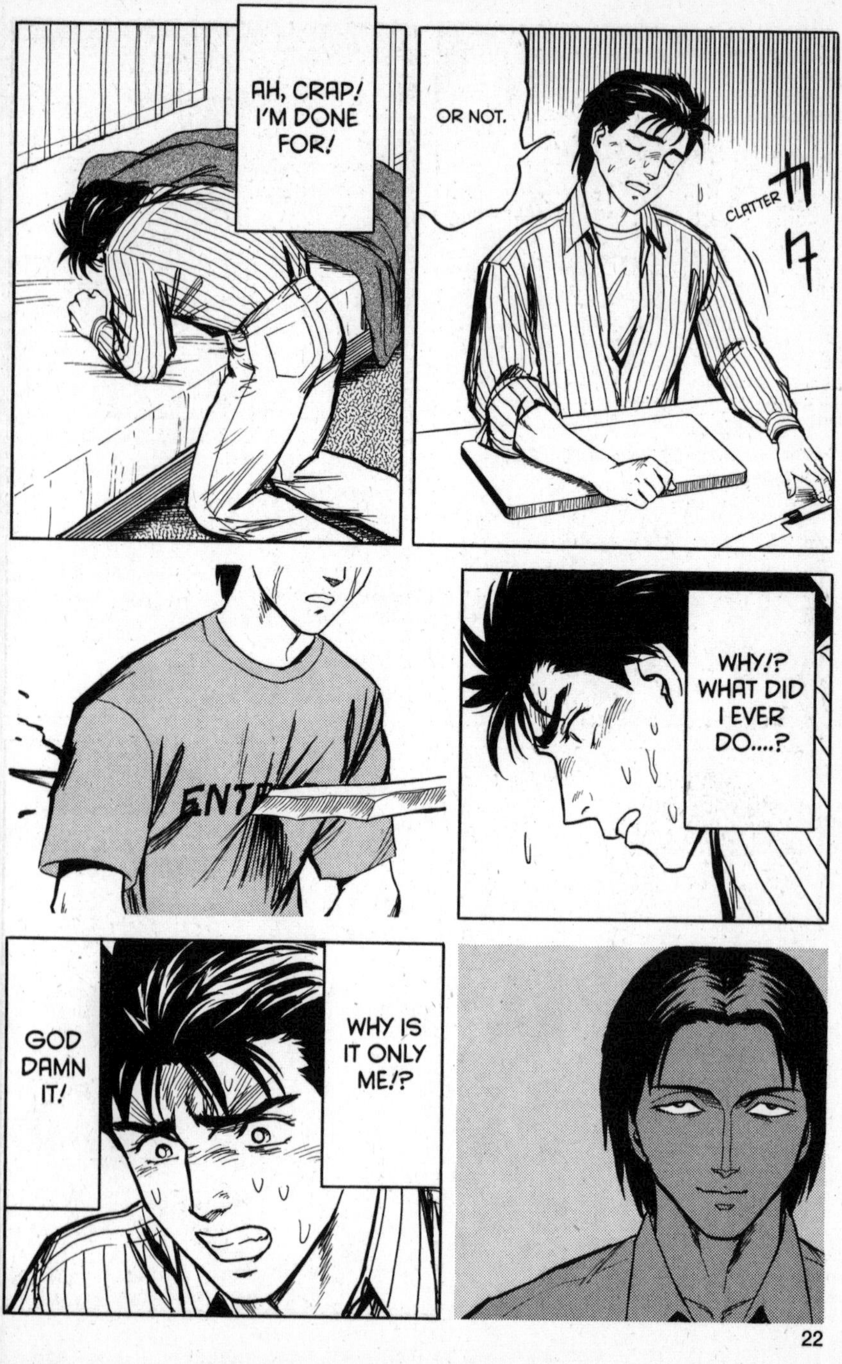
OR NOT.
CLATTER
AH, CRAP! I'M DONE FOR!
WHY!? WHAT DID I EVER DO....?
WHY IS IT ONLY ME!?
GOD DAMN IT!

GET A GRIP.

NO, CALM DOWN.

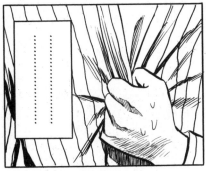

MY FEELINGS ALWAYS SETTLE QUICKLY. MY HEART IS MADE THAT WAY NOW.

SIGH...

OH... MAYBE I SHOULD TALK TO HER, WHILE I STILL CAN.

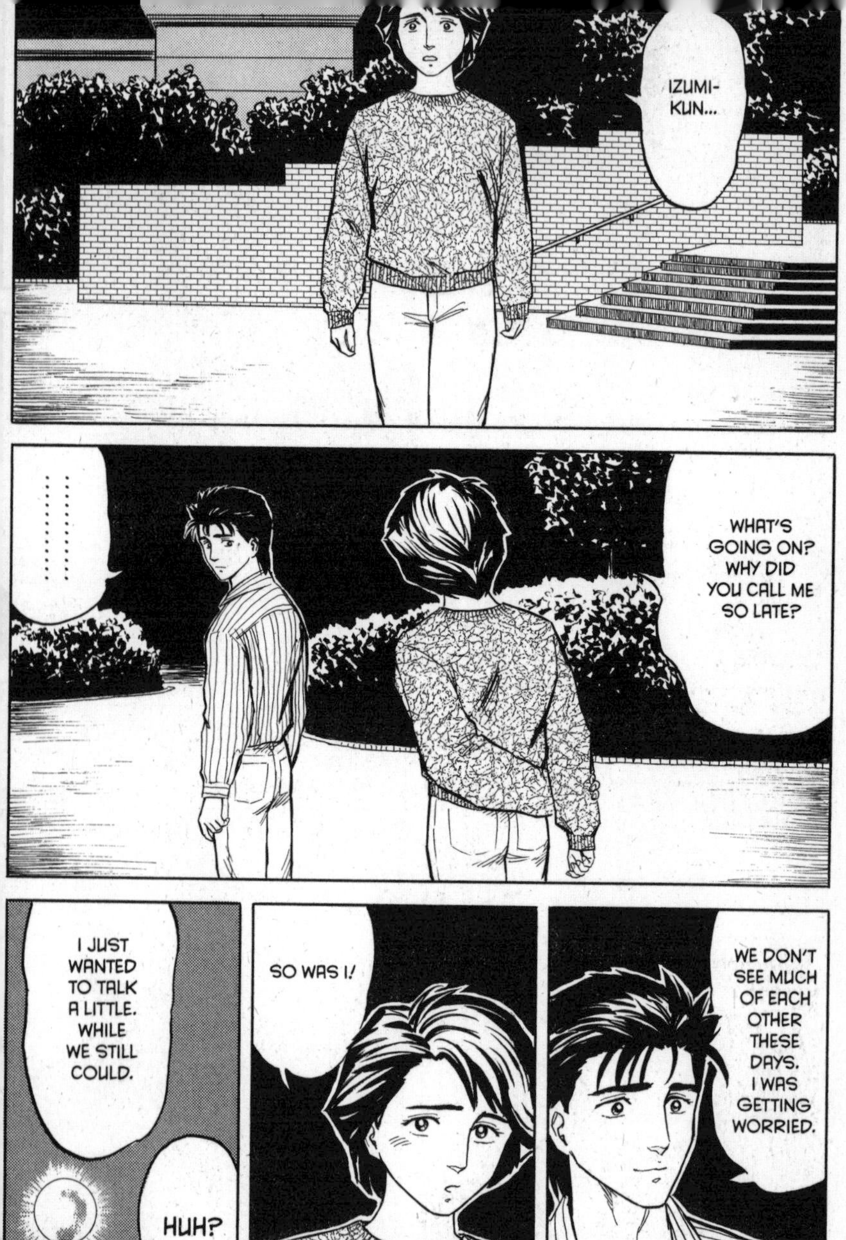
IZUMI-KUN...
WHAT'S GOING ON? WHY DID YOU CALL ME SO LATE?
......
WE DON'T SEE MUCH OF EACH OTHER THESE DAYS. I WAS GETTING WORRIED.
SO WAS I!
I JUST WANTED TO TALK A LITTLE. WHILE WE STILL COULD.
HUH?

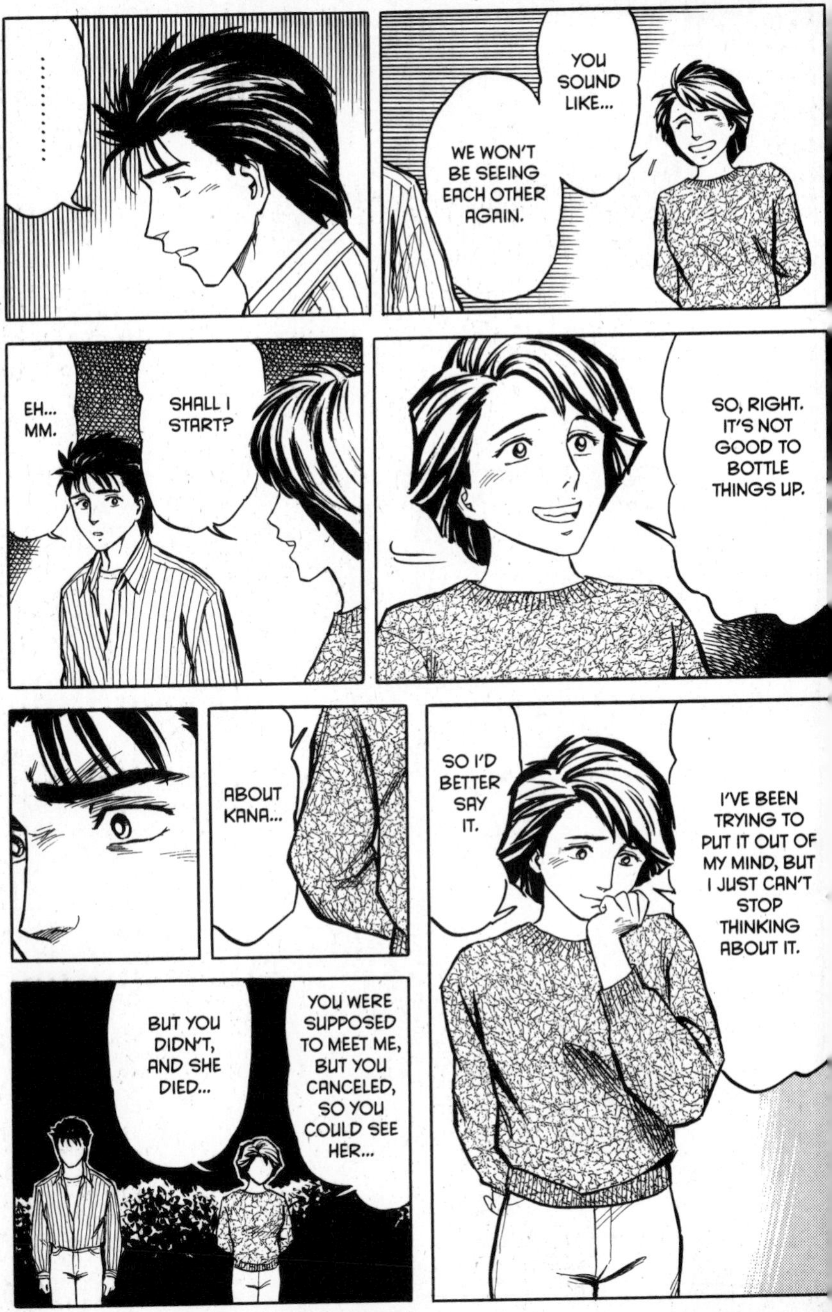
YOU SOUND LIKE...
WE WON'T BE SEEING EACH OTHER AGAIN.
....
SO, RIGHT. IT'S NOT GOOD TO BOTTLE THINGS UP.
SHALL I START?
EH... MM.
I'VE BEEN TRYING TO PUT IT OUT OF MY MIND, BUT I JUST CAN'T STOP THINKING ABOUT IT.
SO I'D BETTER SAY IT.
ABOUT KANA...
YOU WERE SUPPOSED TO MEET ME, BUT YOU CANCELED, SO YOU COULD SEE HER...
BUT YOU DIDN'T, AND SHE DIED...

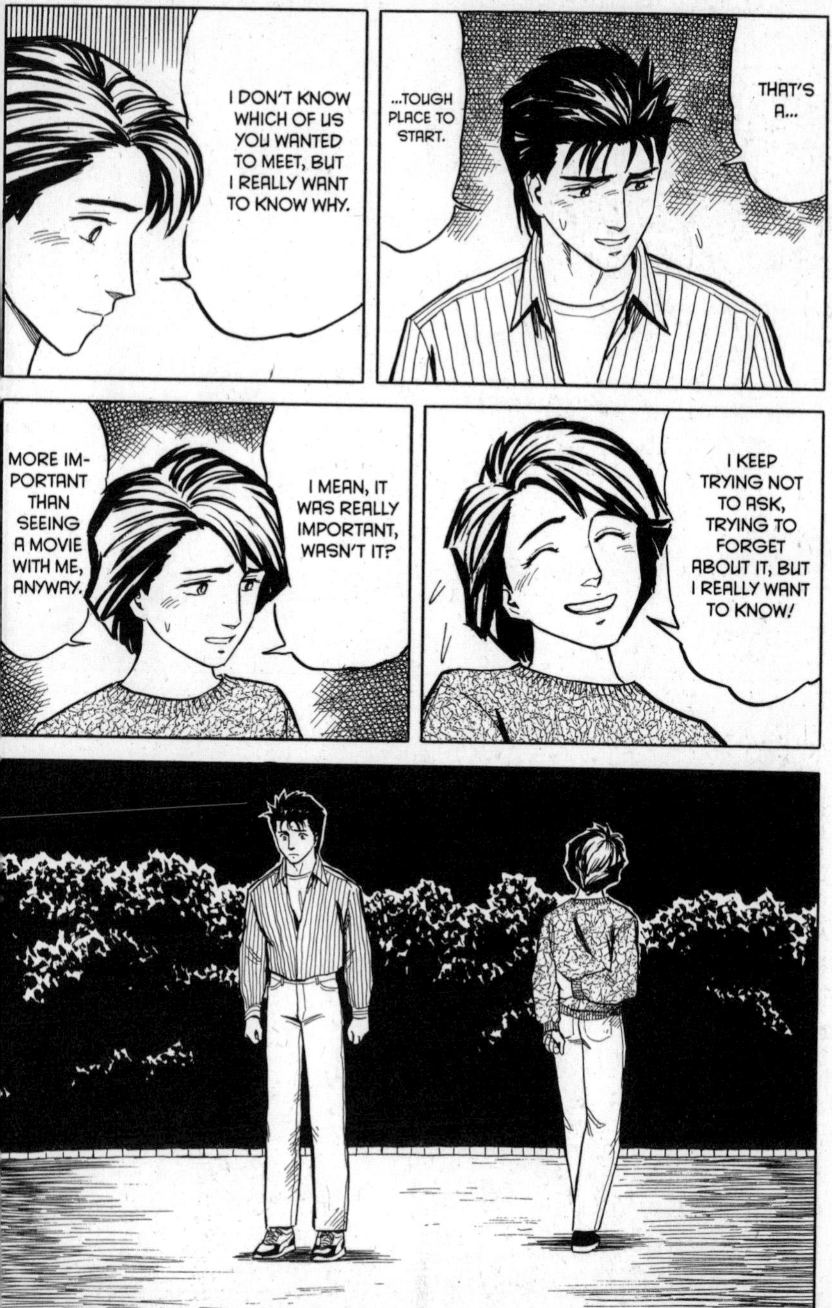
THAT'S A...
...TOUGH PLACE TO START.
I DON'T KNOW WHICH OF US YOU WANTED TO MEET, BUT I REALLY WANT TO KNOW WHY.
I KEEP TRYING NOT TO ASK, TRYING TO FORGET ABOUT IT, BUT I REALLY WANT TO KNOW!
I MEAN, IT WAS REALLY IMPORTANT, WASN'T IT?
MORE IMPORTANT THAN SEEING A MOVIE WITH ME, ANYWAY.

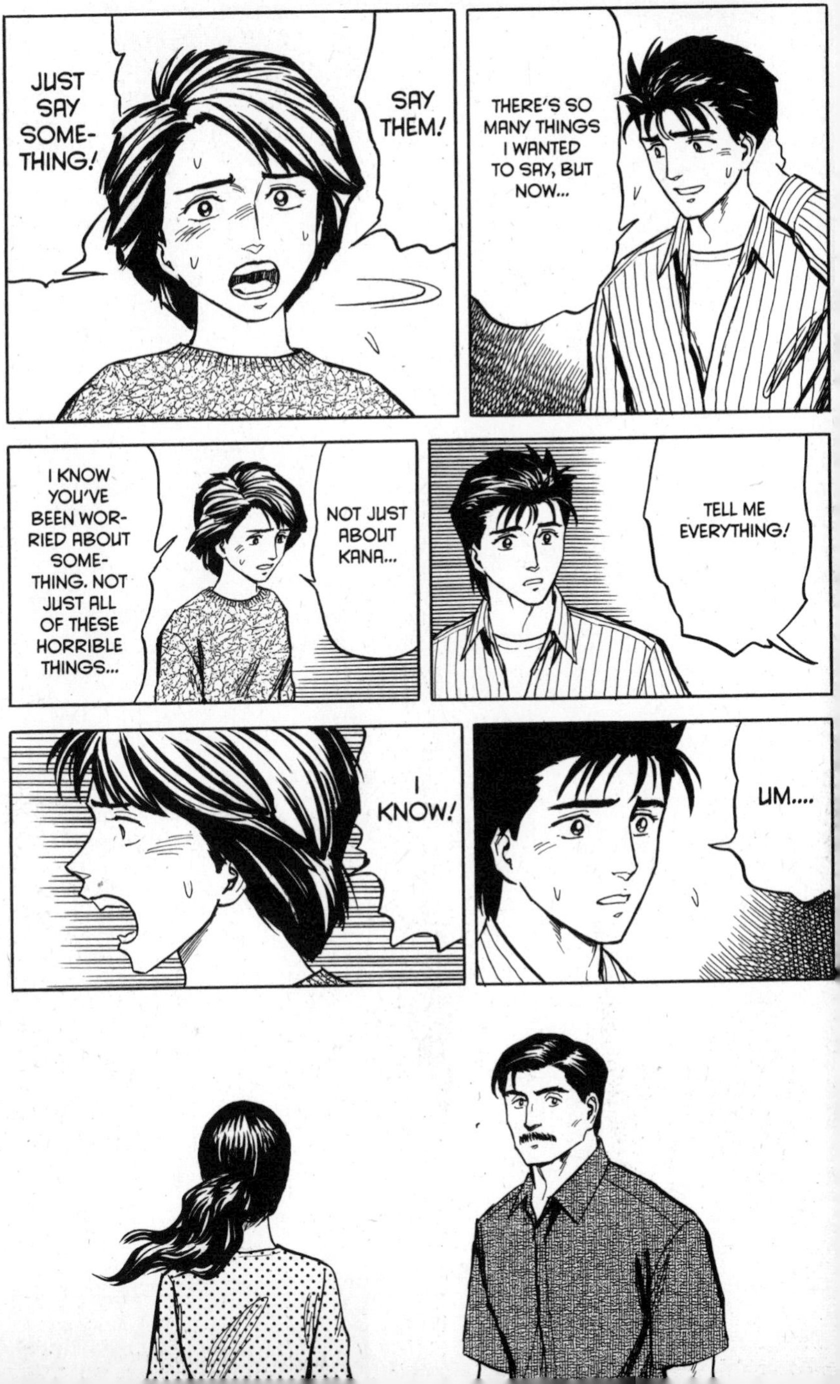
THERE'S SO MANY THINGS I WANTED TO SAY, BUT NOW...
SAY THEM!
JUST SAY SOME-THING!
TELL ME EVERYTHING!
NOT JUST ABOUT KANA...
I KNOW YOU'VE BEEN WOR-RIED ABOUT SOME-THING. NOT JUST ALL OF THESE HORRIBLE THINGS...
UM....
I KNOW!

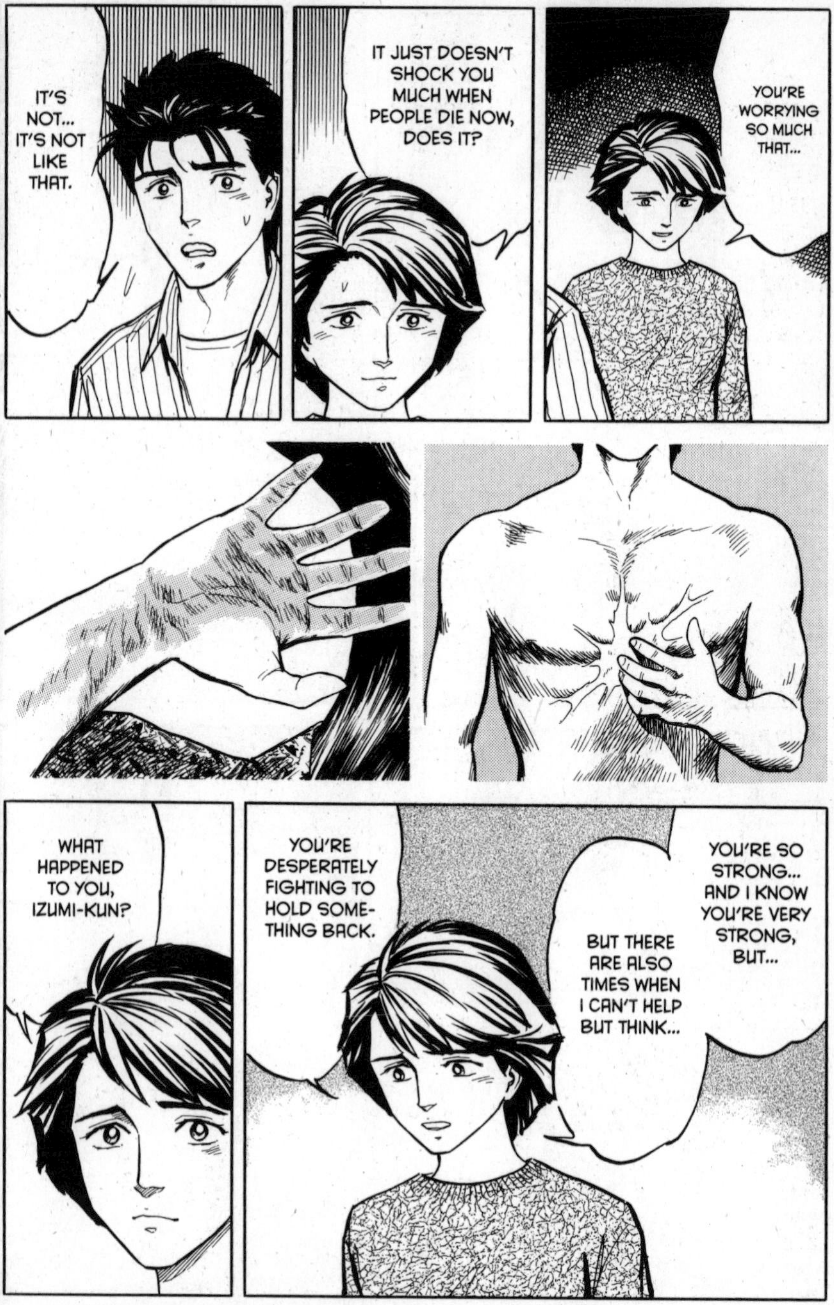
YOU'RE WORRYING SO MUCH THAT...
IT JUST DOESN'T SHOCK YOU MUCH WHEN PEOPLE DIE NOW, DOES IT?
IT'S NOT... IT'S NOT LIKE THAT.
YOU'RE SO STRONG... AND I KNOW YOU'RE VERY STRONG, BUT...
BUT THERE ARE ALSO TIMES WHEN I CAN'T HELP BUT THINK...
YOU'RE DESPERATELY FIGHTING TO HOLD SOME-THING BACK.
WHAT HAPPENED TO YOU, IZUMI-KUN?

IT'S HARD KEEPING IT TO YOUR- SELF, ISN'T IT? TELL ME.

YOU...

MURANO...

NOTHING. NOTHING'S HAPPENED TO ME.

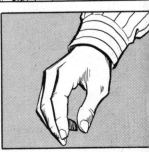

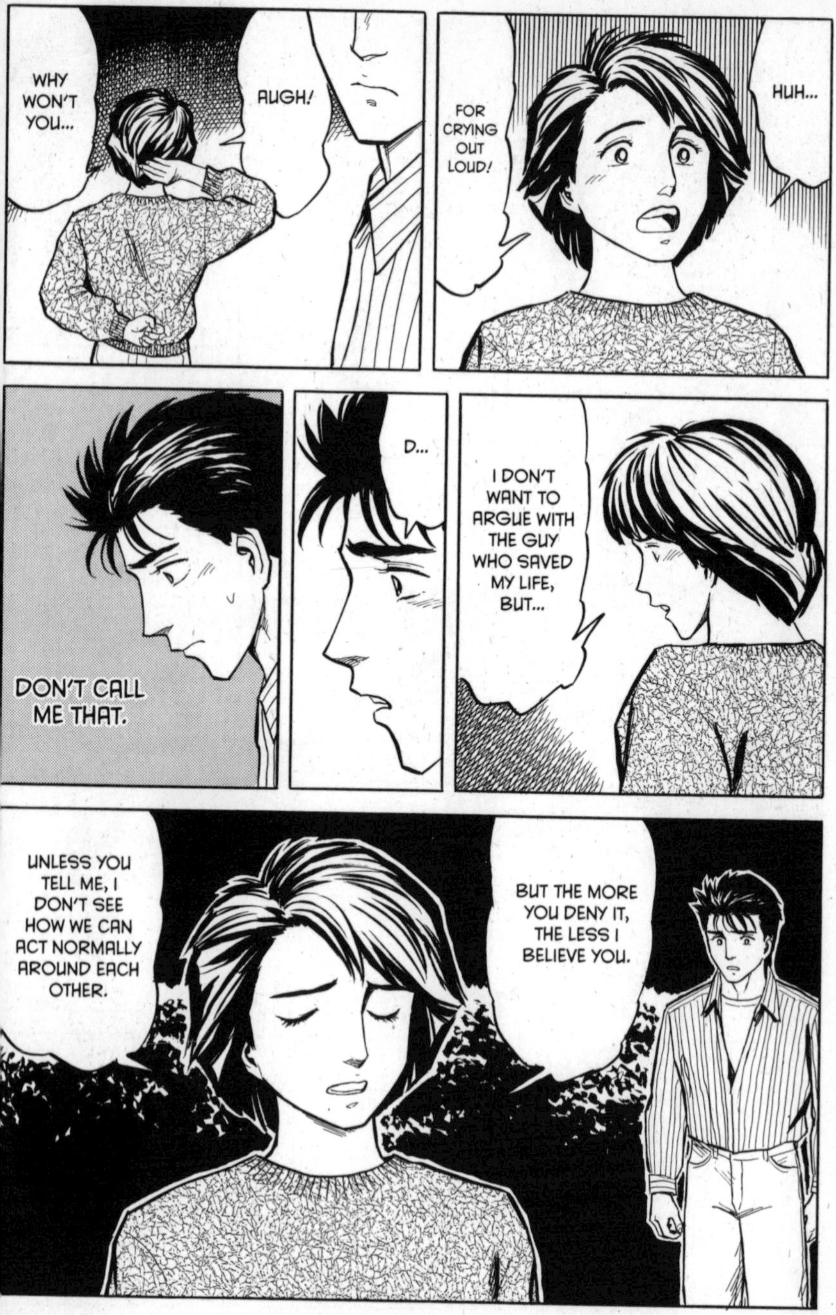
HUH...
FOR CRYING OUT LOUD!
AUGH!
WHY WON'T YOU...
I DON'T WANT TO ARGUE WITH THE GUY WHO SAVED MY LIFE, BUT...
D...
DON'T CALL ME THAT.
BUT THE MORE YOU DENY IT, THE LESS I BELIEVE YOU.
UNLESS YOU TELL ME, I DON'T SEE HOW WE CAN ACT NORMALLY AROUND EACH OTHER.

DON'T TALK LIKE THAT! IF YOU START TALKING LIKE THAT, I...

I WILL!

OKAY, I'LL TELL YOU...

IN MY BODY!!

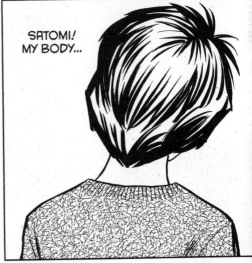

SATOMI! MY BODY...

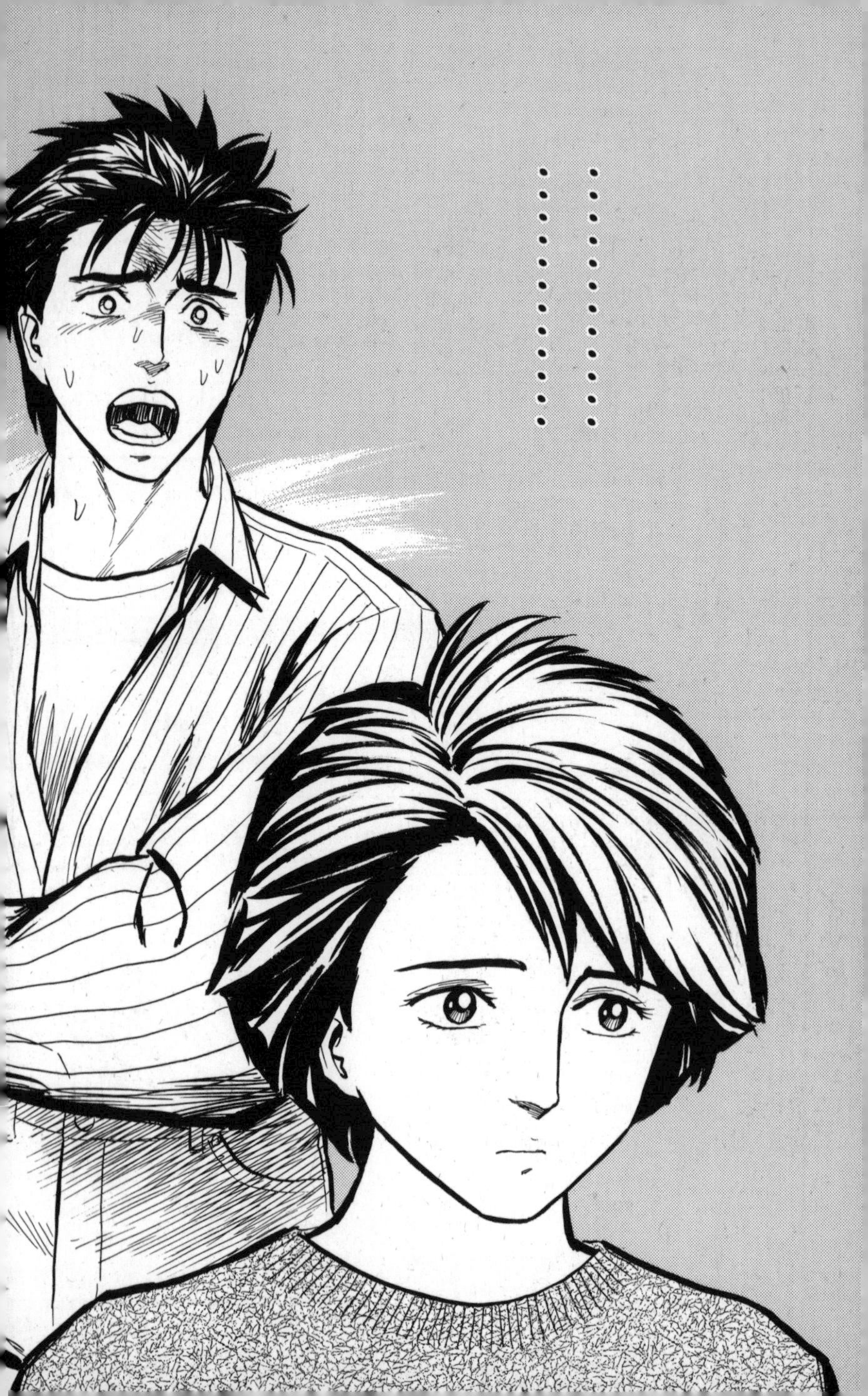

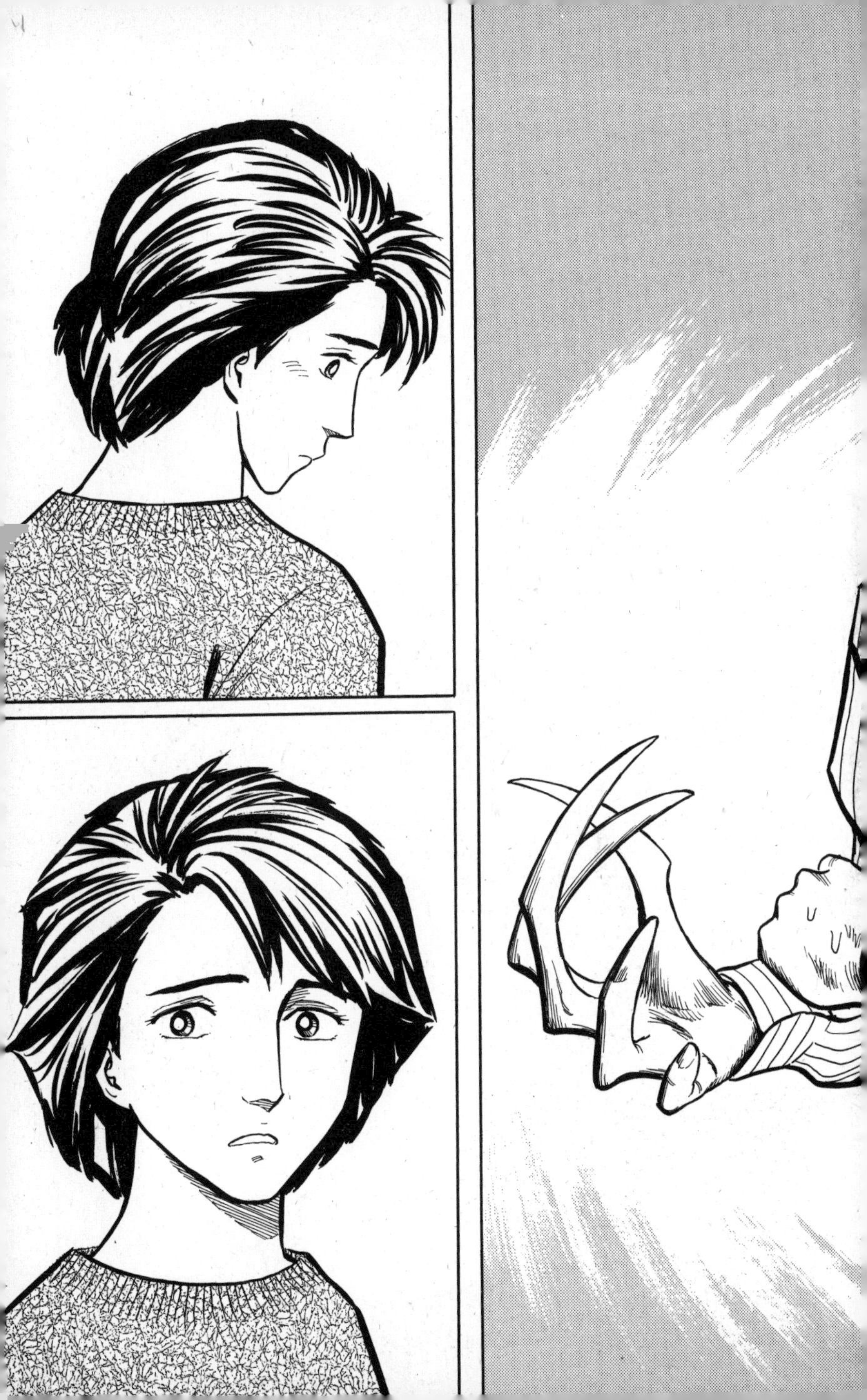

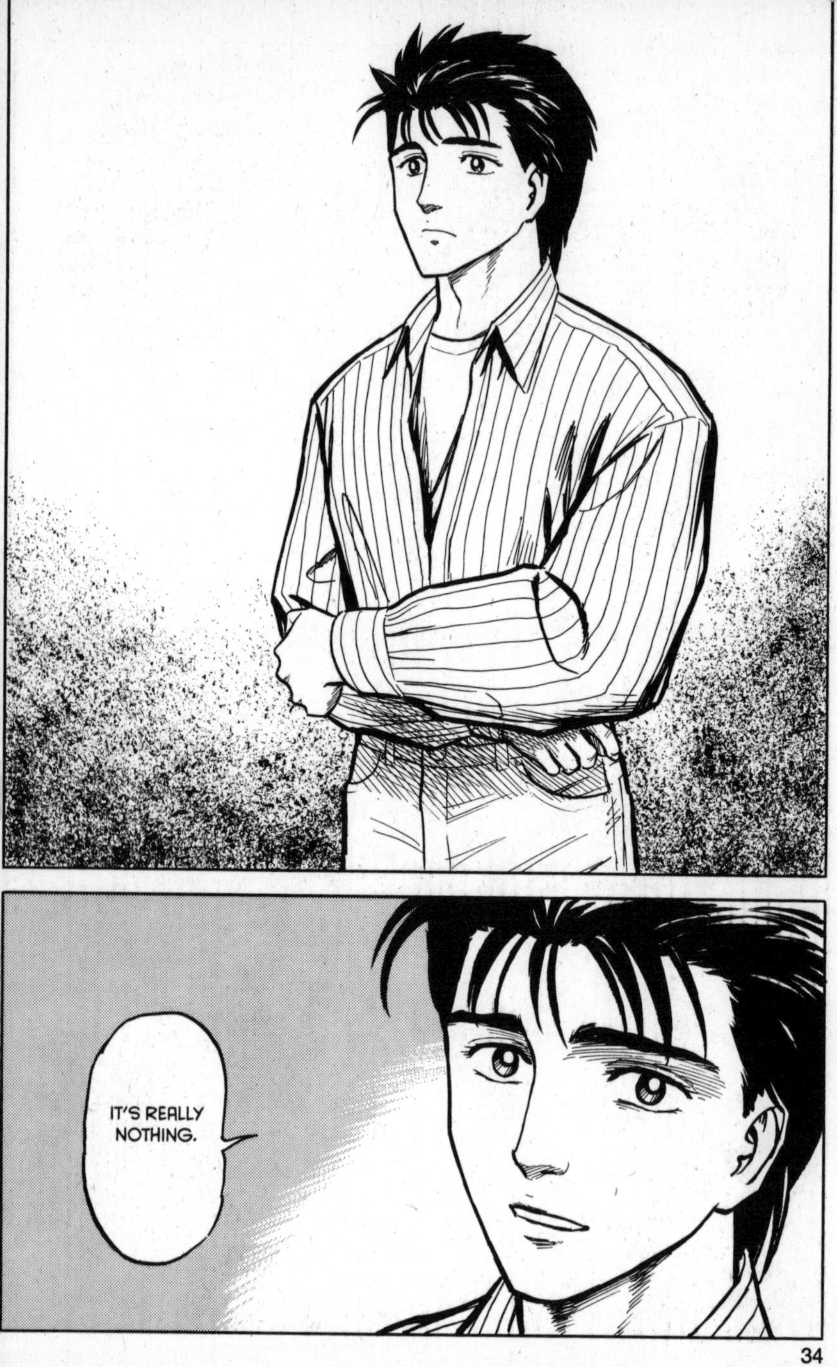
IT'S REALLY NOTHING.

YOU DON'T TRUST ME.
I CAN'T HELP IT IF YOU DON'T BELIEVE ME.
HOW CAN YOUR EYES...
...BE SO DRY?

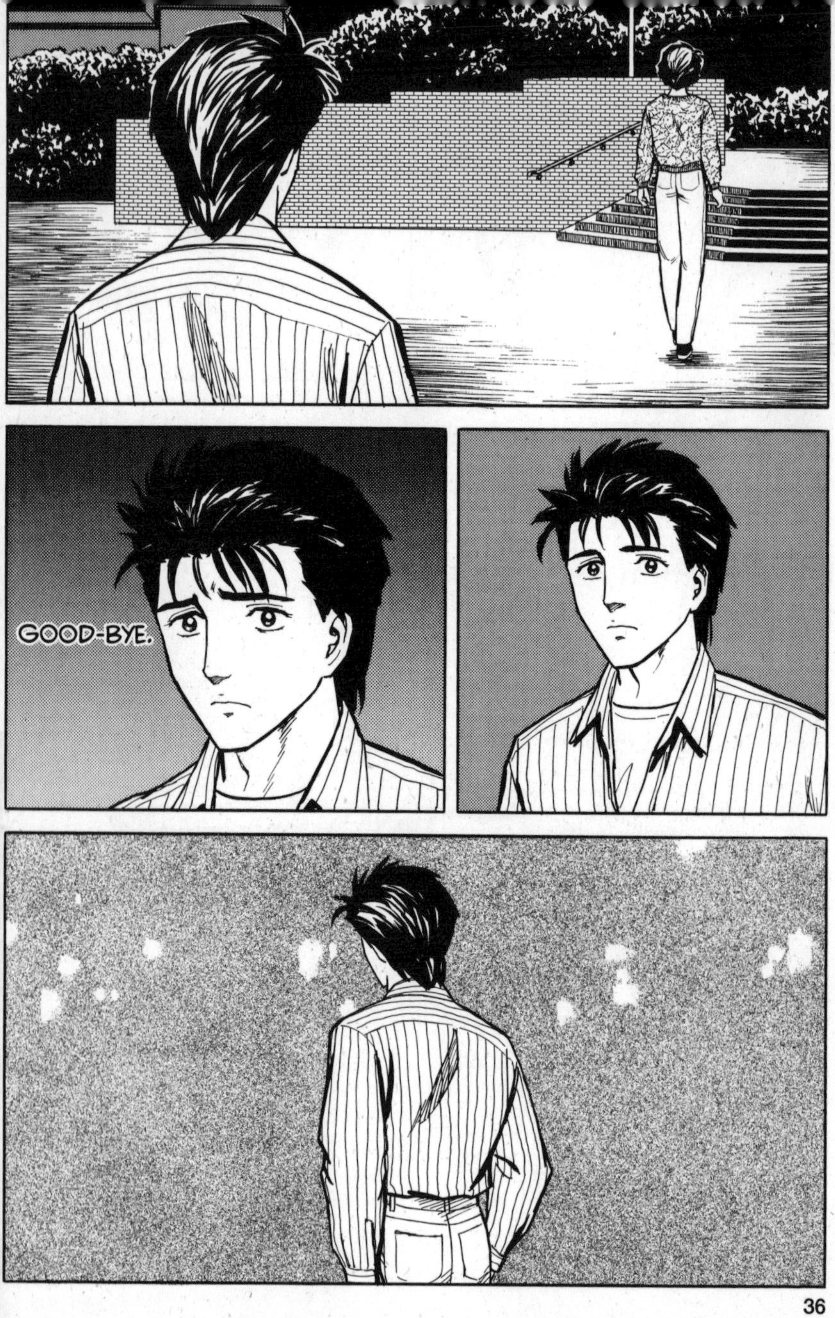
GOOD-BYE.

I GIVE UP.
WHAT HAPPENS HAPPENS.

HMPH!

SHINICHI,
YOU HAD ME
WORRIED.

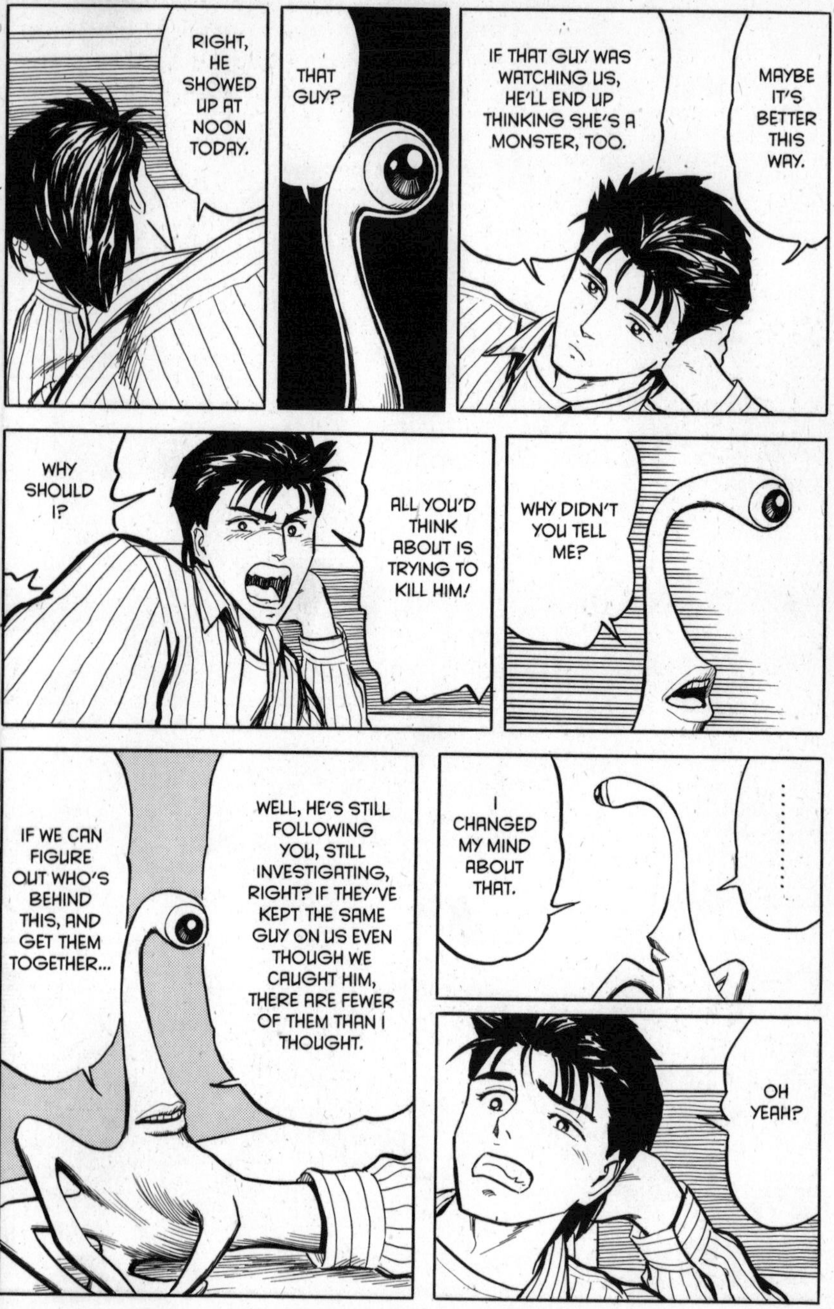
MAYBE IT'S BETTER THIS WAY.
IF THAT GUY WAS WATCHING US, HE'LL END UP THINKING SHE'S A MONSTER, TOO.
THAT GUY?
RIGHT, HE SHOWED UP AT NOON TODAY.
WHY DIDN'T YOU TELL ME?
ALL YOU'D THINK ABOUT IS TRYING TO KILL HIM!
WHY SHOULD I?
......
I CHANGED MY MIND ABOUT THAT.
OH YEAH?
WELL, HE'S STILL FOLLOWING YOU, STILL INVESTIGATING, RIGHT? IF THEY'VE KEPT THE SAME GUY ON US EVEN THOUGH WE CAUGHT HIM, THERE ARE FEWER OF THEM THAN I THOUGHT.
IF WE CAN FIGURE OUT WHO'S BEHIND THIS, AND GET THEM TOGETHER...

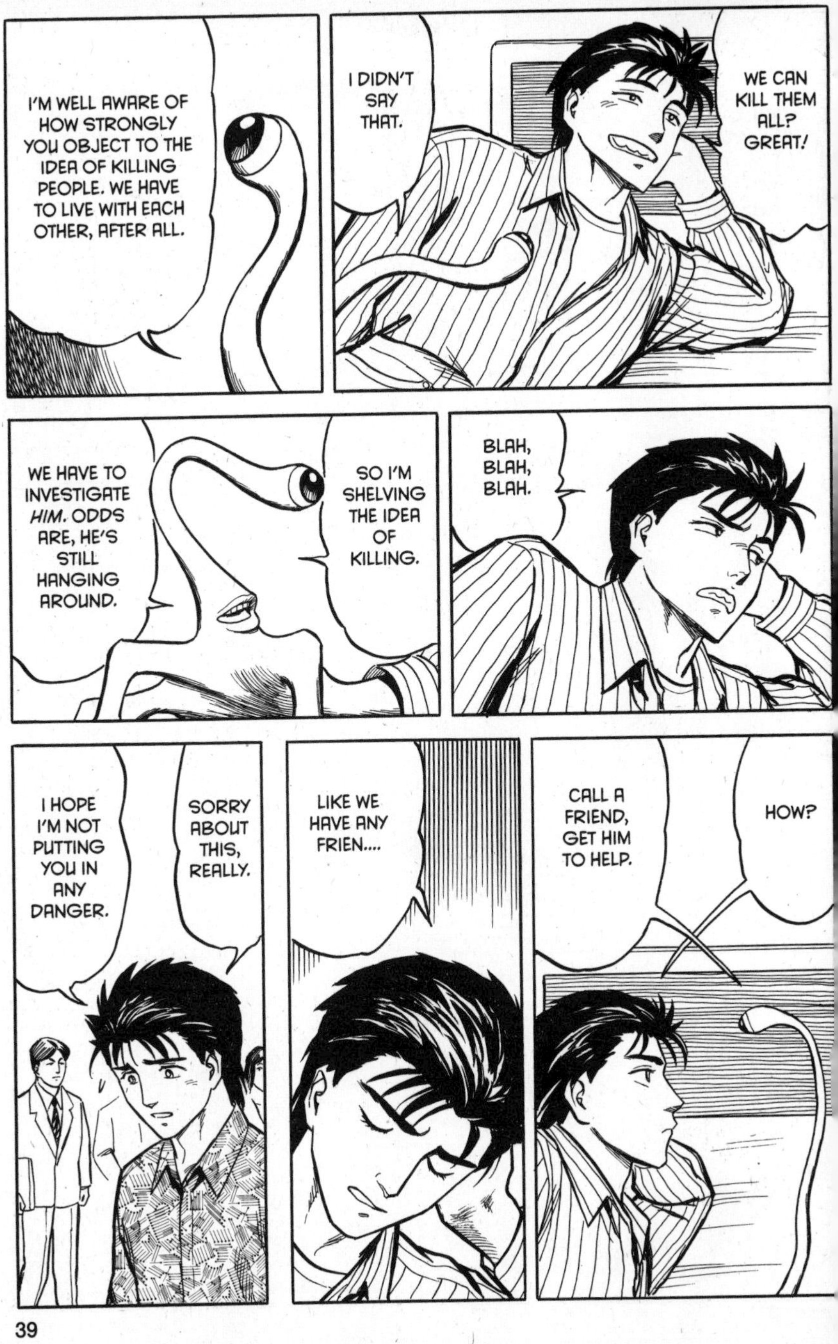
WE CAN KILL THEM ALL? GREAT!
I DIDN'T SAY THAT.
I'M WELL AWARE OF HOW STRONGLY YOU OBJECT TO THE IDEA OF KILLING PEOPLE. WE HAVE TO LIVE WITH EACH OTHER, AFTER ALL.
BLAH, BLAH, BLAH.
SO I'M SHELVING THE IDEA OF KILLING.
WE HAVE TO INVESTIGATE *HIM*. ODDS ARE, HE'S STILL HANGING AROUND.
HOW?
CALL A FRIEND, GET HIM TO HELP.
LIKE WE HAVE ANY FRIEN....
SORRY ABOUT THIS, REALLY.
I HOPE I'M NOT PUTTING YOU IN ANY DANGER.

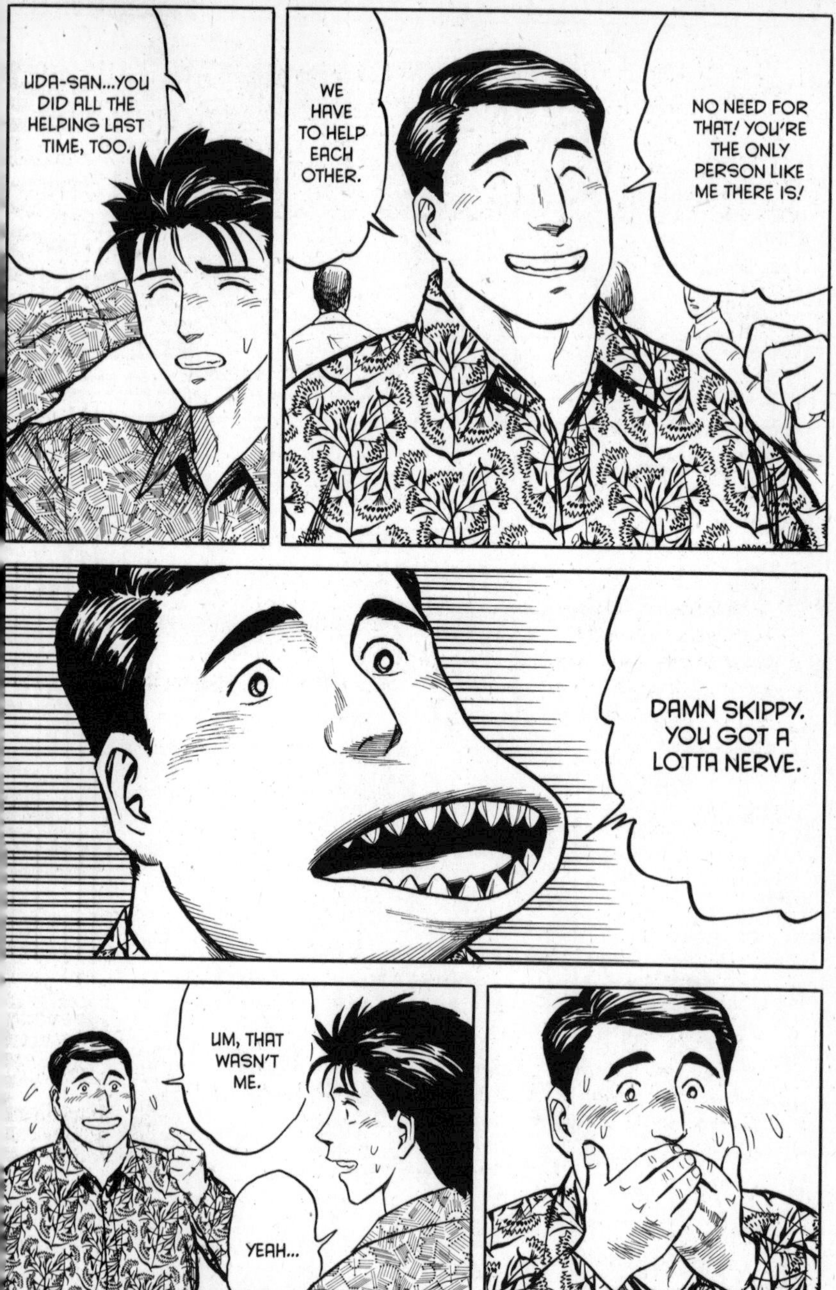
UDA-SAN...YOU DID ALL THE HELPING LAST TIME, TOO.
WE HAVE TO HELP EACH OTHER.
NO NEED FOR THAT! YOU'RE THE ONLY PERSON LIKE ME THERE IS!
DAMN SKIPPY. YOU GOT A LOTTA NERVE.
UM, THAT WASN'T ME.
YEAH...

CHAPTER 34: THE END

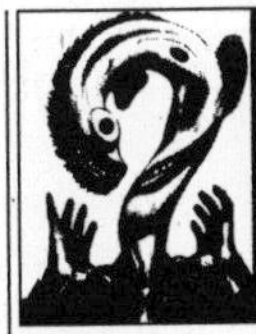

From the Monthly Afternoon Readers' page...

PARASYTE 5 vol. 5

"This is amazing. After I read the February issues, I wanted to talk about the future of mankind so badly I went over to my friend's house in the middle of the night."
(Saitama Prefecture, BE Suzume Boy, 28, Employee)

"You can tell it's *Afternoon* because the cover just stands out. How could I not pick it up?"
(Yamagata Prefecture, Funky Takayama, 29, Employee)

"Drawing the cover for the magazine is different from drawing for the trades—there are so many manga inside. I spent a long time deciding what kind of monster to draw. I mean, if I made it too bloody and grotesque, the bookstores might complain... so I tried to make a monster that was both scary and a little humorous. Did I pull it off?"
(Hitoshi Iwaaki)

(From *Afternoon,* March 1991)

"What would happen if a parasite in larva form planted itself in a parasite human? Would that parasite end up eating only other parasites? This is making my head hurt."
(Kanagawa Prefecture, Gambare!! Sawa Kishu, 34, Employee)

"And if a parasite that ate other parasites was infected by a parasite...this train of thought ends up sounding like mathematics, and is making me sleepy."
(Hitoshi Iwaaki)

(From *Afternoon,* February 1992)

HE READERS ASK. THE AUTHOR ANSWERS.

THE READERS ASK, THE AUTHOR ANSWERS

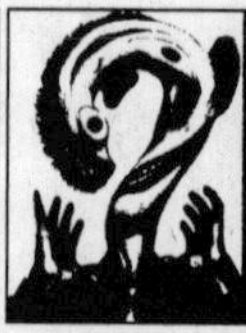

From the Monthly Afternoon Readers' page...

PARASYTE 5 vol. 5

"If Migi had ended up in the left hand, would he have been called Hidari?"
(Saitama Prefecture, Midari, 18)

"Well, of course. But the word Hidari just sounds like Hidari Tonpei or Hidari Bokuzen (do young people know them?) and brings to mind a doddering old man, so that wouldn't have been a good idea. Then again, the first man up Mt. Everest had a name an awful lot like that..."
(Hitoshi Iwaaki)

(From *Afternoon*, September 1992)

"This thing Shinichi's about to do...is it really just?"
(Oita Prefecture, Caterham7, 18, Student)

"Since he will save a number of people, it might be called that. But I believe that all justice is relative, and given how much time Shinichi has spent talking to something that isn't human, his sense of what is just might differ from that of ordinary humans."
(Hitoshi Iwaaki)

(From *Afternoon*, January 1993)

CHAPTER 35: INDIFFERENTLY NAMED

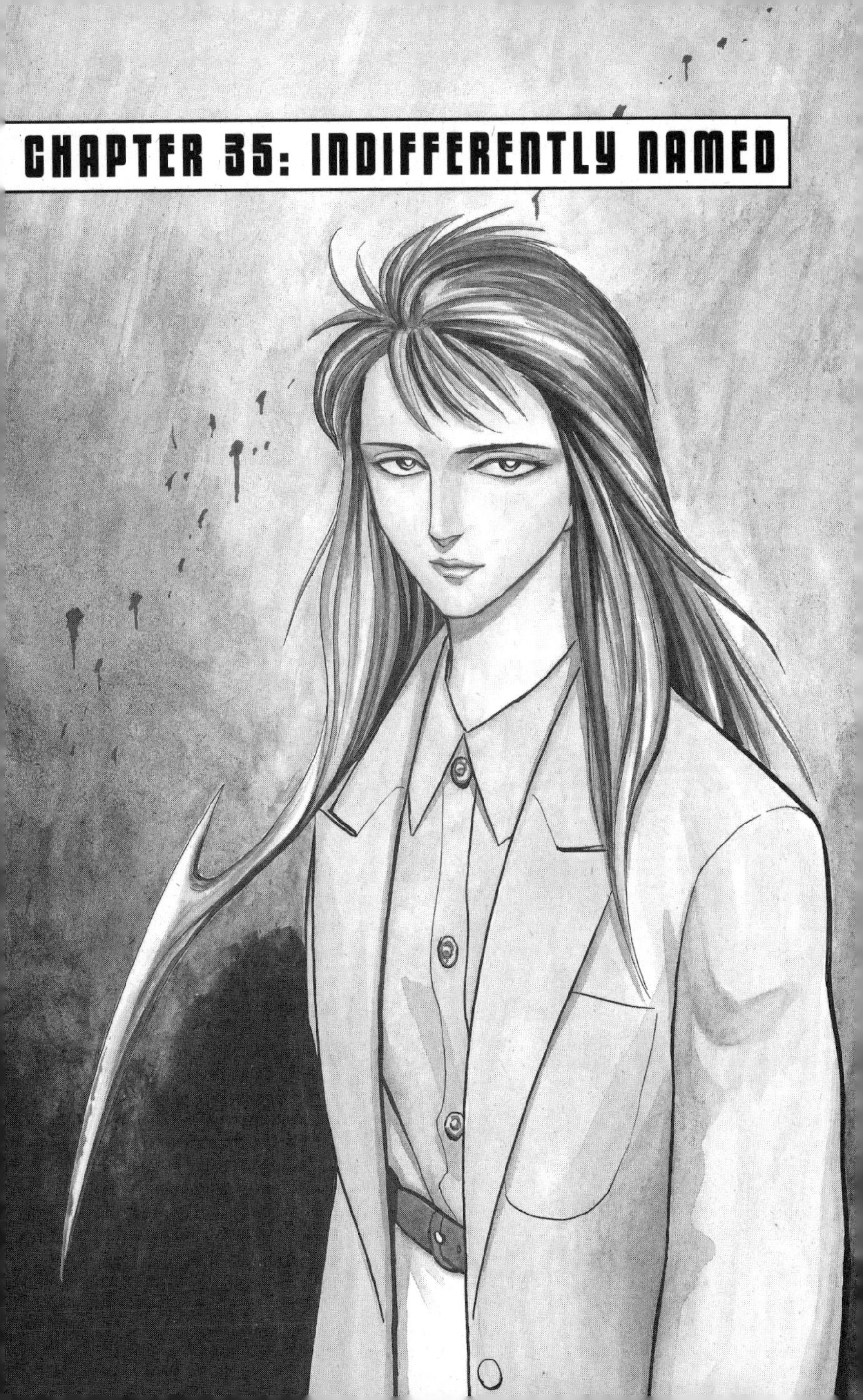

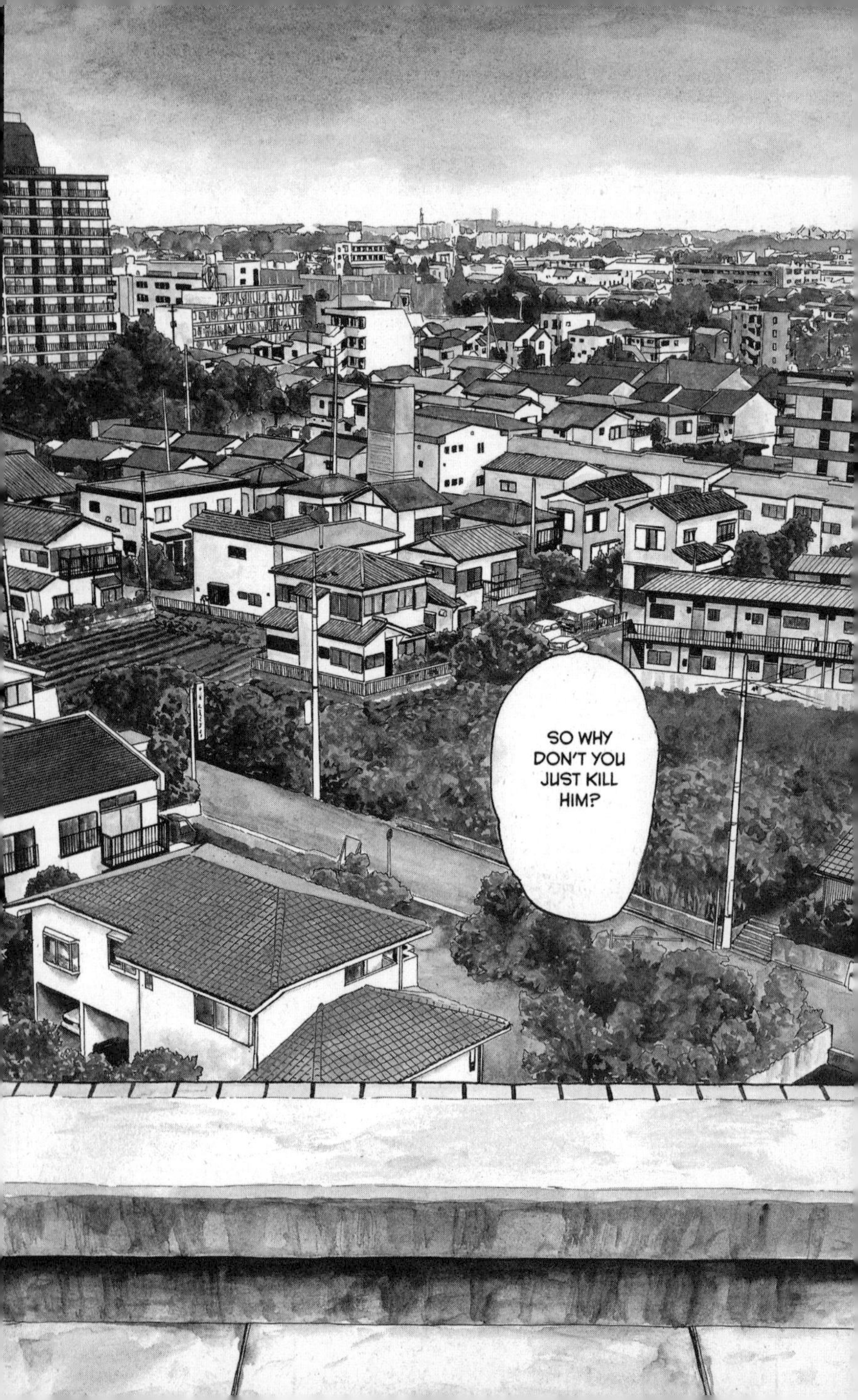
SO WHY DON'T YOU JUST KILL HIM?

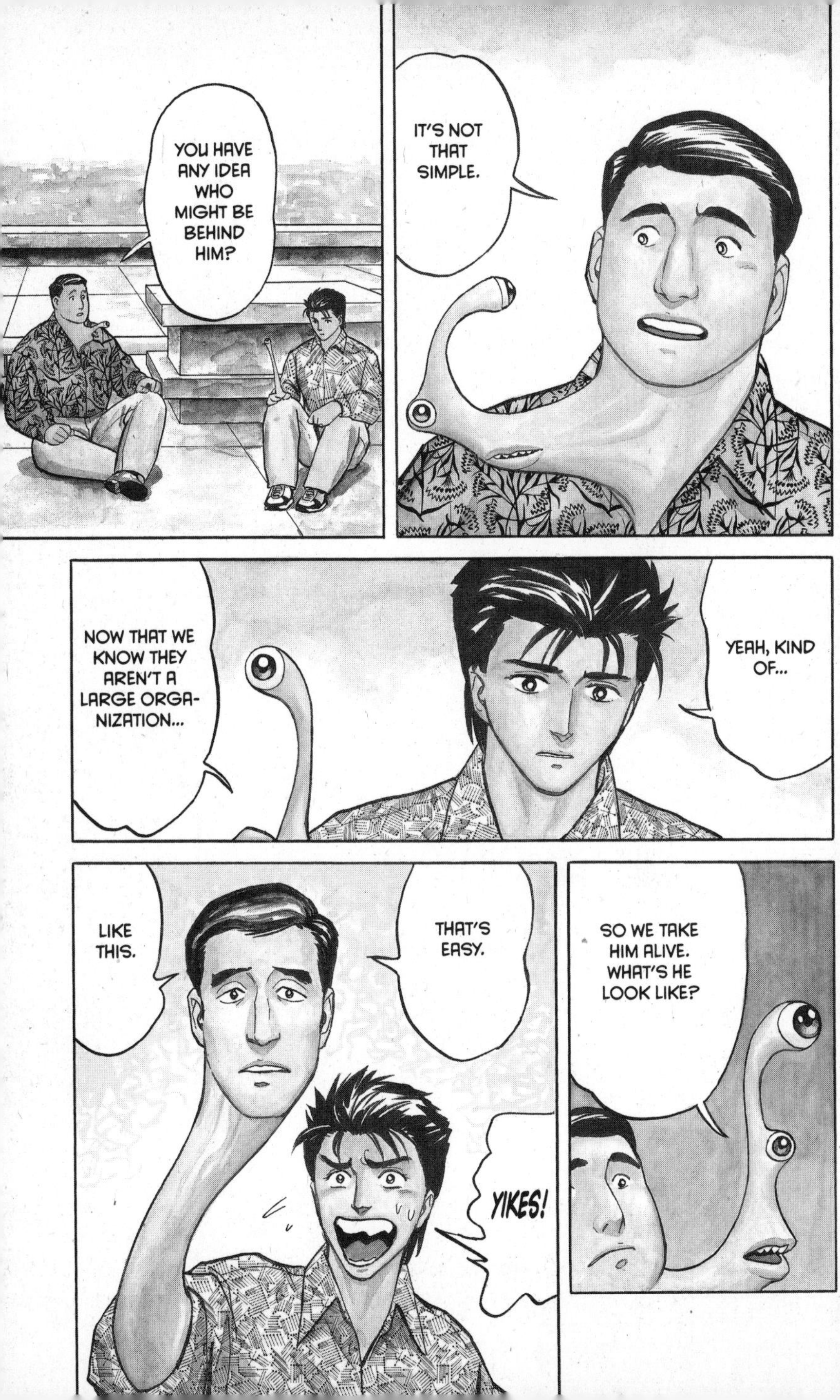
IT'S NOT THAT SIMPLE.
YOU HAVE ANY IDEA WHO MIGHT BE BEHIND HIM?
YEAH, KIND OF...
NOW THAT WE KNOW THEY AREN'T A LARGE ORGA-NIZATION...
SO WE TAKE HIM ALIVE. WHAT'S HE LOOK LIKE?
THAT'S EASY.
LIKE THIS.
YIKES!

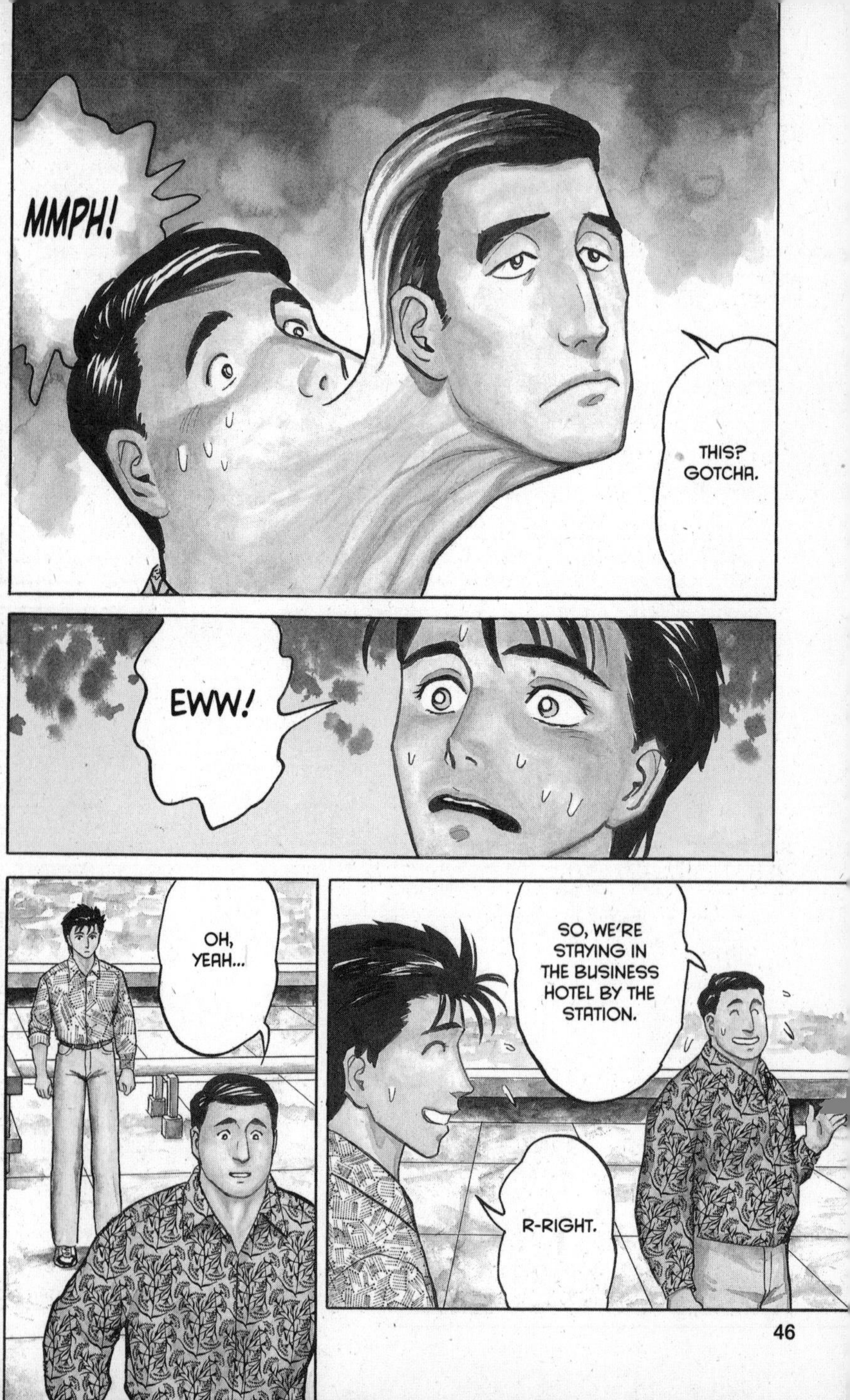
THIS? GOTCHA.
MMPH!
EWW!
SO, WE'RE STAYING IN THE BUSINESS HOTEL BY THE STATION.
R-RIGHT.
OH, YEAH...

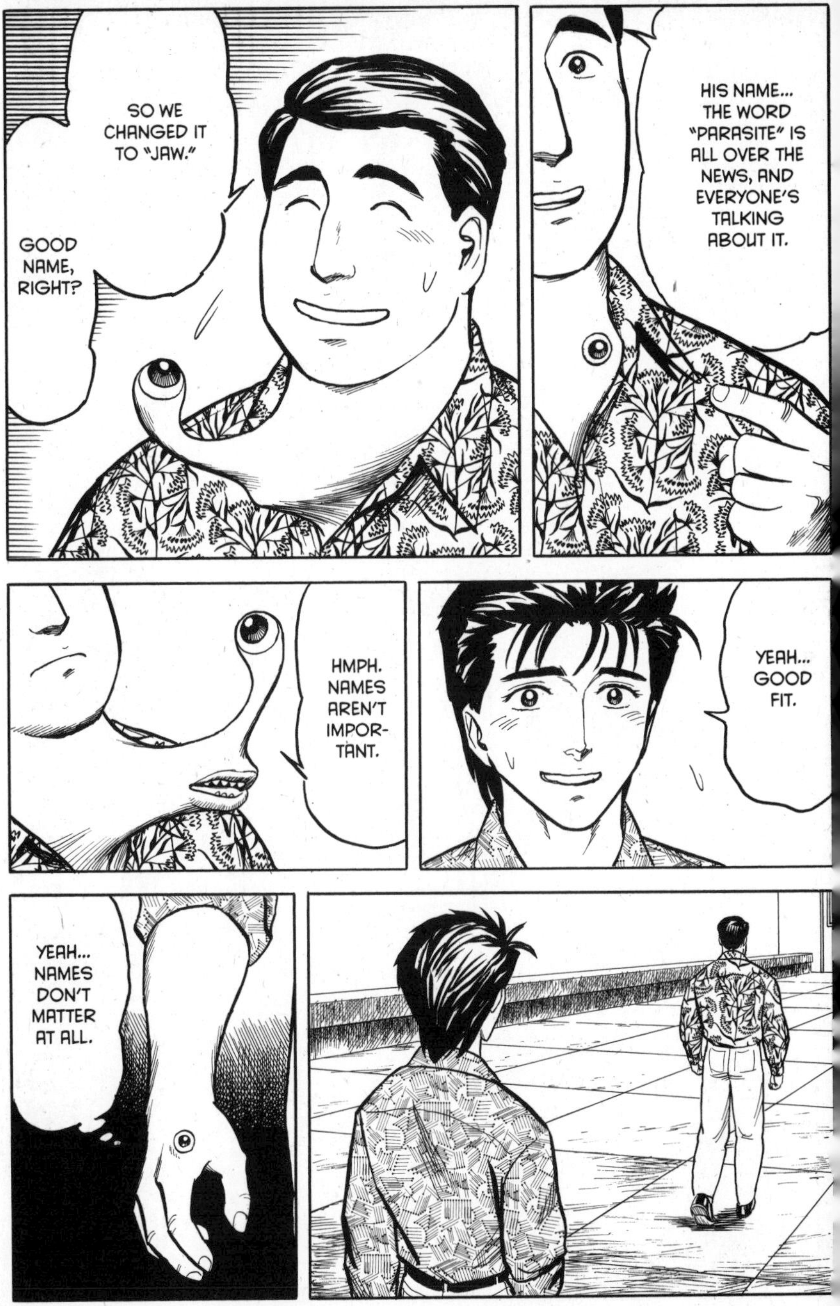
HIS NAME... THE WORD "PARASITE" IS ALL OVER THE NEWS, AND EVERYONE'S TALKING ABOUT IT.
SO WE CHANGED IT TO "JAW."
GOOD NAME, RIGHT?
YEAH... GOOD FIT.
HMPH. NAMES AREN'T IMPOR-TANT.
YEAH... NAMES DON'T MATTER AT ALL.

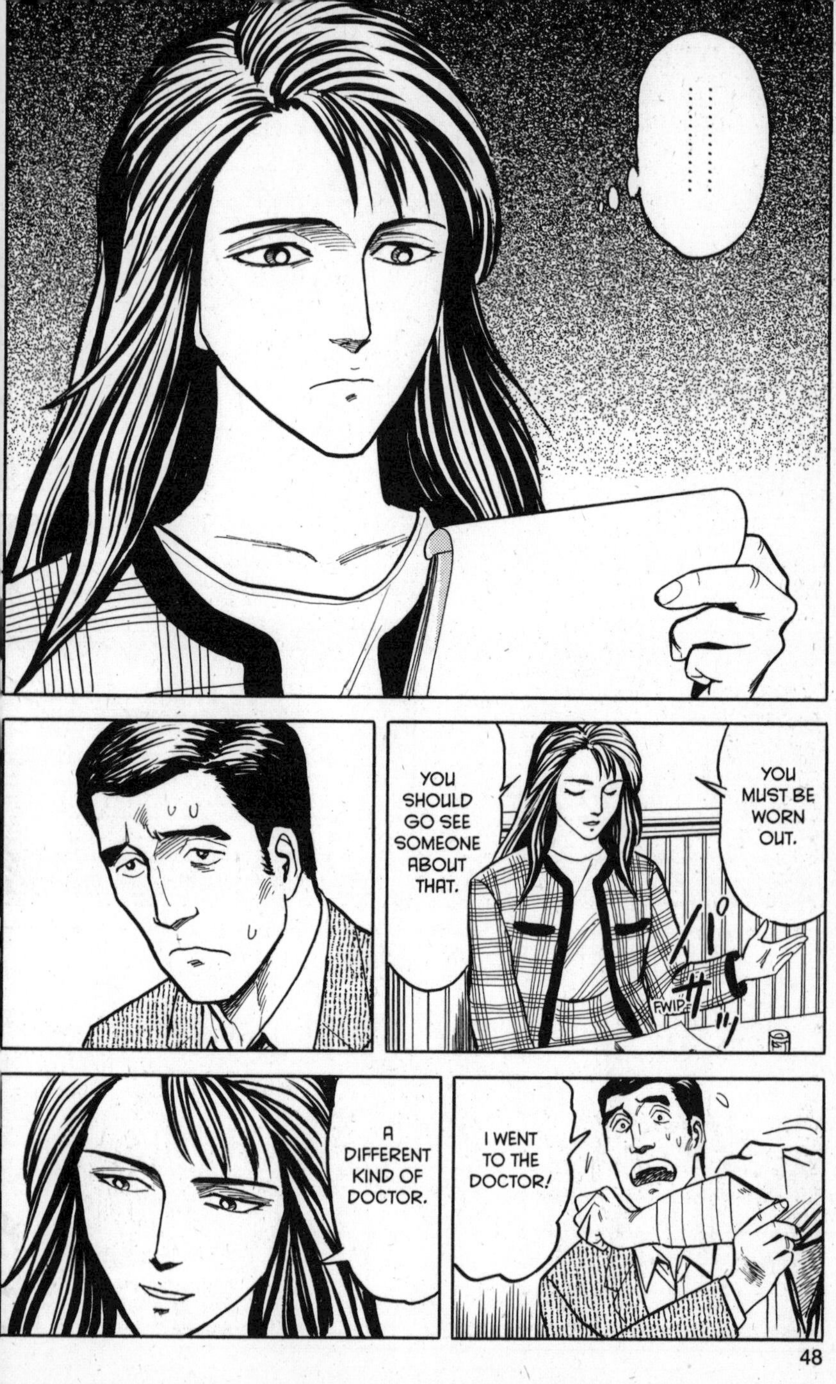
……
YOU MUST BE WORN OUT.
YOU SHOULD GO SEE SOMEONE ABOUT THAT.
FWIP
I WENT TO THE DOCTOR!
A DIFFERENT KIND OF DOCTOR.

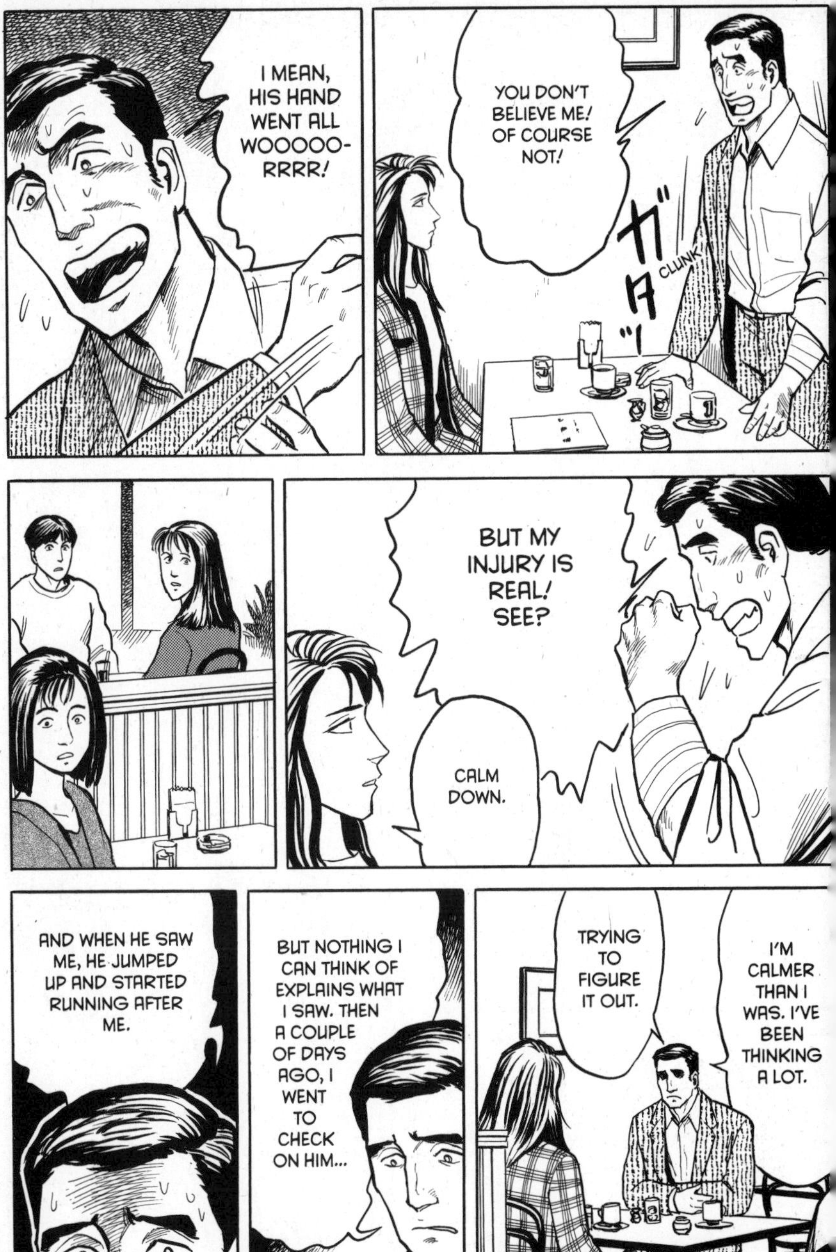

YOU DON'T BELIEVE ME! OF COURSE NOT!
ガタッ
CLUNK
I MEAN, HIS HAND WENT ALL WOOOOO-RRRR!
BUT MY INJURY IS REAL! SEE?
CALM DOWN.
I'M CALMER THAN I WAS. I'VE BEEN THINKING A LOT.
TRYING TO FIGURE IT OUT.
BUT NOTHING I CAN THINK OF EXPLAINS WHAT I SAW. THEN A COUPLE OF DAYS AGO, I WENT TO CHECK ON HIM...
AND WHEN HE SAW ME, HE JUMPED UP AND STARTED RUNNING AFTER ME.

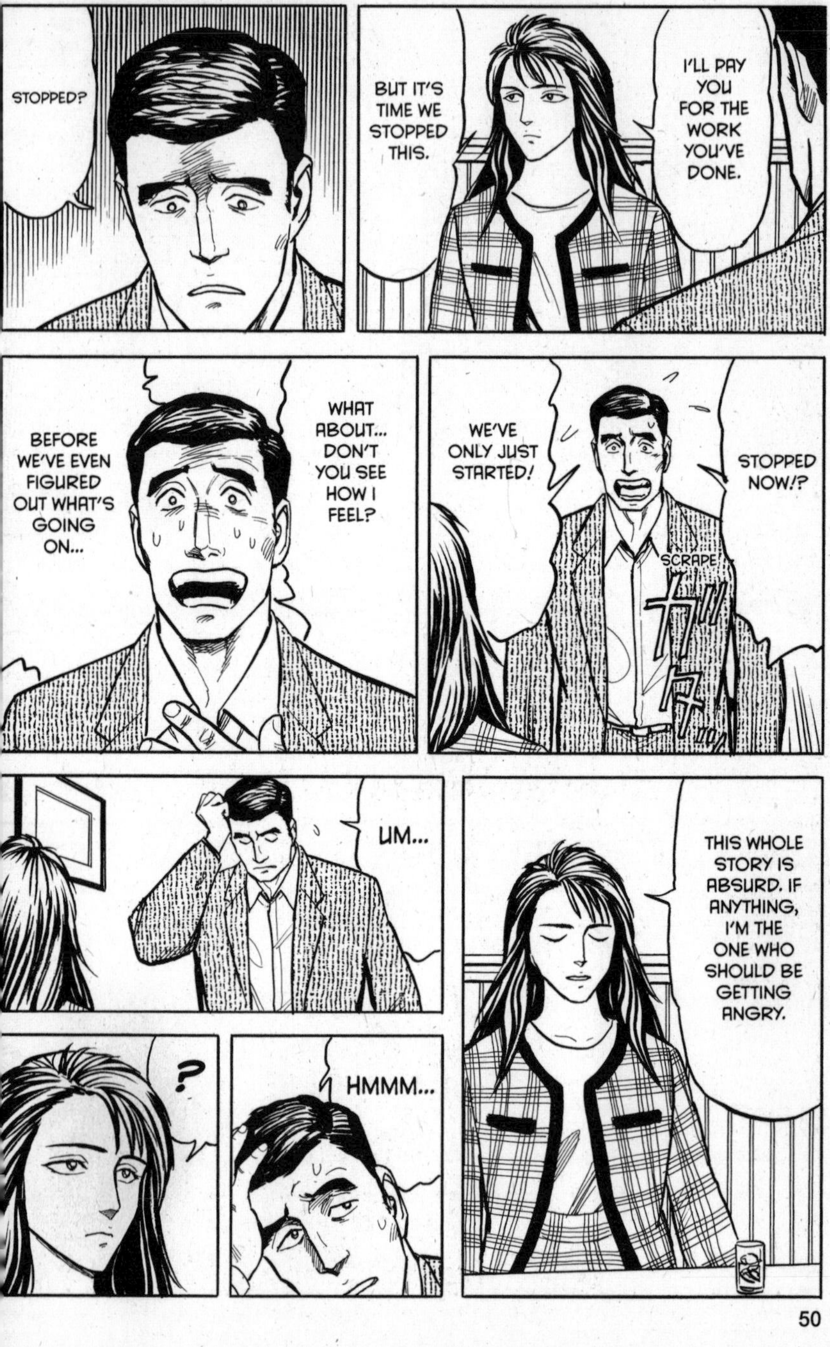
I'LL PAY YOU FOR THE WORK YOU'VE DONE.
BUT IT'S TIME WE STOPPED THIS.
STOPPED?
STOPPED NOW!?
WE'VE ONLY JUST STARTED!
SCRAPE
WHAT ABOUT... DON'T YOU SEE HOW I FEEL?
BEFORE WE'VE EVEN FIGURED OUT WHAT'S GOING ON...
THIS WHOLE STORY IS ABSURD. IF ANYTHING, I'M THE ONE WHO SHOULD BE GETTING ANGRY.
UM...
HMMM...
?

I JUST REMEMBERED!
WHEN IZUMI SHINICHI WAS FIGHTING THOSE DELINQUENTS... YOU ASKED ABOUT THE WAY HIS RIGHT HAND MOVED!
I HAVE NO IDEA WHAT YOU'RE TALKING ABOUT.
YOU SAID IT! I'M SURE OF IT! YOU KNOW SOMETHING!
THAT'S WHY YOU HIRED ME TO LOOK INTO HIM!
WHAT IS THAT THING? YOU WILL TELL ME, WON'T YOU?
I'VE HAD ENOUGH OF THIS.
GOOD DAY.
I'M NOT LETTING YOU OFF THAT EASILY!
ガッ
THUNK

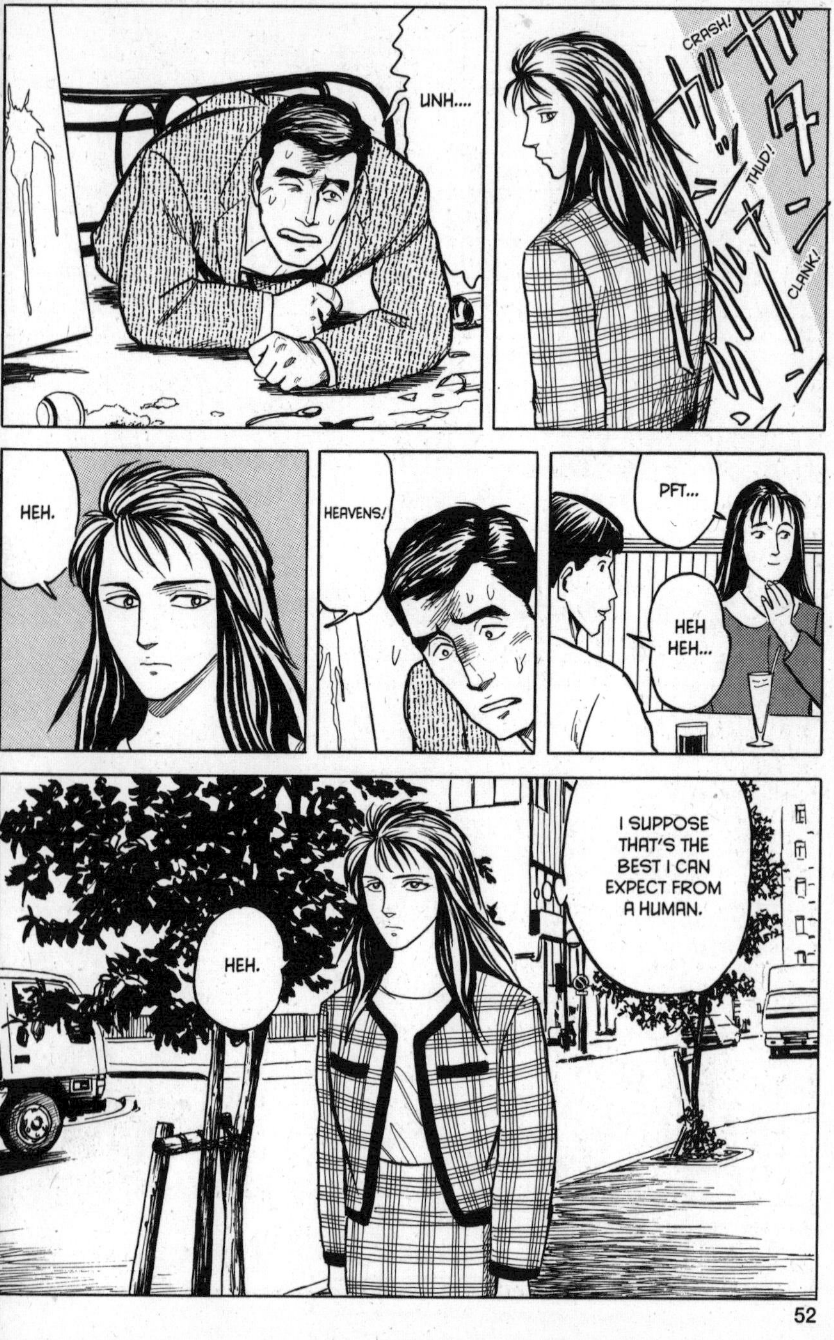
CRASH!
THUD!
CLANK!
UNH....
PFT...
HEH HEH...
HEAVENS!
HEH.
I SUPPOSE THAT'S THE BEST I CAN EXPECT FROM A HUMAN.
HEH.

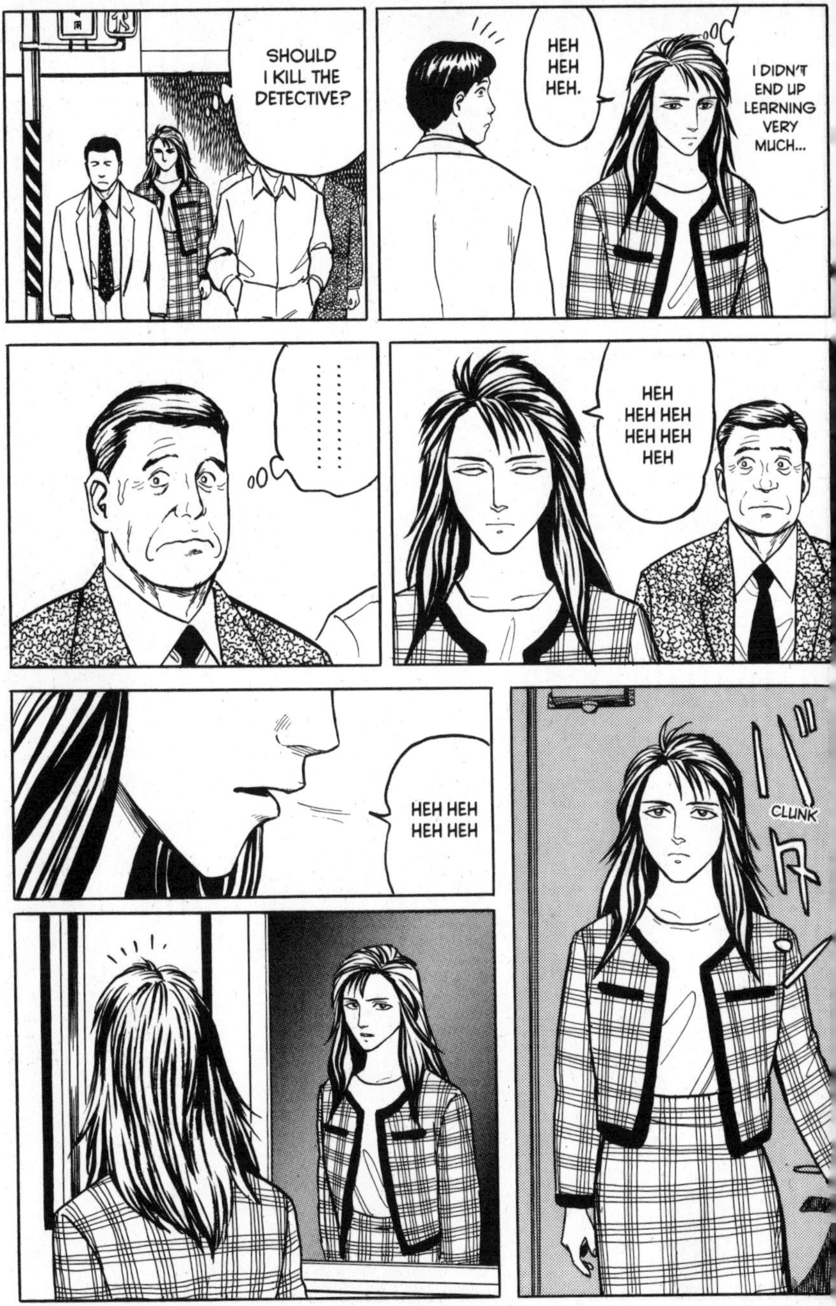
I DIDN'T END UP LEARNING VERY MUCH...
HEH HEH HEH.
SHOULD I KILL THE DETECTIVE?
HEH HEH HEH HEH HEH HEH
......
CLUNK
HEH HEH HEH HEH

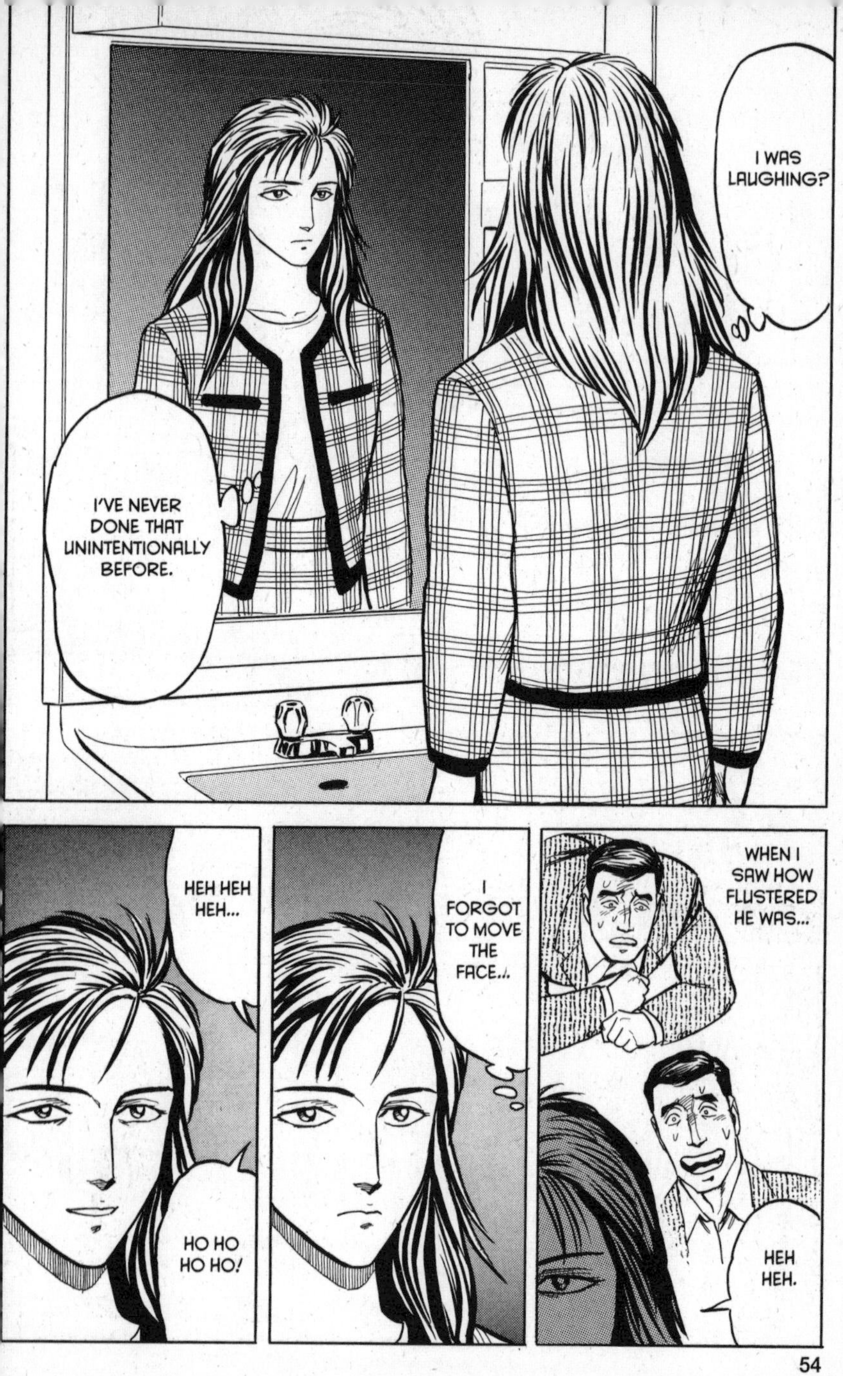
I WAS LAUGHING?
I'VE NEVER DONE THAT UNINTENTIONALLY BEFORE.
WHEN I SAW HOW FLUSTERED HE WAS...
HEH HEH.
I FORGOT TO MOVE THE FACE...
HEH HEH HEH...
HO HO HO HO!

AH
HA HA
HA
HA HA
HA

HA HA
HA
HA HA
HA
HA HA
HA
HA HA

WAA-
AAHH-
HHH!

AAA-
HH-
HHH!

UNH...

AH
HA!
HA!
HA!
HA!

WAAAAAAHH!

ああ
まん
ああ
まん
ああ

AHHHH-
HHH HA
HA HA HA
HA HA

WAAAAAAAHH!

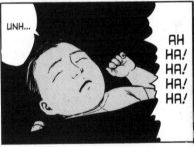

HA!
HA!
HA!
HA!
HA!

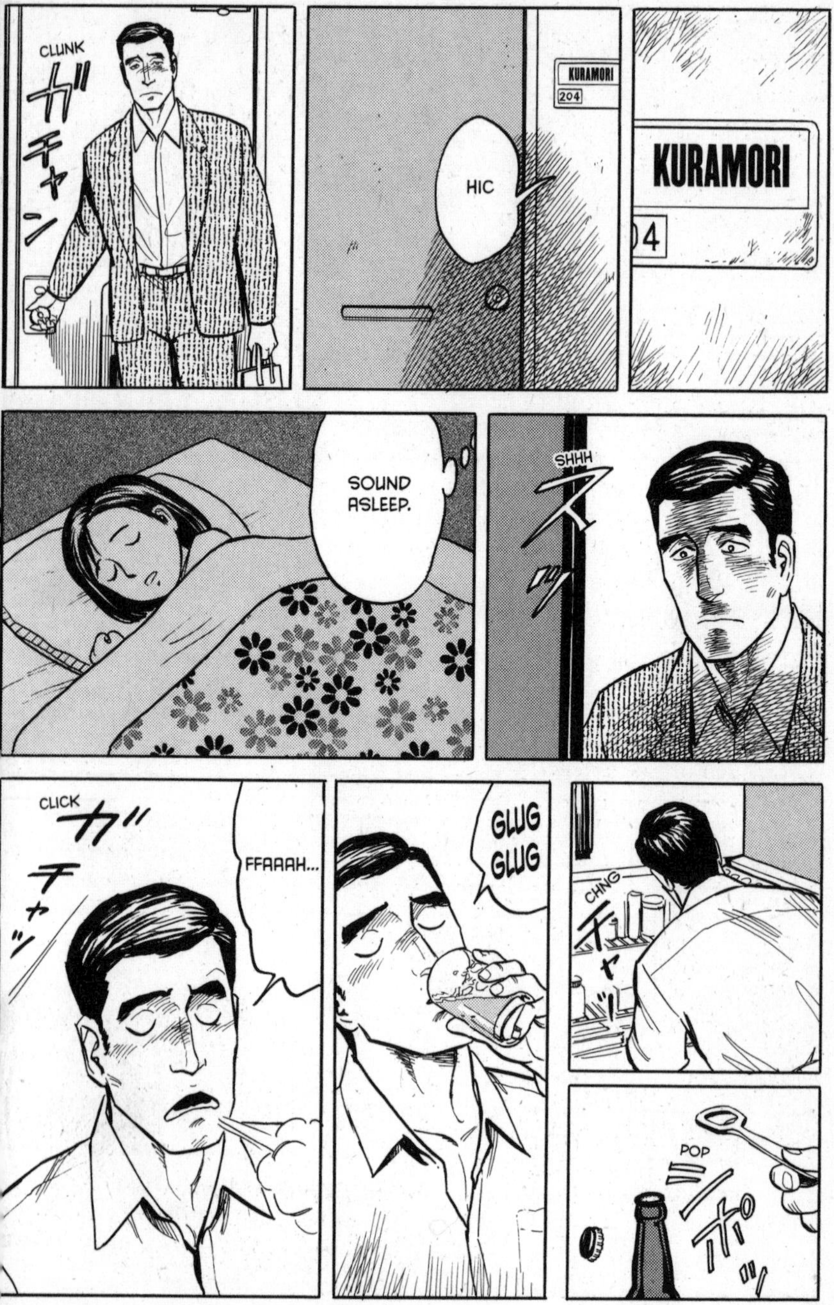
KURAMORI
04
KURAMORI
204
HIC
CLUNK
ガチャン
SHHH
スッ
SOUND ASLEEP.
CHNG
POP
GLUG GLUG
CLICK
カチャッ
FFAAAH...

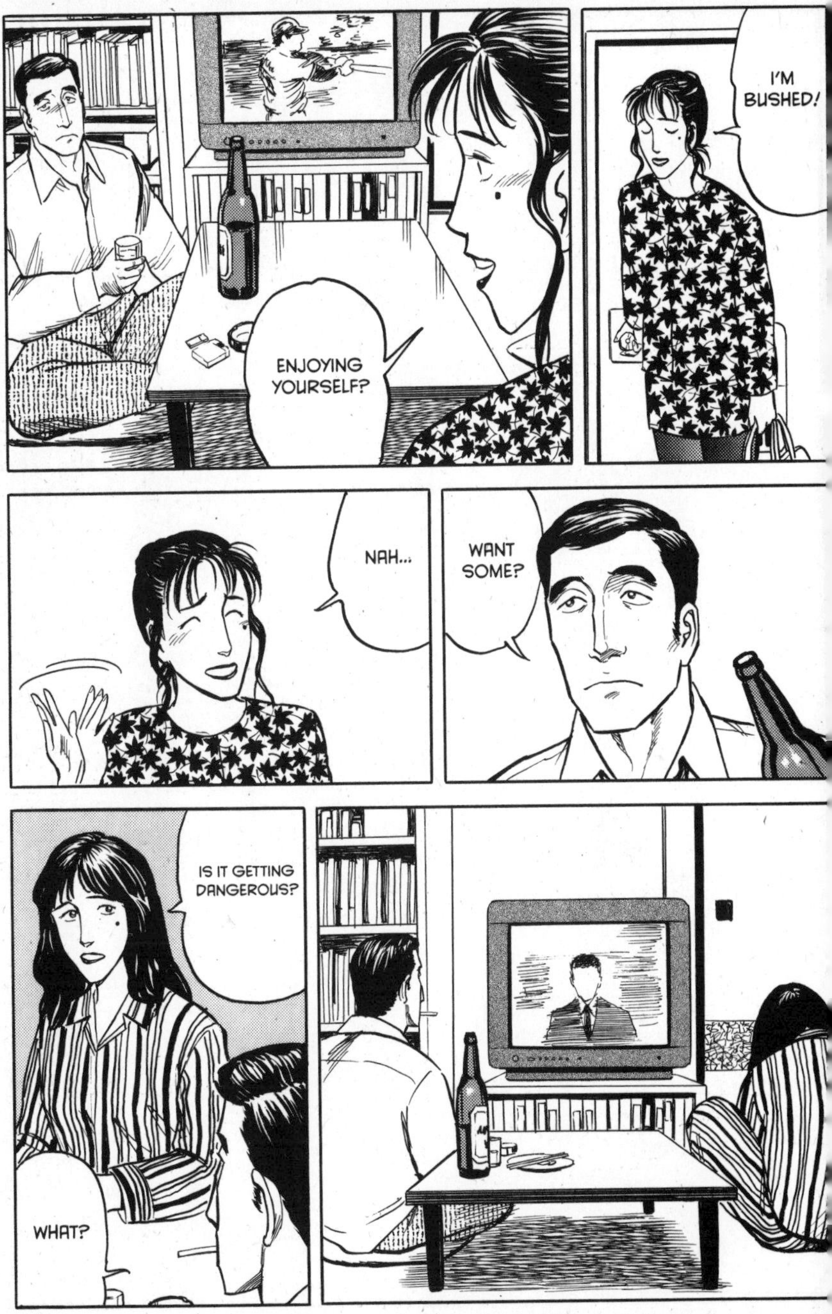
I'M BUSHED!
ENJOYING YOURSELF?
WANT SOME?
NAH...
IS IT GETTING DANGEROUS?
WHAT?

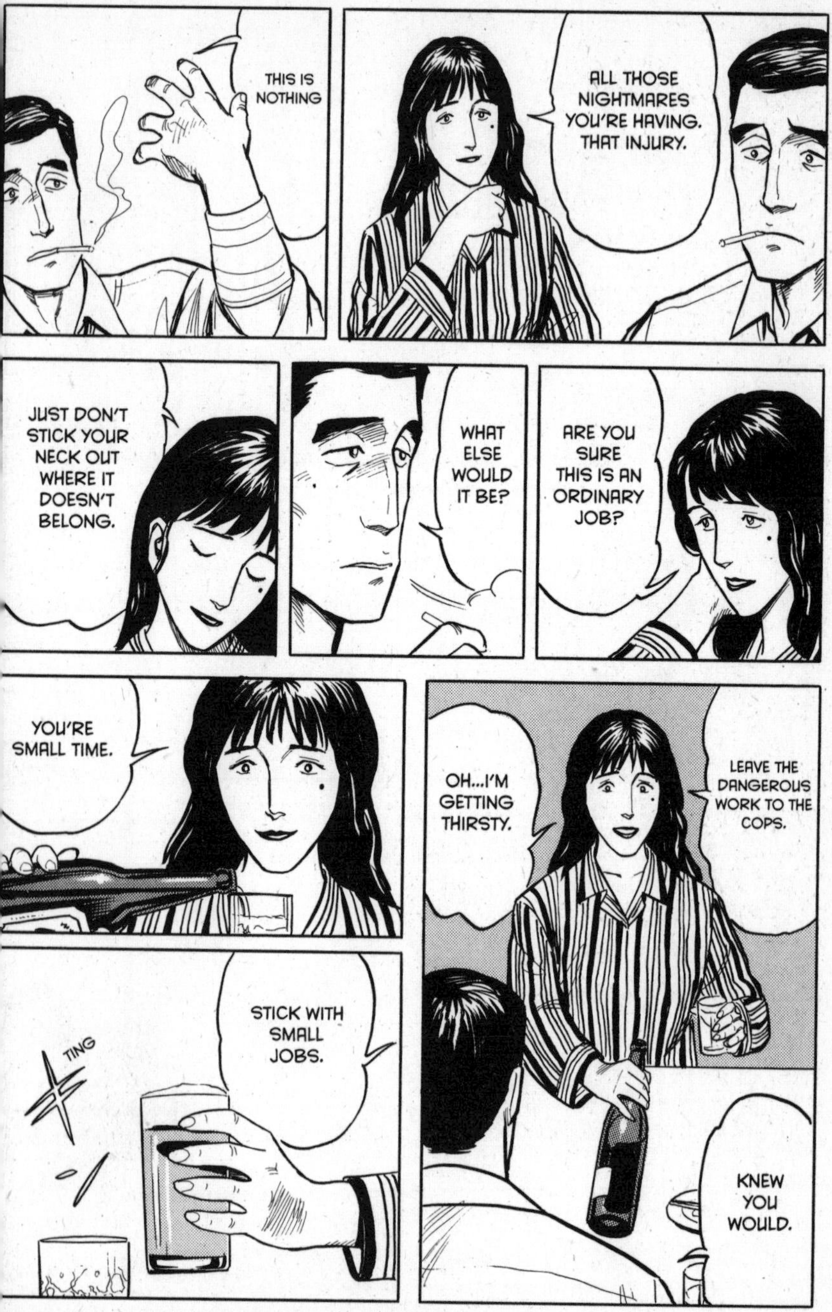
ALL THOSE NIGHTMARES YOU'RE HAVING. THAT INJURY.
THIS IS NOTHING
ARE YOU SURE THIS IS AN ORDINARY JOB?
WHAT ELSE WOULD IT BE?
JUST DON'T STICK YOUR NECK OUT WHERE IT DOESN'T BELONG.
LEAVE THE DANGEROUS WORK TO THE COPS.
OH...I'M GETTING THIRSTY.
KNEW YOU WOULD.
YOU'RE SMALL TIME.
STICK WITH SMALL JOBS.
TING

IS THAT ANY WAY TO TALK TO YOUR HUSBAND?

JUST YOU WATCH. I'LL SHOW YOU ALL.

MURDER MYSTERY

DETECTIVE NOVEL MASTERPIECES
DETECTIVE NOVEL MASTERPIECES
DETECTIVE NOVEL MASTERPIECES
DETECTIVE NOVEL MASTERPIECES
DETECTIVE NOVEL MASTERPIECES

BEST MYSTERY COLLECTION
BEST MYSTERY COLLECTION
BEST MYSTERY COLLECTION

THEY REACT TO THE SLIGHTEST SOUND. WE HAVE TO BE MORE CAREFUL THIS TIME.

59

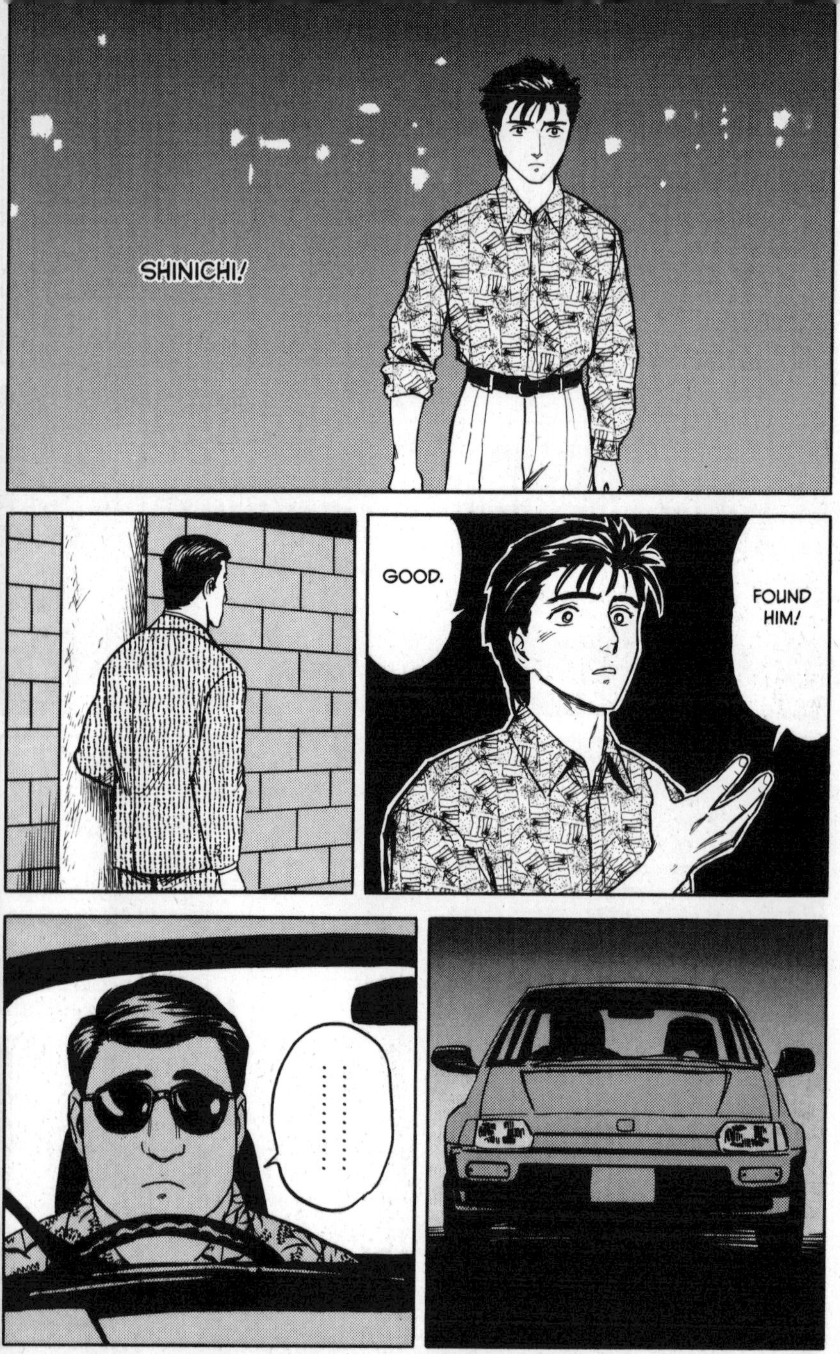
SHINICHI!
FOUND HIM!
GOOD.
......

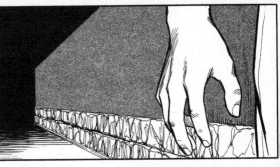

PARASITES SEND OUT A KIND OF SIGNAL THAT ALLOWS THEM TO SENSE EACH OTHER'S PRESENCE.

THEY CAN'T COMMUNICATE, AS IF BY TELEPHONE, BUT THEY CAN ARRANGE PRE-DETERMINED SIGNALS—FOR EXAMPLE, MORSE CODE.

OKAY.

MEET AT THE NEXT CORNER.

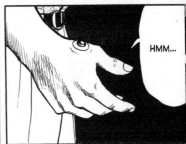

HMM...

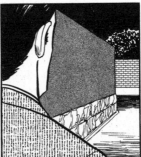

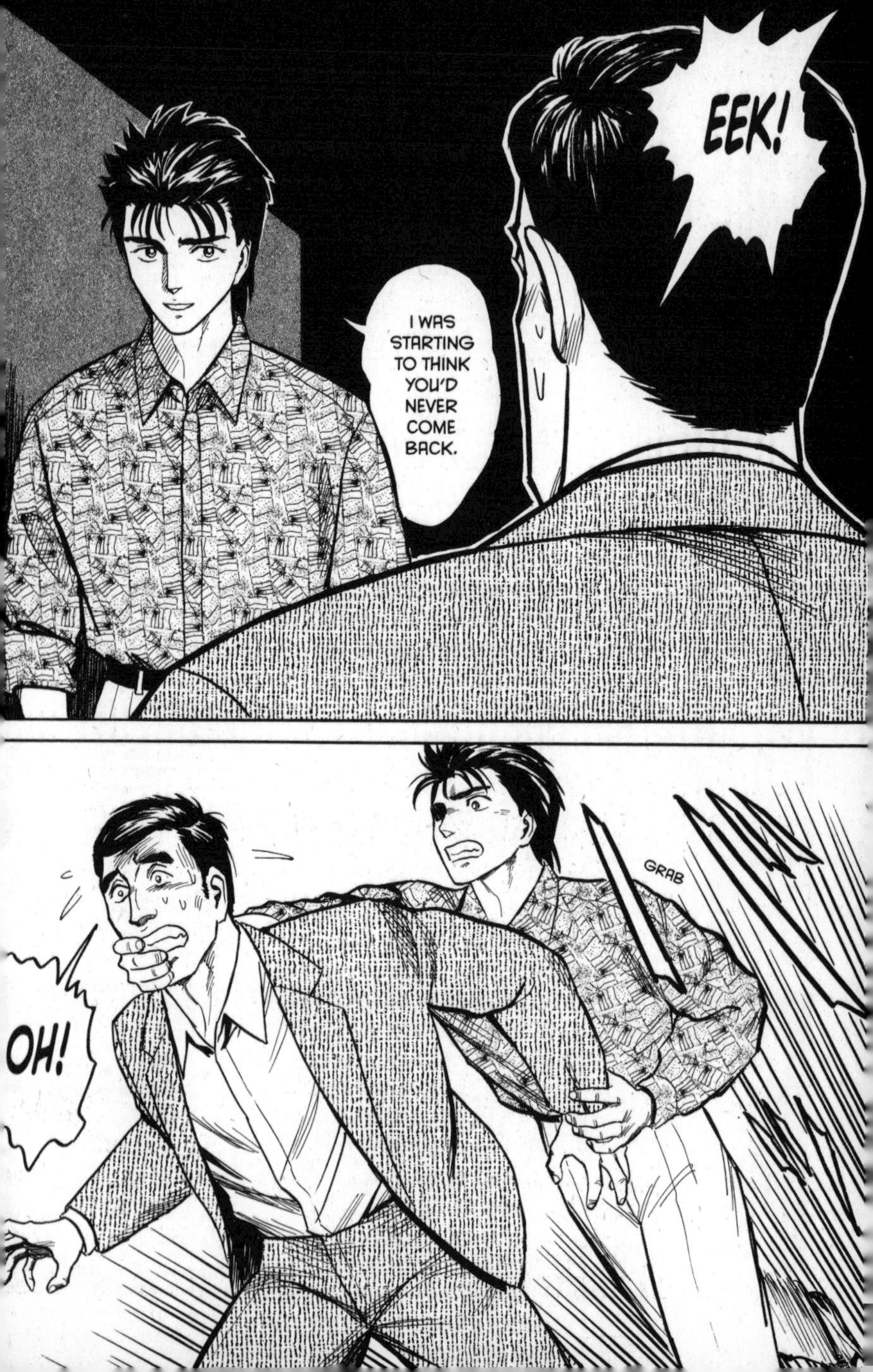
EEK!
I WAS STARTING TO THINK YOU'D NEVER COME BACK.
GRAB
OH!

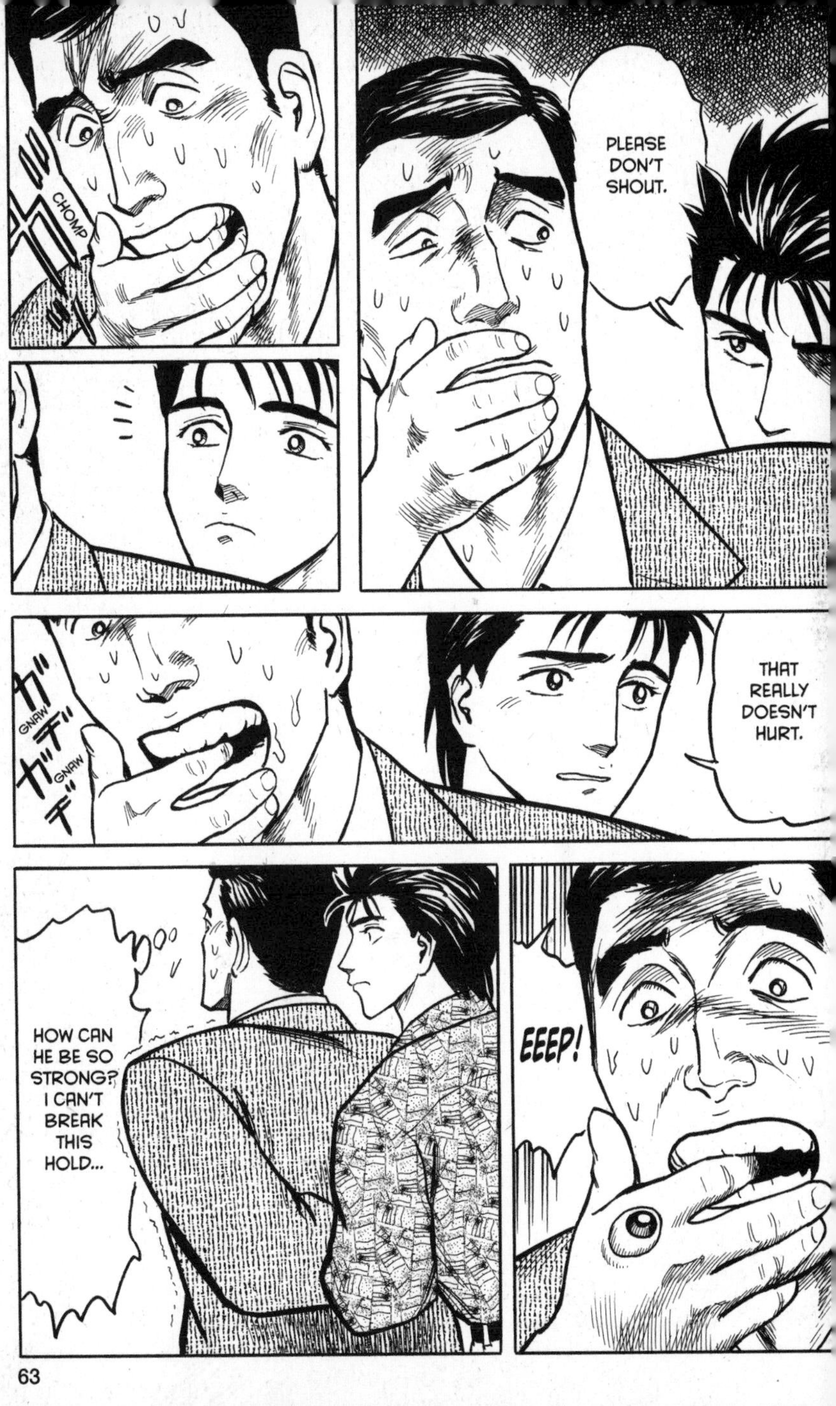
PLEASE DON'T SHOUT.
CHOMP
THAT REALLY DOESN'T HURT.
ガヂ GNAW
ガヂ GNAW
EEEP!
HOW CAN HE BE SO STRONG? I CAN'T BREAK THIS HOLD...

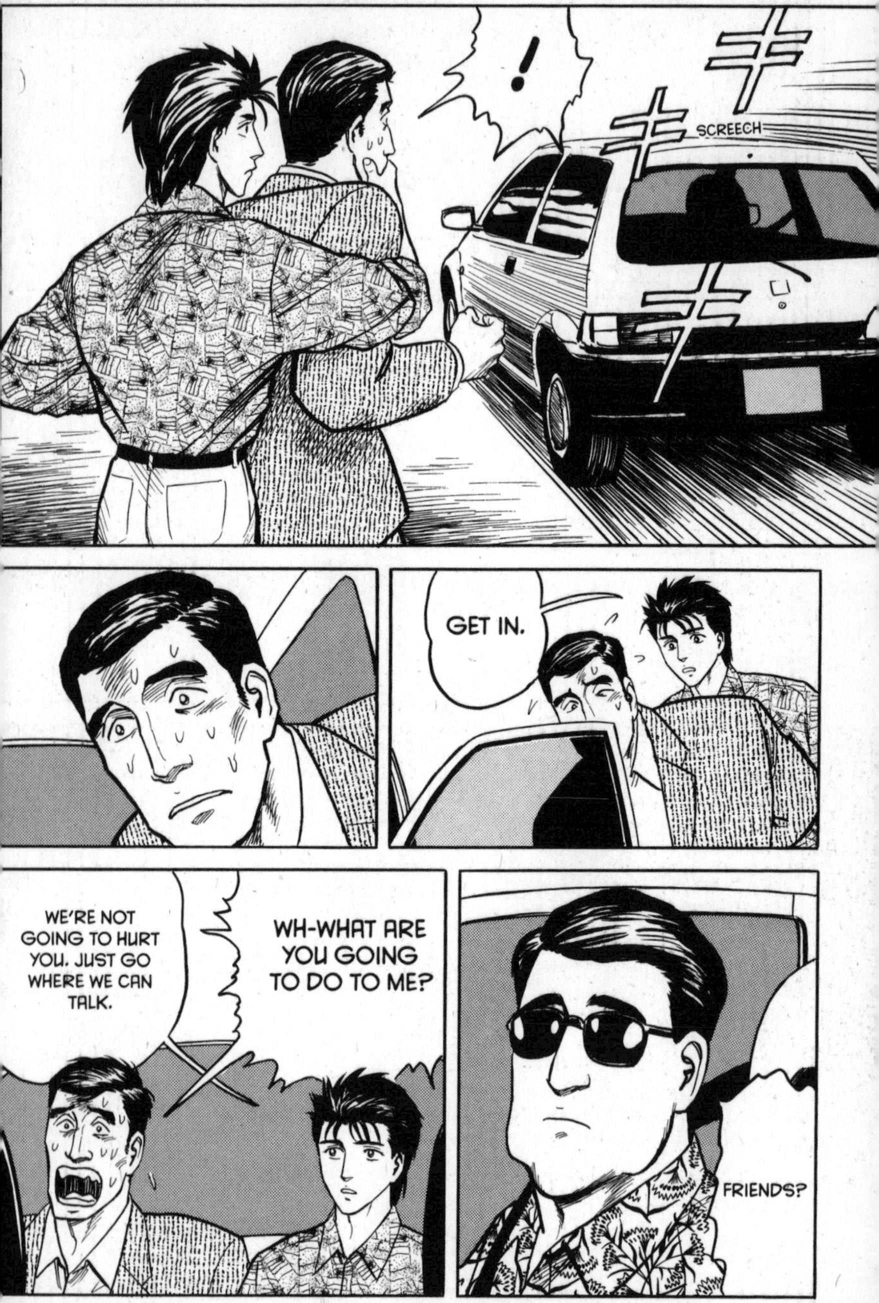
!
キキキ
SCREECH
GET IN.
FRIENDS?
WH-WHAT ARE YOU GOING TO DO TO ME?
WE'RE NOT GOING TO HURT YOU. JUST GO WHERE WE CAN TALK.

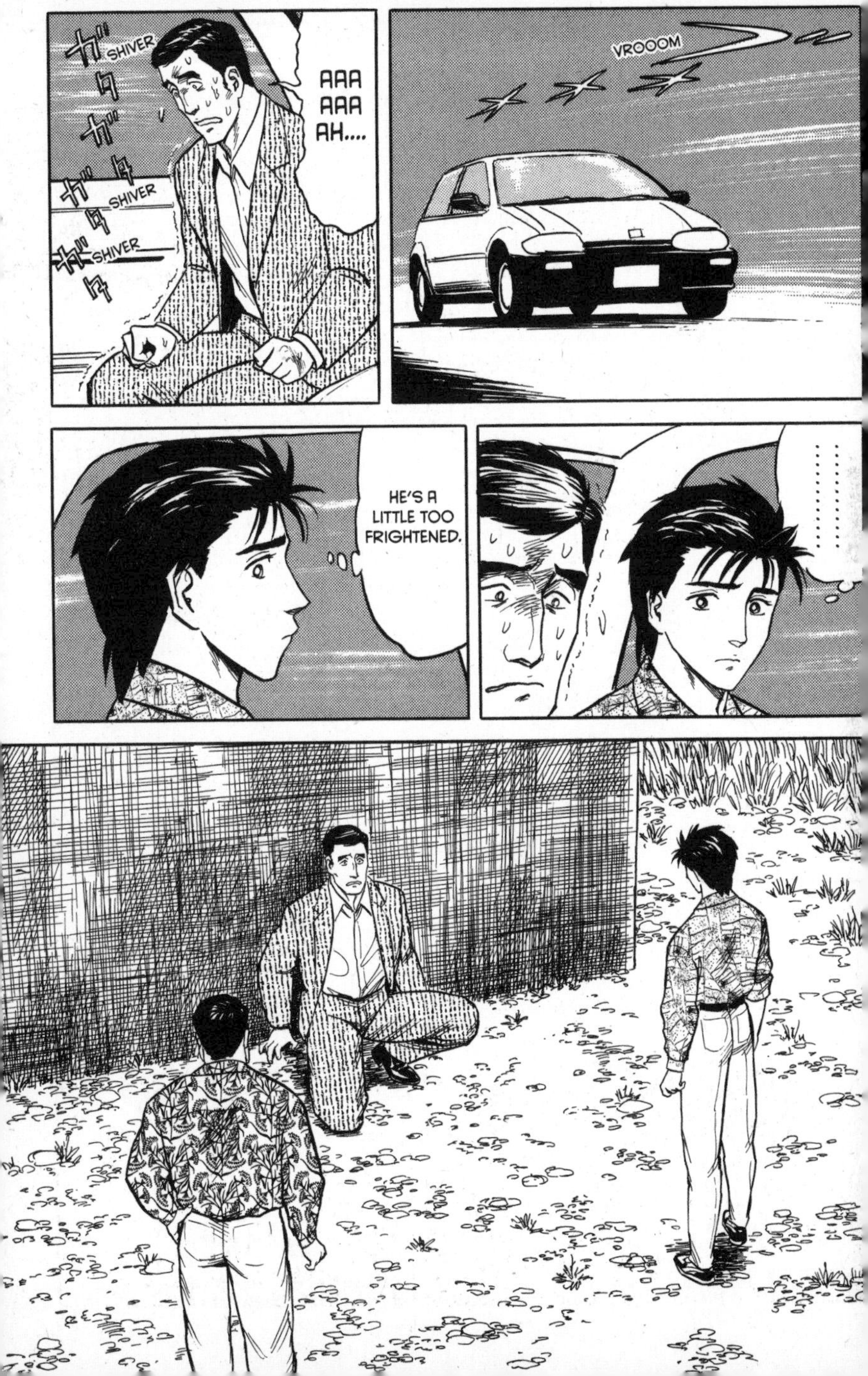

VROOOM
SHIVER
SHIVER
SHIVER
AAA AAA AH....
HE'S A LITTLE TOO FRIGHTENED.

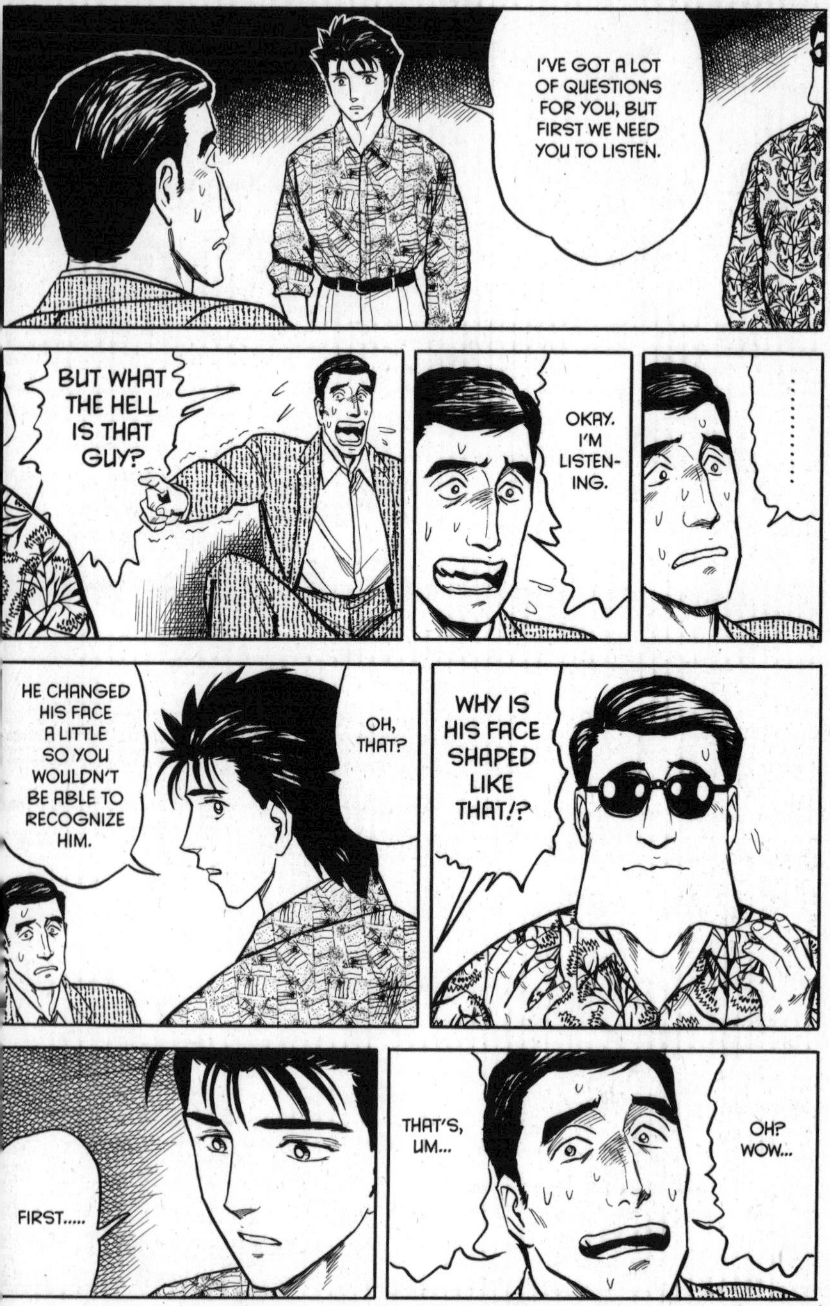
I'VE GOT A LOT OF QUESTIONS FOR YOU, BUT FIRST WE NEED YOU TO LISTEN.
......
OKAY. I'M LISTEN-ING.
BUT WHAT THE HELL IS THAT GUY?
WHY IS HIS FACE SHAPED LIKE THAT!?
OH, THAT?
HE CHANGED HIS FACE A LITTLE SO YOU WOULDN'T BE ABLE TO RECOGNIZE HIM.
OH? WOW...
THAT'S, UM...
FIRST.....

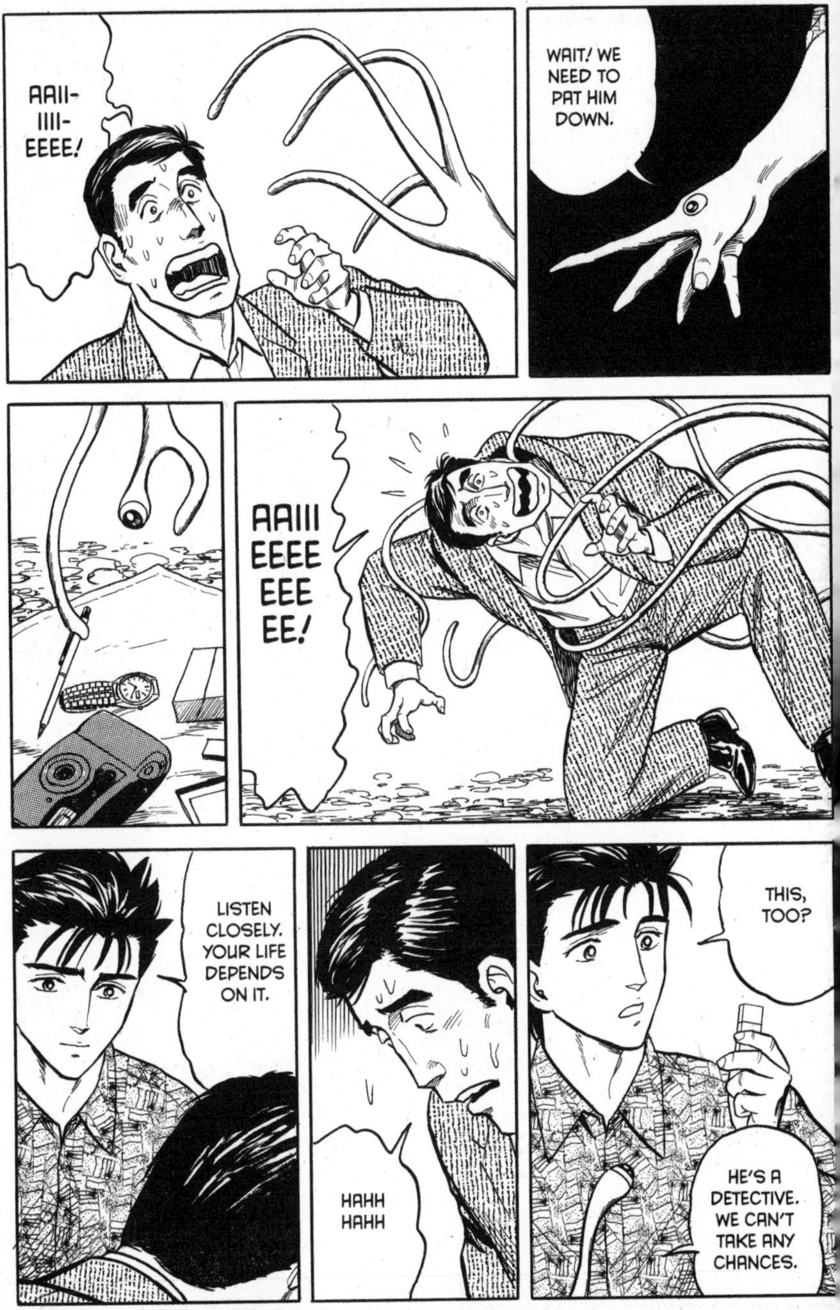
WAIT! WE NEED TO PAT HIM DOWN.
AAII-IIII-EEEE!
AAIIII EEEE EEE EE!
THIS, TOO?
HE'S A DETECTIVE. WE CAN'T TAKE ANY CHANCES.
HAHH HAHH
LISTEN CLOSELY. YOUR LIFE DEPENDS ON IT.

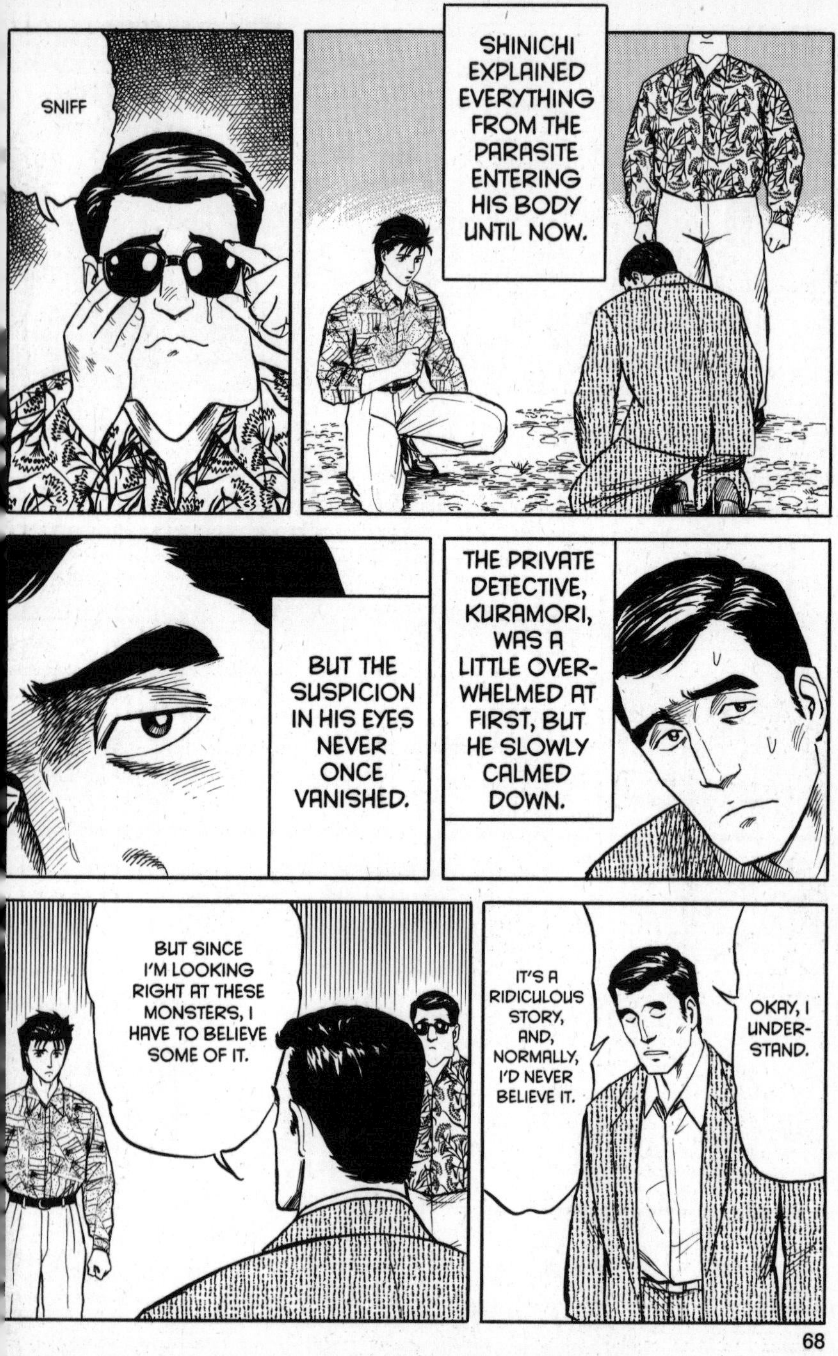
SHINICHI EXPLAINED EVERYTHING FROM THE PARASITE ENTERING HIS BODY UNTIL NOW.
SNIFF
THE PRIVATE DETECTIVE, KURAMORI, WAS A LITTLE OVER-WHELMED AT FIRST, BUT HE SLOWLY CALMED DOWN.
BUT THE SUSPICION IN HIS EYES NEVER ONCE VANISHED.
OKAY, I UNDER-STAND.
IT'S A RIDICULOUS STORY, AND, NORMALLY, I'D NEVER BELIEVE IT.
BUT SINCE I'M LOOKING RIGHT AT THESE MONSTERS, I HAVE TO BELIEVE SOME OF IT.

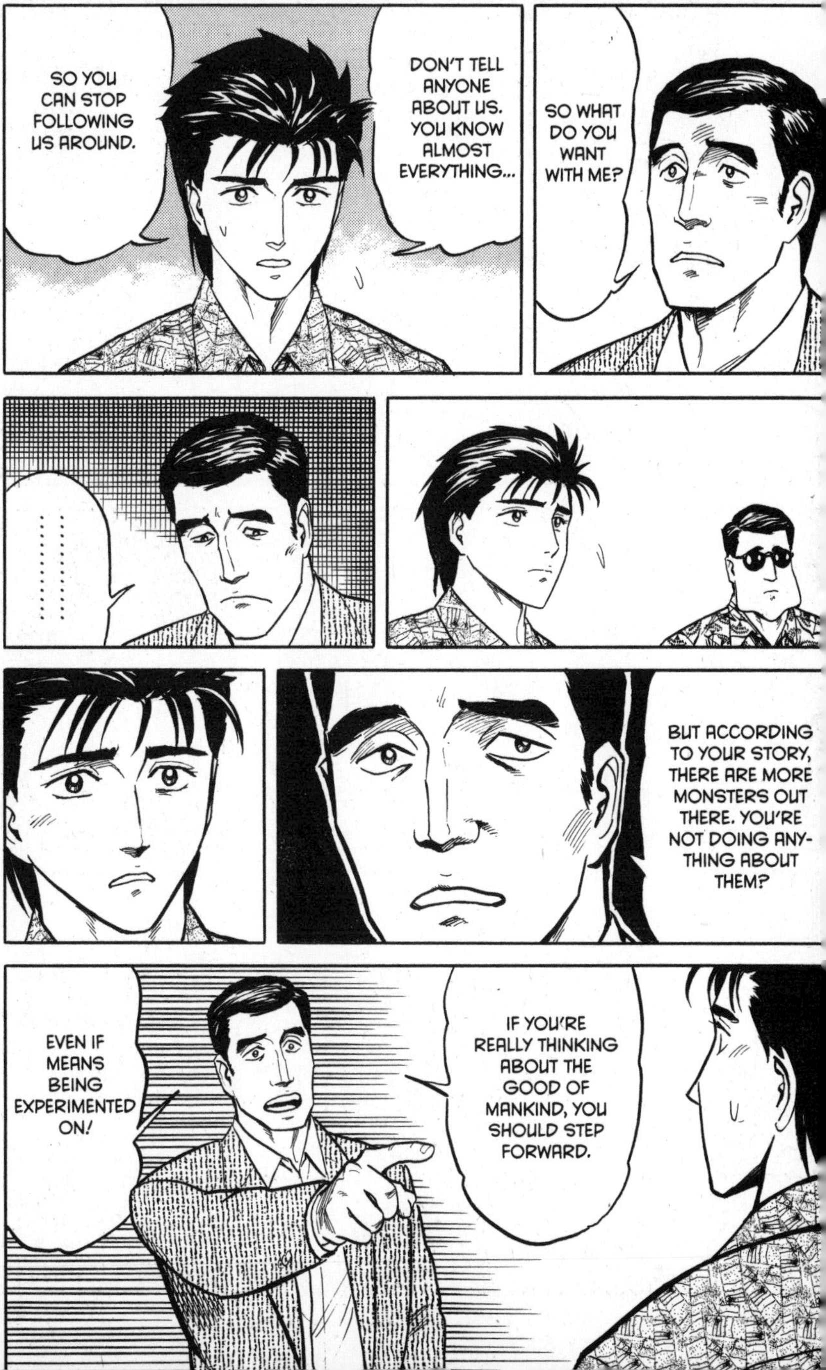
SO WHAT DO YOU WANT WITH ME?
DON'T TELL ANYONE ABOUT US. YOU KNOW ALMOST EVERYTHING...
SO YOU CAN STOP FOLLOWING US AROUND.
......
BUT ACCORDING TO YOUR STORY, THERE ARE MORE MONSTERS OUT THERE. YOU'RE NOT DOING ANY-THING ABOUT THEM?
IF YOU'RE REALLY THINKING ABOUT THE GOOD OF MANKIND, YOU SHOULD STEP FORWARD.
EVEN IF MEANS BEING EXPERIMENTED ON!

SACRIFICE YOURSELF FOR THE COMMON GOOD! THAT'S WHAT BEING HUMAN MEANS!

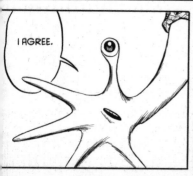

I AGREE.

I TOLD YOU WE SHOULD KILL HIM.

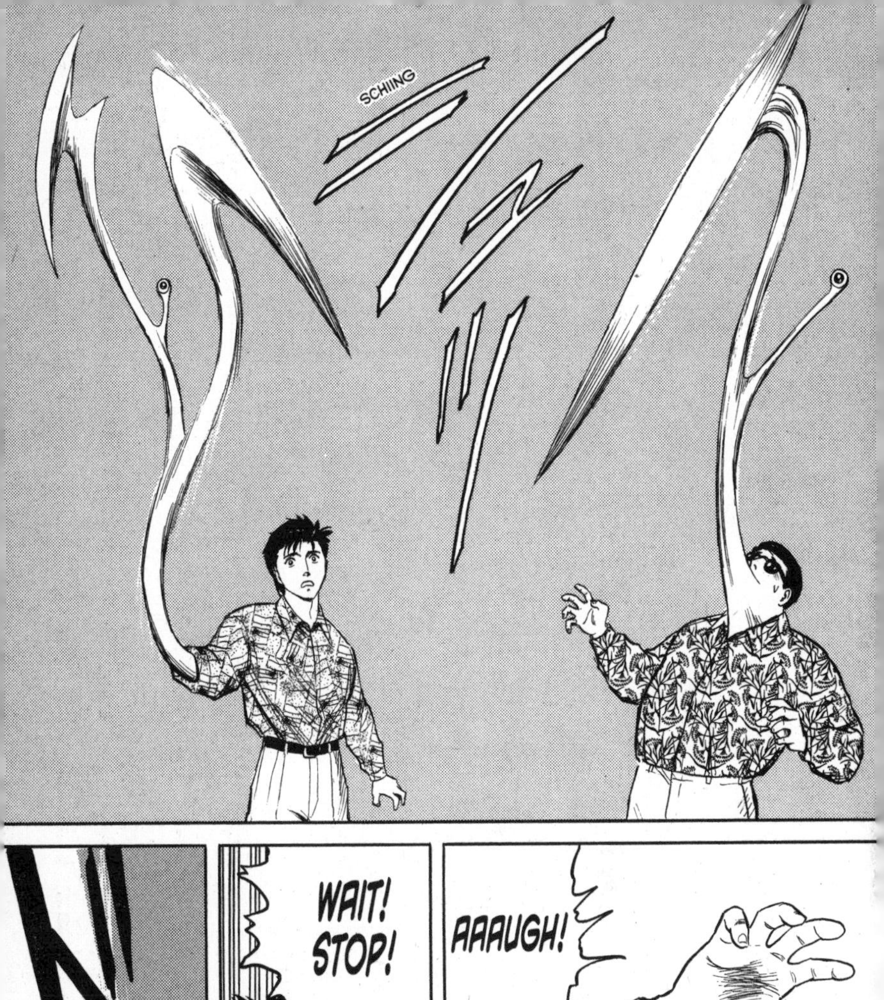
SCHIING
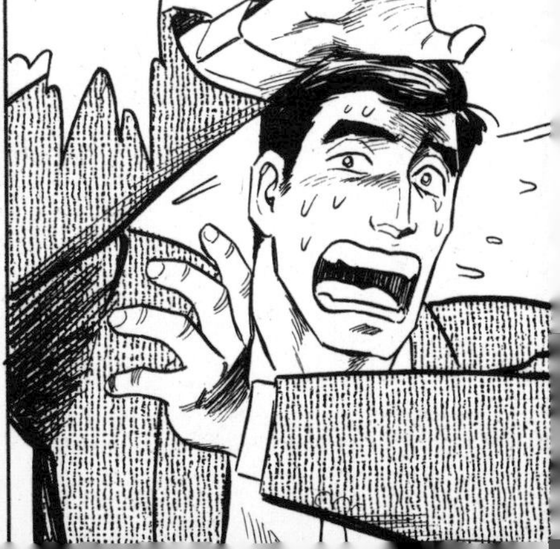
AAAUGH!
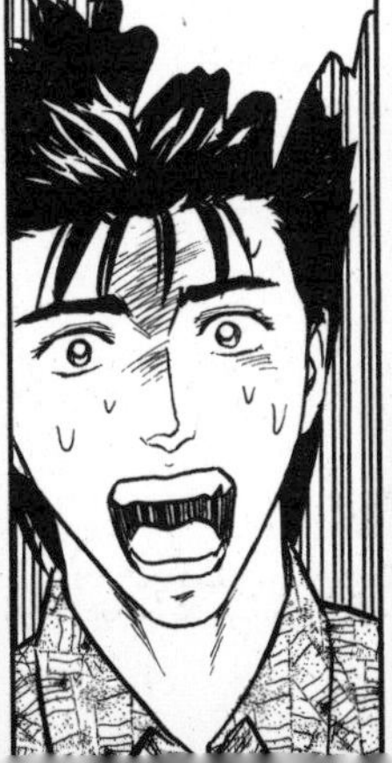
WAIT! STOP!
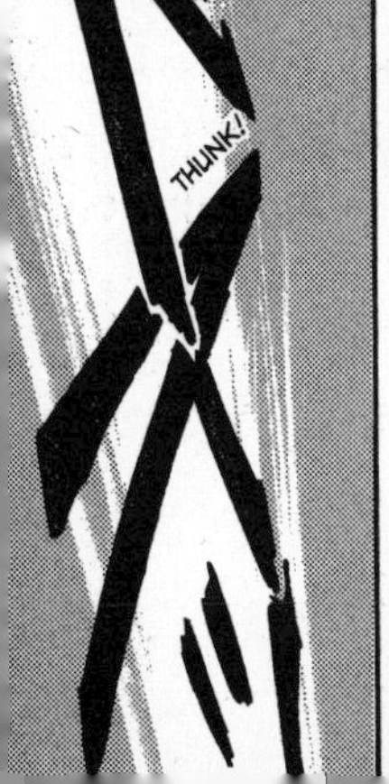
THUNK!

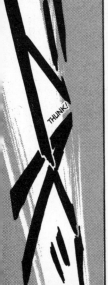

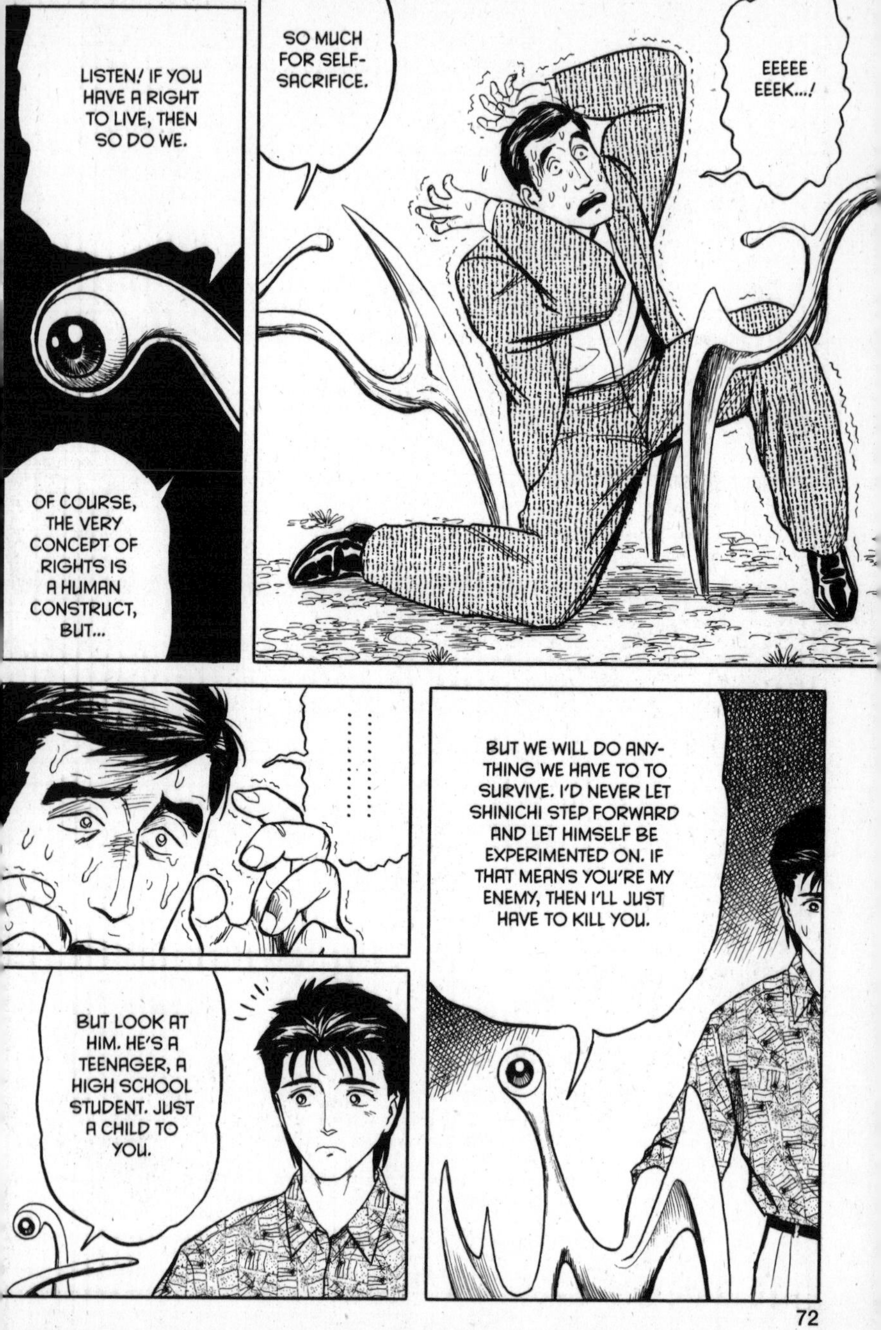
EEEEE EEEK...!
SO MUCH FOR SELF-SACRIFICE.
LISTEN! IF YOU HAVE A RIGHT TO LIVE, THEN SO DO WE.
OF COURSE, THE VERY CONCEPT OF RIGHTS IS A HUMAN CONSTRUCT, BUT...
BUT WE WILL DO ANY-THING WE HAVE TO TO SURVIVE. I'D NEVER LET SHINICHI STEP FORWARD AND LET HIMSELF BE EXPERIMENTED ON. IF THAT MEANS YOU'RE MY ENEMY, THEN I'LL JUST HAVE TO KILL YOU.
......
BUT LOOK AT HIM. HE'S A TEENAGER, A HIGH SCHOOL STUDENT. JUST A CHILD TO YOU.

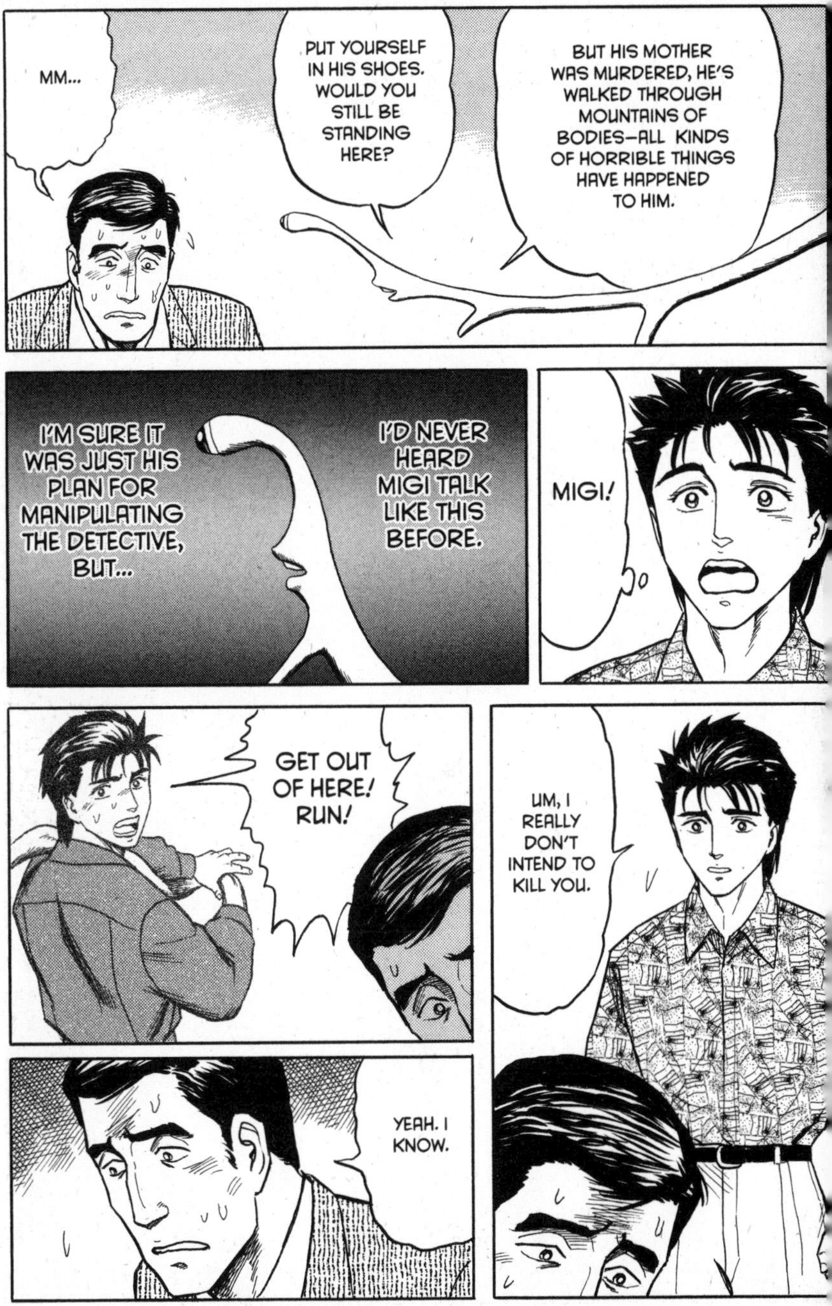
BUT HIS MOTHER WAS MURDERED, HE'S WALKED THROUGH MOUNTAINS OF BODIES—ALL KINDS OF HORRIBLE THINGS HAVE HAPPENED TO HIM.
PUT YOURSELF IN HIS SHOES. WOULD YOU STILL BE STANDING HERE?
MM...
MIGI!
I'D NEVER HEARD MIGI TALK LIKE THIS BEFORE.
I'M SURE IT WAS JUST HIS PLAN FOR MANIPULATING THE DETECTIVE, BUT...
UM, I REALLY DON'T INTEND TO KILL YOU.
GET OUT OF HERE! RUN!
YEAH. I KNOW.

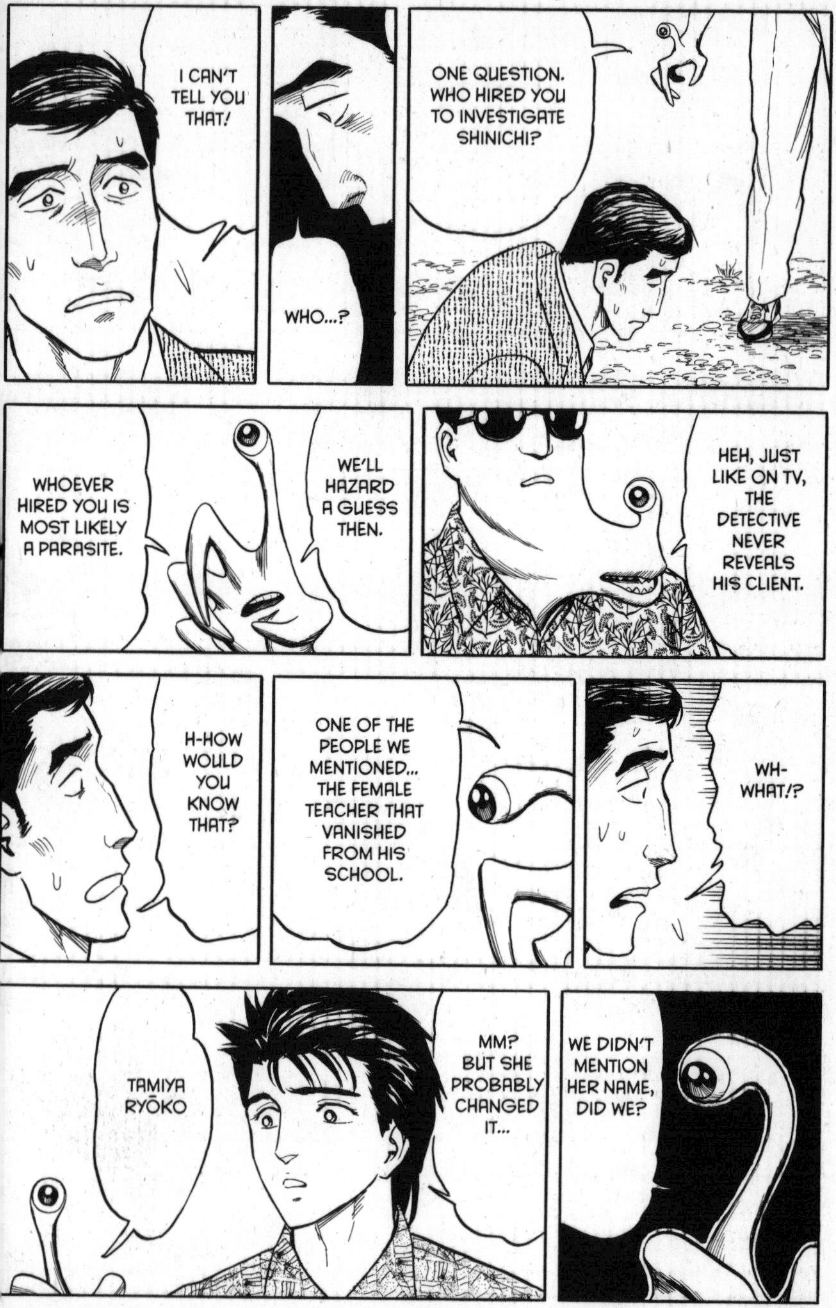
ONE QUESTION. WHO HIRED YOU TO INVESTIGATE SHINICHI?
WHO...?
I CAN'T TELL YOU THAT!
HEH, JUST LIKE ON TV, THE DETECTIVE NEVER REVEALS HIS CLIENT.
WE'LL HAZARD A GUESS THEN.
WHOEVER HIRED YOU IS MOST LIKELY A PARASITE.
WH-WHAT!?
ONE OF THE PEOPLE WE MENTIONED... THE FEMALE TEACHER THAT VANISHED FROM HIS SCHOOL.
H-HOW WOULD YOU KNOW THAT?
WE DIDN'T MENTION HER NAME, DID WE?
MM? BUT SHE PROBABLY CHANGED IT...
TAMIYA RYŌKO

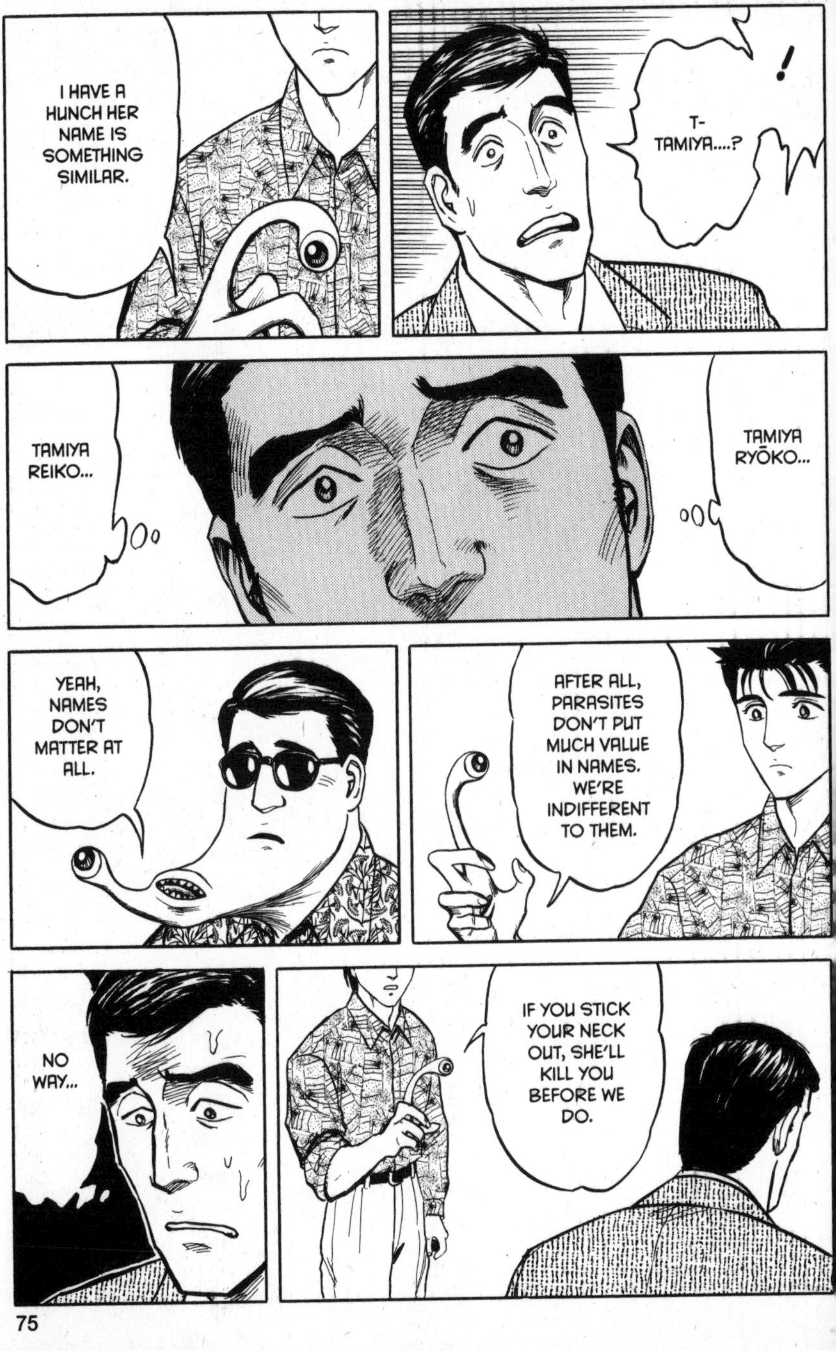
I HAVE A HUNCH HER NAME IS SOMETHING SIMILAR.
!
T-TAMIYA....?
TAMIYA REIKO...
TAMIYA RYŌKO...
YEAH, NAMES DON'T MATTER AT ALL.
AFTER ALL, PARASITES DON'T PUT MUCH VALUE IN NAMES. WE'RE INDIFFERENT TO THEM.
NO WAY...
IF YOU STICK YOUR NECK OUT, SHE'LL KILL YOU BEFORE WE DO.

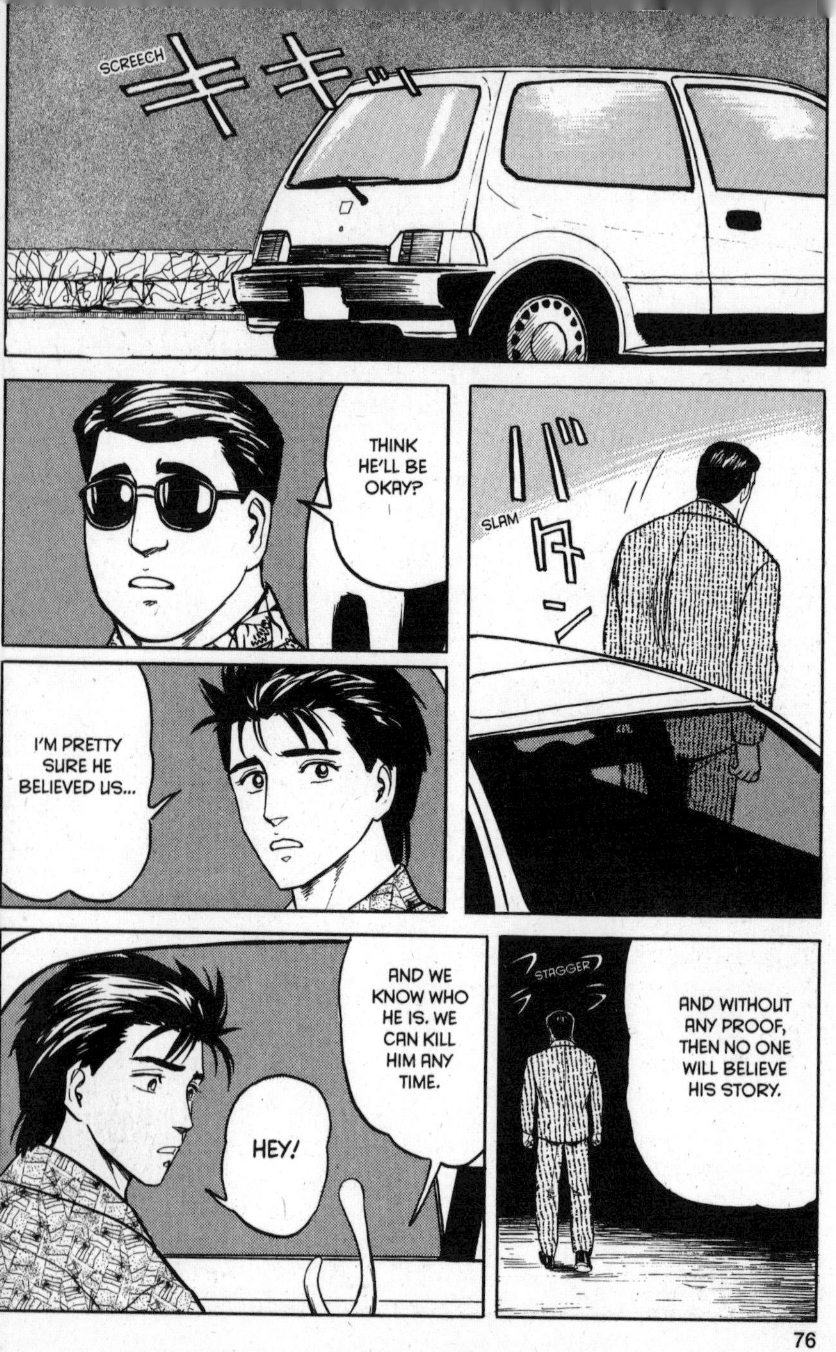
SCREECH
SLAM
THINK HE'LL BE OKAY?
I'M PRETTY SURE HE BELIEVED US...
STAGGER
AND WITHOUT ANY PROOF, THEN NO ONE WILL BELIEVE HIS STORY.
AND WE KNOW WHO HE IS. WE CAN KILL HIM ANY TIME.
HEY!

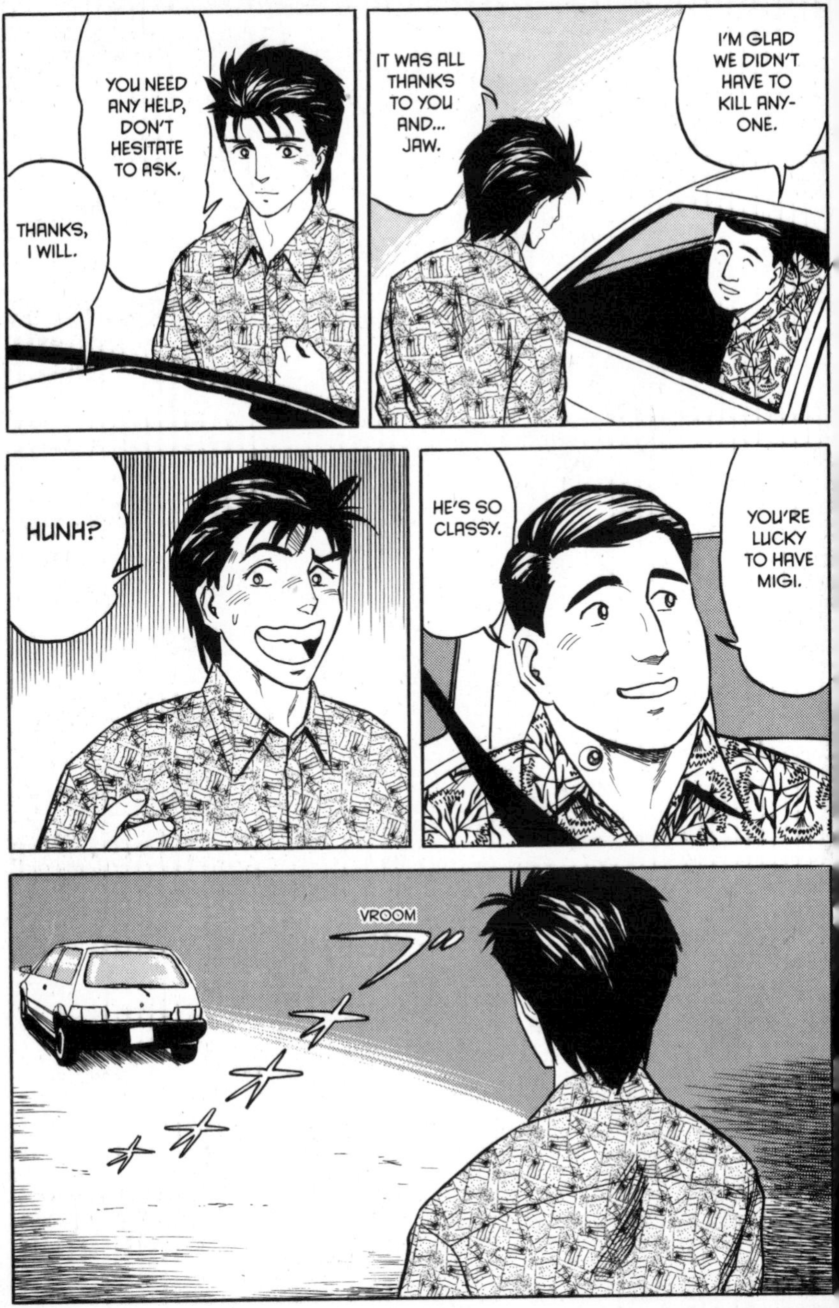
I'M GLAD WE DIDN'T HAVE TO KILL ANY-ONE.
IT WAS ALL THANKS TO YOU AND... JAW.
YOU NEED ANY HELP, DON'T HESITATE TO ASK.
THANKS, I WILL.
YOU'RE LUCKY TO HAVE MIGI.
HE'S SO CLASSY.
HUNH?
VROOM

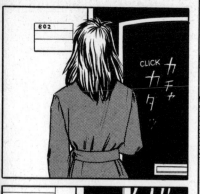

TKK
コッ
TKK
コッ
CLICK
カチャ
カタッ
バタン
THUNK.
THE MISSING HIGH SCHOOL TEACHER?
THIS IS MORE CONVOLUTED THAN A MYSTERY NOVEL! LIKE SOME SORT OF MYSTERY ZONE!
DON'T STICK YOUR NECK OUT WHERE IT DOESN'T BELONG.
......

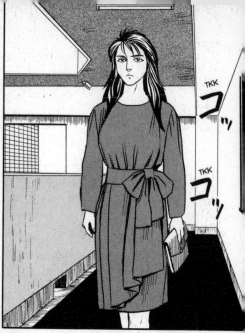

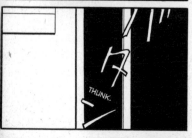

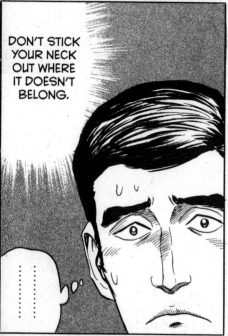

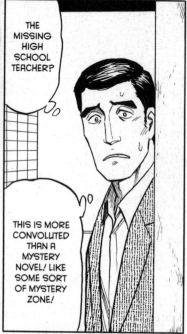

CHAPTER 36: THE DEVIL'S FACE

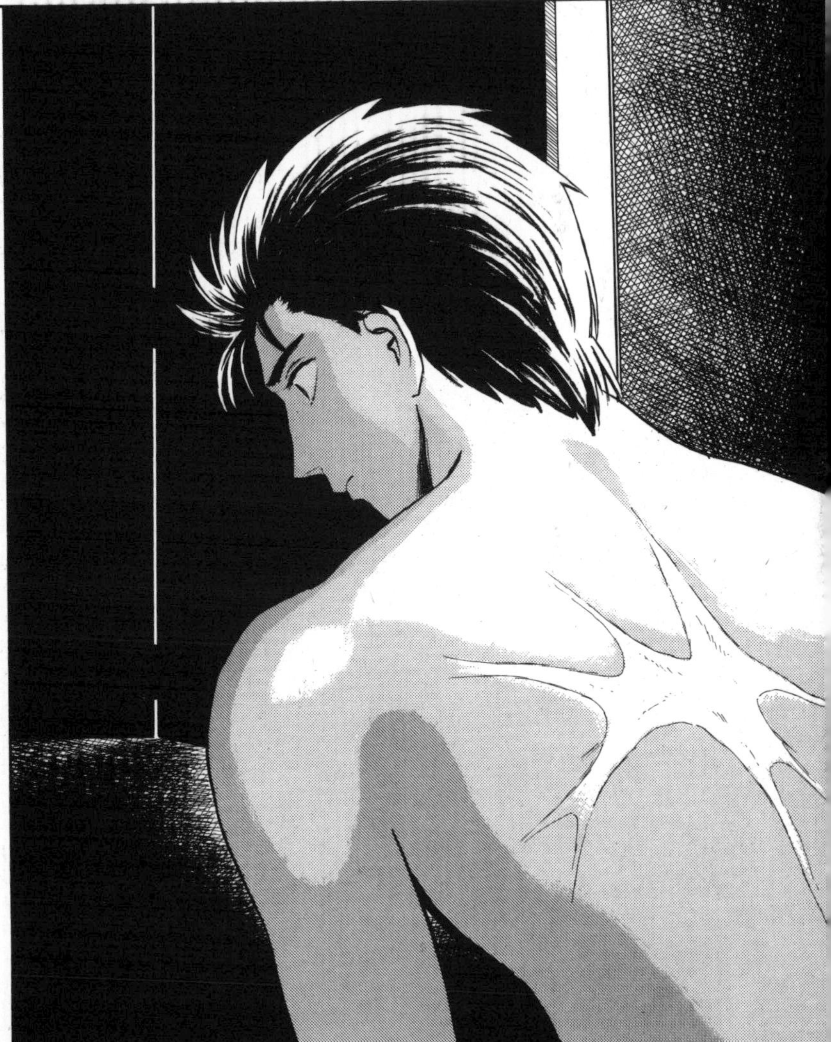

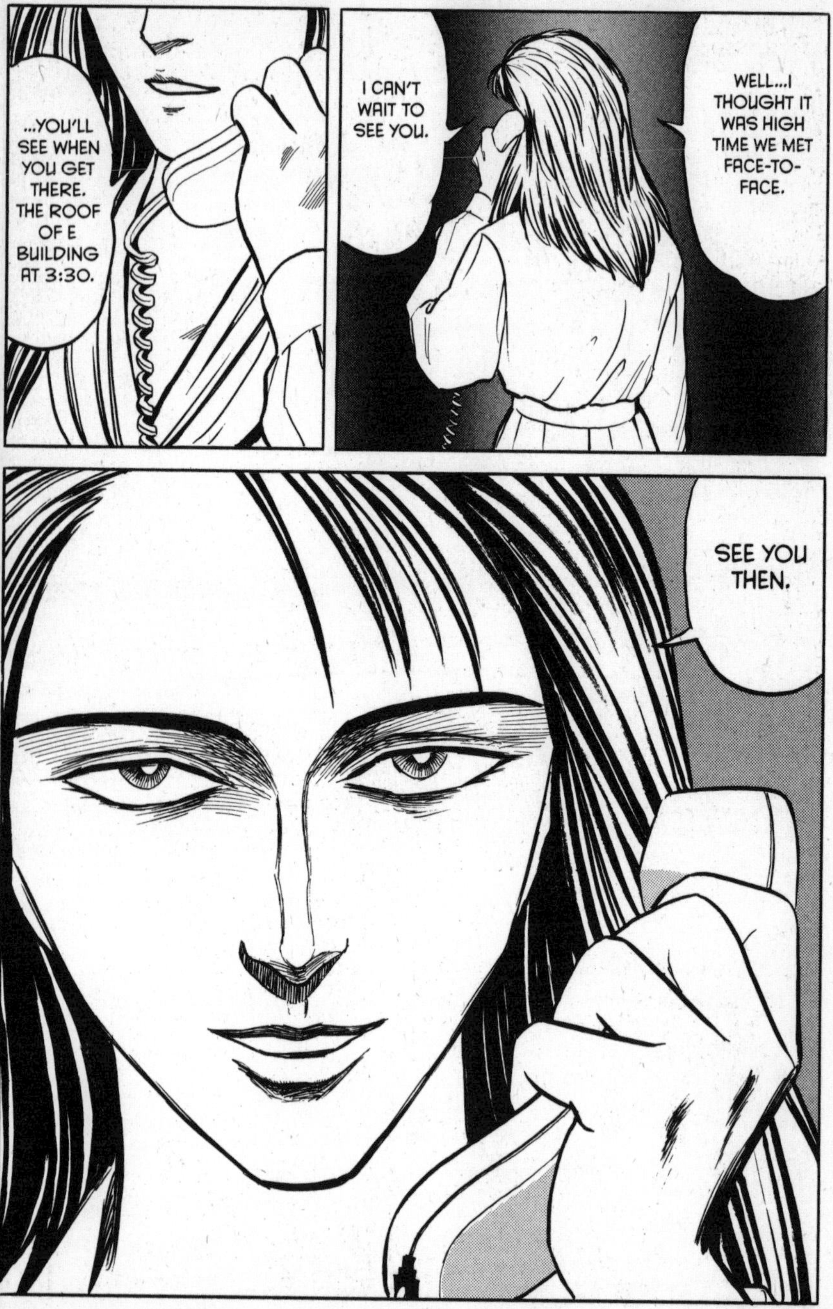
WELL...I THOUGHT IT WAS HIGH TIME WE MET FACE-TO-FACE.
I CAN'T WAIT TO SEE YOU.
...YOU'LL SEE WHEN YOU GET THERE. THE ROOF OF E BUILDING AT 3:30.
SEE YOU THEN.

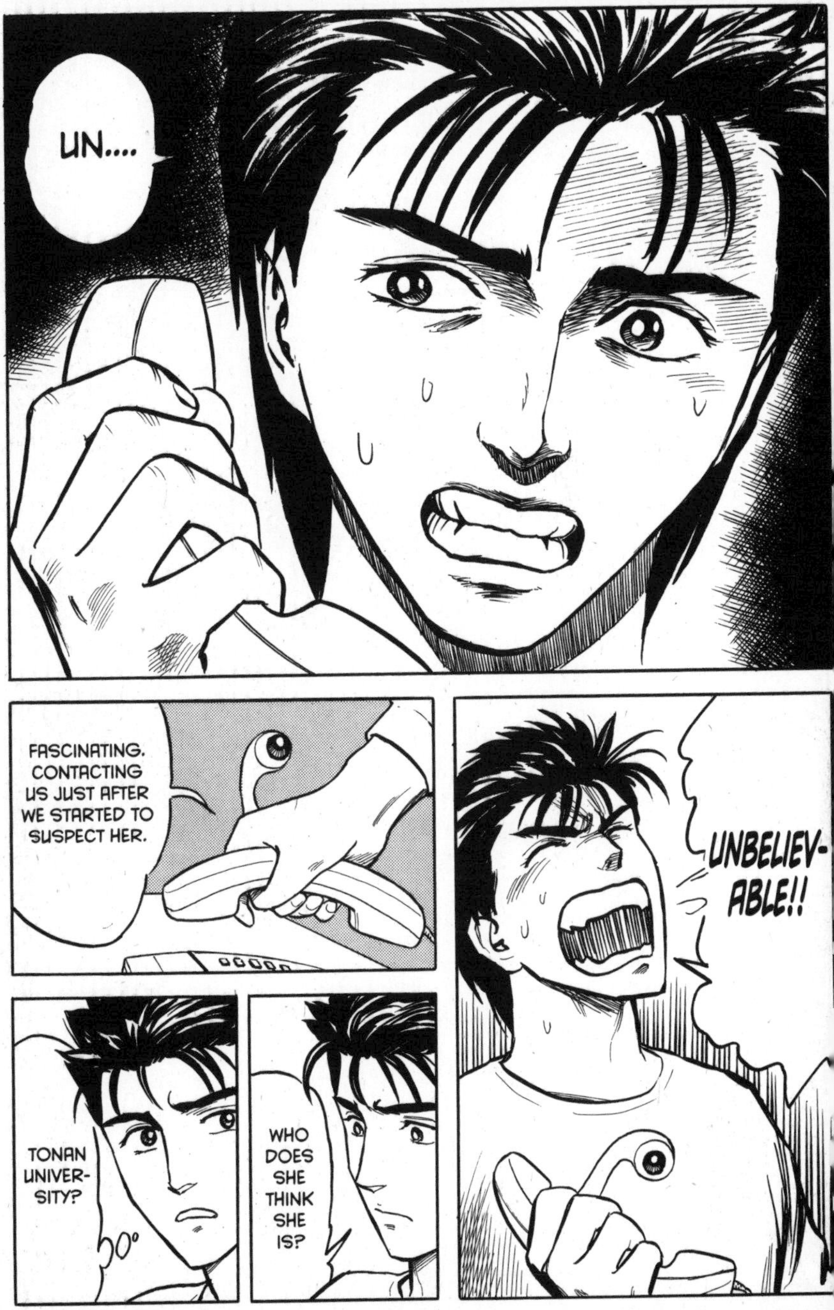
UN....
UNBELIEV-ABLE!!
FASCINATING. CONTACTING US JUST AFTER WE STARTED TO SUSPECT HER.
WHO DOES SHE THINK SHE IS?
TONAN UNIVER-SITY?

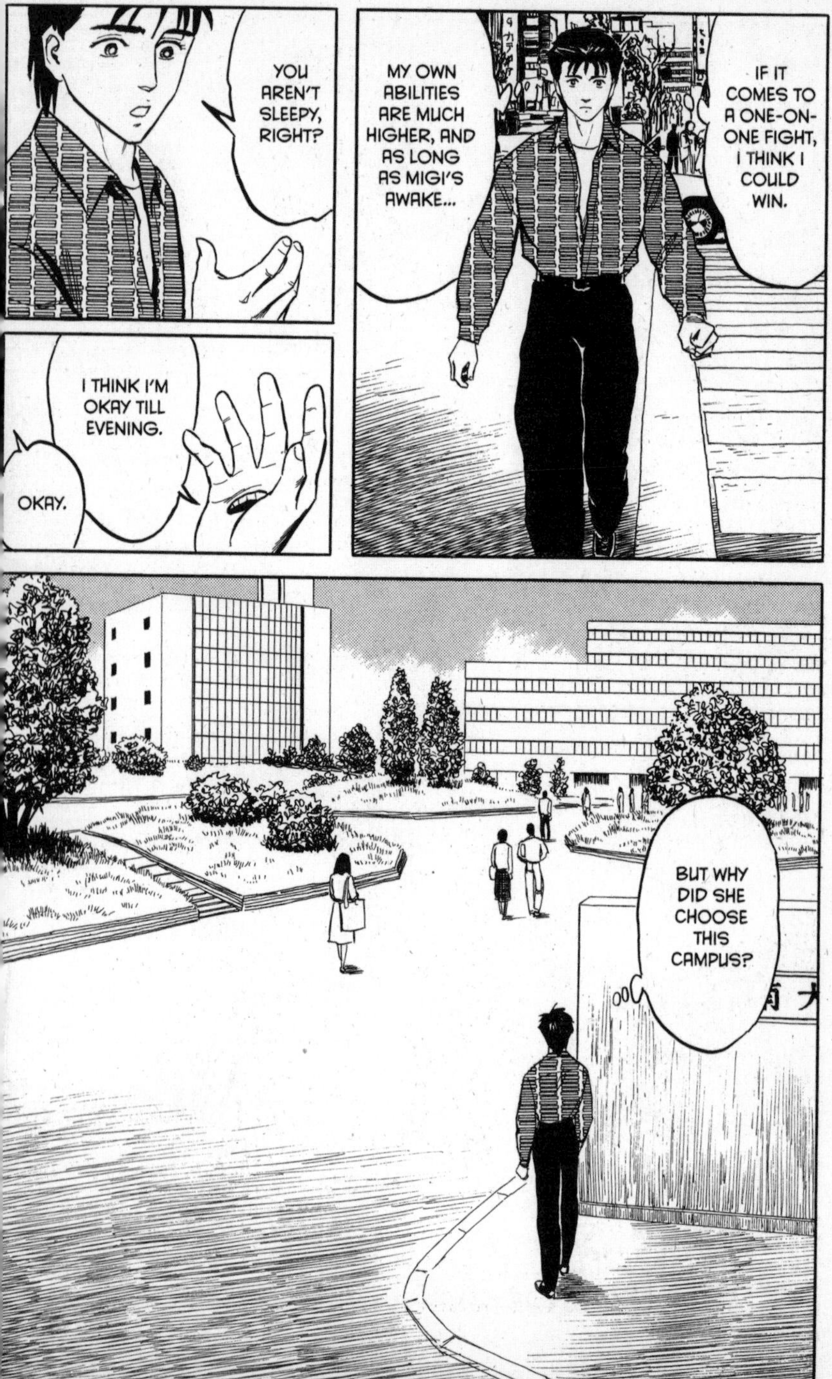
IF IT COMES TO A ONE-ON-ONE FIGHT, I THINK I COULD WIN.
MY OWN ABILITIES ARE MUCH HIGHER, AND AS LONG AS MIGI'S AWAKE...
YOU AREN'T SLEEPY, RIGHT?
I THINK I'M OKAY TILL EVENING.
OKAY.
BUT WHY DID SHE CHOOSE THIS CAMPUS?

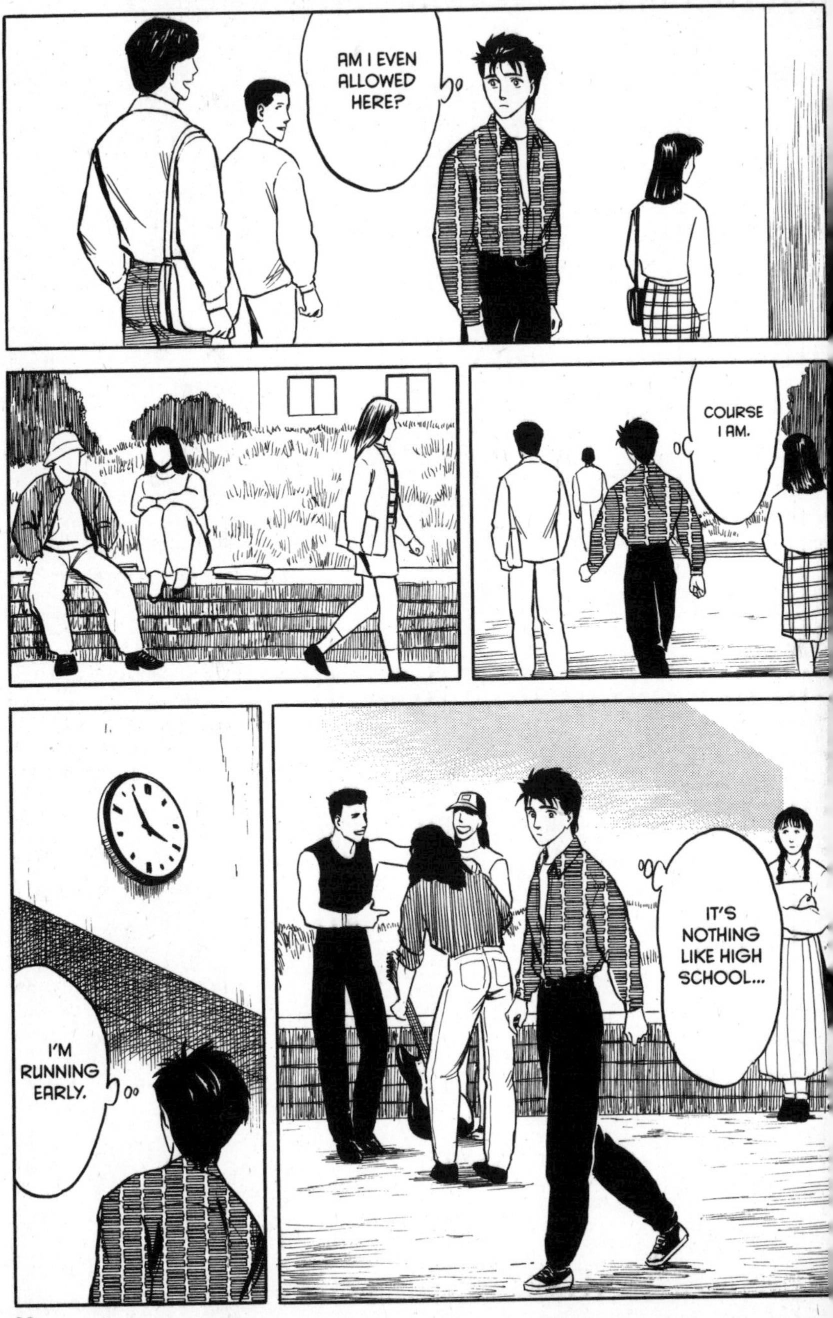
AM I EVEN ALLOWED HERE?
COURSE I AM.
I'M RUNNING EARLY.
IT'S NOTHING LIKE HIGH SCHOOL...

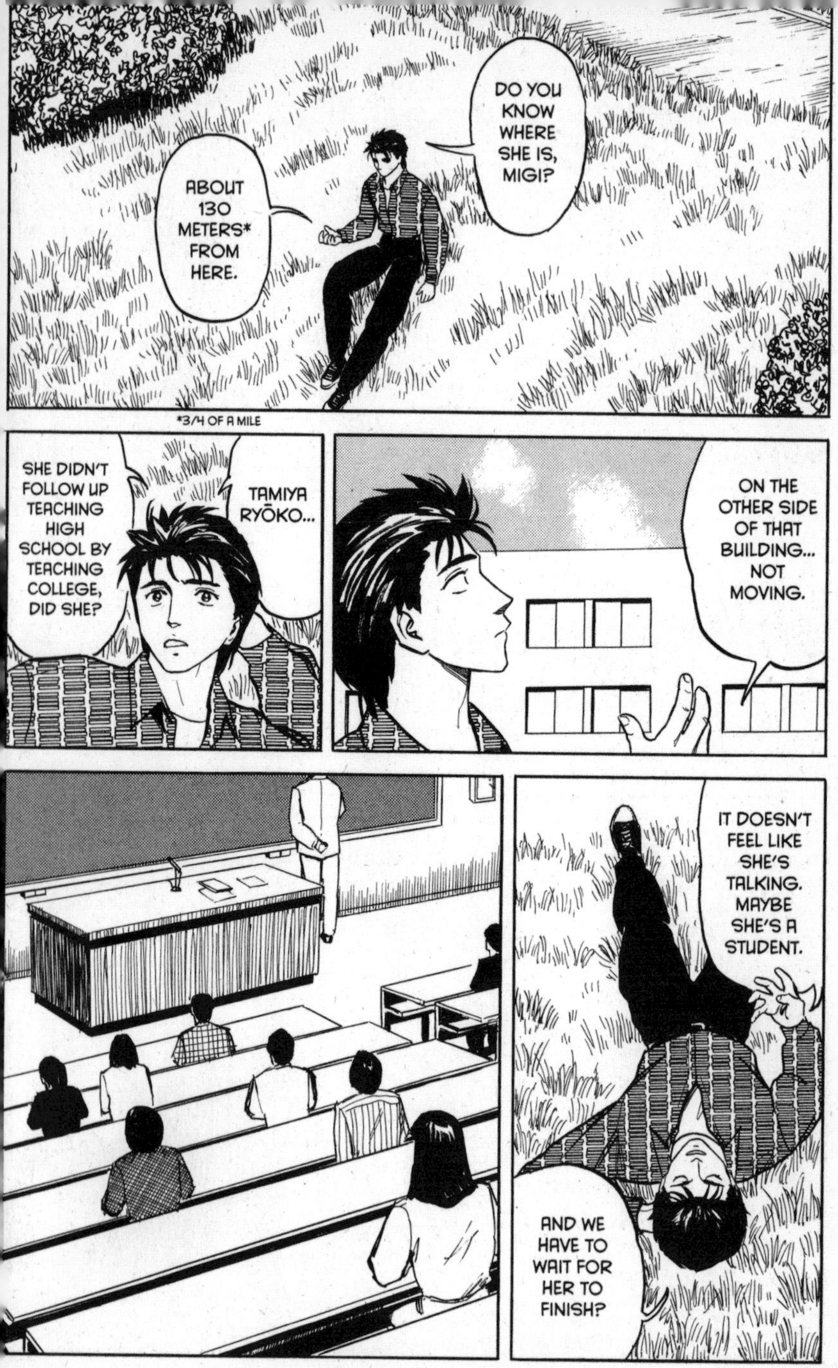
DO YOU KNOW WHERE SHE IS, MIGI?
ABOUT 130 METERS* FROM HERE.
*3/4 OF A MILE
ON THE OTHER SIDE OF THAT BUILDING... NOT MOVING.
TAMIYA RYŌKO...
SHE DIDN'T FOLLOW UP TEACHING HIGH SCHOOL BY TEACHING COLLEGE, DID SHE?
IT DOESN'T FEEL LIKE SHE'S TALKING. MAYBE SHE'S A STUDENT.
AND WE HAVE TO WAIT FOR HER TO FINISH?

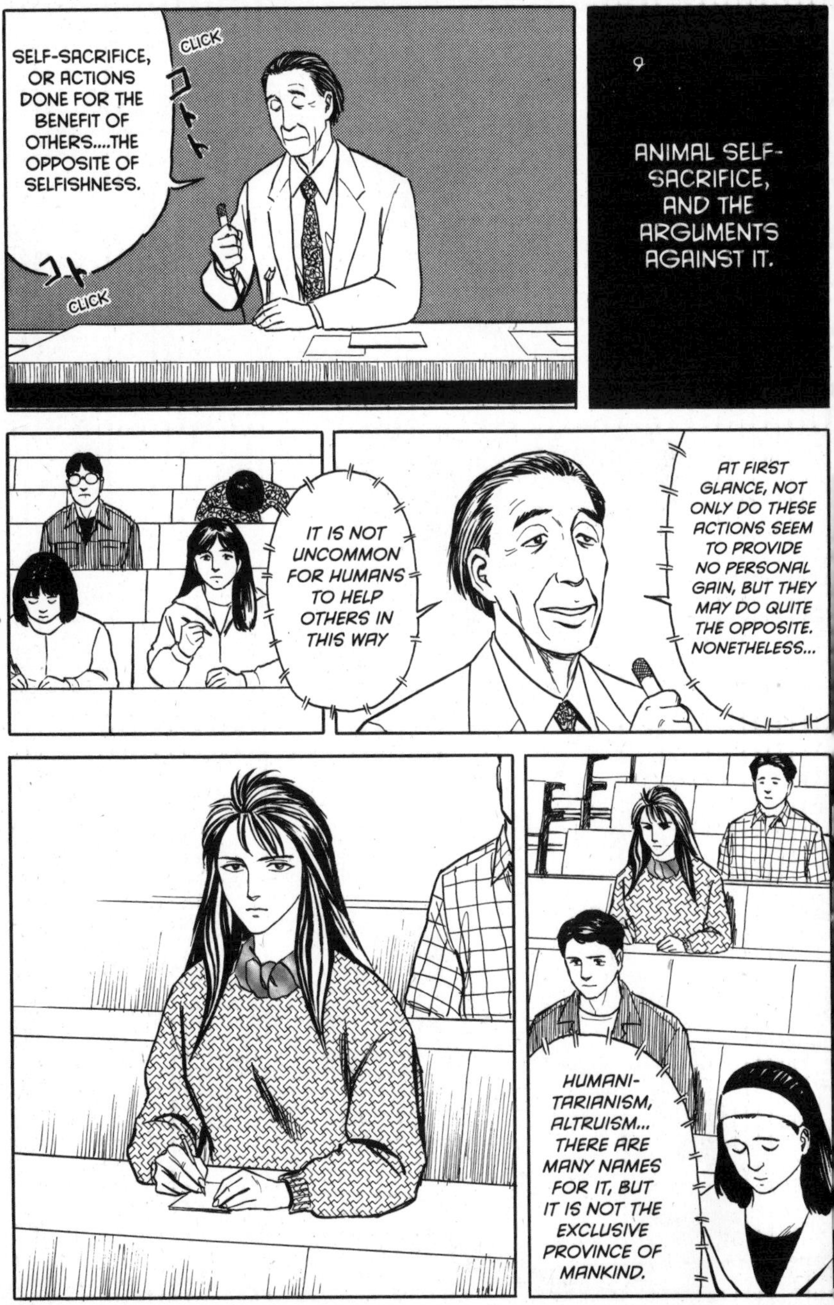
9
ANIMAL SELF-SACRIFICE, AND THE ARGUMENTS AGAINST IT.
CLICK
SELF-SACRIFICE, OR ACTIONS DONE FOR THE BENEFIT OF OTHERS....THE OPPOSITE OF SELFISHNESS.
CLICK
IT IS NOT UNCOMMON FOR HUMANS TO HELP OTHERS IN THIS WAY
AT FIRST GLANCE, NOT ONLY DO THESE ACTIONS SEEM TO PROVIDE NO PERSONAL GAIN, BUT THEY MAY DO QUITE THE OPPOSITE. NONETHELESS...
HUMANITARIANISM, ALTRUISM... THERE ARE MANY NAMES FOR IT, BUT IT IS NOT THE EXCLUSIVE PROVINCE OF MANKIND.

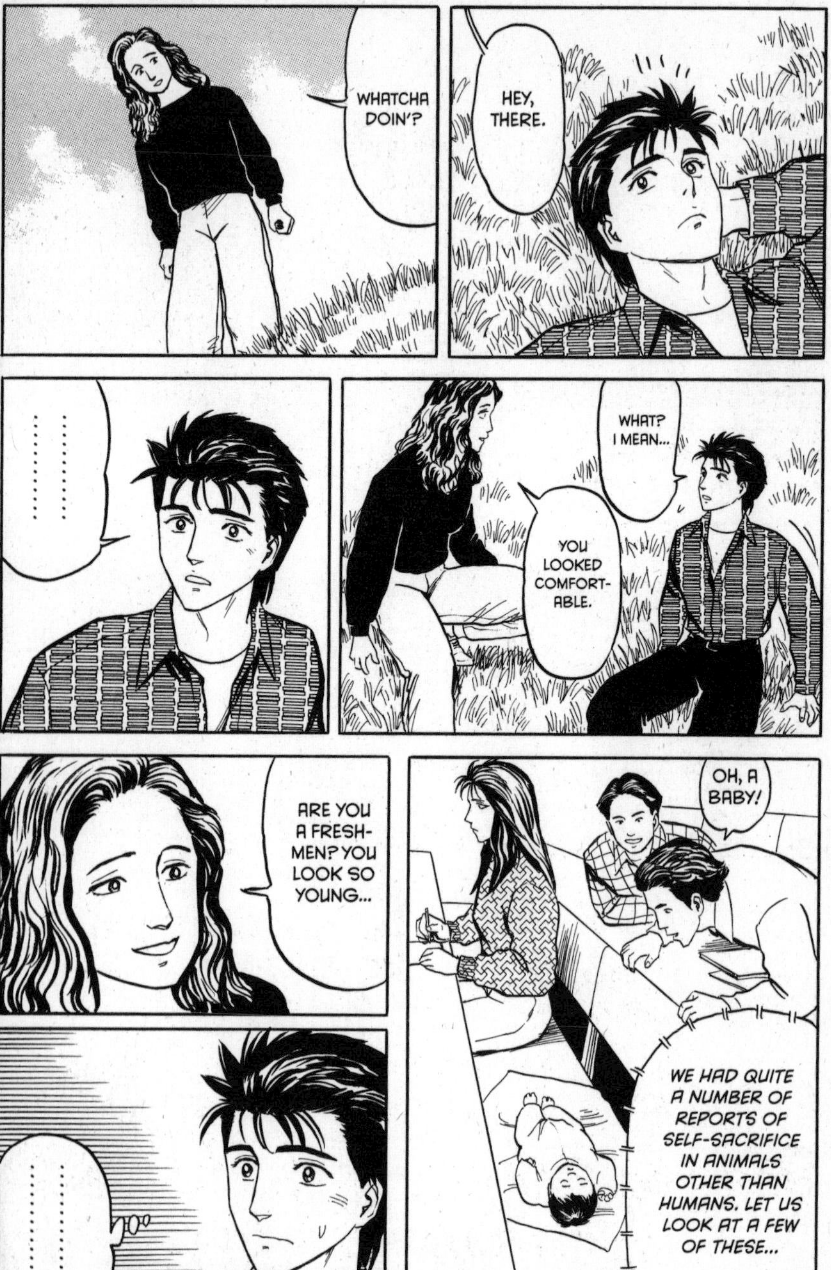
HEY, THERE.
WHATCHA DOIN'?
WHAT? I MEAN...
YOU LOOKED COMFORT-ABLE.
......
OH, A BABY!
WE HAD QUITE A NUMBER OF REPORTS OF SELF-SACRIFICE IN ANIMALS OTHER THAN HUMANS. LET US LOOK AT A FEW OF THESE...
ARE YOU A FRESH-MEN? YOU LOOK SO YOUNG...
......

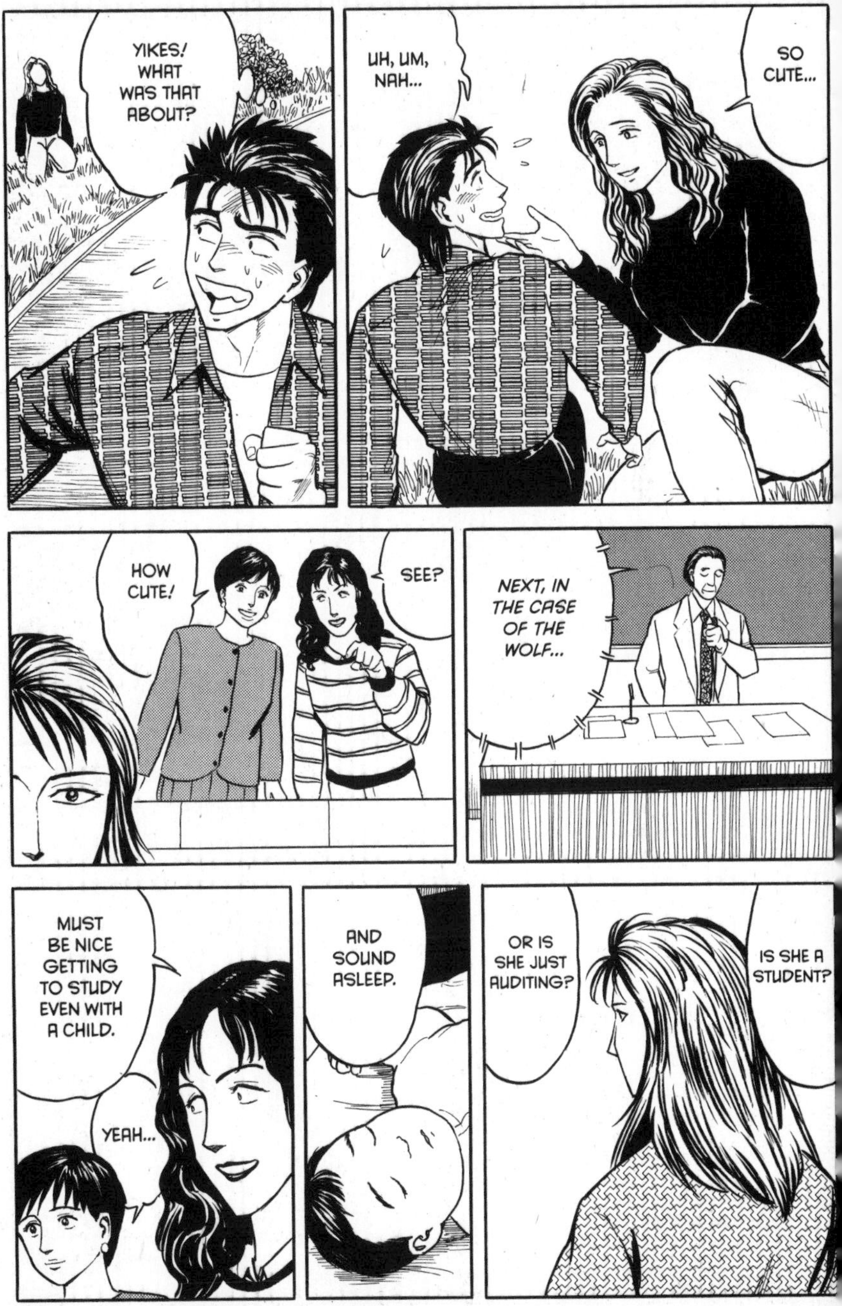
SO CUTE...
UH, UM, NAH...
YIKES! WHAT WAS THAT ABOUT?
NEXT, IN THE CASE OF THE WOLF...
SEE?
HOW CUTE!
IS SHE A STUDENT?
OR IS SHE JUST AUDITING?
AND SOUND ASLEEP.
MUST BE NICE GETTING TO STUDY EVEN WITH A CHILD.
YEAH...

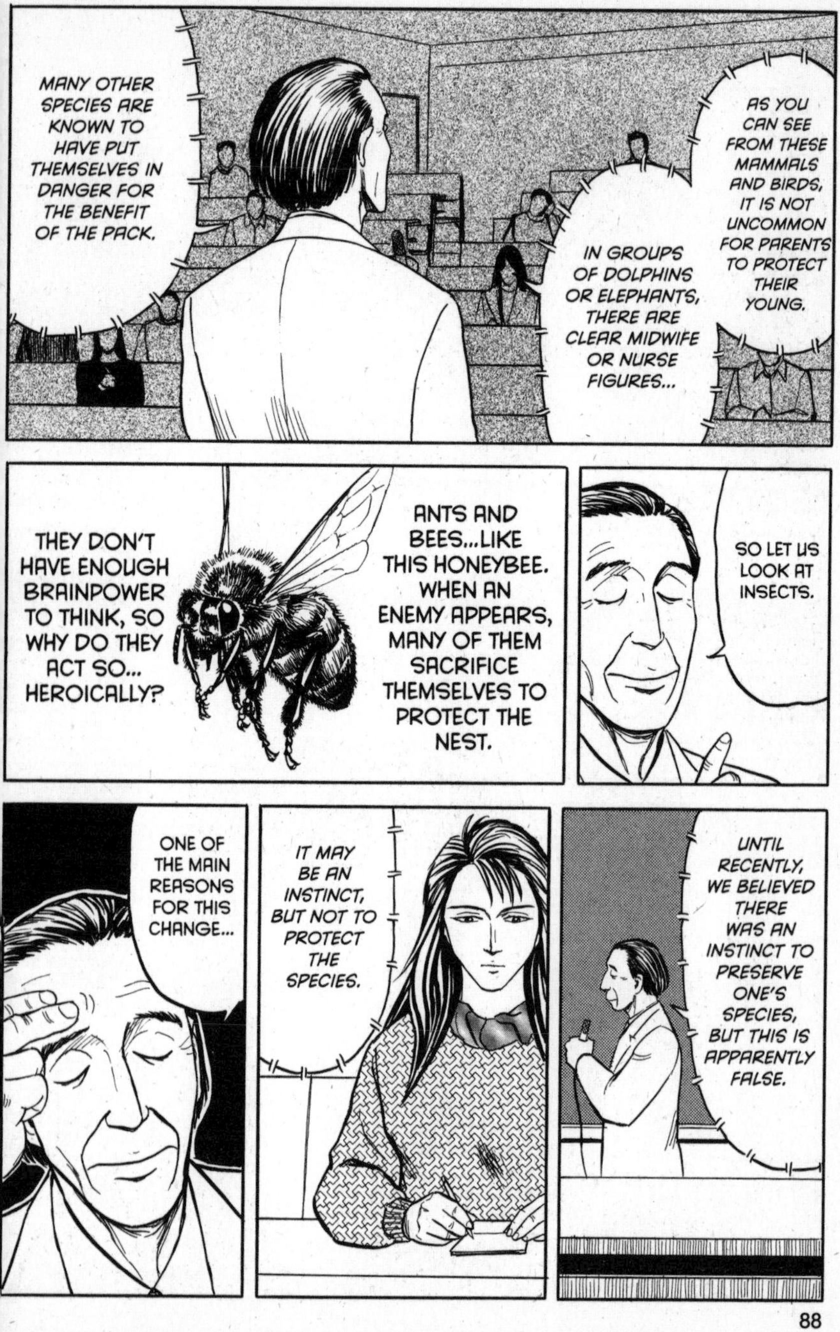
AS YOU CAN SEE FROM THESE MAMMALS AND BIRDS, IT IS NOT UNCOMMON FOR PARENTS TO PROTECT THEIR YOUNG.
IN GROUPS OF DOLPHINS OR ELEPHANTS, THERE ARE CLEAR MIDWIFE OR NURSE FIGURES...
MANY OTHER SPECIES ARE KNOWN TO HAVE PUT THEMSELVES IN DANGER FOR THE BENEFIT OF THE PACK.
SO LET US LOOK AT INSECTS.
ANTS AND BEES...LIKE THIS HONEYBEE. WHEN AN ENEMY APPEARS, MANY OF THEM SACRIFICE THEMSELVES TO PROTECT THE NEST.
THEY DON'T HAVE ENOUGH BRAINPOWER TO THINK, SO WHY DO THEY ACT SO... HEROICALLY?
UNTIL RECENTLY, WE BELIEVED THERE WAS AN INSTINCT TO PRESERVE ONE'S SPECIES, BUT THIS IS APPARENTLY FALSE.
IT MAY BE AN INSTINCT, BUT NOT TO PROTECT THE SPECIES.
ONE OF THE MAIN REASONS FOR THIS CHANGE...

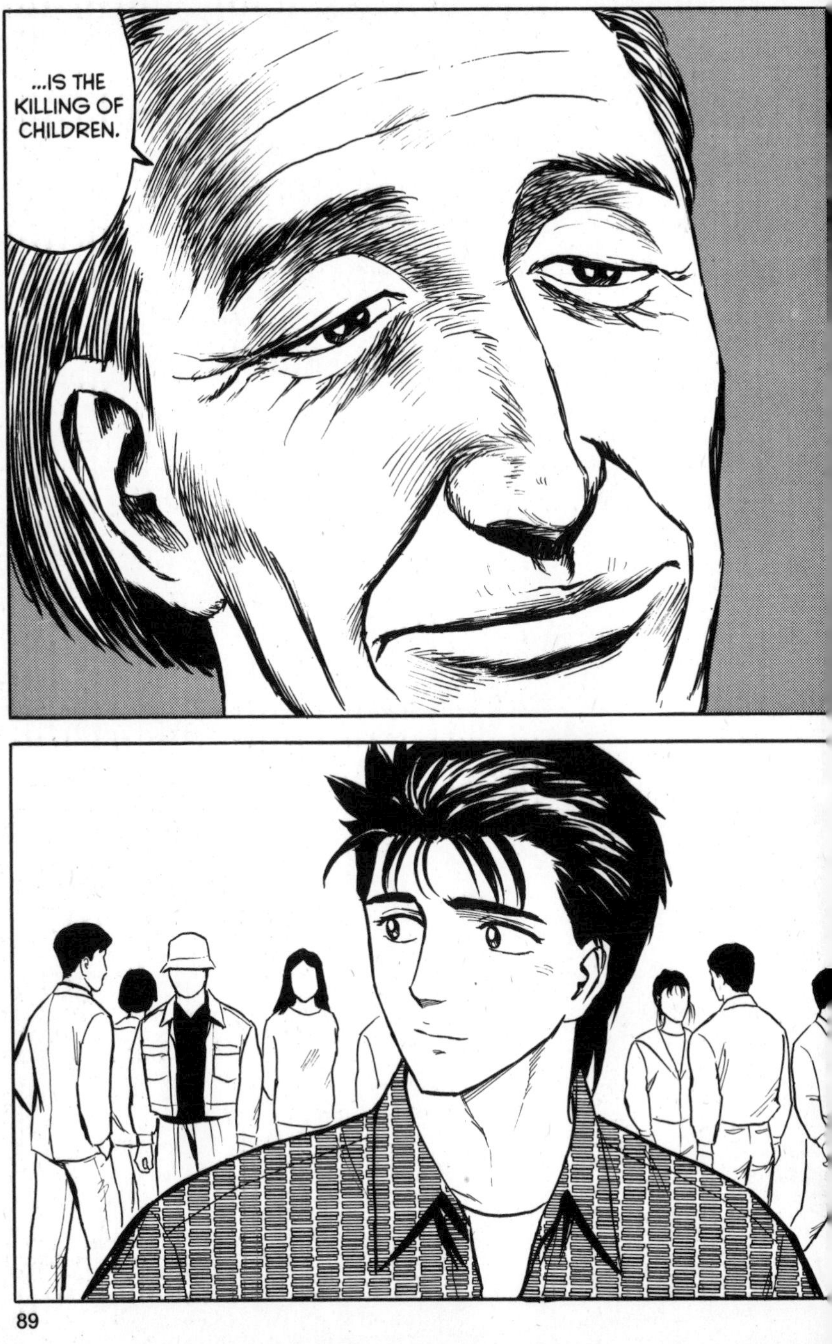
...IS THE KILLING OF CHILDREN.

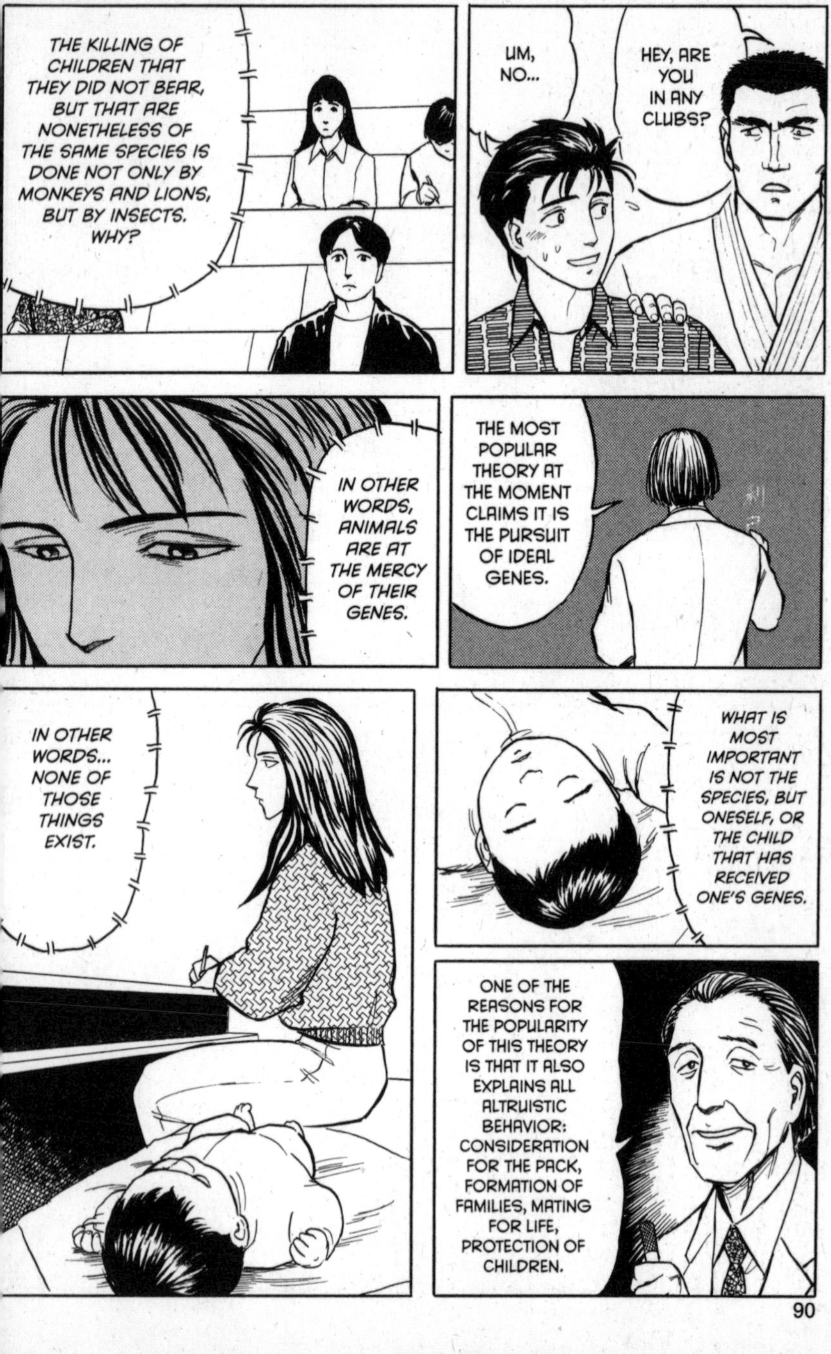
HEY, ARE YOU IN ANY CLUBS?
UM, NO...
THE KILLING OF CHILDREN THAT THEY DID NOT BEAR, BUT THAT ARE NONETHELESS OF THE SAME SPECIES IS DONE NOT ONLY BY MONKEYS AND LIONS, BUT BY INSECTS. WHY?
THE MOST POPULAR THEORY AT THE MOMENT CLAIMS IT IS THE PURSUIT OF IDEAL GENES.
IN OTHER WORDS, ANIMALS ARE AT THE MERCY OF THEIR GENES.
WHAT IS MOST IMPORTANT IS NOT THE SPECIES, BUT ONESELF, OR THE CHILD THAT HAS RECEIVED ONE'S GENES.
ONE OF THE REASONS FOR THE POPULARITY OF THIS THEORY IS THAT IT ALSO EXPLAINS ALL ALTRUISTIC BEHAVIOR: CONSIDERATION FOR THE PACK, FORMATION OF FAMILIES, MATING FOR LIFE, PROTECTION OF CHILDREN.
IN OTHER WORDS... NONE OF THOSE THINGS EXIST.

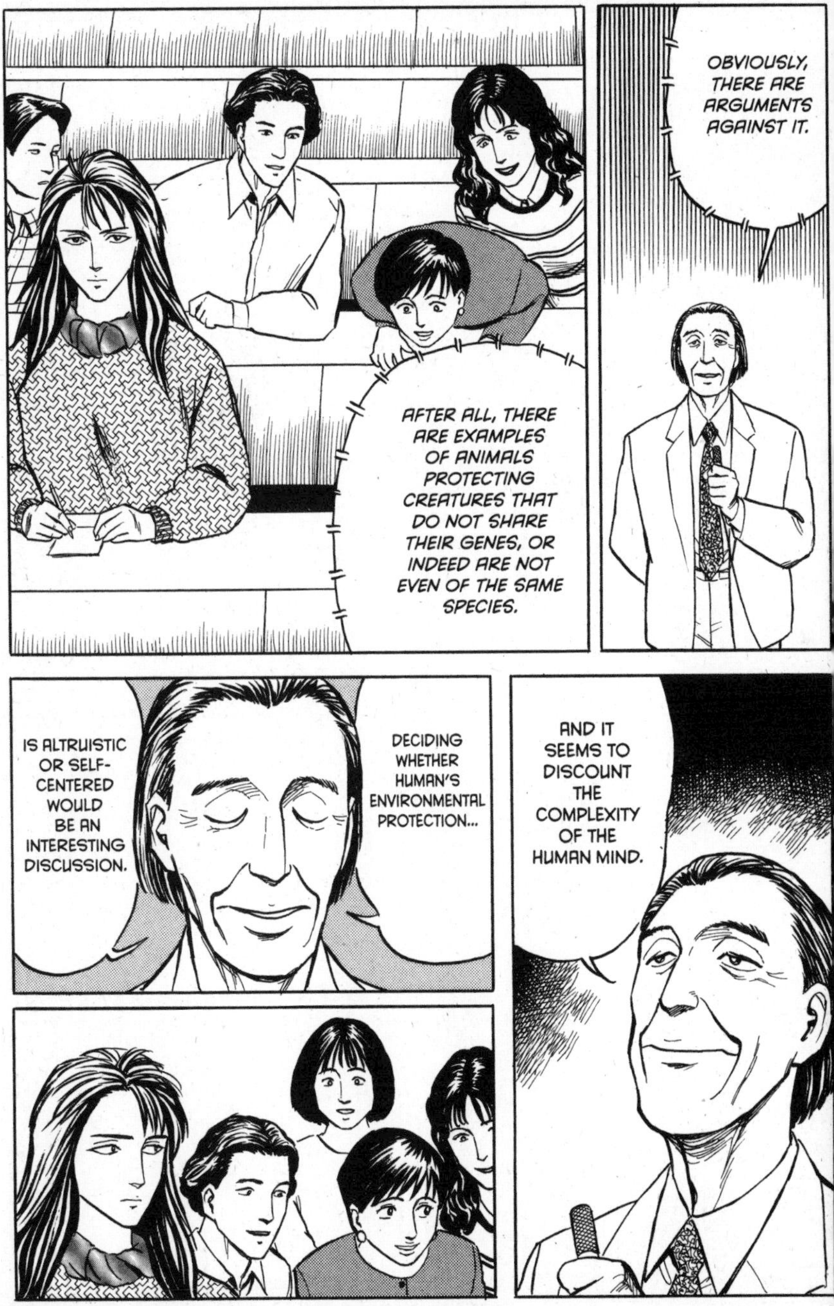
OBVIOUSLY, THERE ARE ARGUMENTS AGAINST IT.
AFTER ALL, THERE ARE EXAMPLES OF ANIMALS PROTECTING CREATURES THAT DO NOT SHARE THEIR GENES, OR INDEED ARE NOT EVEN OF THE SAME SPECIES.
AND IT SEEMS TO DISCOUNT THE COMPLEXITY OF THE HUMAN MIND.
DECIDING WHETHER HUMAN'S ENVIRONMENTAL PROTECTION...
IS ALTRUISTIC OR SELF-CENTERED WOULD BE AN INTERESTING DISCUSSION.

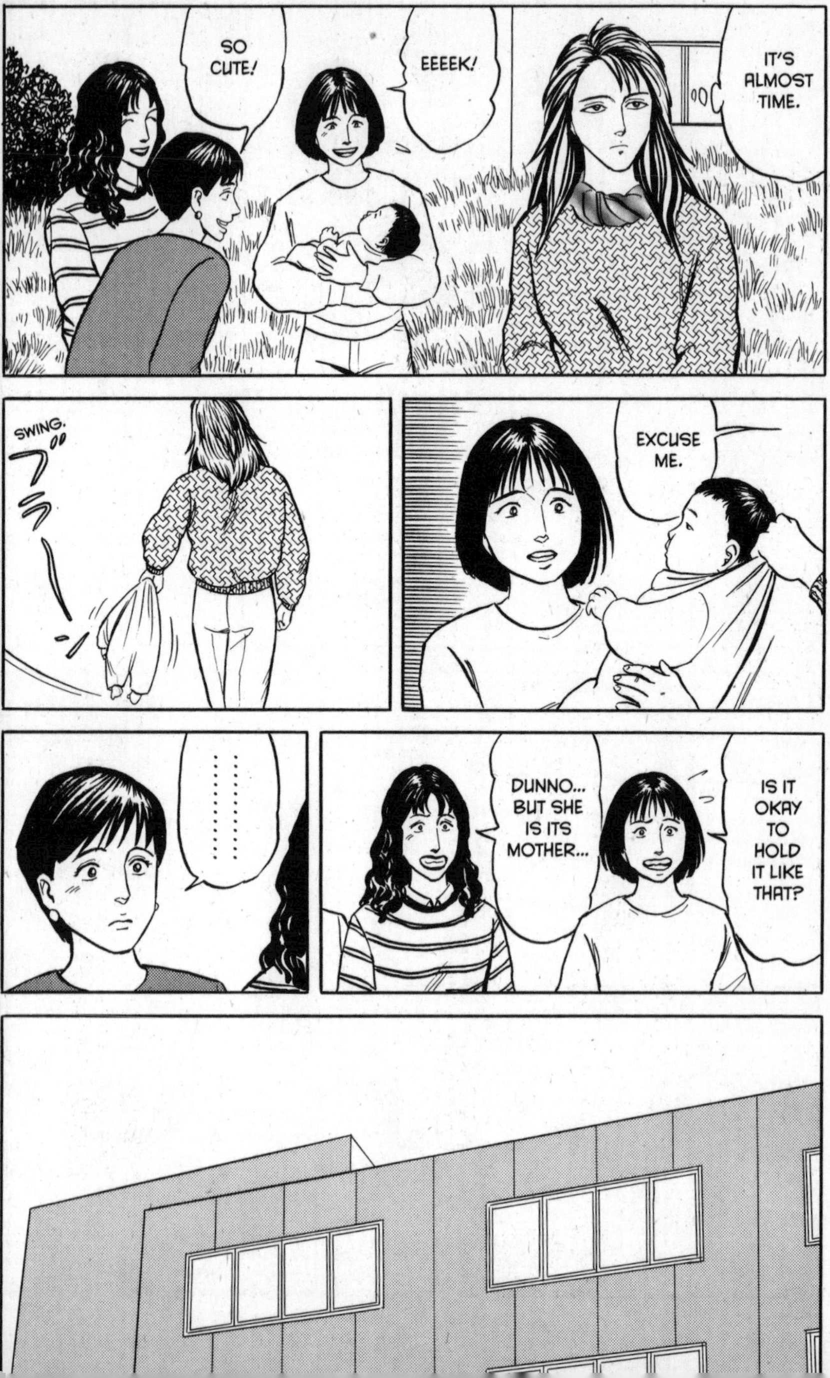
IT'S ALMOST TIME.
EEEEK!
SO CUTE!
EXCUSE ME.
SWING.
IS IT OKAY TO HOLD IT LIKE THAT?
DUNNO... BUT SHE IS ITS MOTHER...
......

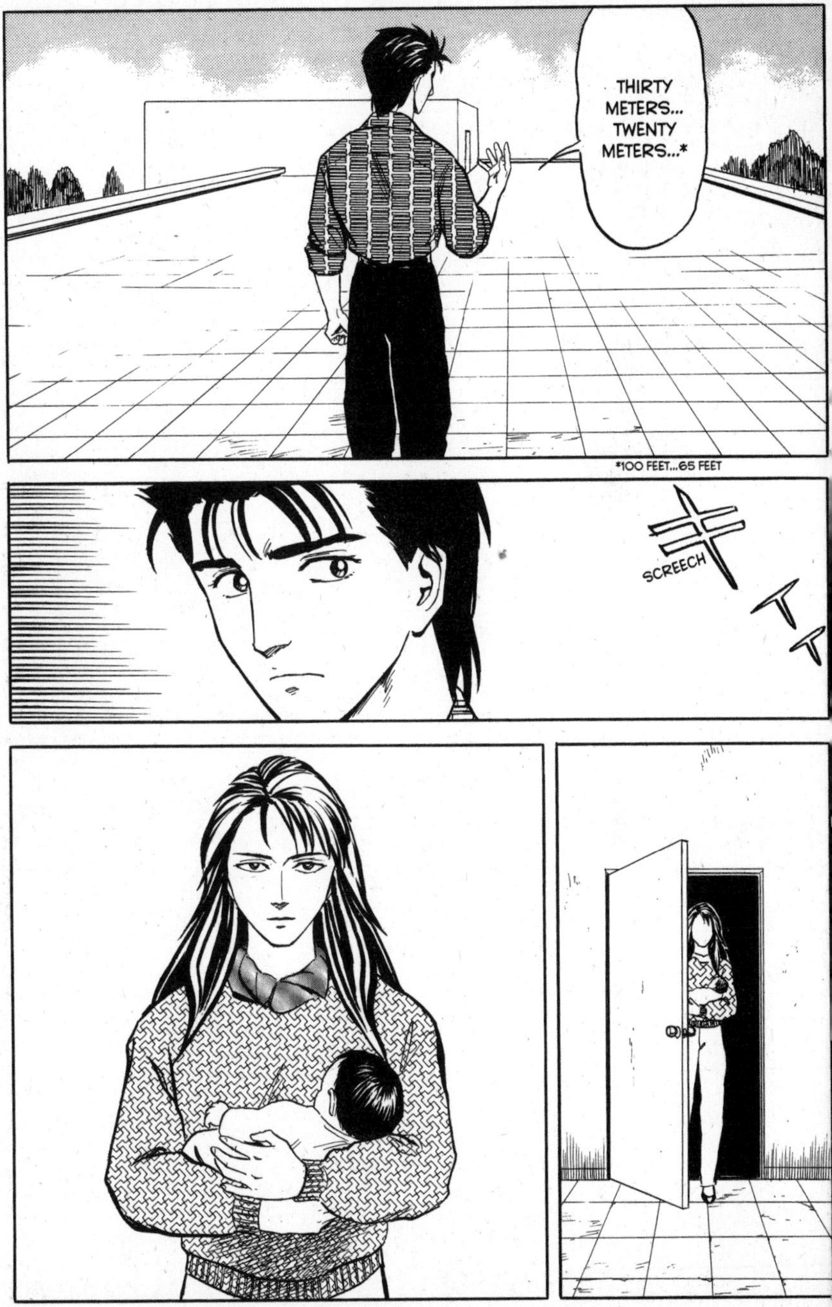
THIRTY METERS... TWENTY METERS...*
*100 FEET...65 FEET
SCREECH

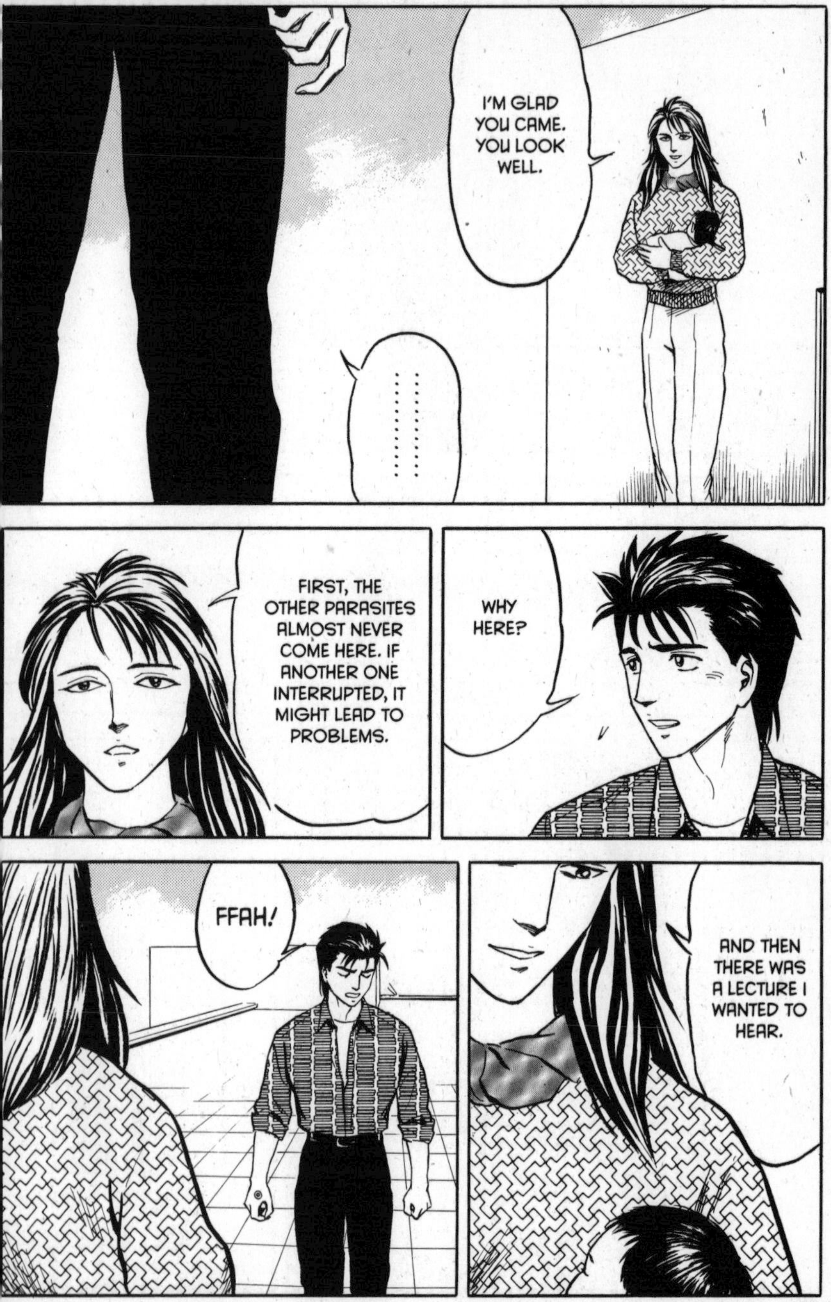
I'M GLAD YOU CAME. YOU LOOK WELL.
......
WHY HERE?
FIRST, THE OTHER PARASITES ALMOST NEVER COME HERE. IF ANOTHER ONE INTERRUPTED, IT MIGHT LEAD TO PROBLEMS.
AND THEN THERE WAS A LECTURE I WANTED TO HEAR.
FFAH!

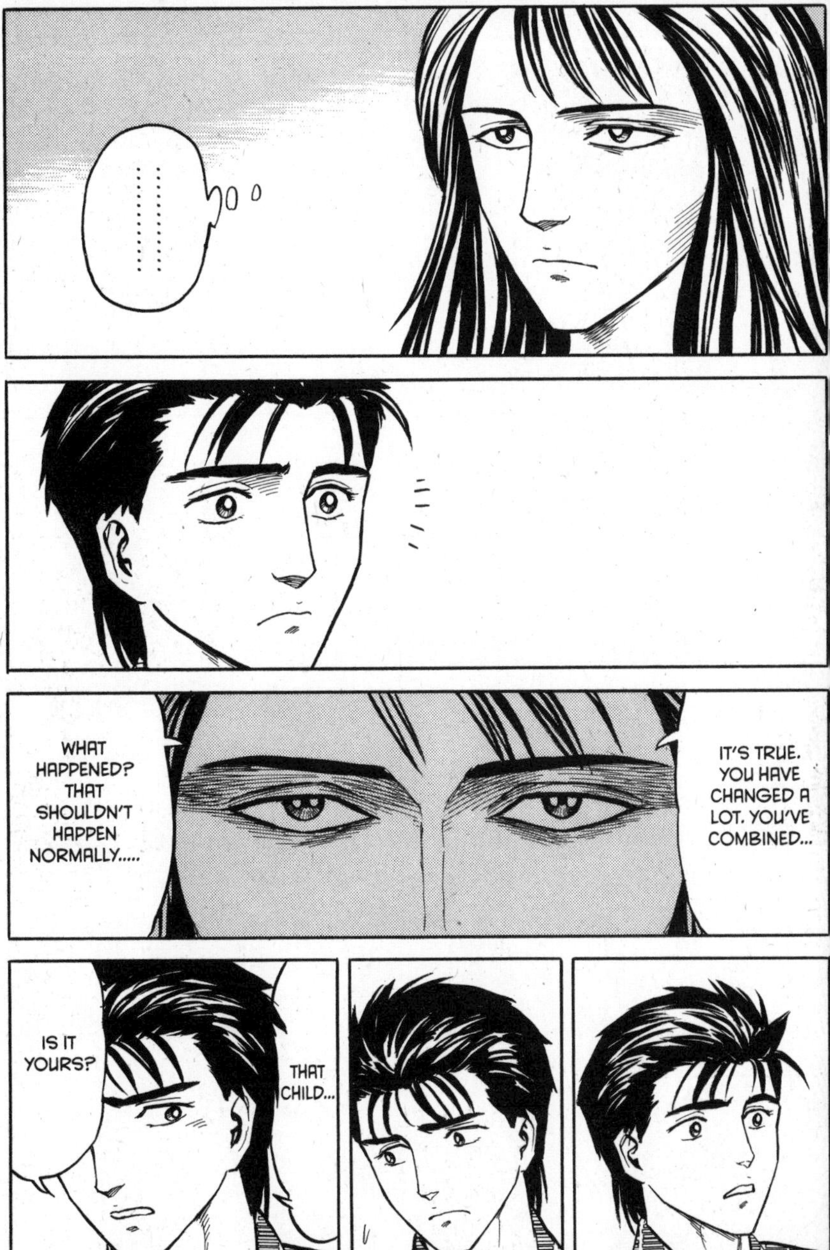
......
IT'S TRUE. YOU HAVE CHANGED A LOT. YOU'VE COMBINED...
WHAT HAPPENED? THAT SHOULDN'T HAPPEN NORMALLY.....
THAT CHILD...
IS IT YOURS?

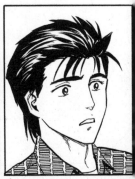

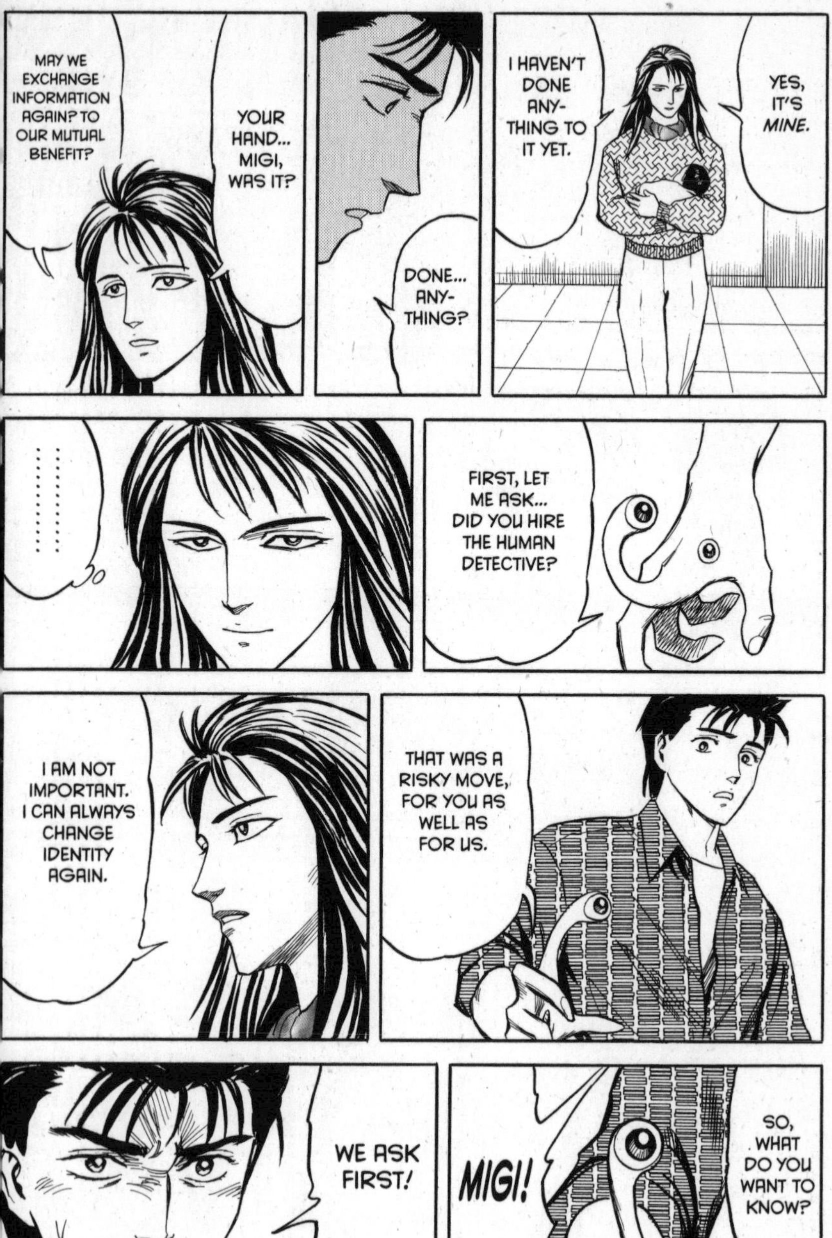
YES, IT'S *MINE.*
I HAVEN'T DONE ANYTHING TO IT YET.
DONE... ANYTHING?
YOUR HAND... MIGI, WAS IT?
MAY WE EXCHANGE INFORMATION AGAIN? TO OUR MUTUAL BENEFIT?
FIRST, LET ME ASK... DID YOU HIRE THE HUMAN DETECTIVE?
......
THAT WAS A RISKY MOVE, FOR YOU AS WELL AS FOR US.
I AM NOT IMPORTANT. I CAN ALWAYS CHANGE IDENTITY AGAIN.
SO, WHAT DO YOU WANT TO KNOW?
MIGI!
WE ASK FIRST!

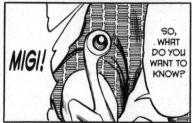

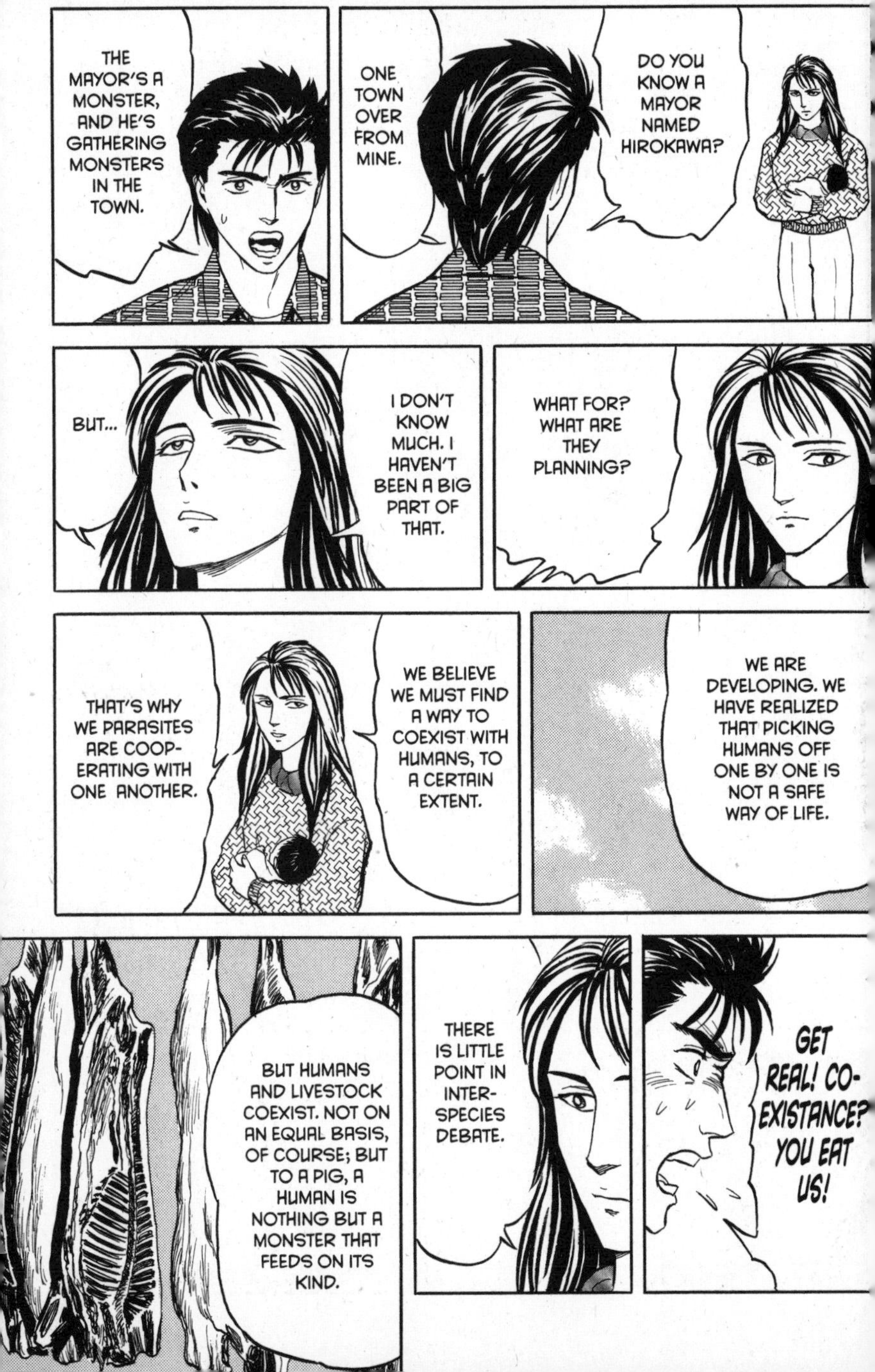
DO YOU KNOW A MAYOR NAMED HIROKAWA?
ONE TOWN OVER FROM MINE.
THE MAYOR'S A MONSTER, AND HE'S GATHERING MONSTERS IN THE TOWN.
WHAT FOR? WHAT ARE THEY PLANNING?
I DON'T KNOW MUCH. I HAVEN'T BEEN A BIG PART OF THAT.
BUT...
WE ARE DEVELOPING. WE HAVE REALIZED THAT PICKING HUMANS OFF ONE BY ONE IS NOT A SAFE WAY OF LIFE.
WE BELIEVE WE MUST FIND A WAY TO COEXIST WITH HUMANS, TO A CERTAIN EXTENT.
THAT'S WHY WE PARASITES ARE COOP-ERATING WITH ONE ANOTHER.
GET REAL! CO-EXISTANCE? YOU EAT US!
THERE IS LITTLE POINT IN INTER-SPECIES DEBATE.
BUT HUMANS AND LIVESTOCK COEXIST. NOT ON AN EQUAL BASIS, OF COURSE; BUT TO A PIG, A HUMAN IS NOTHING BUT A MONSTER THAT FEEDS ON ITS KIND.

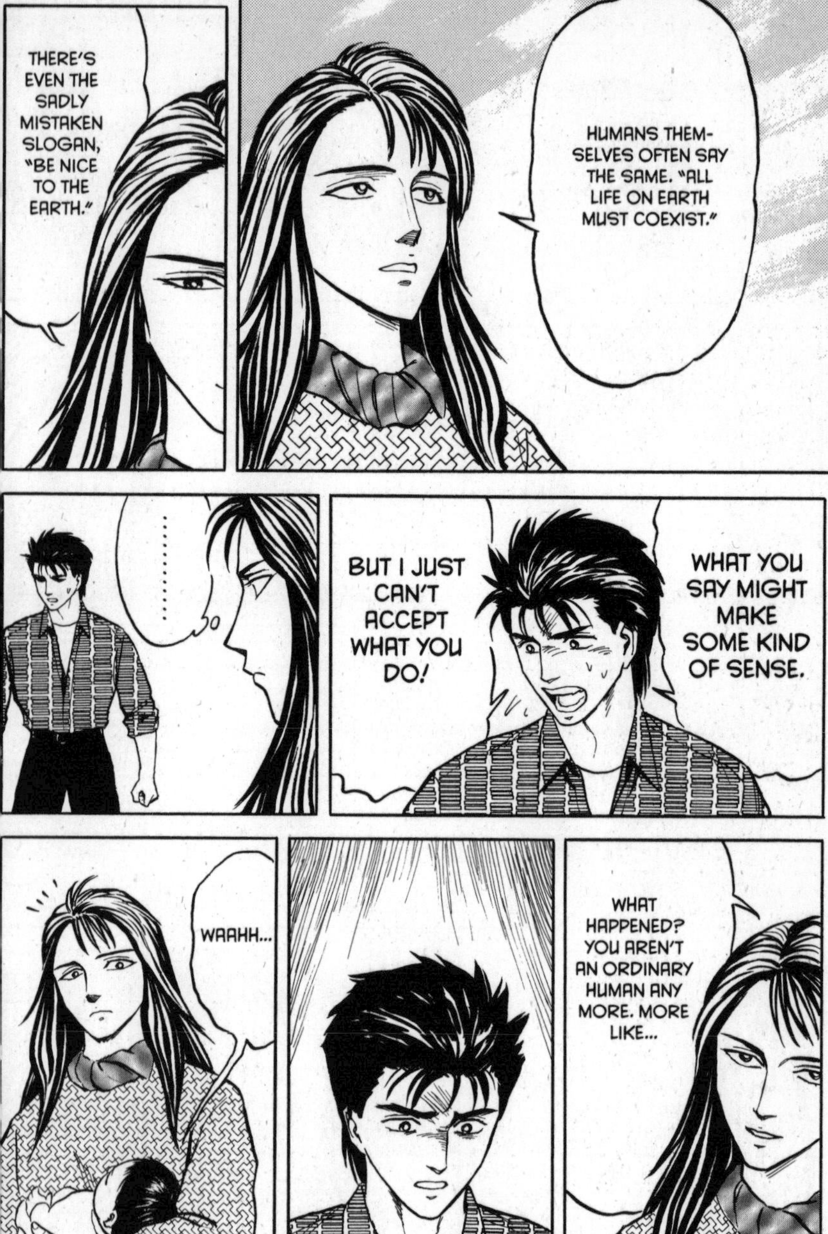
HUMANS THEMSELVES OFTEN SAY THE SAME. "ALL LIFE ON EARTH MUST COEXIST."
THERE'S EVEN THE SADLY MISTAKEN SLOGAN, "BE NICE TO THE EARTH."
WHAT YOU SAY MIGHT MAKE SOME KIND OF SENSE.
BUT I JUST CAN'T ACCEPT WHAT YOU DO!
......
WHAT HAPPENED? YOU AREN'T AN ORDINARY HUMAN ANY MORE. MORE LIKE...
WAAHH...

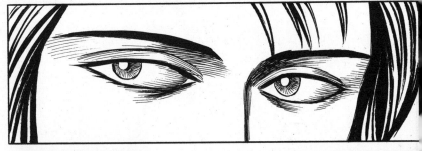

YOUR MOTHER IS MISSING.

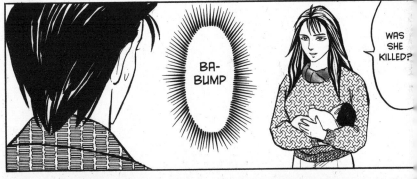

BA-BUMP

WAS SHE KILLED?

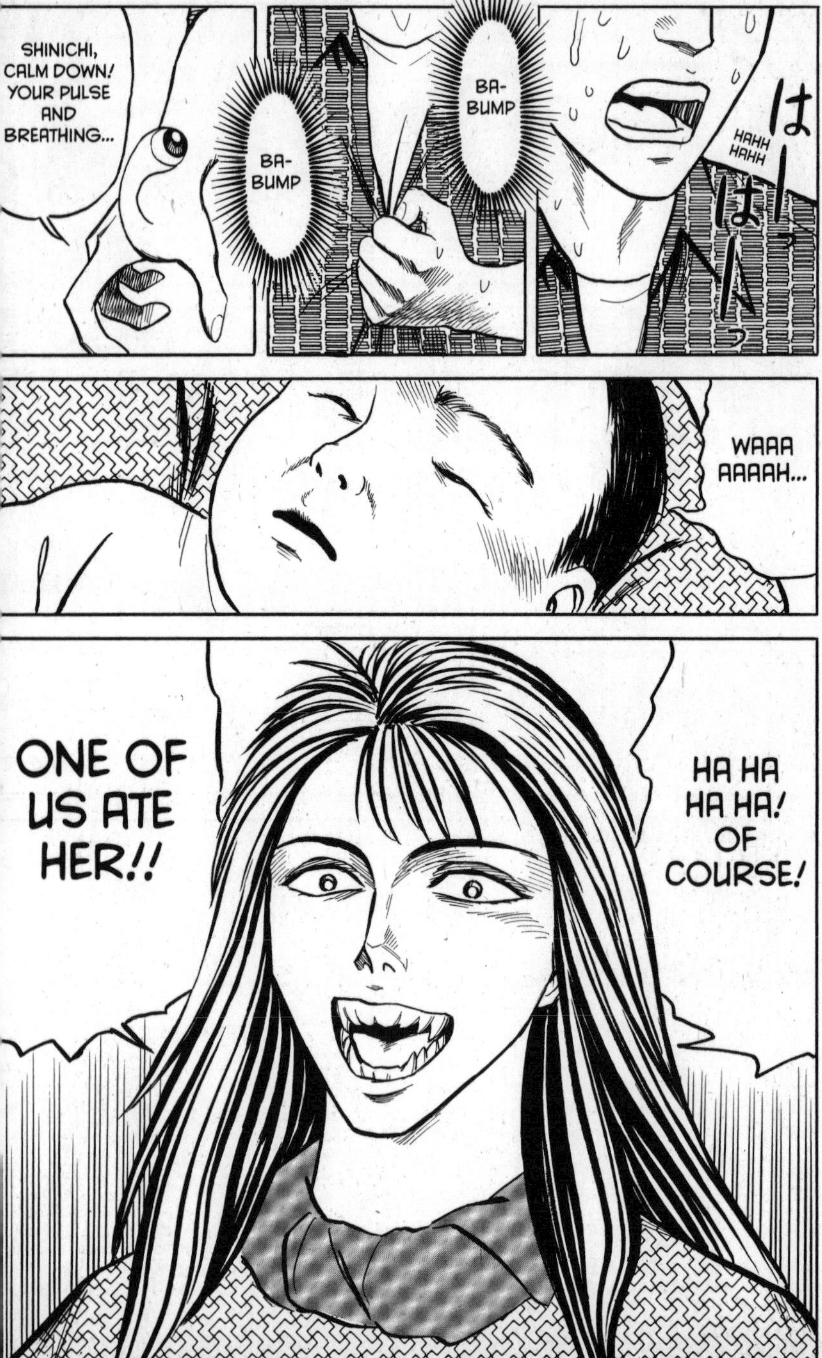
HAHH HAHH
BA-BUMP
BA-BUMP
SHINICHI, CALM DOWN! YOUR PULSE AND BREATHING...
WAAA AAAAH...
HA HA HA HA! OF COURSE!
ONE OF US ATE HER!!

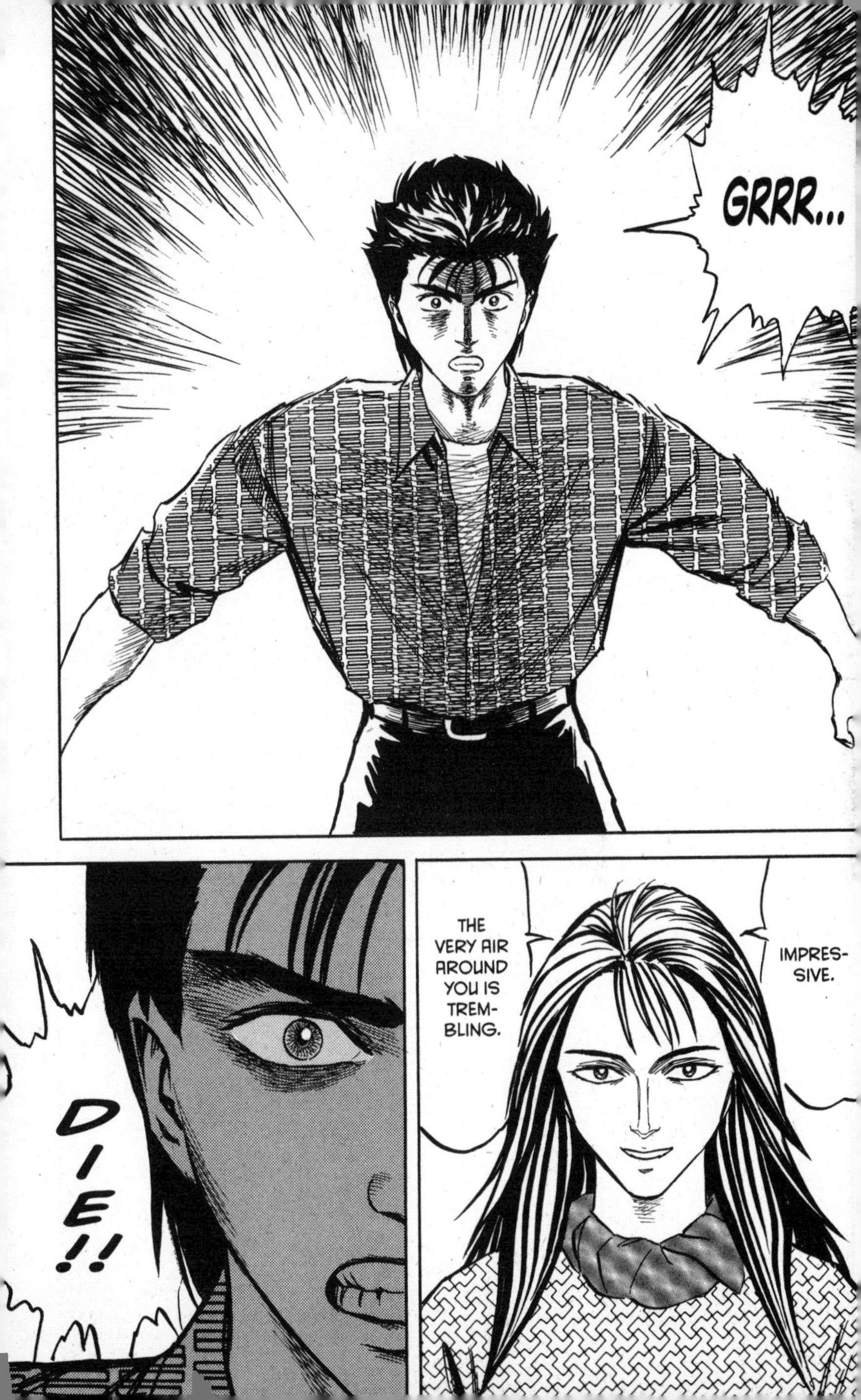
GRRR...
IMPRES-SIVE.
THE VERY AIR AROUND YOU IS TREM-BLING.
DIE!!

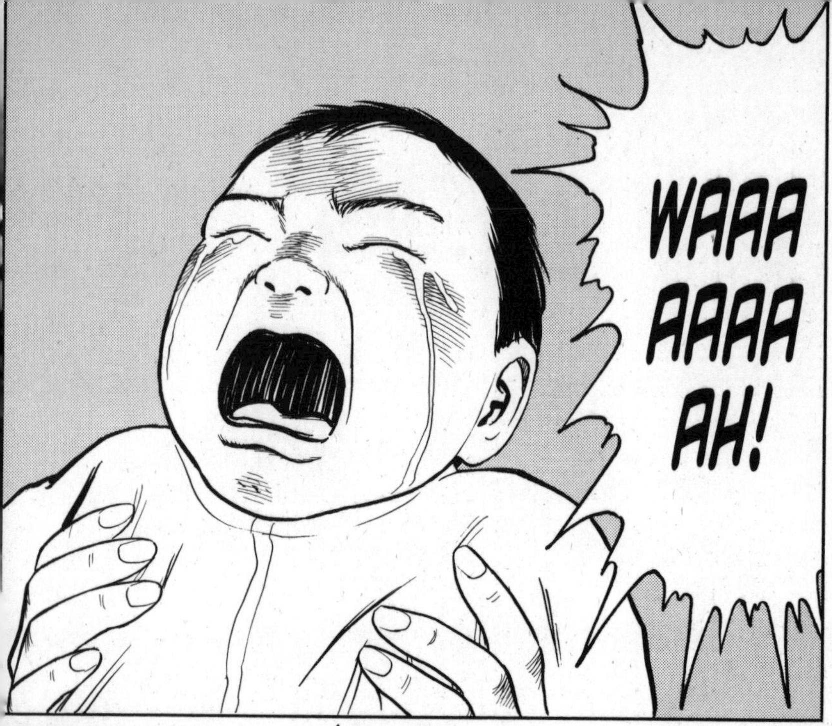
WAAA AAAA AH!

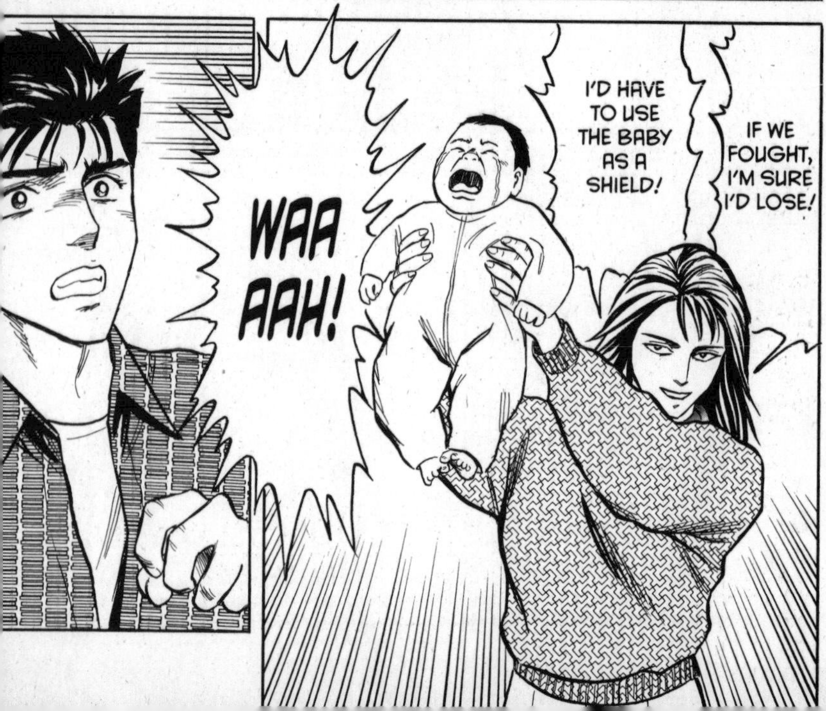
IF WE FOUGHT, I'M SURE I'D LOSE!
I'D HAVE TO USE THE BABY AS A SHIELD!
WAA AAH!

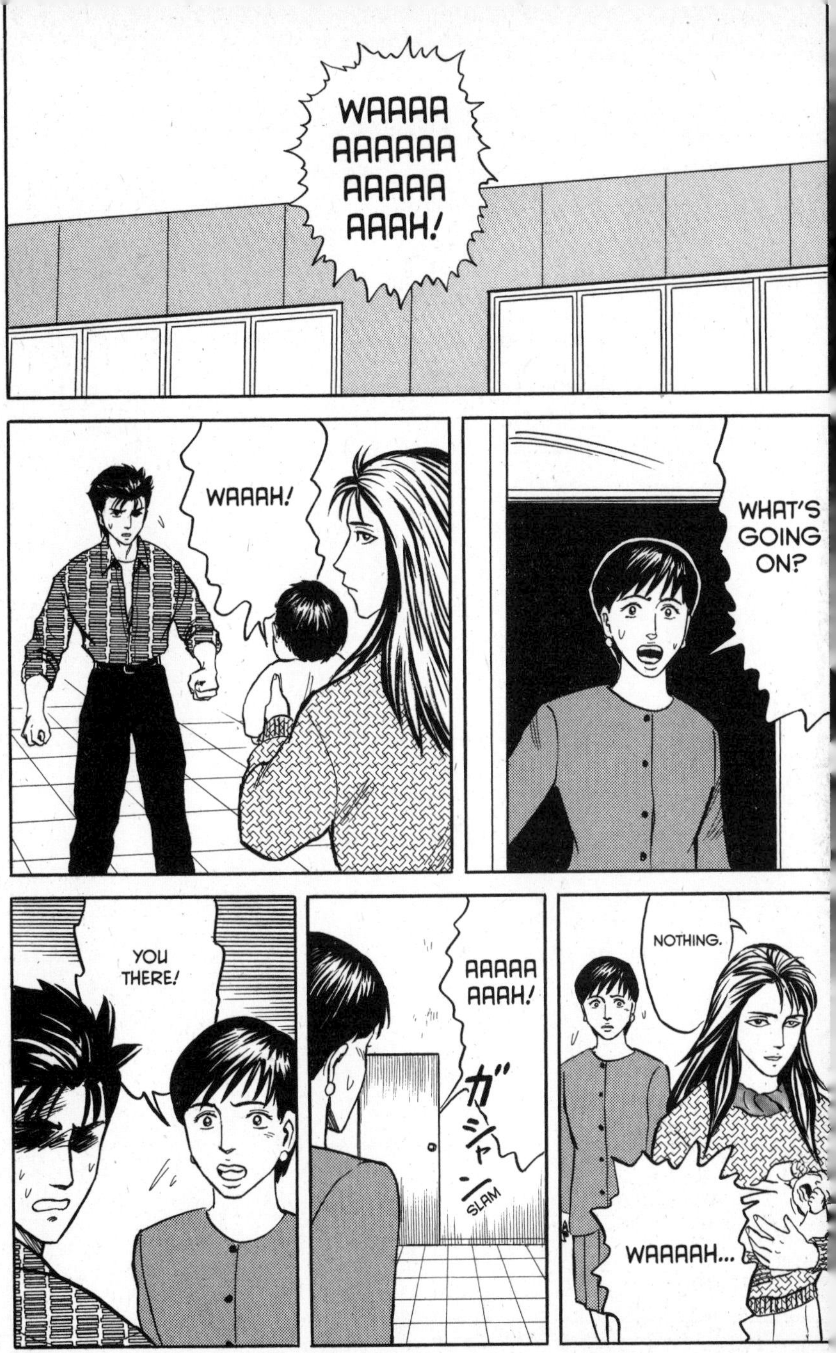
WAAAA AAAAAA AAAAA AAAH!
WHAT'S GOING ON?
WAAAH!
NOTHING.
WAAAAH...
AAAAA AAAH!
ガシャン
SLAM
YOU THERE!

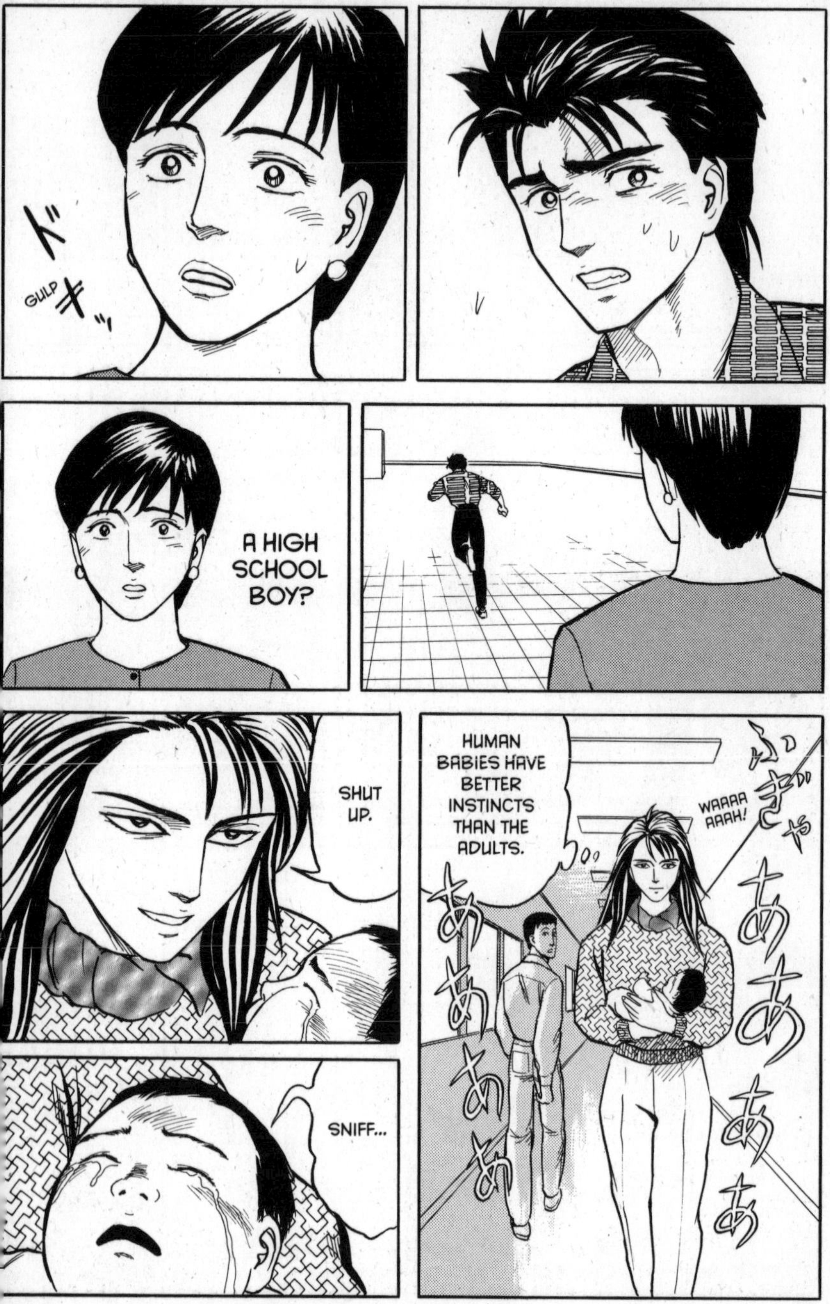
GULP
ドキッ
A HIGH SCHOOL BOY?
HUMAN BABIES HAVE BETTER INSTINCTS THAN THE ADULTS.
WAAAA AAAH!
SHUT UP.
SNIFF...

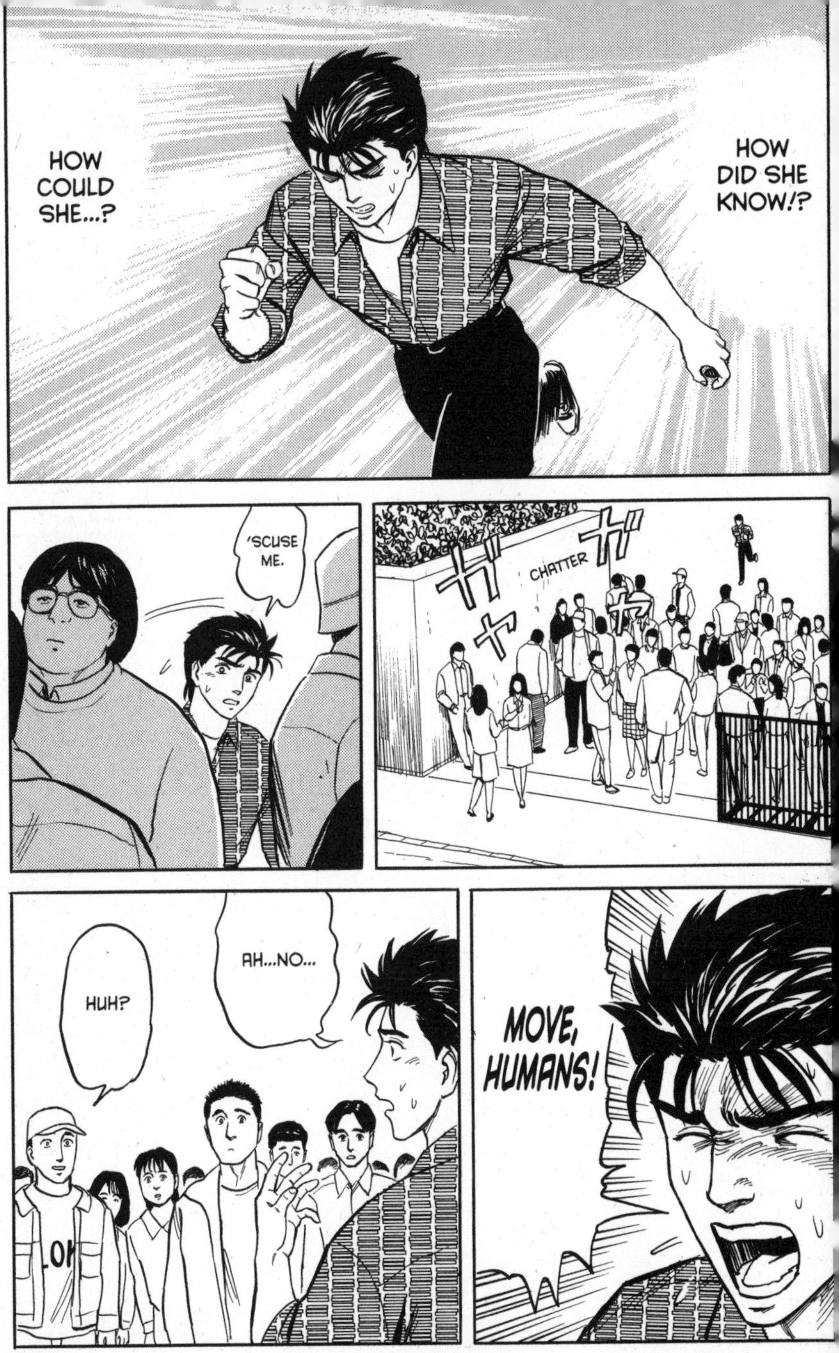
HOW DID SHE KNOW!?
HOW COULD SHE...?
ガヤガヤ
CHATTER
'SCUSE ME.
MOVE, HUMANS!
AH...NO...
HUH?

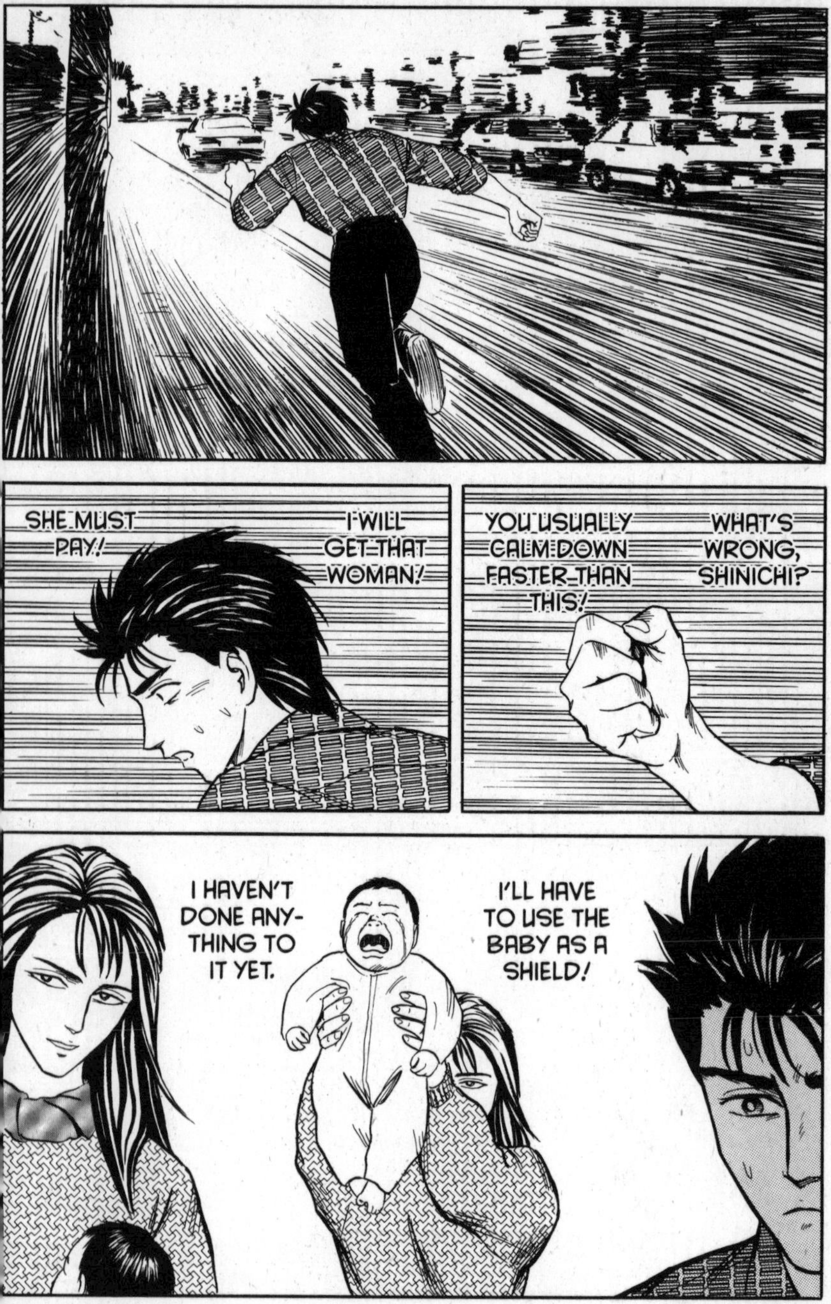
WHAT'S WRONG, SHINICHI?
YOU USUALLY CALM DOWN FASTER THAN THIS!
I WILL GET THAT WOMAN!
SHE MUST PAY!
I'LL HAVE TO USE THE BABY AS A SHIELD!
I HAVEN'T DONE ANY-THING TO IT YET.

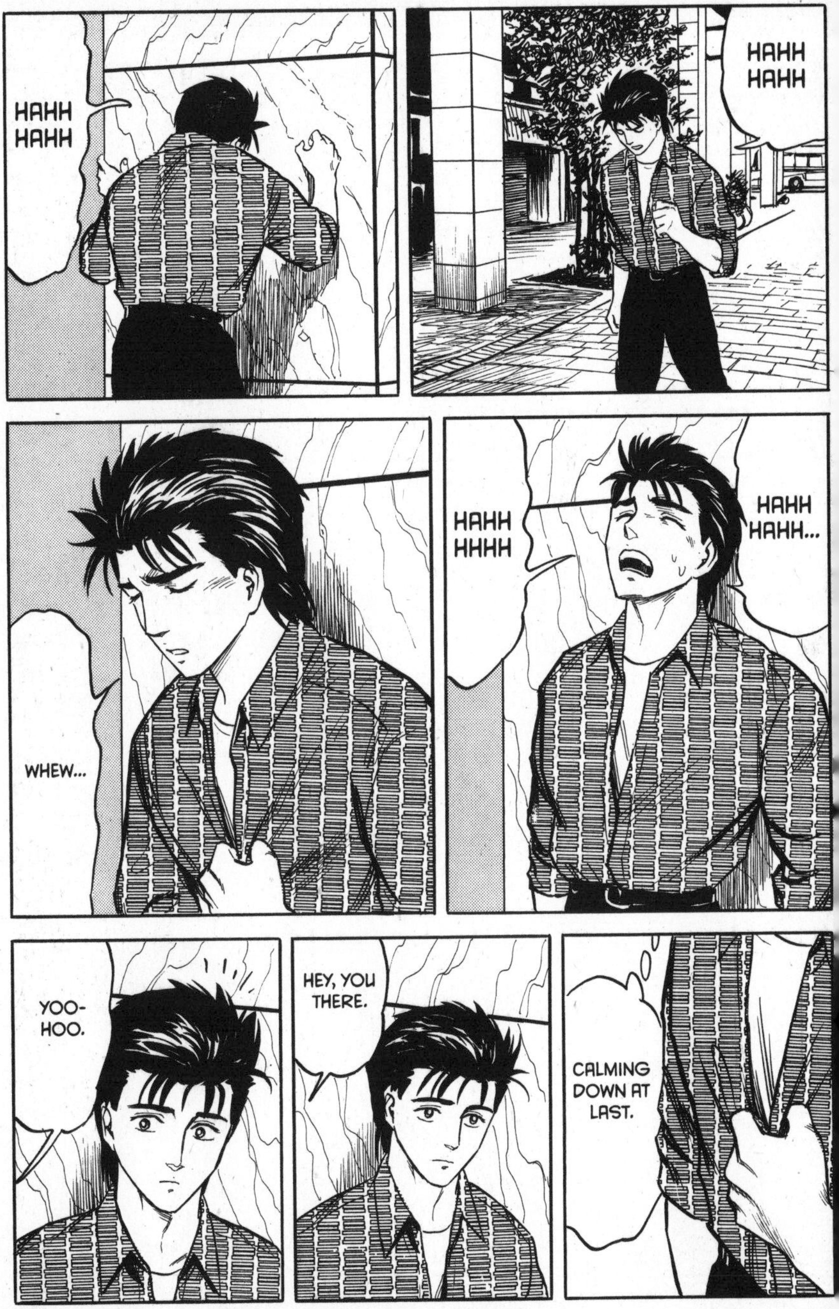

HAHH HAHH
HAHH HAHH
HAHH HAHH...
HAHH HHHH
WHEW...
CALMING DOWN AT LAST.
HEY, YOU THERE.
YOO-HOO.

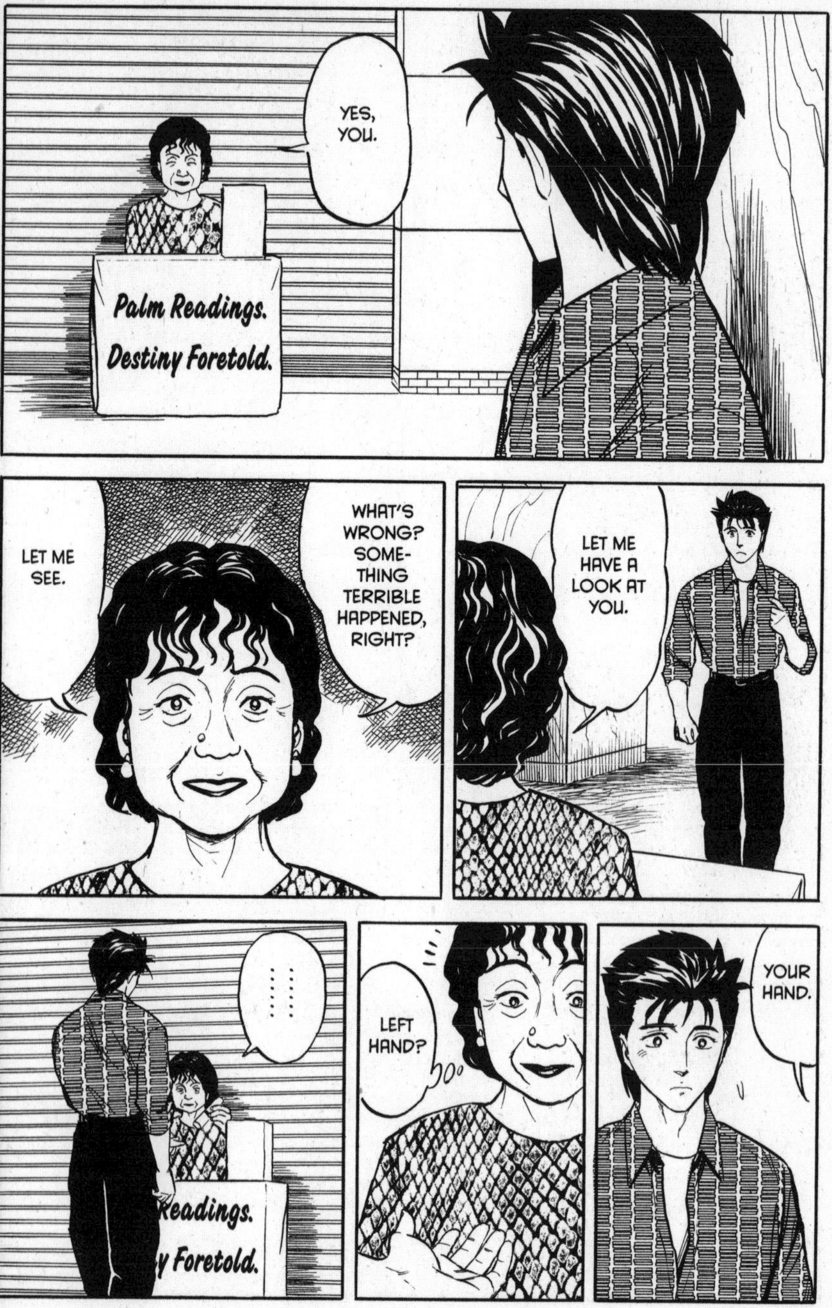
YES, YOU.
Palm Readings.
Destiny Foretold.
LET ME HAVE A LOOK AT YOU.
WHAT'S WRONG? SOME-THING TERRIBLE HAPPENED, RIGHT?
LET ME SEE.
YOUR HAND.
LEFT HAND?
......
Readings.

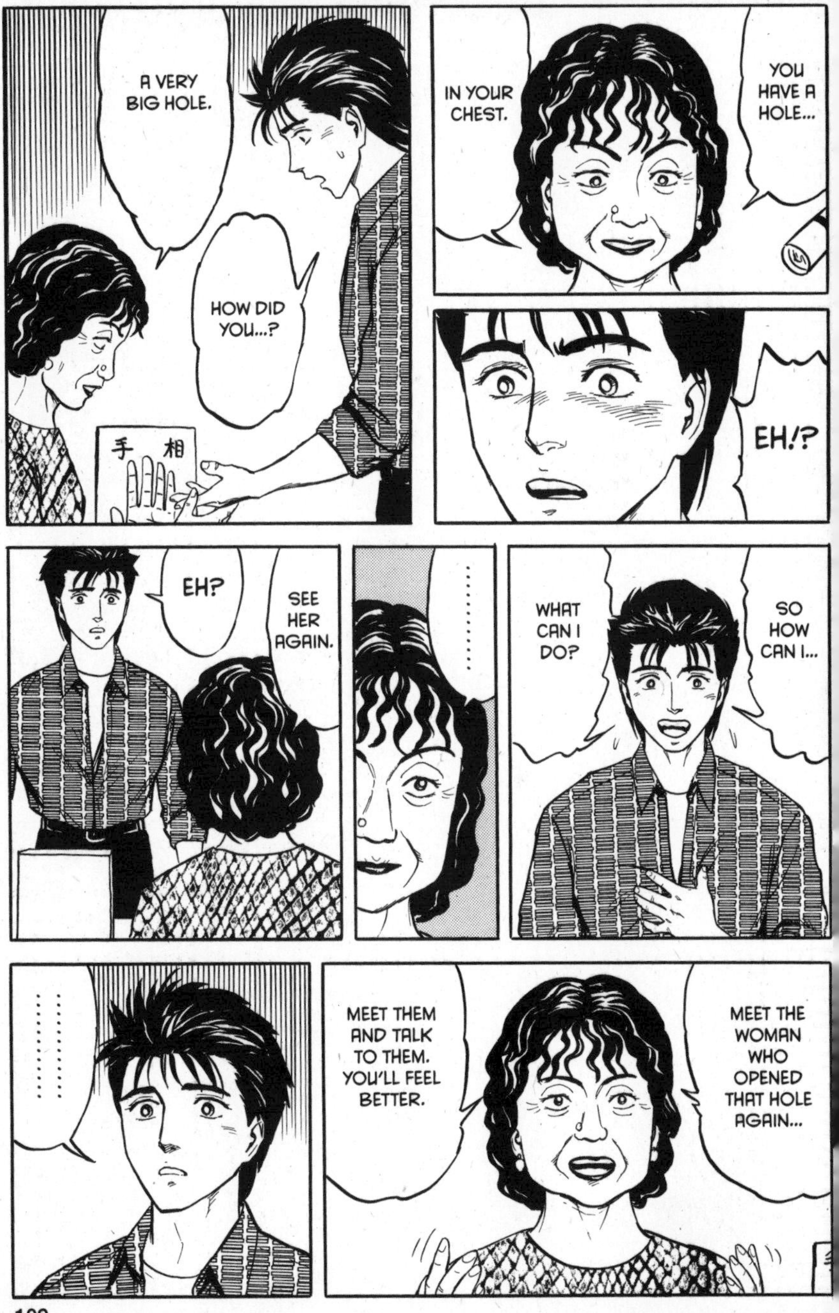
YOU HAVE A HOLE...
IN YOUR CHEST.
EH!?
A VERY BIG HOLE.
HOW DID YOU...?
手相
SO HOW CAN I...
WHAT CAN I DO?
......
SEE HER AGAIN.
EH?
MEET THE WOMAN WHO OPENED THAT HOLE AGAIN...
MEET THEM AND TALK TO THEM. YOU'LL FEEL BETTER.
......

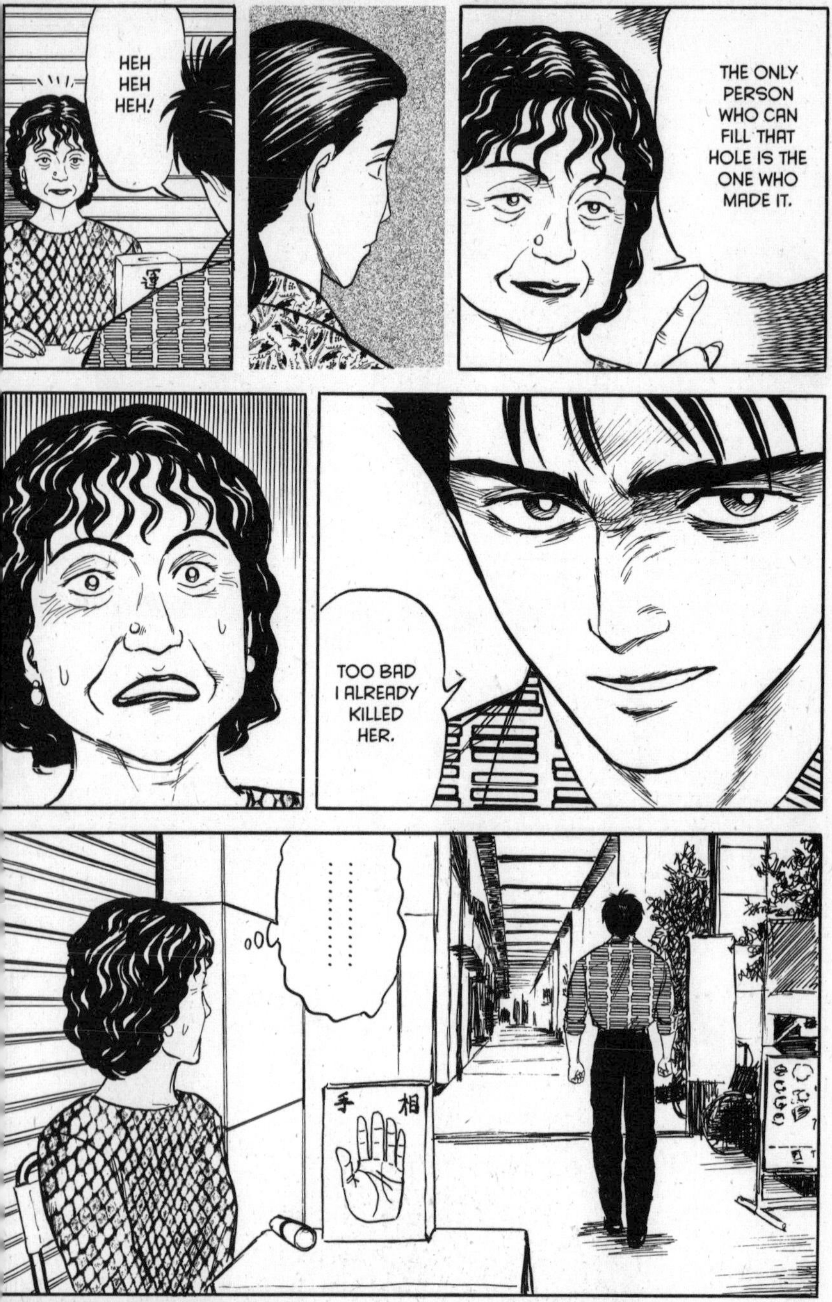
THE ONLY PERSON WHO CAN FILL THAT HOLE IS THE ONE WHO MADE IT.
HEH HEH HEH!
TOO BAD I ALREADY KILLED HER.
手 相

CHAPTER 37: DINING ROOM

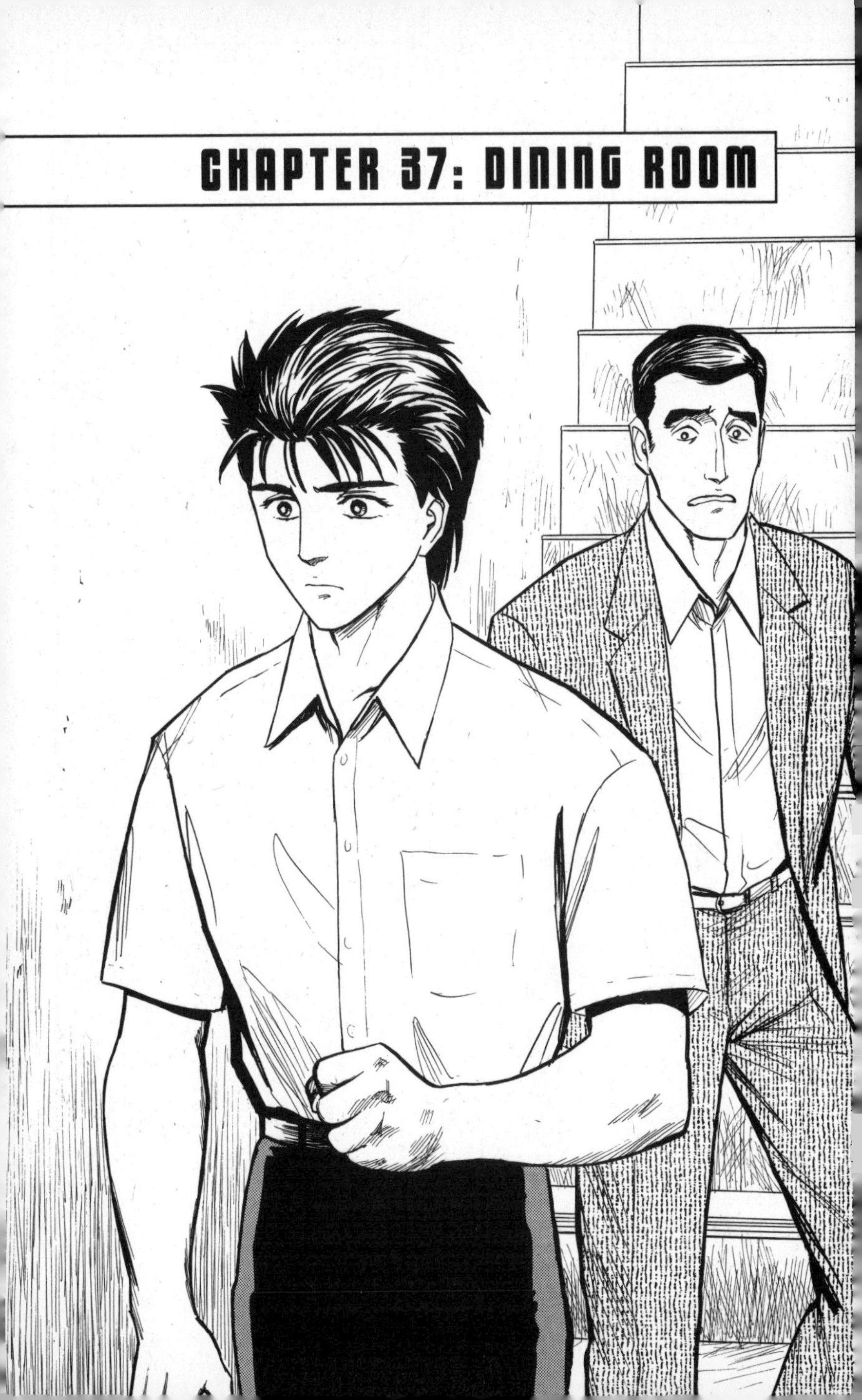

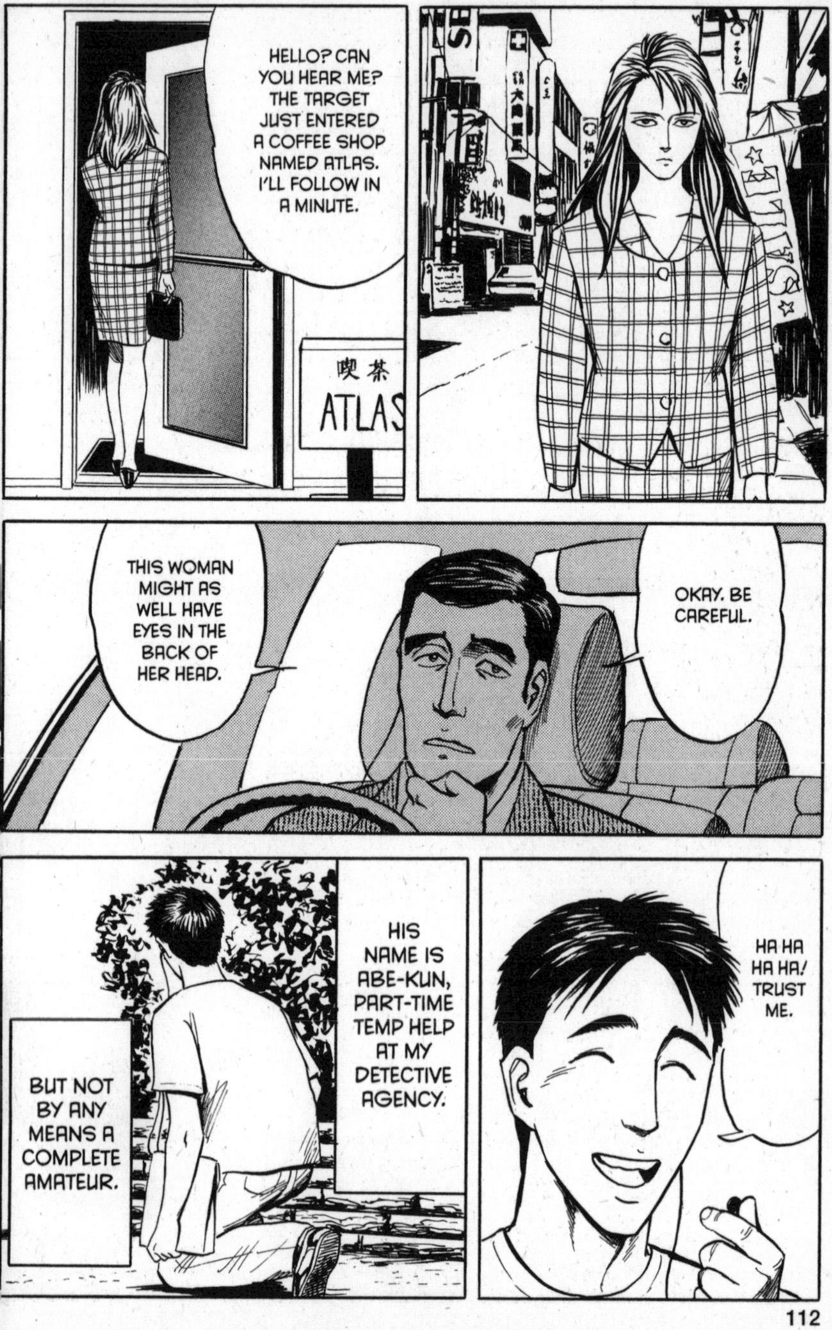
HELLO? CAN YOU HEAR ME? THE TARGET JUST ENTERED A COFFEE SHOP NAMED ATLAS. I'LL FOLLOW IN A MINUTE.
喫茶
ATLAS
OKAY. BE CAREFUL.
THIS WOMAN MIGHT AS WELL HAVE EYES IN THE BACK OF HER HEAD.
HA HA HA HA! TRUST ME.
HIS NAME IS ABE-KUN, PART-TIME TEMP HELP AT MY DETECTIVE AGENCY.
BUT NOT BY ANY MEANS A COMPLETE AMATEUR.

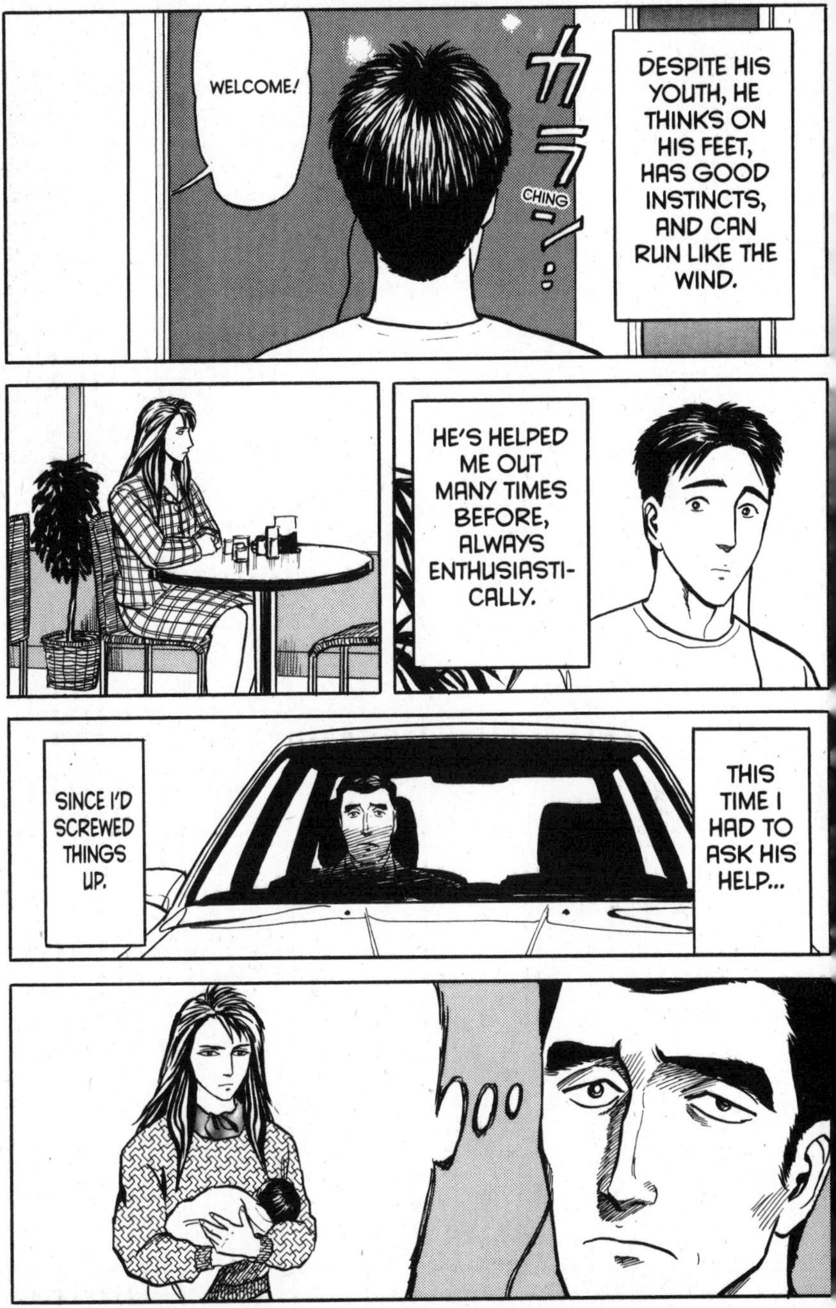
DESPITE HIS YOUTH, HE THINKS ON HIS FEET, HAS GOOD INSTINCTS, AND CAN RUN LIKE THE WIND.
カラーン
CHING
WELCOME!
HE'S HELPED ME OUT MANY TIMES BEFORE, ALWAYS ENTHUSIASTI-CALLY.
THIS TIME I HAD TO ASK HIS HELP...
SINCE I'D SCREWED THINGS UP.

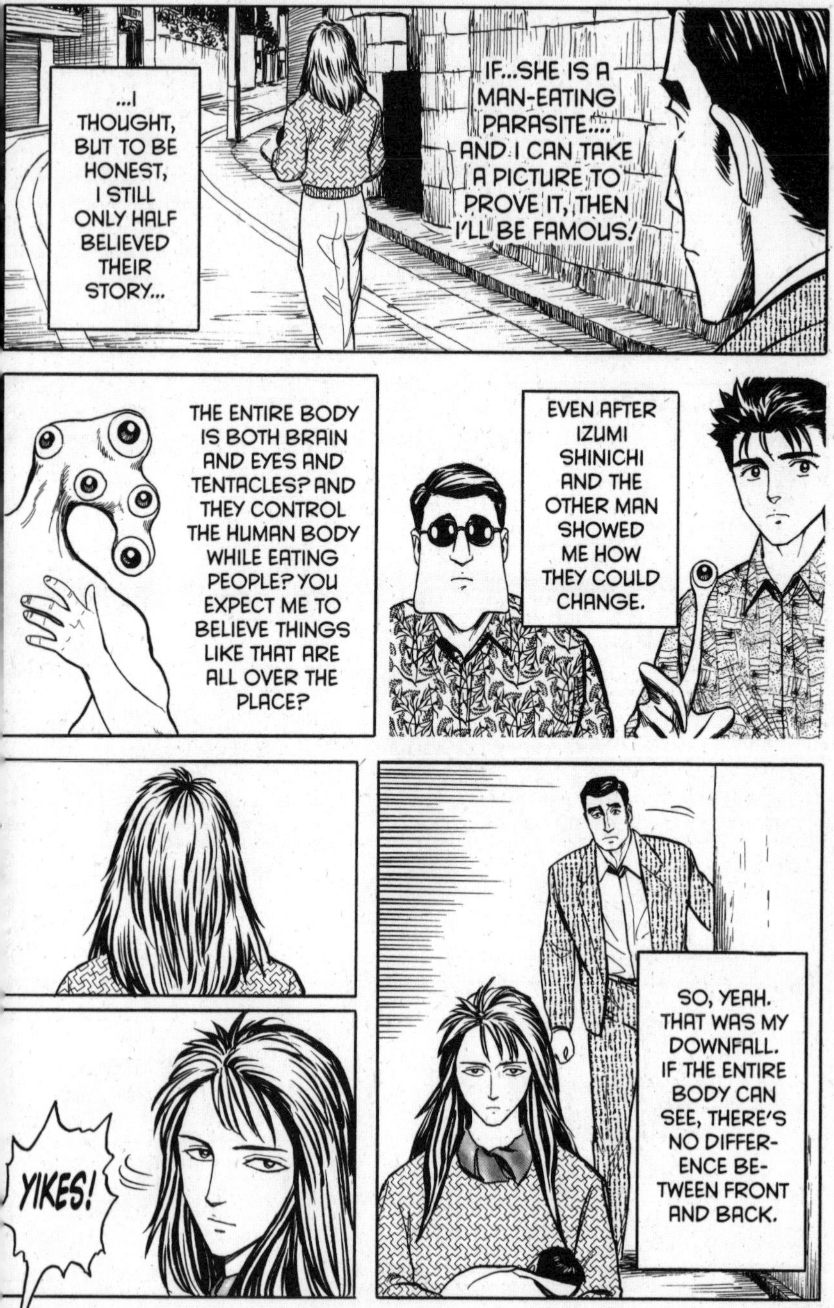
IF...SHE IS A MAN-EATING PARASITE.... AND I CAN TAKE A PICTURE TO PROVE IT, THEN I'LL BE FAMOUS!
...I THOUGHT, BUT TO BE HONEST, I STILL ONLY HALF BELIEVED THEIR STORY...
EVEN AFTER IZUMI SHINICHI AND THE OTHER MAN SHOWED ME HOW THEY COULD CHANGE.
THE ENTIRE BODY IS BOTH BRAIN AND EYES AND TENTACLES? AND THEY CONTROL THE HUMAN BODY WHILE EATING PEOPLE? YOU EXPECT ME TO BELIEVE THINGS LIKE THAT ARE ALL OVER THE PLACE?
SO, YEAH. THAT WAS MY DOWNFALL. IF THE ENTIRE BODY CAN SEE, THERE'S NO DIFFER-ENCE BE-TWEEN FRONT AND BACK.
YIKES!

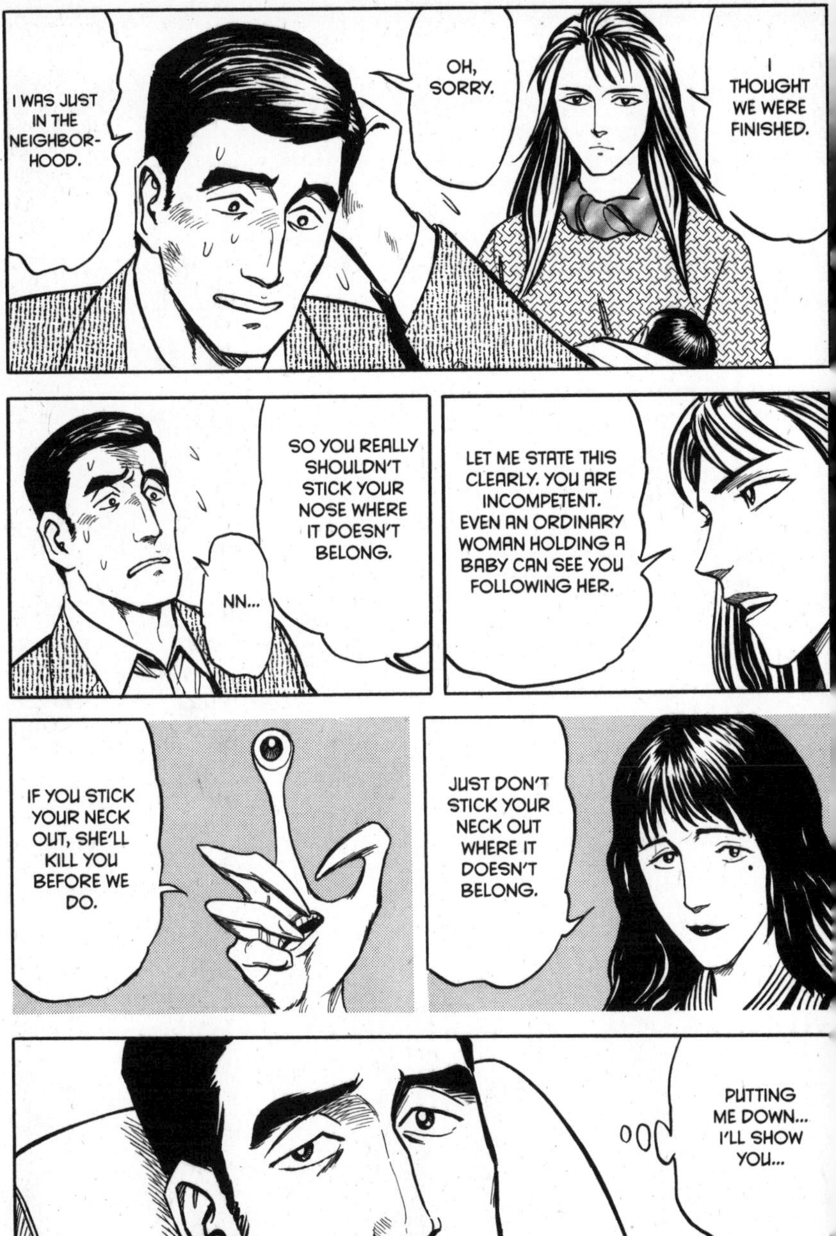

I THOUGHT WE WERE FINISHED.
OH, SORRY.
I WAS JUST IN THE NEIGHBOR-HOOD.
LET ME STATE THIS CLEARLY. YOU ARE INCOMPETENT. EVEN AN ORDINARY WOMAN HOLDING A BABY CAN SEE YOU FOLLOWING HER.
SO YOU REALLY SHOULDN'T STICK YOUR NOSE WHERE IT DOESN'T BELONG.
NN...
JUST DON'T STICK YOUR NECK OUT WHERE IT DOESN'T BELONG.
IF YOU STICK YOUR NECK OUT, SHE'LL KILL YOU BEFORE WE DO.
PUTTING ME DOWN... I'LL SHOW YOU...

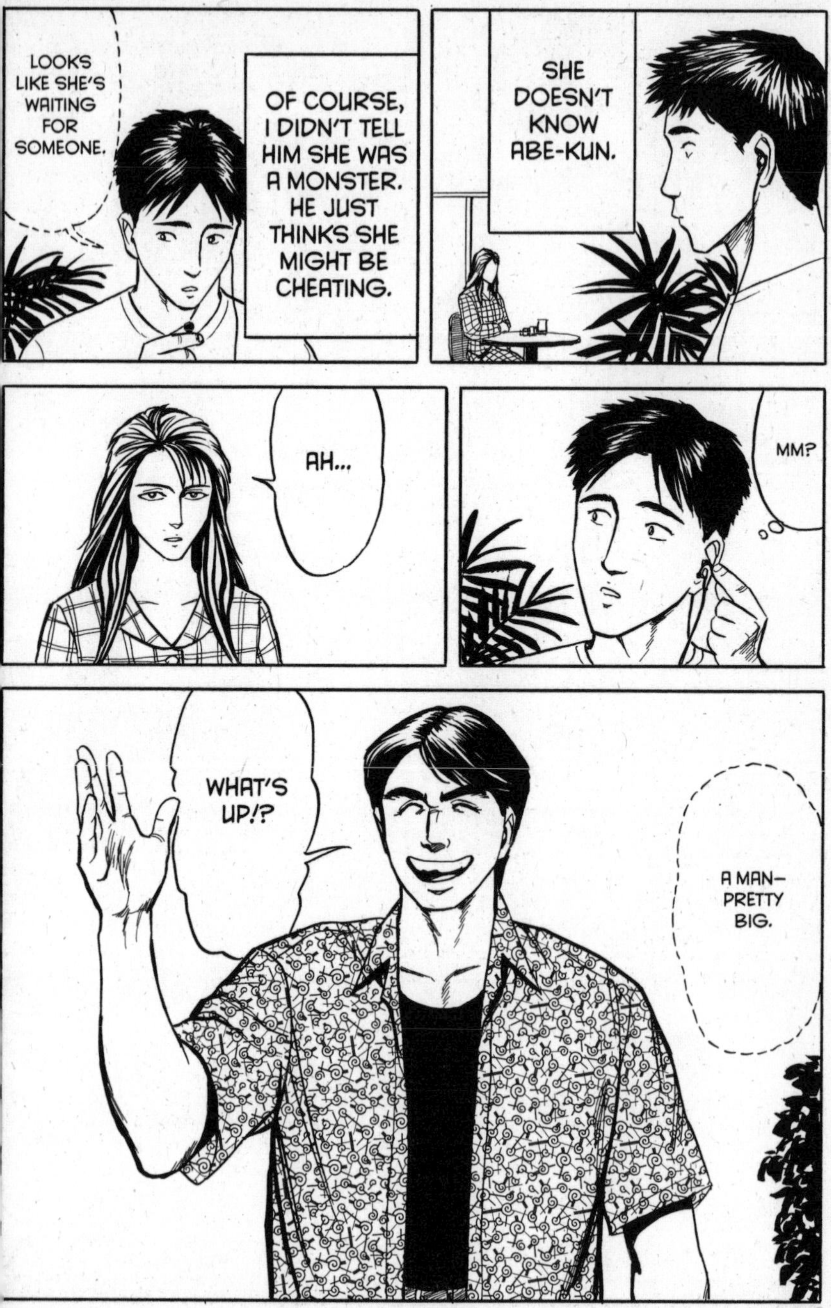
SHE DOESN'T KNOW ABE-KUN.
OF COURSE, I DIDN'T TELL HIM SHE WAS A MONSTER. HE JUST THINKS SHE MIGHT BE CHEATING.
LOOKS LIKE SHE'S WAITING FOR SOMEONE.
MM?
AH...
A MAN—PRETTY BIG.
WHAT'S UP!?

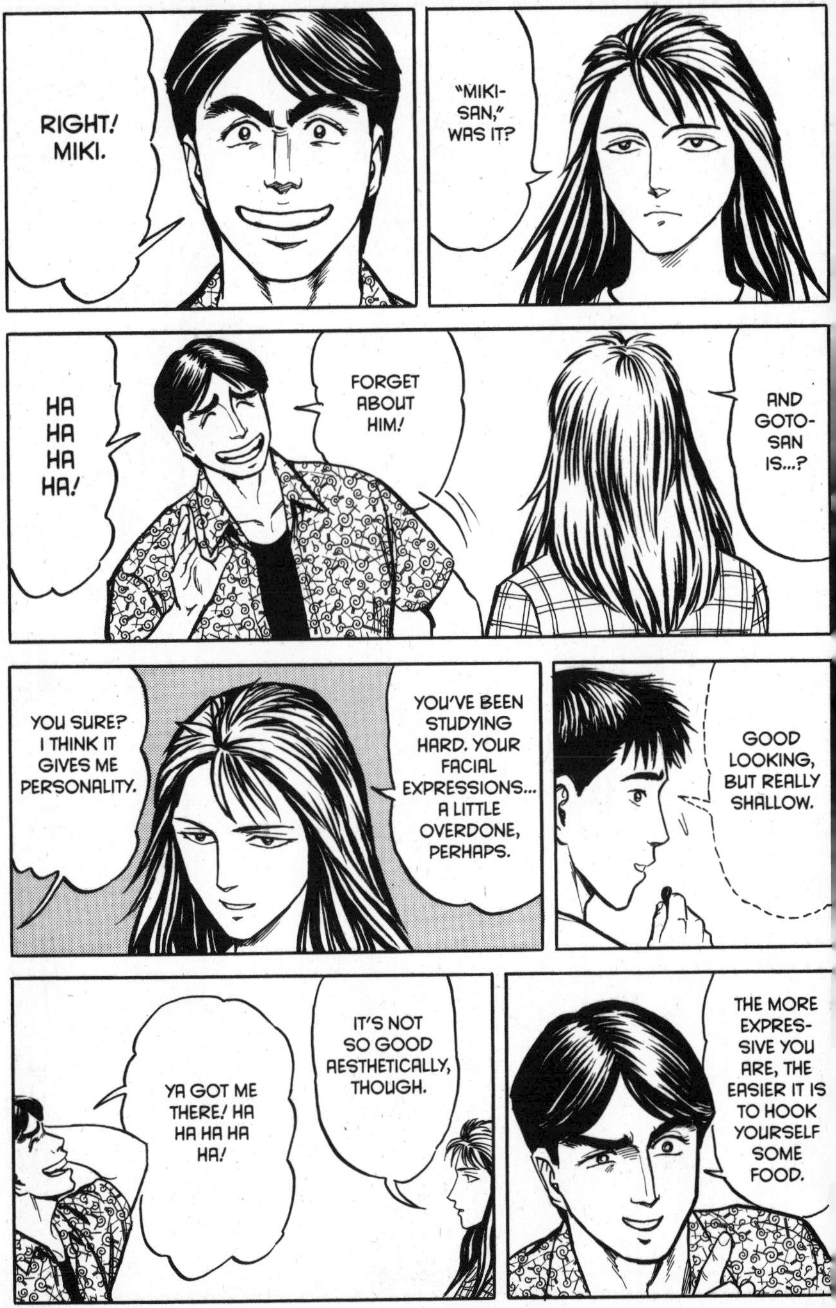
"MIKI-SAN," WAS IT?
RIGHT! MIKI.
AND GOTO-SAN IS...?
FORGET ABOUT HIM!
HA HA HA HA!
GOOD LOOKING, BUT REALLY SHALLOW.
YOU'VE BEEN STUDYING HARD. YOUR FACIAL EXPRESSIONS... A LITTLE OVERDONE, PERHAPS.
YOU SURE? I THINK IT GIVES ME PERSONALITY.
THE MORE EXPRESSIVE YOU ARE, THE EASIER IT IS TO HOOK YOURSELF SOME FOOD.
IT'S NOT SO GOOD AESTHETICALLY, THOUGH.
YA GOT ME THERE! HA HA HA HA HA!

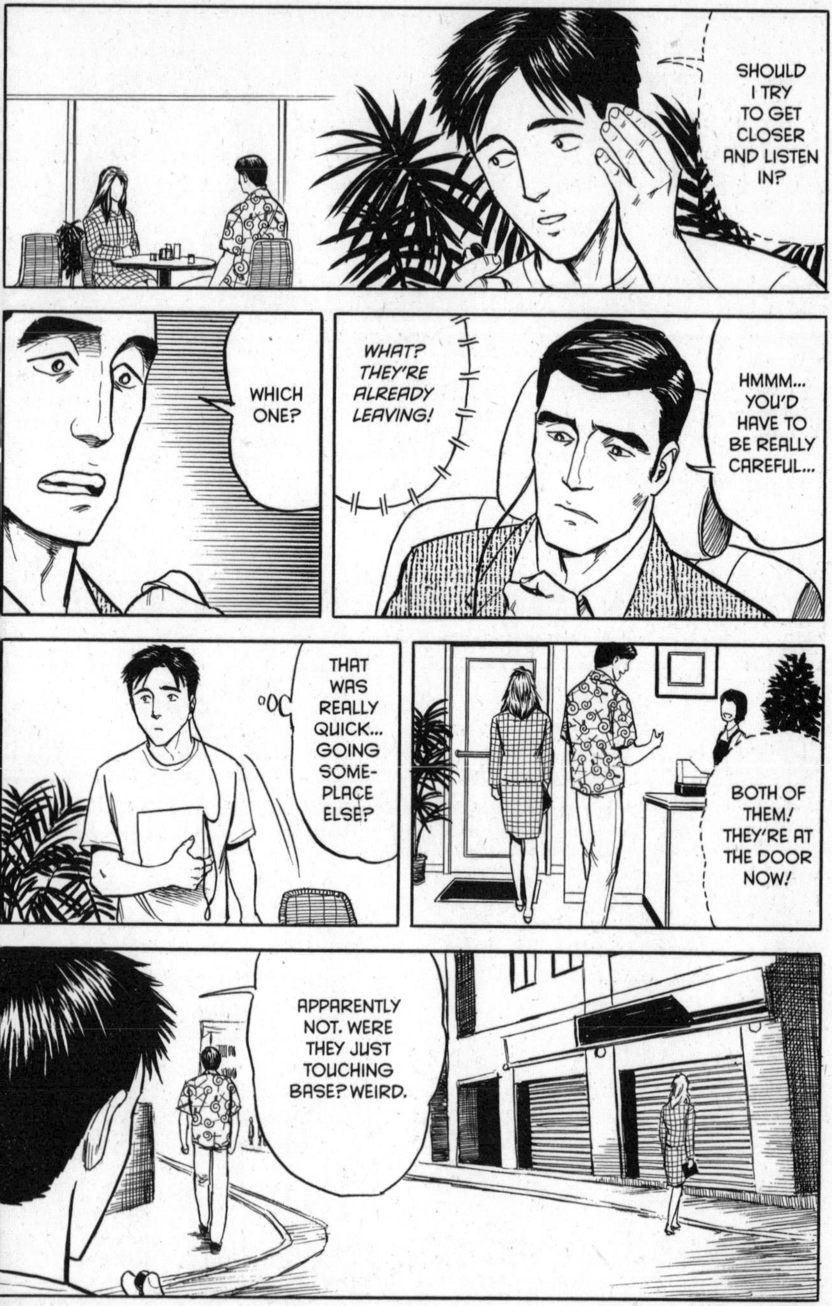
SHOULD I TRY TO GET CLOSER AND LISTEN IN?
HMMM... YOU'D HAVE TO BE REALLY CAREFUL...
WHAT? THEY'RE ALREADY LEAVING!
WHICH ONE?
BOTH OF THEM! THEY'RE AT THE DOOR NOW!
THAT WAS REALLY QUICK... GOING SOME-PLACE ELSE?
APPARENTLY NOT. WERE THEY JUST TOUCHING BASE? WEIRD.

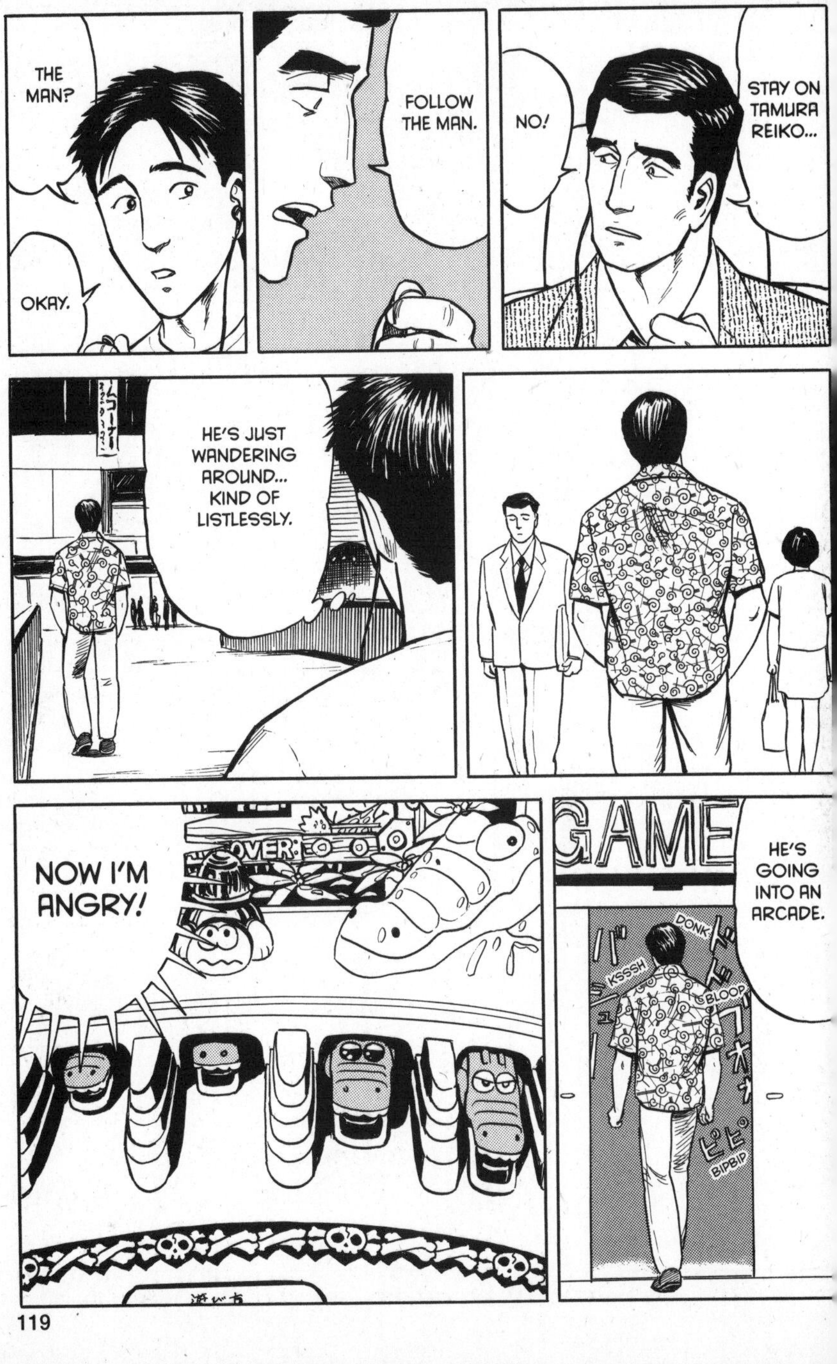
STAY ON TAMURA REIKO...
NO!
FOLLOW THE MAN.
THE MAN?
OKAY.
HE'S JUST WANDERING AROUND... KIND OF LISTLESSLY.
GAME
HE'S GOING INTO AN ARCADE.
DONK
KSSSH
BLOOP
BIPBIP
OVER
NOW I'M ANGRY!

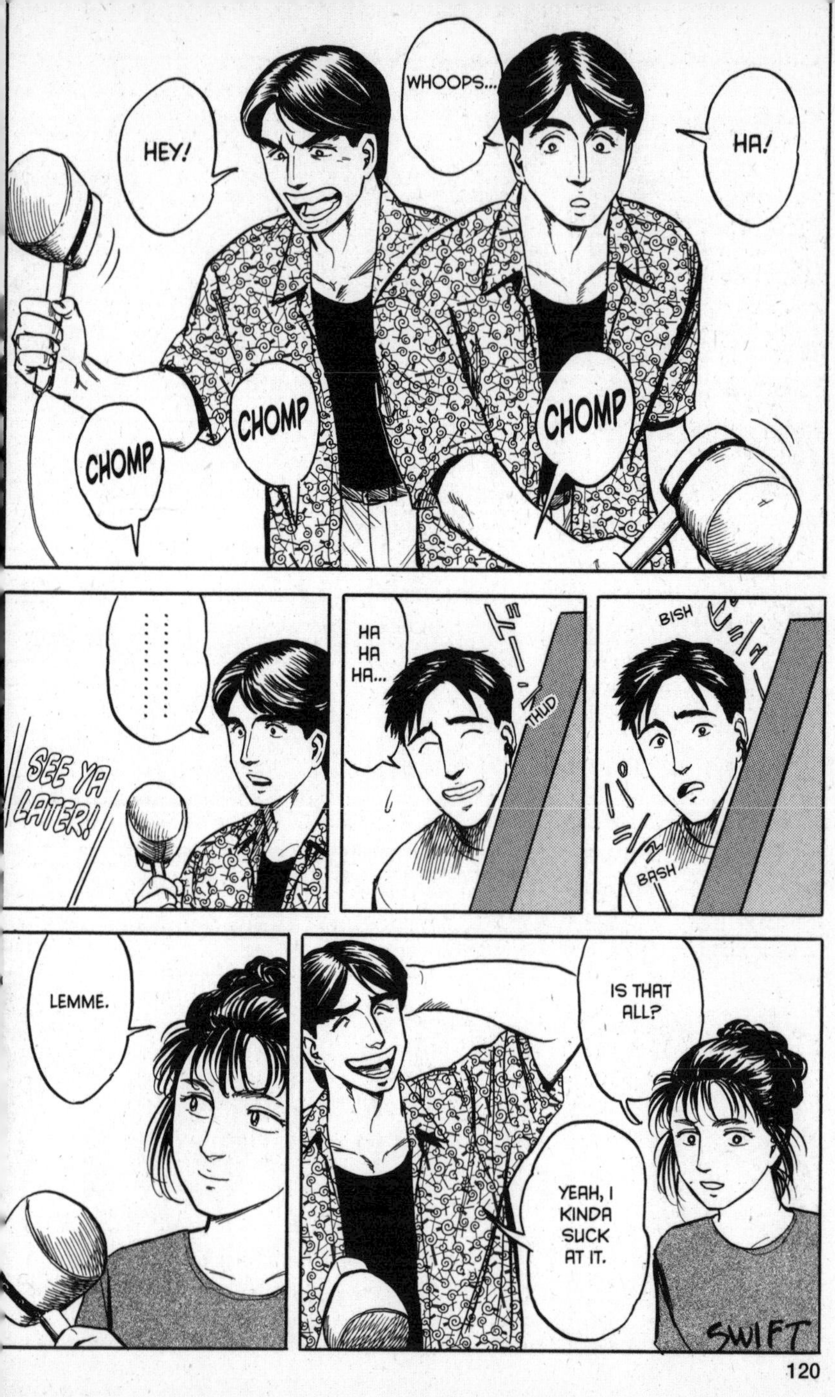
HA!
WHOOPS...
HEY!
CHOMP
CHOMP
CHOMP
BISH
BASH
HA
HA
HA...
THUD
......
SEE YA LATER!
IS THAT ALL?
YEAH, I KINDA SUCK AT IT.
SWIFT
LEMME.

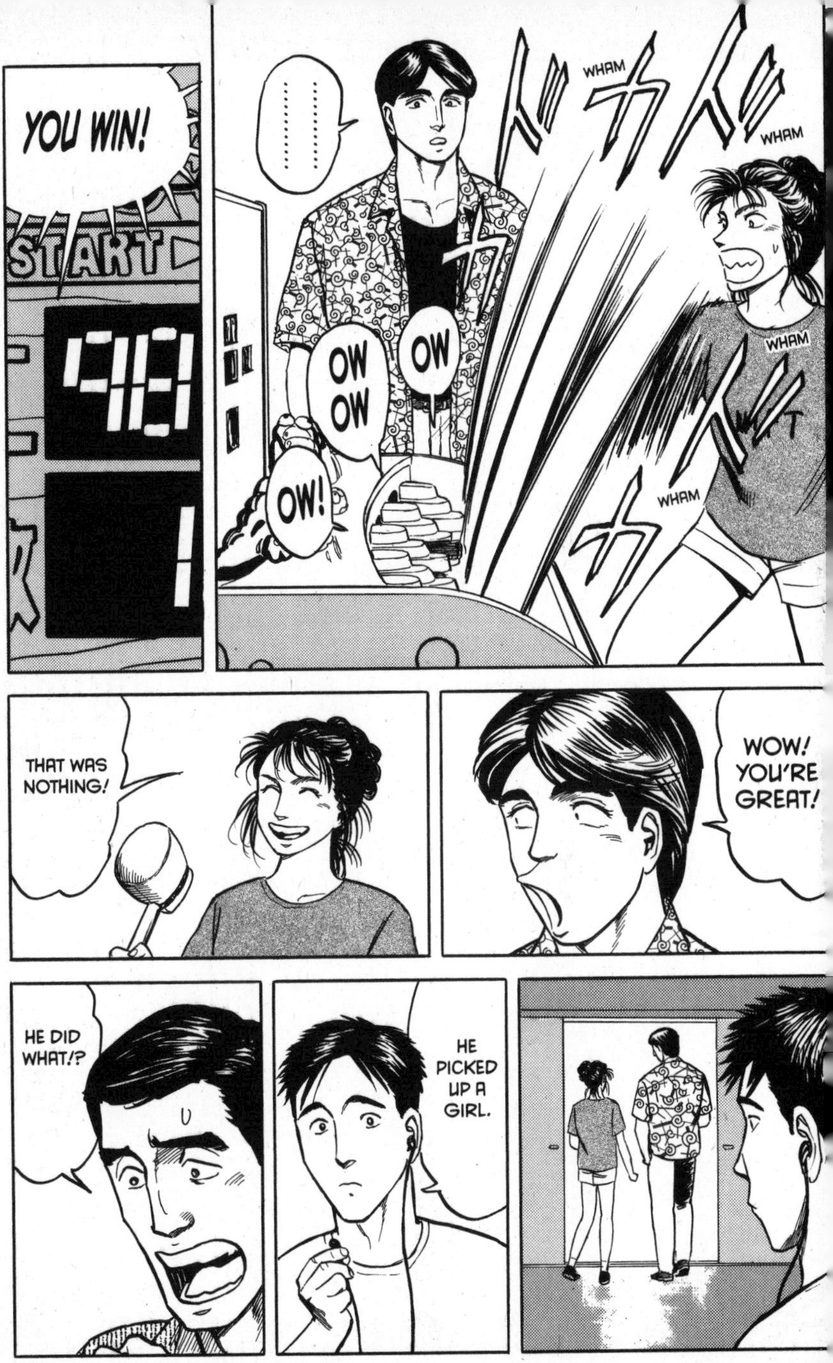
WHAM
WHAM
WHAM
WHAM
......
OW
OW OW
OW!
YOU WIN!
START
WOW! YOU'RE GREAT!
THAT WAS NOTHING!
HE PICKED UP A GIRL.
HE DID WHAT!?

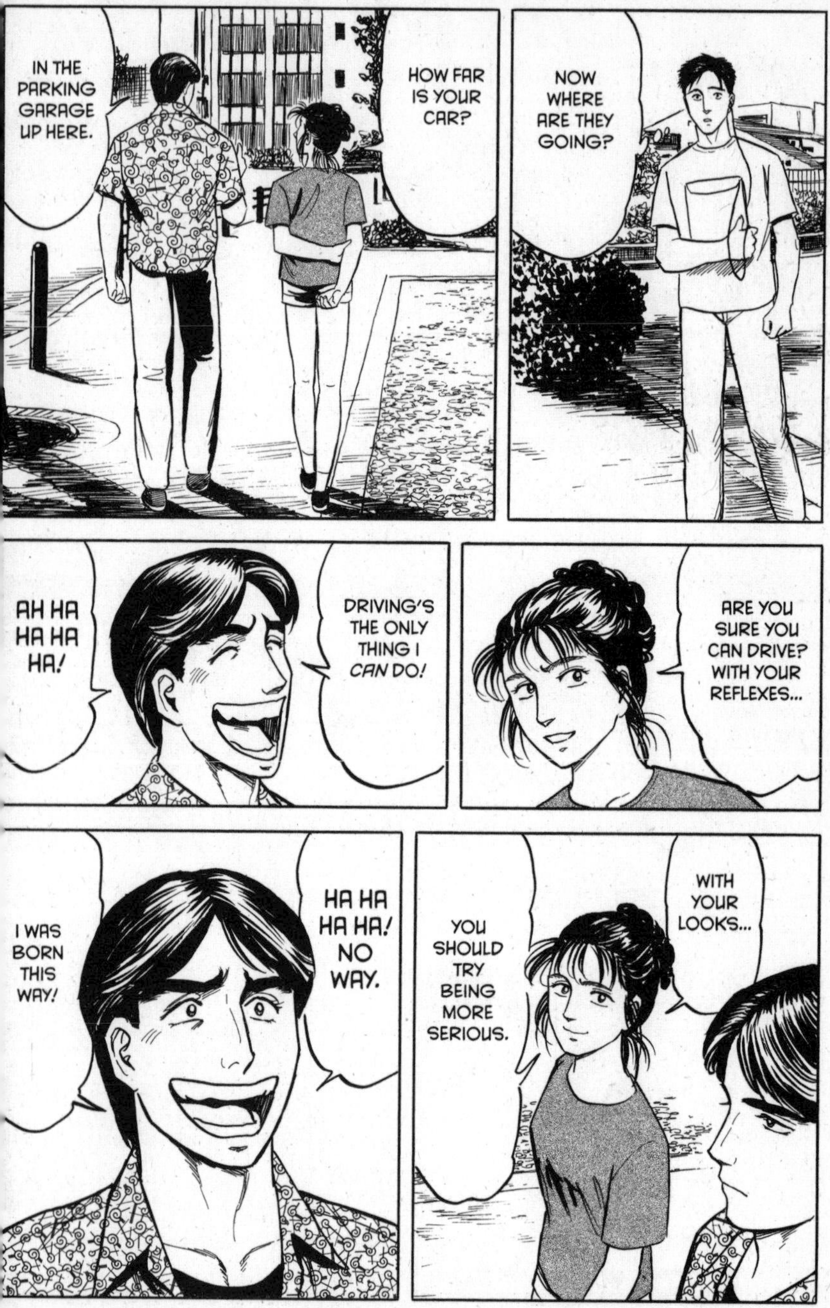
NOW WHERE ARE THEY GOING?
HOW FAR IS YOUR CAR?
IN THE PARKING GARAGE UP HERE.
ARE YOU SURE YOU CAN DRIVE? WITH YOUR REFLEXES...
DRIVING'S THE ONLY THING I *CAN* DO!
AH HA HA HA HA!
WITH YOUR LOOKS...
YOU SHOULD TRY BEING MORE SERIOUS.
HA HA HA HA! NO WAY.
I WAS BORN THIS WAY!

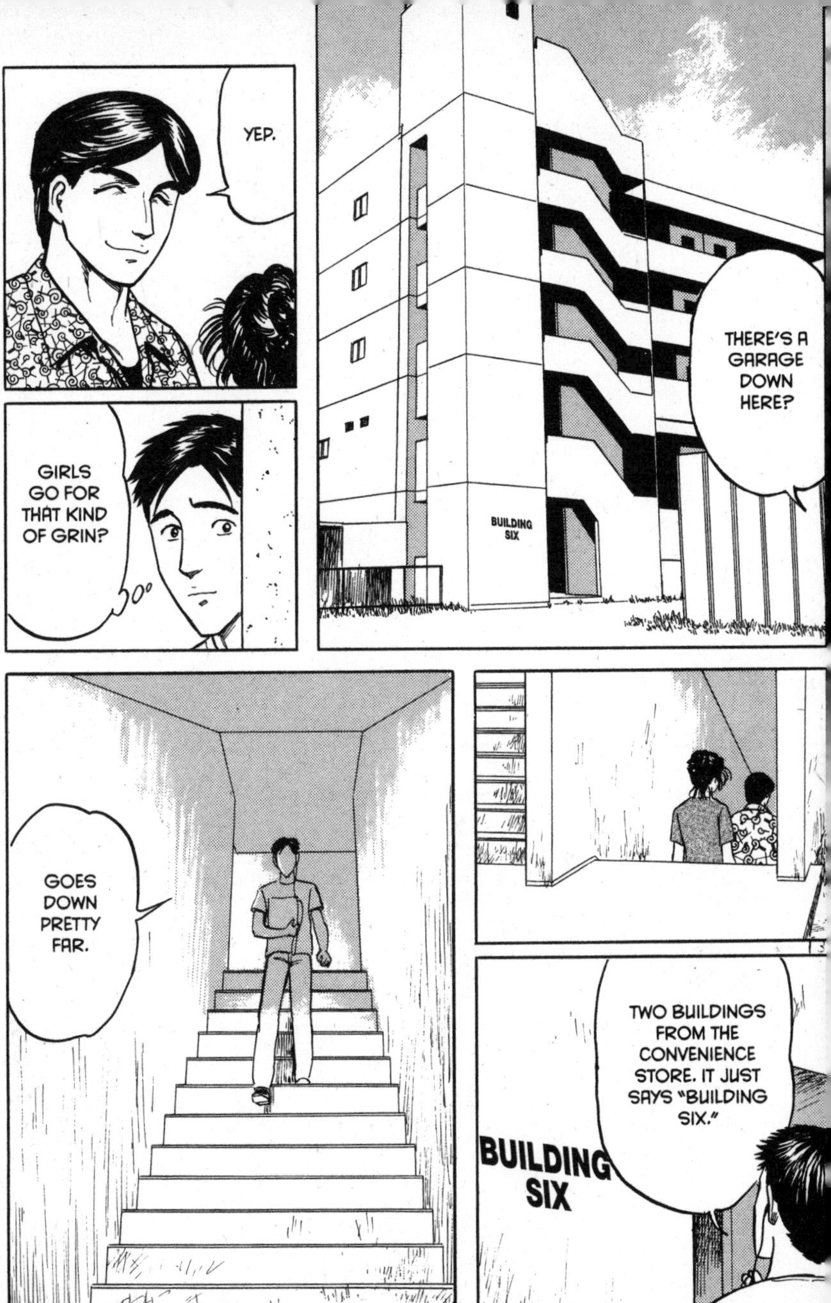
THERE'S A GARAGE DOWN HERE?
BUILDING SIX
YEP.
GIRLS GO FOR THAT KIND OF GRIN?
TWO BUILDINGS FROM THE CONVENIENCE STORE. IT JUST SAYS "BUILDING SIX."
BUILDING SIX
GOES DOWN PRETTY FAR.

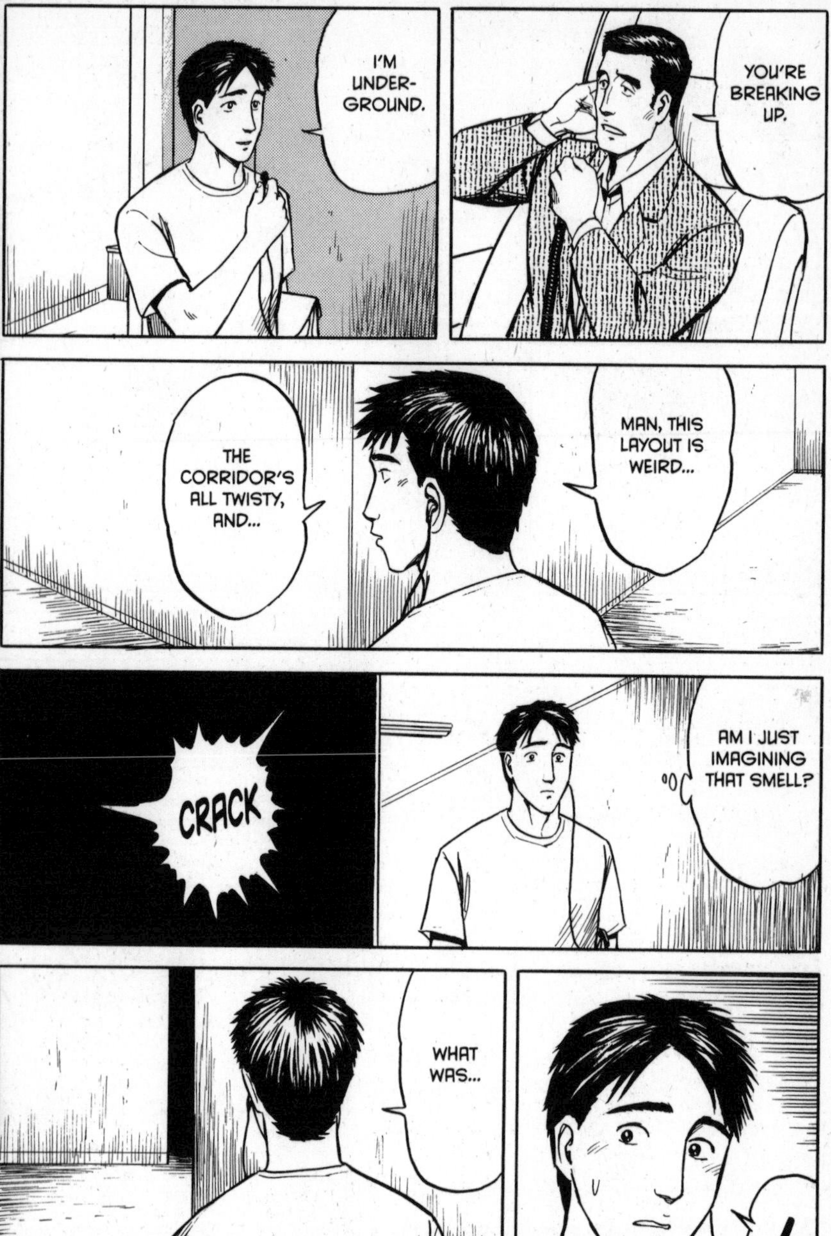
YOU'RE BREAKING UP.
I'M UNDER-GROUND.
MAN, THIS LAYOUT IS WEIRD...
THE CORRIDOR'S ALL TWISTY, AND...
AM I JUST IMAGINING THAT SMELL?
CRACK
!
WHAT WAS...

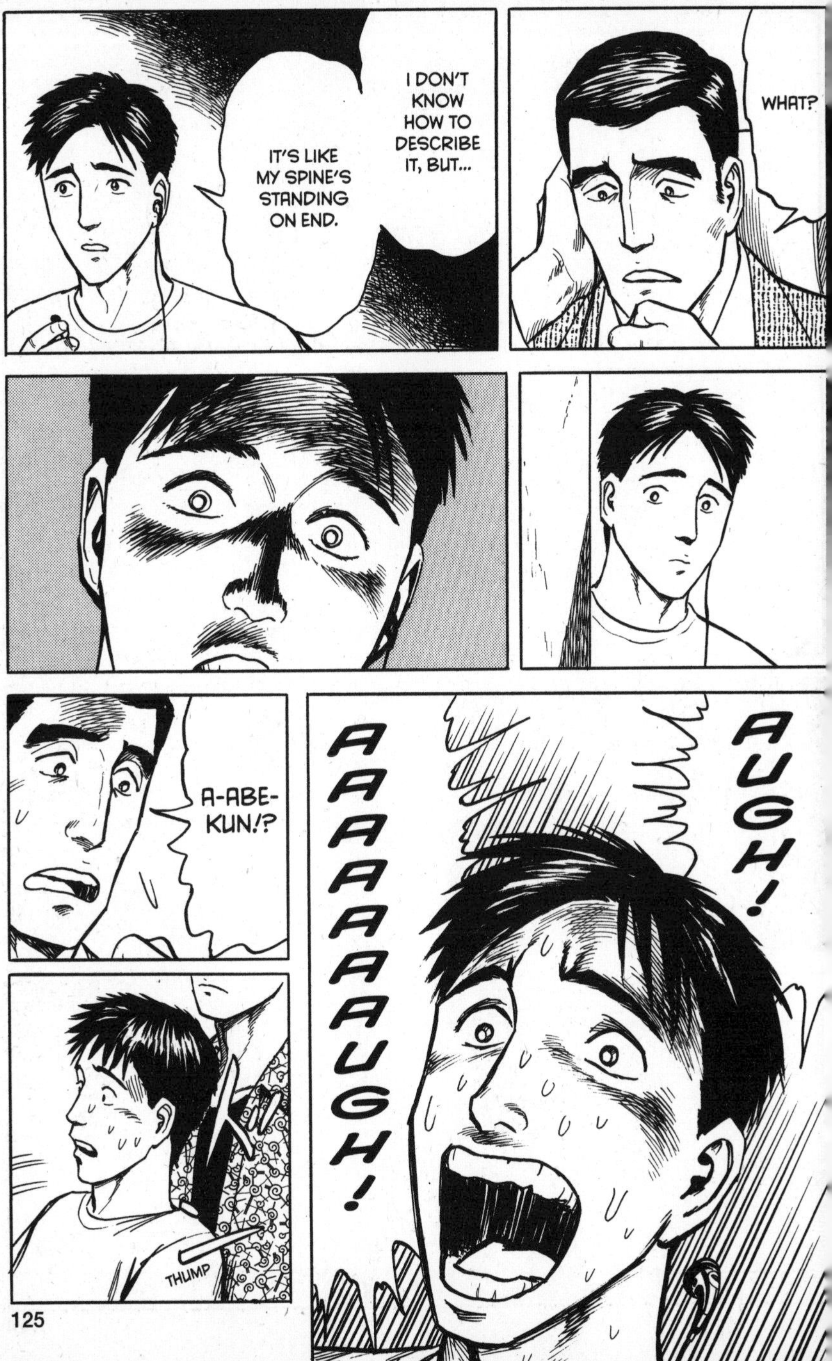
WHAT?
I DON'T KNOW HOW TO DESCRIBE IT, BUT...
IT'S LIKE MY SPINE'S STANDING ON END.
AUGH!
AAAAAAAUGH!
A-ABE-KUN!?
THUMP

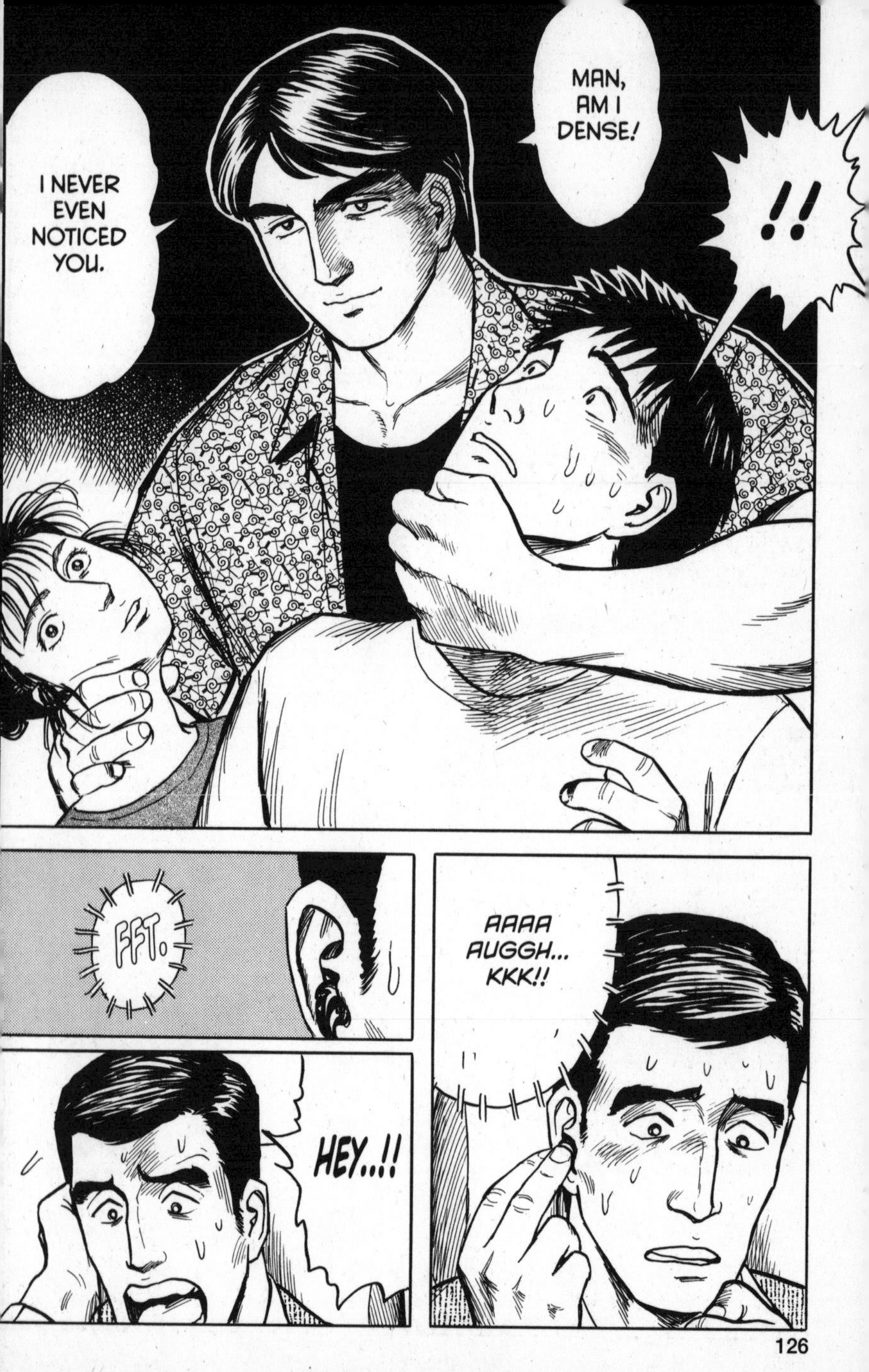
!!
MAN, AM I DENSE!
I NEVER EVEN NOTICED YOU.
AAAA AUGGH... KKK!!
FFT.
HEY...!!

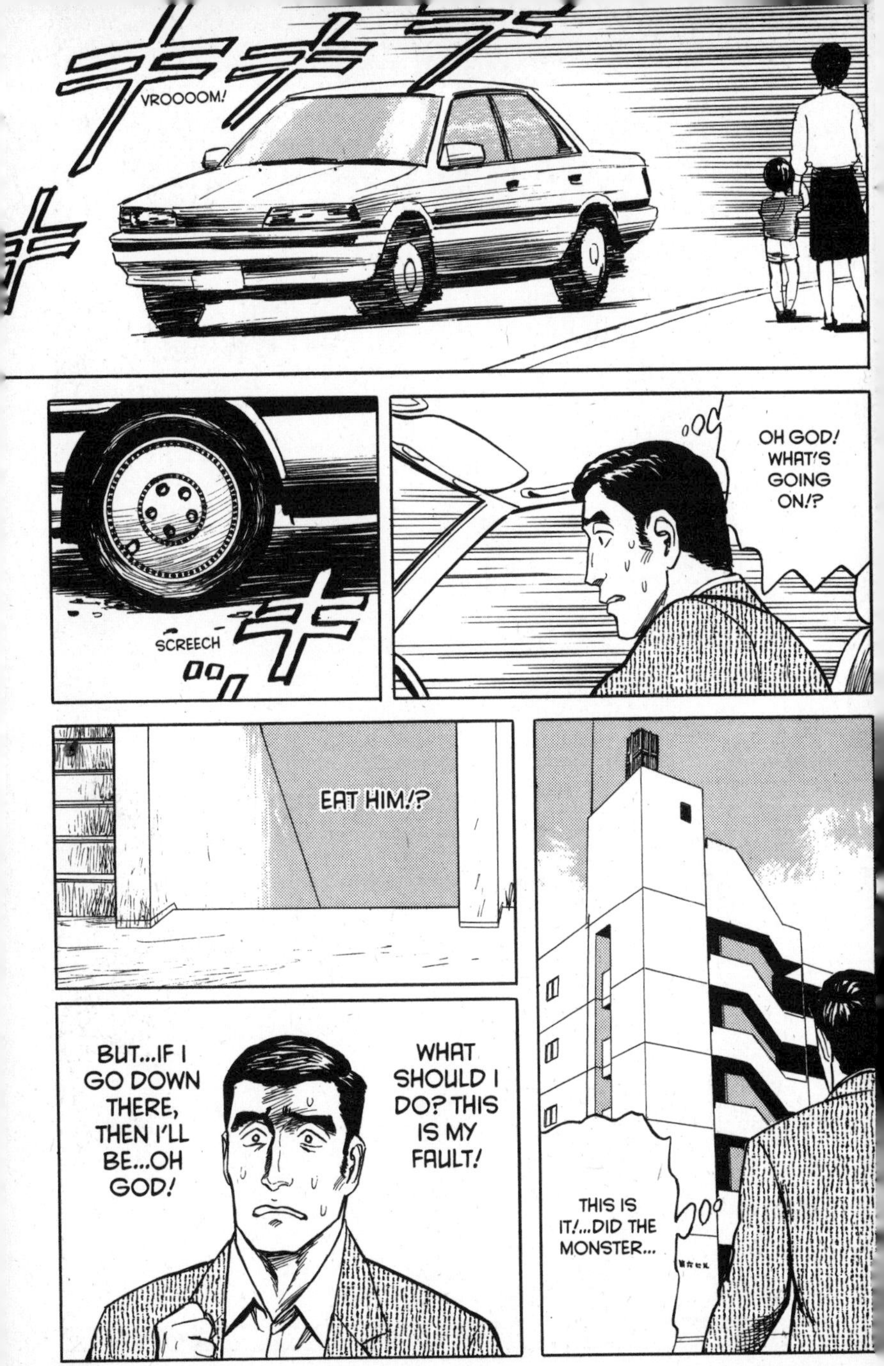
VROOOOM!
OH GOD! WHAT'S GOING ON!?
SCREECH
THIS IS IT!...DID THE MONSTER...
EAT HIM!?
WHAT SHOULD I DO? THIS IS MY FAULT!
BUT...IF I GO DOWN THERE, THEN I'LL BE...OH GOD!

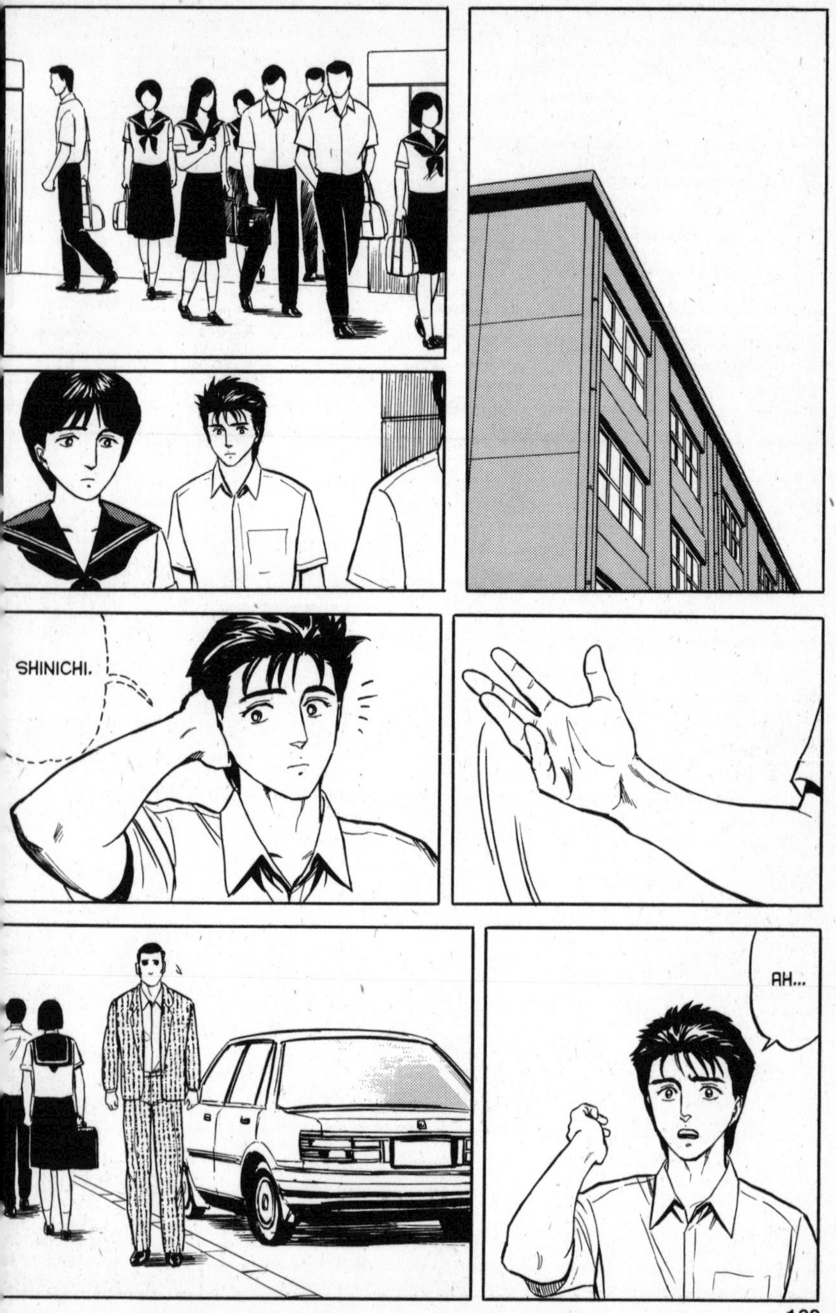
SHINICHI.
AH...

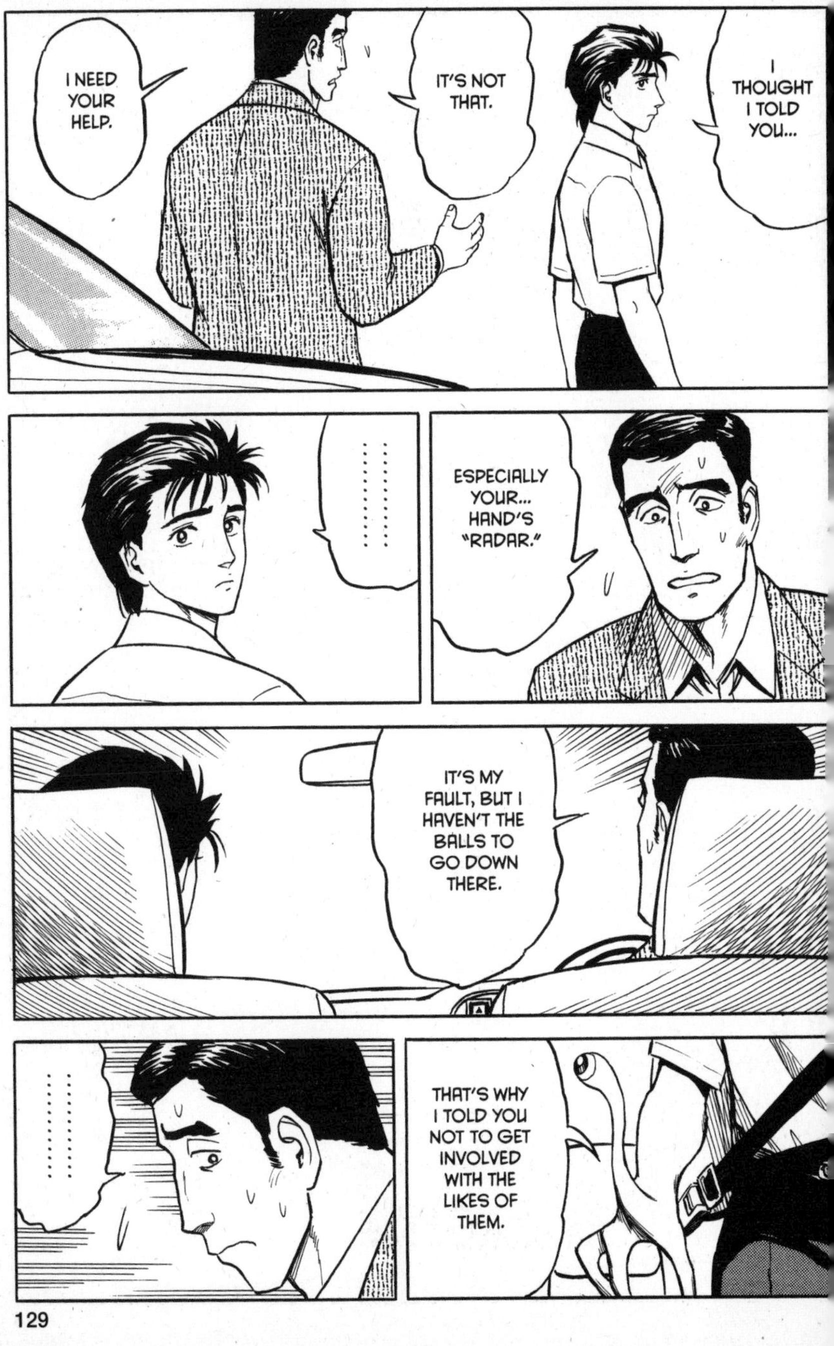
I THOUGHT I TOLD YOU...
IT'S NOT THAT.
I NEED YOUR HELP.
ESPECIALLY YOUR... HAND'S "RADAR."
......
IT'S MY FAULT, BUT I HAVEN'T THE BALLS TO GO DOWN THERE.
THAT'S WHY I TOLD YOU NOT TO GET INVOLVED WITH THE LIKES OF THEM.
......

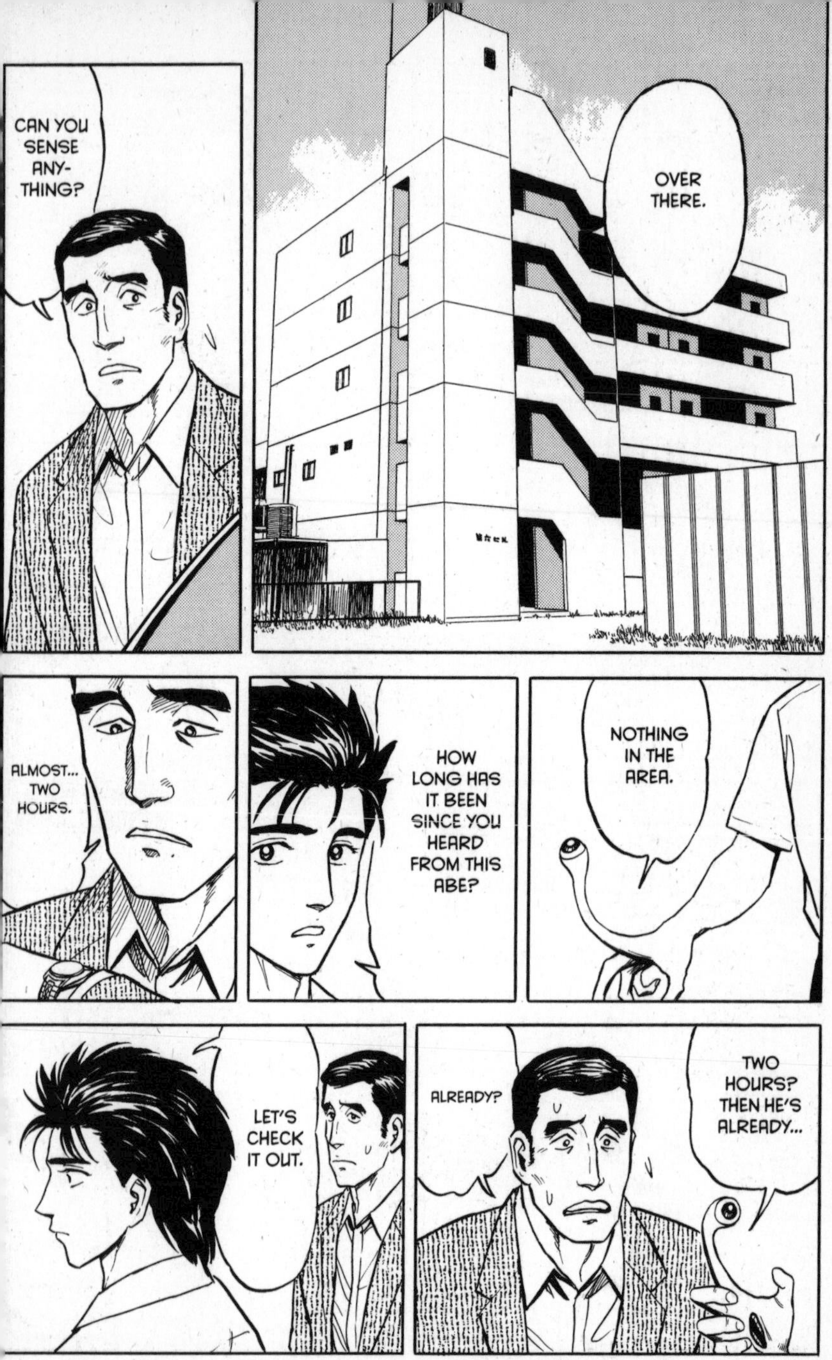
OVER THERE.
CAN YOU SENSE ANYTHING?
NOTHING IN THE AREA.
HOW LONG HAS IT BEEN SINCE YOU HEARD FROM THIS ABE?
ALMOST... TWO HOURS.
TWO HOURS? THEN HE'S ALREADY...
ALREADY?
LET'S CHECK IT OUT.

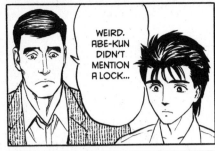

IT'S LOCKED.
WEIRD. ABE-KUN DIDN'T MENTION A LOCK...
IT DOESN'T MATTER.
......
......
......
カチッ
CLICK
IT'S OPEN.
WOW! YOU COULD BE A GREAT TH... DETECTIVE!
DETECTIVES PICK LOCKS?
UM, WELL...

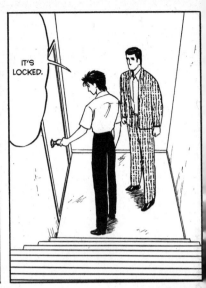

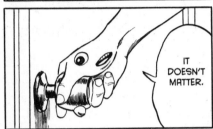

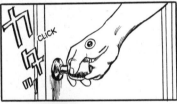

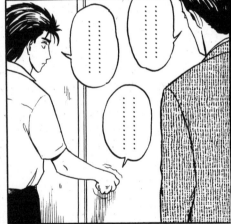

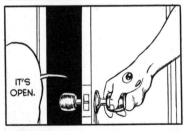

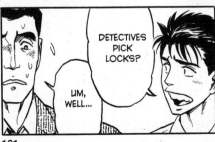

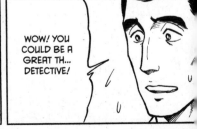

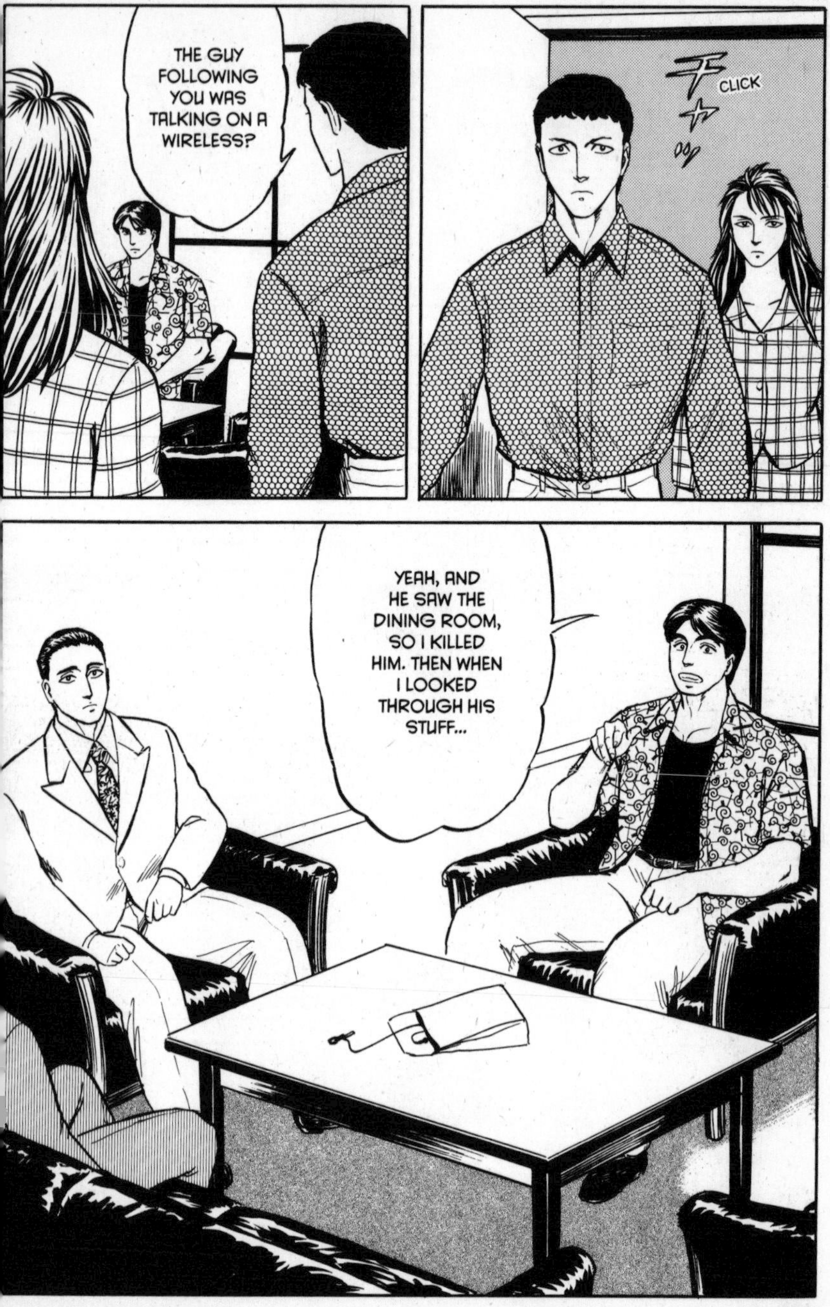
チャッ
CLICK
THE GUY FOLLOWING YOU WAS TALKING ON A WIRELESS?
YEAH, AND HE SAW THE DINING ROOM, SO I KILLED HIM. THEN WHEN I LOOKED THROUGH HIS STUFF...

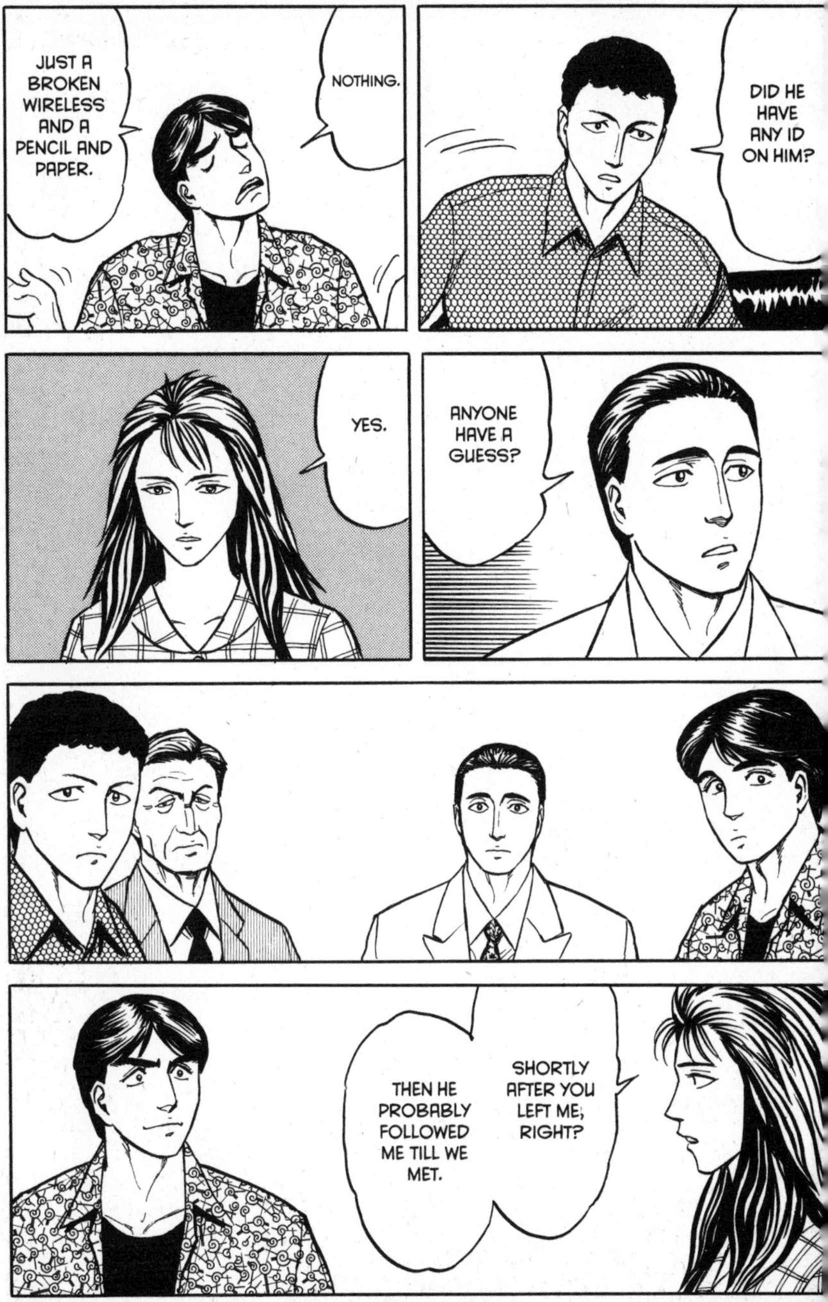
DID HE HAVE ANY ID ON HIM?
NOTHING.
JUST A BROKEN WIRELESS AND A PENCIL AND PAPER.
ANYONE HAVE A GUESS?
YES.
SHORTLY AFTER YOU LEFT ME; RIGHT?
THEN HE PROBABLY FOLLOWED ME TILL WE MET.

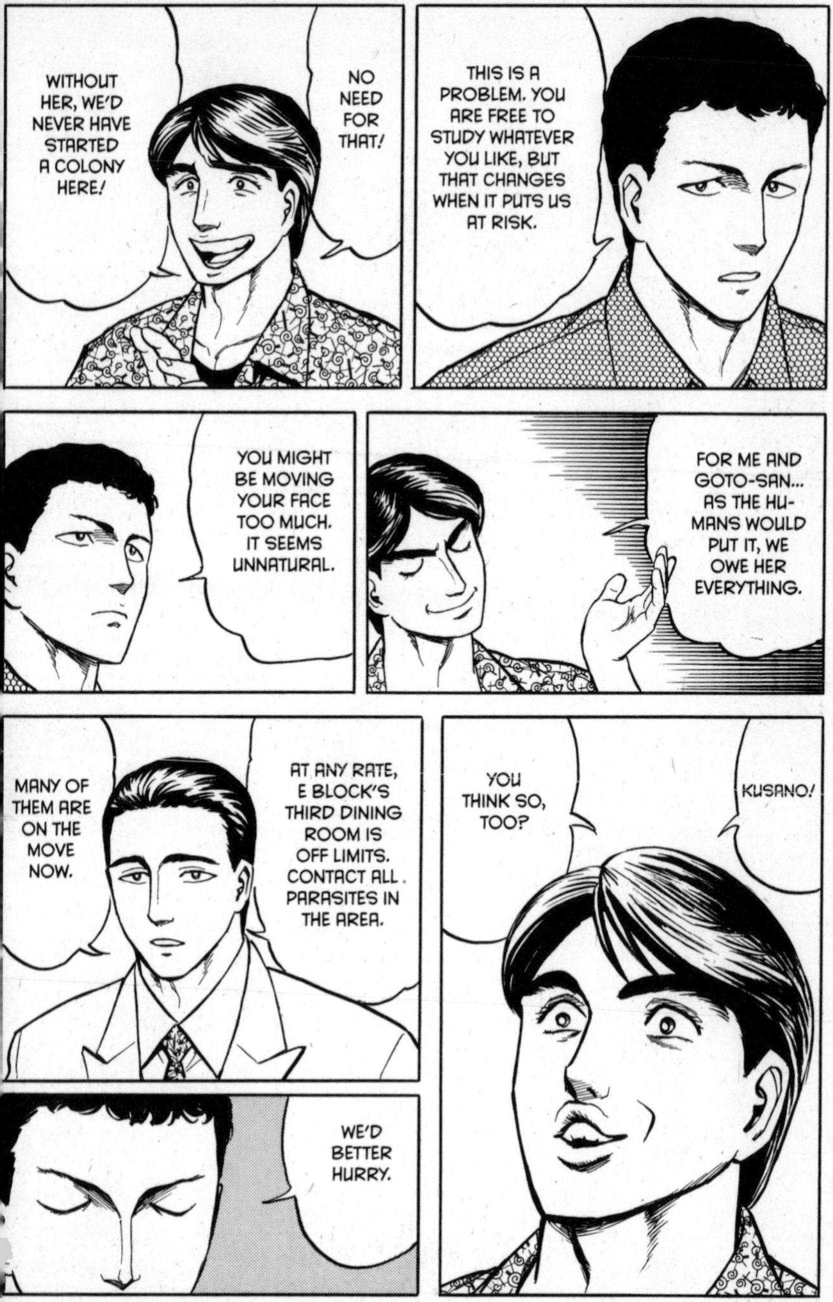
THIS IS A PROBLEM. YOU ARE FREE TO STUDY WHATEVER YOU LIKE, BUT THAT CHANGES WHEN IT PUTS US AT RISK.
NO NEED FOR THAT!
WITHOUT HER, WE'D NEVER HAVE STARTED A COLONY HERE!
FOR ME AND GOTO-SAN... AS THE HU-MANS WOULD PUT IT, WE OWE HER EVERYTHING.
YOU MIGHT BE MOVING YOUR FACE TOO MUCH. IT SEEMS UNNATURAL.
KUSANO!
YOU THINK SO, TOO?
AT ANY RATE, E BLOCK'S THIRD DINING ROOM IS OFF LIMITS. CONTACT ALL PARASITES IN THE AREA.
MANY OF THEM ARE ON THE MOVE NOW.
WE'D BETTER HURRY.

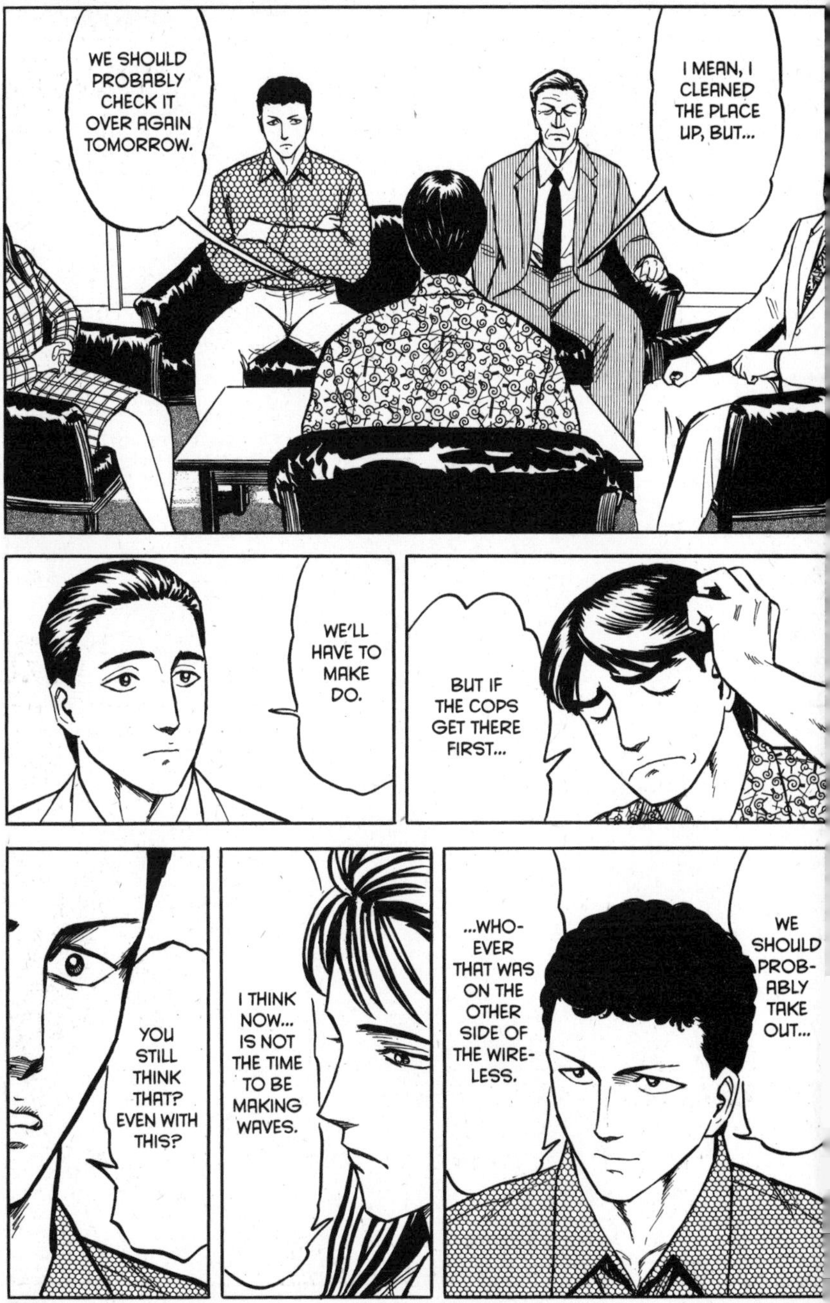
I MEAN, I CLEANED THE PLACE UP, BUT...
WE SHOULD PROBABLY CHECK IT OVER AGAIN TOMORROW.
BUT IF THE COPS GET THERE FIRST...
WE'LL HAVE TO MAKE DO.
WE SHOULD PROBABLY TAKE OUT...
...WHOEVER THAT WAS ON THE OTHER SIDE OF THE WIRELESS.
I THINK NOW... IS NOT THE TIME TO BE MAKING WAVES.
YOU STILL THINK THAT? EVEN WITH THIS?

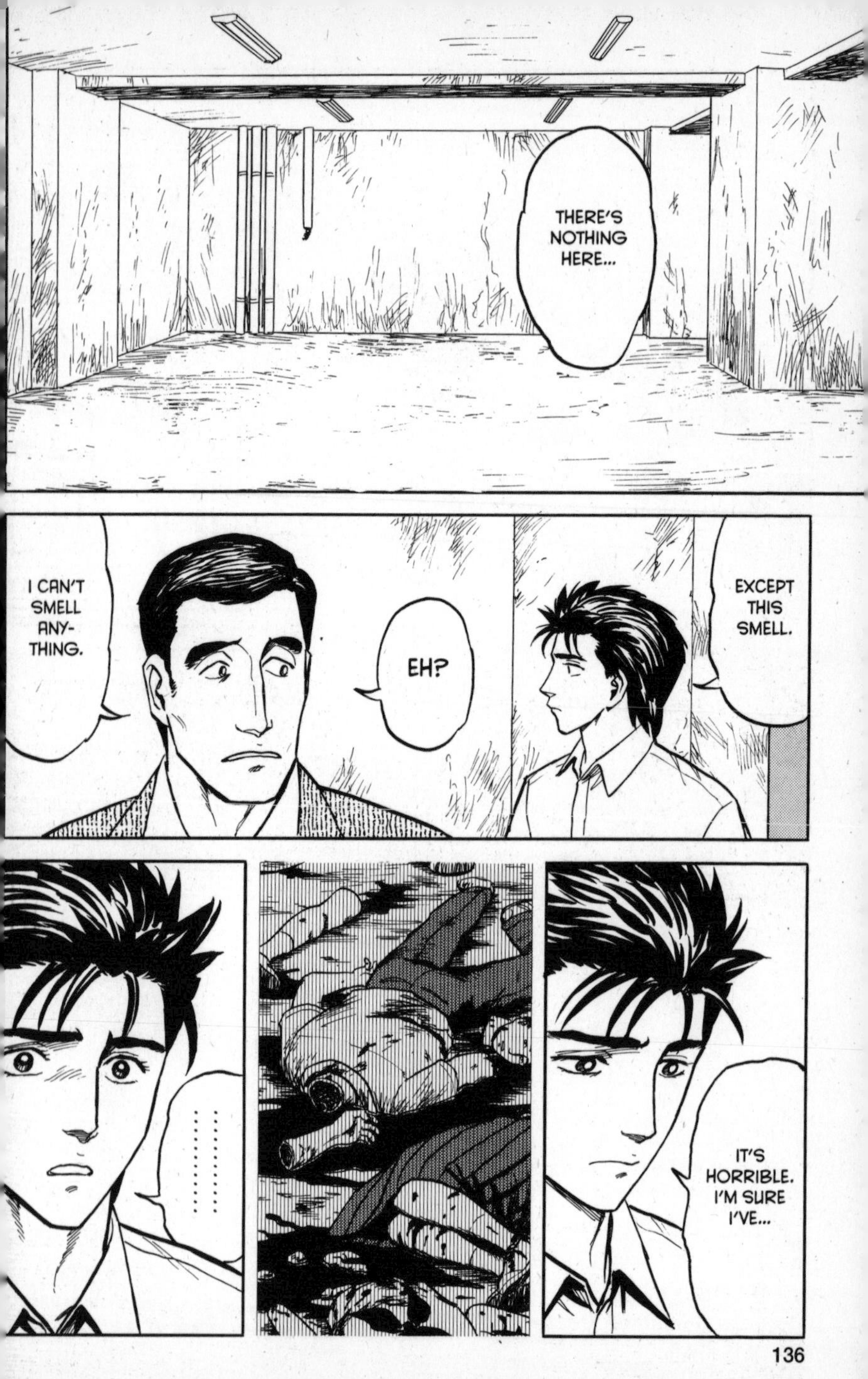
THERE'S NOTHING HERE...
EXCEPT THIS SMELL.
EH?
I CAN'T SMELL ANY-THING.
IT'S HORRIBLE. I'M SURE I'VE...
......

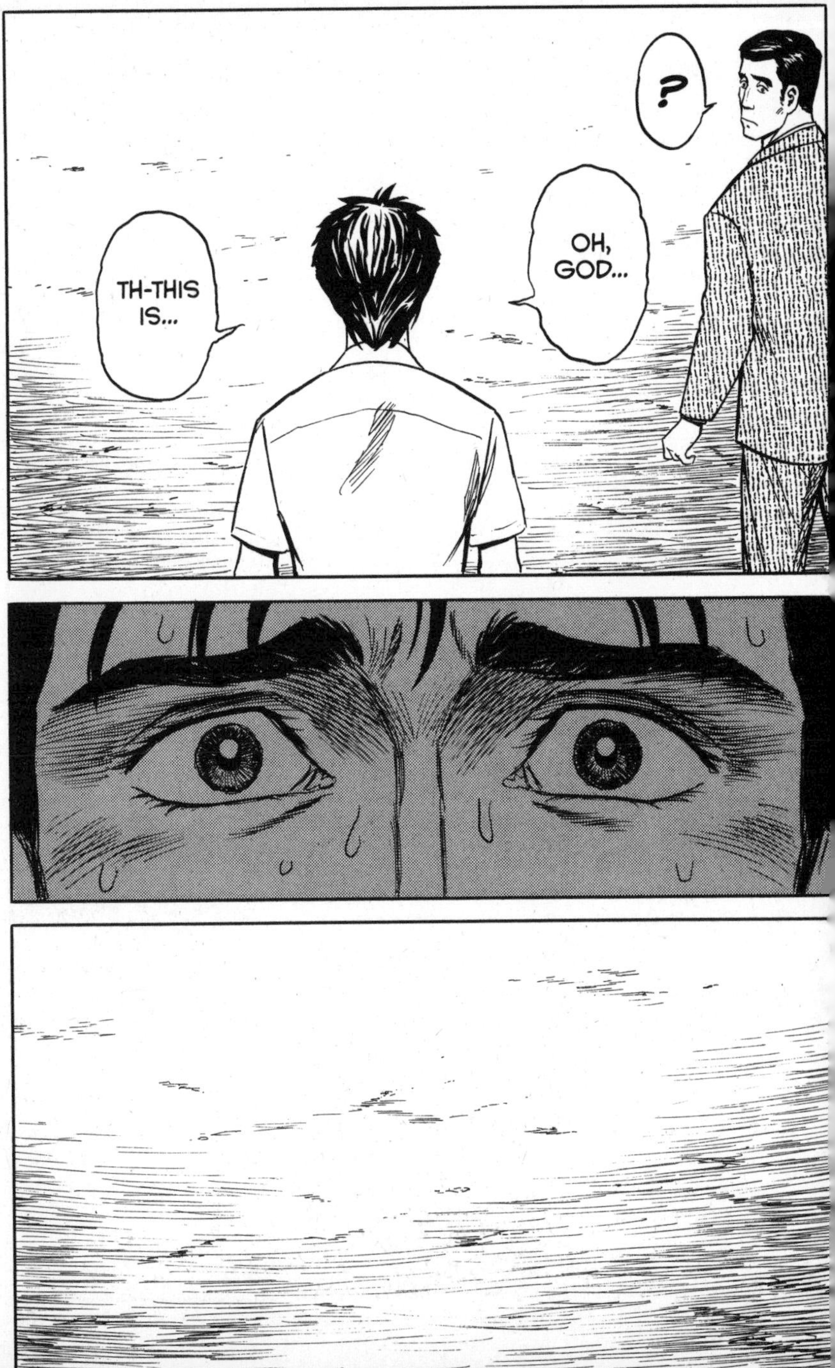
?
OH, GOD...
TH-THIS IS...

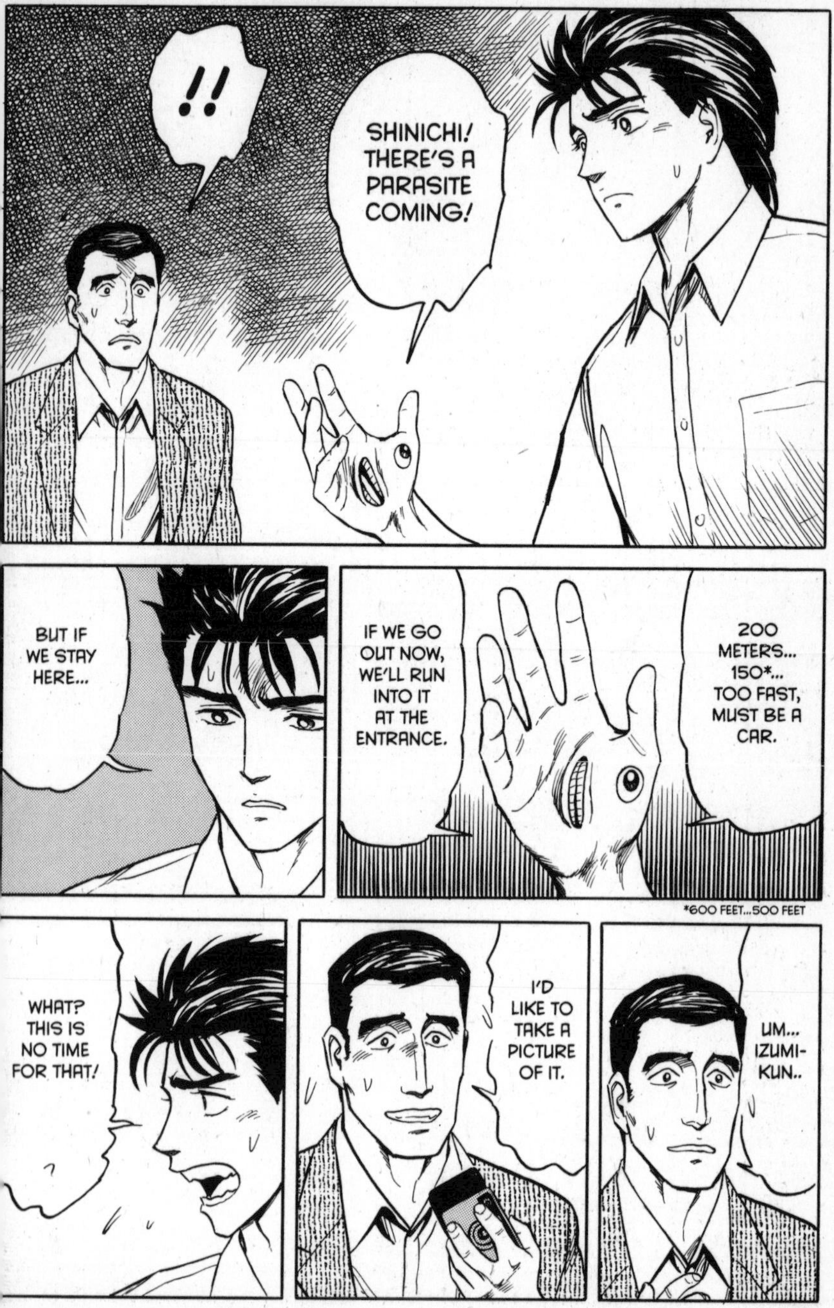
SHINICHI! THERE'S A PARASITE COMING!
!!
200 METERS... 150*... TOO FAST, MUST BE A CAR.
IF WE GO OUT NOW, WE'LL RUN INTO IT AT THE ENTRANCE.
BUT IF WE STAY HERE...
UM... IZUMI-KUN..
I'D LIKE TO TAKE A PICTURE OF IT.
WHAT? THIS IS NO TIME FOR THAT!

*600 FEET...500 FEET

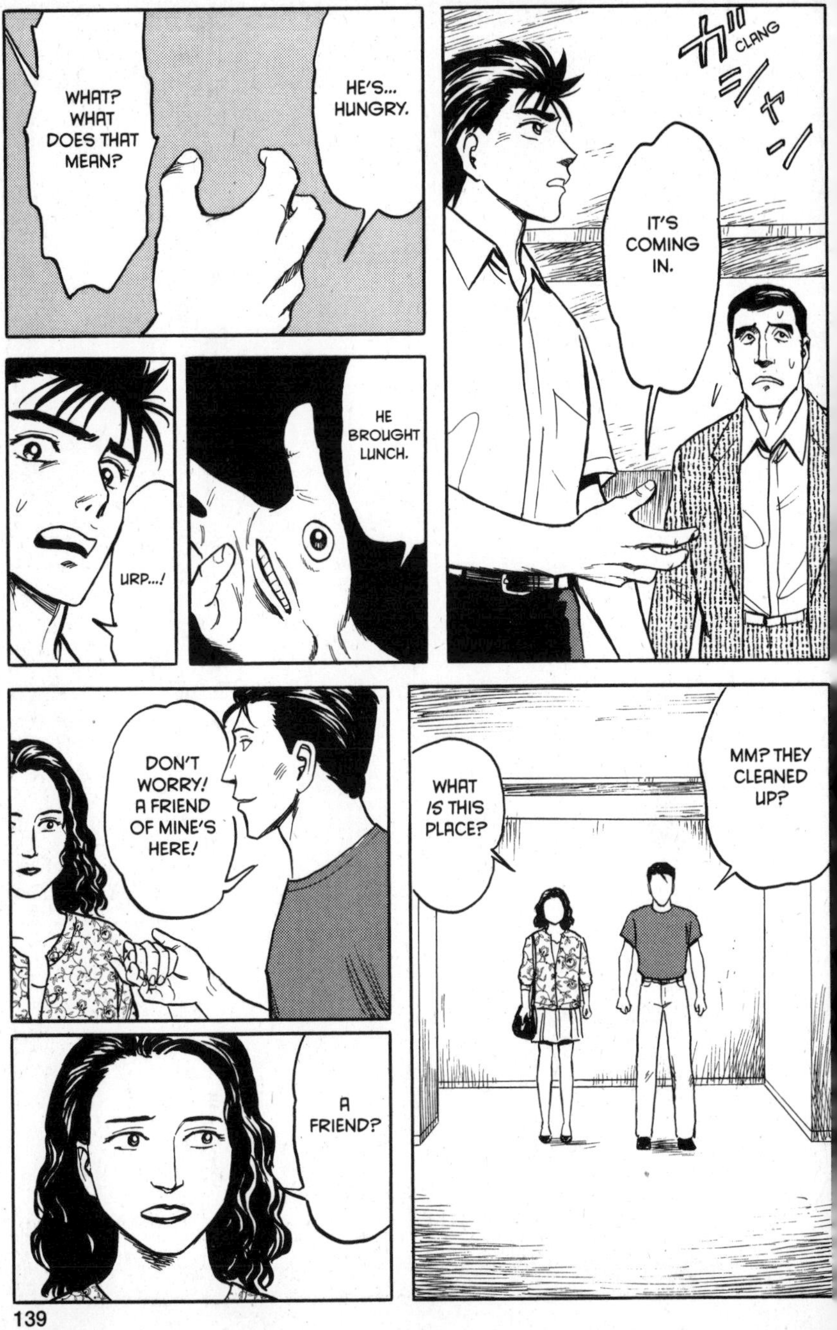
CLANG
IT'S COMING IN.
HE'S... HUNGRY.
WHAT? WHAT DOES THAT MEAN?
HE BROUGHT LUNCH.
URP...!
MM? THEY CLEANED UP?
WHAT *IS* THIS PLACE?
DON'T WORRY! A FRIEND OF MINE'S HERE!
A FRIEND?

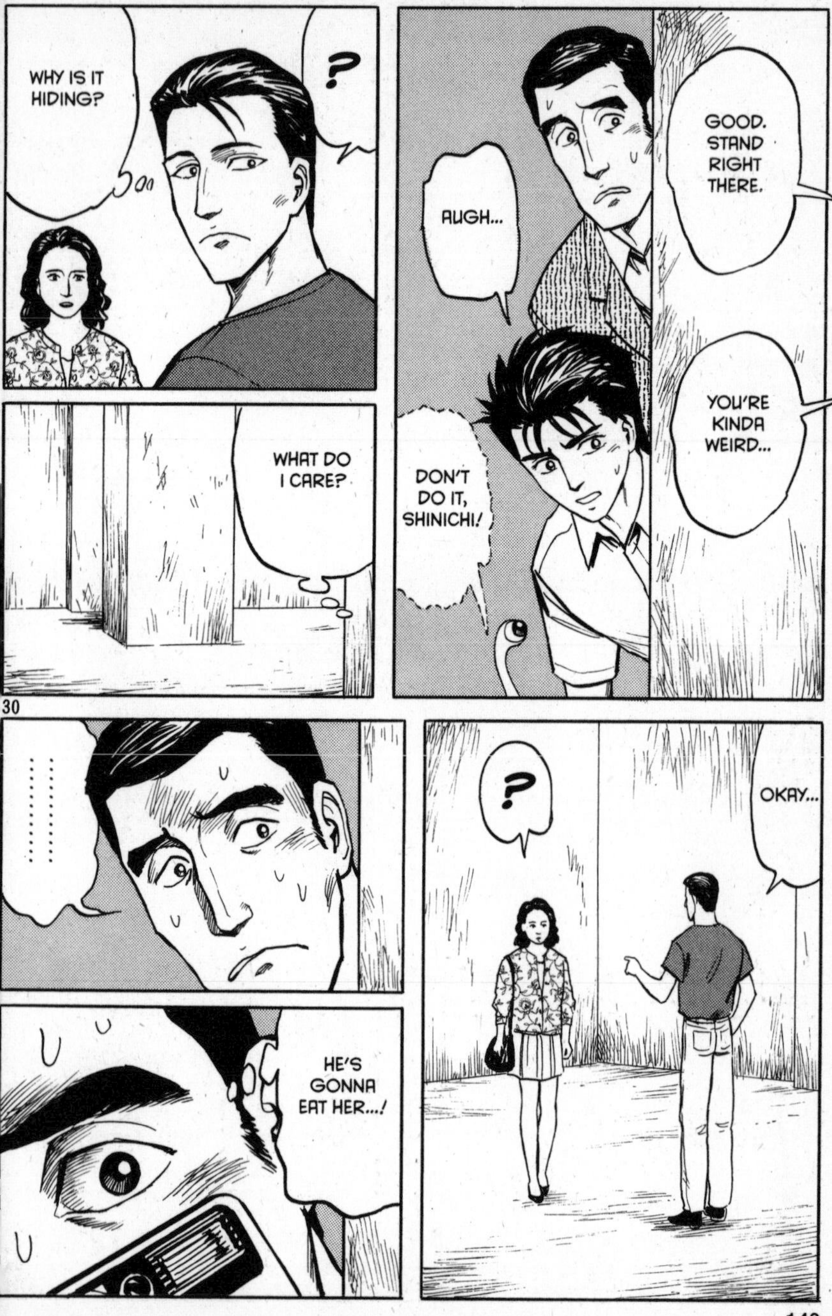
GOOD. STAND RIGHT THERE.
AUGH...
YOU'RE KINDA WEIRD...
DON'T DO IT, SHINICHI!
?
WHY IS IT HIDING?
WHAT DO I CARE?
OKAY...
?
......
HE'S GONNA EAT HER...!

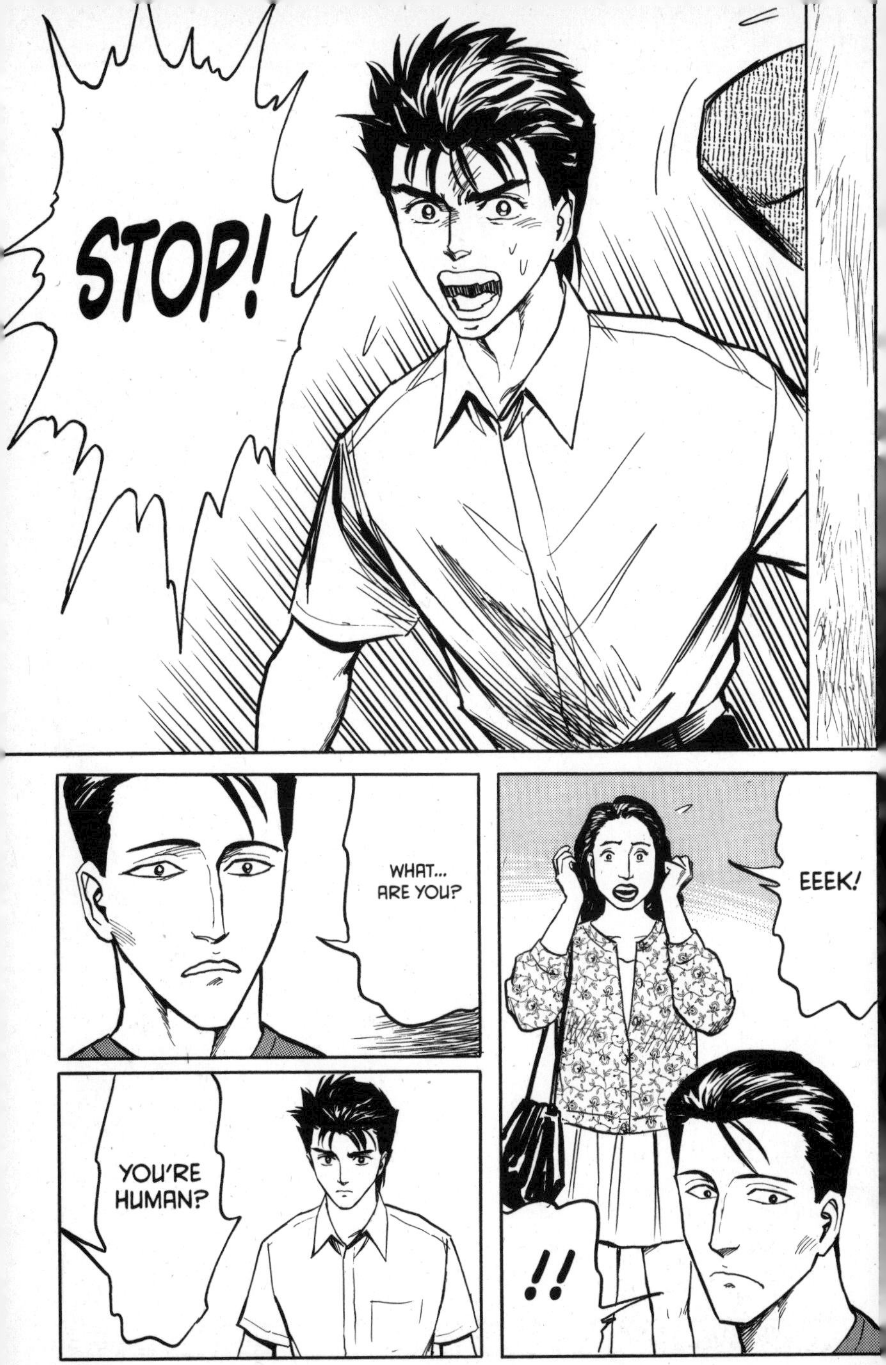
STOP!
EEEK!
!!
WHAT... ARE YOU?
YOU'RE HUMAN?

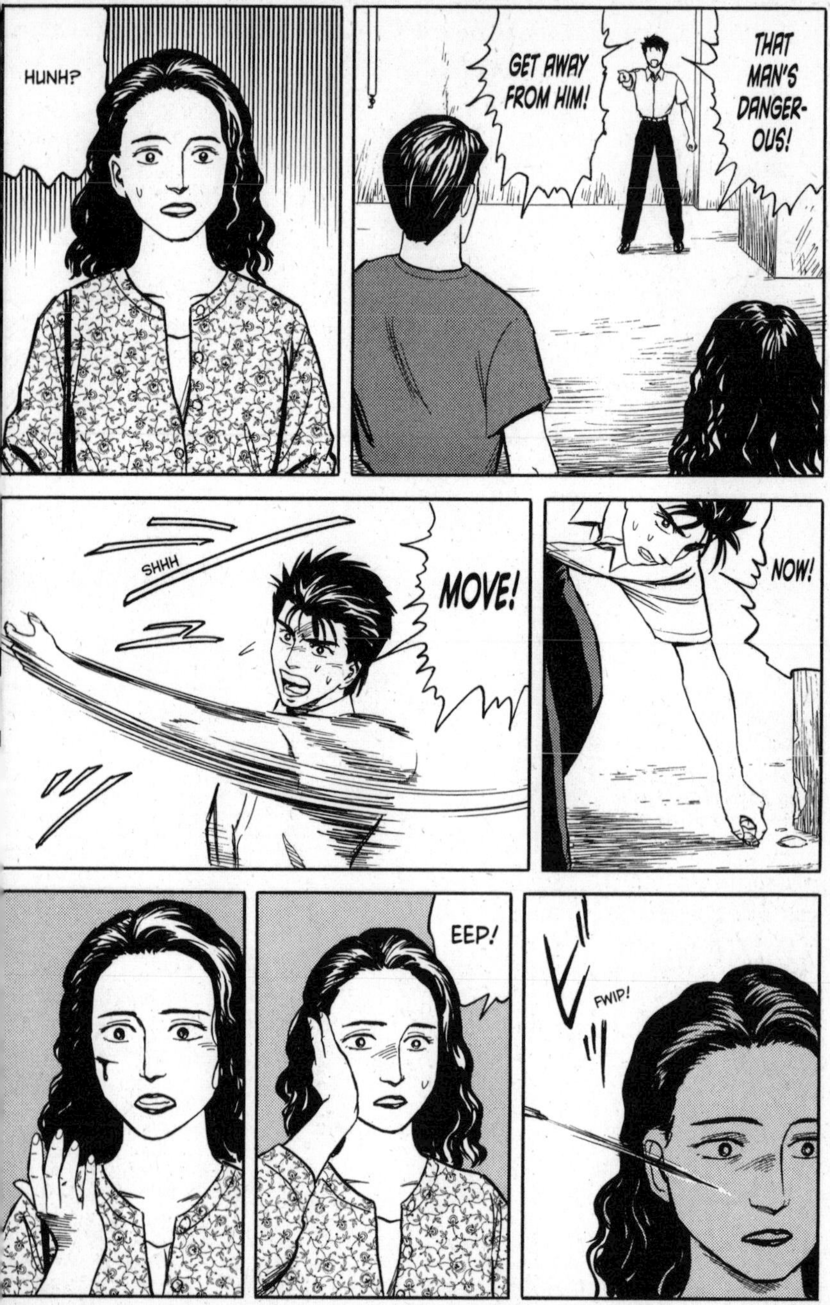
THAT MAN'S DANGER-OUS!
GET AWAY FROM HIM!
HUNH?
NOW!
MOVE!
SHHH
FWIP!
EEP!

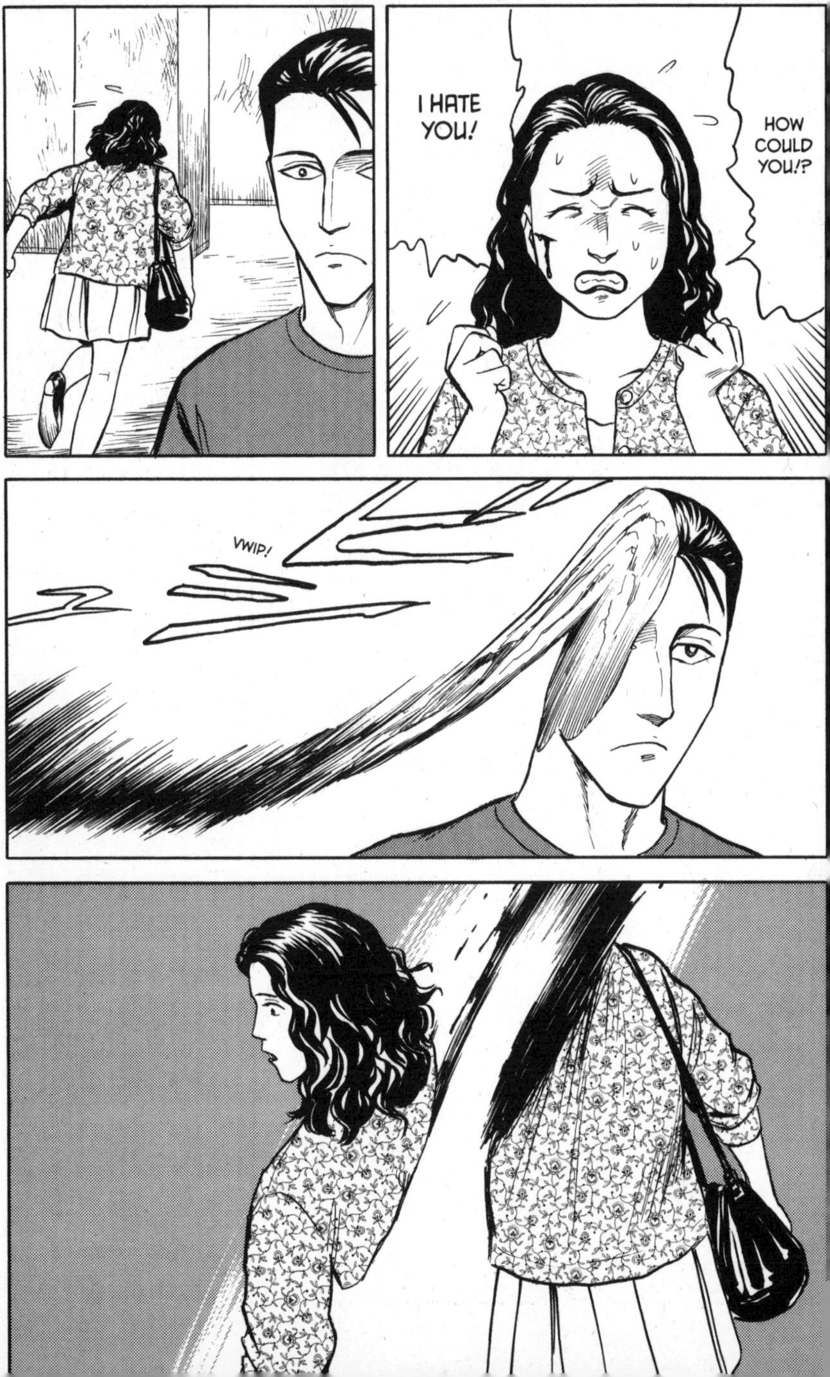
HOW COULD YOU!?
I HATE YOU!
VWIP!

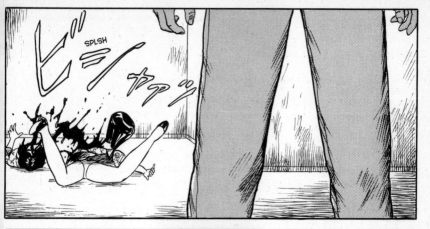

SPLSH

...SON OF A BITCH!

YOU...

HUMANS....!

CHAPTER 37: THE END

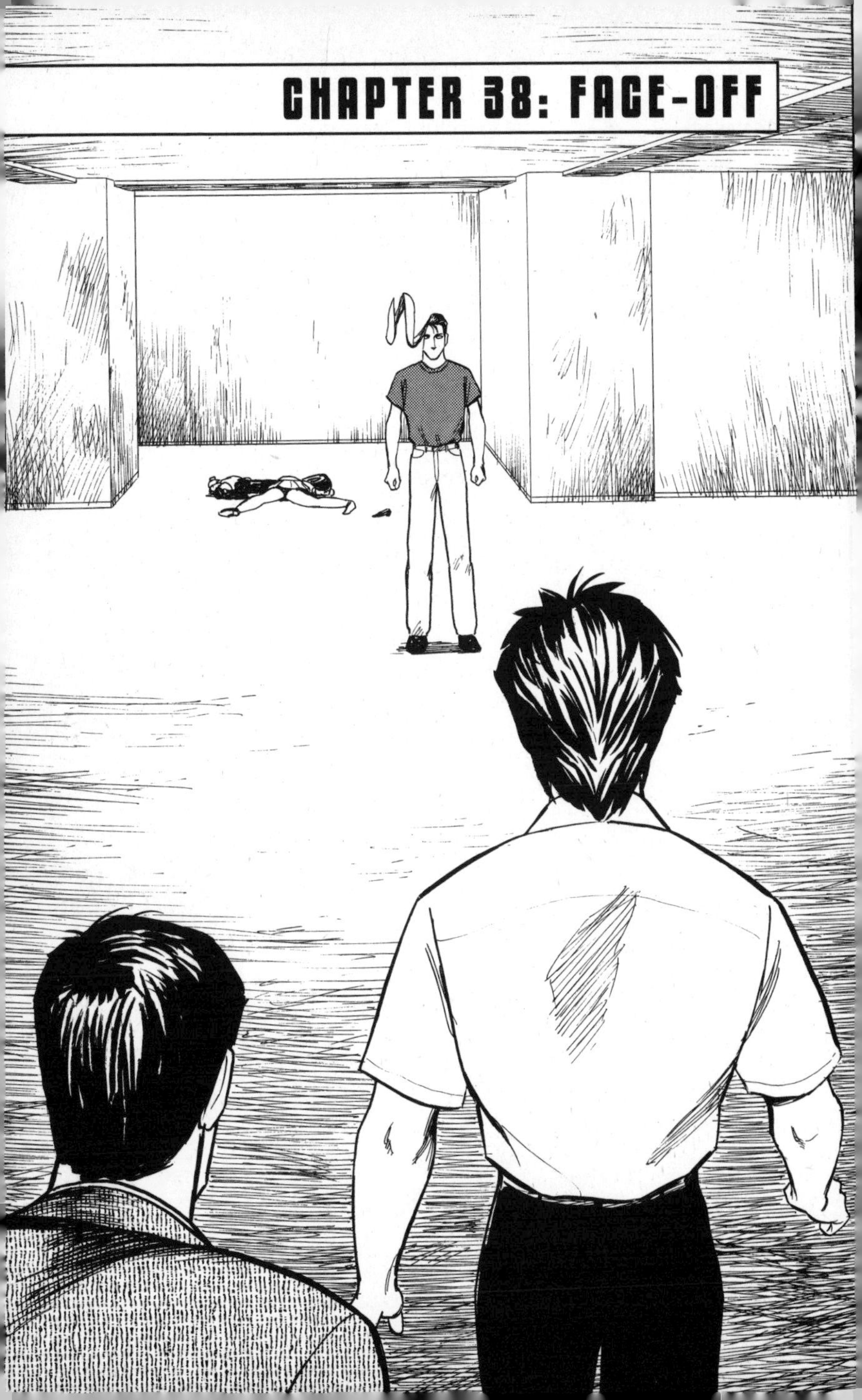
CHAPTER 38: FACE-OFF

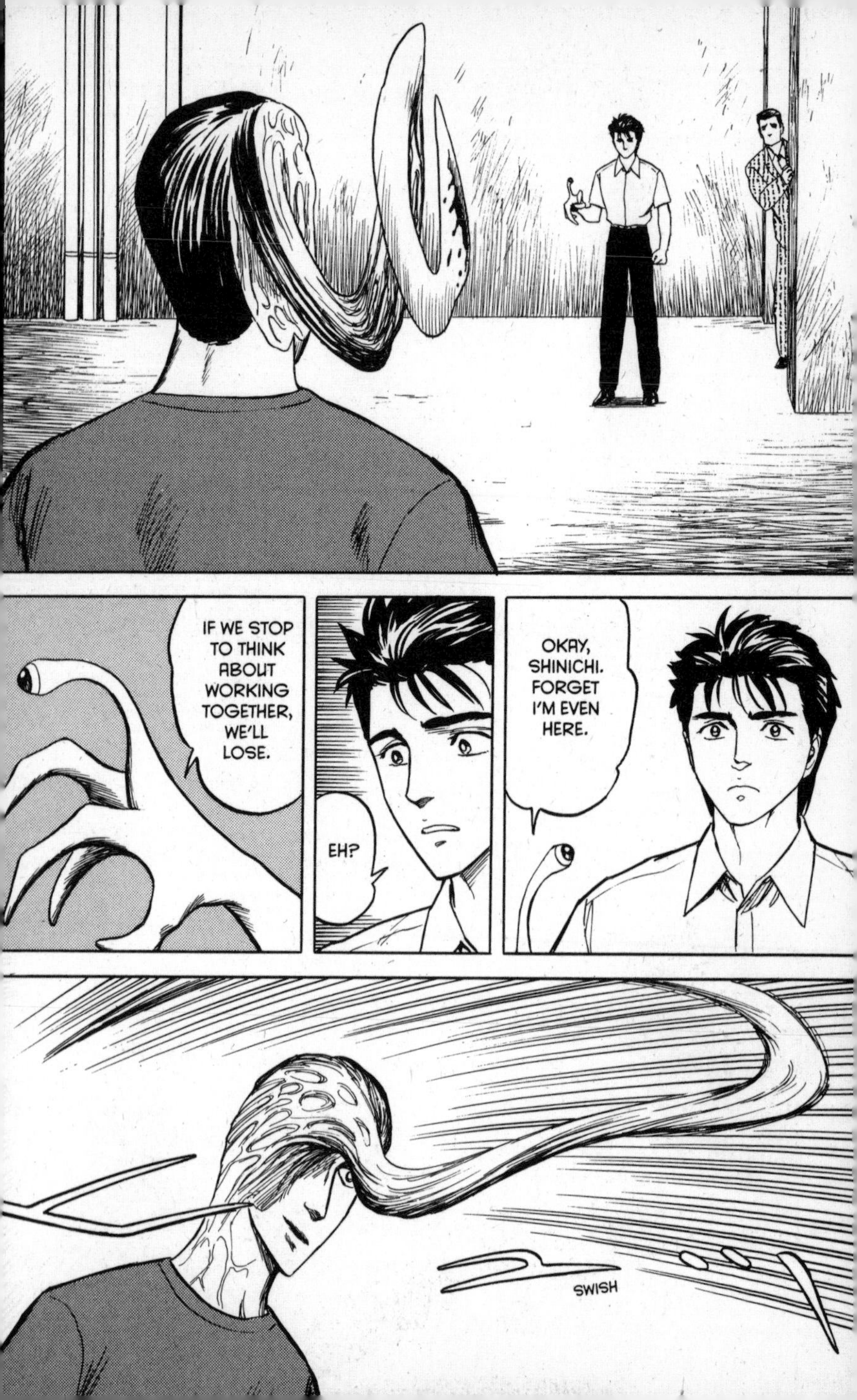
OKAY, SHINICHI. FORGET I'M EVEN HERE.
EH?
IF WE STOP TO THINK ABOUT WORKING TOGETHER, WE'LL LOSE.
SWISH

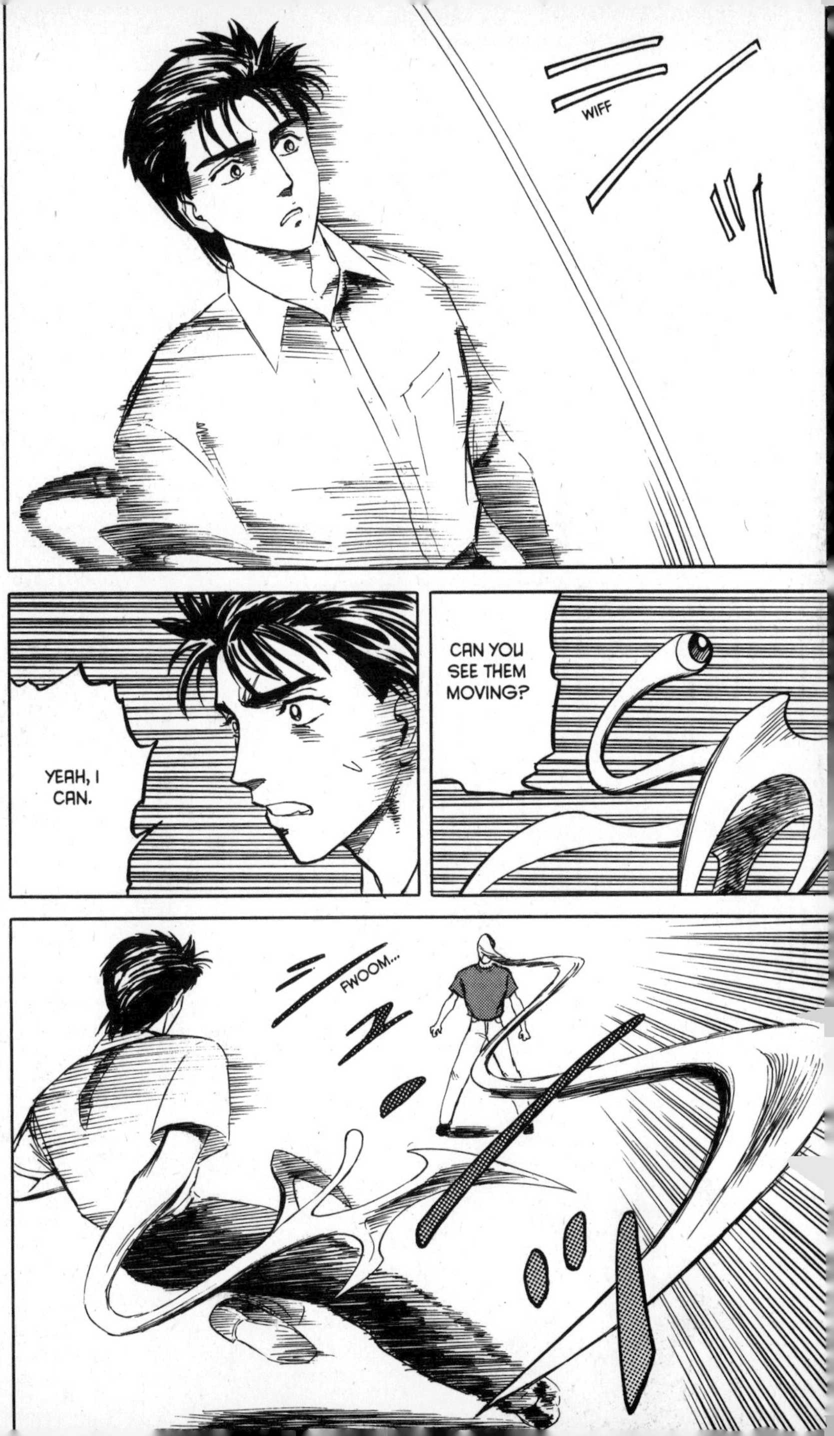
WIFF
CAN YOU SEE THEM MOVING?
YEAH, I CAN.
FWOOM...

CLICK

CLICK

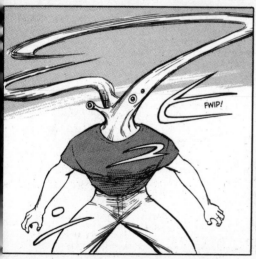

FWIP!

M-MY GOD! THEY'RE SO FAST!

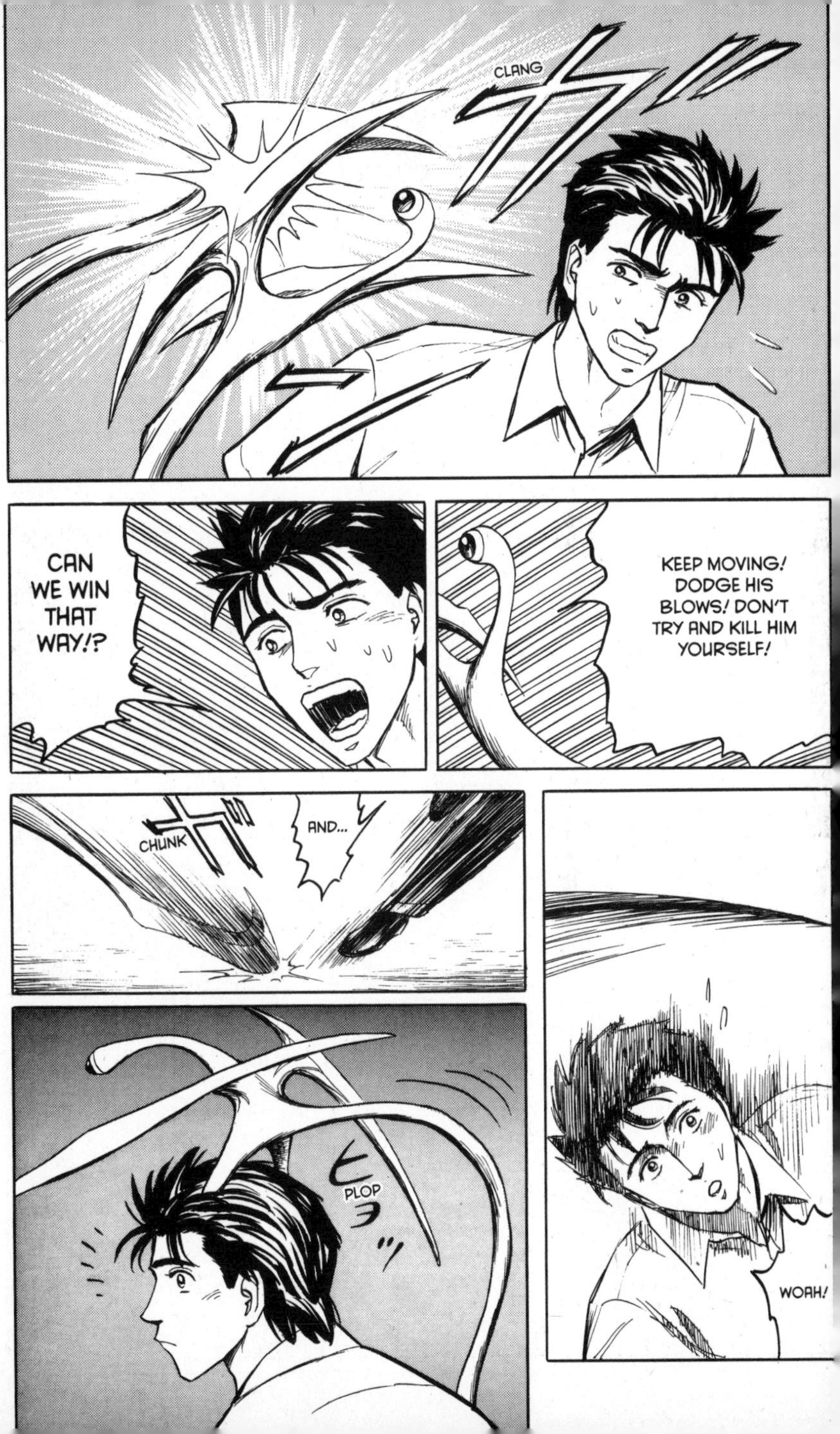
CLANG
KEEP MOVING! DODGE HIS BLOWS! DON'T TRY AND KILL HIM YOURSELF!
CAN WE WIN THAT WAY!?
WOAH!
CHUNK
AND...
PLOP

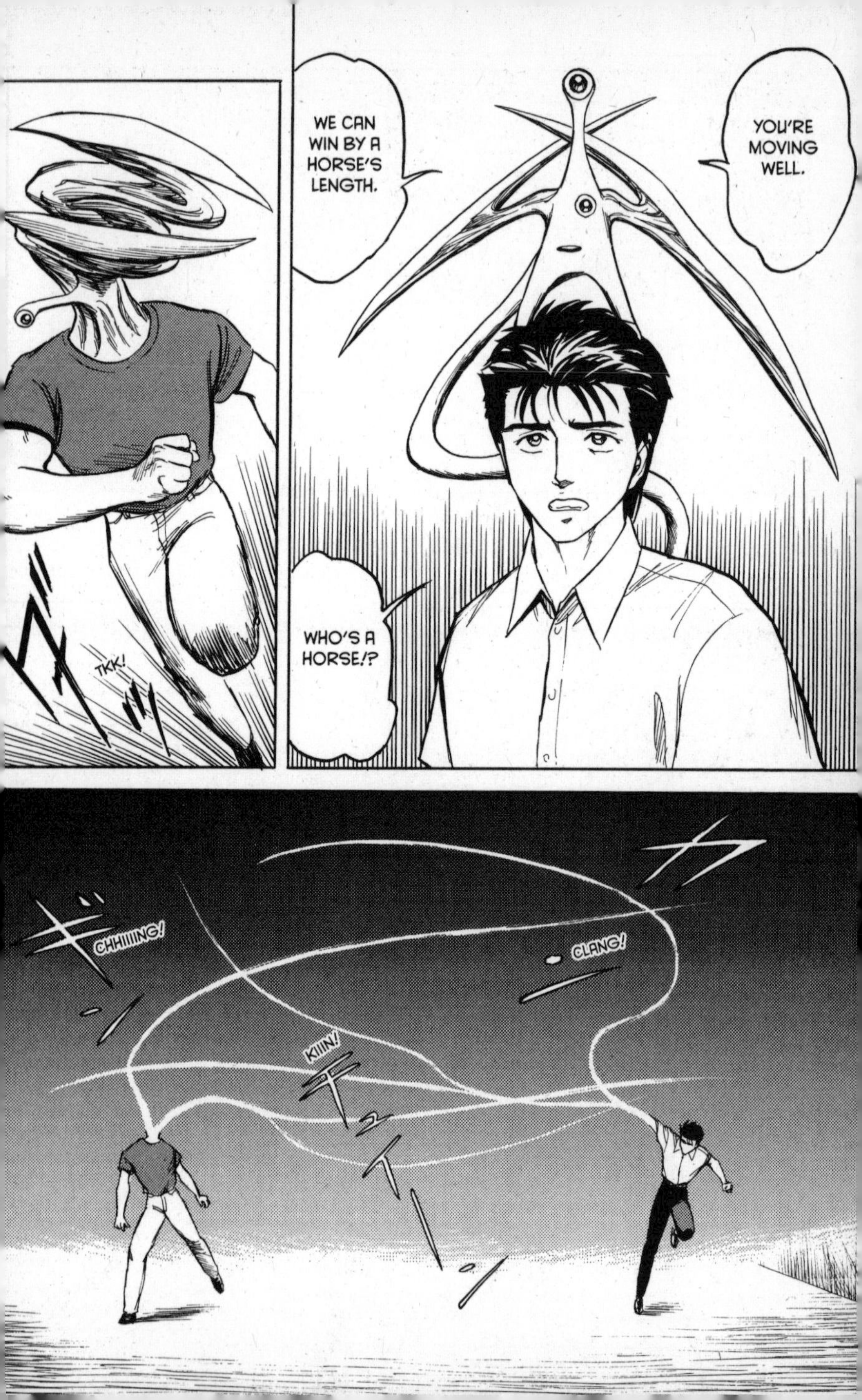
YOU'RE MOVING WELL.
WE CAN WIN BY A HORSE'S LENGTH.
WHO'S A HORSE!?
TKK!
CLANG!
CHHIIIIING!
KIIIN!

SCHUNCH!
GAH!
SPLAT!

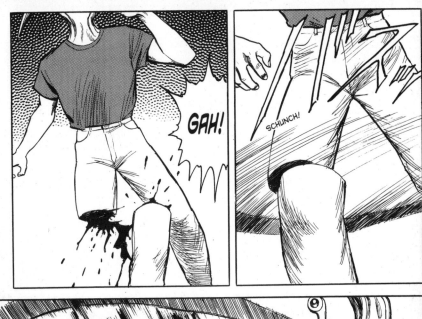

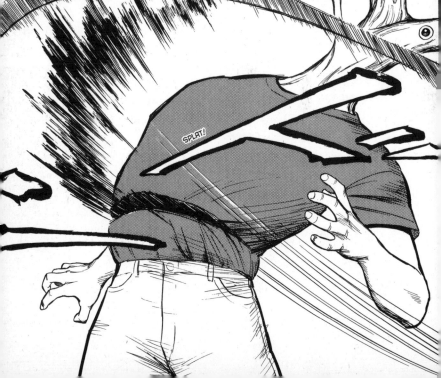

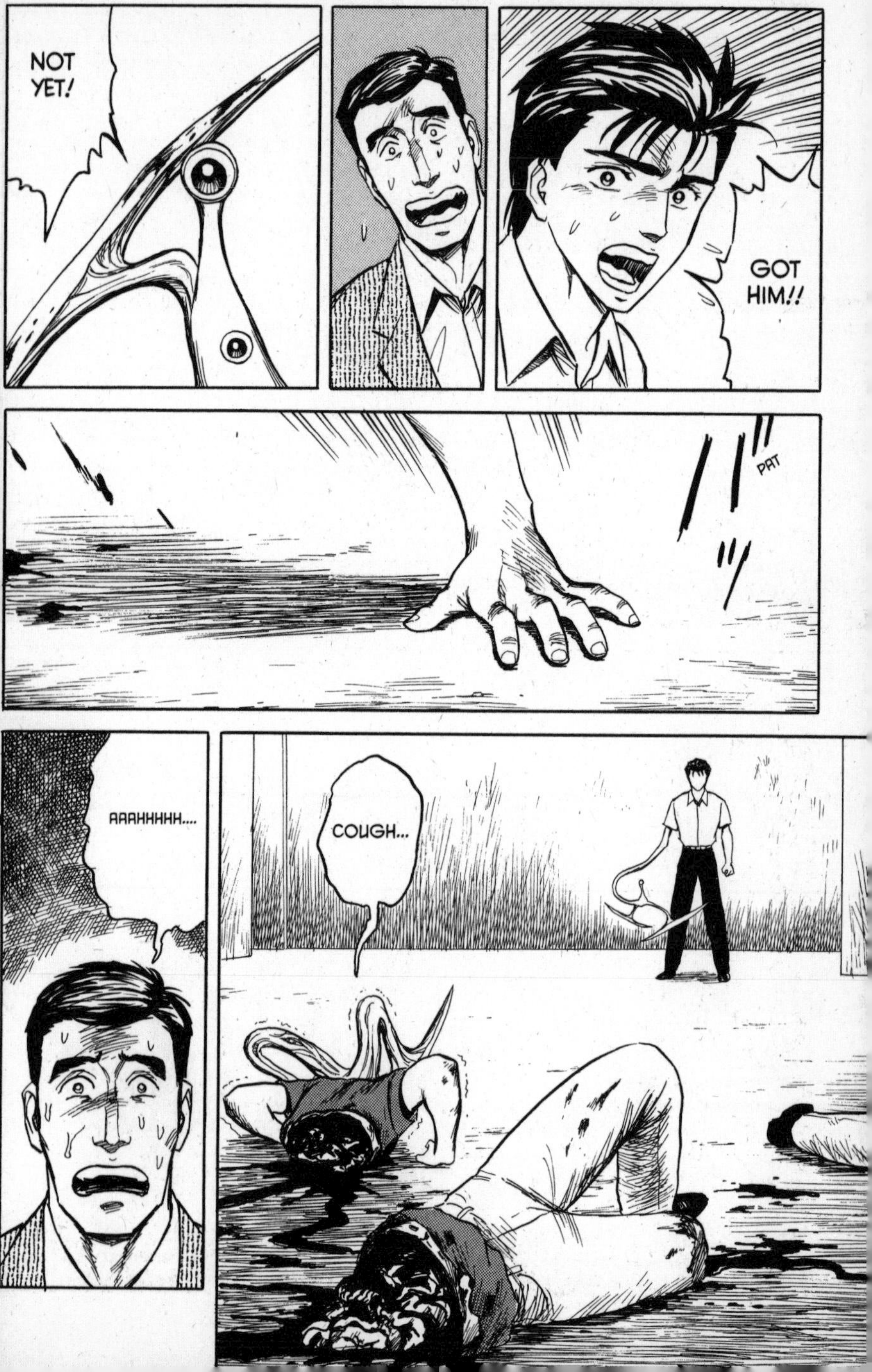
GOT HIM!!
NOT YET!
PAT
COUGH...
AAAHHHHH....

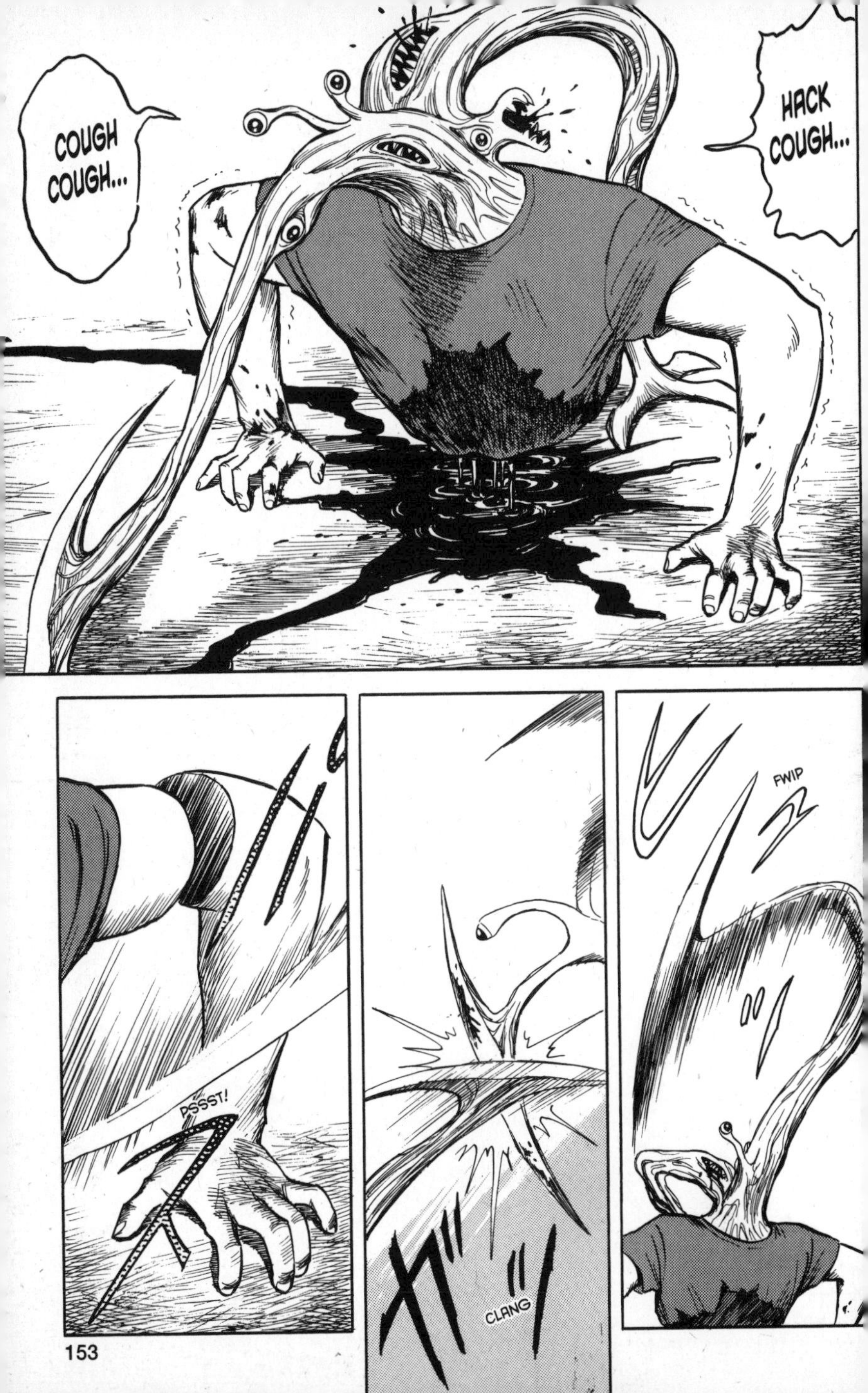
HACK COUGH...
COUGH COUGH...
FWIP
CLANG
PSSST!

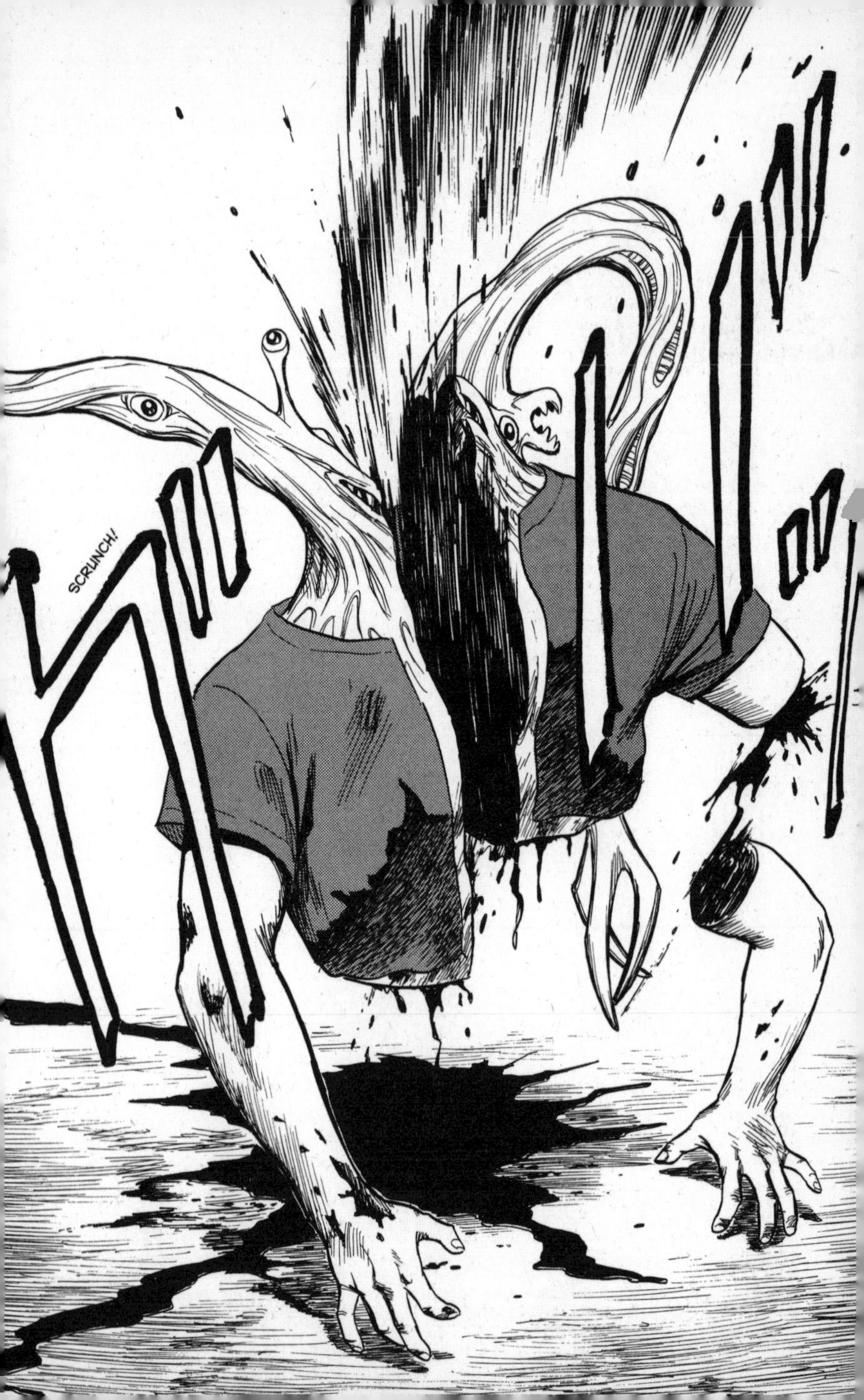
SCRUNCH!

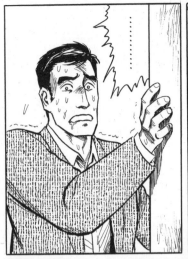

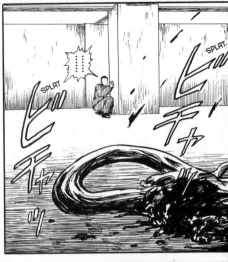

SPLAT
......
SPLAT
......
HAHH HAH-HH HAH-HH
NO MATTER WHAT YOU DO, BELOW THE NECK—THE HUMAN PART—IS THEIR WEAK POINT. AS LONG AS WE PROTECT OURS, WE'LL WIN.
GLURP

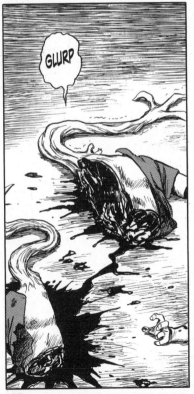

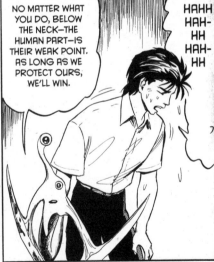

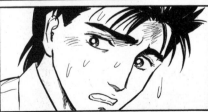

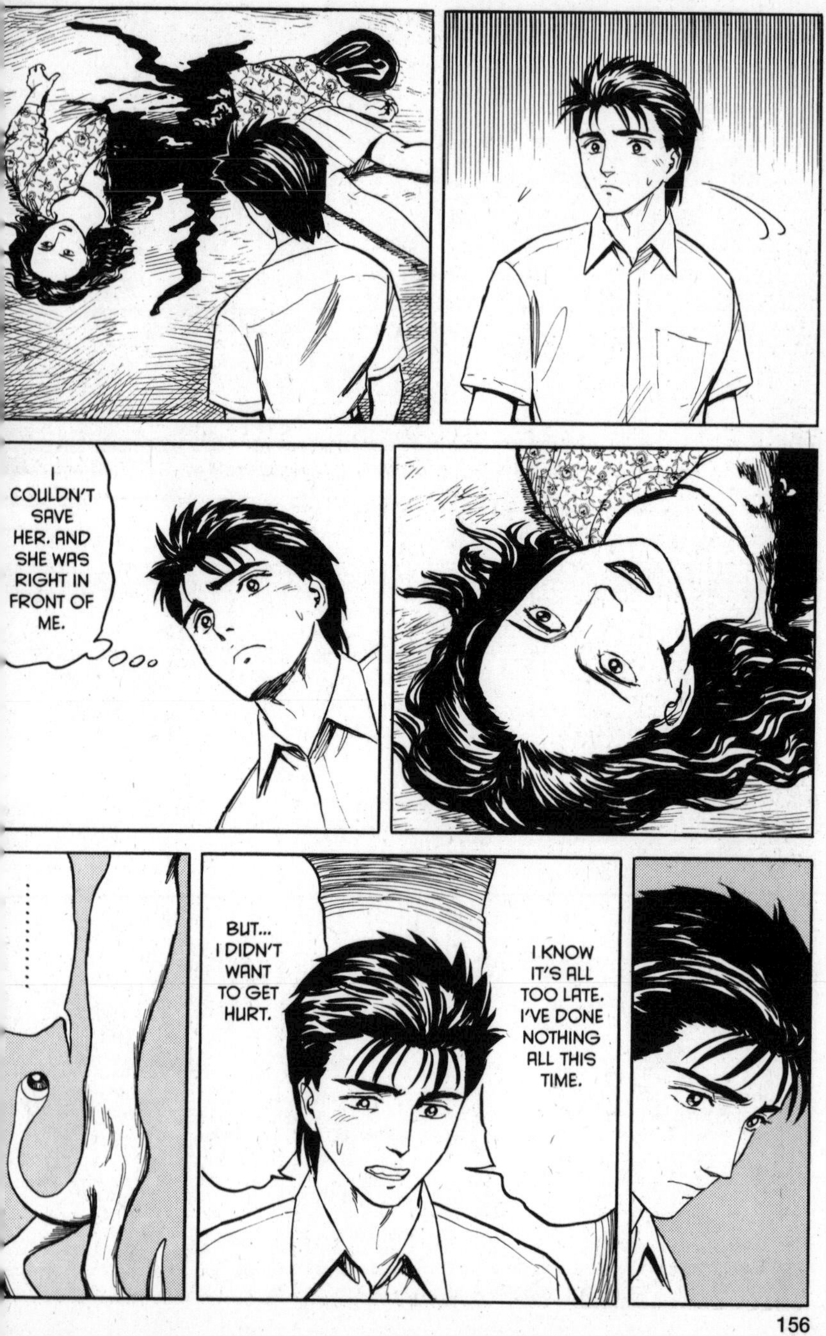
I COULDN'T SAVE HER. AND SHE WAS RIGHT IN FRONT OF ME.
I KNOW IT'S ALL TOO LATE. I'VE DONE NOTHING ALL THIS TIME.
BUT... I DIDN'T WANT TO GET HURT.
......

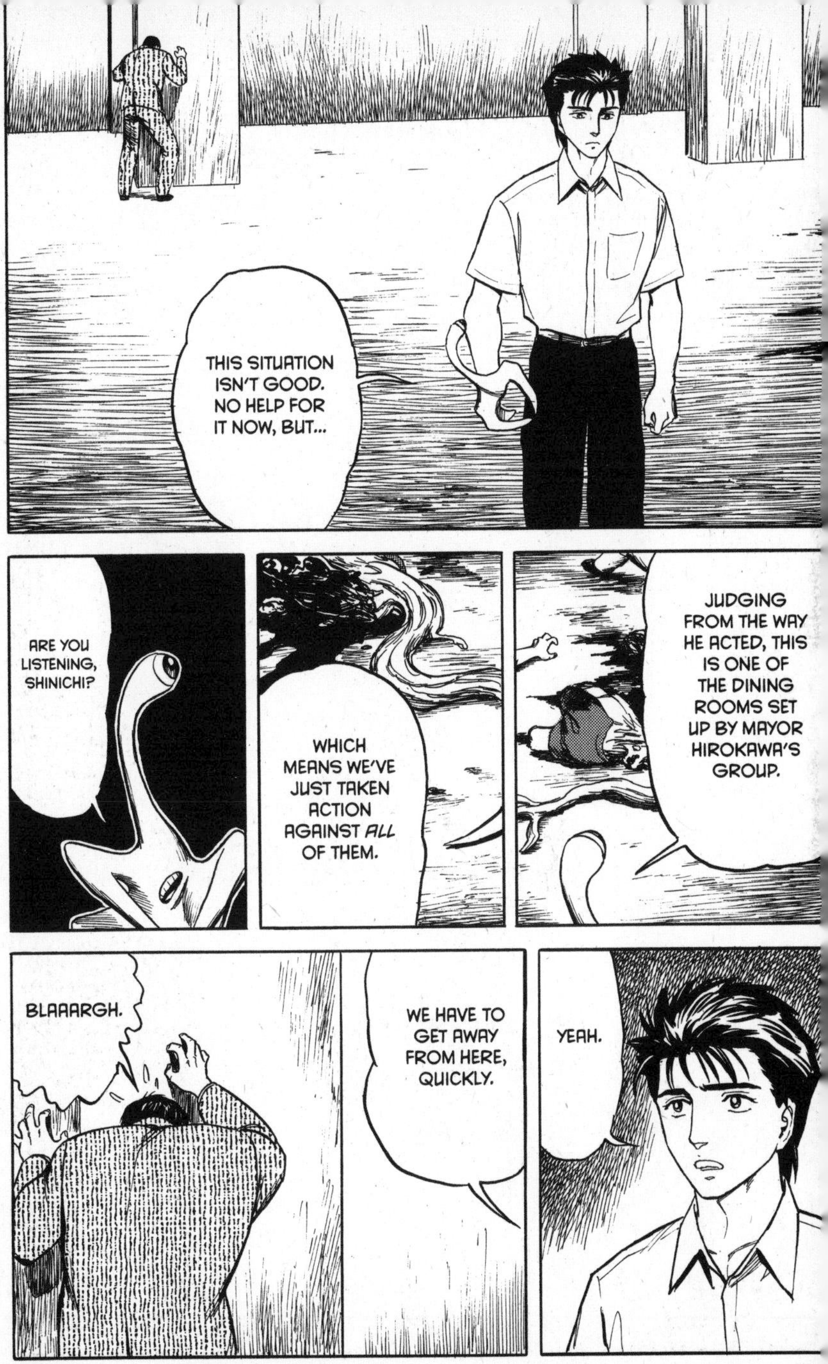
THIS SITUATION ISN'T GOOD. NO HELP FOR IT NOW, BUT...
JUDGING FROM THE WAY HE ACTED, THIS IS ONE OF THE DINING ROOMS SET UP BY MAYOR HIROKAWA'S GROUP.
WHICH MEANS WE'VE JUST TAKEN ACTION AGAINST *ALL* OF THEM.
ARE YOU LISTENING, SHINICHI?
YEAH.
WE HAVE TO GET AWAY FROM HERE, QUICKLY.
BLAAARGH.

The Cure

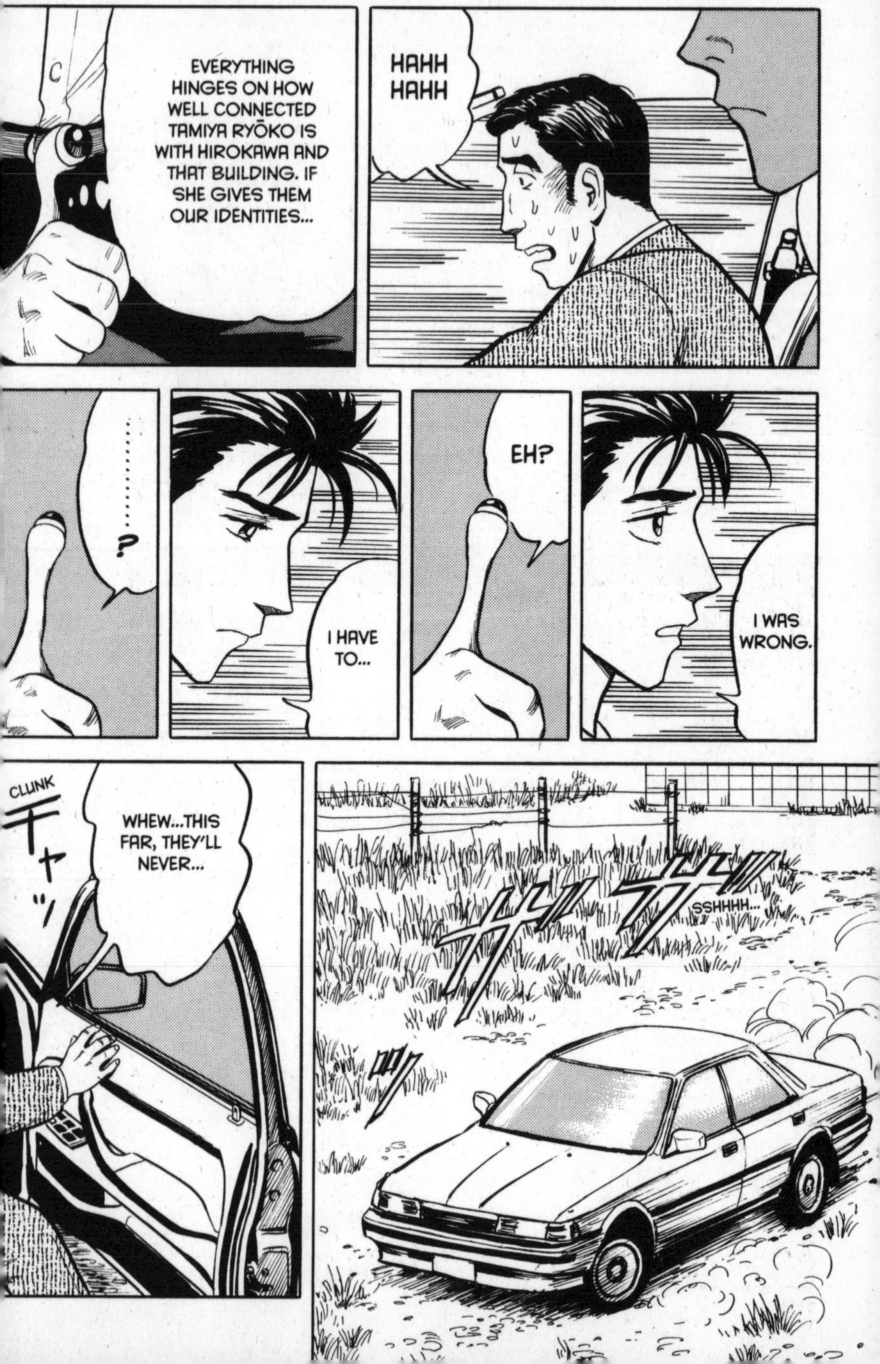
HAHH HAHH
EVERYTHING HINGES ON HOW WELL CONNECTED TAMIYA RYŌKO IS WITH HIROKAWA AND THAT BUILDING. IF SHE GIVES THEM OUR IDENTITIES...
I WAS WRONG.
EH?
I HAVE TO...
......?
SSHHHH...
CLUNK
WHEW...THIS FAR, THEY'LL NEVER...

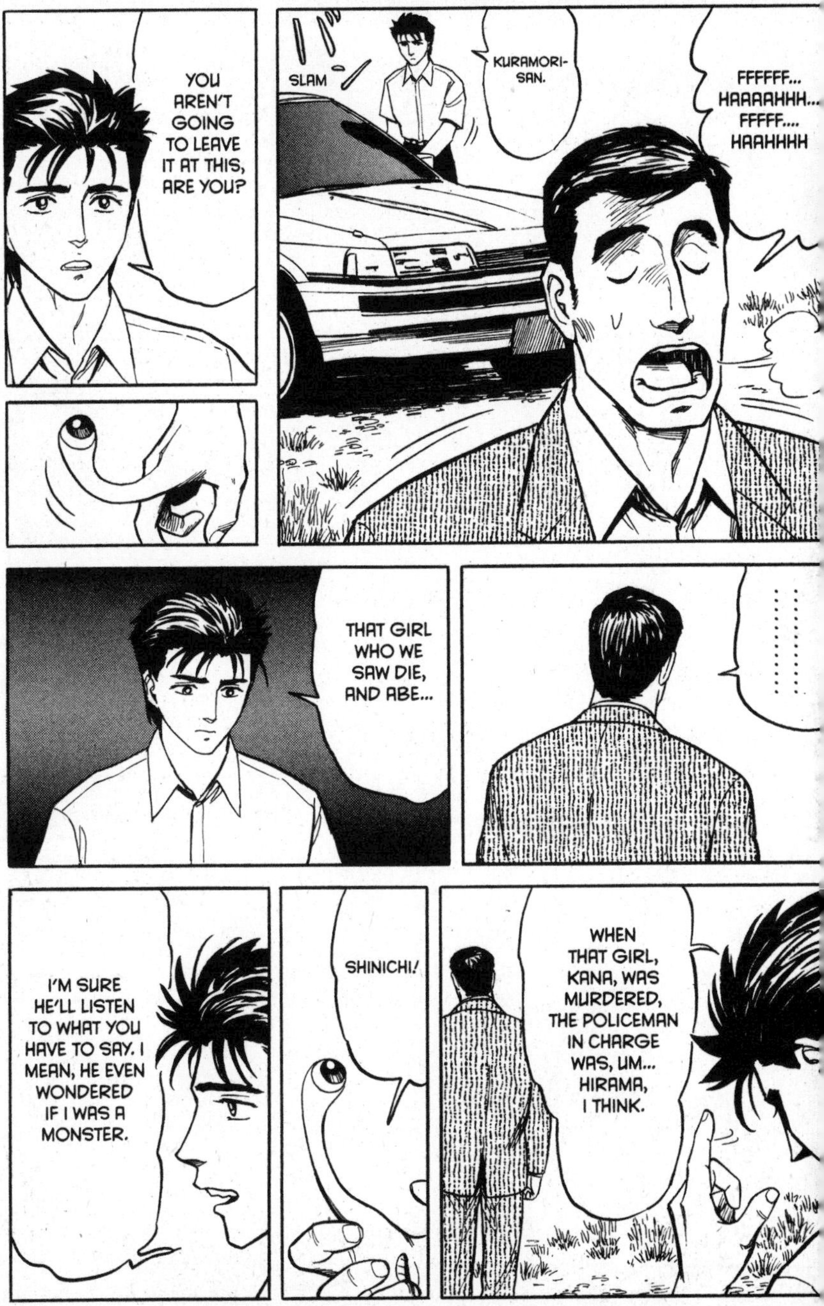
FFFFFF... HAAAAHHH... FFFFF.... HAAHHHH
KURAMORI-SAN.
SLAM
YOU AREN'T GOING TO LEAVE IT AT THIS, ARE YOU?
......
THAT GIRL WHO WE SAW DIE, AND ABE...
WHEN THAT GIRL, KANA, WAS MURDERED, THE POLICEMAN IN CHARGE WAS, UM... HIRAMA, I THINK.
SHINICHI!
I'M SURE HE'LL LISTEN TO WHAT YOU HAVE TO SAY. I MEAN, HE EVEN WONDERED IF I WAS A MONSTER.

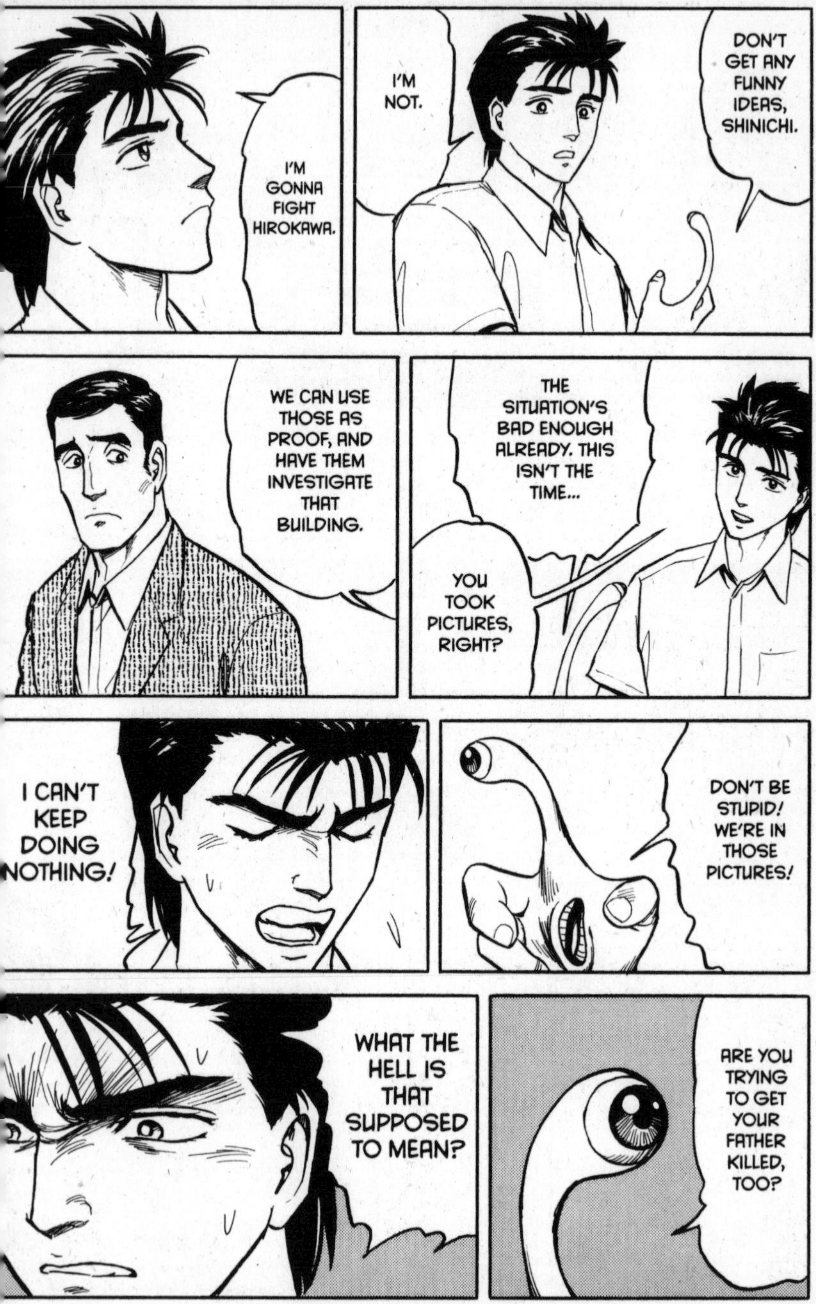
DON'T GET ANY FUNNY IDEAS, SHINICHI.
I'M NOT.
I'M GONNA FIGHT HIROKAWA.
THE SITUATION'S BAD ENOUGH ALREADY. THIS ISN'T THE TIME...
YOU TOOK PICTURES, RIGHT?
WE CAN USE THOSE AS PROOF, AND HAVE THEM INVESTIGATE THAT BUILDING.
DON'T BE STUPID! WE'RE IN THOSE PICTURES!
I CAN'T KEEP DOING NOTHING!
ARE YOU TRYING TO GET YOUR FATHER KILLED, TOO?
WHAT THE HELL IS THAT SUPPOSED TO MEAN?

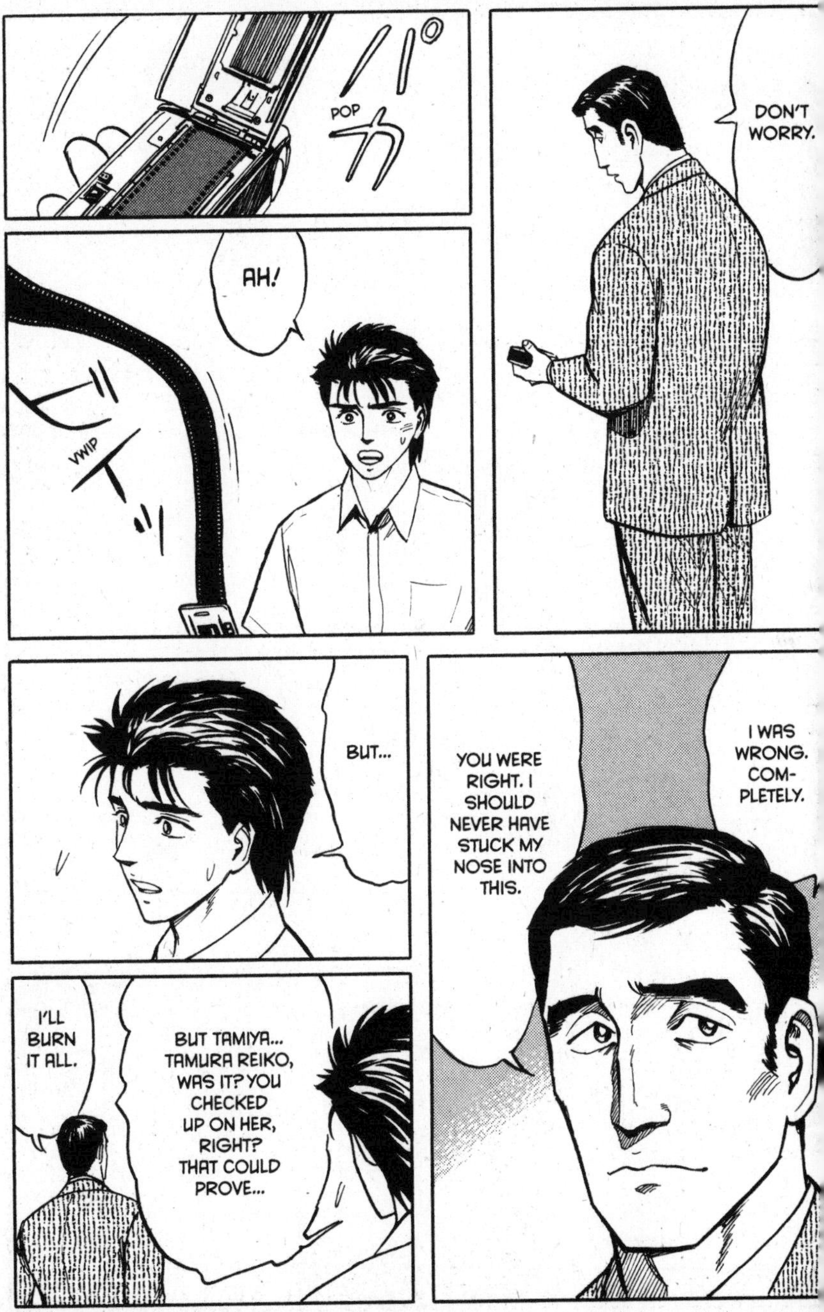
DON'T WORRY.
パ
カ
POP
AH!
VWIP
I WAS WRONG. COMPLETELY.
YOU WERE RIGHT. I SHOULD NEVER HAVE STUCK MY NOSE INTO THIS.
BUT...
BUT TAMIYA... TAMURA REIKO, WAS IT? YOU CHECKED UP ON HER, RIGHT? THAT COULD PROVE...
I'LL BURN IT ALL.

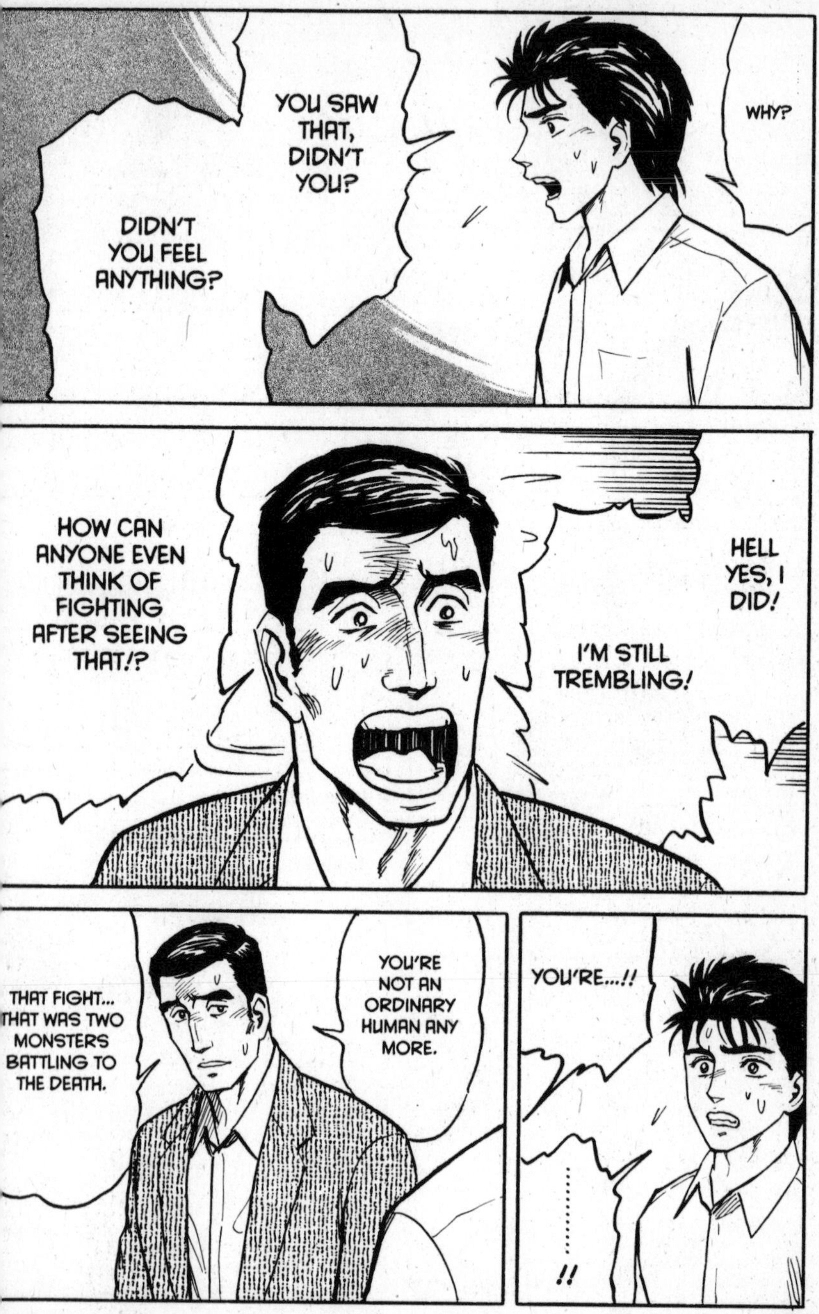

WHY?
YOU SAW THAT, DIDN'T YOU?
DIDN'T YOU FEEL ANYTHING?
HELL YES, I DID!
I'M STILL TREMBLING!
HOW CAN ANYONE EVEN THINK OF FIGHTING AFTER SEEING THAT!?
YOU'RE...!!
......!!
YOU'RE NOT AN ORDINARY HUMAN ANY MORE.
THAT FIGHT... THAT WAS TWO MONSTERS BATTLING TO THE DEATH.

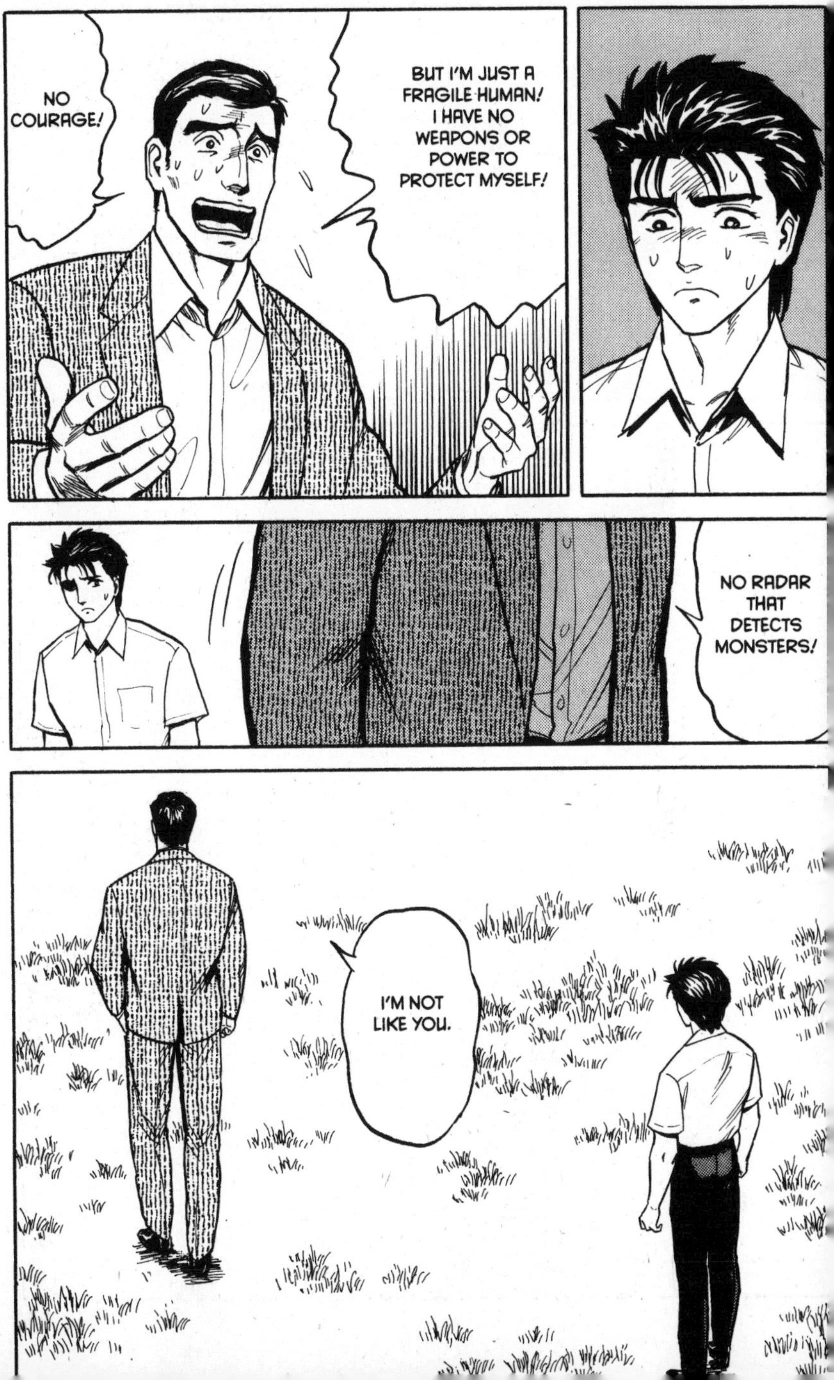
BUT I'M JUST A FRAGILE HUMAN! I HAVE NO WEAPONS OR POWER TO PROTECT MYSELF!
NO COURAGE!
NO RADAR THAT DETECTS MONSTERS!
I'M NOT LIKE YOU.

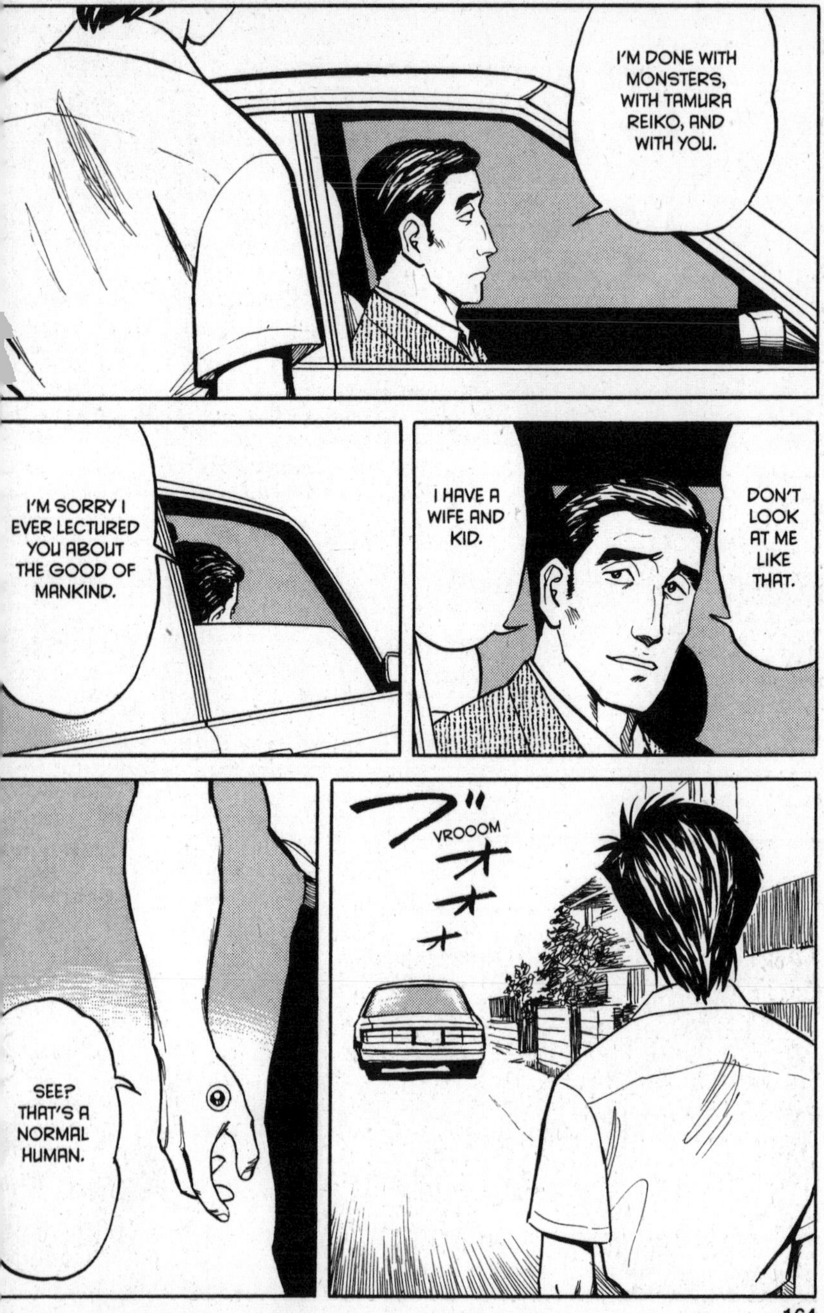
I'M DONE WITH MONSTERS, WITH TAMURA REIKO, AND WITH YOU.
DON'T LOOK AT ME LIKE THAT.
I HAVE A WIFE AND KID.
I'M SORRY I EVER LECTURED YOU ABOUT THE GOOD OF MANKIND.
ブオオオ
VROOOM
SEE? THAT'S A NORMAL HUMAN.

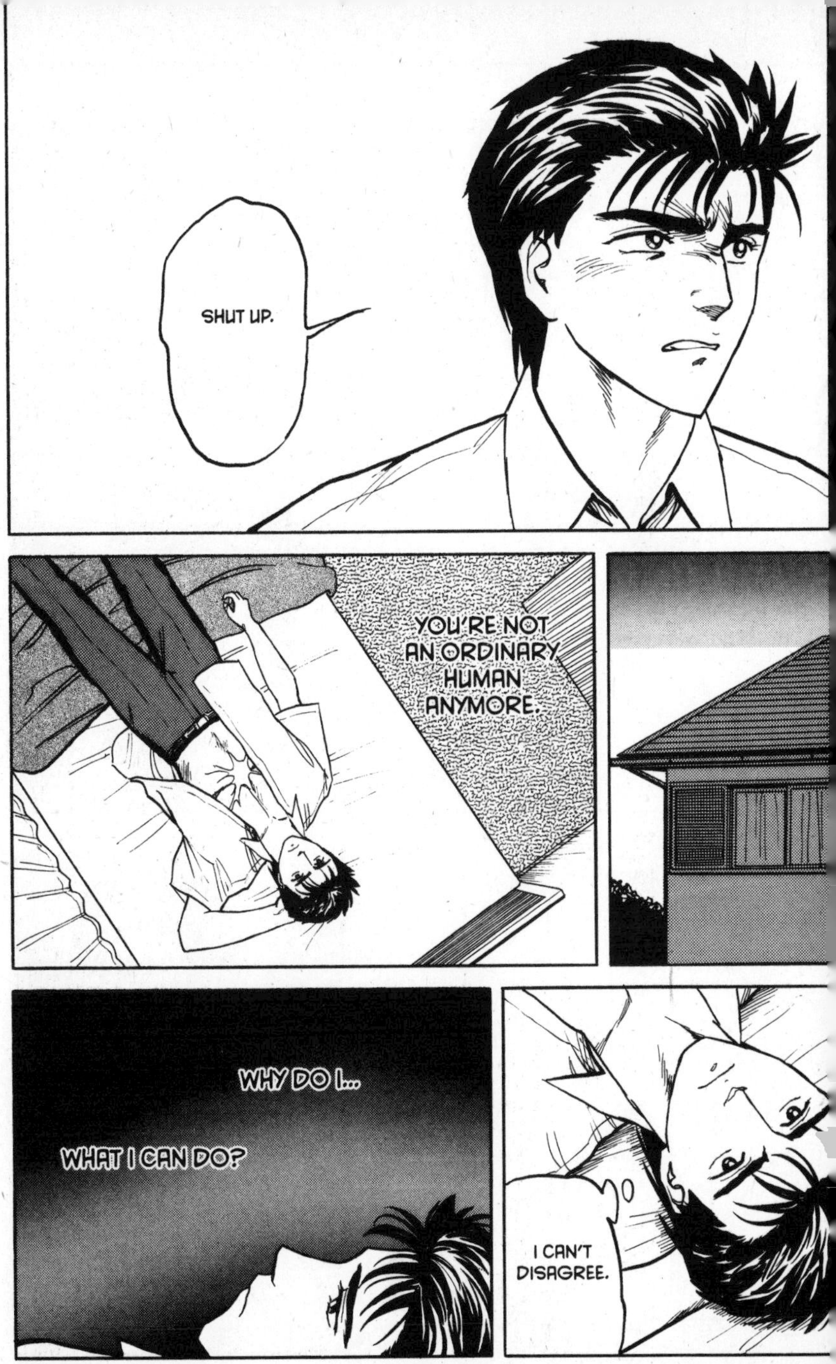
SHUT UP.
YOU'RE NOT AN ORDINARY HUMAN ANYMORE.
I CAN'T DISAGREE.
WHY DO I...
WHAT I CAN DO?

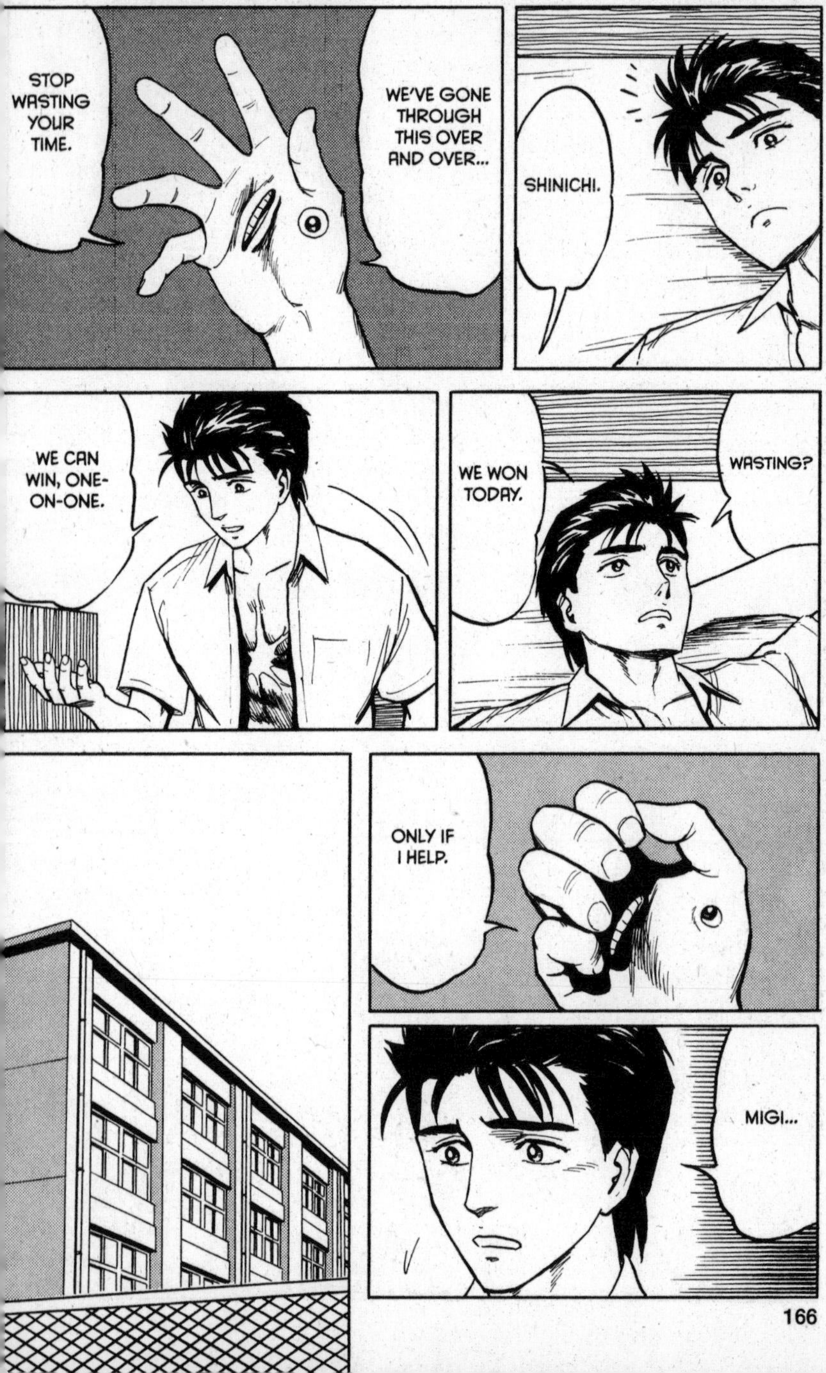
SHINICHI.
WE'VE GONE THROUGH THIS OVER AND OVER...
STOP WASTING YOUR TIME.
WASTING?
WE WON TODAY.
WE CAN WIN, ONE-ON-ONE.
ONLY IF I HELP.
MIGI...

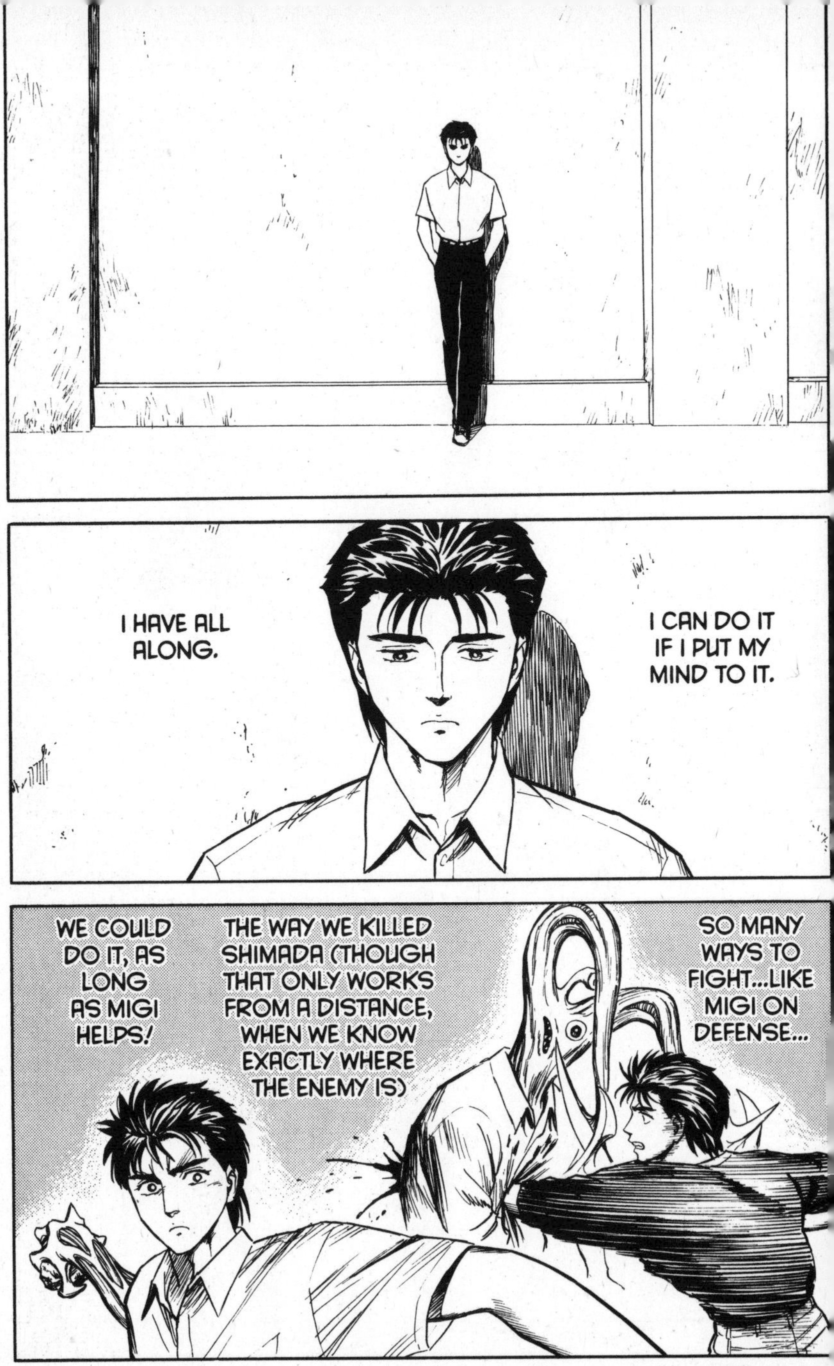
I CAN DO IT IF I PUT MY MIND TO IT.
I HAVE ALL ALONG.
SO MANY WAYS TO FIGHT...LIKE MIGI ON DEFENSE...
THE WAY WE KILLED SHIMADA (THOUGH THAT ONLY WORKS FROM A DISTANCE, WHEN WE KNOW EXACTLY WHERE THE ENEMY IS)
WE COULD DO IT, AS LONG AS MIGI HELPS!

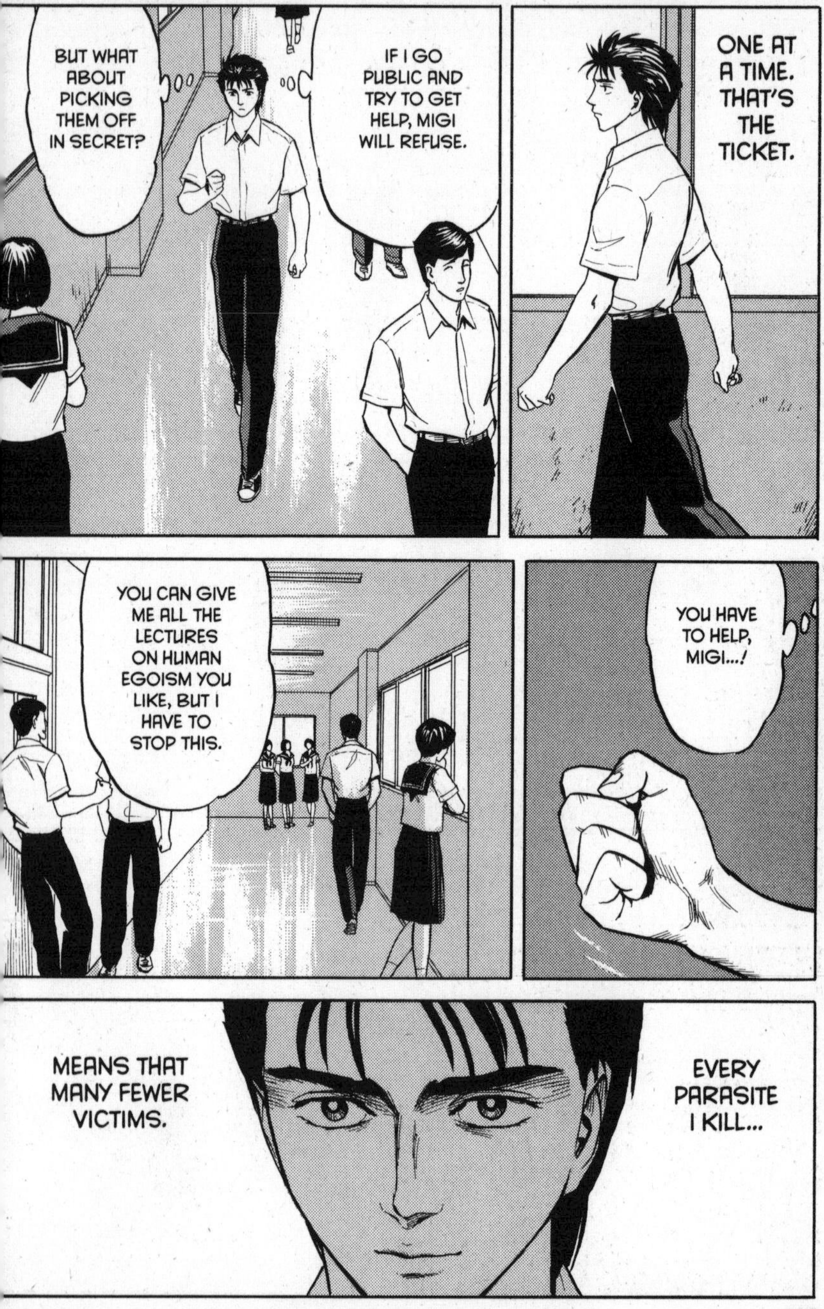
ONE AT A TIME. THAT'S THE TICKET.
IF I GO PUBLIC AND TRY TO GET HELP, MIGI WILL REFUSE.
BUT WHAT ABOUT PICKING THEM OFF IN SECRET?
YOU HAVE TO HELP, MIGI...!
YOU CAN GIVE ME ALL THE LECTURES ON HUMAN EGOISM YOU LIKE, BUT I HAVE TO STOP THIS.
EVERY PARASITE I KILL...
MEANS THAT MANY FEWER VICTIMS.

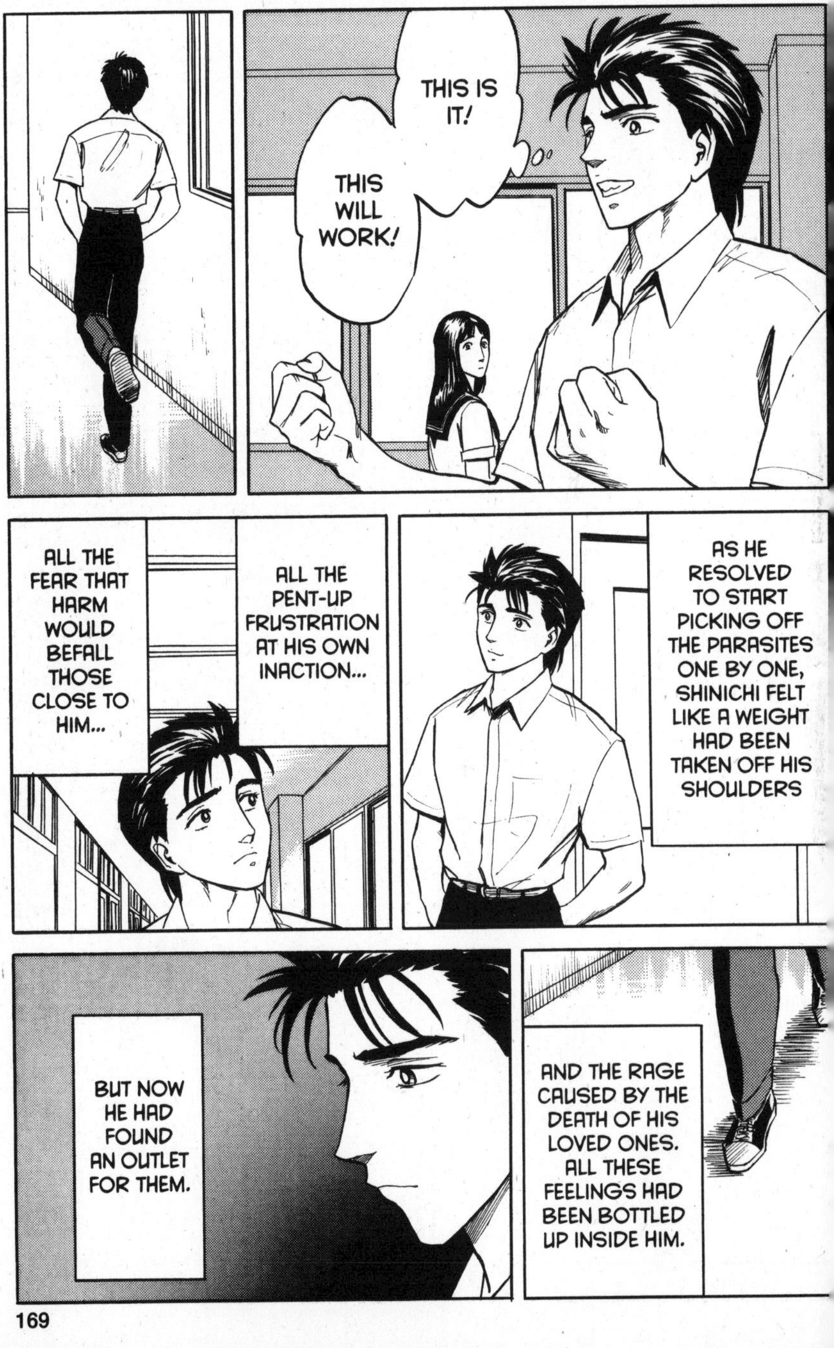
THIS IS IT!
THIS WILL WORK!
AS HE RESOLVED TO START PICKING OFF THE PARASITES ONE BY ONE, SHINICHI FELT LIKE A WEIGHT HAD BEEN TAKEN OFF HIS SHOULDERS
ALL THE PENT-UP FRUSTRATION AT HIS OWN INACTION...
ALL THE FEAR THAT HARM WOULD BEFALL THOSE CLOSE TO HIM...
AND THE RAGE CAUSED BY THE DEATH OF HIS LOVED ONES. ALL THESE FEELINGS HAD BEEN BOTTLED UP INSIDE HIM.
BUT NOW HE HAD FOUND AN OUTLET FOR THEM.

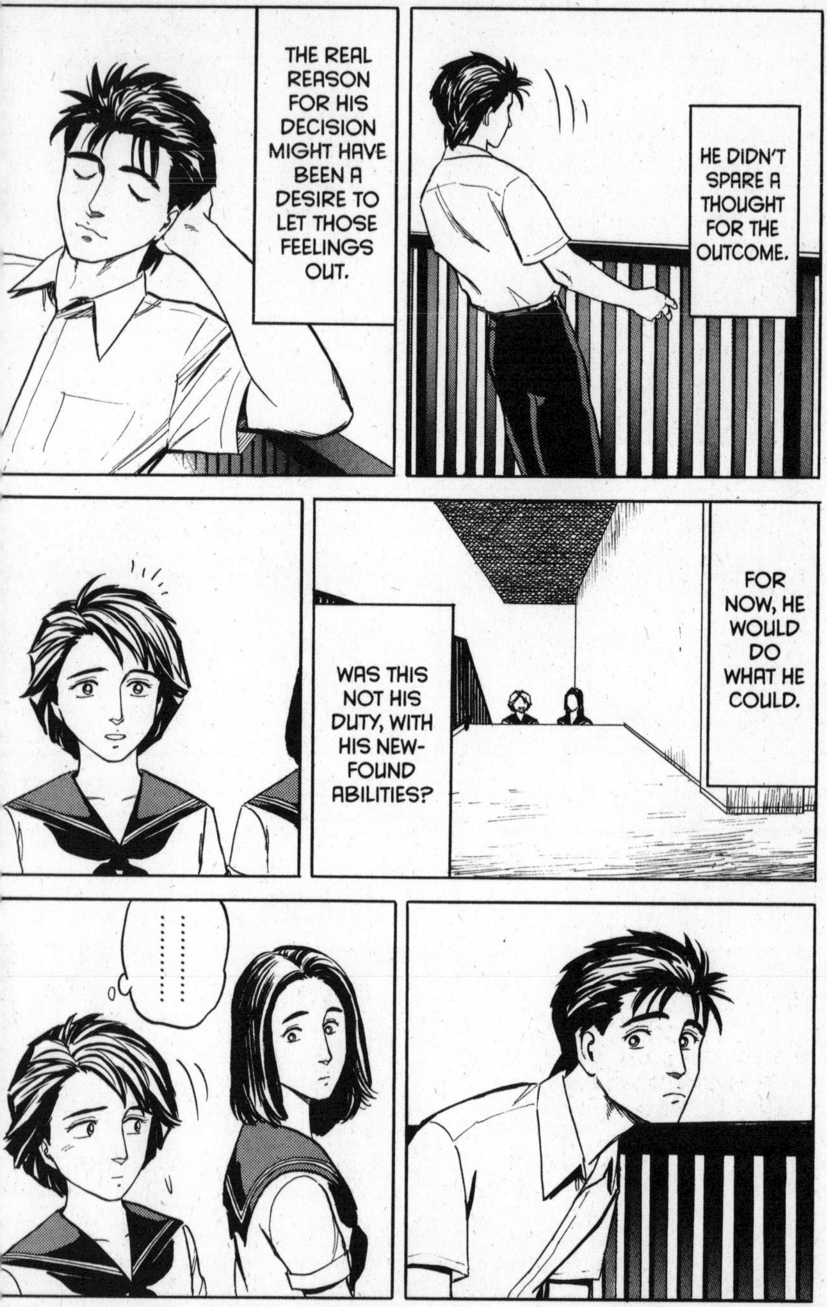
HE DIDN'T SPARE A THOUGHT FOR THE OUTCOME.
THE REAL REASON FOR HIS DECISION MIGHT HAVE BEEN A DESIRE TO LET THOSE FEELINGS OUT.
FOR NOW, HE WOULD DO WHAT HE COULD.
WAS THIS NOT HIS DUTY, WITH HIS NEW-FOUND ABILITIES?
......

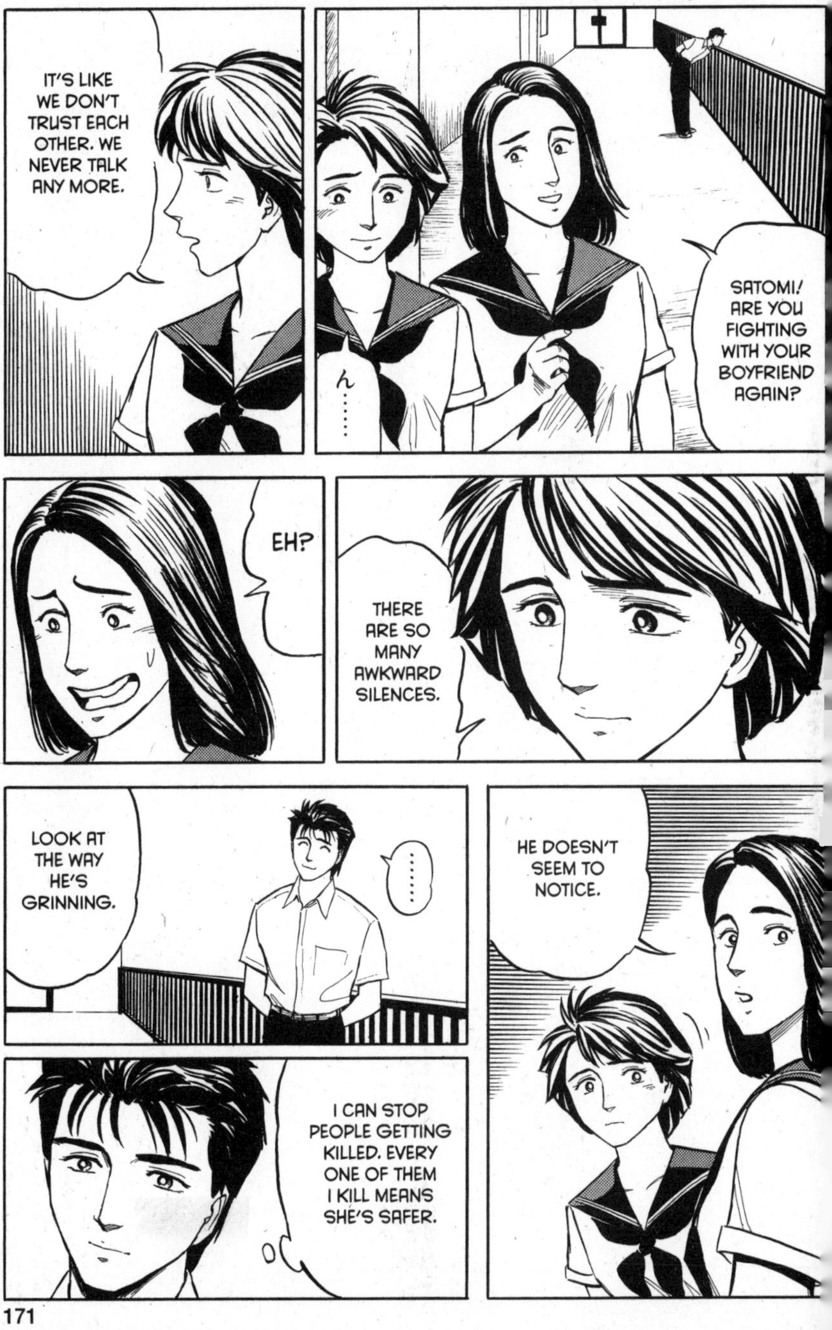
SATOMI! ARE YOU FIGHTING WITH YOUR BOYFRIEND AGAIN?
ん……
IT'S LIKE WE DON'T TRUST EACH OTHER. WE NEVER TALK ANY MORE.
THERE ARE SO MANY AWKWARD SILENCES.
EH?
HE DOESN'T SEEM TO NOTICE.
LOOK AT THE WAY HE'S GRINNING.
……
I CAN STOP PEOPLE GETTING KILLED. EVERY ONE OF THEM I KILL MEANS SHE'S SAFER.

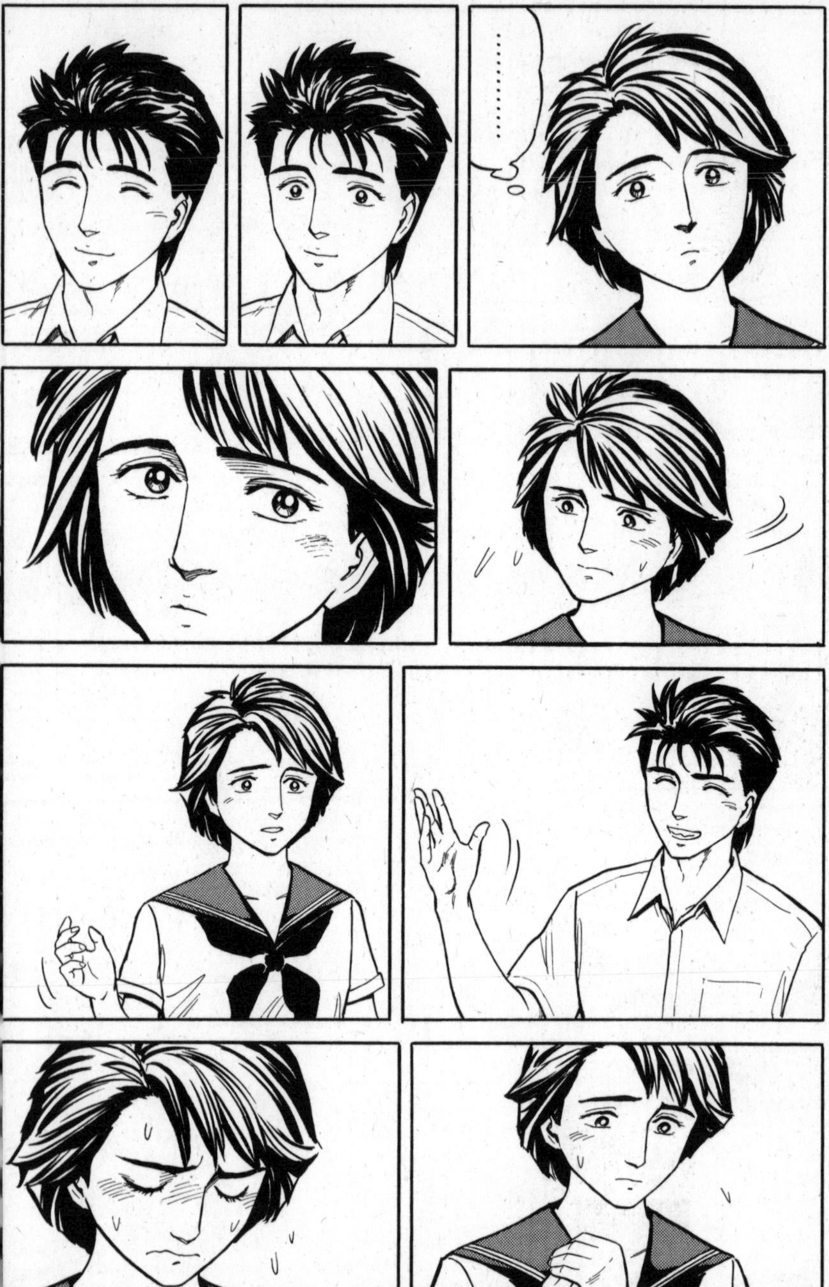
……

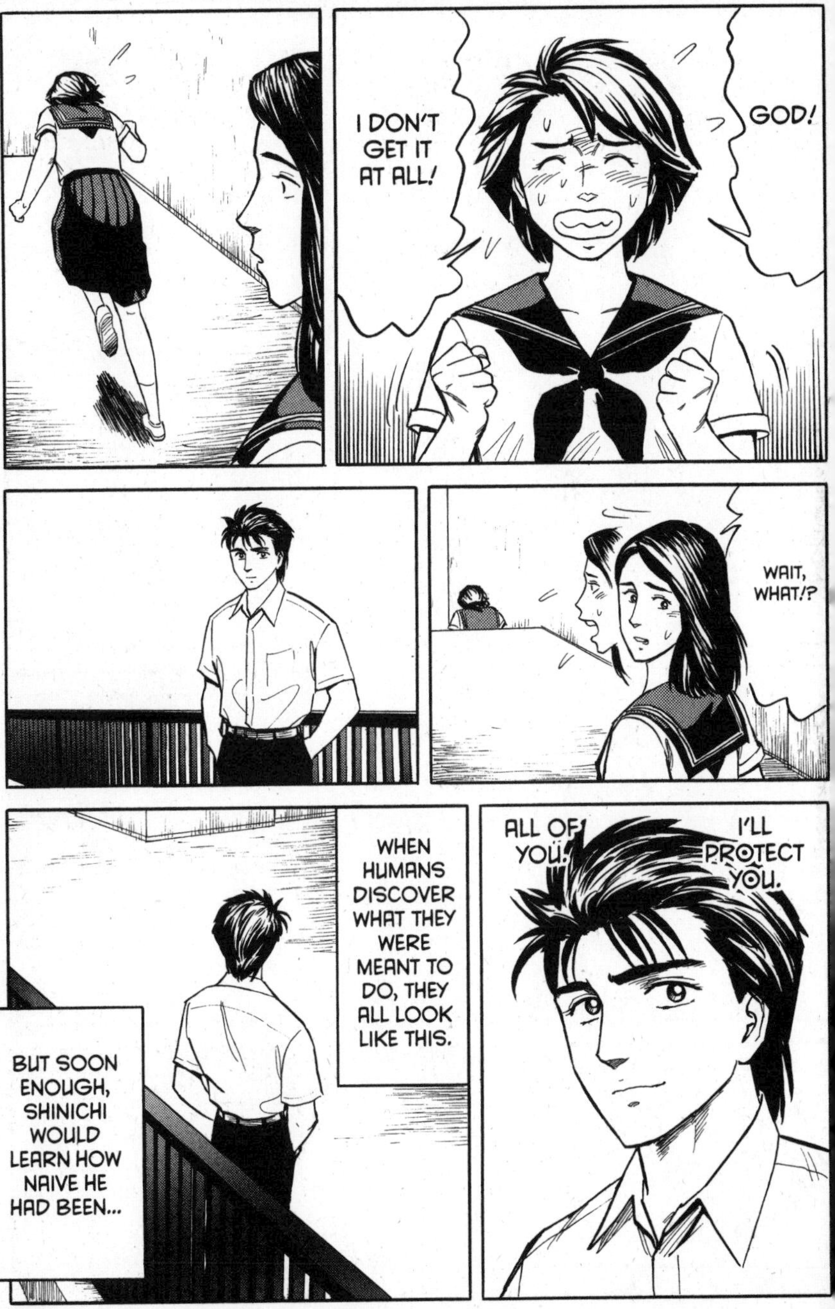
GOD!
I DON'T GET IT AT ALL!
WAIT, WHAT!?
I'LL PROTECT YOU.
ALL OF YOU.
WHEN HUMANS DISCOVER WHAT THEY WERE MEANT TO DO, THEY ALL LOOK LIKE THIS.
BUT SOON ENOUGH, SHINICHI WOULD LEARN HOW NAIVE HE HAD BEEN...

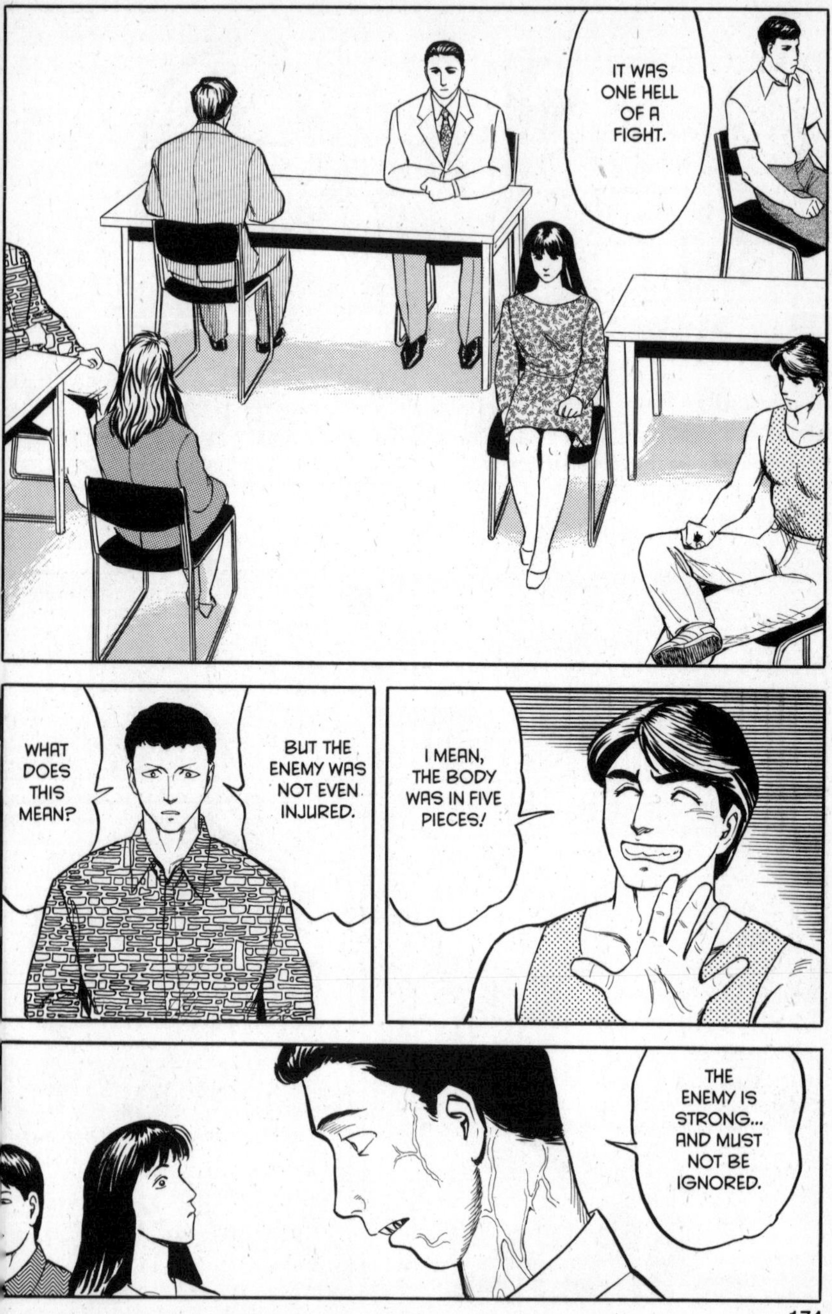
IT WAS ONE HELL OF A FIGHT.
I MEAN, THE BODY WAS IN FIVE PIECES!
BUT THE ENEMY WAS NOT EVEN INJURED.
WHAT DOES THIS MEAN?
THE ENEMY IS STRONG... AND MUST NOT BE IGNORED.

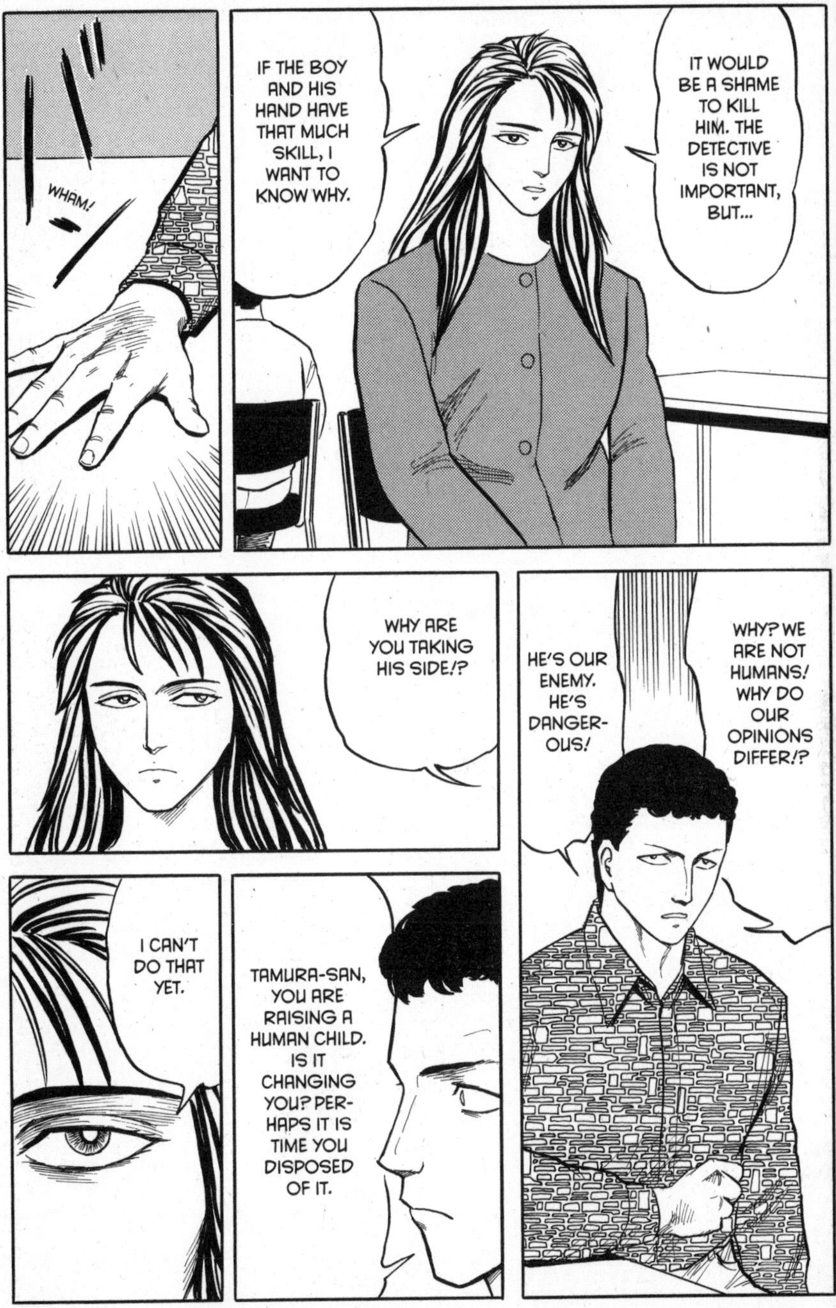
IT WOULD BE A SHAME TO KILL HIM. THE DETECTIVE IS NOT IMPORTANT, BUT...
IF THE BOY AND HIS HAND HAVE THAT MUCH SKILL, I WANT TO KNOW WHY.
WHAM!
WHY? WE ARE NOT HUMANS! WHY DO OUR OPINIONS DIFFER!?
HE'S OUR ENEMY. HE'S DANGER-OUS!
WHY ARE YOU TAKING HIS SIDE!?
TAMURA-SAN, YOU ARE RAISING A HUMAN CHILD. IS IT CHANGING YOU? PER-HAPS IT IS TIME YOU DISPOSED OF IT.
I CAN'T DO THAT YET.

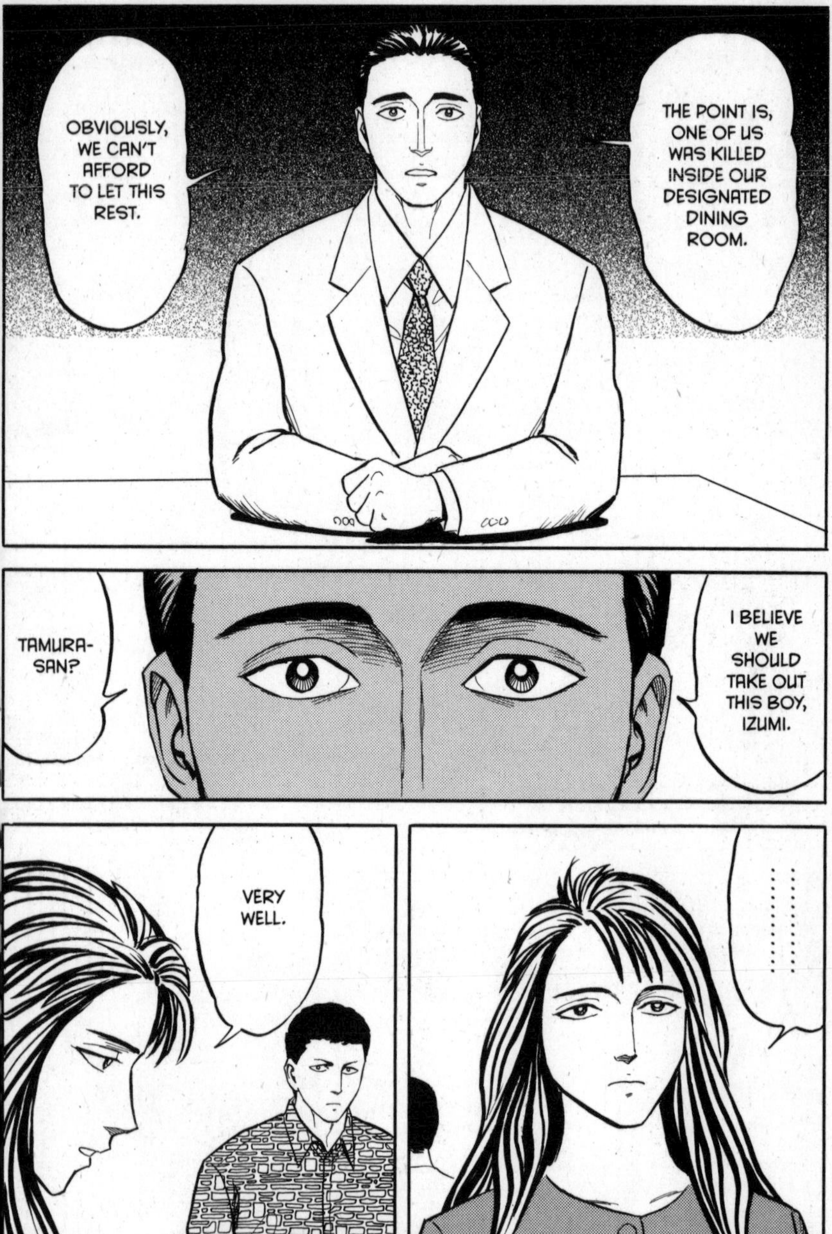
THE POINT IS, ONE OF US WAS KILLED INSIDE OUR DESIGNATED DINING ROOM.
OBVIOUSLY, WE CAN'T AFFORD TO LET THIS REST.
I BELIEVE WE SHOULD TAKE OUT THIS BOY, IZUMI.
TAMURA-SAN?
......
VERY WELL.

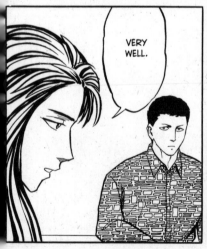

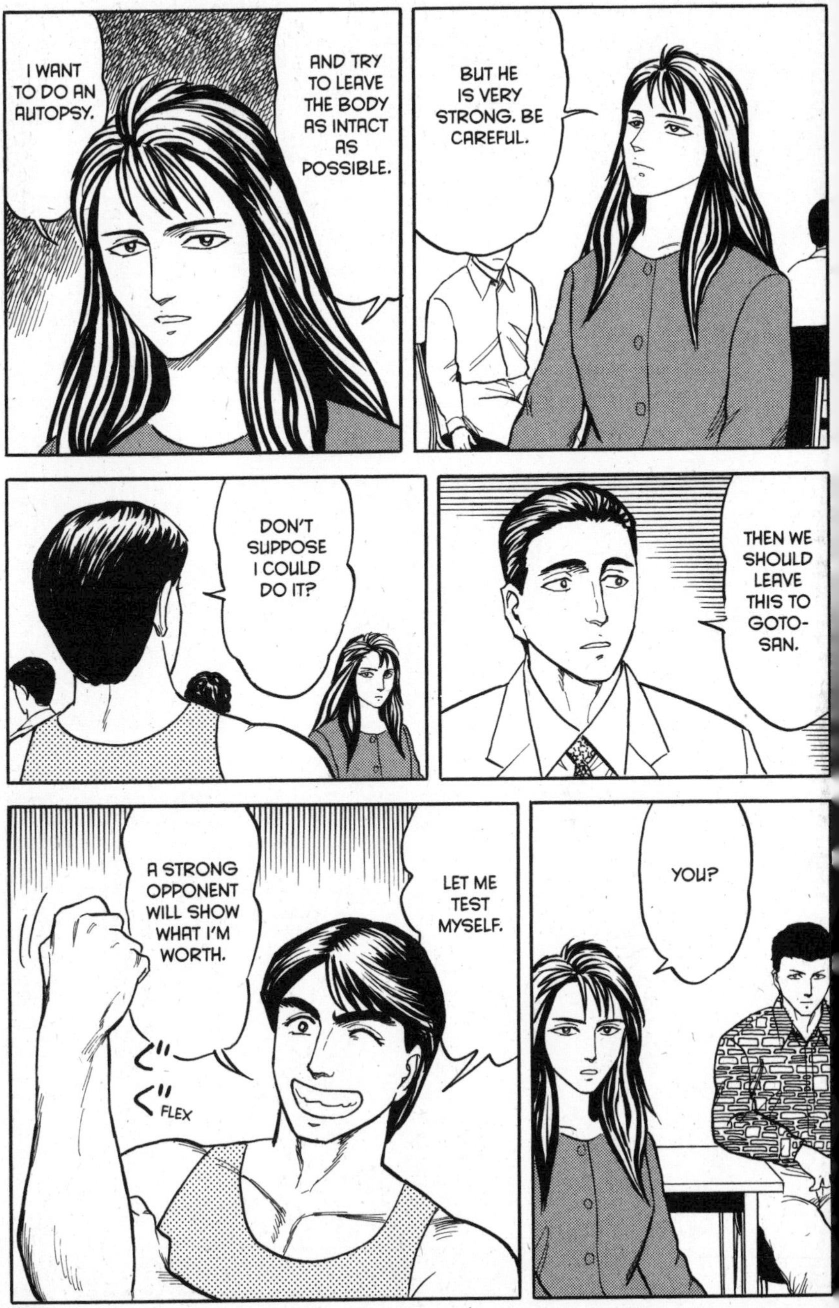
BUT HE IS VERY STRONG. BE CAREFUL.
AND TRY TO LEAVE THE BODY AS INTACT AS POSSIBLE.
I WANT TO DO AN AUTOPSY.
THEN WE SHOULD LEAVE THIS TO GOTO-SAN.
DON'T SUPPOSE I COULD DO IT?
YOU?
LET ME TEST MYSELF.
A STRONG OPPONENT WILL SHOW WHAT I'M WORTH.
ぐ
ぐ FLEX

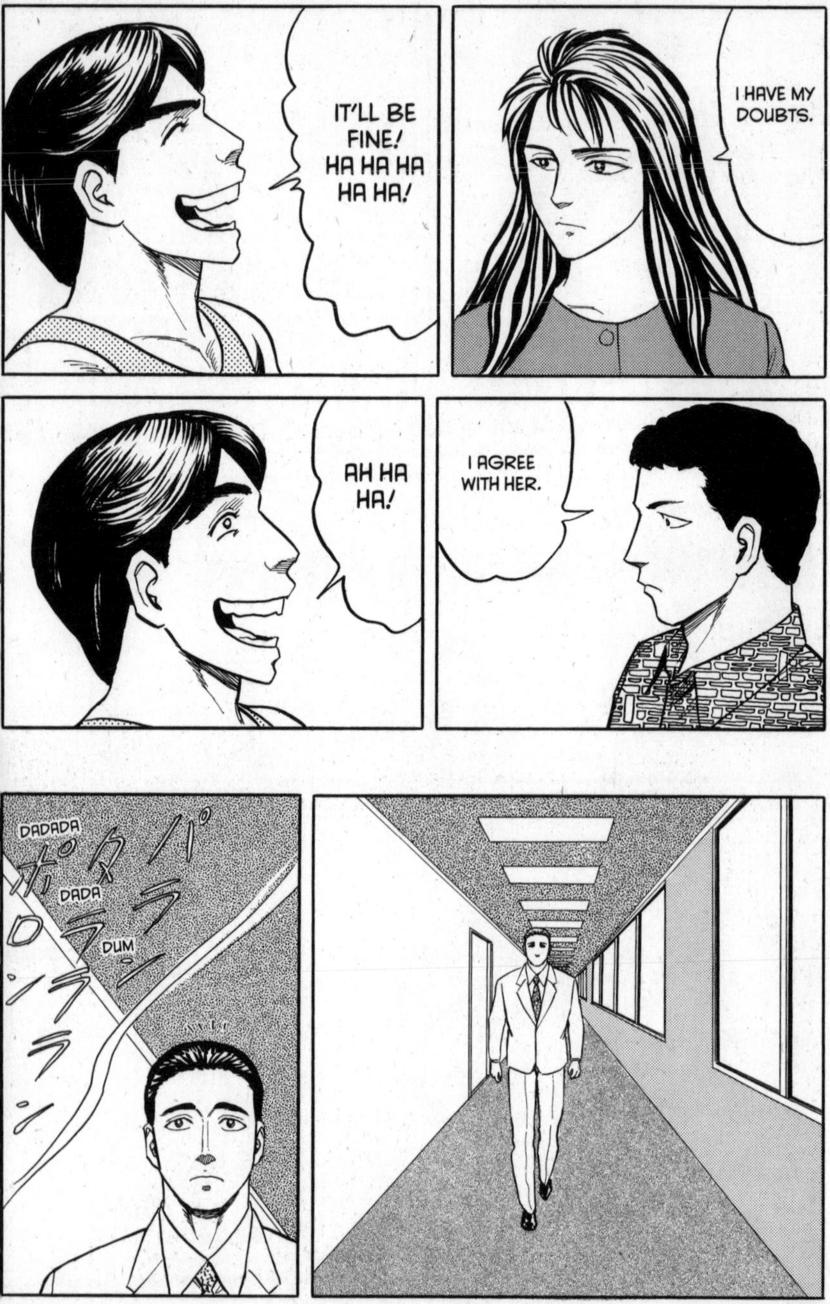
I HAVE MY DOUBTS.
IT'LL BE FINE! HA HA HA HA HA!
I AGREE WITH HER.
AH HA HA!
DADADA
DADA
DUM

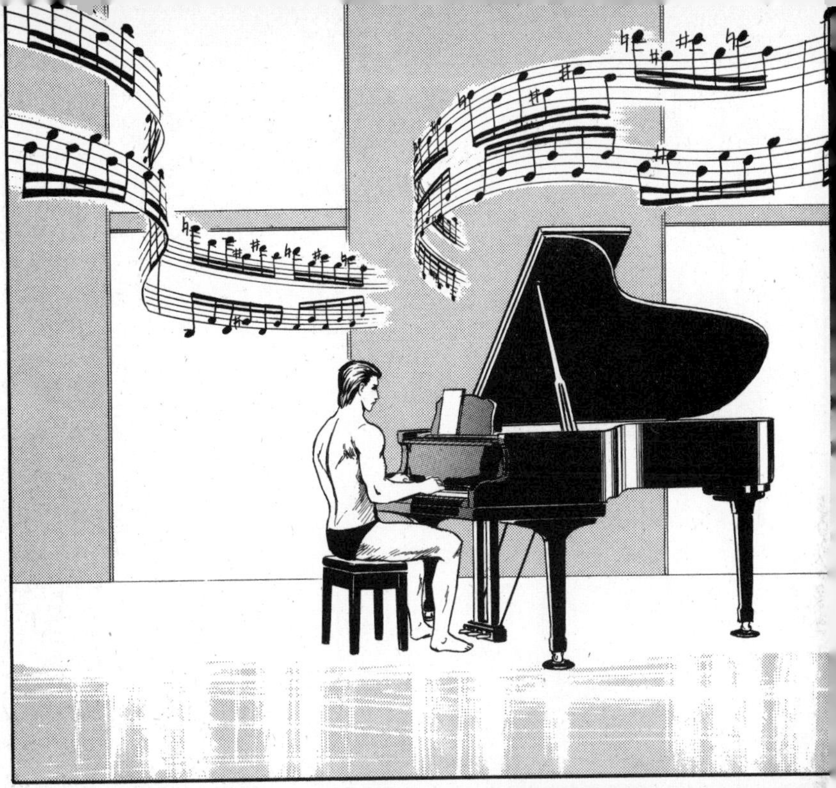

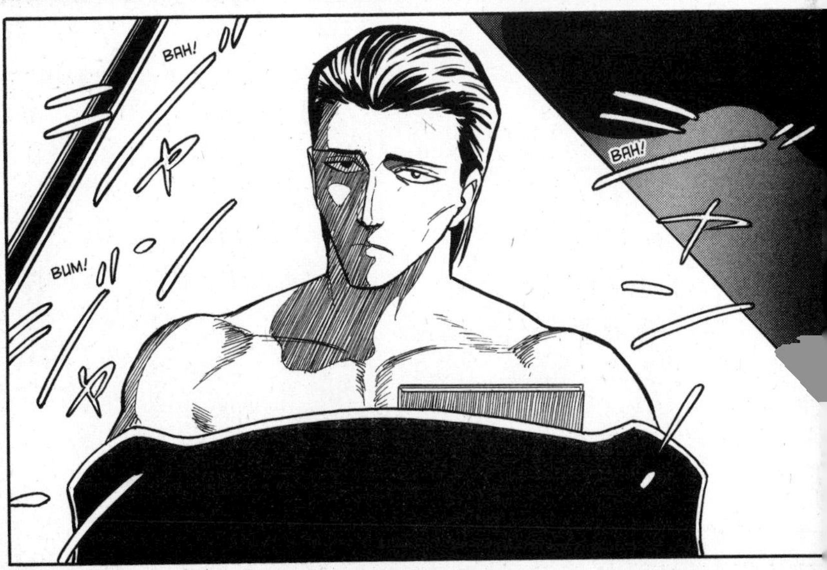
BAH!
BAH!
BUM!

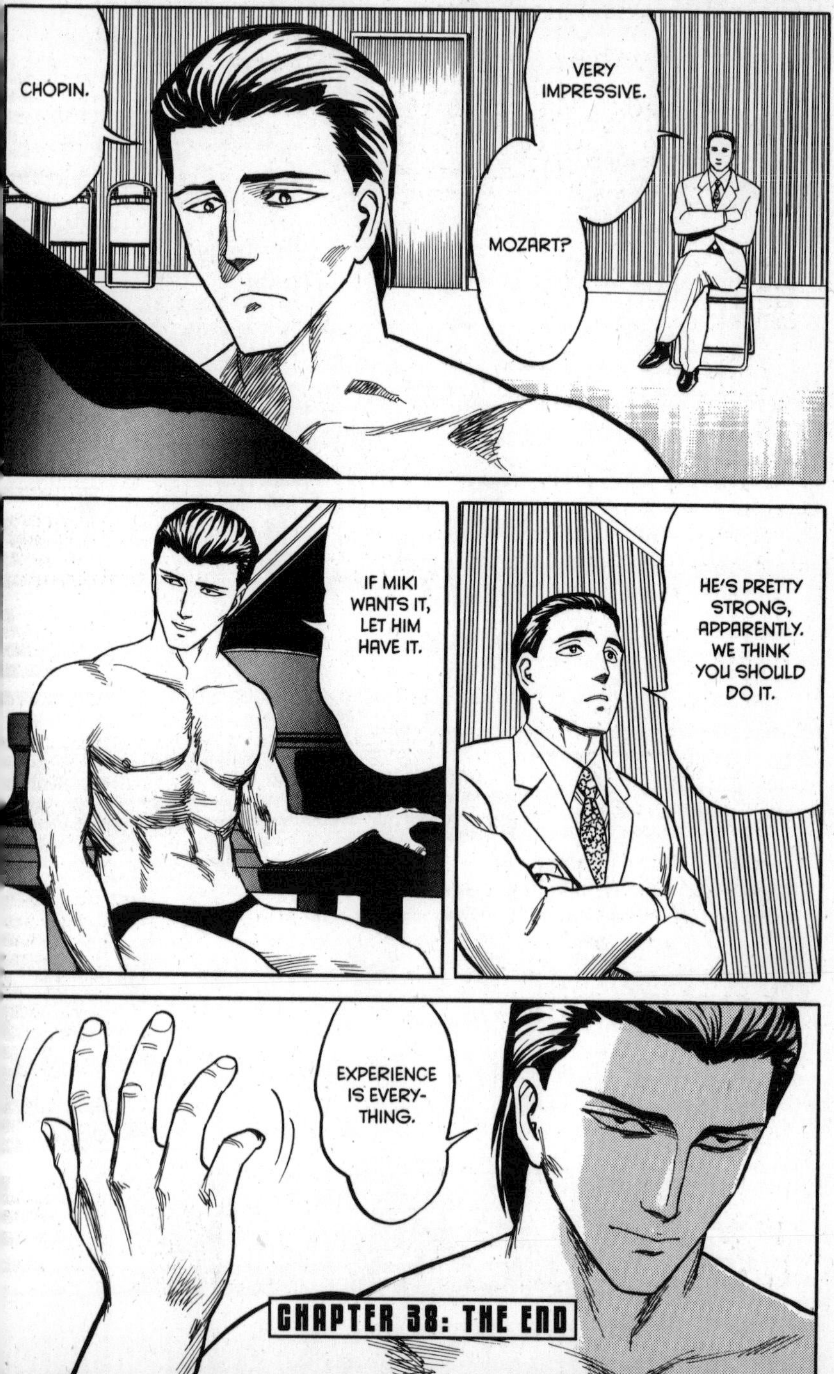
VERY IMPRESSIVE.
MOZART?
CHOPIN.
HE'S PRETTY STRONG, APPARENTLY. WE THINK YOU SHOULD DO IT.
IF MIKI WANTS IT, LET HIM HAVE IT.
EXPERIENCE IS EVERY-THING.
CHAPTER 38: THE END

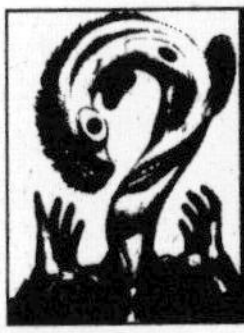

From the Monthly Afternoon Readers' page...

PARASYTE 5

vol. 5

THE READERS ASK. THE AUTHOR ANSWERS.

"Every time I see Shinichi and Migi moving together, it amazes me."
(Tokushima Prefecture, Ueno Takehiko, 22)

"At first glance, Migi appears to be Shinichi's weapon, but when they start fighting, he's the one in control. Not that many stories have the weapon in charge of strategy. Shinichi is still young, and does need guidance, which is why this works. If Migi had been trapped in a company president or a politician, they would have ended up arguing all the time."
(Hitoshi Iwaaki)

(From *Afternoon*, March 1993)

"Shinichi is about to be killed, but still so calm. He's not human anymore!"
(Fukuoka Prefecture, Harada Masanori, 20, Student)

"Shinichi's getting used to close calls. Possible because, no matter how bloody things get, Migi is right next to him, speaking calmly. Remaining clearheaded while scared of death and bits of flying flesh may not be very human, but the fact that this takes place in a peaceful country like Japan might be making it seem even more out of the ordinary."
(Hitoshi Iwaaki)

(From *Afternoon*, April 1993)

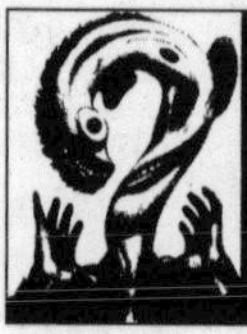

Interview with Hitoshi Iwaaki, recipient of the 17th Kodansha Manga Award

PARASYTE 5

KODANSHA MANGA AWARD / RECIPIENT INTERVIEW

Q. Congratulations. How do you feel?
Iwaaki: Extremely happy. I have to make sure the book doesn't fizzle out now, but that was always the case anyway.

Q. Why did you start drawing *Parasyte*?
Iwaaki: That's too long ago to remember. (Laughs.) But I wanted to make a story that was never boring. With this story, I was sure I could do that.

Q. The parasites initially fall from the sky, so are they intended to be alien?
Iwaaki: Almost every write-up of the series has said so, but if you actually read the narration, they were intended to have been created somewhere on the Earth. But since they did fall out of the sky, I can see why people thought that...but they were just being carried by the wind. When I thought them up, I decided they should be carried like dandelion seeds. But then again, I first started thinking about this story long before I started work at Kodansha...almost ten years ago now, so the exact details are a little fuzzy.

CHAPTER 39: ASSASSIN

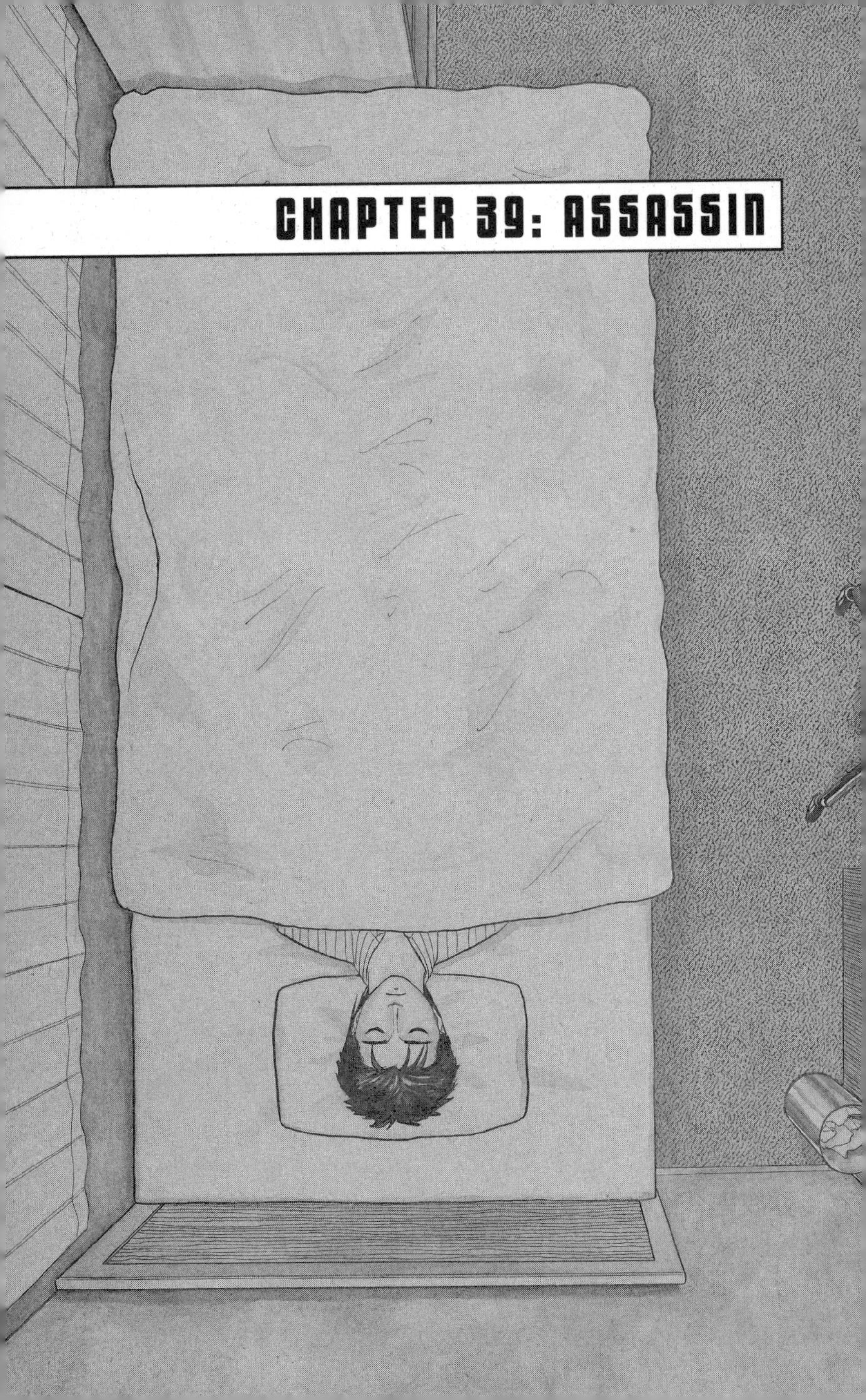

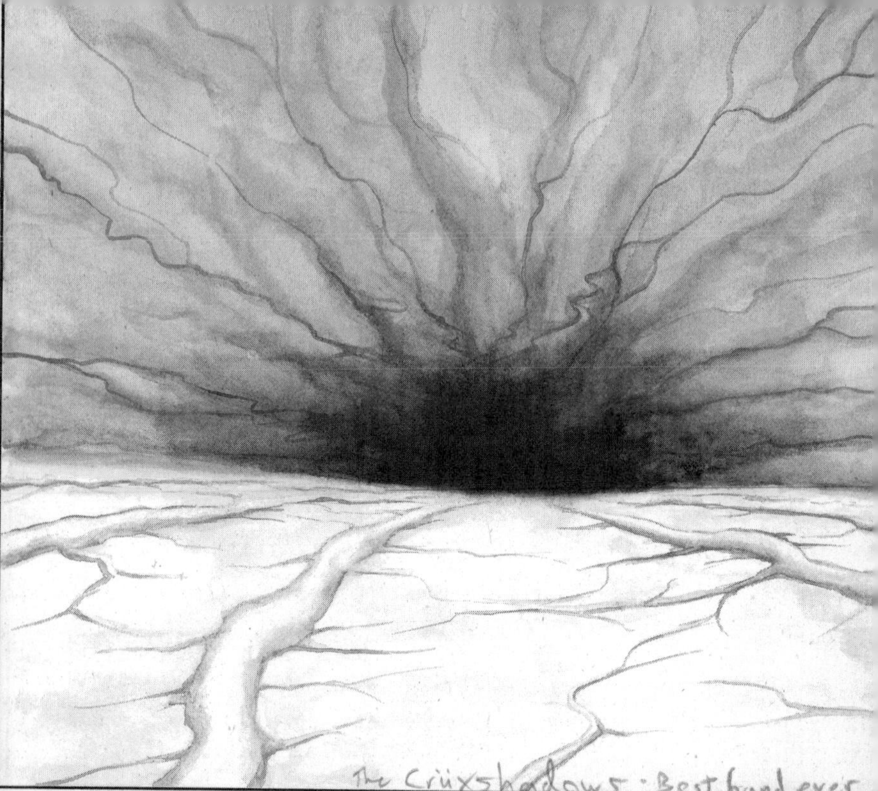
The Crüxshadows - Best band ever
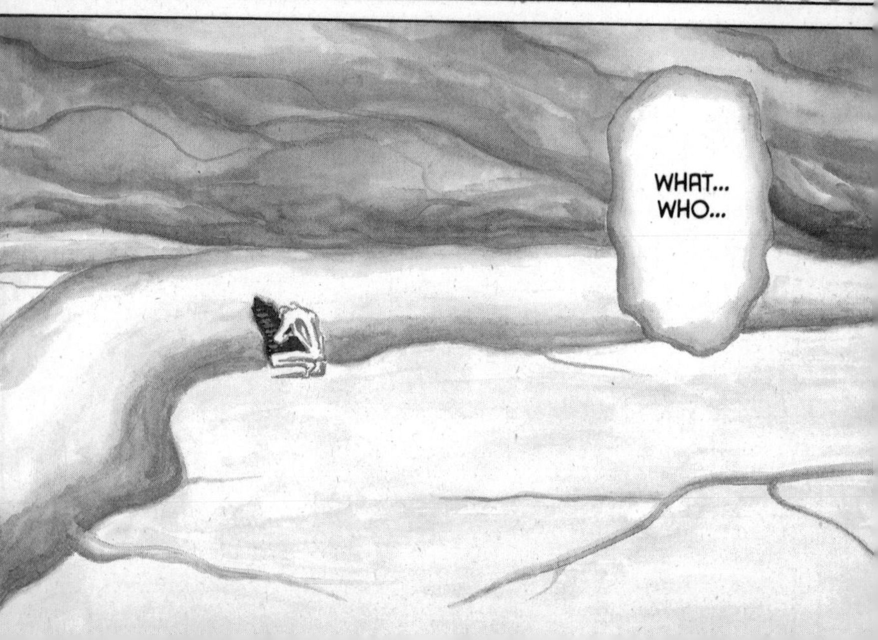
WHAT...
WHO...

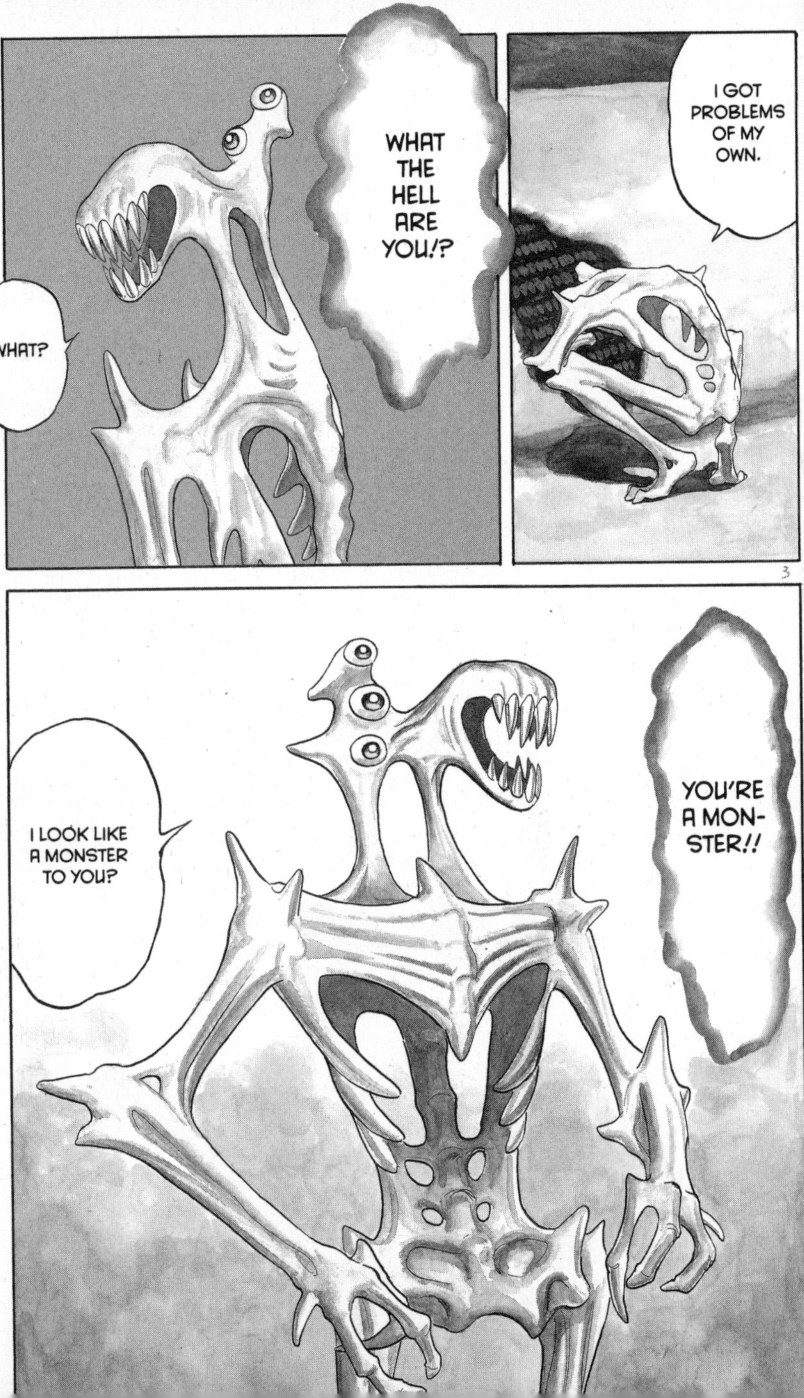
I GOT PROBLEMS OF MY OWN.
WHAT THE HELL ARE YOU!?
WHAT?
YOU'RE A MONSTER!!
I LOOK LIKE A MONSTER TO YOU?

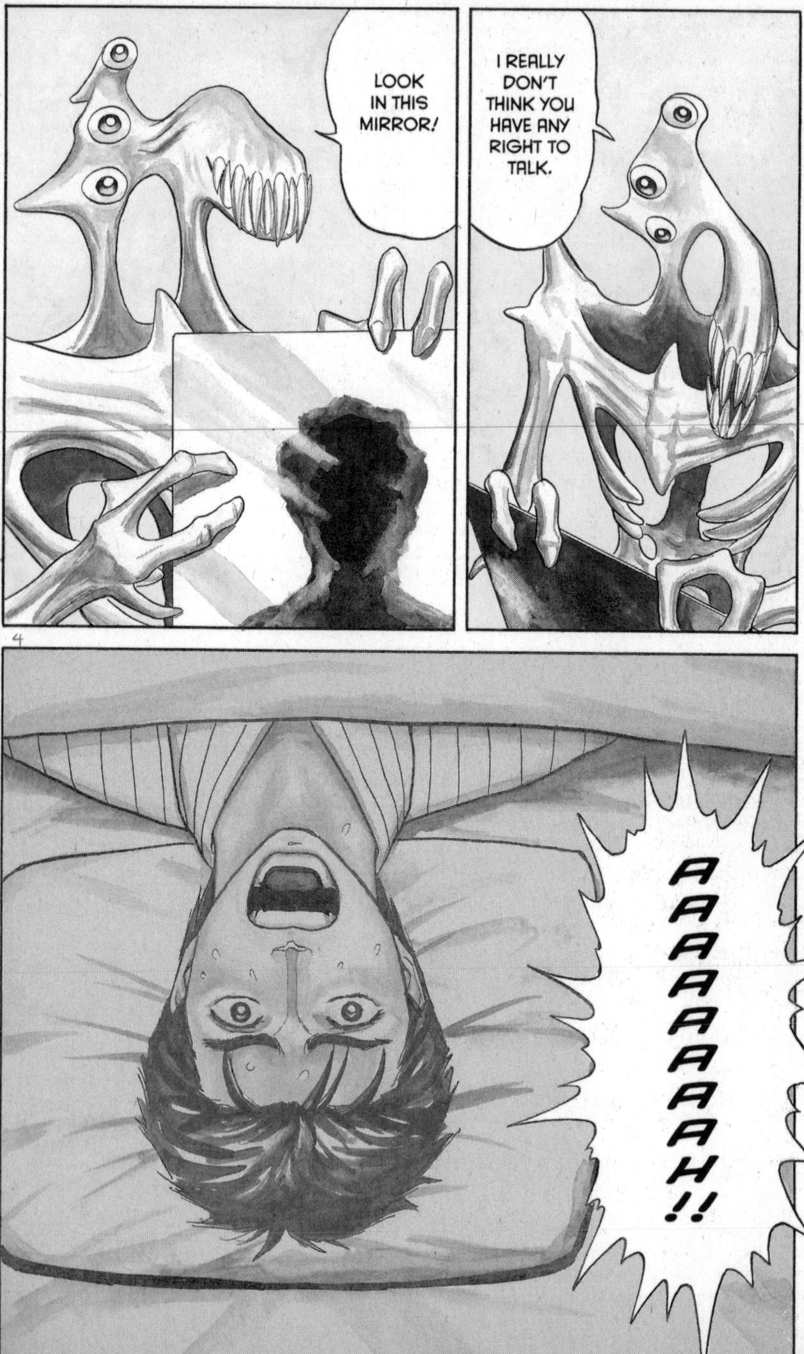
I REALLY DON'T THINK YOU HAVE ANY RIGHT TO TALK.
LOOK IN THIS MIRROR!
AAAAAAAAAAH!!

GOD! WHAT A HOR- RIBLE DREAM!

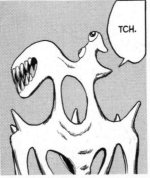

TCH.

I'VE SEEN THAT MONSTER...

IN A DIFFERENT DREAM.

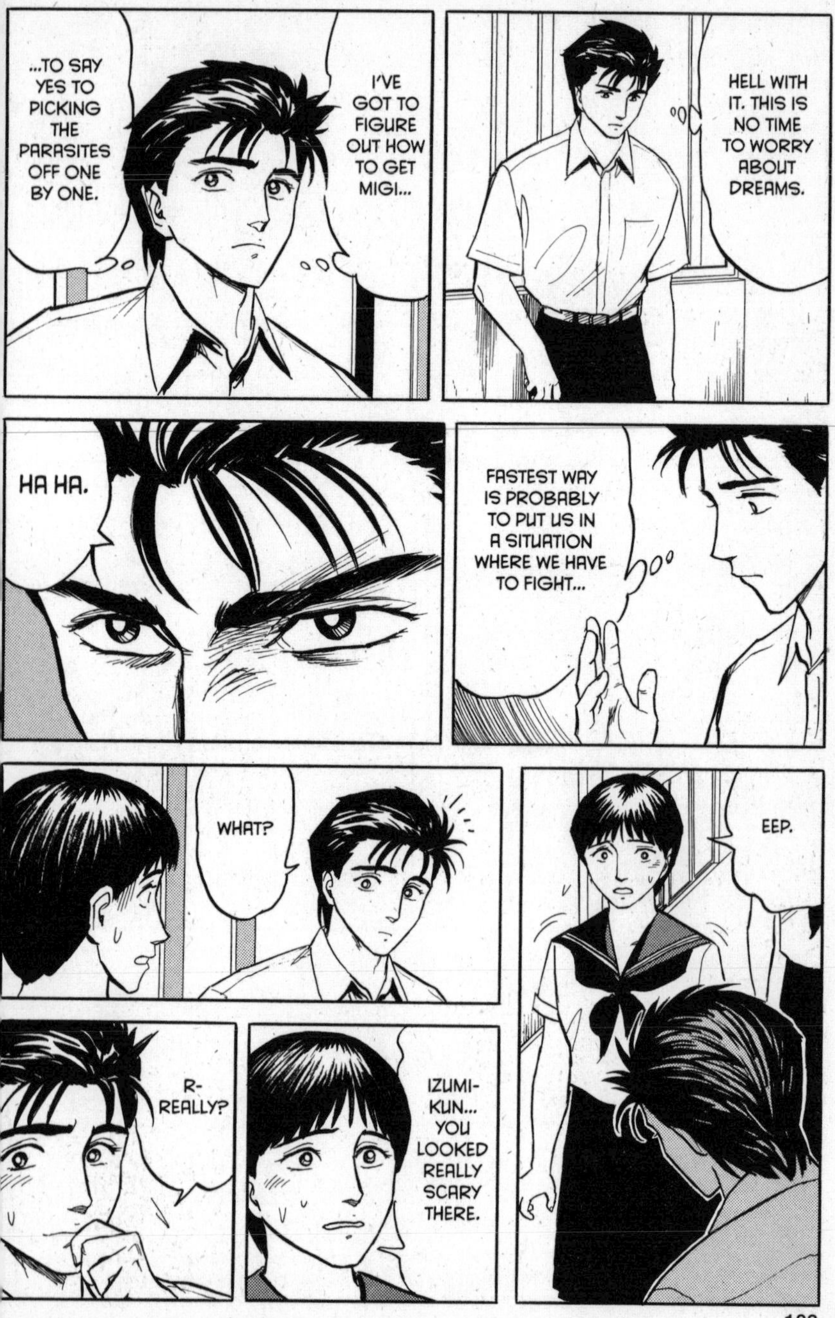
HELL WITH IT. THIS IS NO TIME TO WORRY ABOUT DREAMS.
I'VE GOT TO FIGURE OUT HOW TO GET MIGI...
...TO SAY YES TO PICKING THE PARASITES OFF ONE BY ONE.
FASTEST WAY IS PROBABLY TO PUT US IN A SITUATION WHERE WE HAVE TO FIGHT...
HA HA.
EEP.
WHAT?
IZUMI-KUN... YOU LOOKED REALLY SCARY THERE.
R- REALLY?

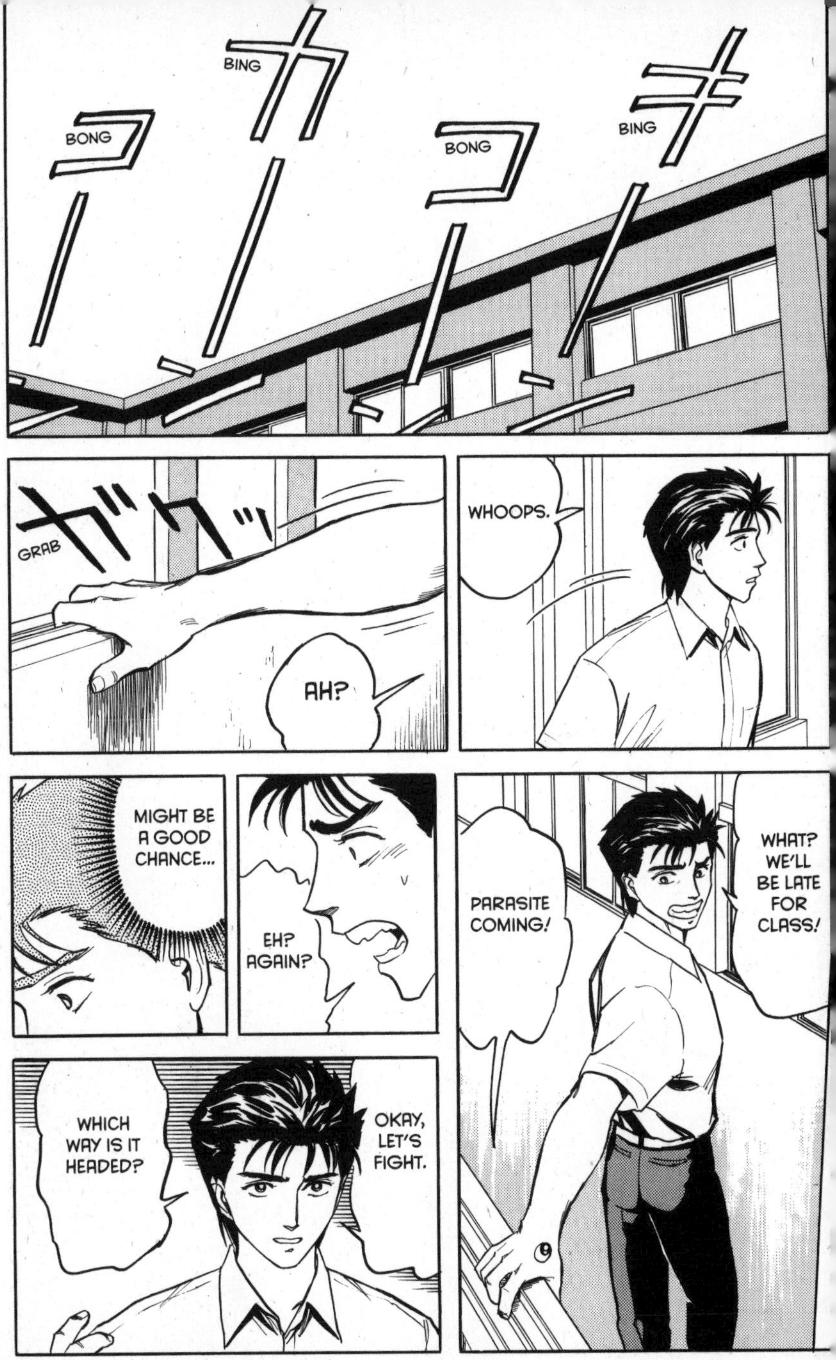
BING
BONG
BING
BONG
WHOOPS.
GRAB
AH?
WHAT? WE'LL BE LATE FOR CLASS!
PARASITE COMING!
EH? AGAIN?
MIGHT BE A GOOD CHANCE...
OKAY, LET'S FIGHT.
WHICH WAY IS IT HEADED?

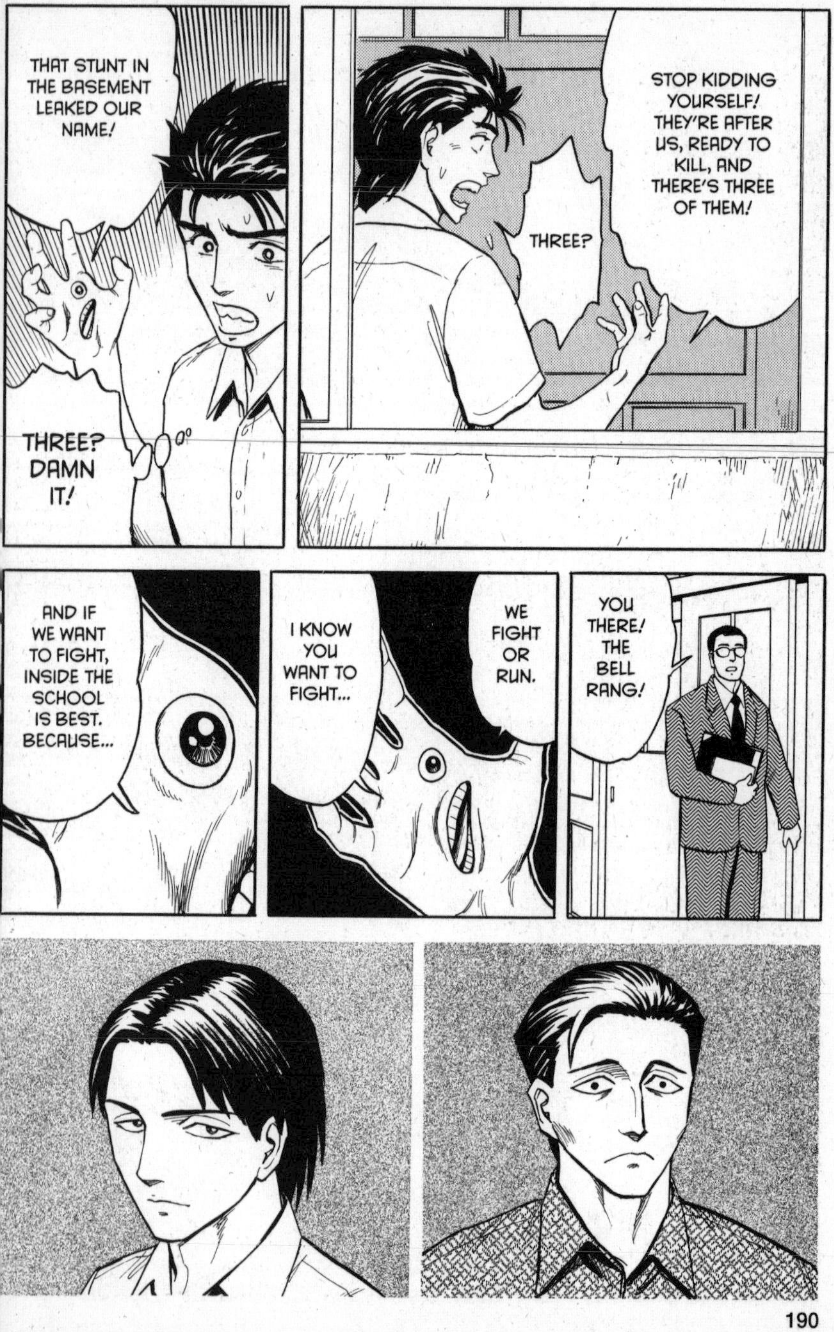
STOP KIDDING YOURSELF! THEY'RE AFTER US, READY TO KILL, AND THERE'S THREE OF THEM!
THREE?
THAT STUNT IN THE BASEMENT LEAKED OUR NAME!
THREE? DAMN IT!
YOU THERE! THE BELL RANG!
WE FIGHT OR RUN.
I KNOW YOU WANT TO FIGHT...
AND IF WE WANT TO FIGHT, INSIDE THE SCHOOL IS BEST. BECAUSE...

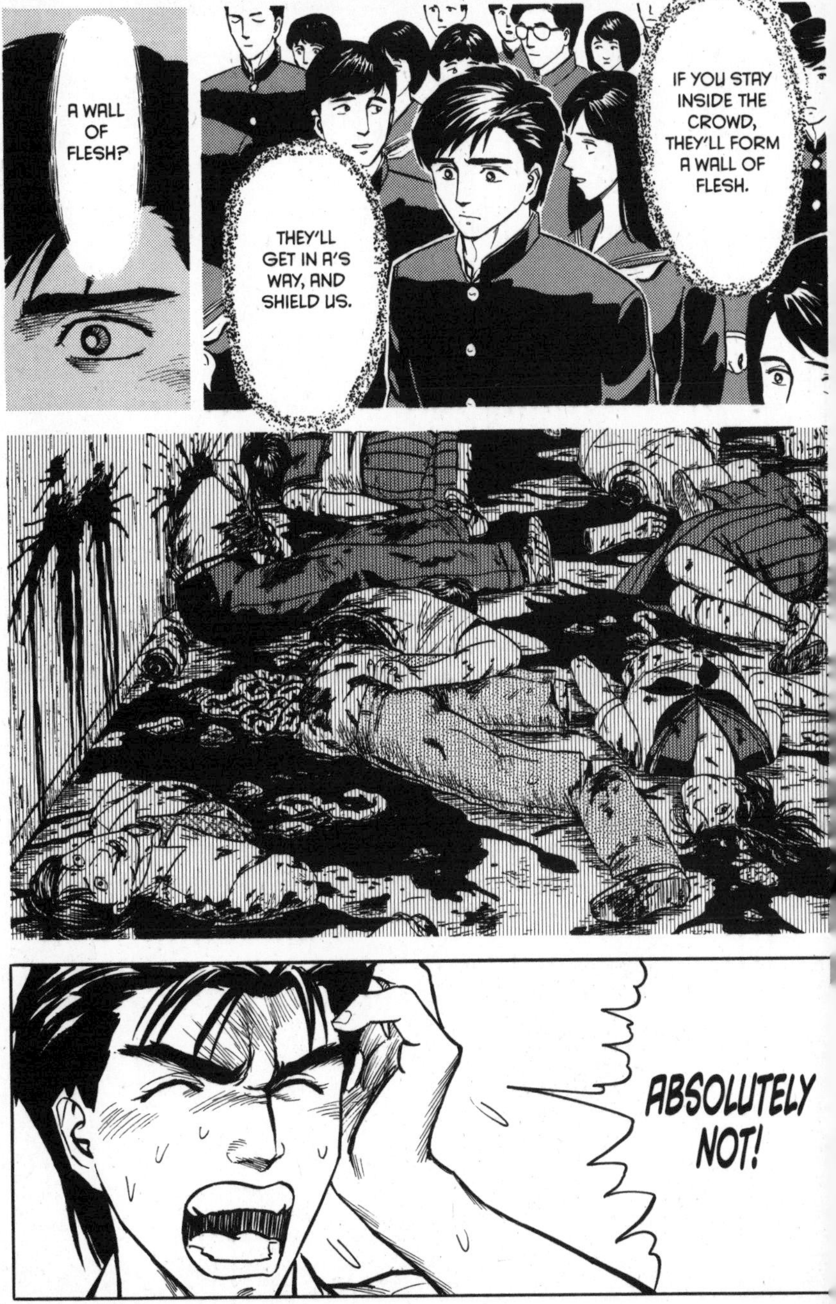
IF YOU STAY INSIDE THE CROWD, THEY'LL FORM A WALL OF FLESH.
THEY'LL GET IN A'S WAY, AND SHIELD US.
A WALL OF FLESH?
ABSOLUTELY NOT!

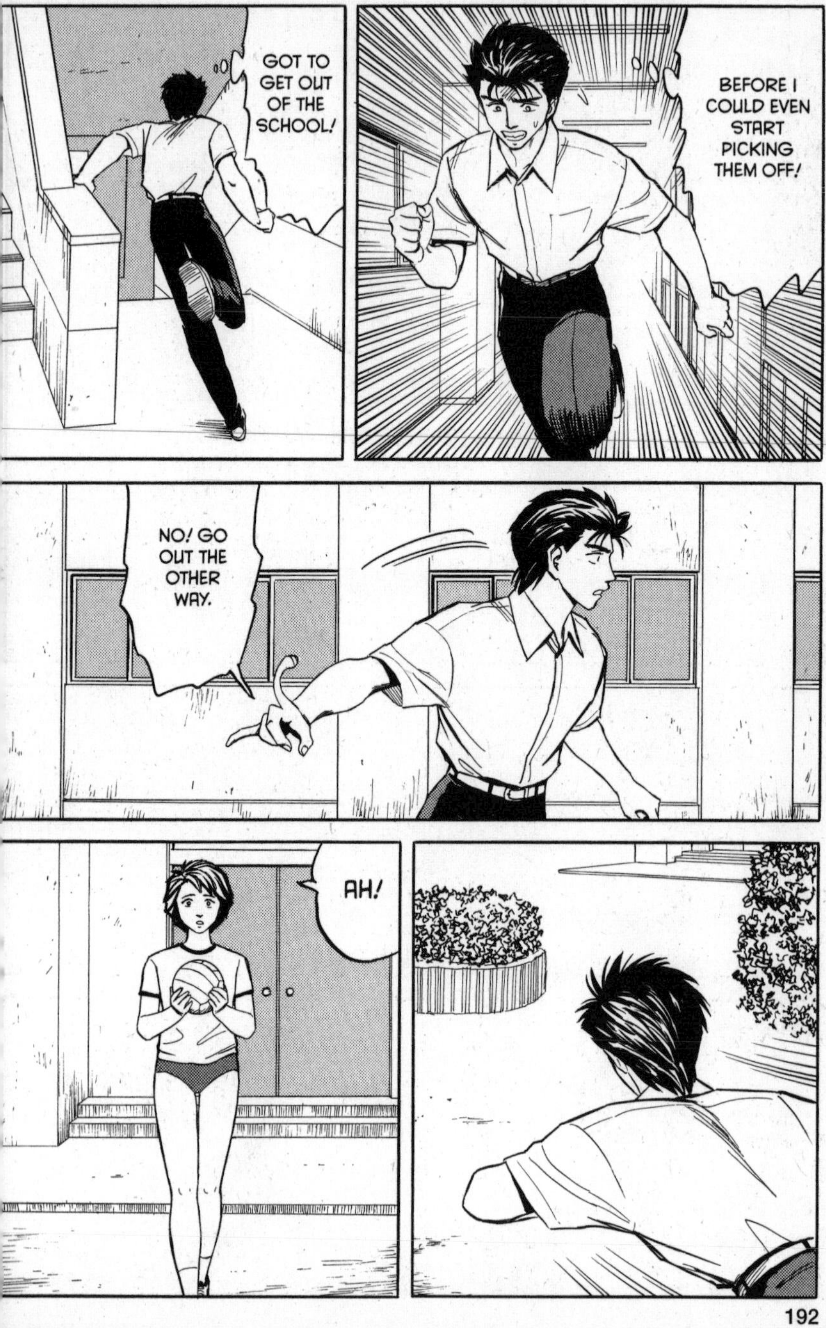
BEFORE I COULD EVEN START PICKING THEM OFF!
GOT TO GET OUT OF THE SCHOOL!
NO! GO OUT THE OTHER WAY.
AH!

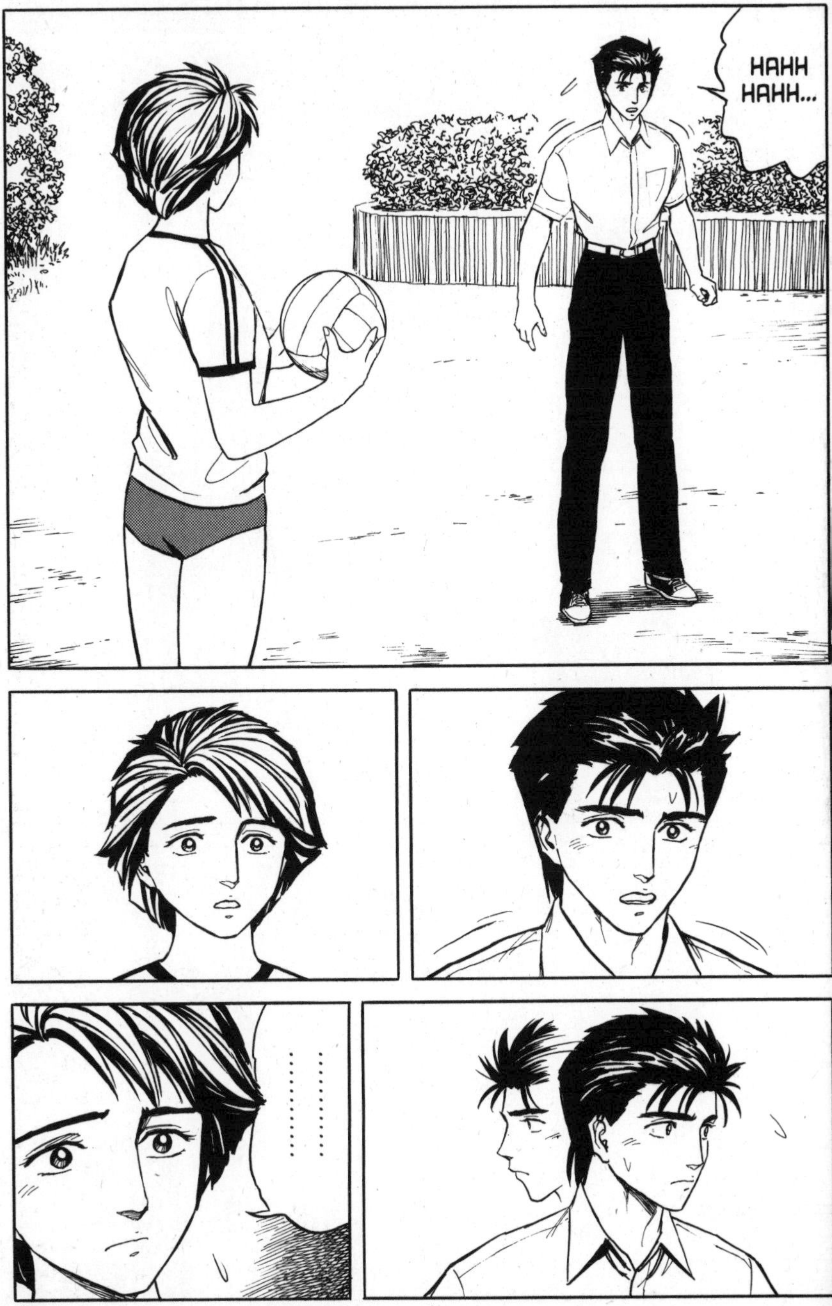
HAHH
HAHH...
......

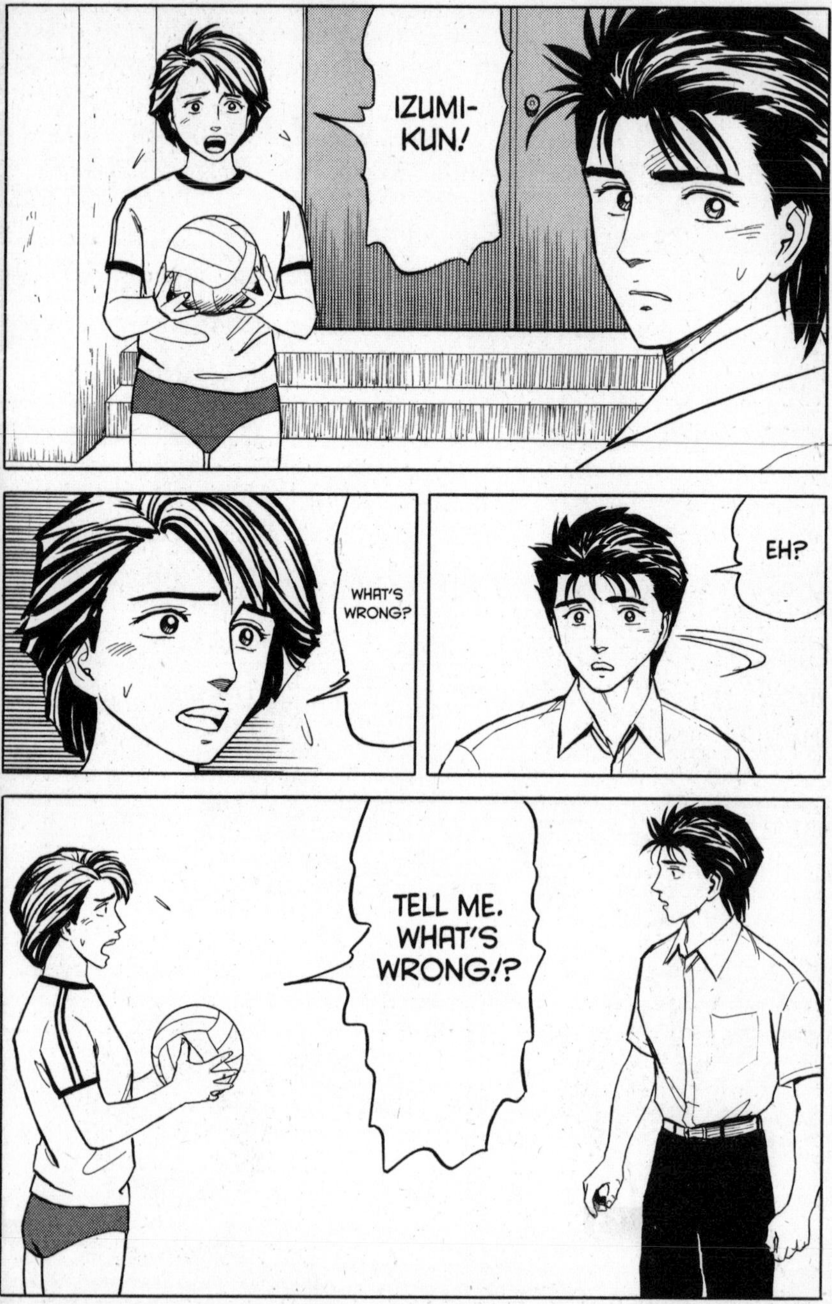
IZUMI-KUN!
EH?
WHAT'S WRONG?
TELL ME. WHAT'S WRONG!?

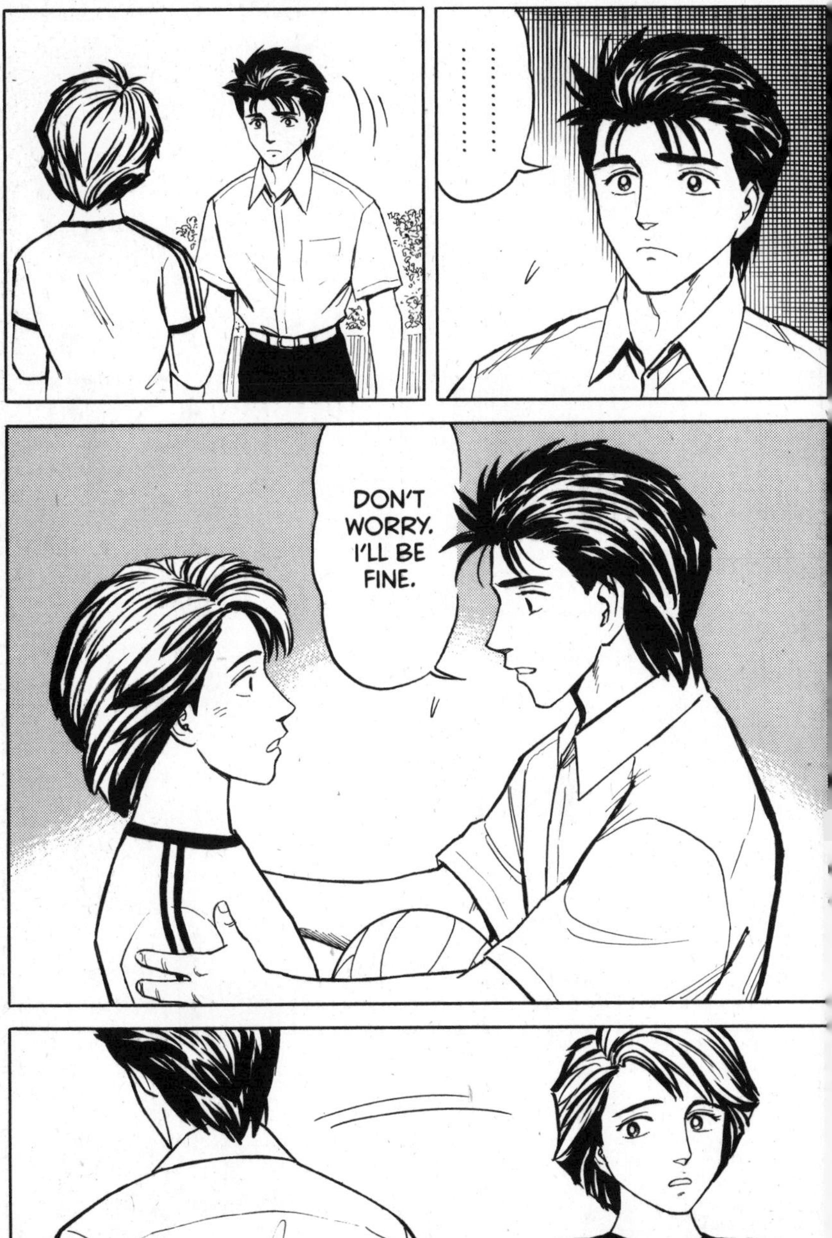
......
DON'T WORRY. I'LL BE FINE.

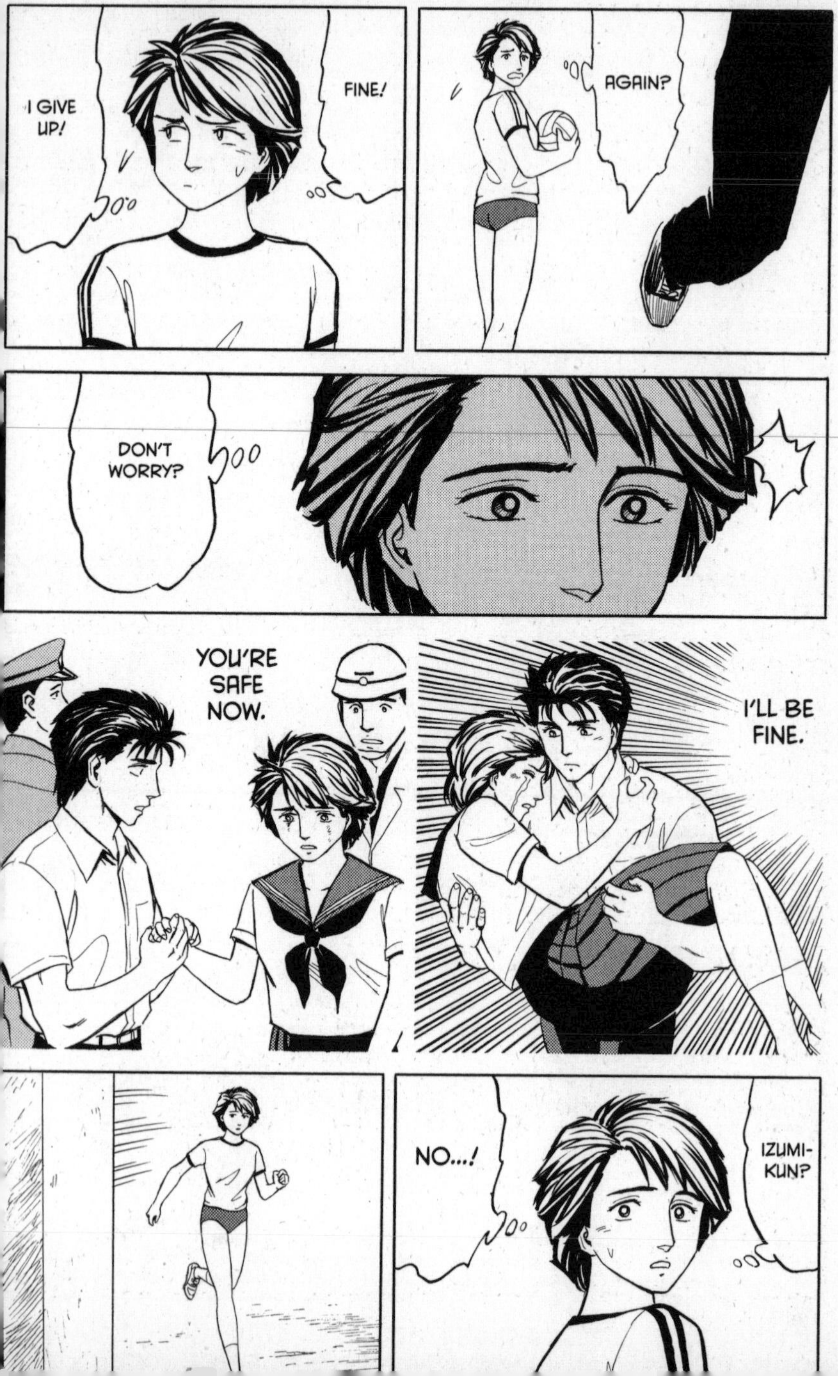
AGAIN?
FINE!
I GIVE UP!
DON'T WORRY?
I'LL BE FINE.
YOU'RE SAFE NOW.
IZUMI-KUN?
NO...!

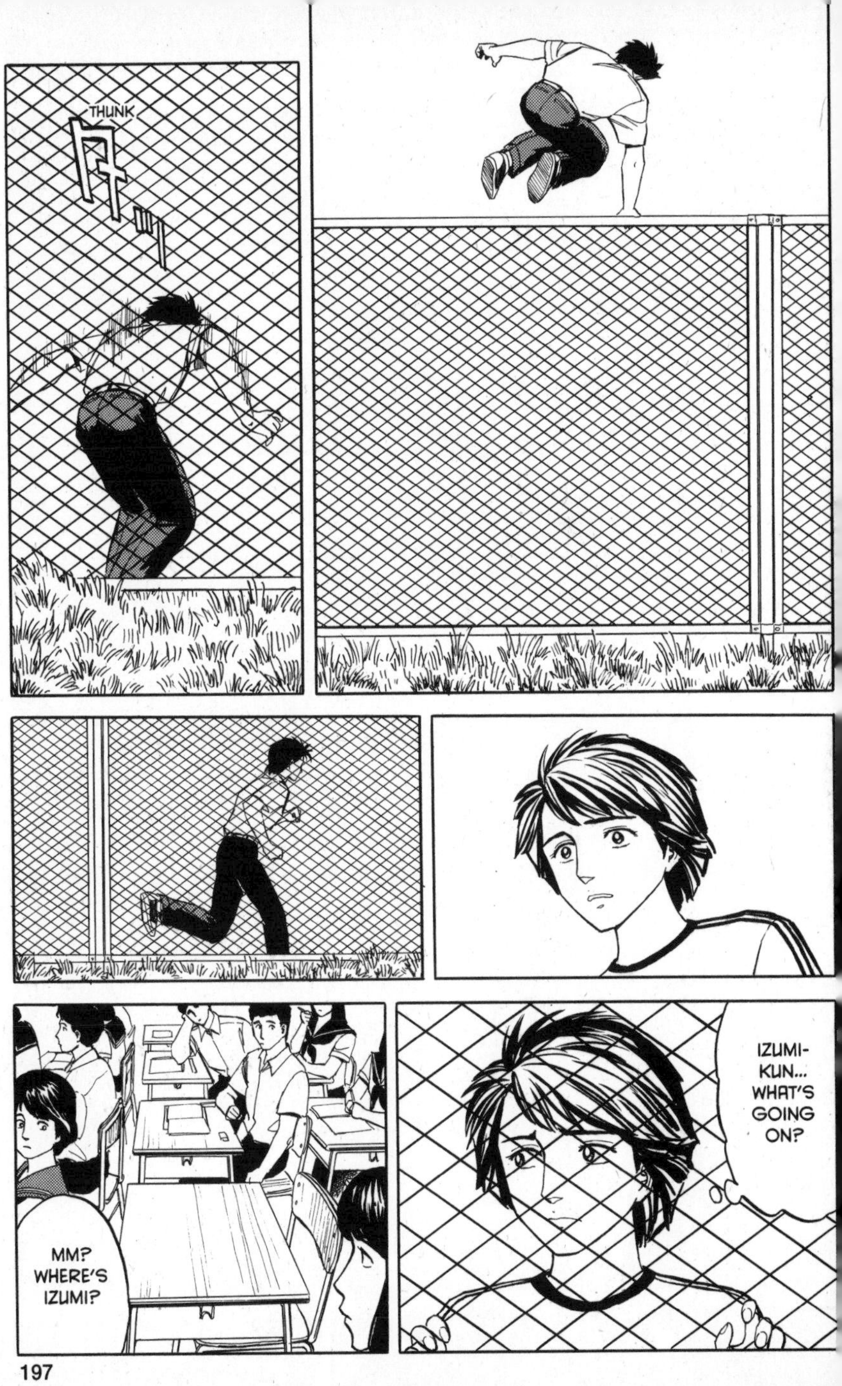
THUNK
IZUMI-KUN... WHAT'S GOING ON?
MM? WHERE'S IZUMI?

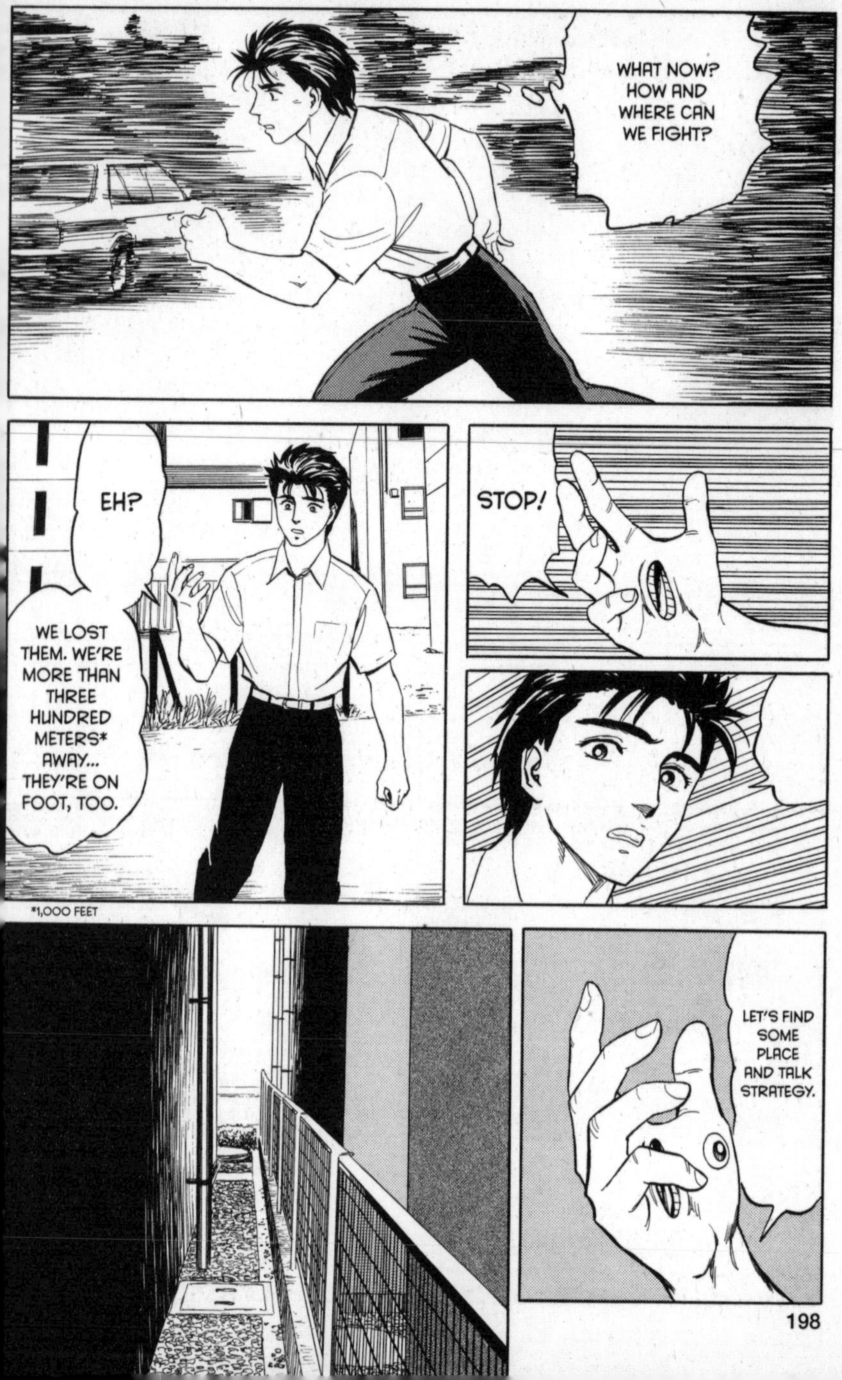
WHAT NOW? HOW AND WHERE CAN WE FIGHT?
STOP!
EH?
WE LOST THEM. WE'RE MORE THAN THREE HUNDRED METERS* AWAY... THEY'RE ON FOOT, TOO.
*1,000 FEET
LET'S FIND SOME PLACE AND TALK STRATEGY.

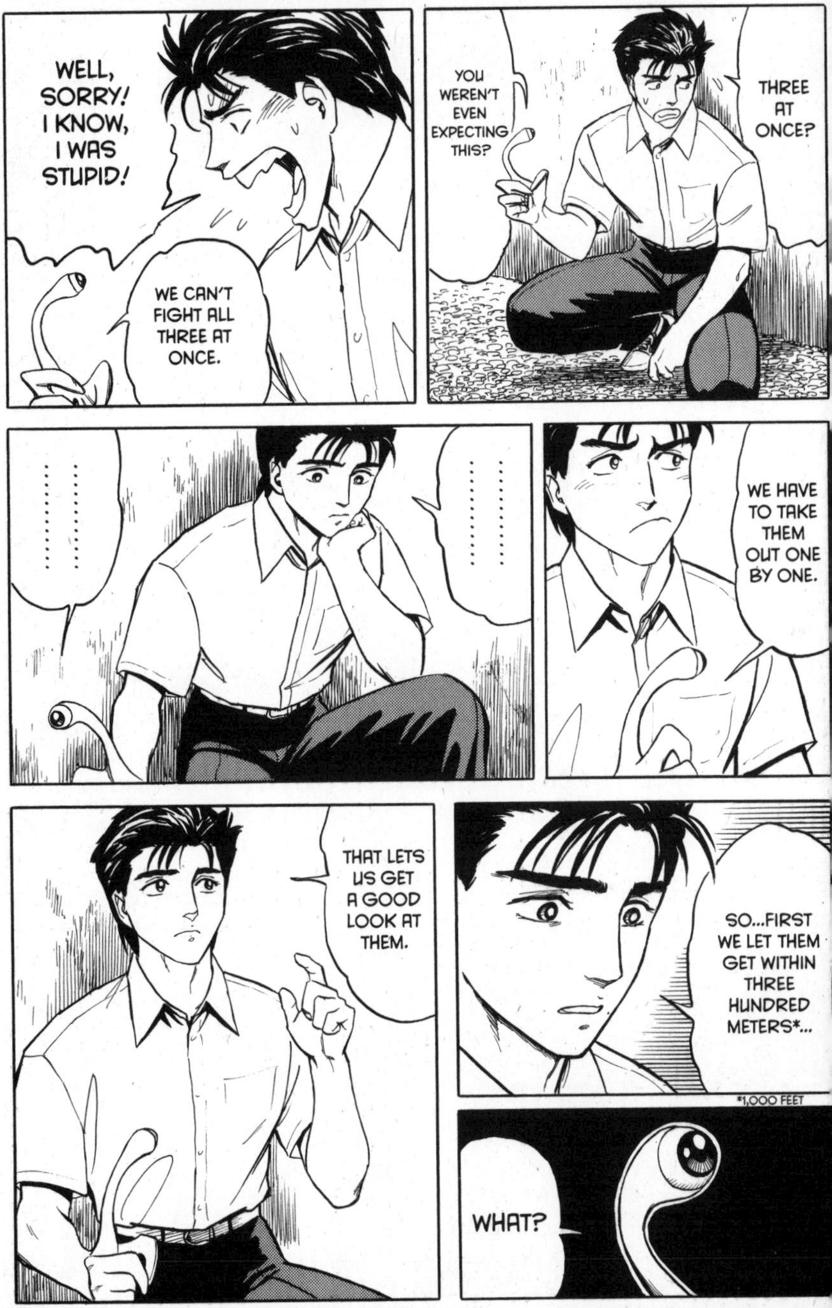
THREE AT ONCE?
YOU WEREN'T EVEN EXPECTING THIS?
WELL, SORRY! I KNOW, I WAS STUPID!
WE CAN'T FIGHT ALL THREE AT ONCE.
WE HAVE TO TAKE THEM OUT ONE BY ONE.
......
......
SO...FIRST WE LET THEM GET WITHIN THREE HUNDRED METERS*...
*1,000 FEET
WHAT?
THAT LETS US GET A GOOD LOOK AT THEM.

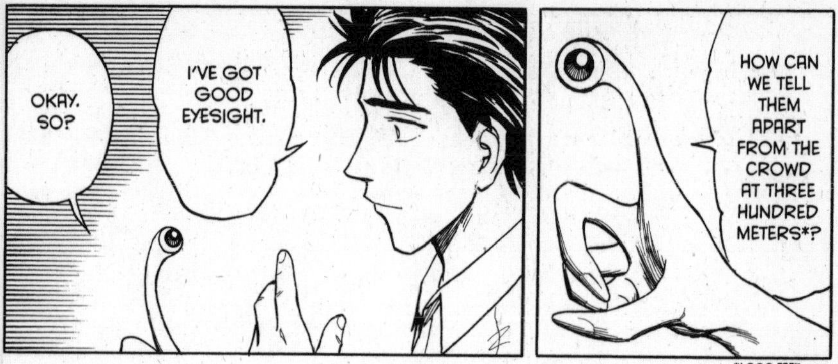
HOW CAN WE TELL THEM APART FROM THE CROWD AT THREE HUNDRED METERS*?
I'VE GOT GOOD EYESIGHT.
OKAY. SO?

*1,000 FEET

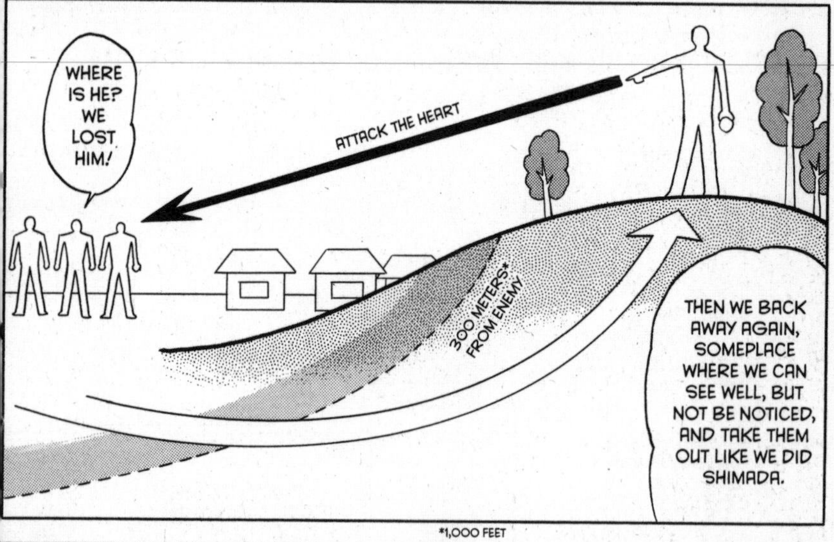
ATTACK THE HEART
WHERE IS HE? WE LOST HIM!
300 METERS* FROM ENEMY
THEN WE BACK AWAY AGAIN, SOMEPLACE WHERE WE CAN SEE WELL, BUT NOT BE NOTICED, AND TAKE THEM OUT LIKE WE DID SHIMADA.

*1,000 FEET

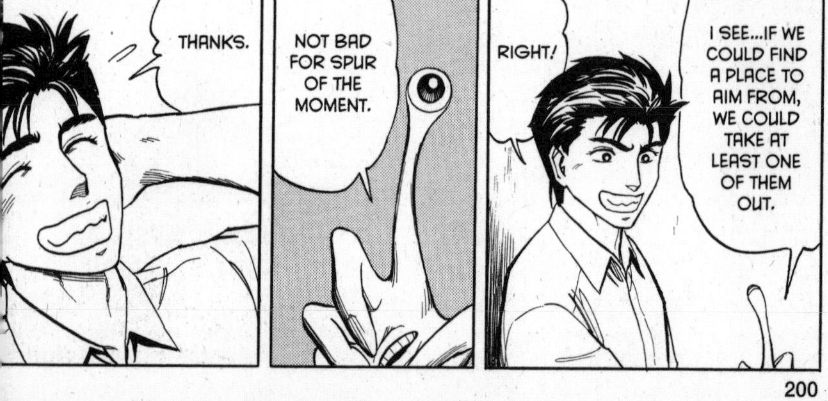
I SEE...IF WE COULD FIND A PLACE TO AIM FROM, WE COULD TAKE AT LEAST ONE OF THEM OUT.
RIGHT!
NOT BAD FOR SPUR OF THE MOMENT.
THANKS.

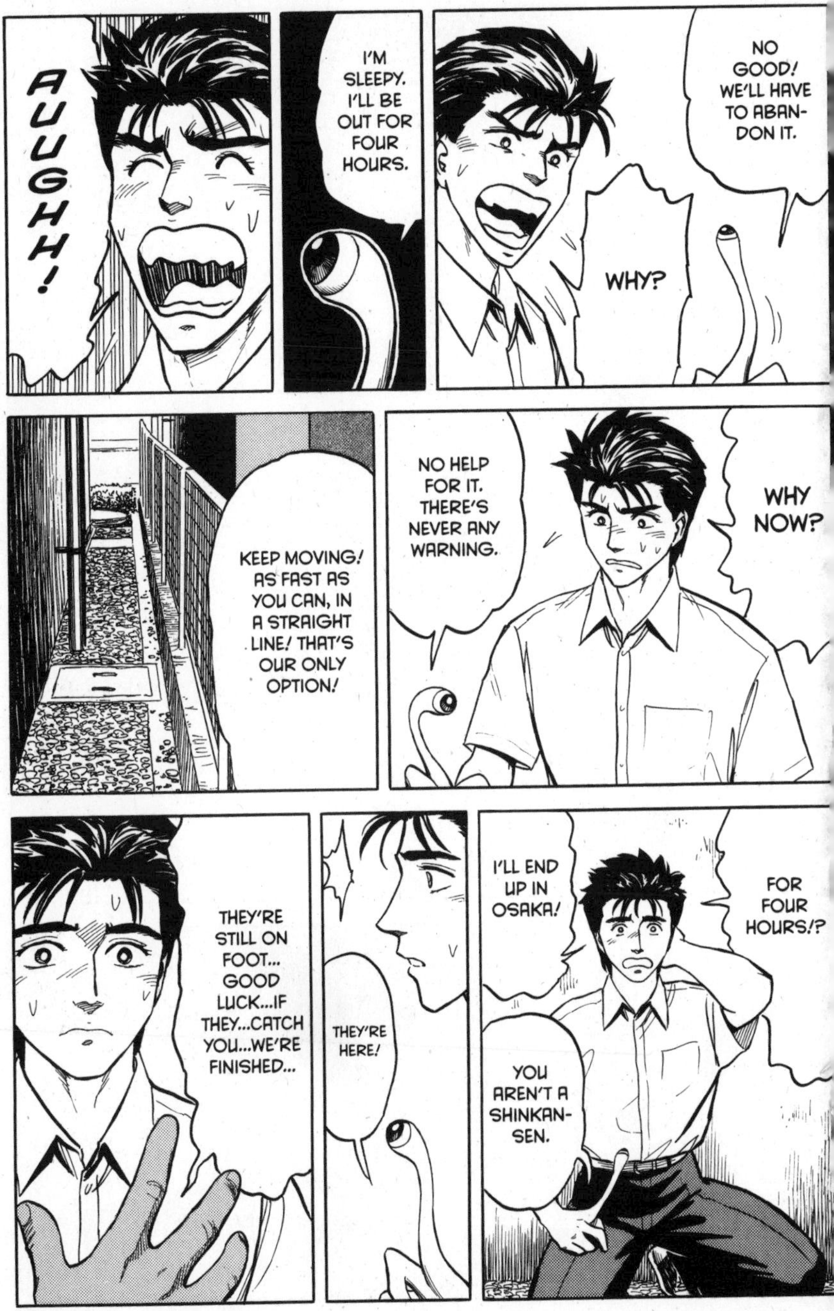
NO GOOD! WE'LL HAVE TO ABANDON IT.
WHY?
I'M SLEEPY. I'LL BE OUT FOR FOUR HOURS.
AUUGHH!
WHY NOW?
NO HELP FOR IT. THERE'S NEVER ANY WARNING.
KEEP MOVING! AS FAST AS YOU CAN, IN A STRAIGHT LINE! THAT'S OUR ONLY OPTION!
FOR FOUR HOURS!?
I'LL END UP IN OSAKA!
YOU AREN'T A SHINKANSEN.
THEY'RE HERE!
THEY'RE STILL ON FOOT... GOOD LUCK...IF THEY...CATCH YOU...WE'RE FINISHED...

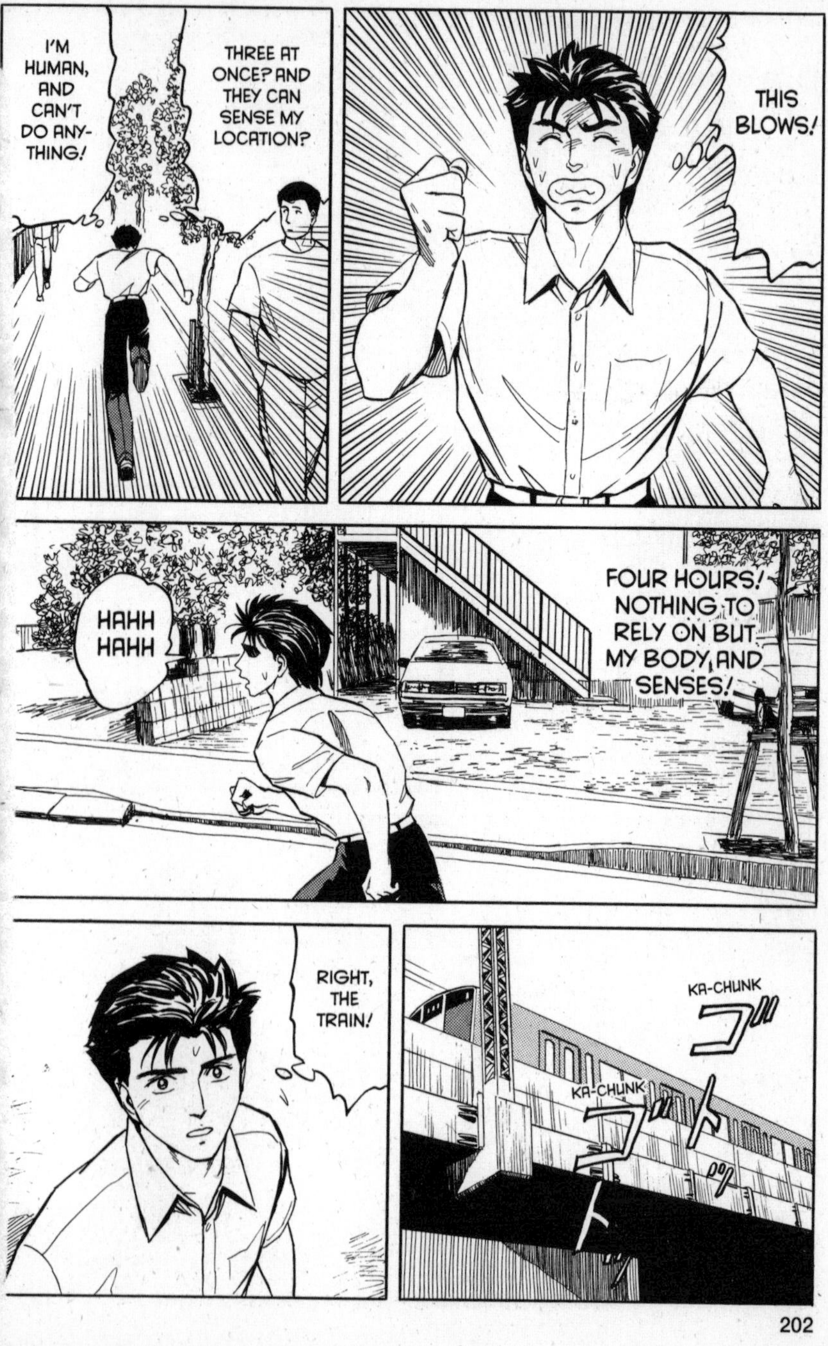
THIS BLOWS!
THREE AT ONCE? AND THEY CAN SENSE MY LOCATION?
I'M HUMAN, AND CAN'T DO ANYTHING!
FOUR HOURS! NOTHING TO RELY ON BUT MY BODY AND SENSES!
HAHH HAHH
KA-CHUNK
KA-CHUNK
RIGHT, THE TRAIN!

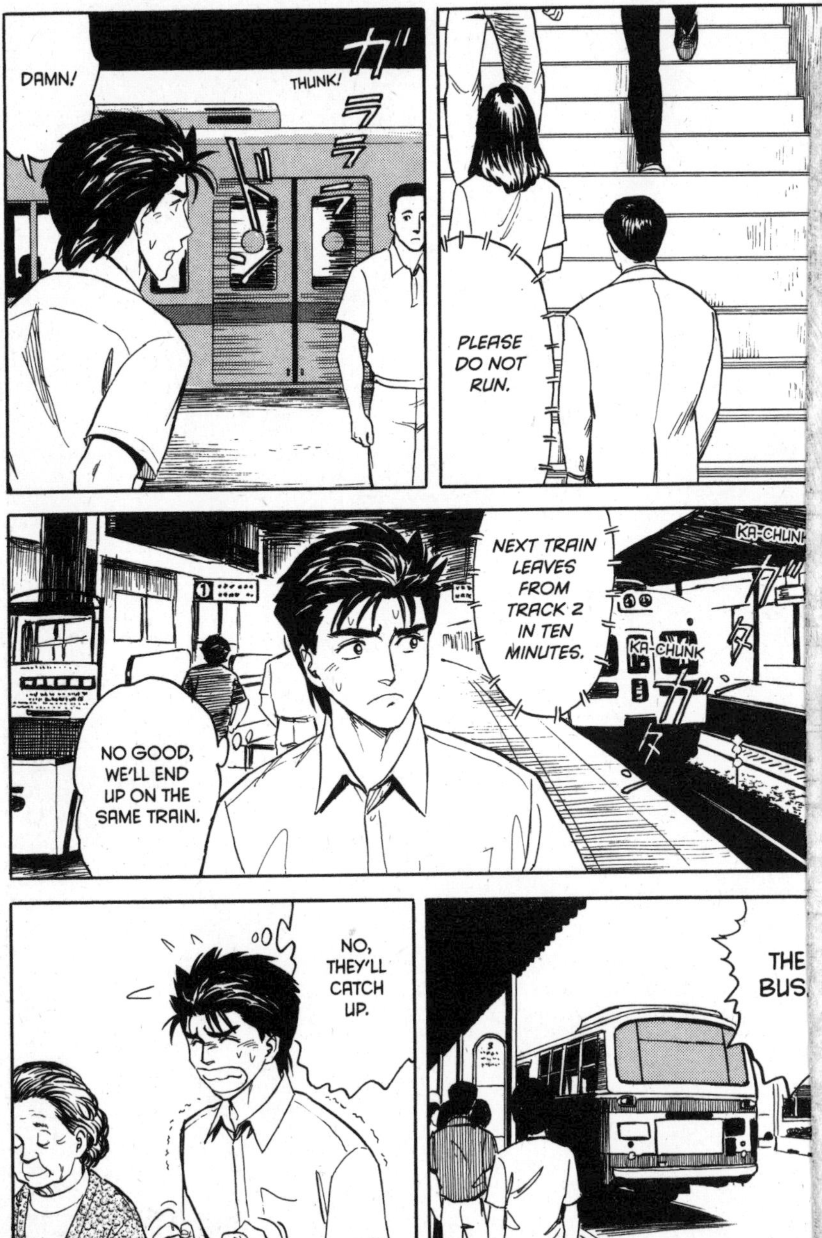
PLEASE DO NOT RUN.
THUNK!
DAMN!
KA-CHUNK
KA-CHUNK
NEXT TRAIN LEAVES FROM TRACK 2 IN TEN MINUTES.
NO GOOD, WE'LL END UP ON THE SAME TRAIN.
THE BUS.
NO, THEY'LL CATCH UP.

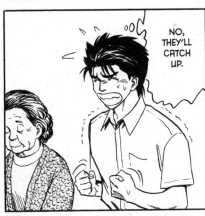

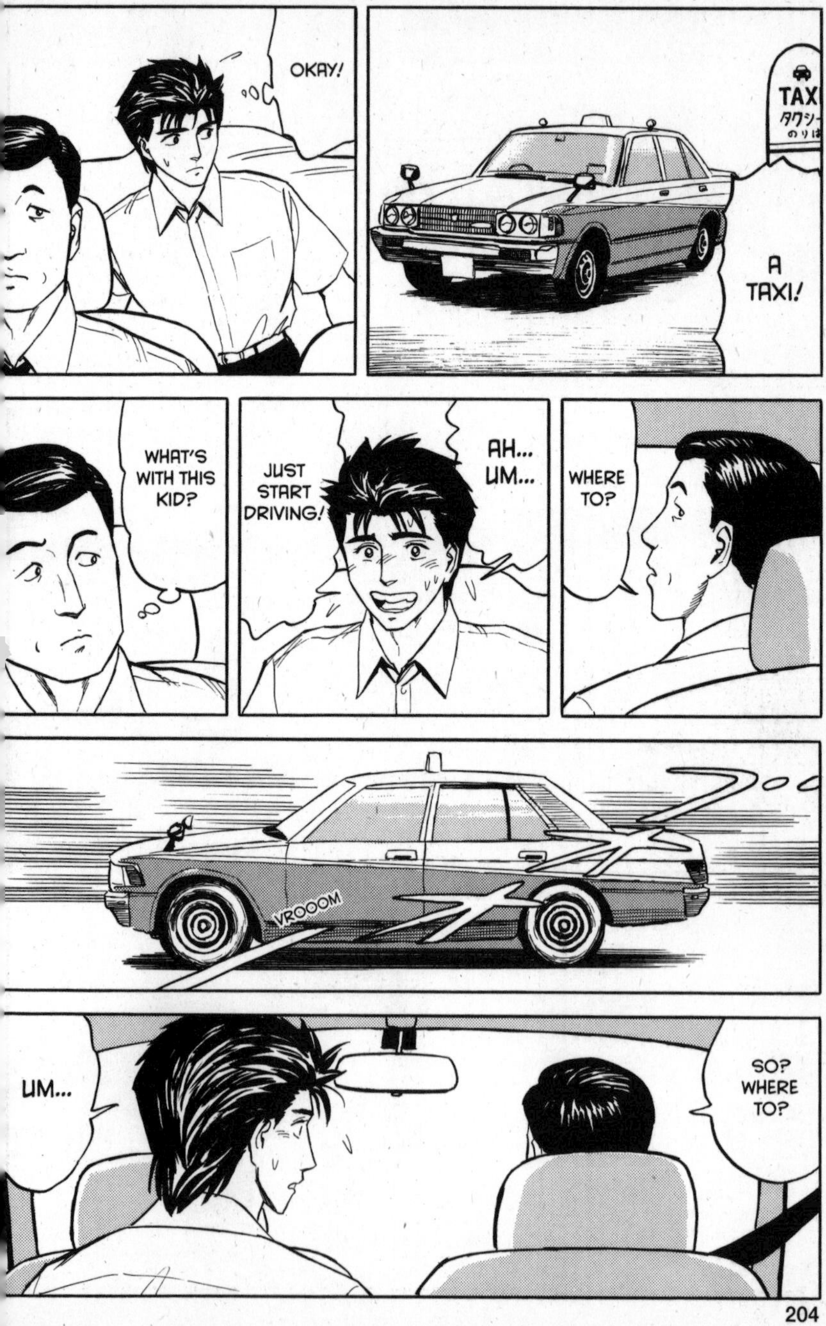
A TAXI!
OKAY!
WHERE TO?
AH... UM...
JUST START DRIVING!
WHAT'S WITH THIS KID?
VROOOM
SO? WHERE TO?
UM...

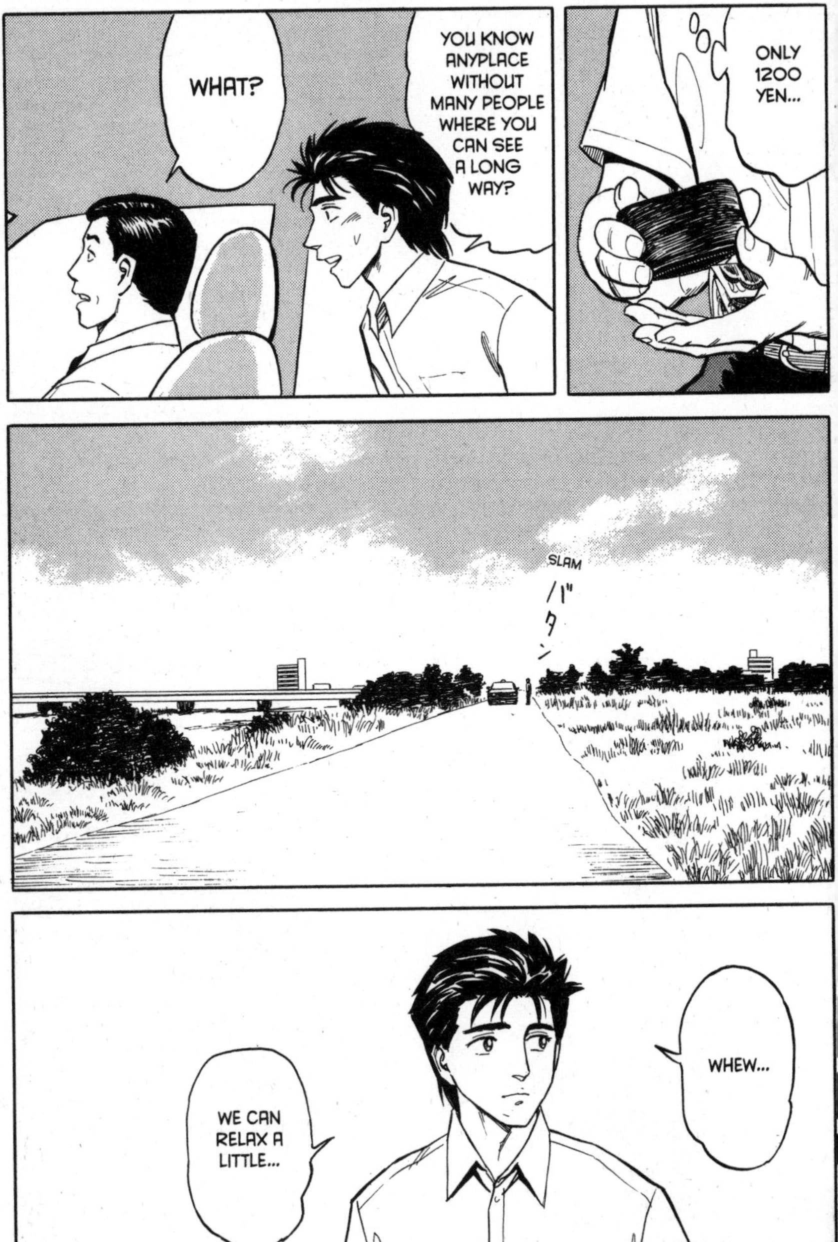
ONLY 1200 YEN...
YOU KNOW ANYPLACE WITHOUT MANY PEOPLE WHERE YOU CAN SEE A LONG WAY?
WHAT?
SLAM
バタン
WHEW...
WE CAN RELAX A LITTLE...

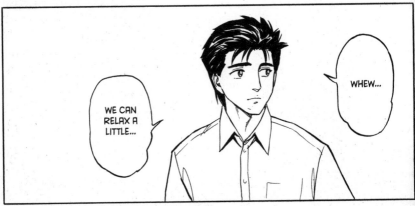

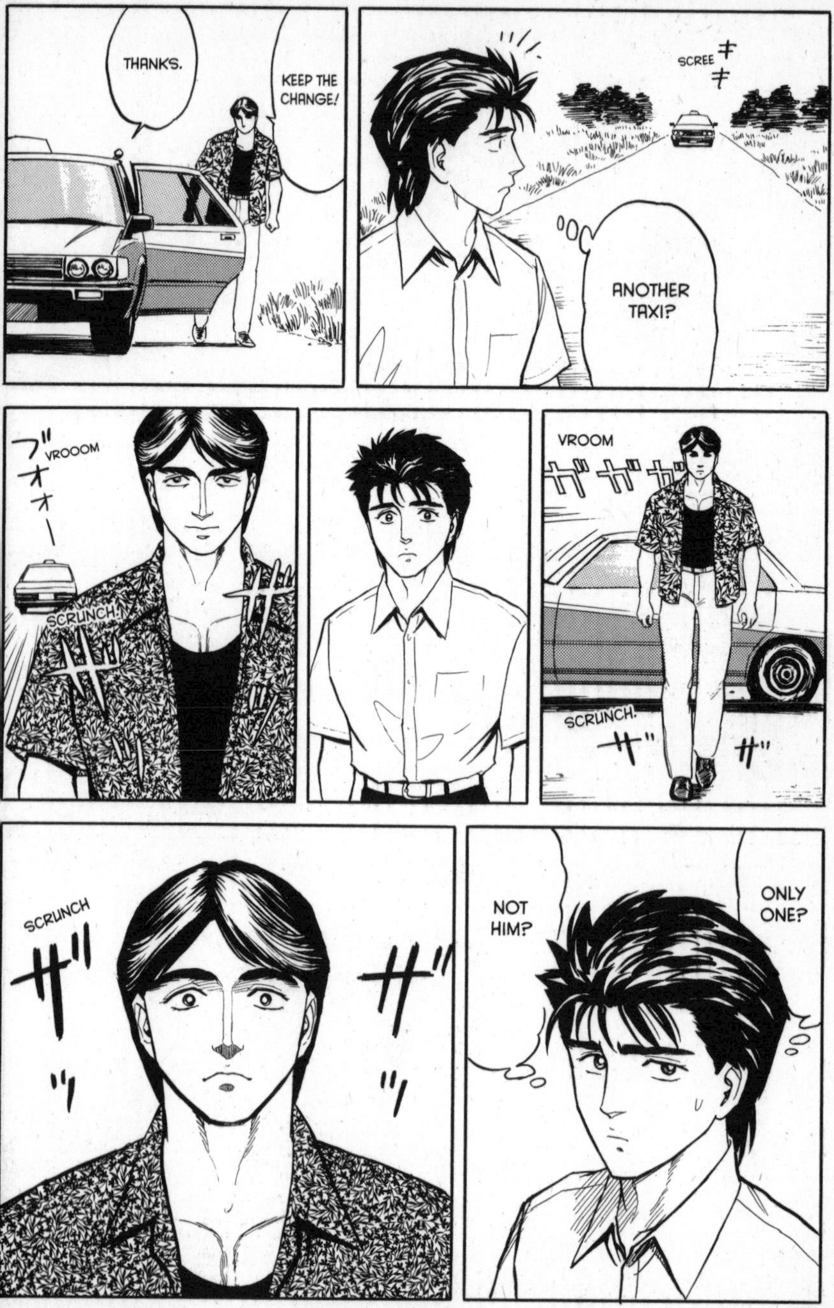
SCREE キキ
ANOTHER TAXI?
KEEP THE CHANGE!
THANKS.
VROOM ガガガ
SCRUNCH. ザ ザ
VROOOM ブオオー
SCRUNCH. ザザ
ONLY ONE?
NOT HIM?
ザッ
SCRUNCH ザッ

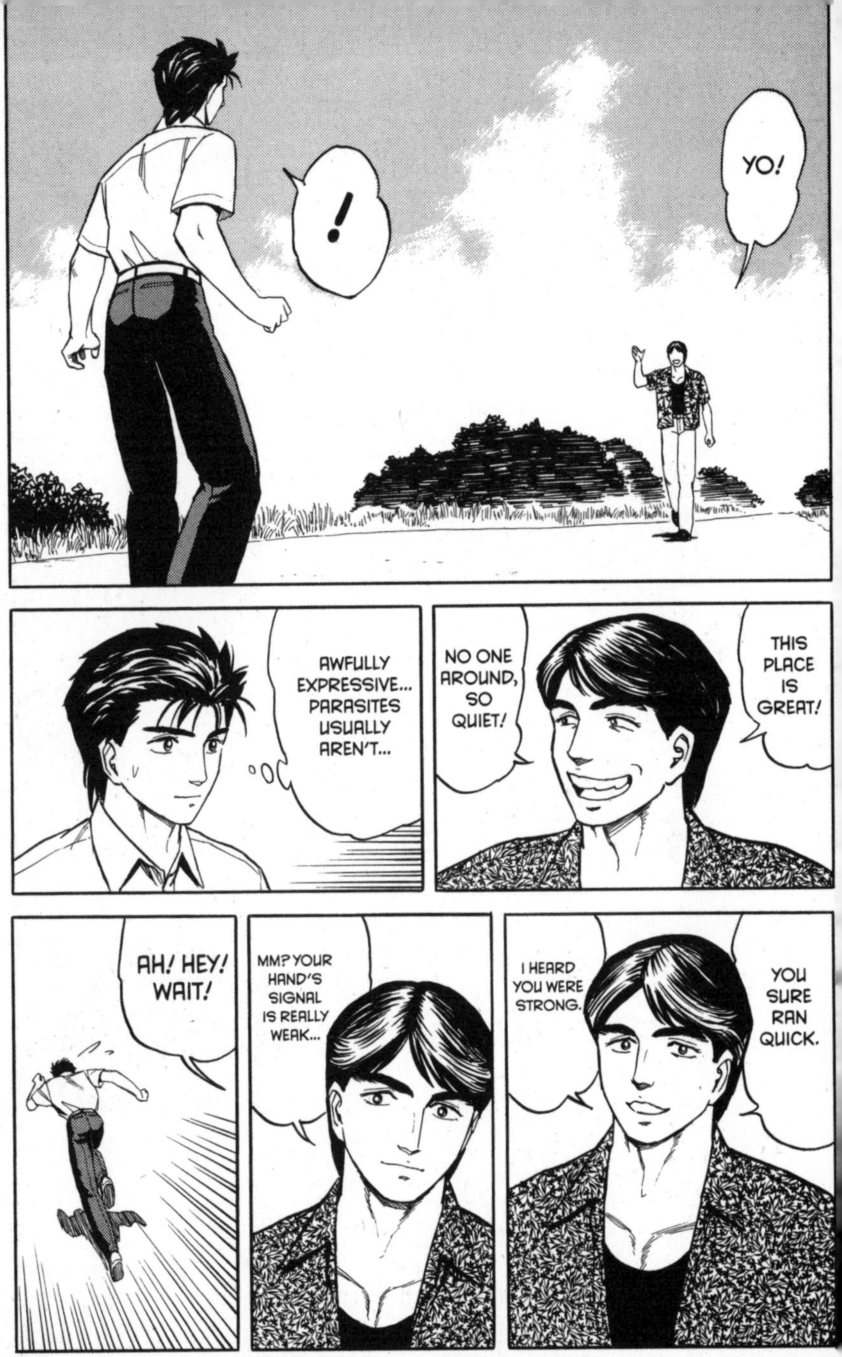
YO!
!
THIS PLACE IS GREAT!
NO ONE AROUND, SO QUIET!
AWFULLY EXPRESSIVE... PARASITES USUALLY AREN'T...
YOU SURE RAN QUICK.
I HEARD YOU WERE STRONG.
MM? YOUR HAND'S SIGNAL IS REALLY WEAK...
AH! HEY! WAIT!

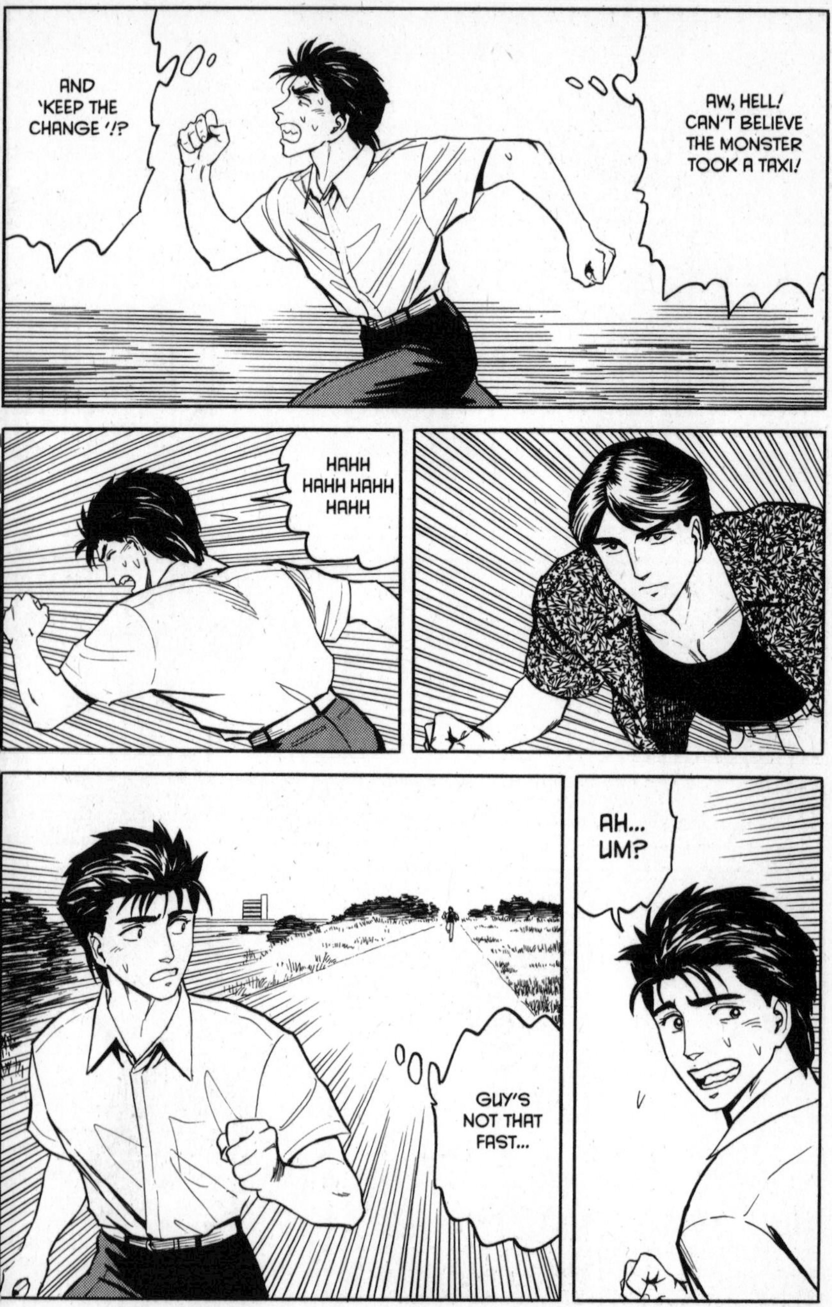
AW, HELL! CAN'T BELIEVE THE MONSTER TOOK A TAXI!
AND 'KEEP THE CHANGE'!?
HAHH HAHH HAHH HAHH
AH... UM?
GUY'S NOT THAT FAST...

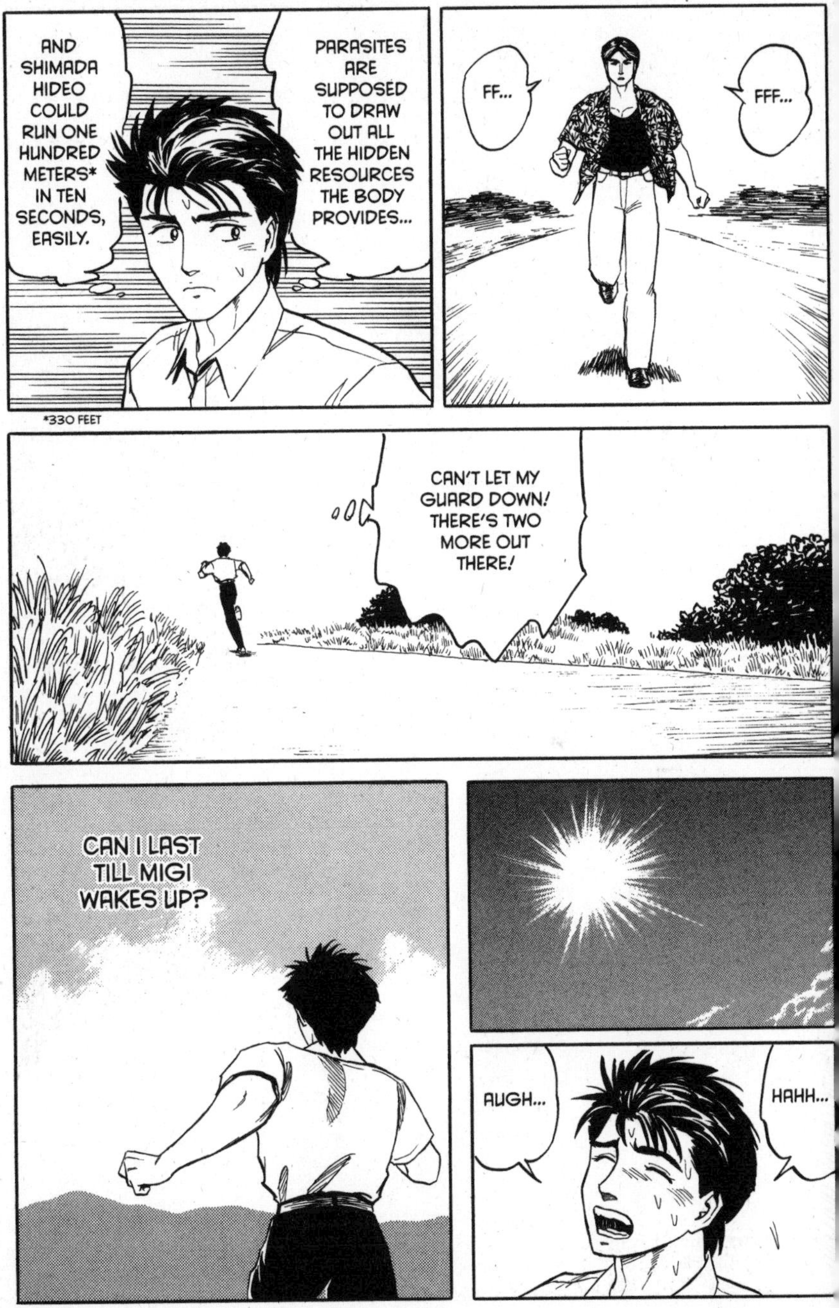
FFF...
FF...
PARASITES ARE SUPPOSED TO DRAW OUT ALL THE HIDDEN RESOURCES THE BODY PROVIDES...
AND SHIMADA HIDEO COULD RUN ONE HUNDRED METERS* IN TEN SECONDS, EASILY.
CAN'T LET MY GUARD DOWN! THERE'S TWO MORE OUT THERE!
HAHH...
AUGH...
CAN I LAST TILL MIGI WAKES UP?

*330 FEET

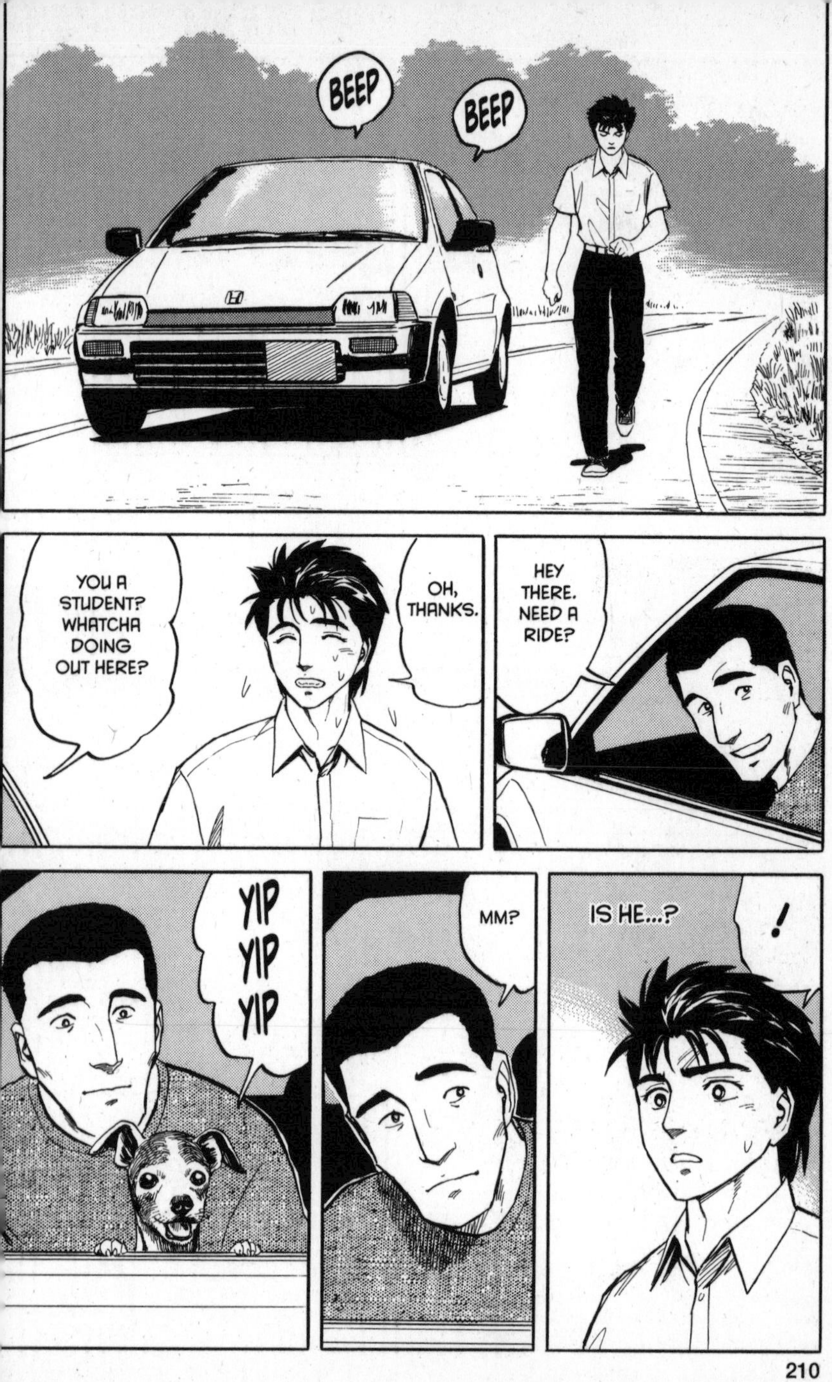
BEEP
BEEP
HEY THERE. NEED A RIDE?
OH, THANKS.
YOU A STUDENT? WHATCHA DOING OUT HERE?
!
IS HE...?
MM?
YIP YIP YIP

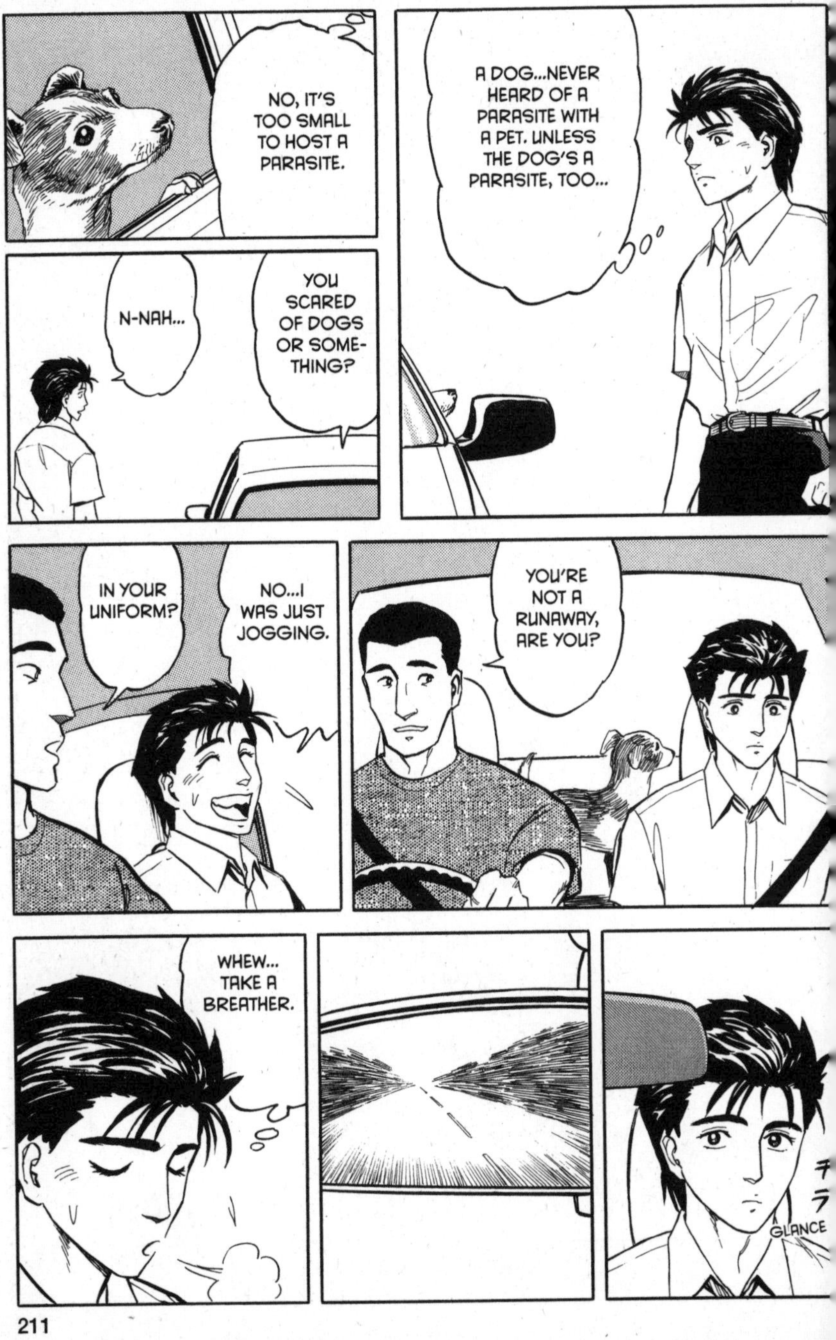
A DOG...NEVER HEARD OF A PARASITE WITH A PET. UNLESS THE DOG'S A PARASITE, TOO...
NO, IT'S TOO SMALL TO HOST A PARASITE.
YOU SCARED OF DOGS OR SOME-THING?
N-NAH...
YOU'RE NOT A RUNAWAY, ARE YOU?
NO...I WAS JUST JOGGING.
IN YOUR UNIFORM?
チラ
GLANCE
WHEW... TAKE A BREATHER.

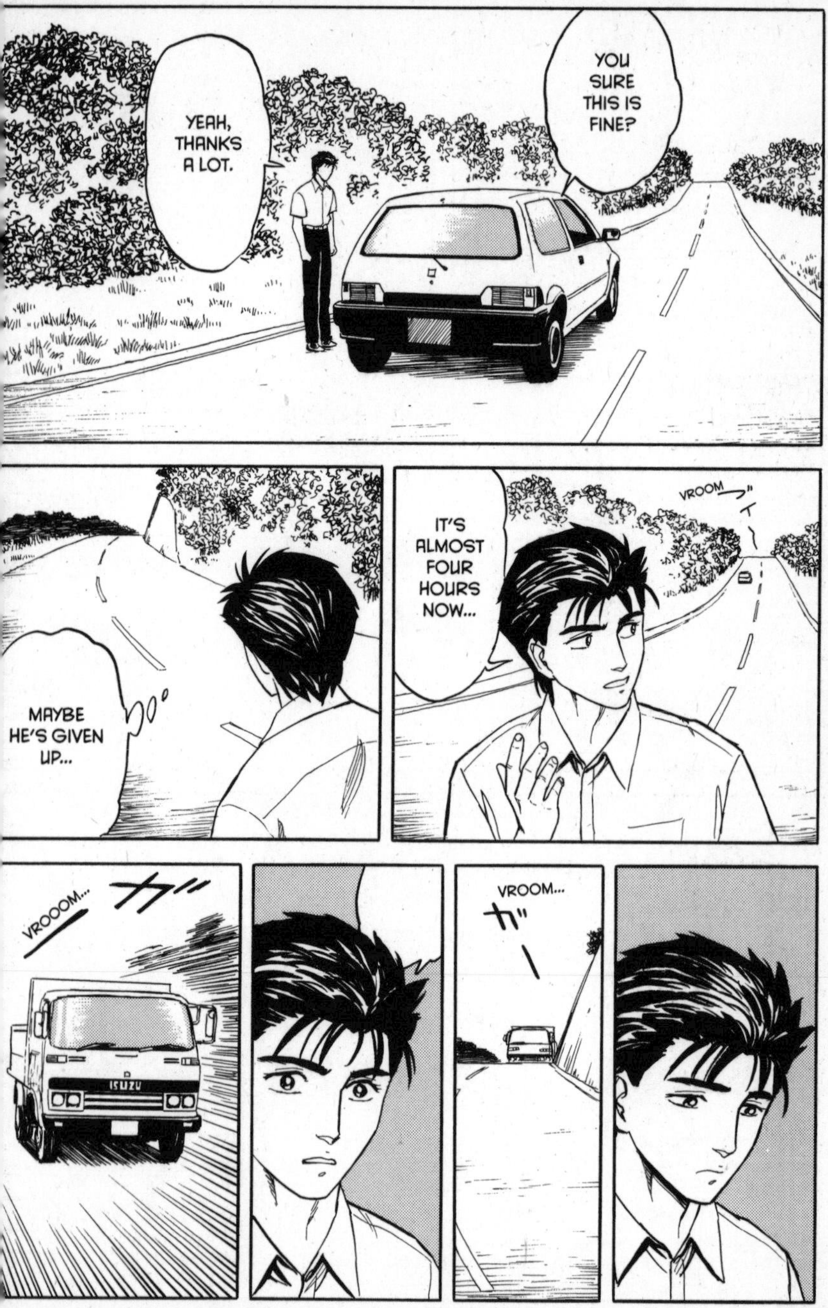
YOU SURE THIS IS FINE?
YEAH, THANKS A LOT.
VROOM
IT'S ALMOST FOUR HOURS NOW...
MAYBE HE'S GIVEN UP...
VROOM...
VROOOM...

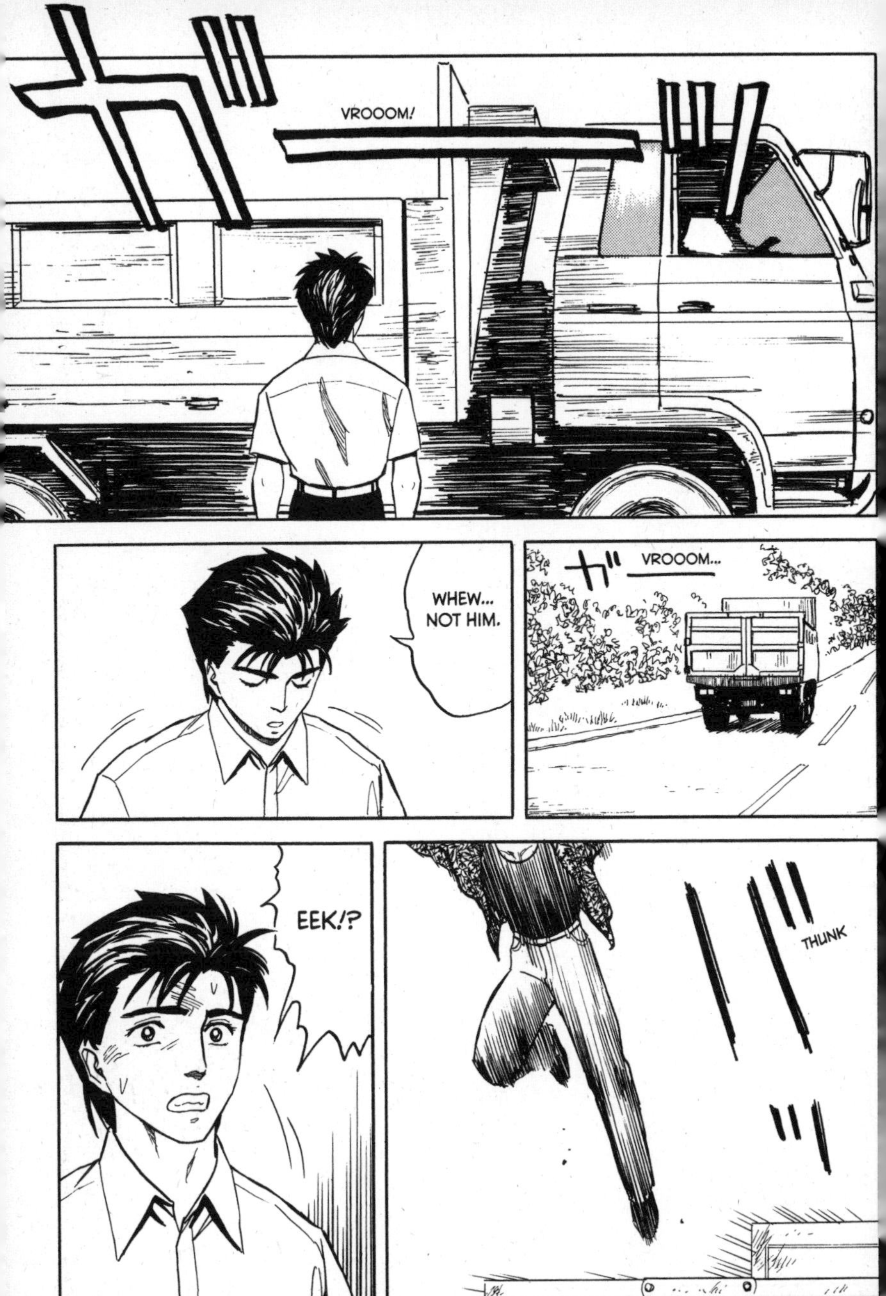
VROOOM!
VROOOM...
WHEW... NOT HIM.
THUNK
EEK!?

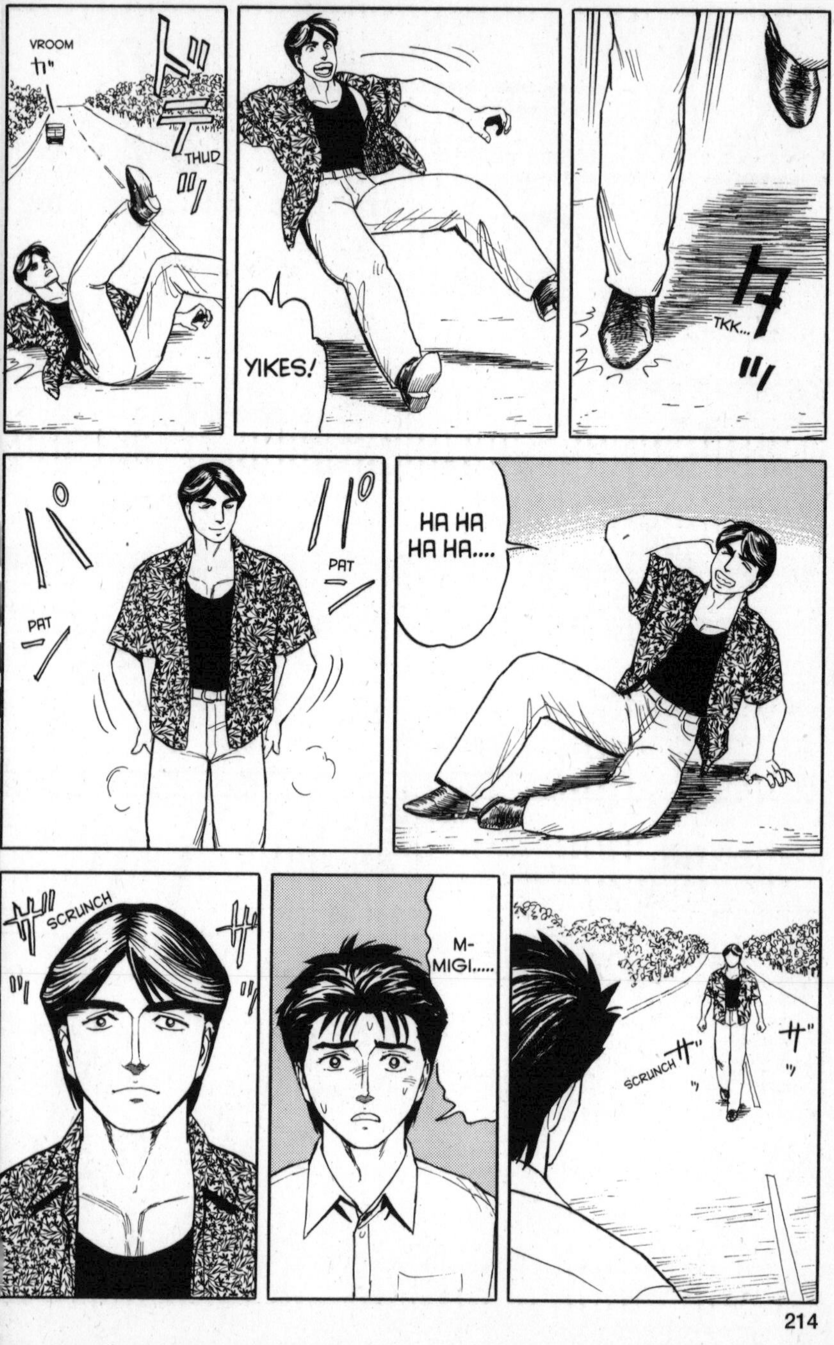
トッ
TKK...
YIKES!
VROOM
ガー
ドテッ
THUD
HA HA
HA HA....
パッ
PAT
パッ
PAT
ザッ
SCRUNCH
ザッ
M-
MIGI.....
ザッ
SCRUNCH
ザッ

MM...

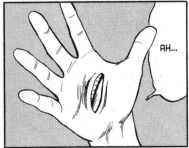

AH...

M/G/!!

THREE?

!!

AH HA HA HA HA.

SHINICHI. STILL ALIVE, I SEE.

DON'T KNOW WHERE THE OTHER TWO ARE...

YEAH...

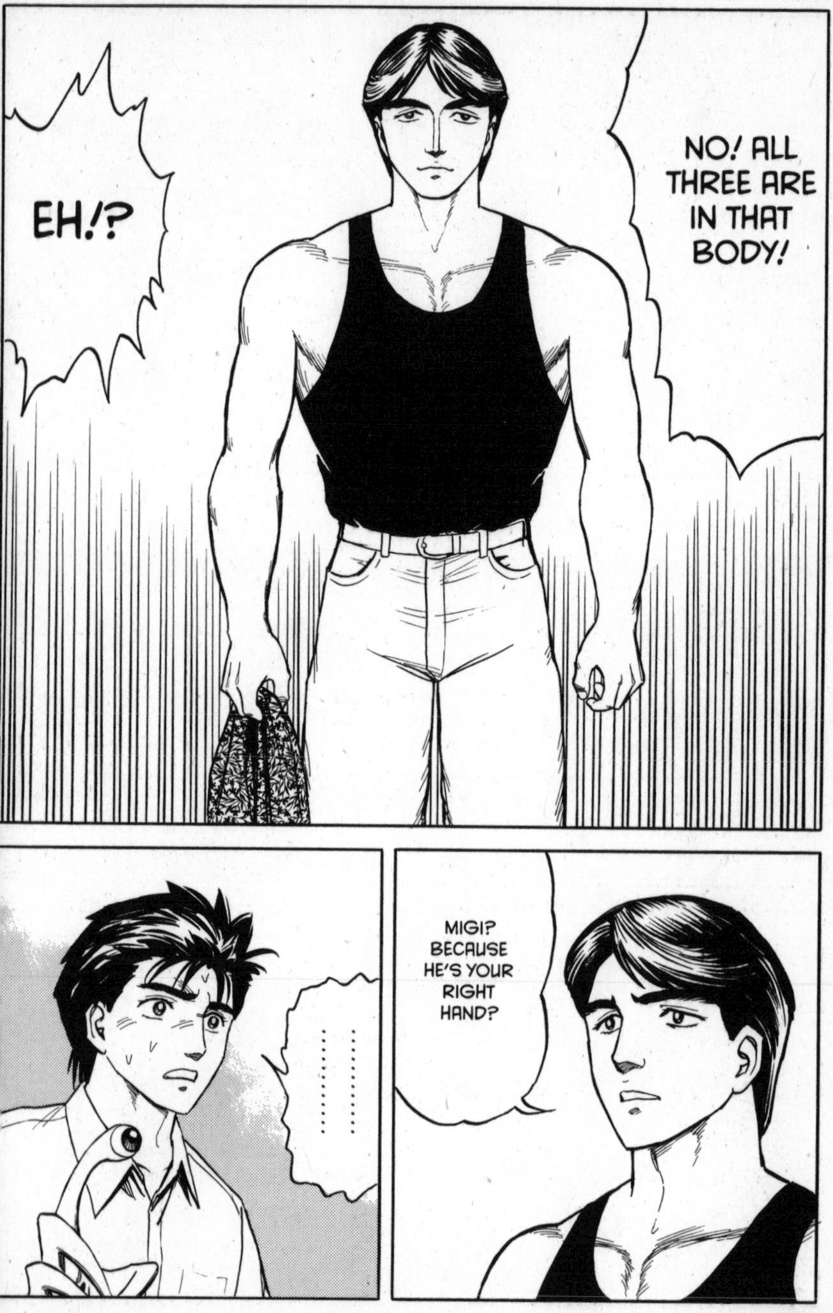
NO! ALL THREE ARE IN THAT BODY!
EH!?
MIGI? BECAUSE HE'S YOUR RIGHT HAND?
......

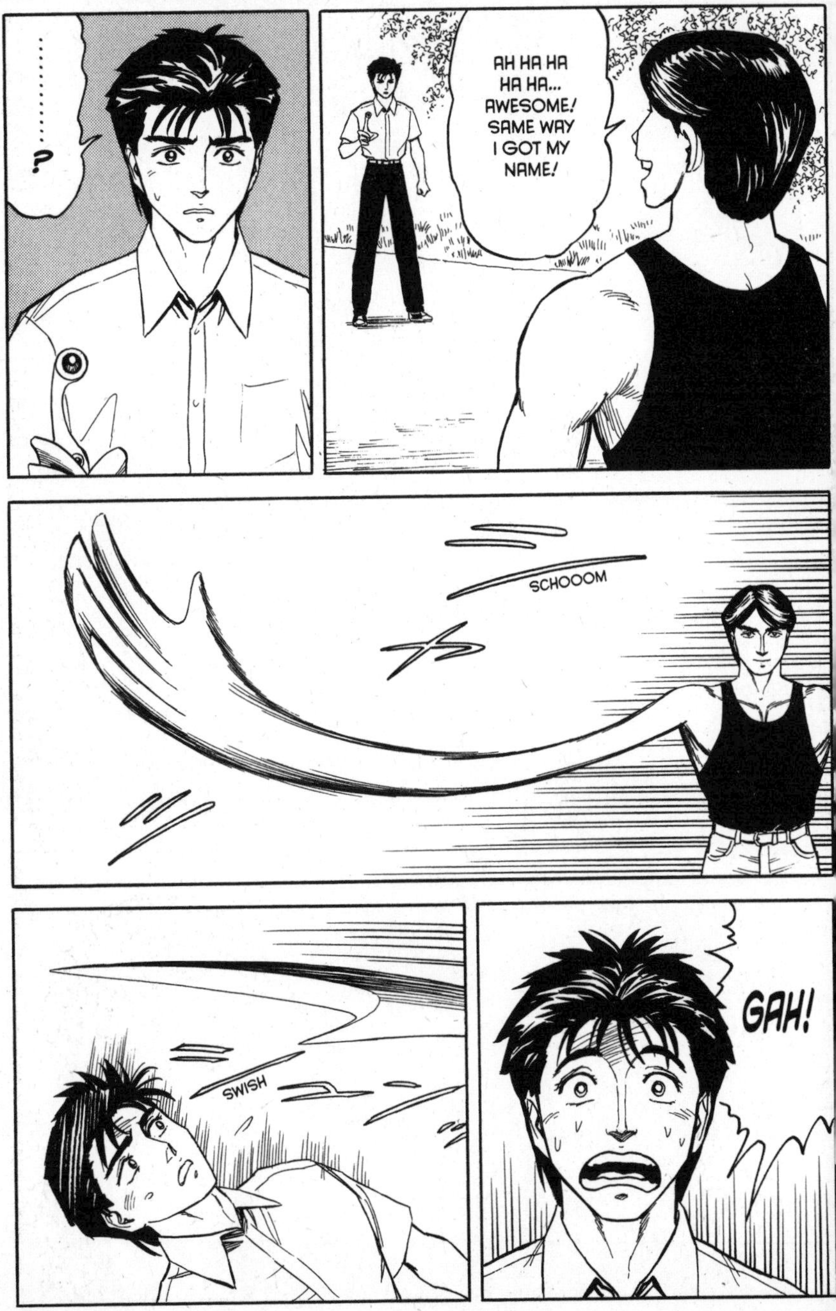
AH HA HA HA HA... AWESOME! SAME WAY I GOT MY NAME!
......?
SCHOOOM
GAH!
SWISH

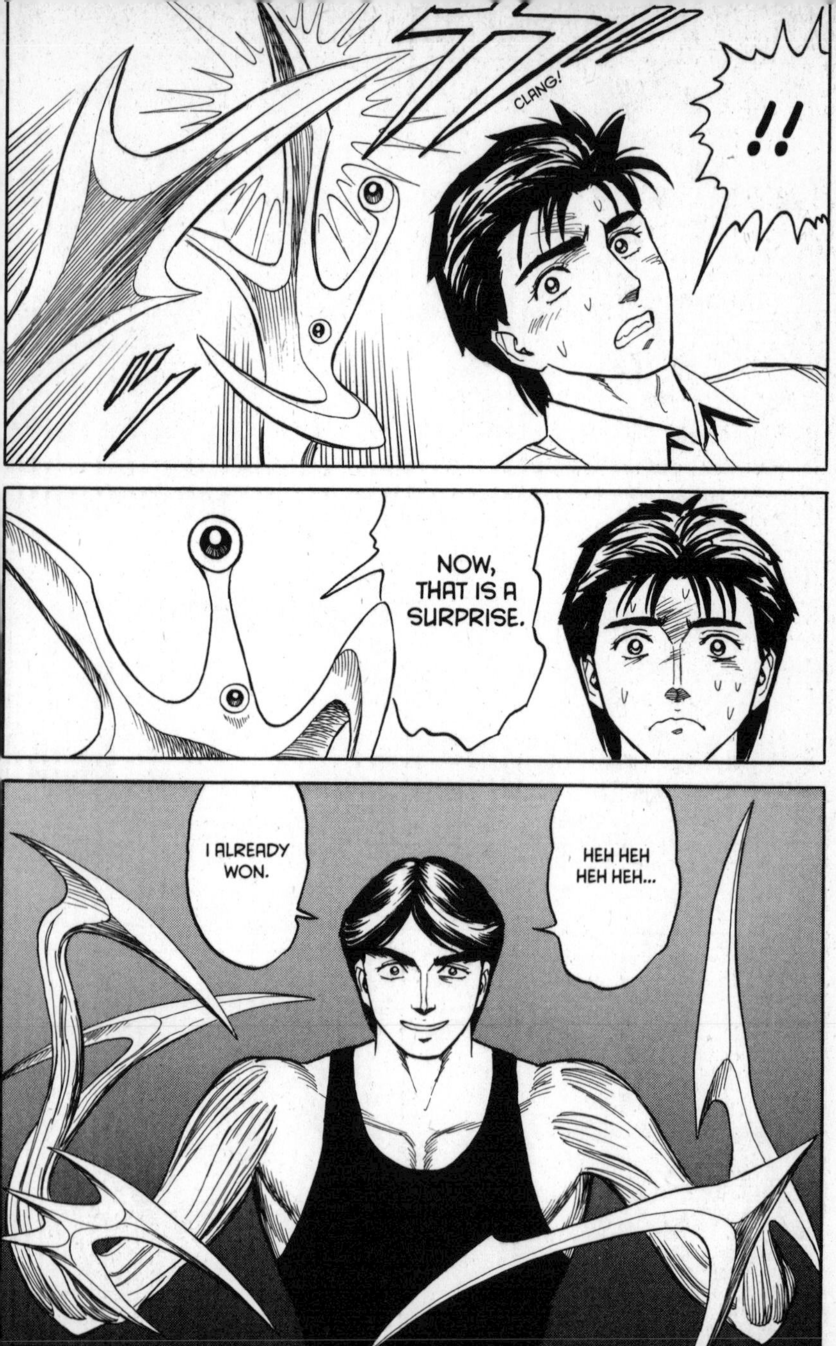
!!
CLANG!
NOW, THAT IS A SURPRISE.
HEH HEH HEH HEH...
I ALREADY WON.
CHAPTER 39: THE END

CHAPTER 40: COMMAND TOWER

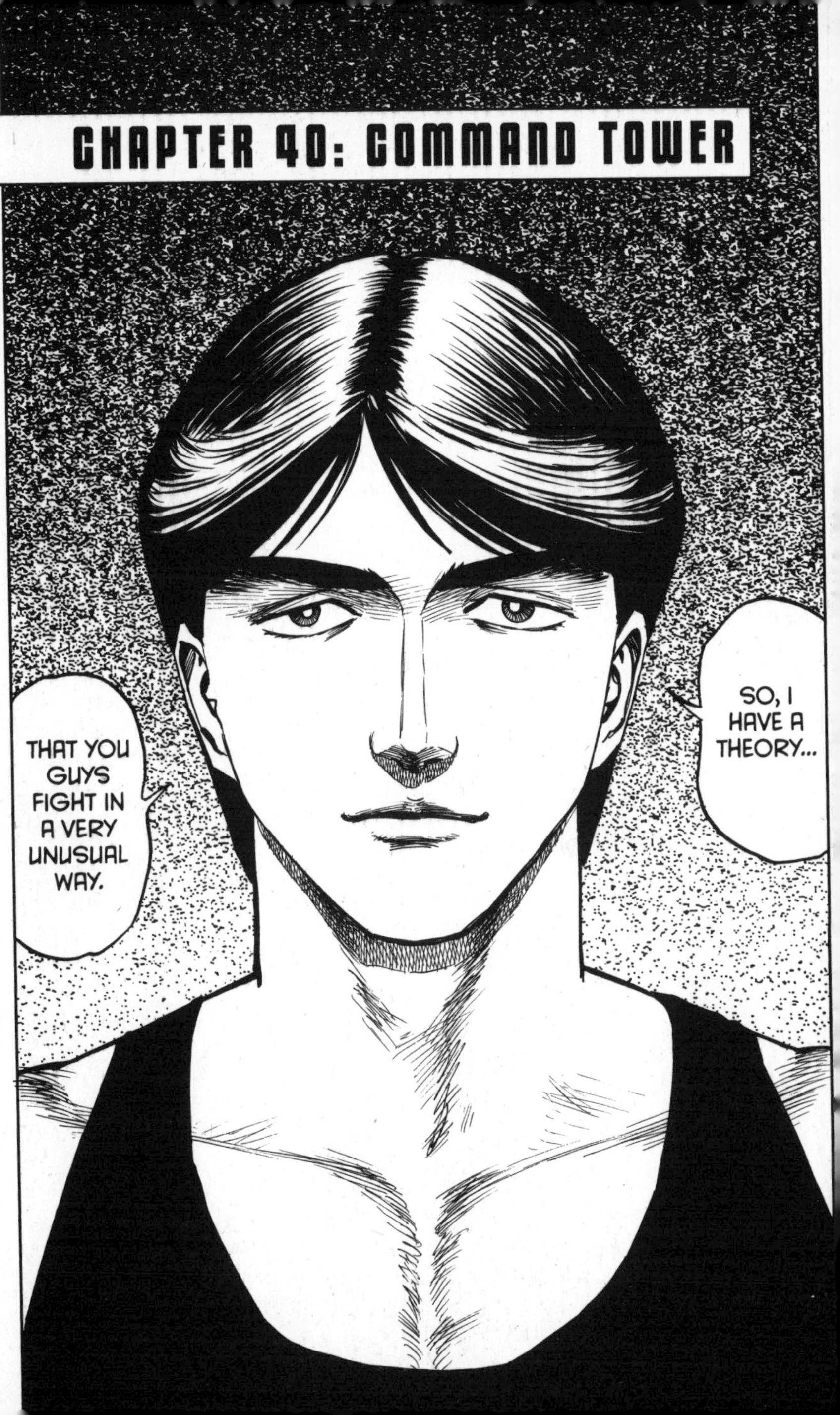
SO, I HAVE A THEORY...
THAT YOU GUYS FIGHT IN A VERY UNUSUAL WAY.

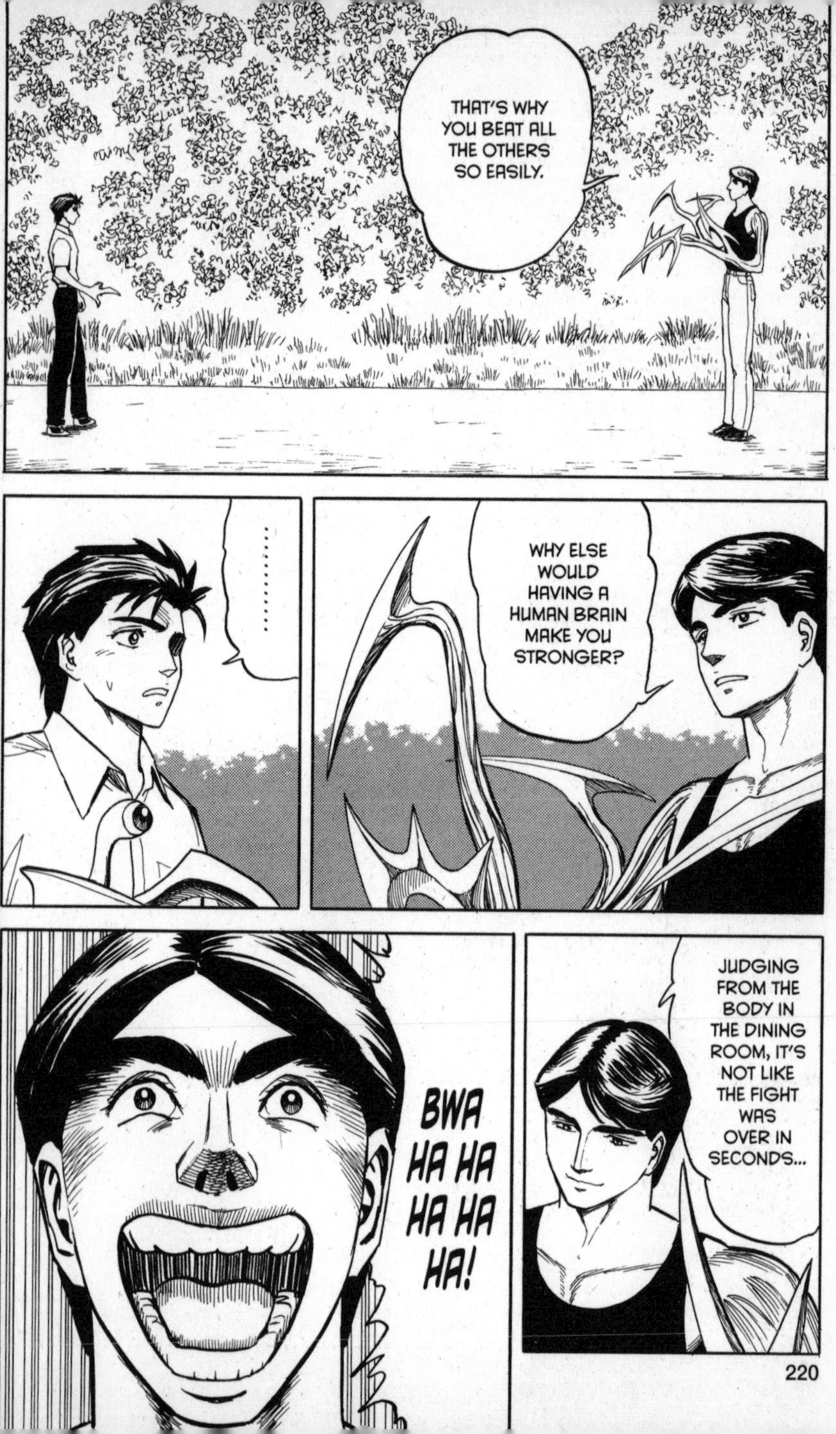
THAT'S WHY YOU BEAT ALL THE OTHERS SO EASILY.
WHY ELSE WOULD HAVING A HUMAN BRAIN MAKE YOU STRONGER?
......
JUDGING FROM THE BODY IN THE DINING ROOM, IT'S NOT LIKE THE FIGHT WAS OVER IN SECONDS...
BWA HA HA HA HA HA!

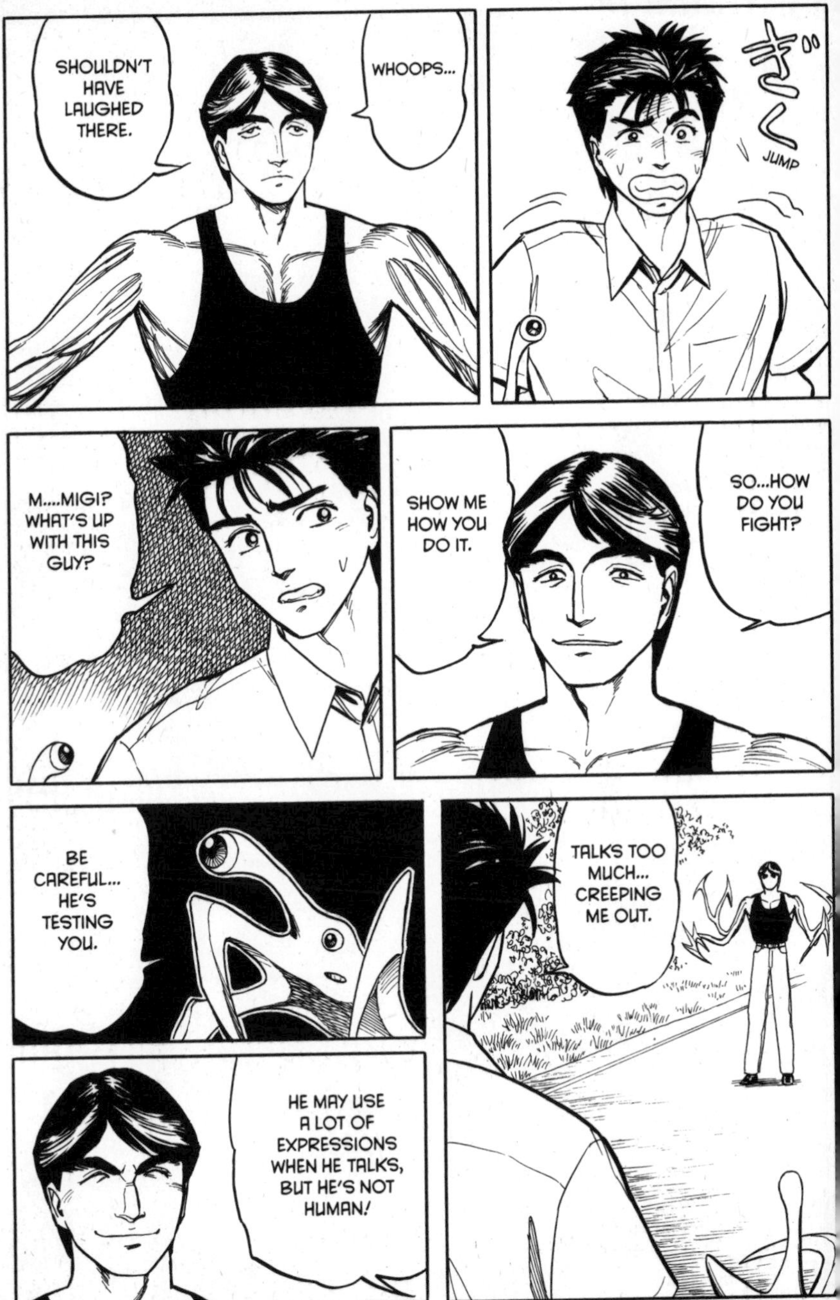
ぎく
JUMP
WHOOPS...
SHOULDN'T HAVE LAUGHED THERE.
SO...HOW DO YOU FIGHT?
SHOW ME HOW YOU DO IT.
M....MIGI? WHAT'S UP WITH THIS GUY?
TALKS TOO MUCH... CREEPING ME OUT.
BE CAREFUL... HE'S TESTING YOU.
HE MAY USE A LOT OF EXPRESSIONS WHEN HE TALKS, BUT HE'S NOT HUMAN!

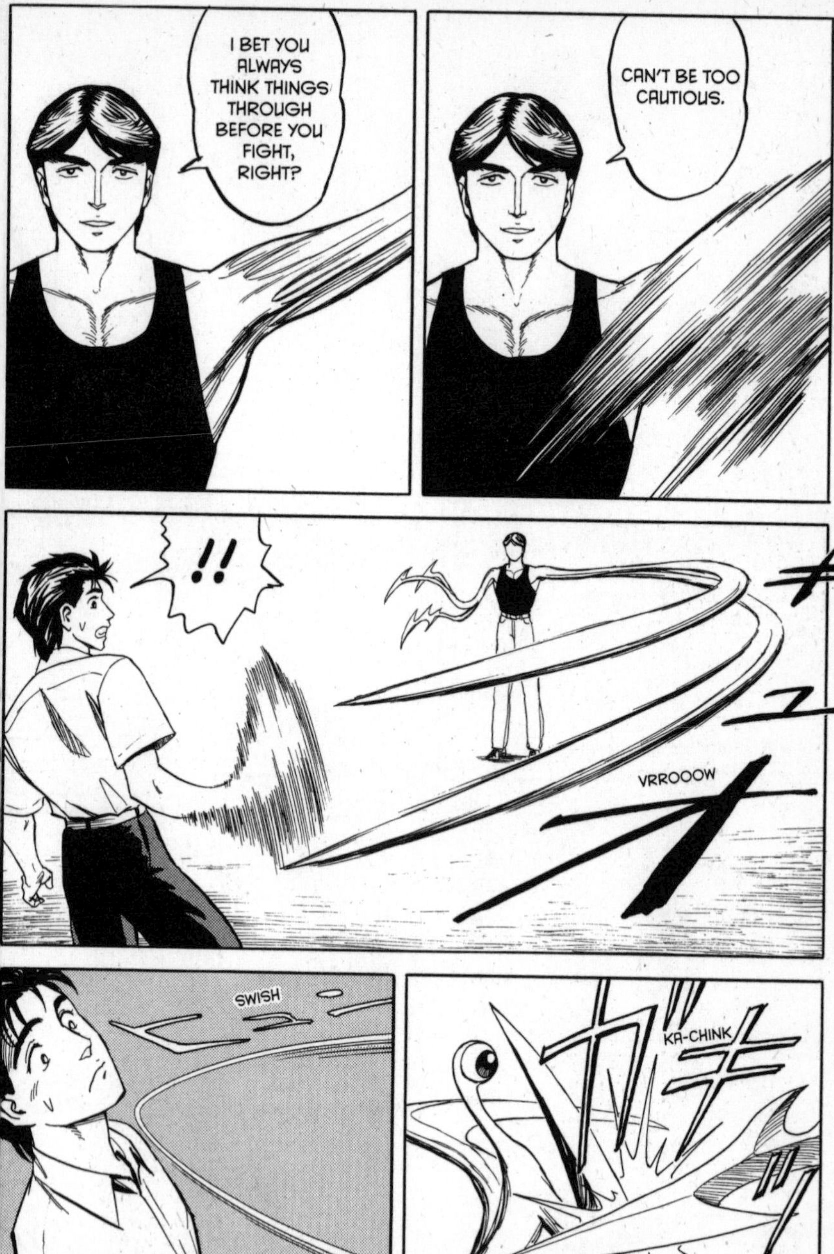
CAN'T BE TOO CAUTIOUS.
I BET YOU ALWAYS THINK THINGS THROUGH BEFORE YOU FIGHT, RIGHT?
!!
VRROOOW
KA-CHINK
SWISH

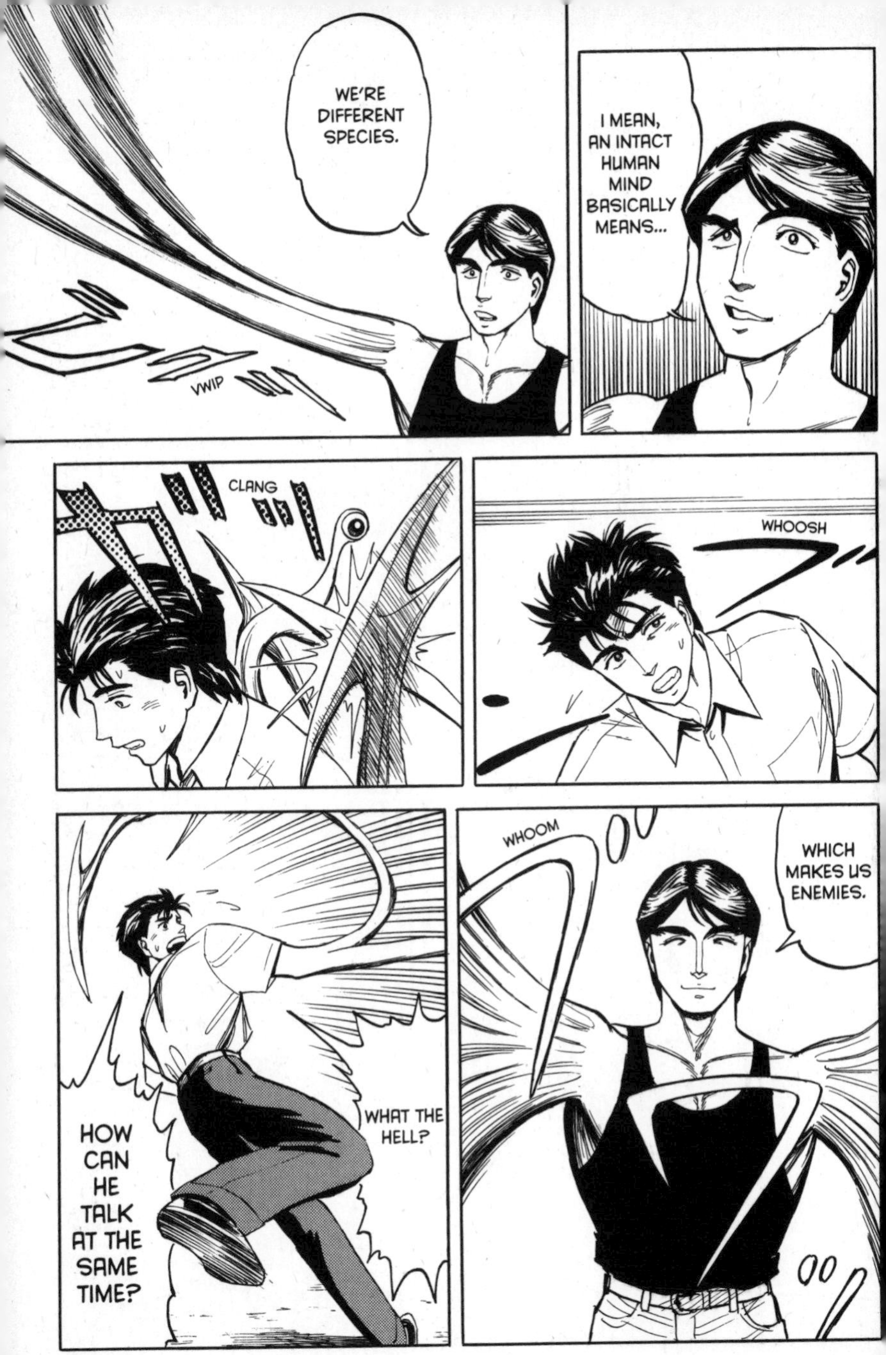
I MEAN, AN INTACT HUMAN MIND BASICALLY MEANS...
WE'RE DIFFERENT SPECIES.
VWIP
WHOOSH
CLANG
WHOOM
WHICH MAKES US ENEMIES.
WHAT THE HELL?
HOW CAN HE TALK AT THE SAME TIME?

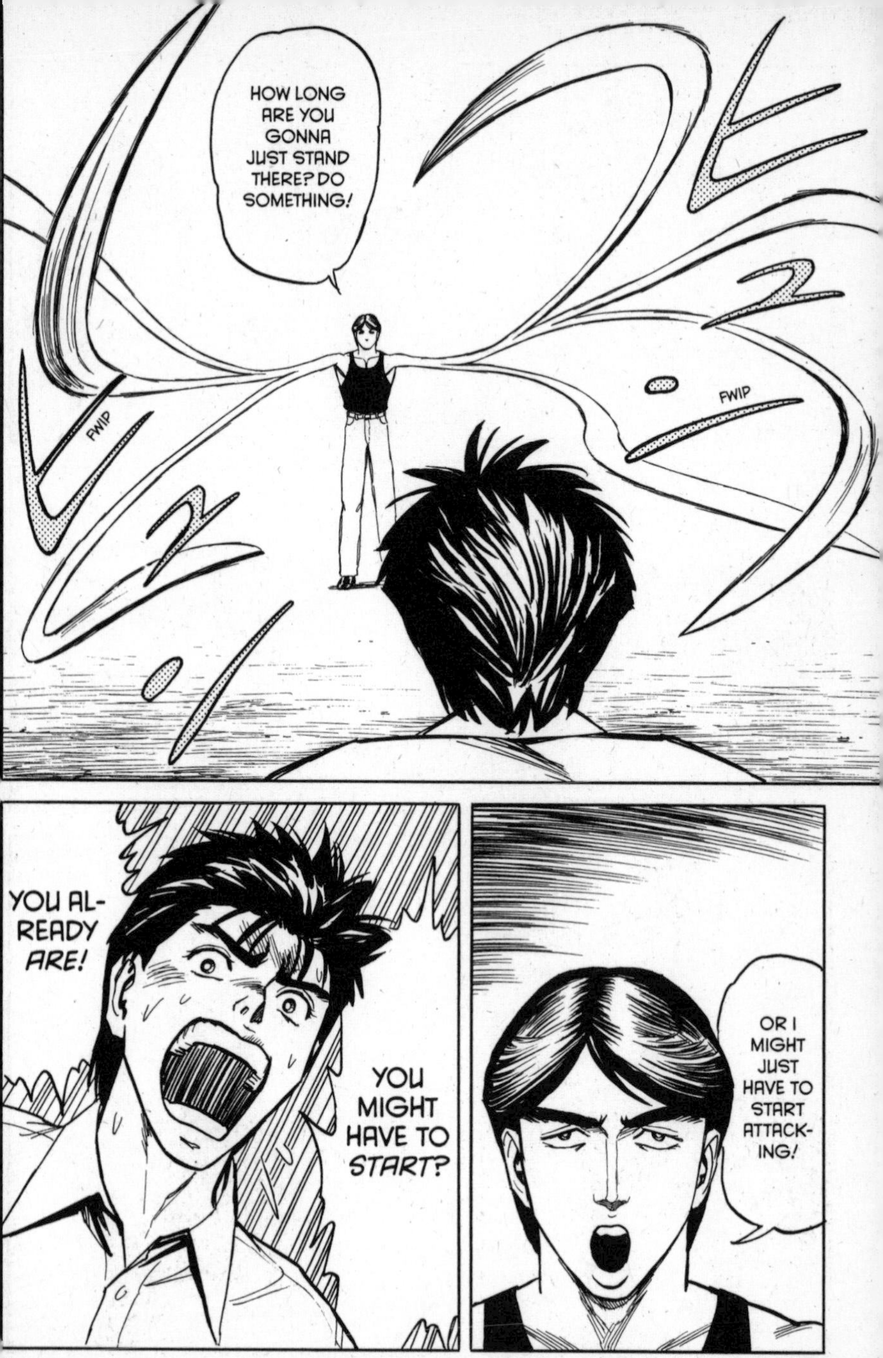
HOW LONG ARE YOU GONNA JUST STAND THERE? DO SOMETHING!
FWIP
FWIP
OR I MIGHT JUST HAVE TO START ATTACK-ING!
YOU MIGHT HAVE TO *START*?
YOU AL-READY *ARE*!

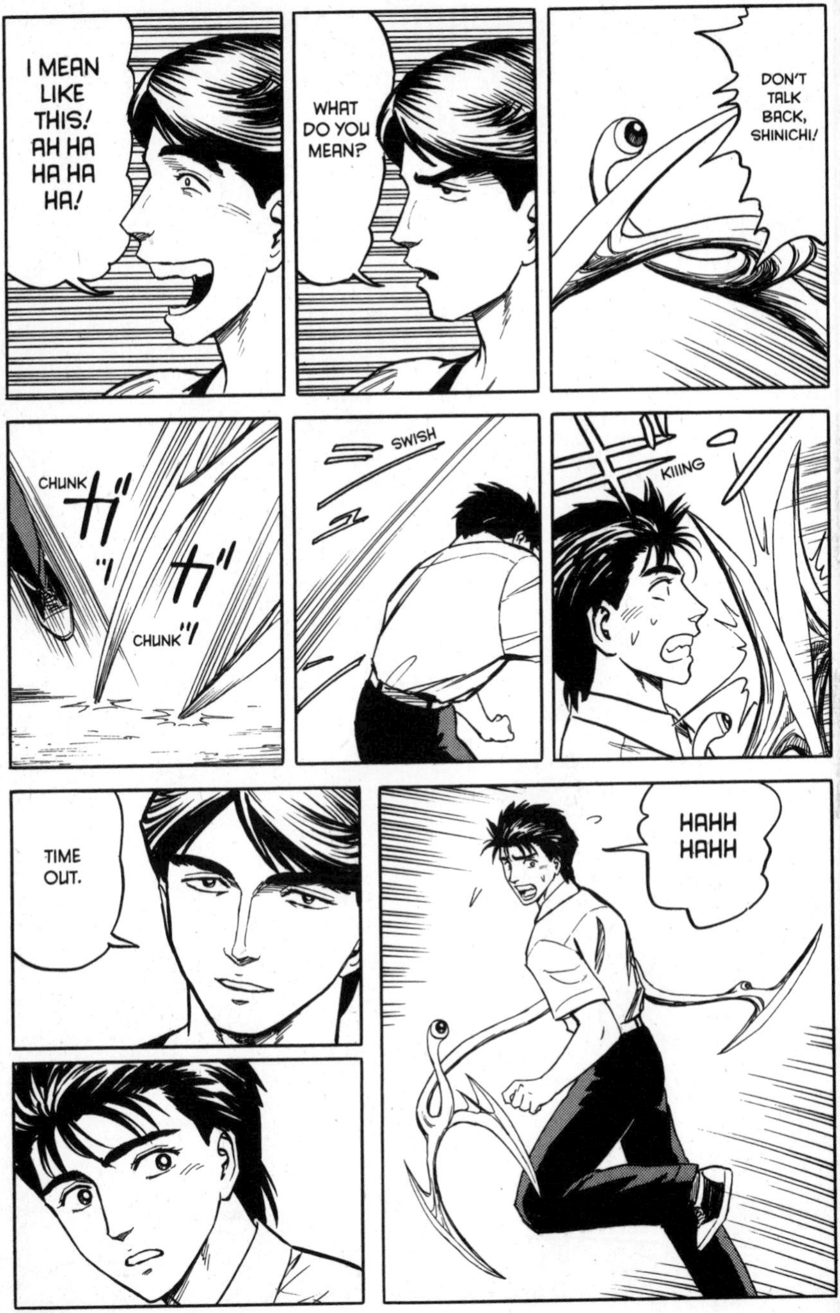
DON'T TALK BACK, SHINICHI!
WHAT DO YOU MEAN?
I MEAN LIKE THIS! AH HA HA HA HA!
KIIING
SWISH
CHUNK
ガ
ガ
CHUNK
HAHH HAHH
TIME OUT.

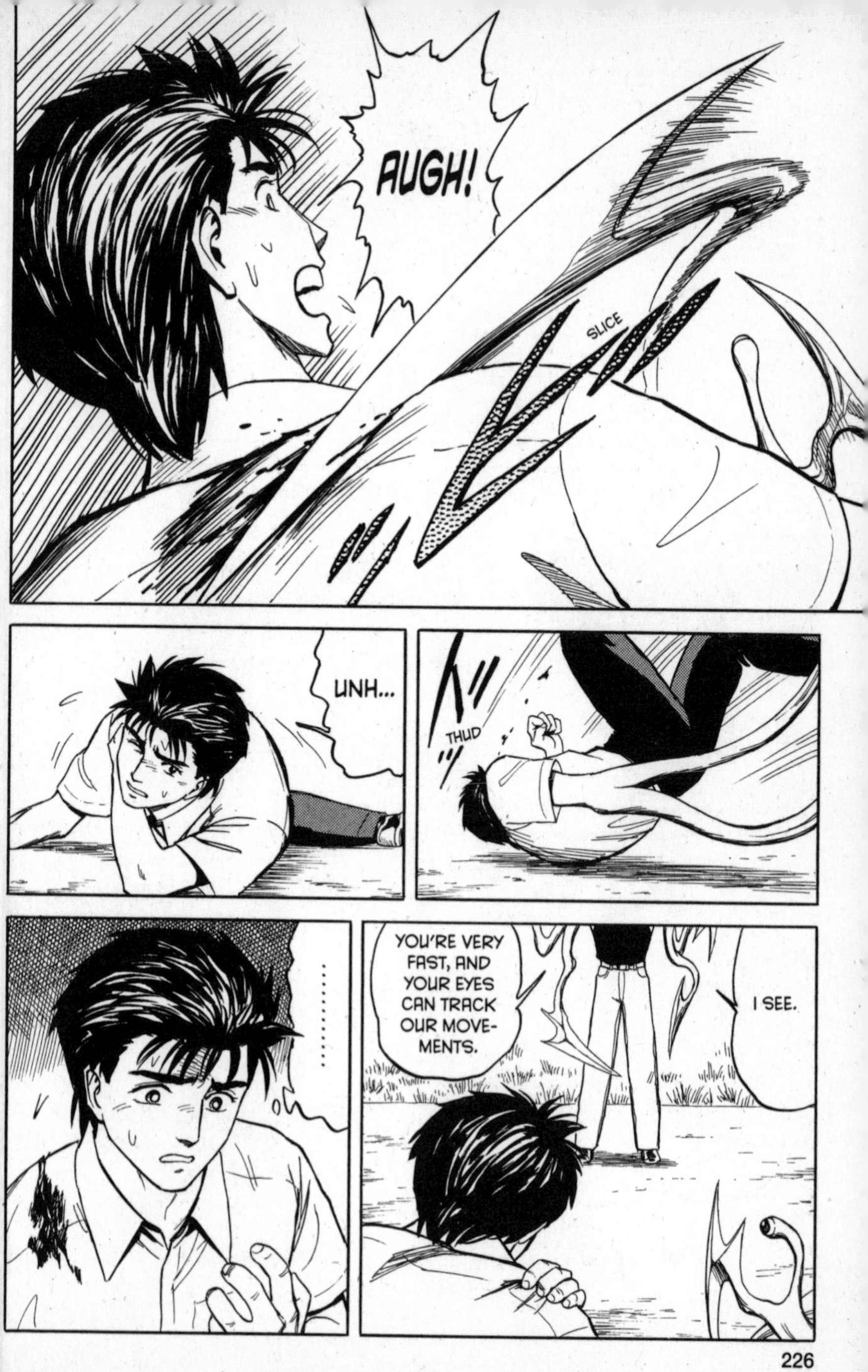
AUGH!
SLICE
THUD
UNH...
YOU'RE VERY FAST, AND YOUR EYES CAN TRACK OUR MOVEMENTS.
I SEE.
......

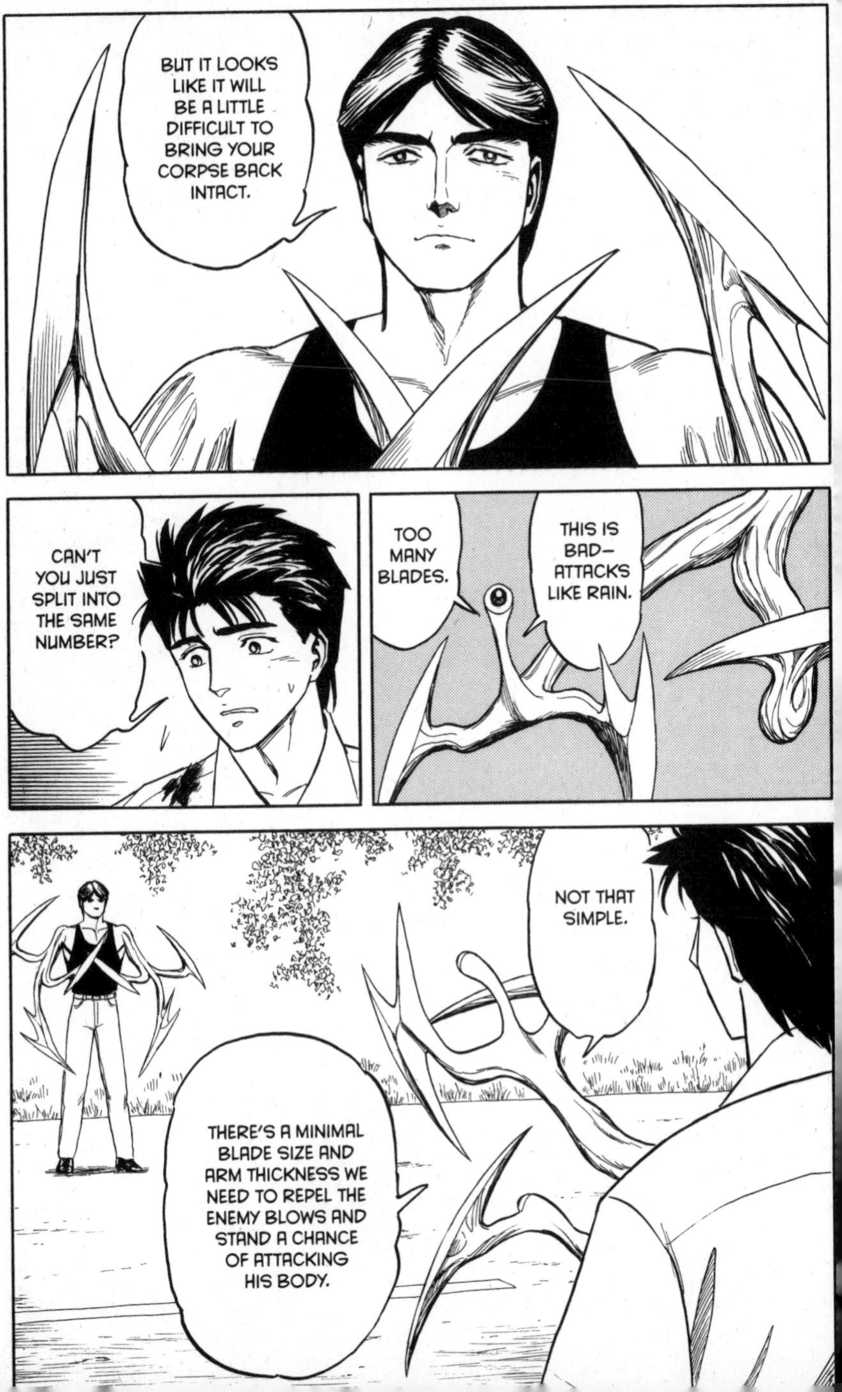
BUT IT LOOKS LIKE IT WILL BE A LITTLE DIFFICULT TO BRING YOUR CORPSE BACK INTACT.
THIS IS BAD—ATTACKS LIKE RAIN.
TOO MANY BLADES.
CAN'T YOU JUST SPLIT INTO THE SAME NUMBER?
NOT THAT SIMPLE.
THERE'S A MINIMAL BLADE SIZE AND ARM THICKNESS WE NEED TO REPEL THE ENEMY BLOWS AND STAND A CHANCE OF ATTACKING HIS BODY.

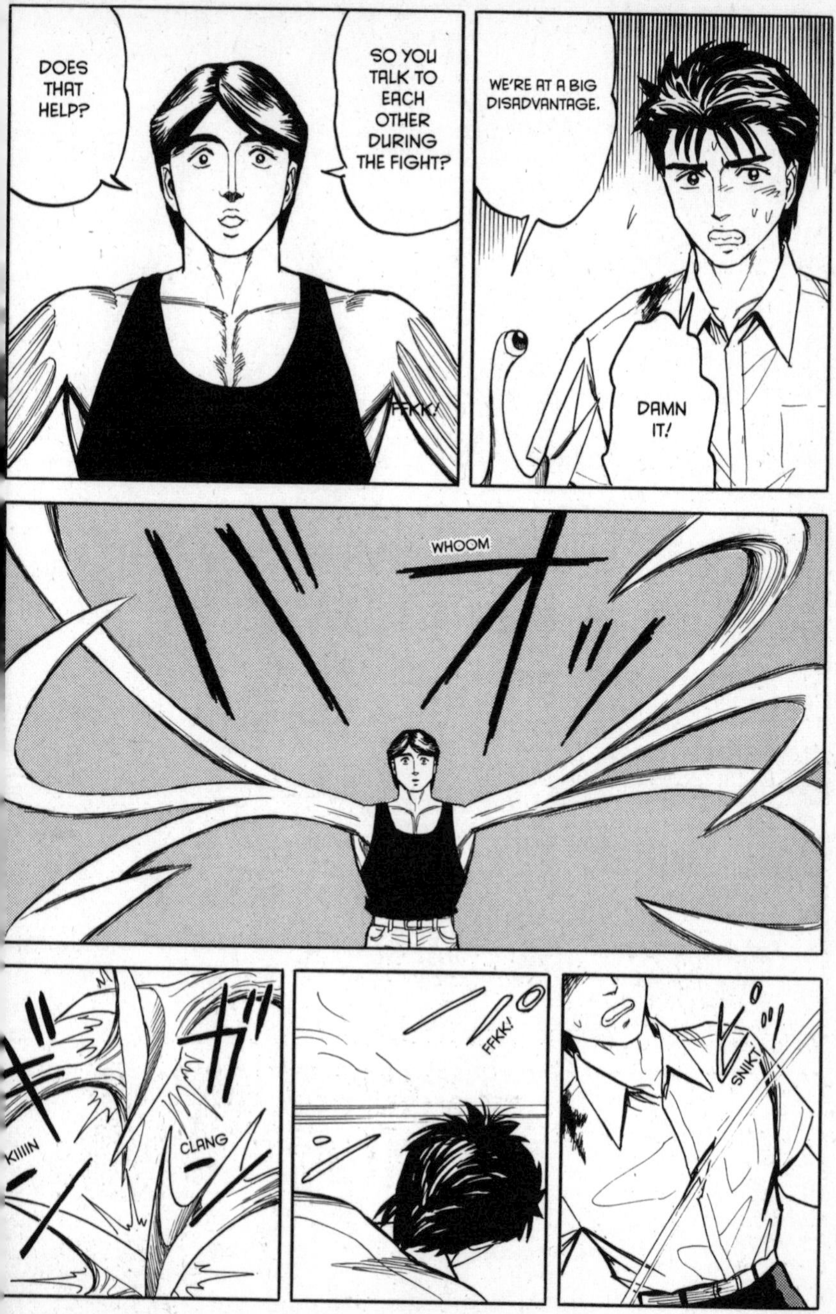
WE'RE AT A BIG DISADVANTAGE.
DAMN IT!
SO YOU TALK TO EACH OTHER DURING THE FIGHT?
DOES THAT HELP?
FFKK!
WHOOM
SNIKT!
FFKK!
CLANG
KIIIN

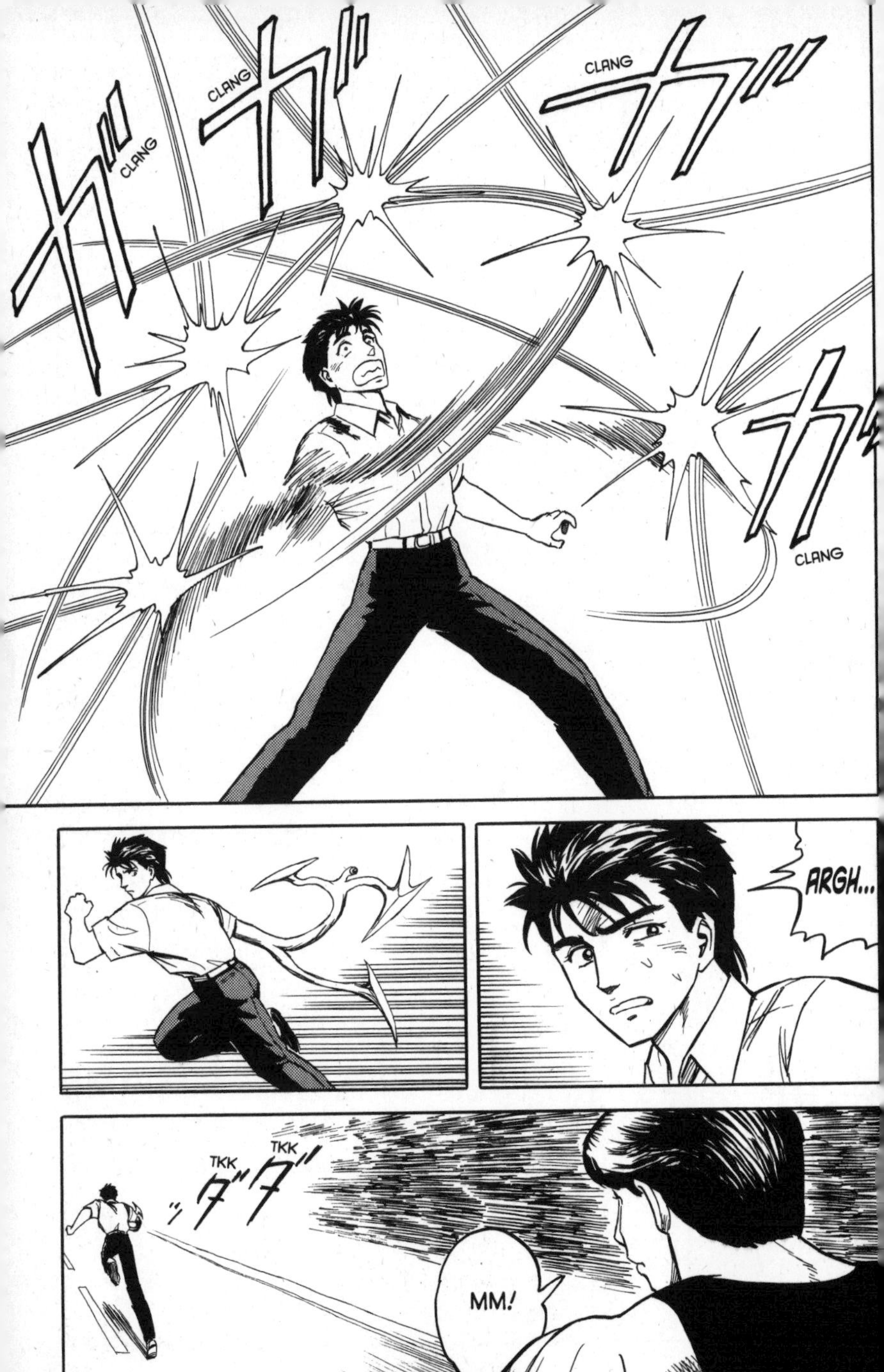
ガ
CLANG
ガ
CLANG
ガ
CLANG
ガ
CLANG
ARGH...
ッダダ
TKK TKK
MM!

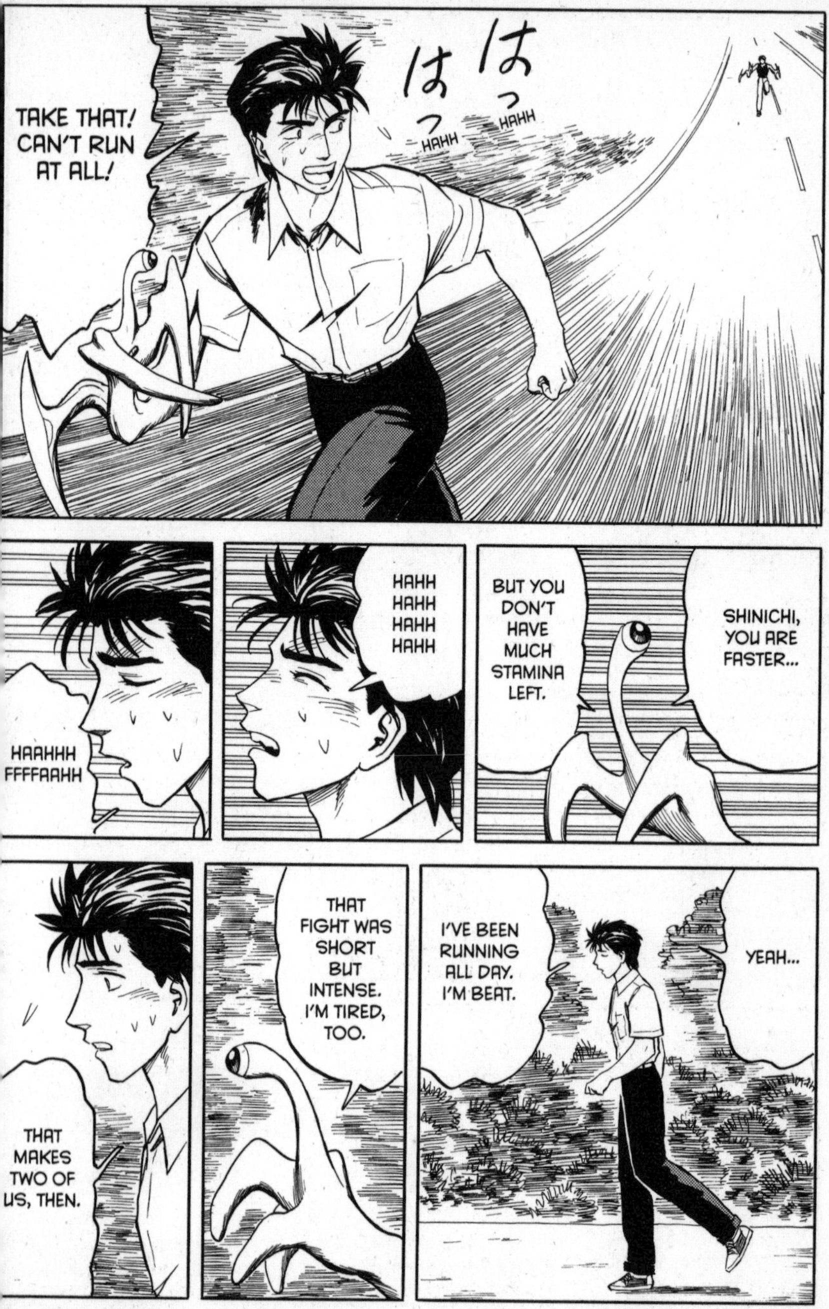
はっ
HAHH
はっ
HAHH
TAKE THAT! CAN'T RUN AT ALL!
SHINICHI, YOU ARE FASTER...
BUT YOU DON'T HAVE MUCH STAMINA LEFT.
HAHH HAHH HAHH HAHH
HAAHHH FFFFAAHH
YEAH...
I'VE BEEN RUNNING ALL DAY. I'M BEAT.
THAT FIGHT WAS SHORT BUT INTENSE. I'M TIRED, TOO.
THAT MAKES TWO OF US, THEN.

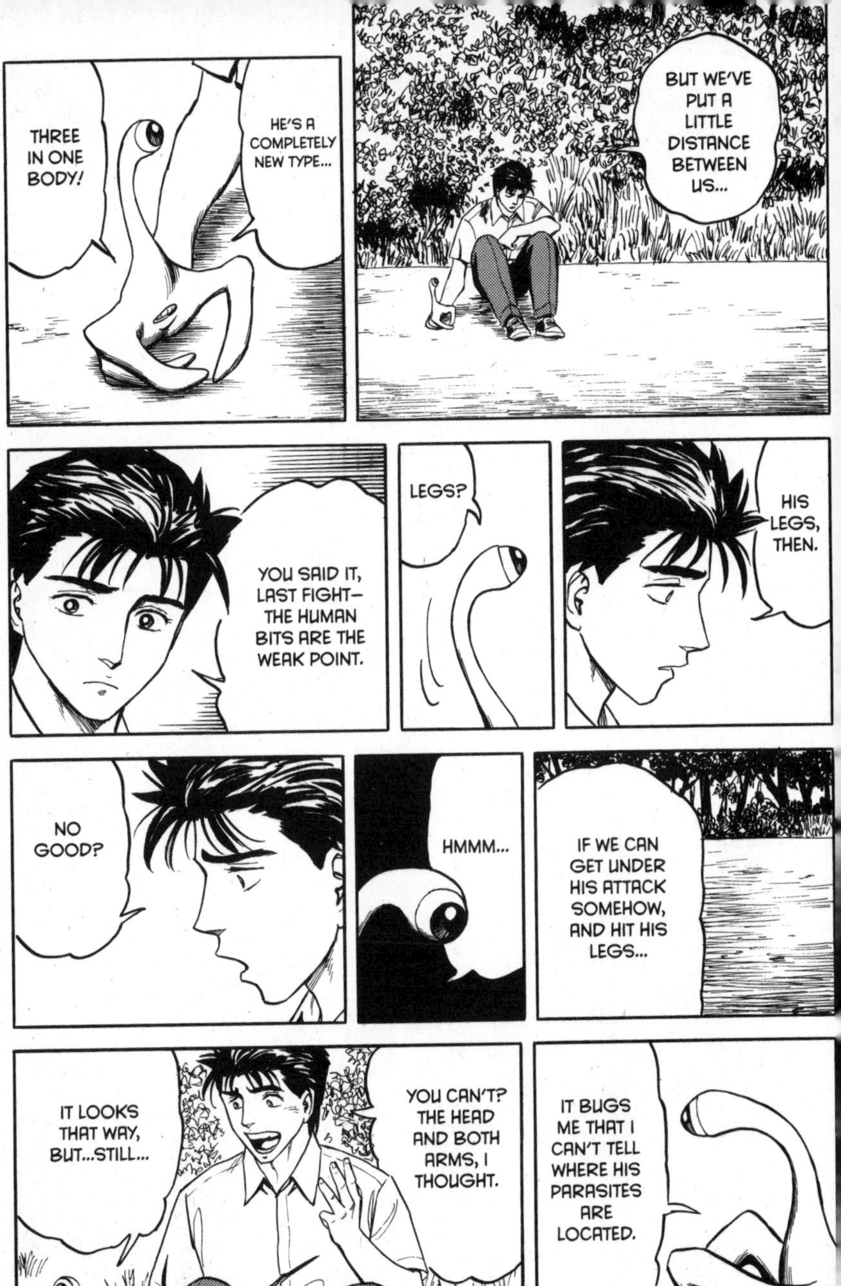
BUT WE'VE PUT A LITTLE DISTANCE BETWEEN US...
HE'S A COMPLETELY NEW TYPE...
THREE IN ONE BODY!
HIS LEGS, THEN.
LEGS?
YOU SAID IT, LAST FIGHT— THE HUMAN BITS ARE THE WEAK POINT.
IF WE CAN GET UNDER HIS ATTACK SOMEHOW, AND HIT HIS LEGS...
HMMM...
NO GOOD?
IT BUGS ME THAT I CAN'T TELL WHERE HIS PARASITES ARE LOCATED.
YOU CAN'T? THE HEAD AND BOTH ARMS, I THOUGHT.
IT LOOKS THAT WAY, BUT...STILL...

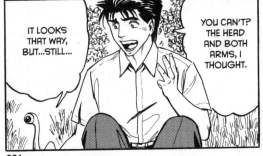

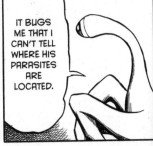

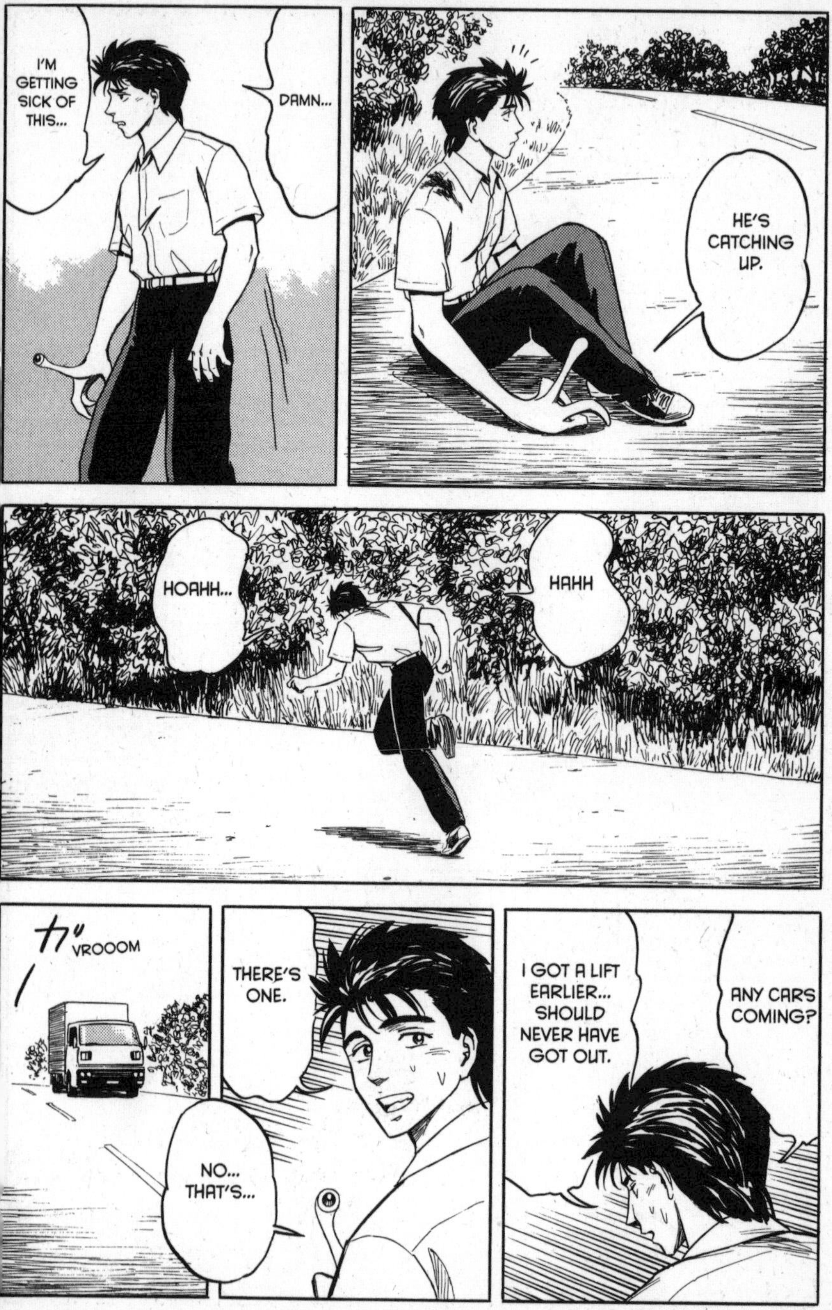
HE'S CATCHING UP.
DAMN...
I'M GETTING SICK OF THIS...
HAHH
HOAHH...
ANY CARS COMING?
I GOT A LIFT EARLIER... SHOULD NEVER HAVE GOT OUT.
THERE'S ONE.
NO... THAT'S...
VROOOM

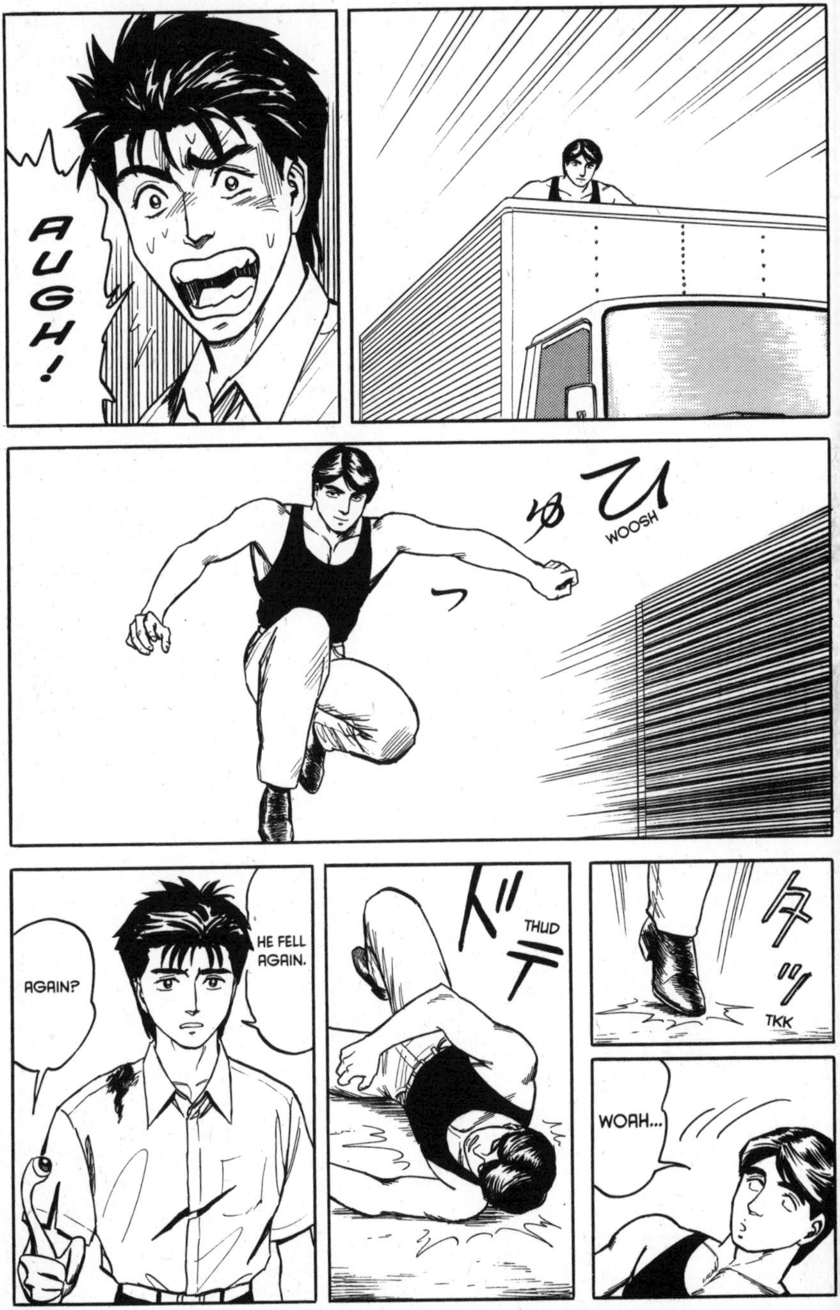
AUGH!
ひゅっ
WOOSH
タッ
TKK
WOAH...
ドテ
THUD
HE FELL AGAIN.
AGAIN?

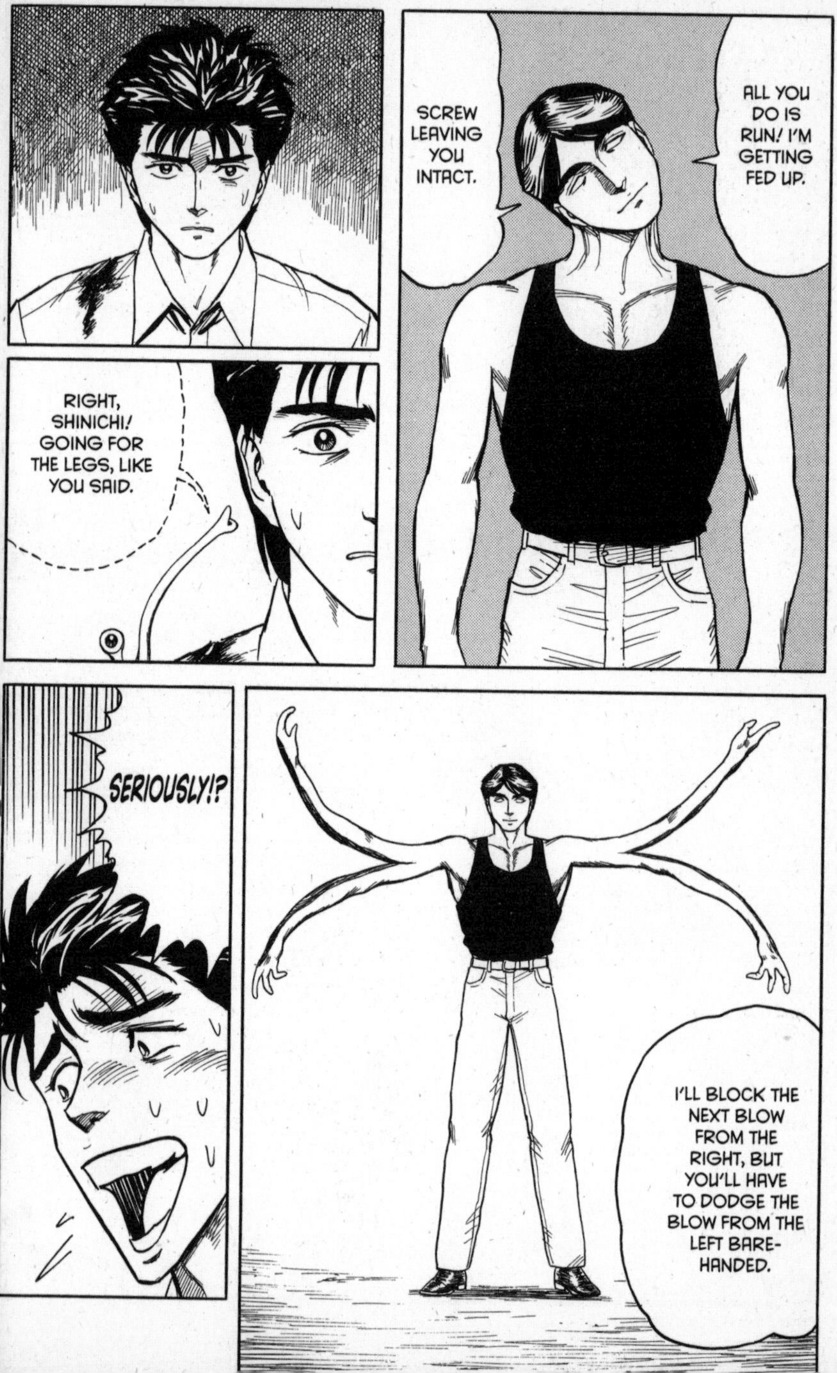
ALL YOU DO IS RUN! I'M GETTING FED UP.
SCREW LEAVING YOU INTACT.
RIGHT, SHINICHI! GOING FOR THE LEGS, LIKE YOU SAID.
I'LL BLOCK THE NEXT BLOW FROM THE RIGHT, BUT YOU'LL HAVE TO DODGE THE BLOW FROM THE LEFT BARE-HANDED.
SERIOUSLY!?

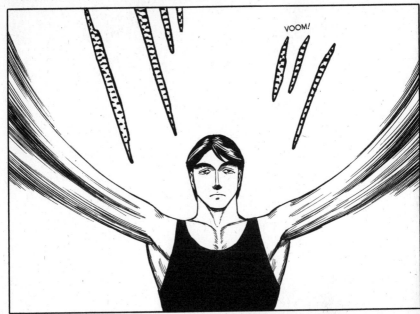

VOOM!

235

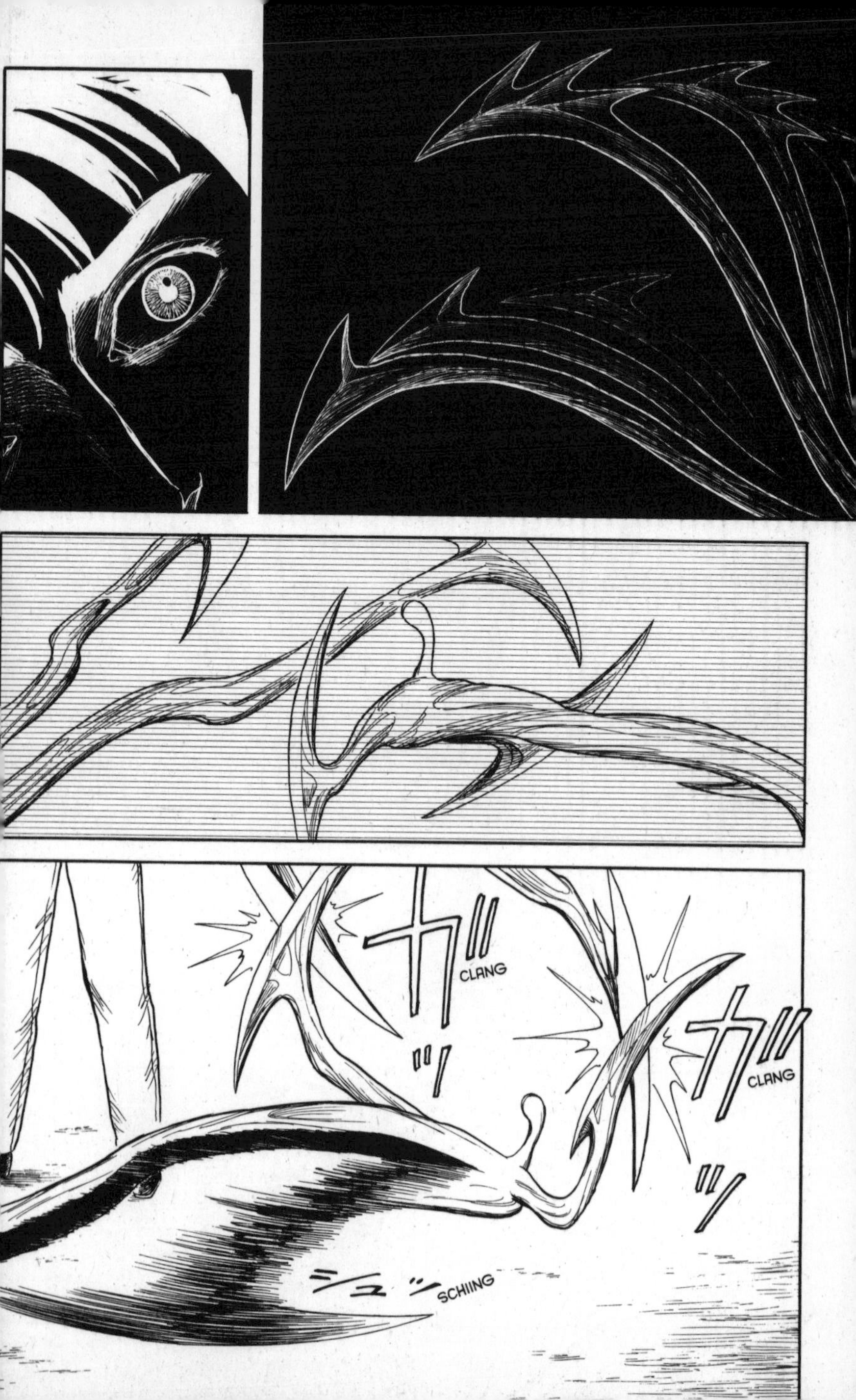
カッ
CLANG
カッ
CLANG
シュッ
SCHIING

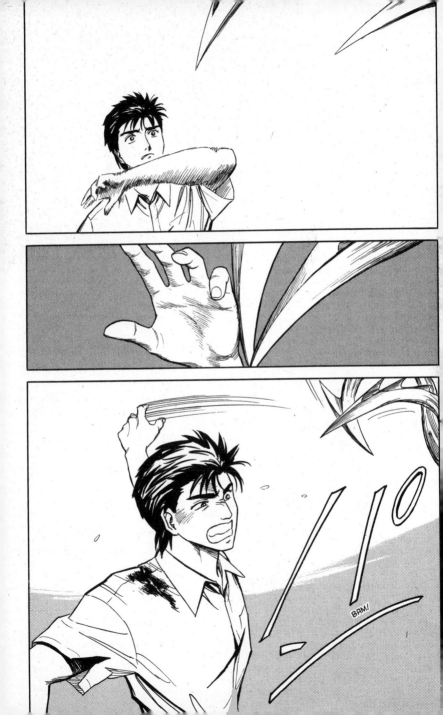

BAM!

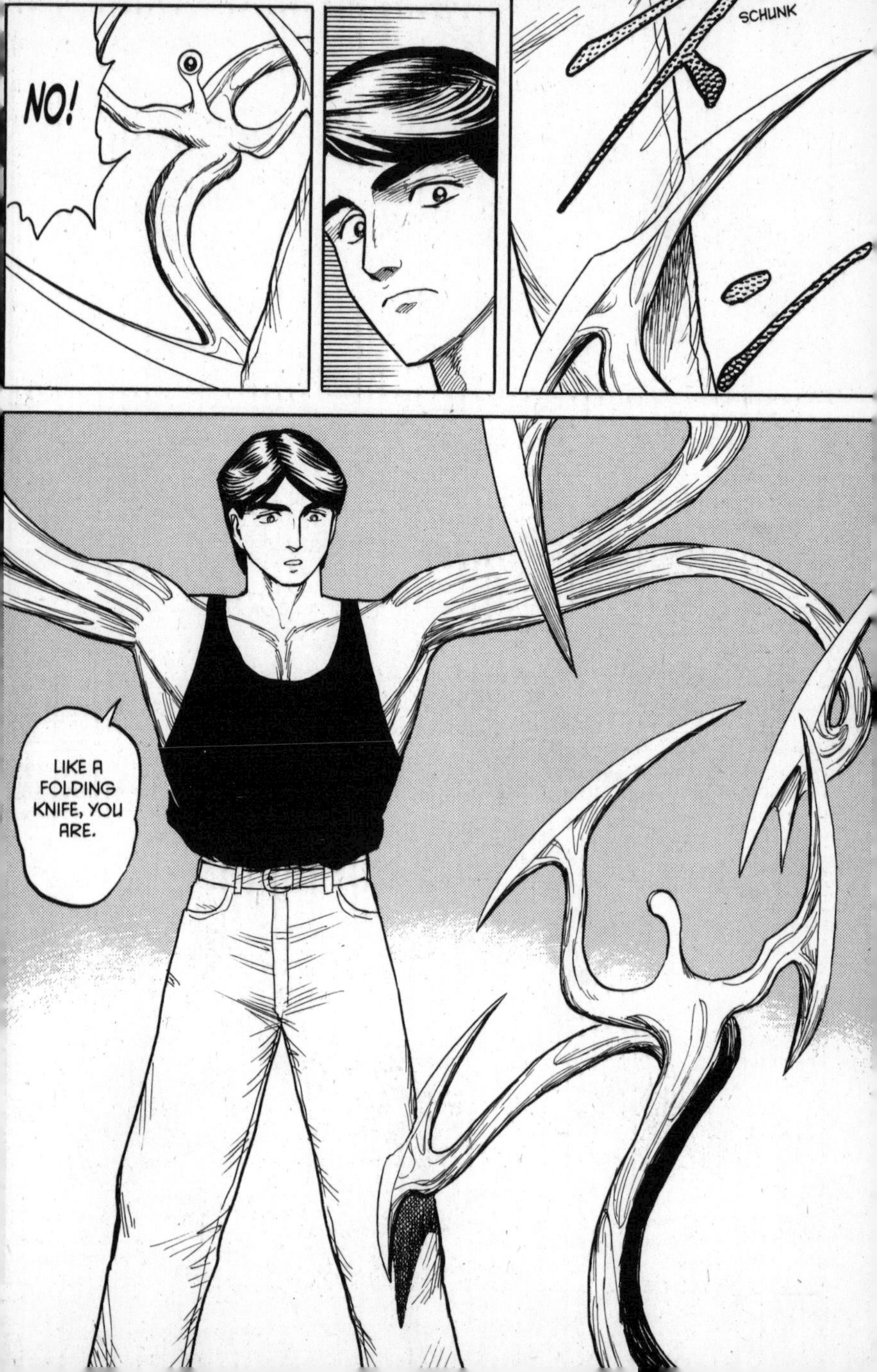
SCHUNK
NO!
LIKE A FOLDING KNIFE, YOU ARE.

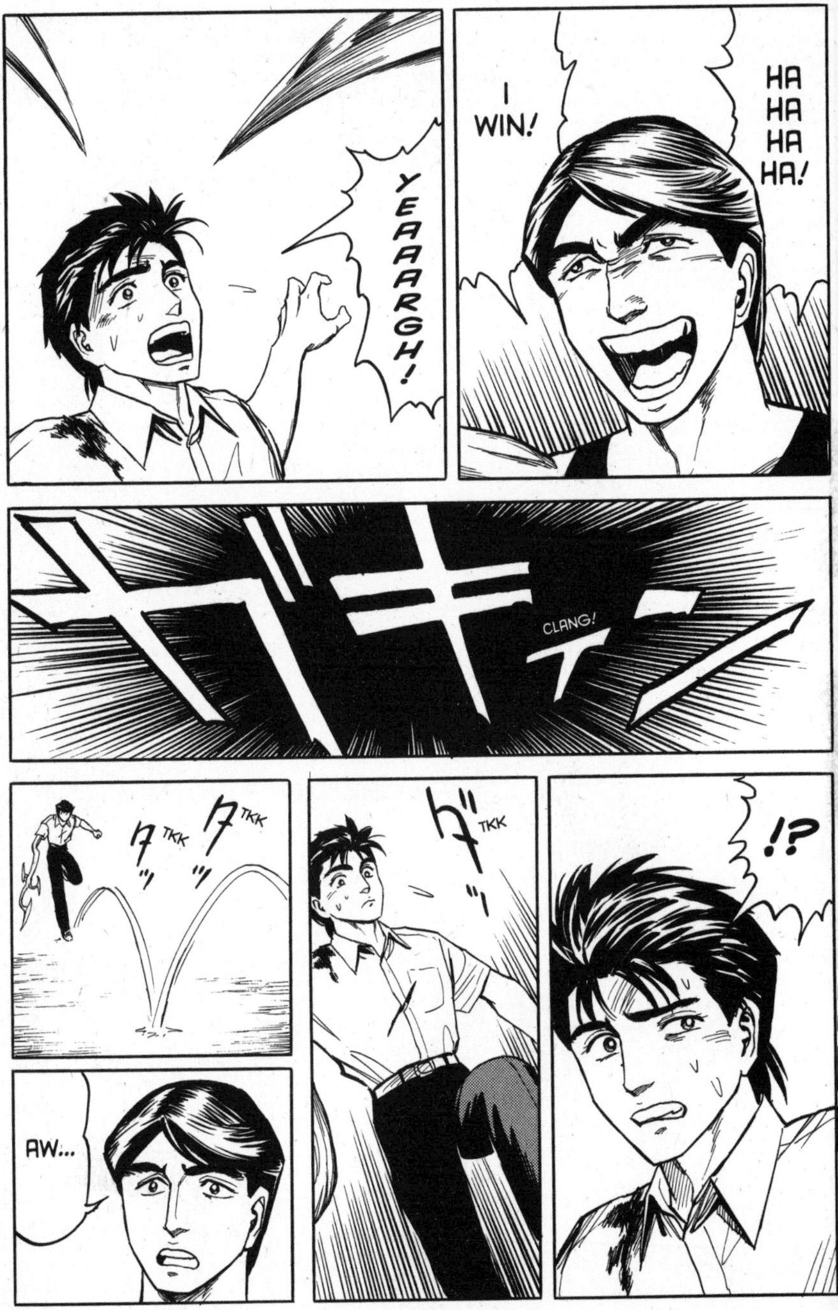
HA HA HA HA!
I WIN!
YEAAAARGH!
CLANG!
!?
TKK
TKK
TKK
AW...

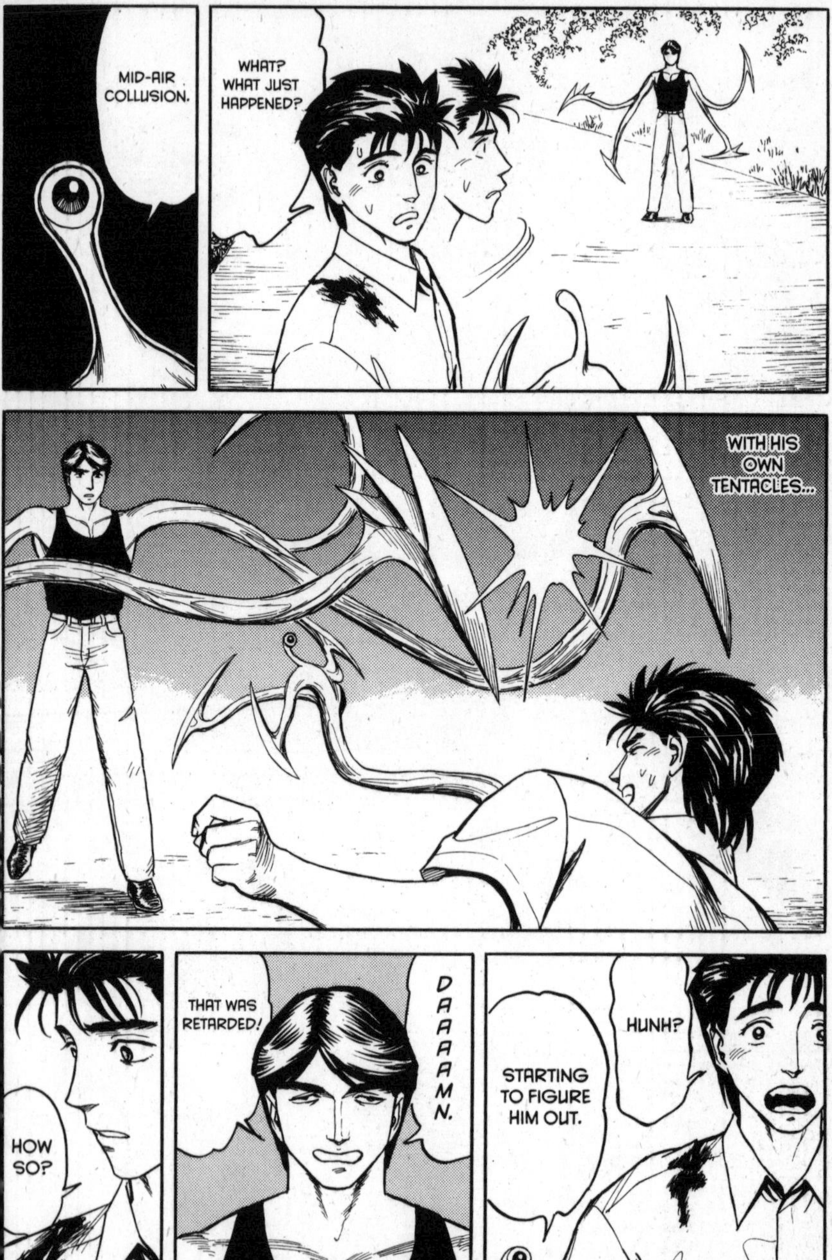
WHAT? WHAT JUST HAPPENED?
MID-AIR COLLUSION.
WITH HIS OWN TENTACLES...
HUNH?
STARTING TO FIGURE HIM OUT.
DAAAAAMN.
THAT WAS RETARDED!
HOW SO?

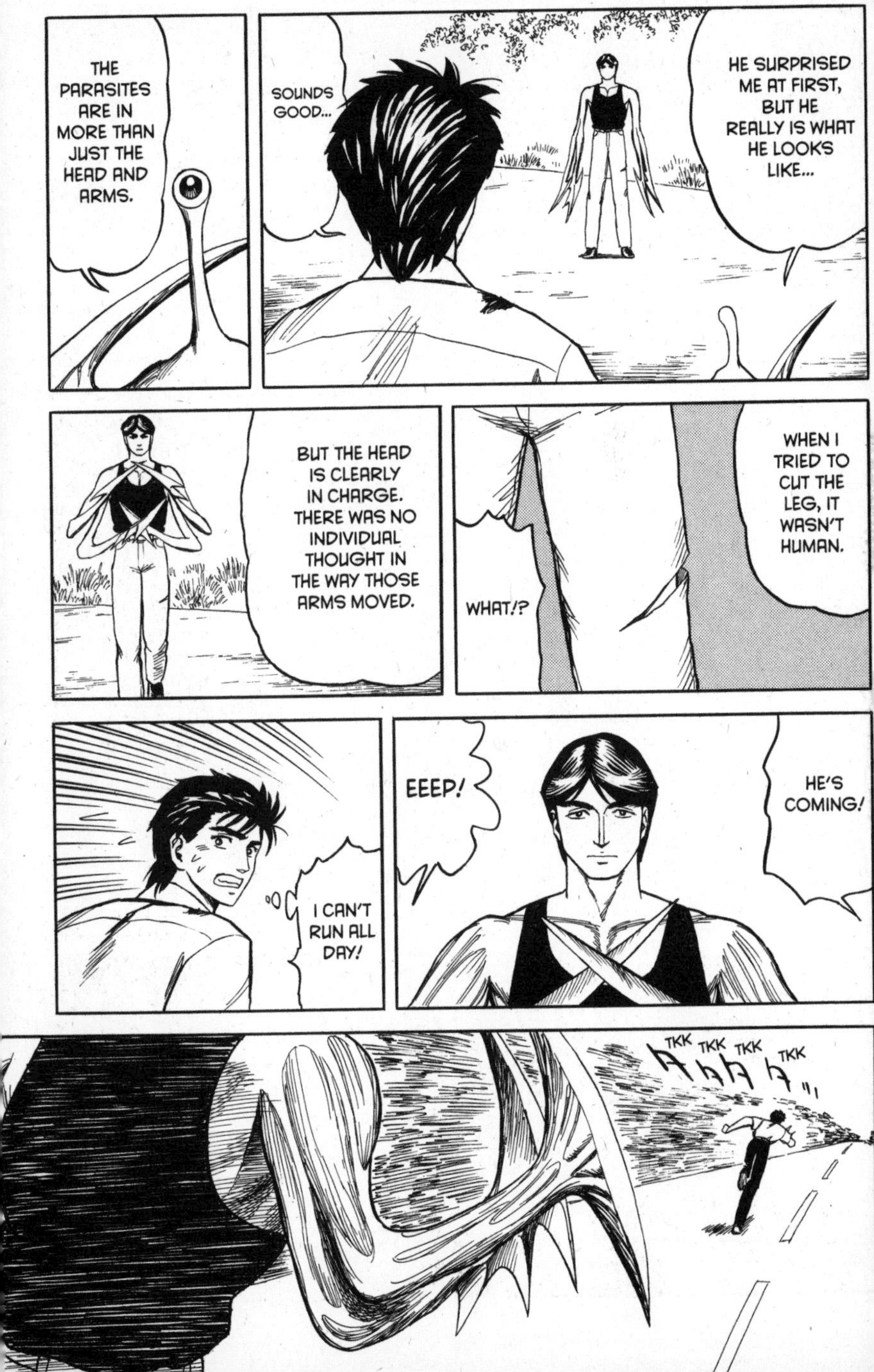
HE SURPRISED ME AT FIRST, BUT HE REALLY IS WHAT HE LOOKS LIKE...
SOUNDS GOOD...
THE PARASITES ARE IN MORE THAN JUST THE HEAD AND ARMS.
WHEN I TRIED TO CUT THE LEG, IT WASN'T HUMAN.
WHAT!?
BUT THE HEAD IS CLEARLY IN CHARGE. THERE WAS NO INDIVIDUAL THOUGHT IN THE WAY THOSE ARMS MOVED.
HE'S COMING!
EEEP!
I CAN'T RUN ALL DAY!
TKK TKK TKK TKK

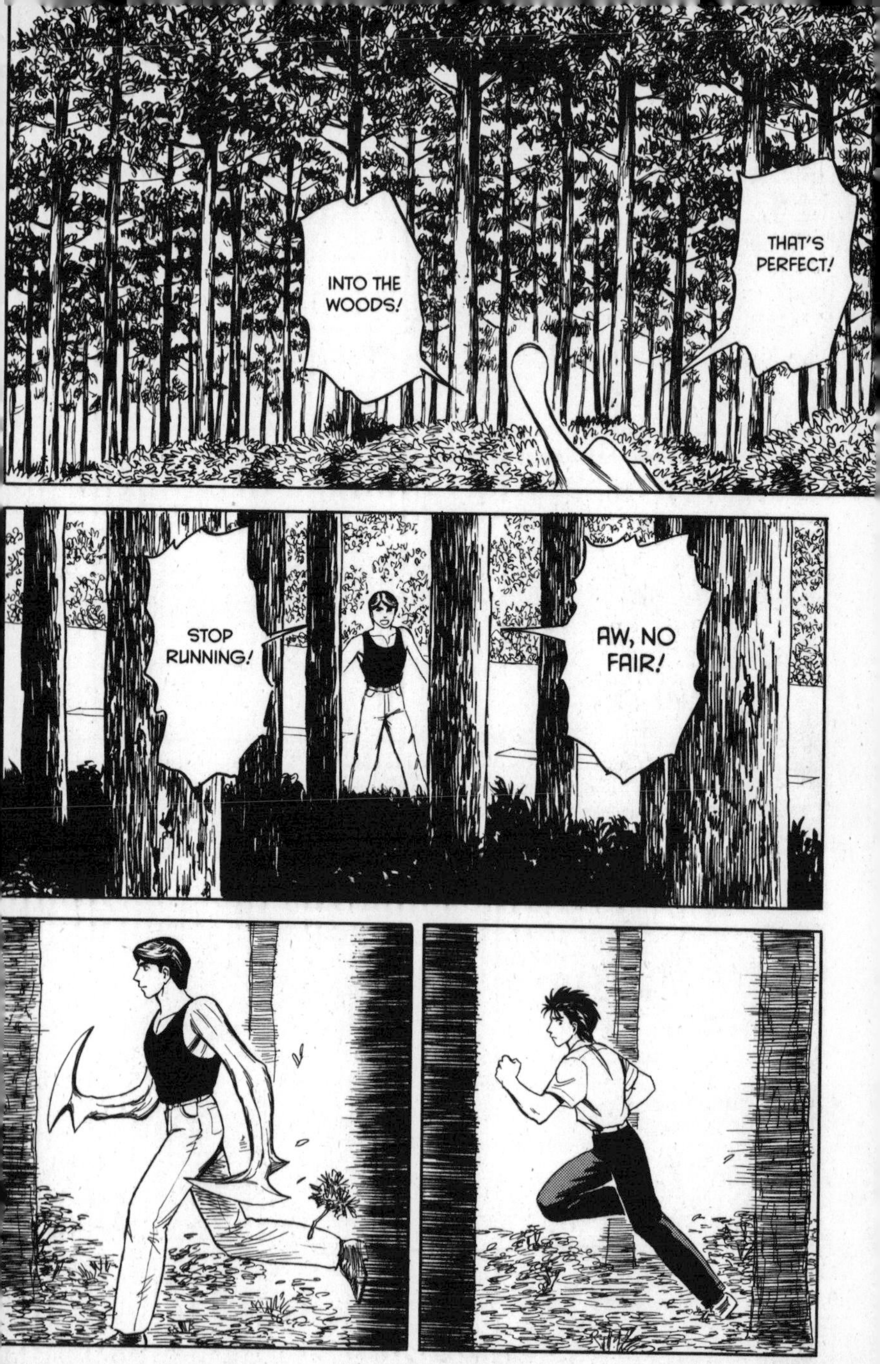
THAT'S PERFECT!
INTO THE WOODS!
AW, NO FAIR!
STOP RUNNING!

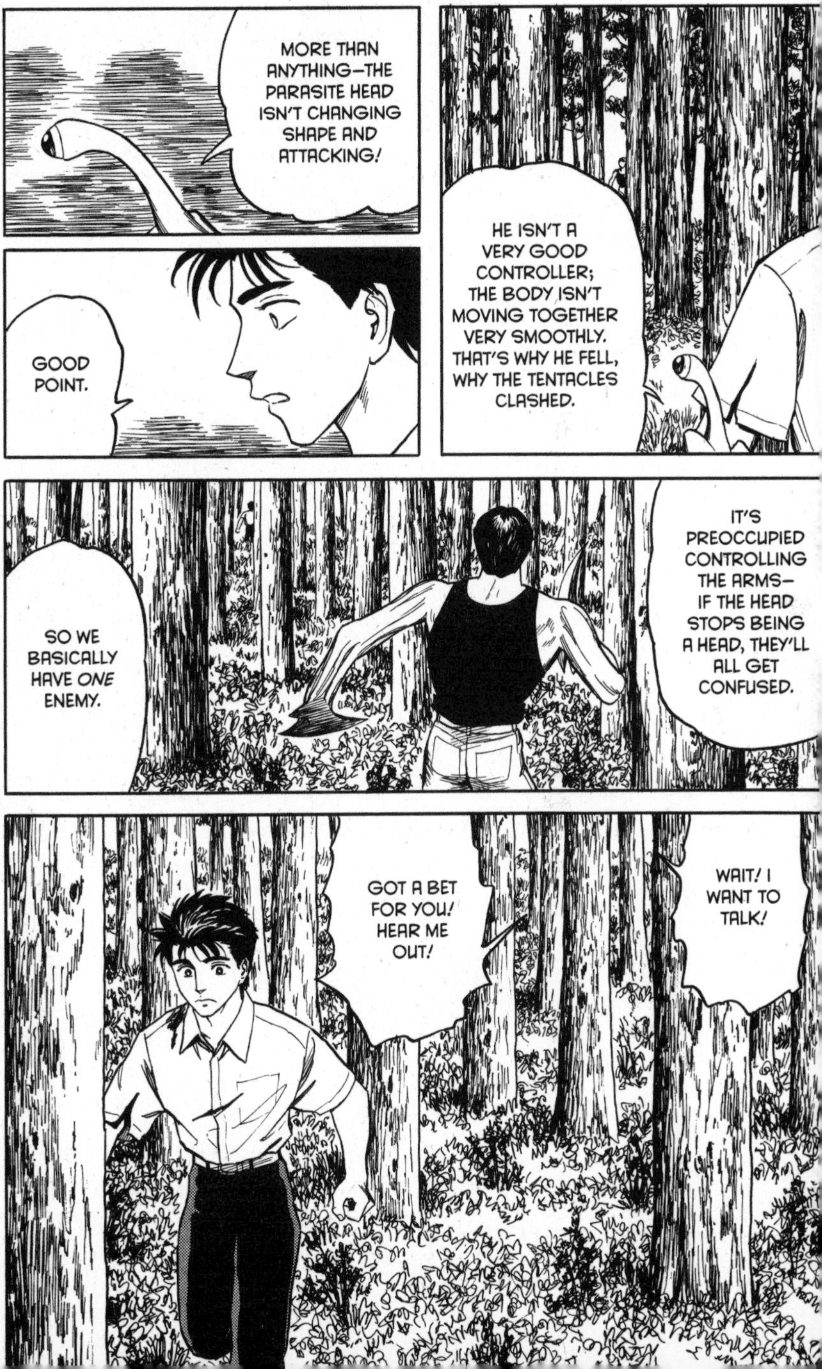
HE ISN'T A VERY GOOD CONTROLLER; THE BODY ISN'T MOVING TOGETHER VERY SMOOTHLY. THAT'S WHY HE FELL, WHY THE TENTACLES CLASHED.
MORE THAN ANYTHING—THE PARASITE HEAD ISN'T CHANGING SHAPE AND ATTACKING!
GOOD POINT.
IT'S PREOCCUPIED CONTROLLING THE ARMS— IF THE HEAD STOPS BEING A HEAD, THEY'LL ALL GET CONFUSED.
SO WE BASICALLY HAVE *ONE* ENEMY.
WAIT! I WANT TO TALK!
GOT A BET FOR YOU! HEAR ME OUT!

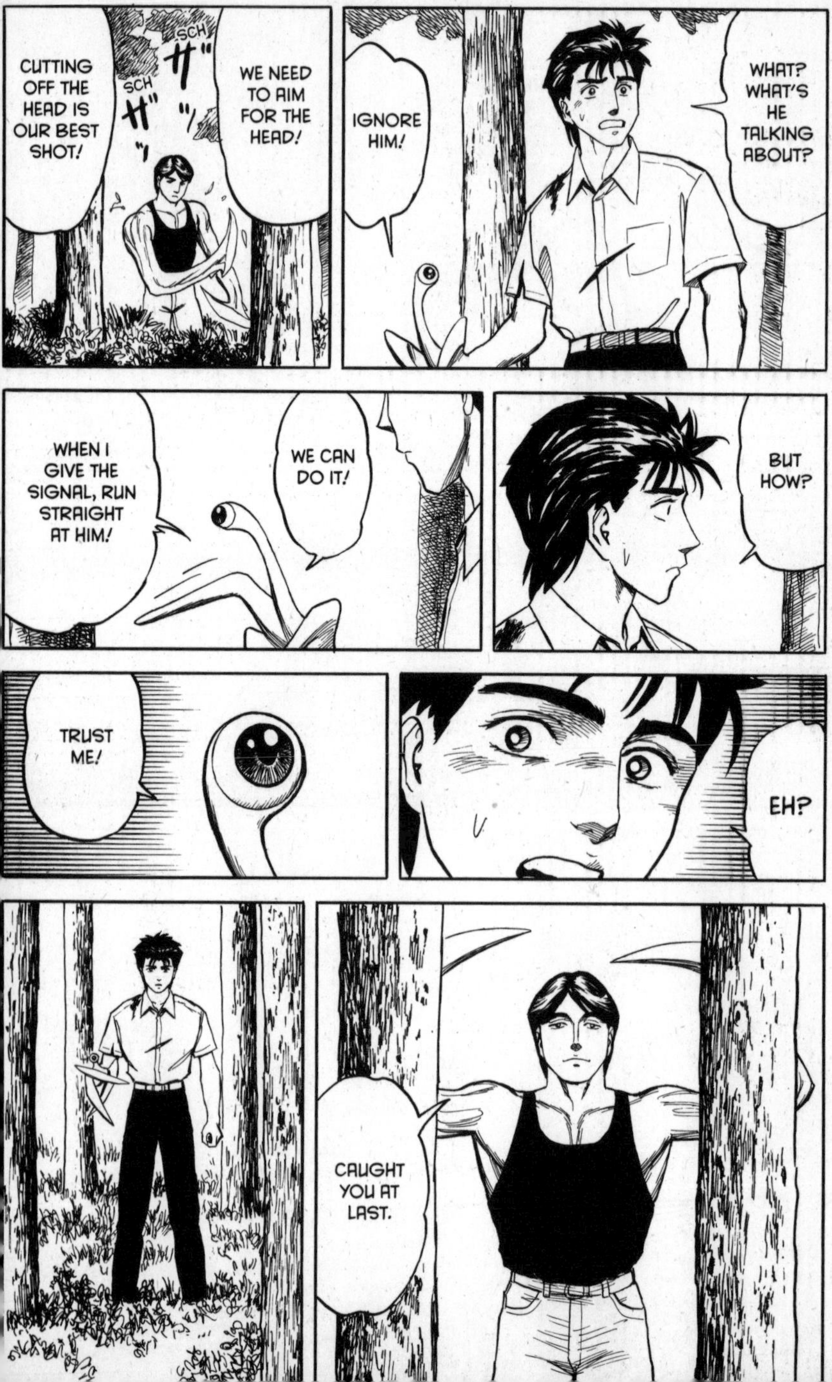
WHAT? WHAT'S HE TALKING ABOUT?
IGNORE HIM!
WE NEED TO AIM FOR THE HEAD!
SCH
SCH
CUTTING OFF THE HEAD IS OUR BEST SHOT!
BUT HOW?
WE CAN DO IT!
WHEN I GIVE THE SIGNAL, RUN STRAIGHT AT HIM!
EH?
TRUST ME!
CAUGHT YOU AT LAST.

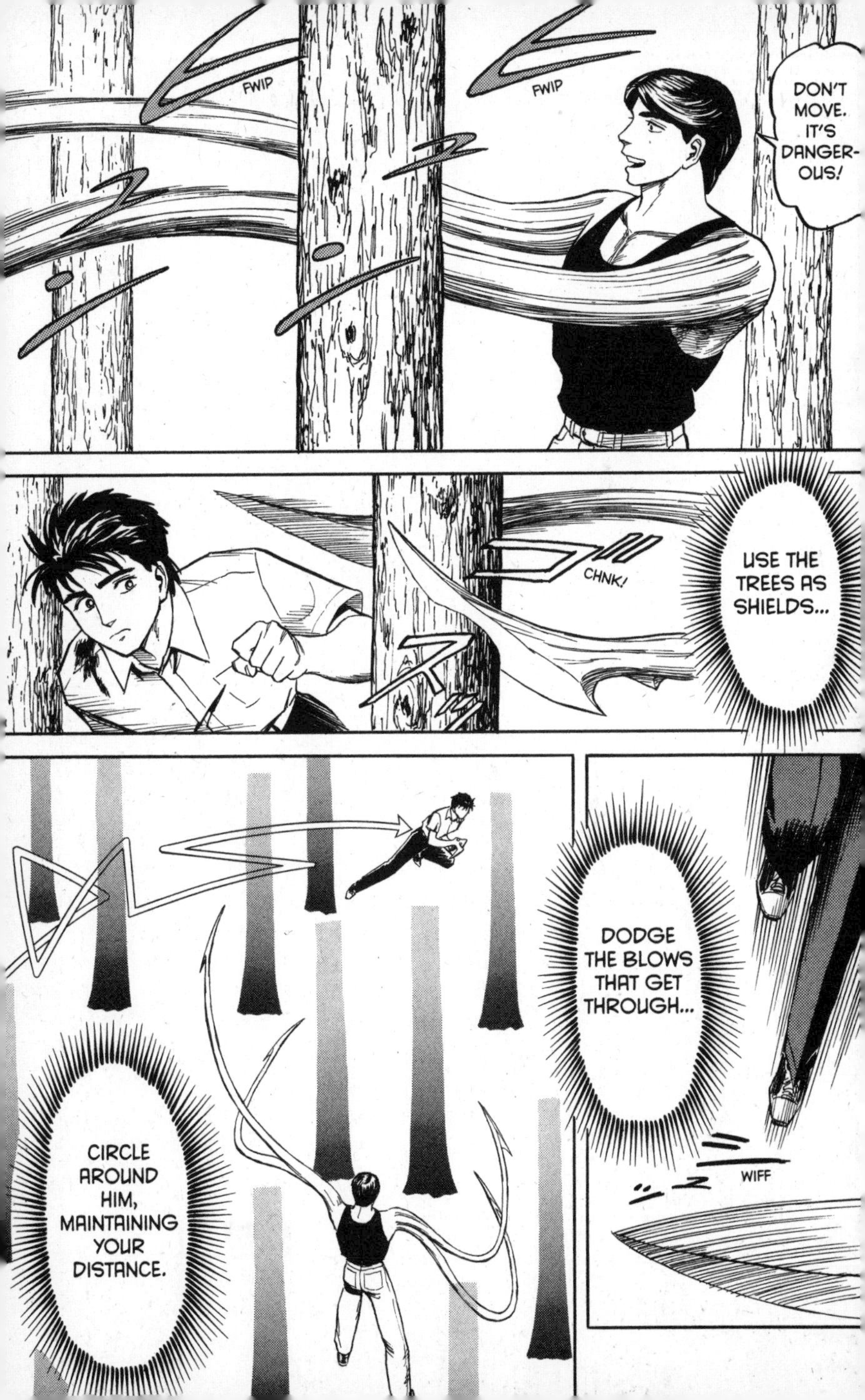
DON'T MOVE. IT'S DANGER-OUS!
FWIP
FWIP
USE THE TREES AS SHIELDS...
CHNK!
DODGE THE BLOWS THAT GET THROUGH...
WIFF
CIRCLE AROUND HIM, MAINTAINING YOUR DISTANCE.

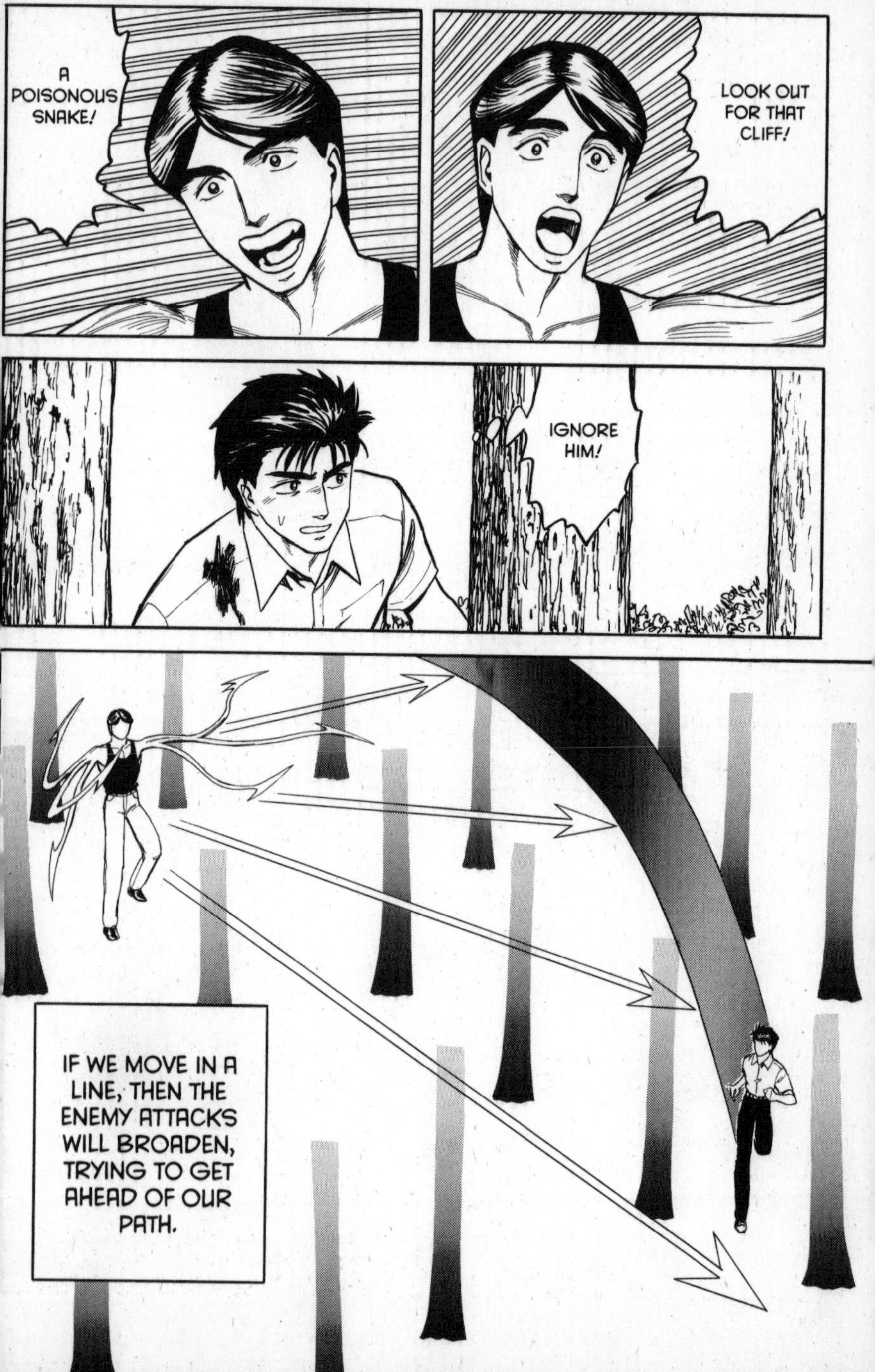
LOOK OUT FOR THAT CLIFF!
A POISONOUS SNAKE!
IGNORE HIM!
IF WE MOVE IN A LINE, THEN THE ENEMY ATTACKS WILL BROADEN, TRYING TO GET AHEAD OF OUR PATH.

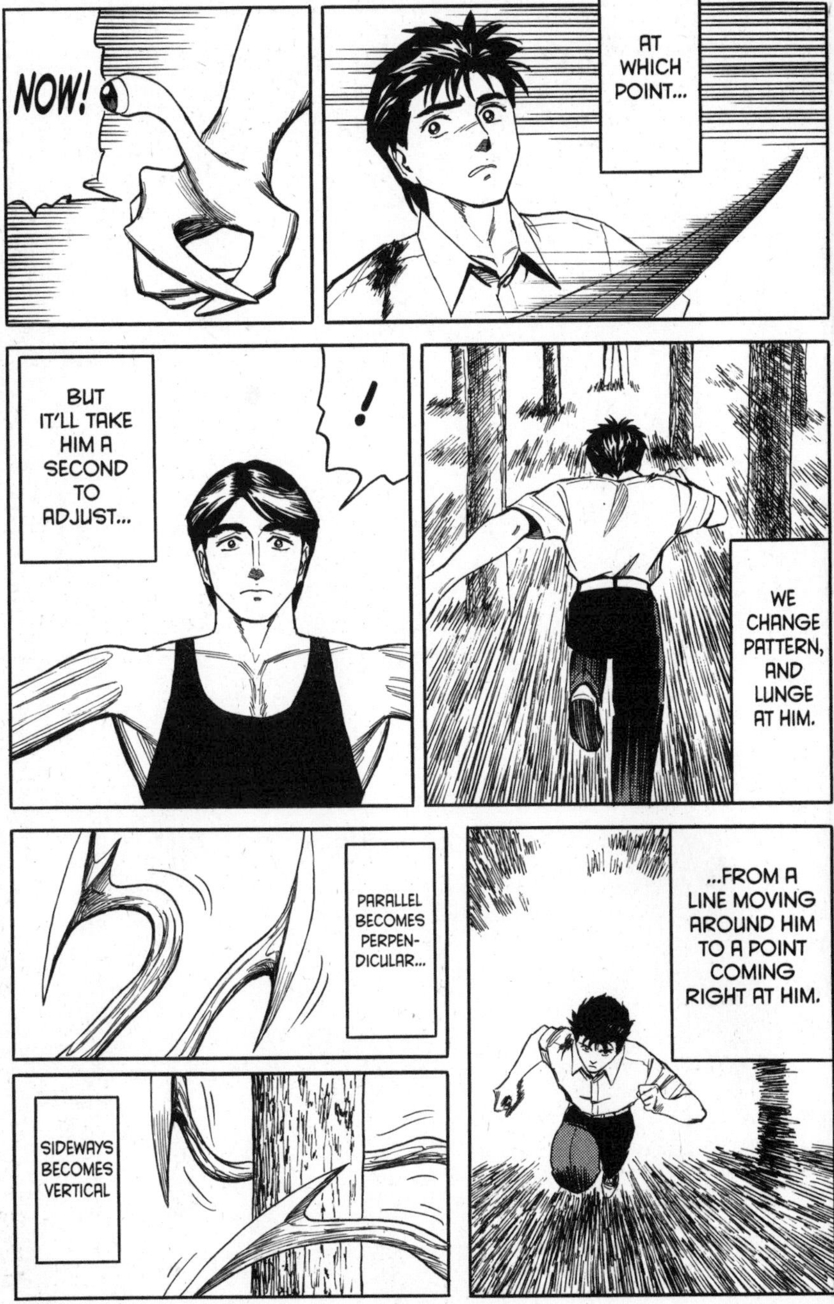
AT WHICH POINT...
NOW!
WE CHANGE PATTERN, AND LUNGE AT HIM.
!
BUT IT'LL TAKE HIM A SECOND TO ADJUST...
...FROM A LINE MOVING AROUND HIM TO A POINT COMING RIGHT AT HIM.
PARALLEL BECOMES PERPEN-DICULAR...
SIDEWAYS BECOMES VERTICAL

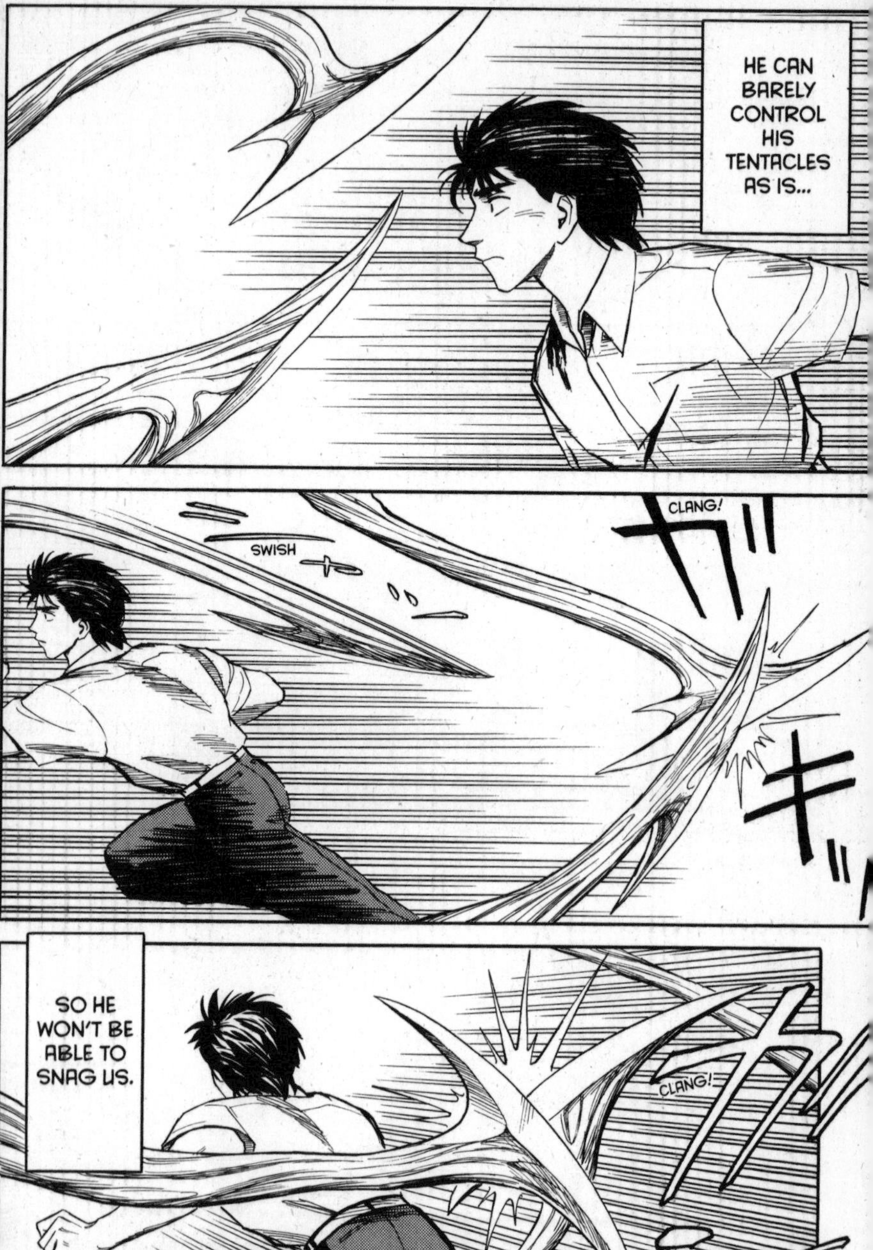
HE CAN BARELY CONTROL HIS TENTACLES AS IS...
CLANG!
SWISH
CLANG!
SO HE WON'T BE ABLE TO SNAG US.

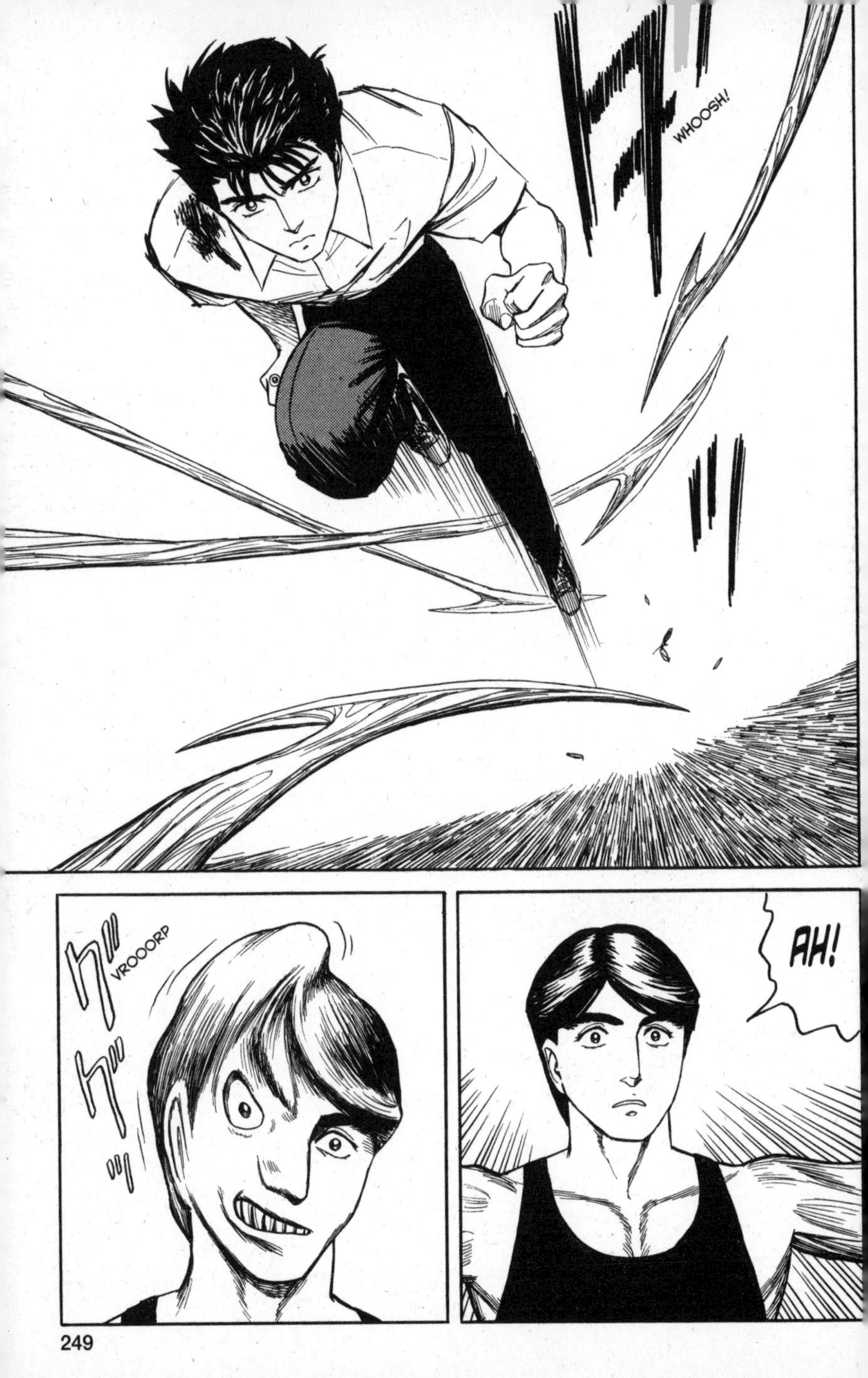
WHOOSH!
AH!
VROOORP

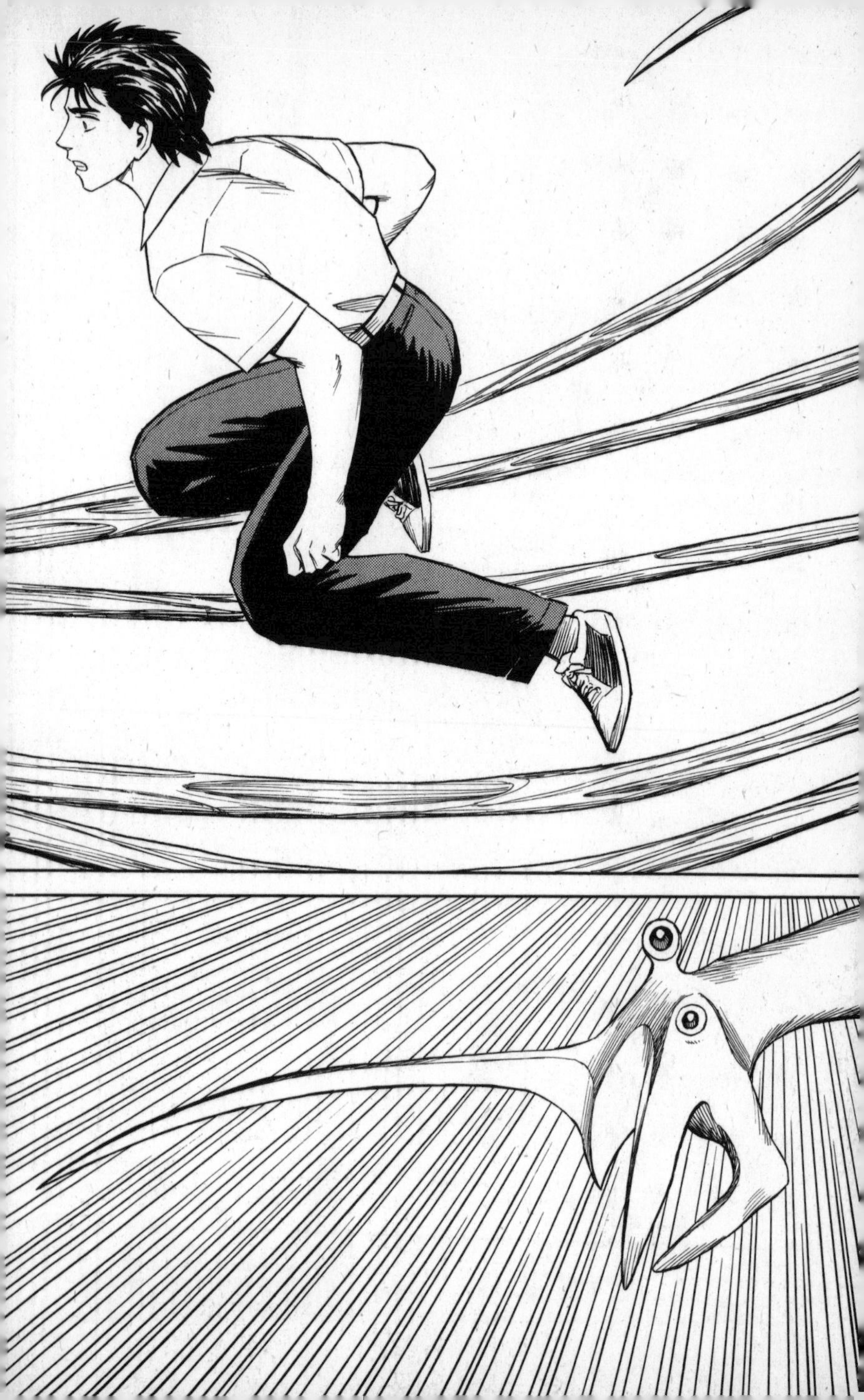

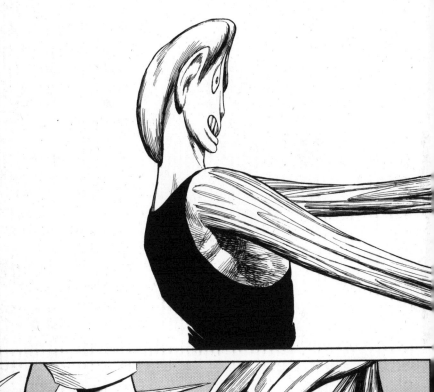
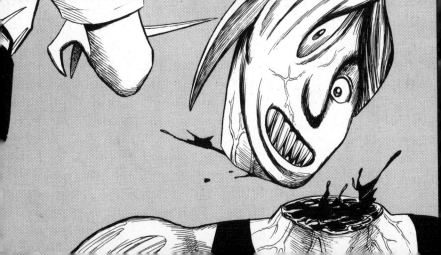

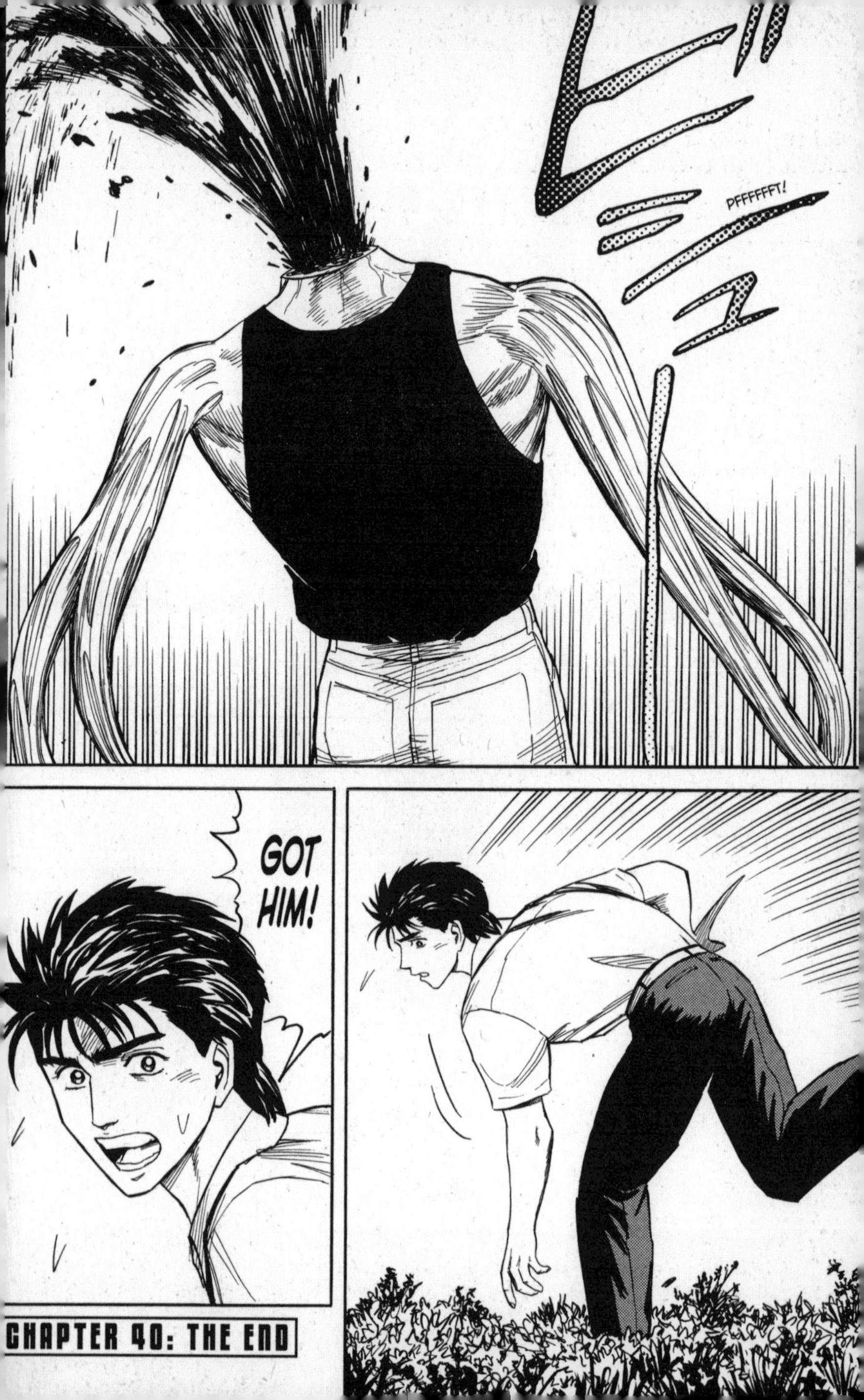
PFFFFFFT!
GOT HIM!
CHAPTER 40: THE END

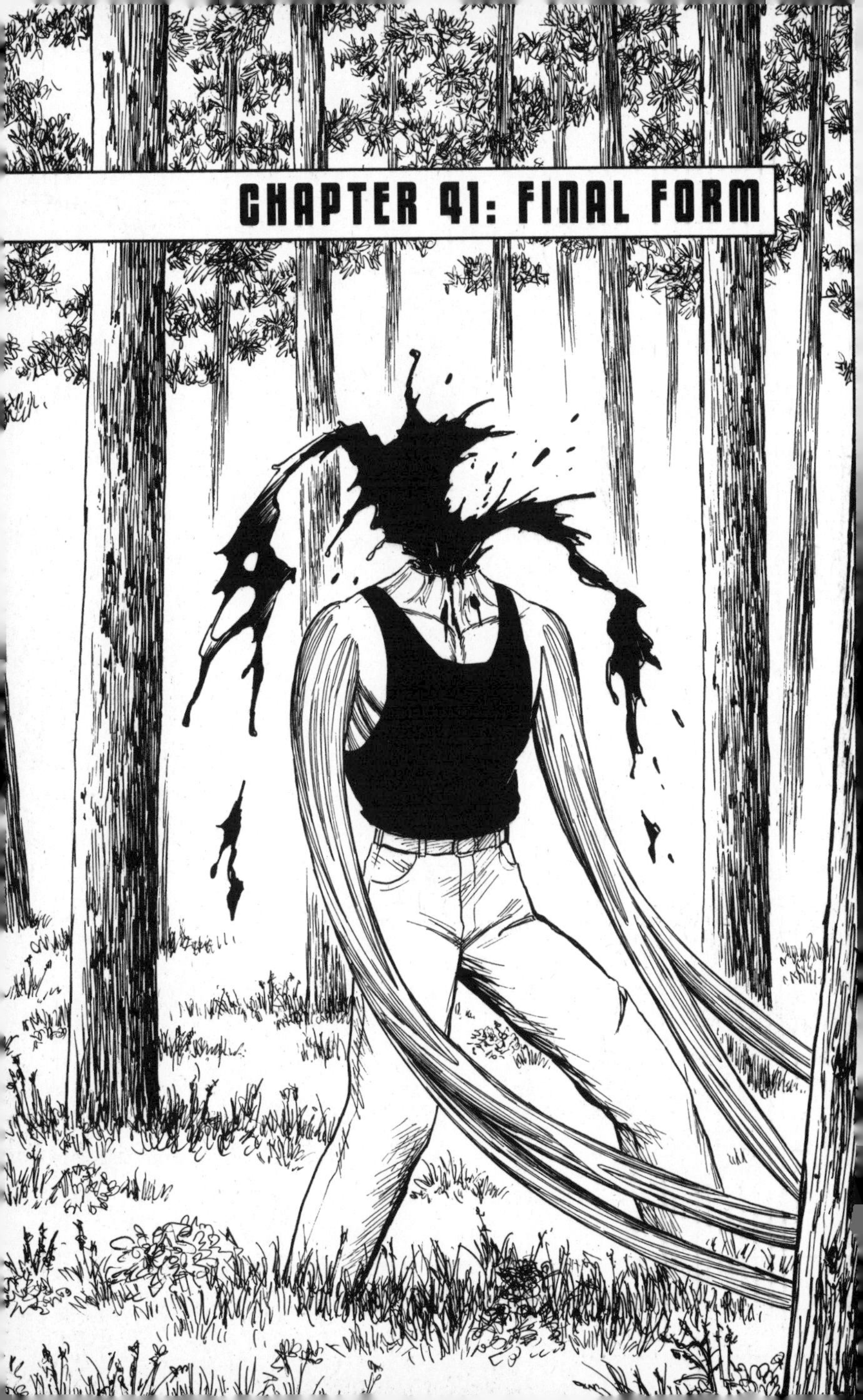
CHAPTER 41: FINAL FORM

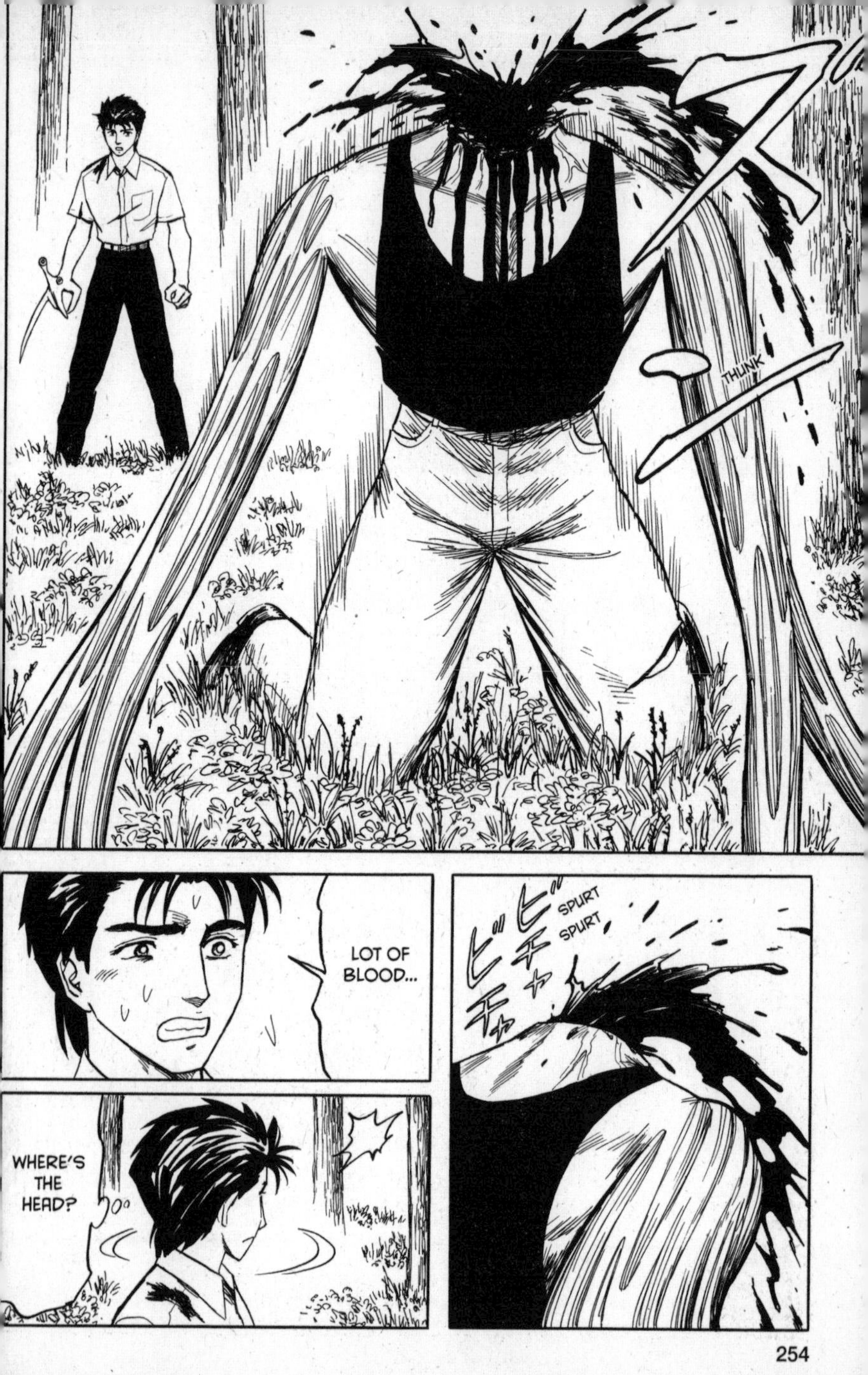
THUNK
ビチャ ビチャ
SPURT SPURT
LOT OF BLOOD...
WHERE'S THE HEAD?

AH!

MM?

AH......

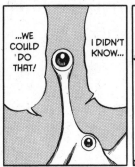

...WE COULD DO THAT!

I DIDN'T KNOW...

OH...

WHAT?

VRROO...

VROOOP

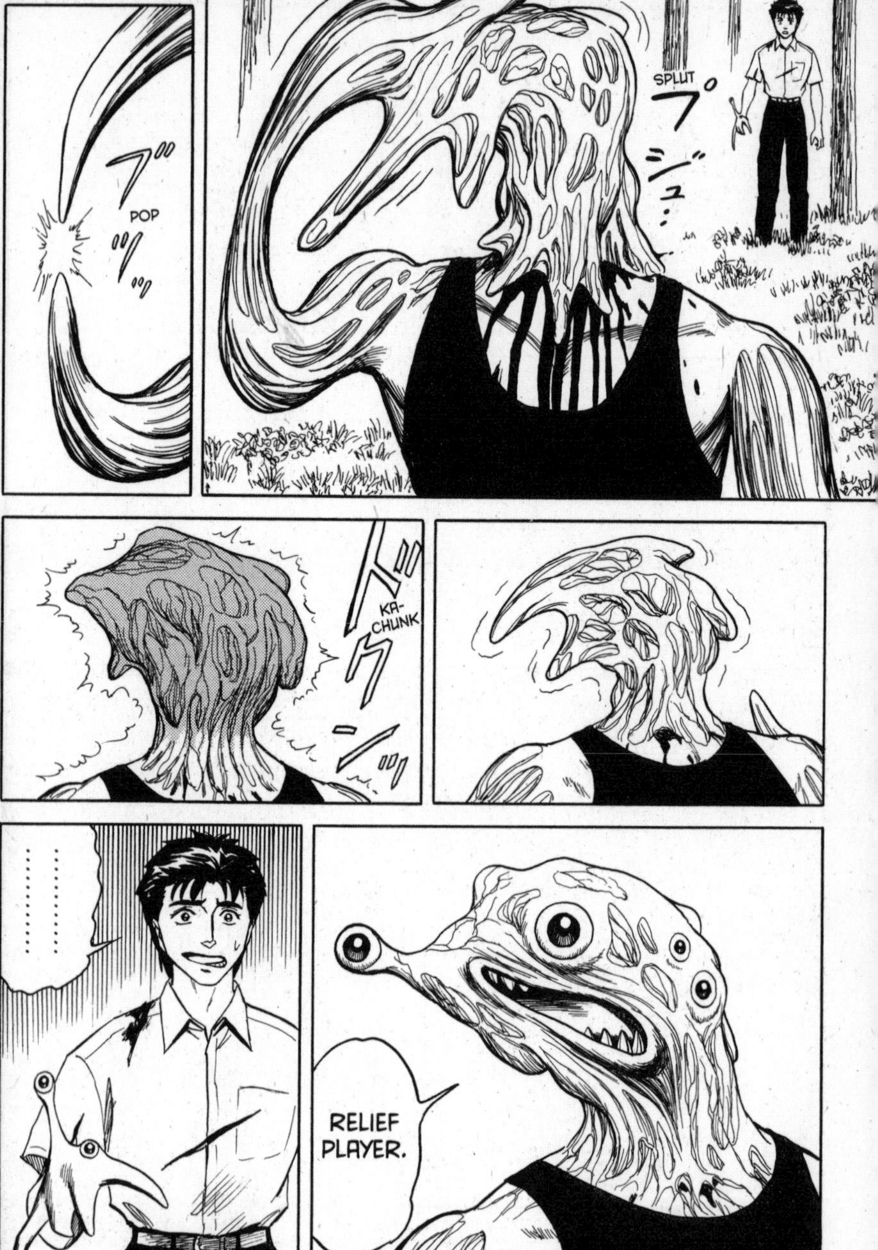
SPLUT
POP
KA-CHUNK
RELIEF PLAYER.
......

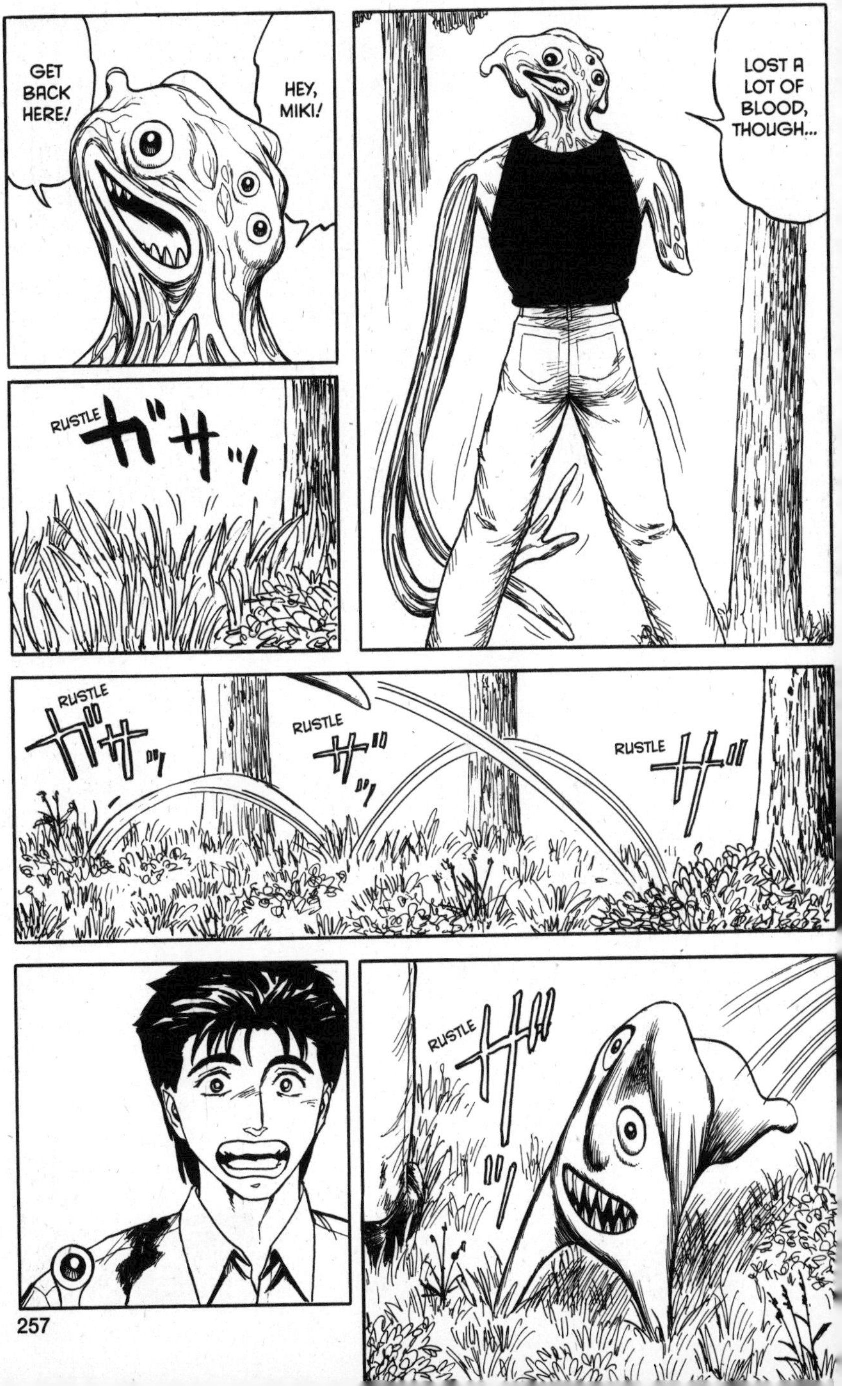
LOST A LOT OF BLOOD, THOUGH...
HEY, MIKI!
GET BACK HERE!
RUSTLE
ガサッ
RUSTLE
ザッ
RUSTLE
ザッ
RUSTLE
ガサッ
RUSTLE
ザッ

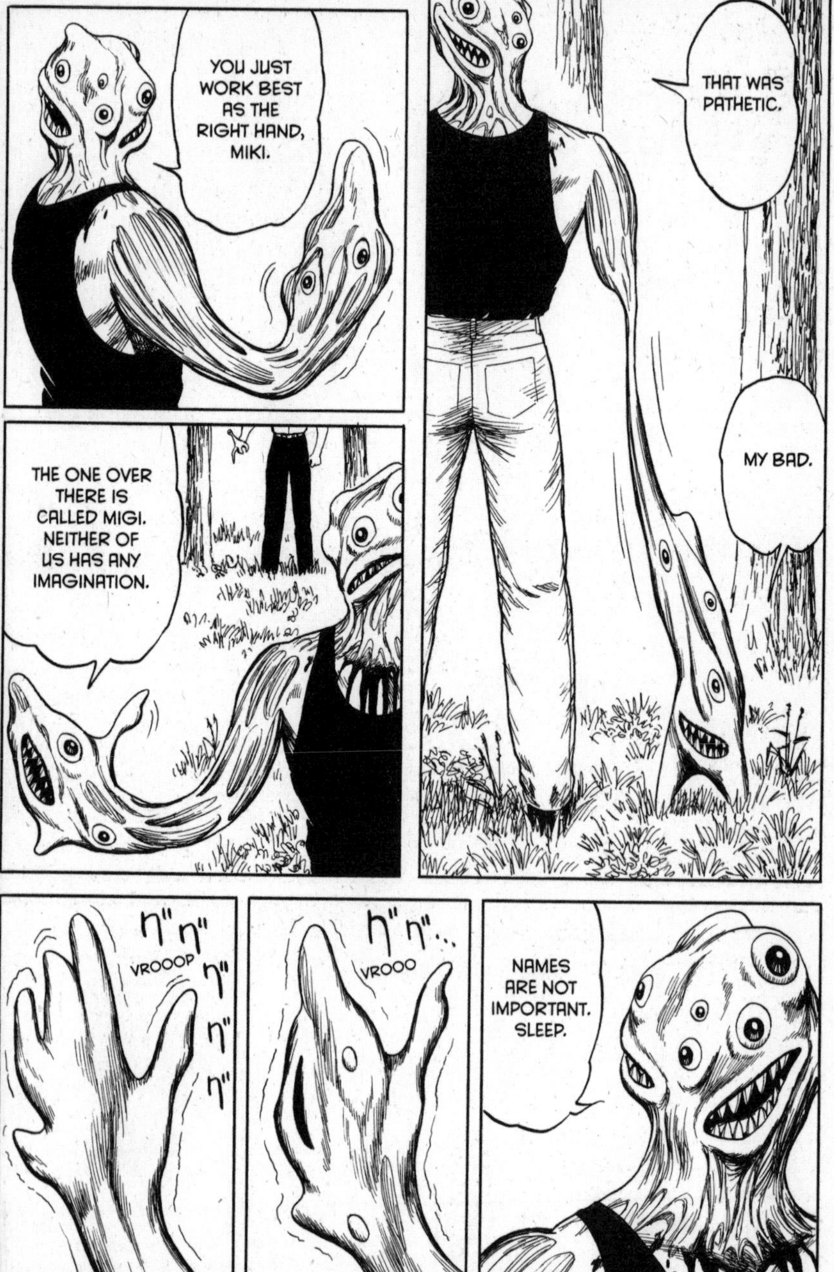
THAT WAS PATHETIC.
MY BAD.
YOU JUST WORK BEST AS THE RIGHT HAND, MIKI.
THE ONE OVER THERE IS CALLED MIGI. NEITHER OF US HAS ANY IMAGINATION.
NAMES ARE NOT IMPORTANT. SLEEP.
VROOO
VROOOP

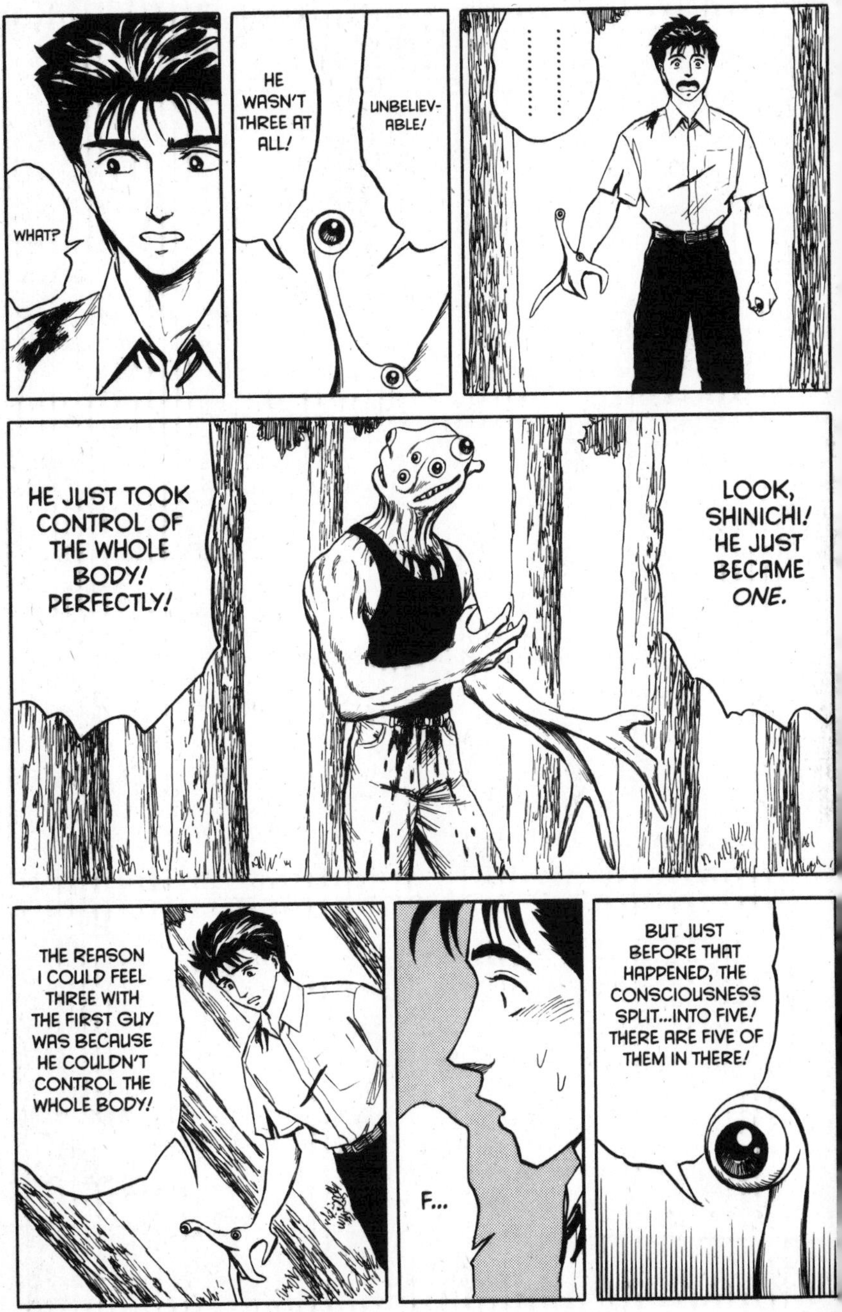
......
UNBELIEVABLE!
HE WASN'T THREE AT ALL!
WHAT?
LOOK, SHINICHI! HE JUST BECAME *ONE.*
HE JUST TOOK CONTROL OF THE WHOLE BODY! PERFECTLY!
BUT JUST BEFORE THAT HAPPENED, THE CONSCIOUSNESS SPLIT...INTO FIVE! THERE ARE FIVE OF THEM IN THERE!
F...
THE REASON I COULD FEEL THREE WITH THE FIRST GUY WAS BECAUSE HE COULDN'T CONTROL THE WHOLE BODY!

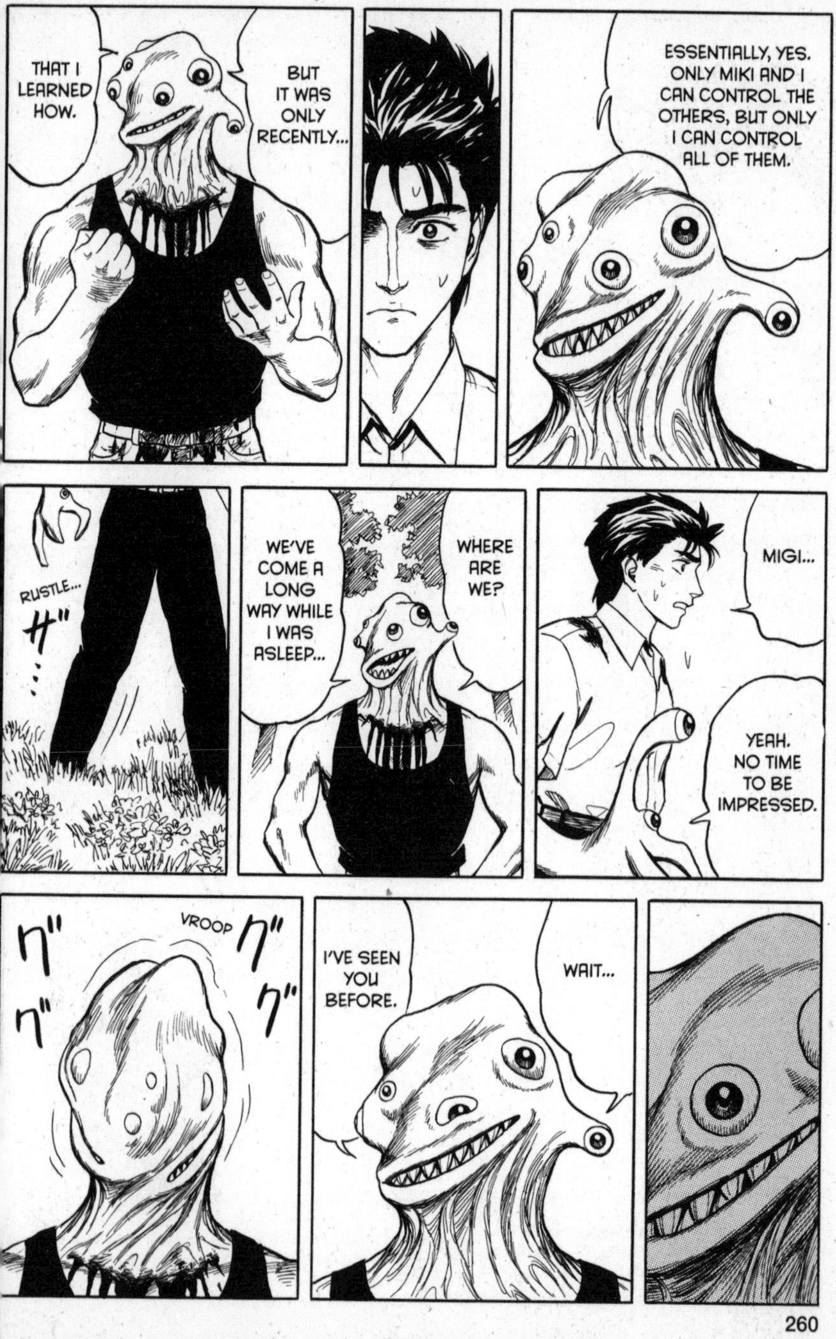
ESSENTIALLY, YES. ONLY MIKI AND I CAN CONTROL THE OTHERS, BUT ONLY I CAN CONTROL ALL OF THEM.
BUT IT WAS ONLY RECENTLY...
THAT I LEARNED HOW.
MIGI...
YEAH. NO TIME TO BE IMPRESSED.
WHERE ARE WE?
WE'VE COME A LONG WAY WHILE I WAS ASLEEP...
RUSTLE...
ザ...
WAIT...
I'VE SEEN YOU BEFORE.
VROOP
グ グ グ グ

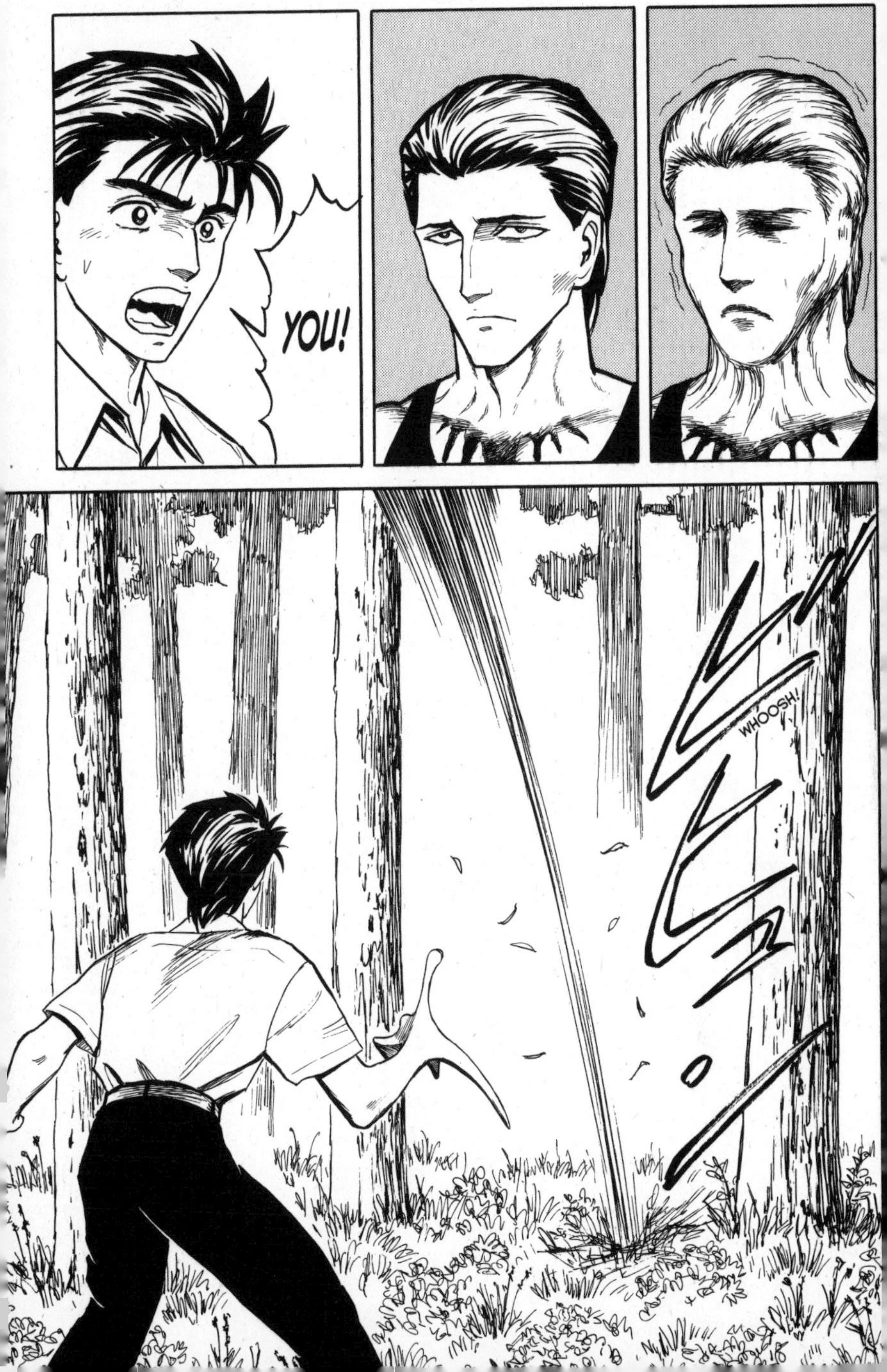
YOU!
WHOOSH!

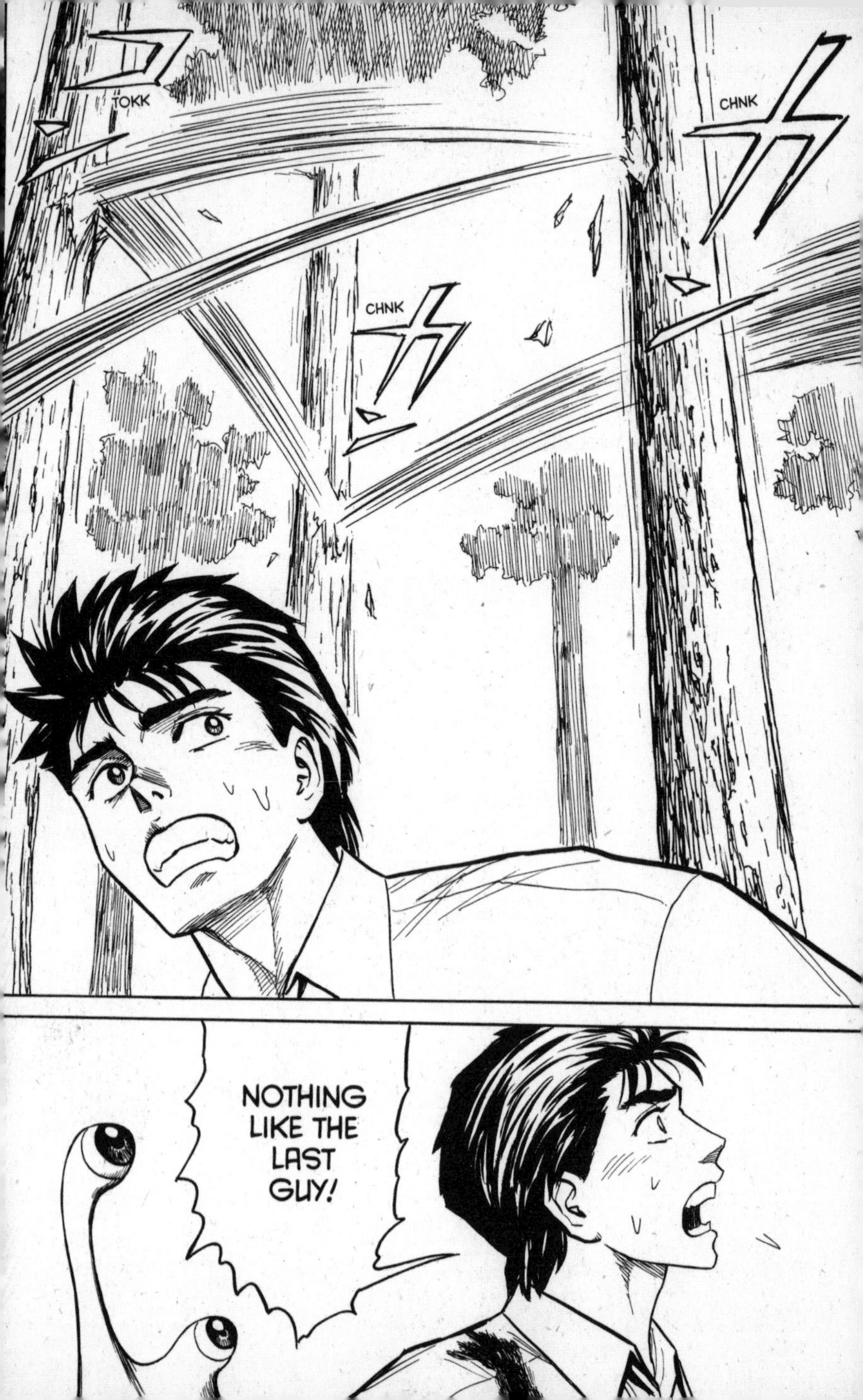

CHNK
CHNK
TOKK
NOTHING LIKE THE LAST GUY!

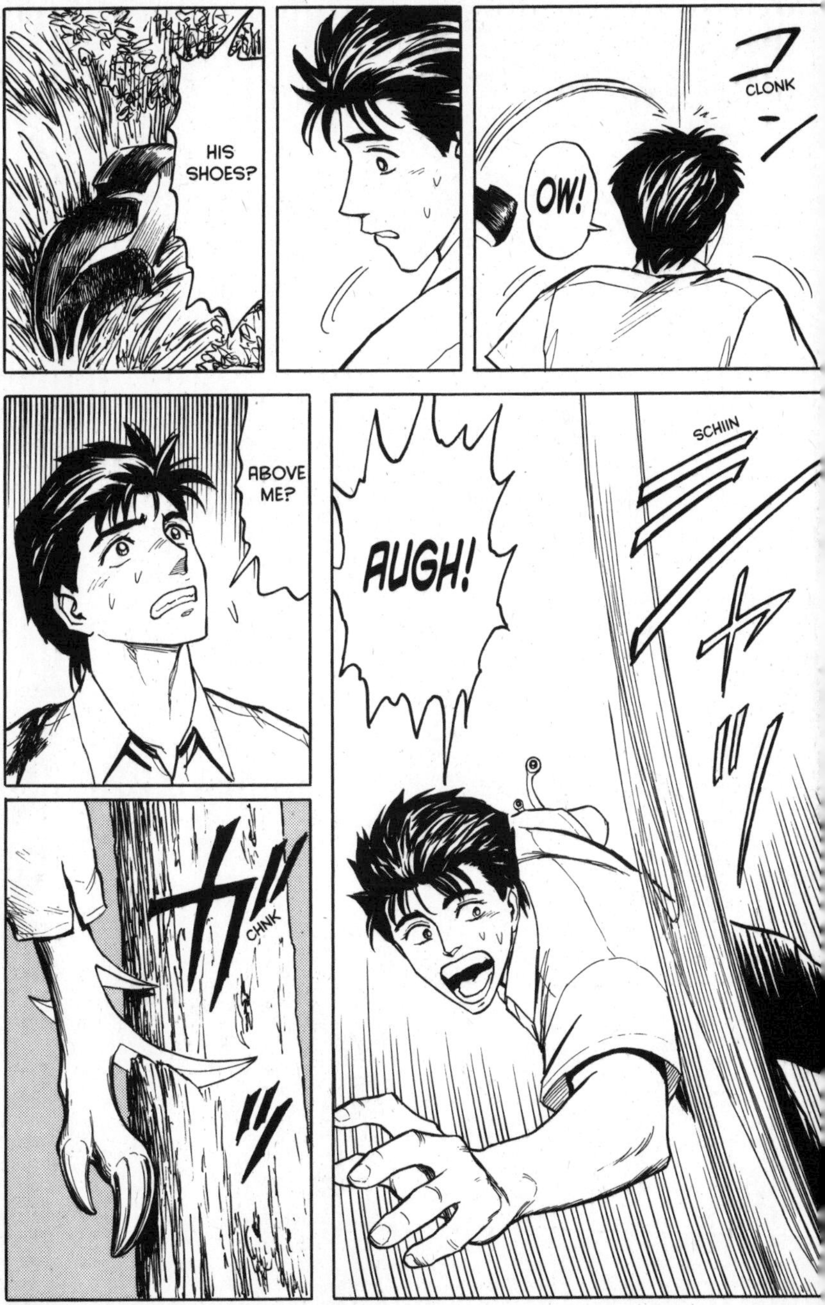
CLONK
OW!
HIS SHOES?
SCHIIN
AUGH!
ABOVE ME?
CHNK

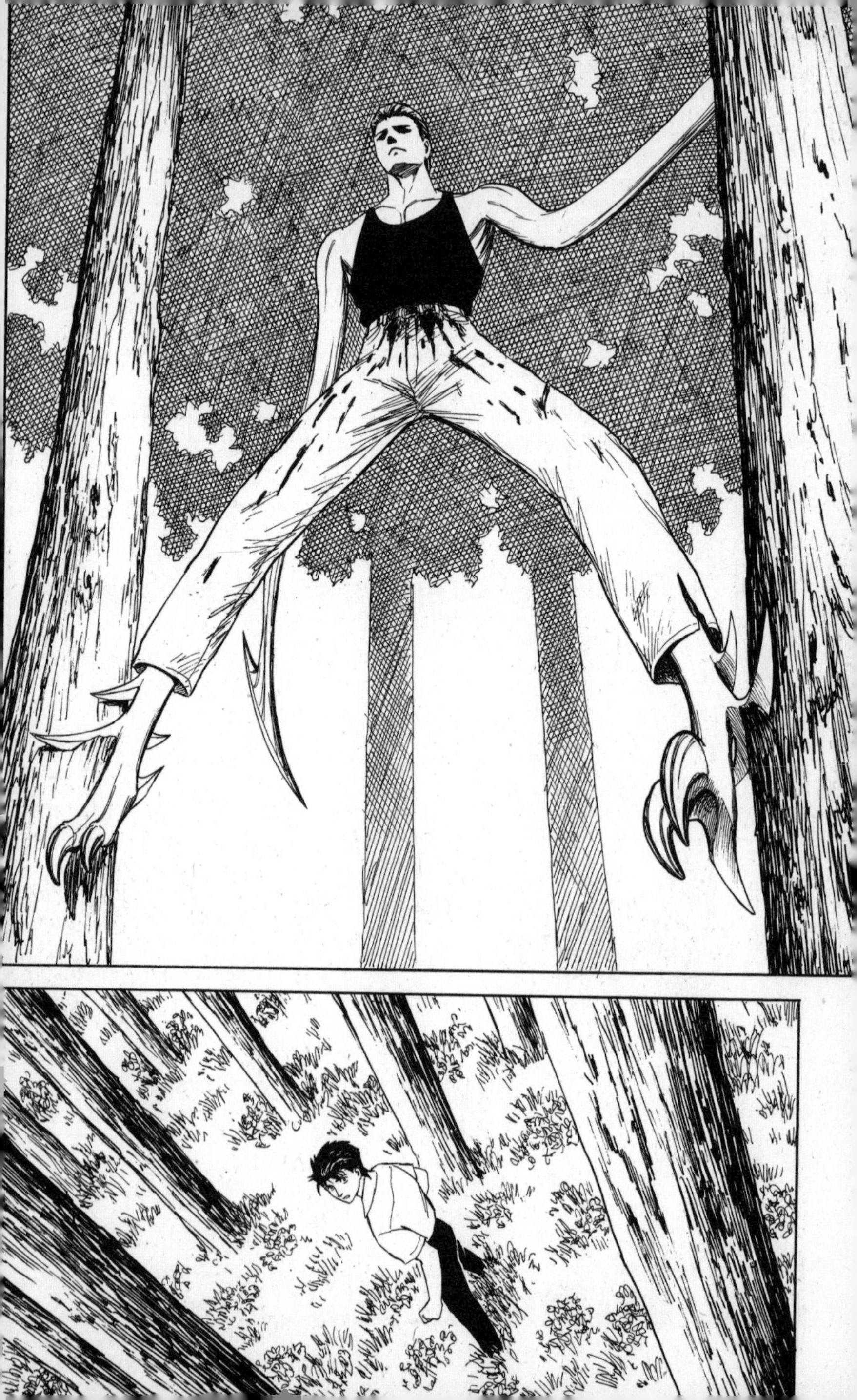

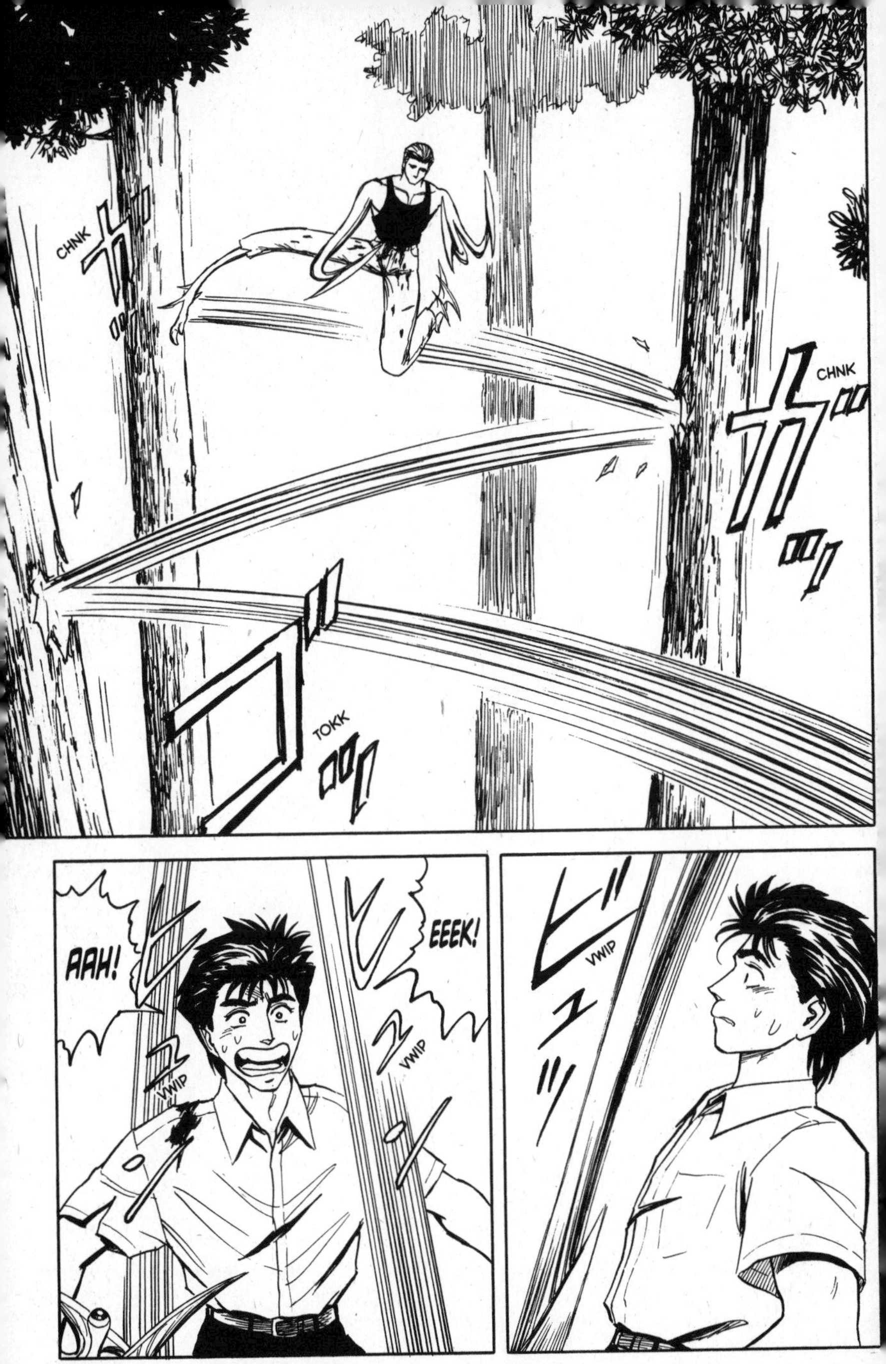
CHNK
CHNK
TOKK
VWIP
EEEK!
VWIP
AAH!
VWIP

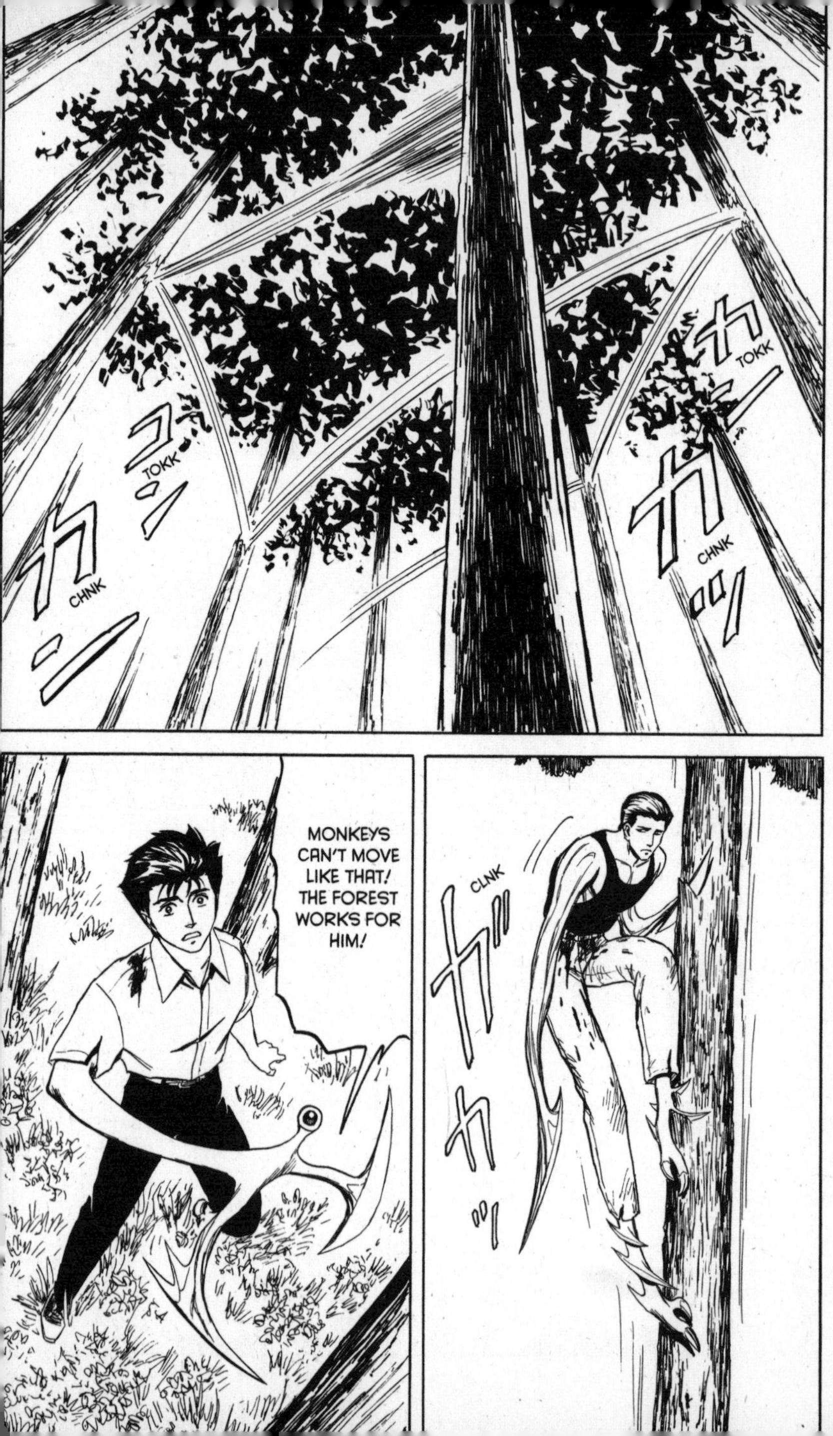
TOKK
CHNK
TOKK
CHNK
CLNK
MONKEYS CAN'T MOVE LIKE THAT! THE FOREST WORKS FOR HIM!

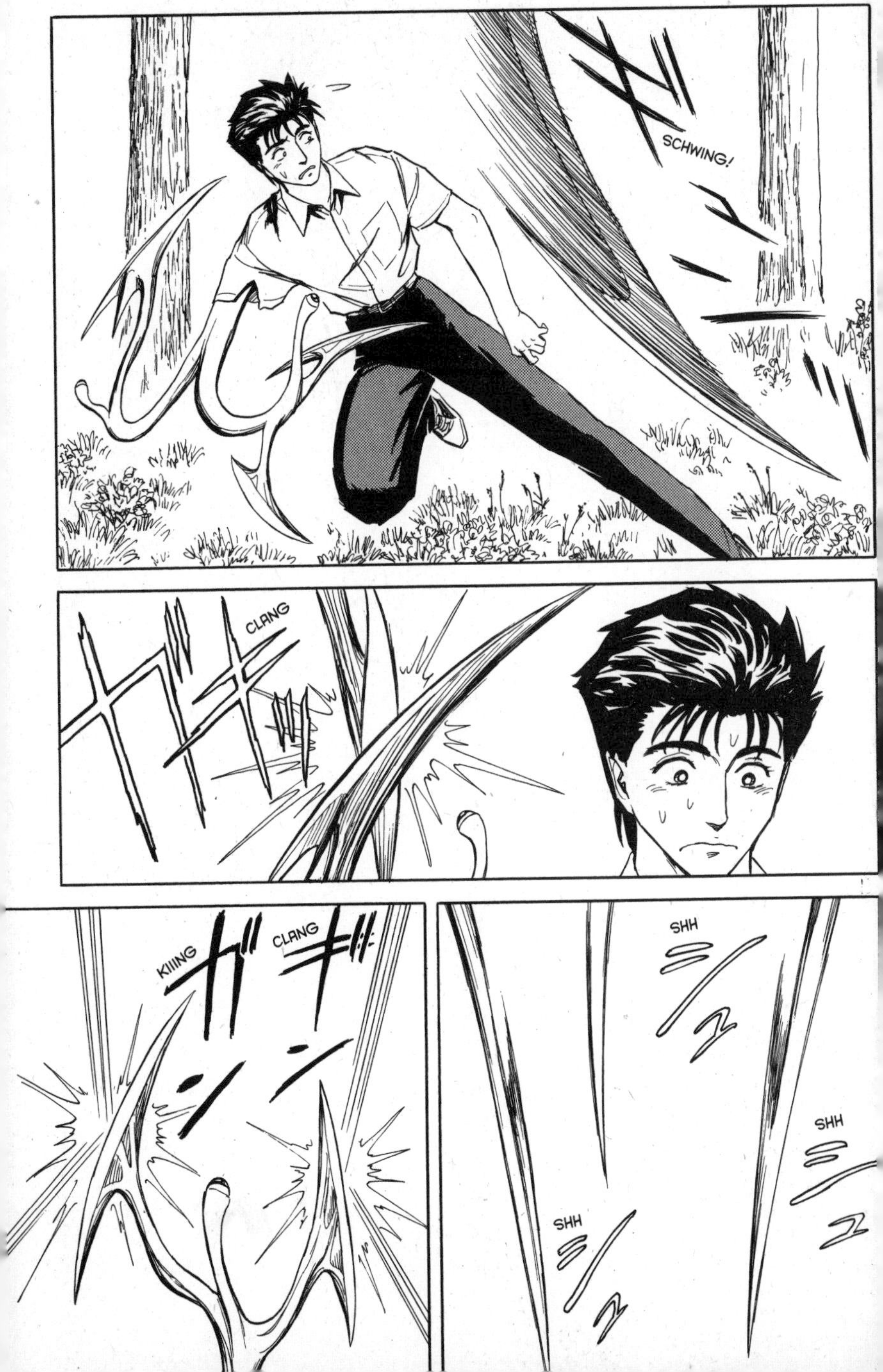
SCHWING!
CLANG
SHH
SHH
SHH
CLANG
KIIING

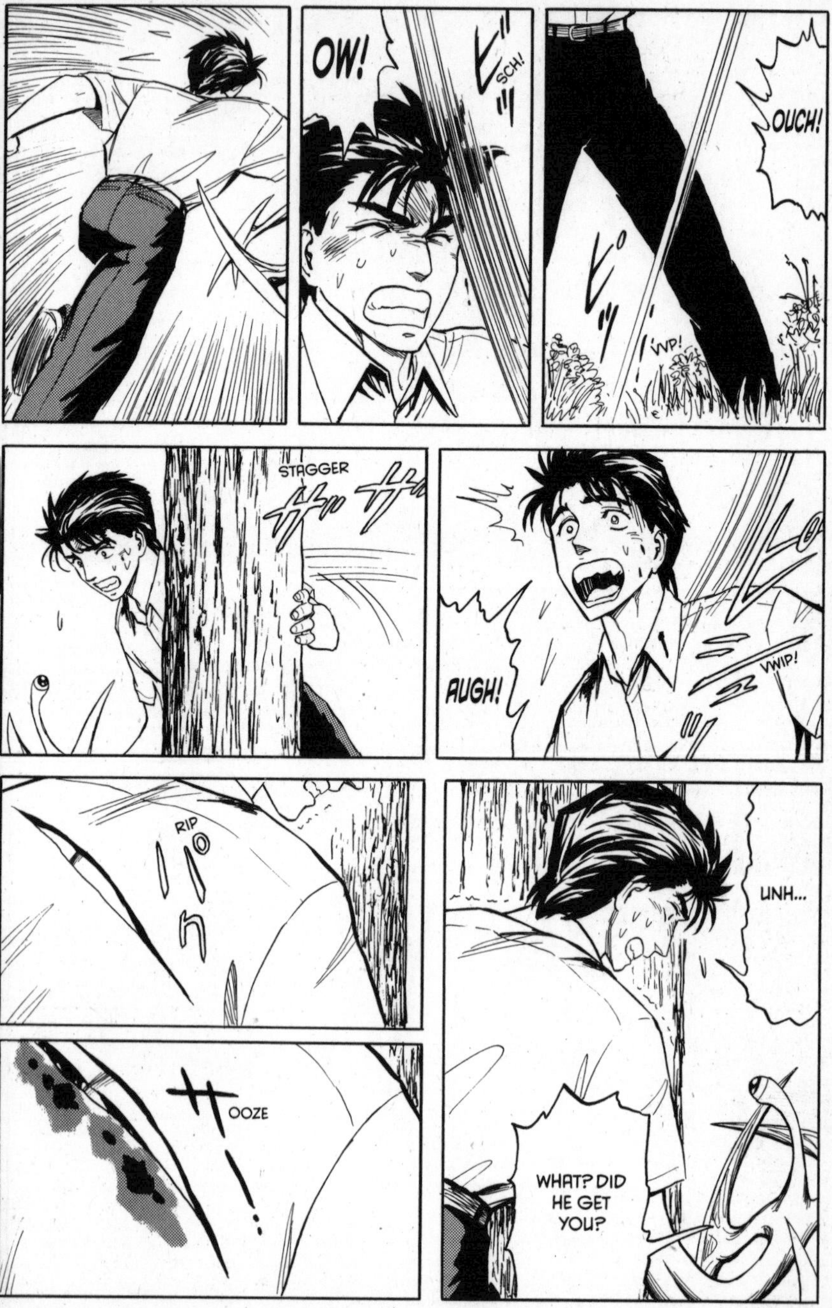
OUCH!
VVP!
OW!
SCH!
AUGH!
VWIP!
STAGGER
UNH...
WHAT? DID HE GET YOU?
RIP
OOZE

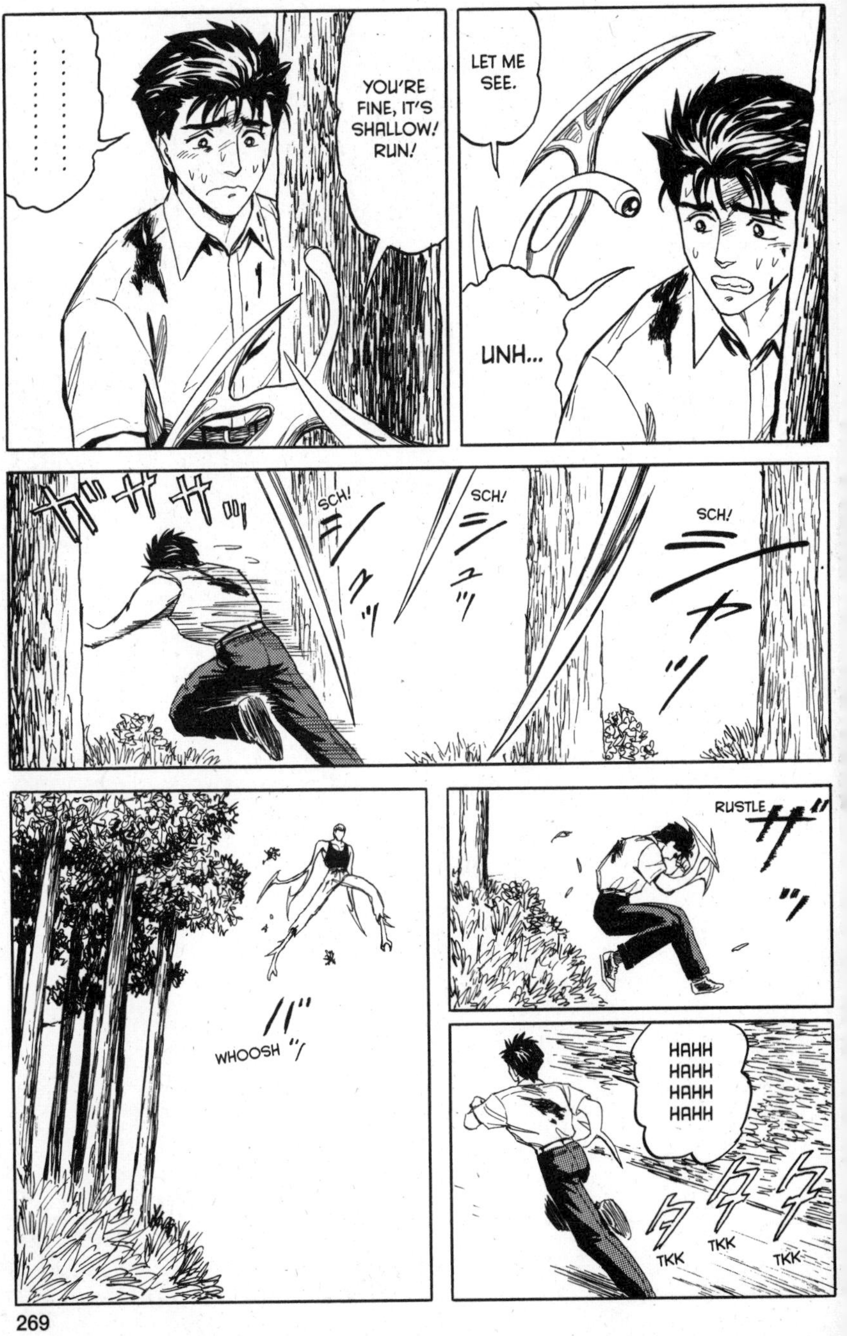
LET ME SEE.
UNH...
YOU'RE FINE, IT'S SHALLOW! RUN!
......
SCH!
SCH!
SCH!
RUSTLE
HAHH
HAHH
HAHH
HAHH
TKK
TKK
TKK
WHOOSH

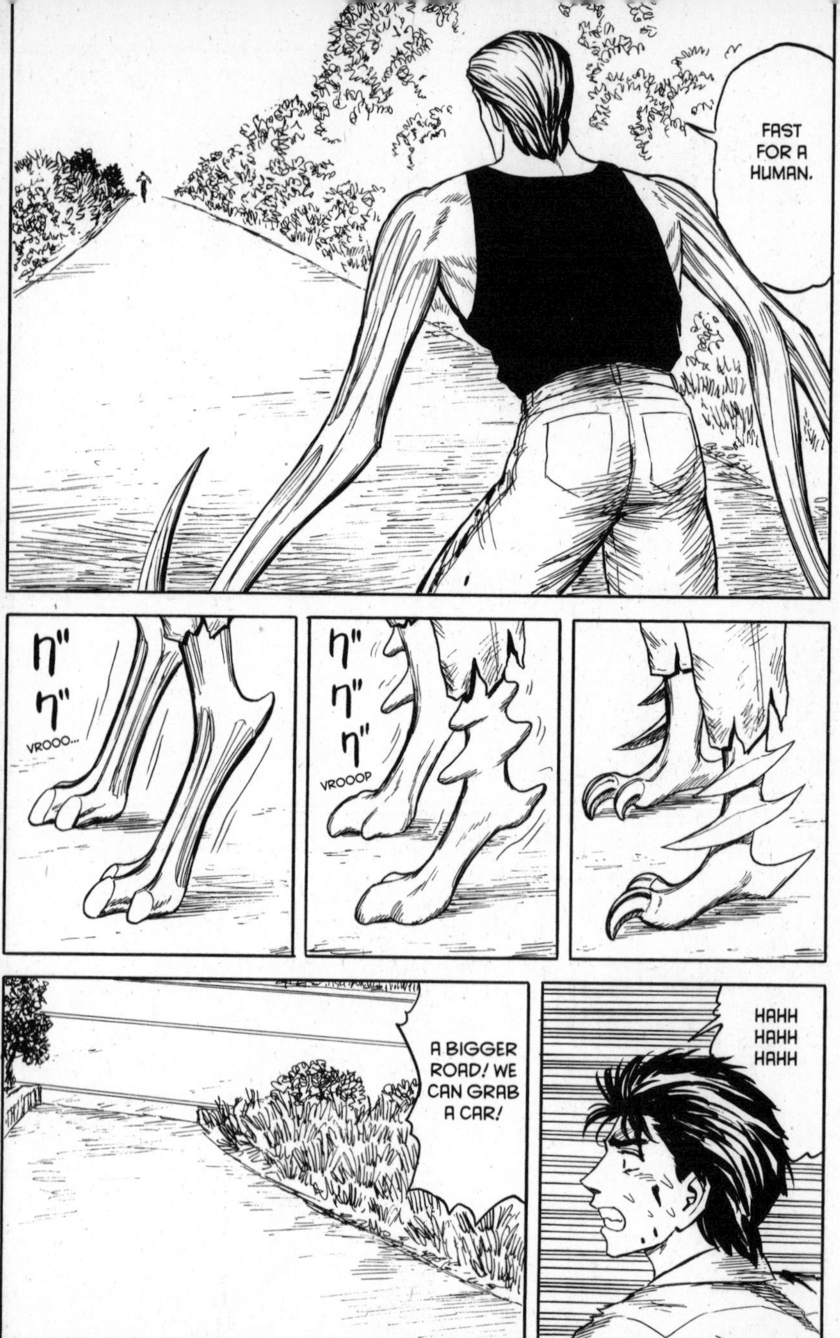
FAST FOR A HUMAN.
グググ
VROOOP
ググ
VROOO...
HAHH HAHH HAHH
A BIGGER ROAD! WE CAN GRAB A CAR!

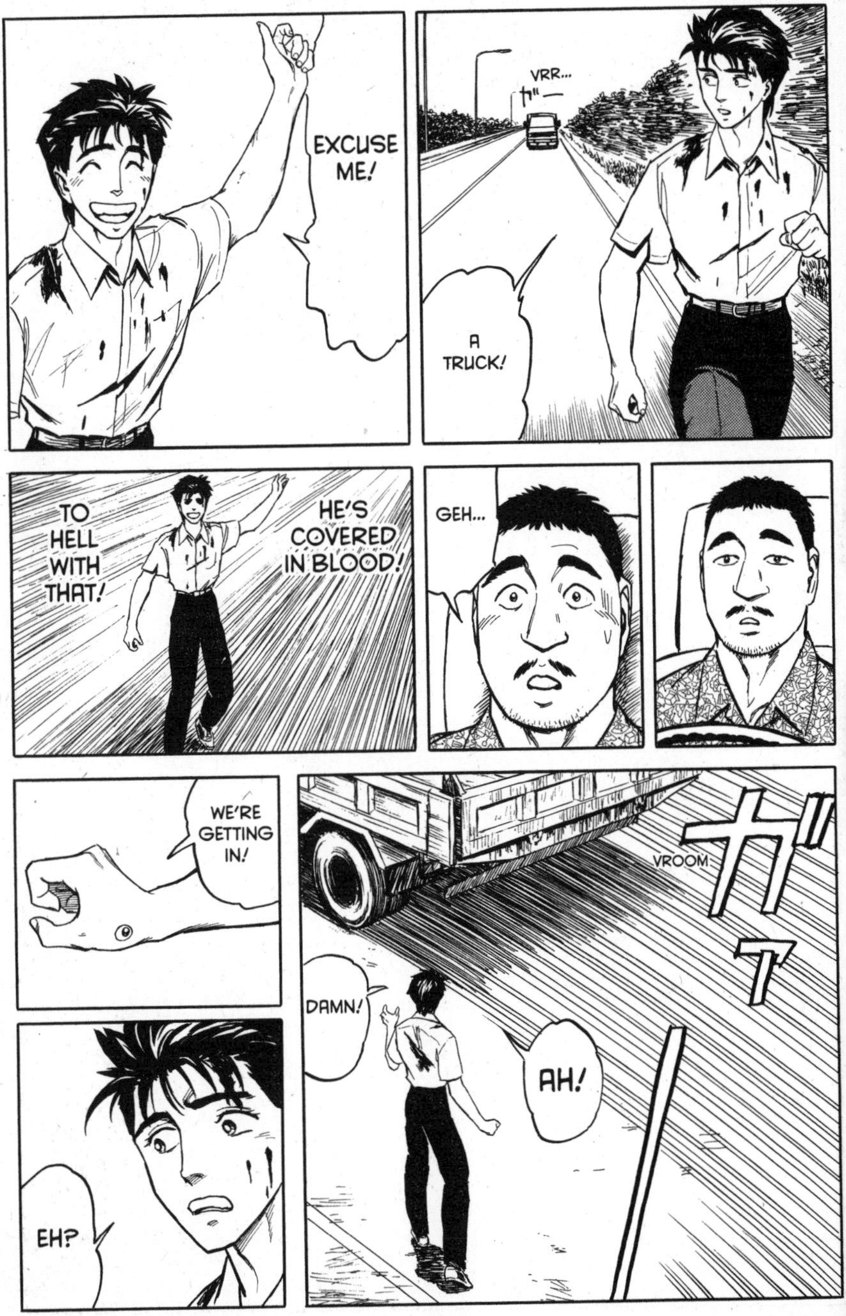
VRR...
ガー
A TRUCK!
EXCUSE ME!
GEH...
HE'S COVERED IN BLOOD!
TO HELL WITH THAT!
VROOM
ガァ
DAMN!
AH!
WE'RE GETTING IN!
EH?

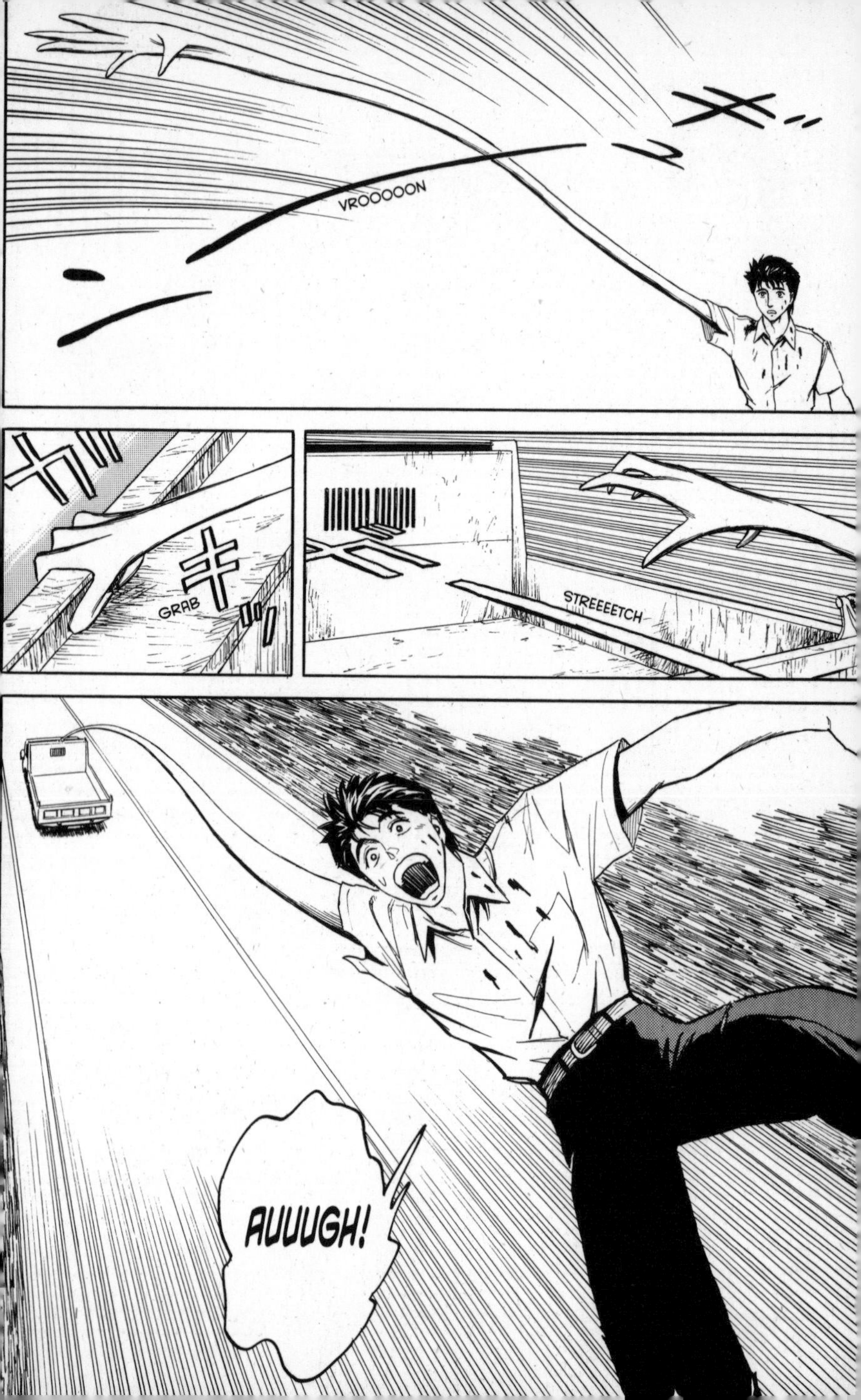
VROOOOON
STREEEETCH
GRAB
AUUUGH!

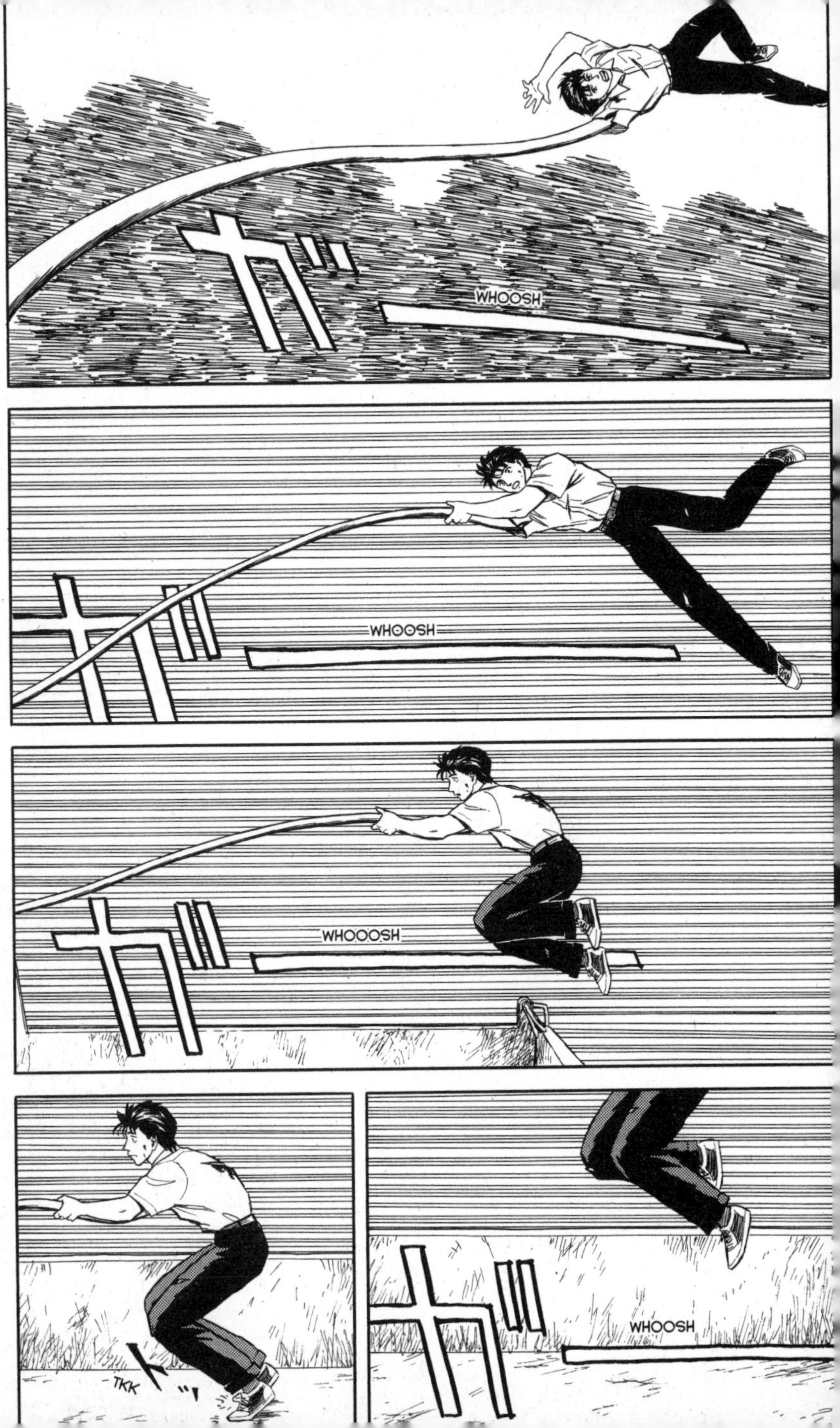
WHOOSH
WHOOSH
WHOOOSH
WHOOSH
TKK

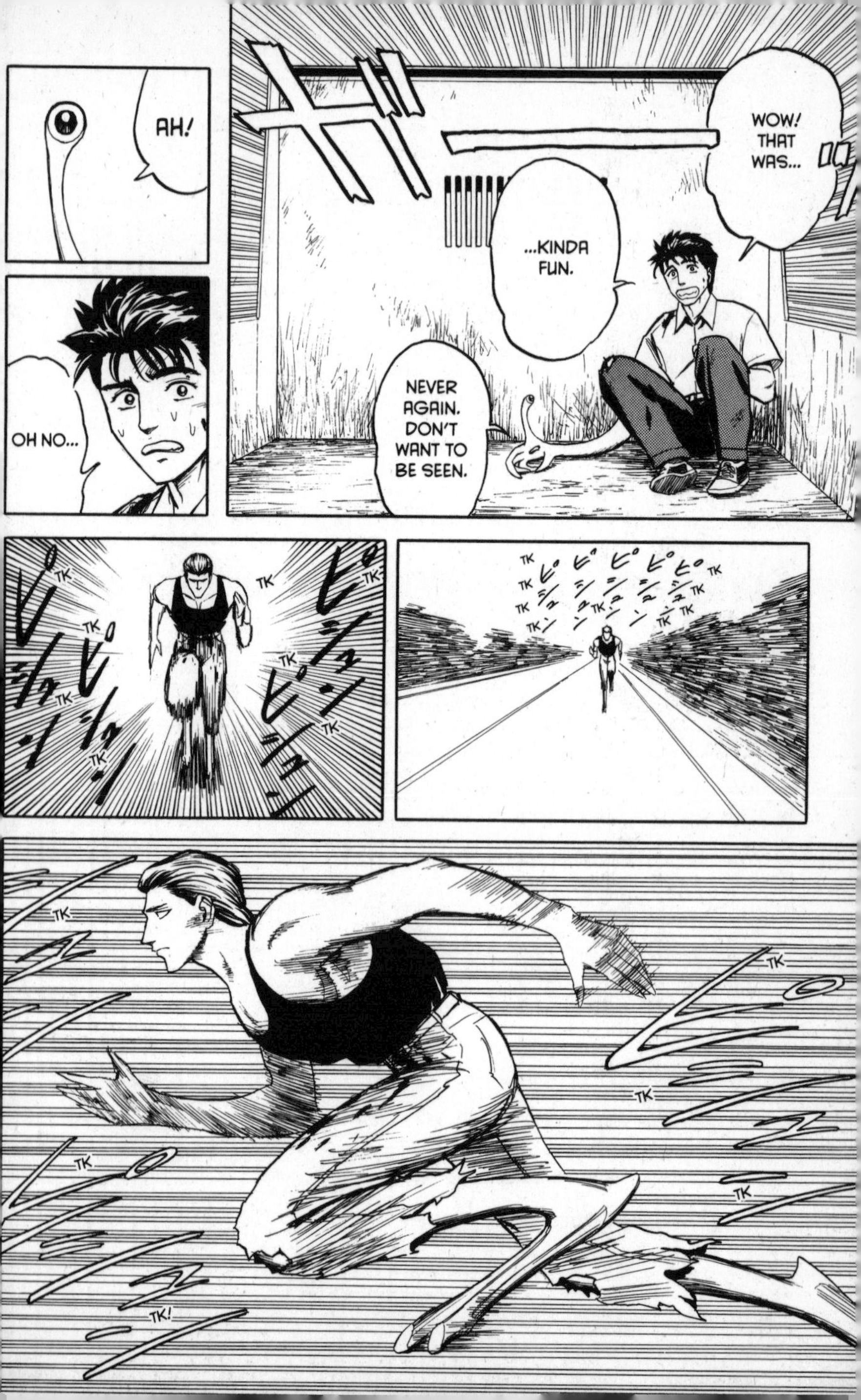
WOW! THAT WAS...
...KINDA FUN.
NEVER AGAIN. DON'T WANT TO BE SEEN.
AH!
OH NO...
TK TK TK TK TK TK TK TK TK TK TK
TK TK TK TK TK TK TK
TK TK TK TK TK
TK!

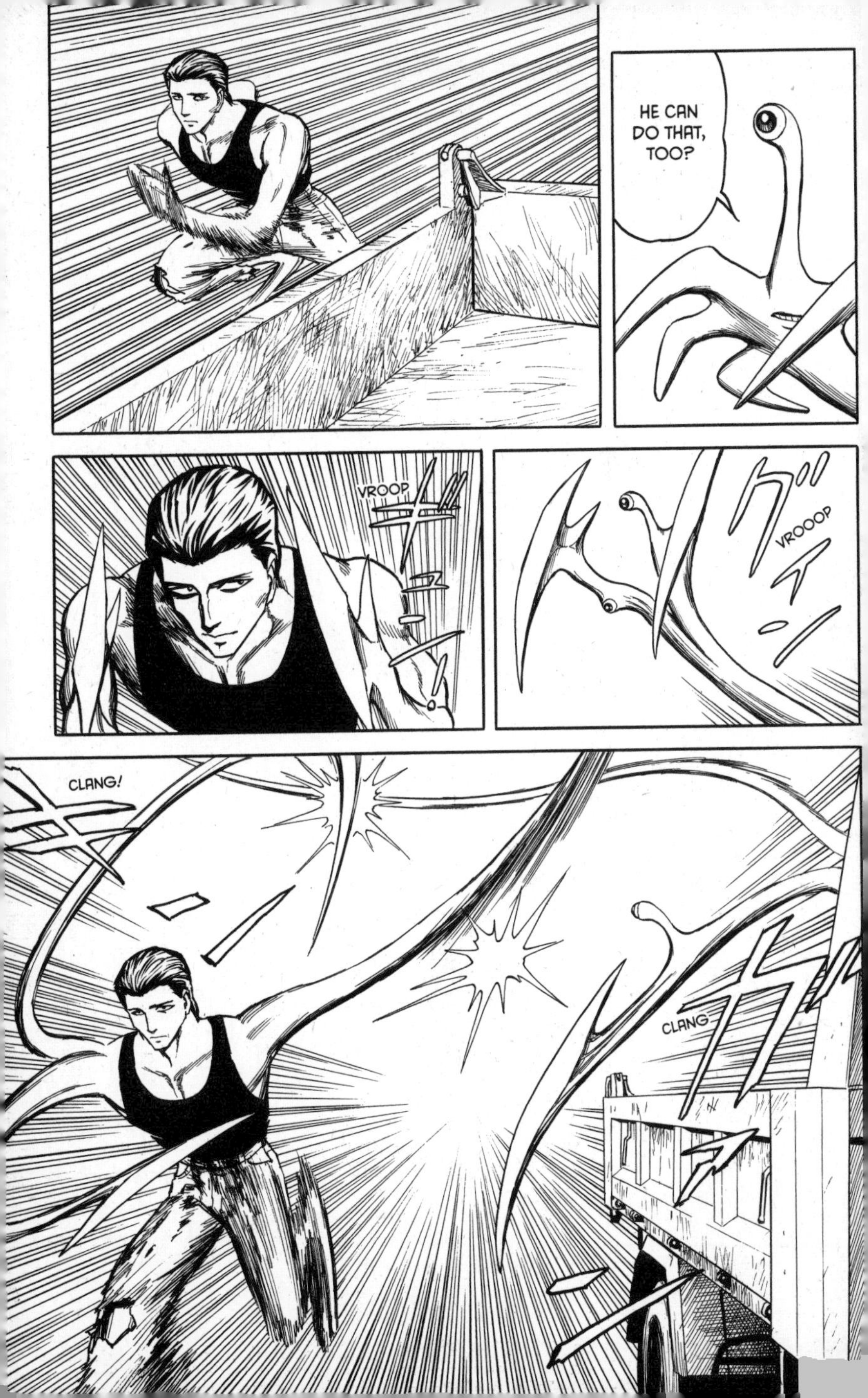
HE CAN DO THAT, TOO?
VROOOP
VROOP
CLANG!
CLANG

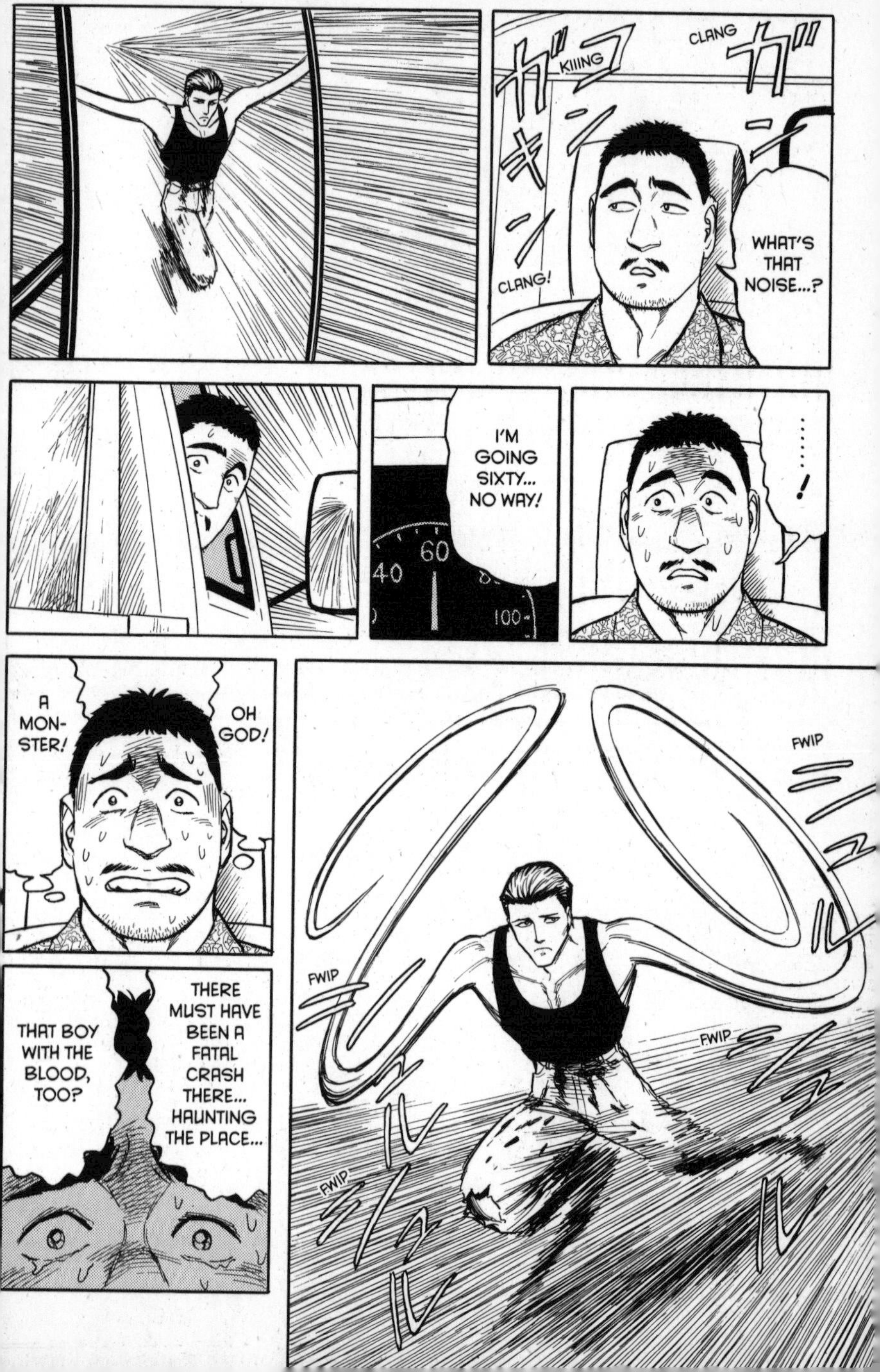
CLANG
KIIING
CLANG!
WHAT'S THAT NOISE...?
......!
I'M GOING SIXTY... NO WAY!
60
40
100
FWIP
FWIP
FWIP
FWIP
OH GOD!
A MONSTER!
THERE MUST HAVE BEEN A FATAL CRASH THERE... HAUNTING THE PLACE...
THAT BOY WITH THE BLOOD, TOO?

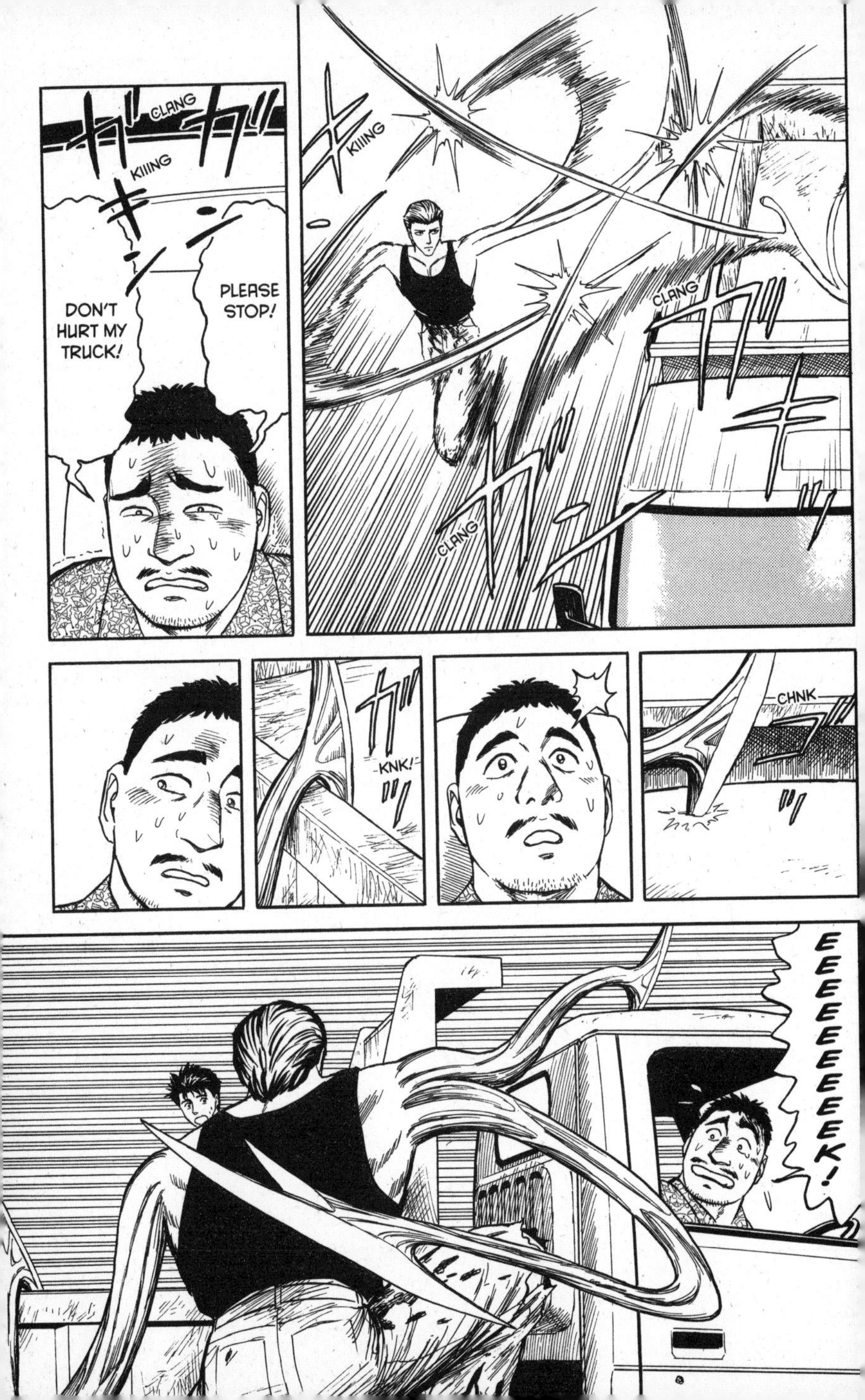
KIIING
CLANG
CLANG
CLANG
KIIING
PLEASE STOP!
DON'T HURT MY TRUCK!
CHNK
KNK!
EEEEEEEEEEK!

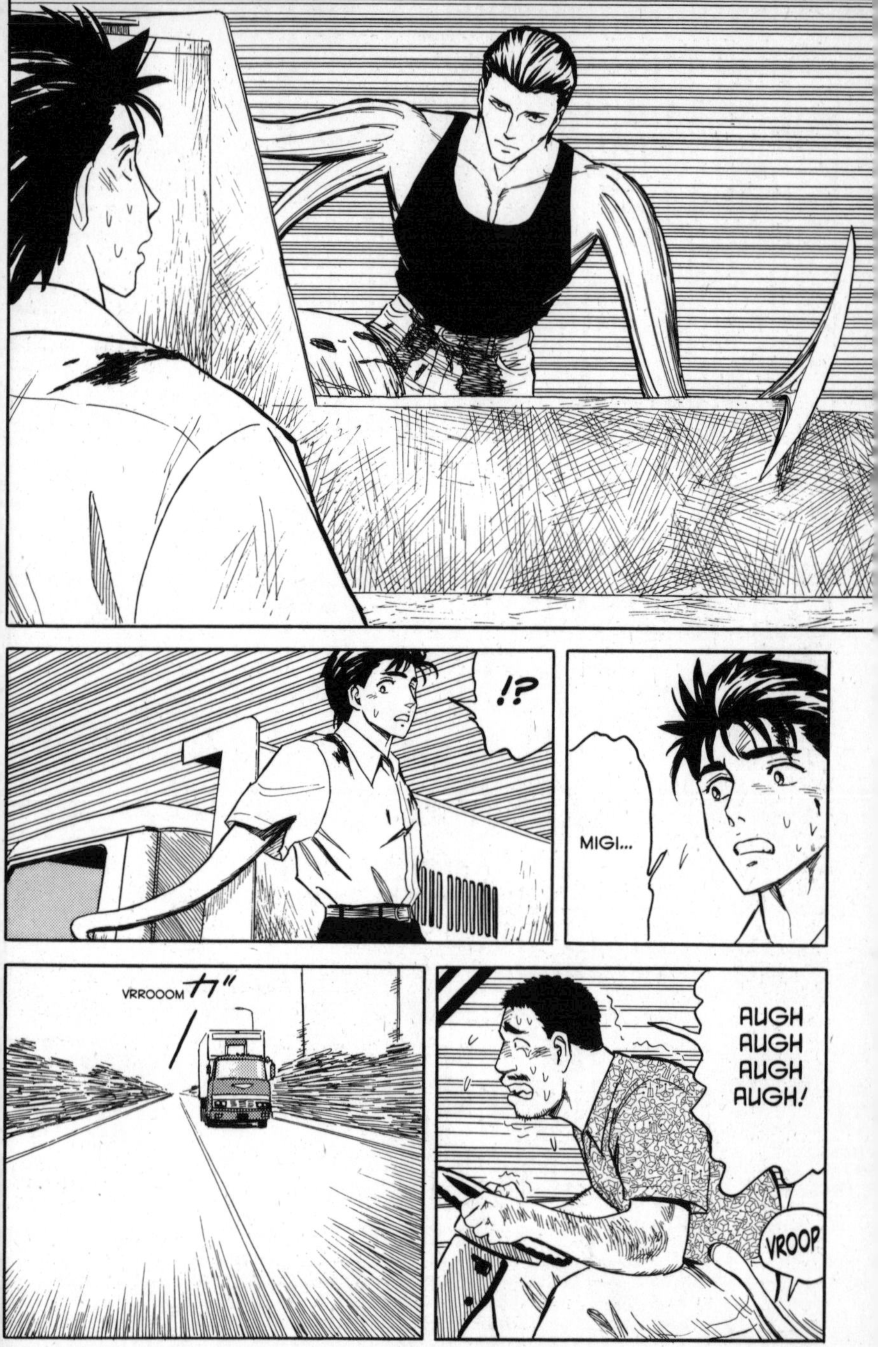
MIGI...
!?
AUGH AUGH AUGH AUGH!
VROOP
VRROOOM ガ"

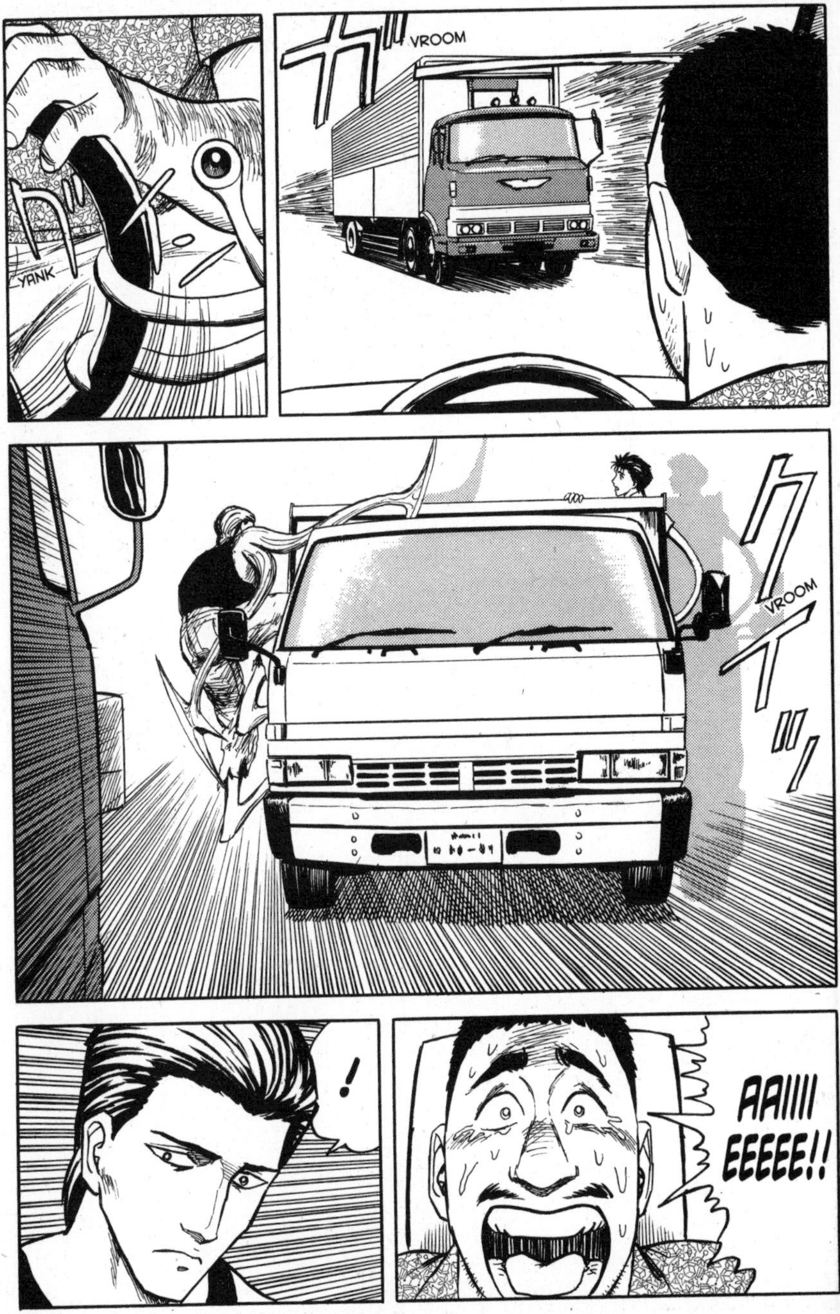
VROOM
YANK
VROOM
AAIIII EEEEE!!
!

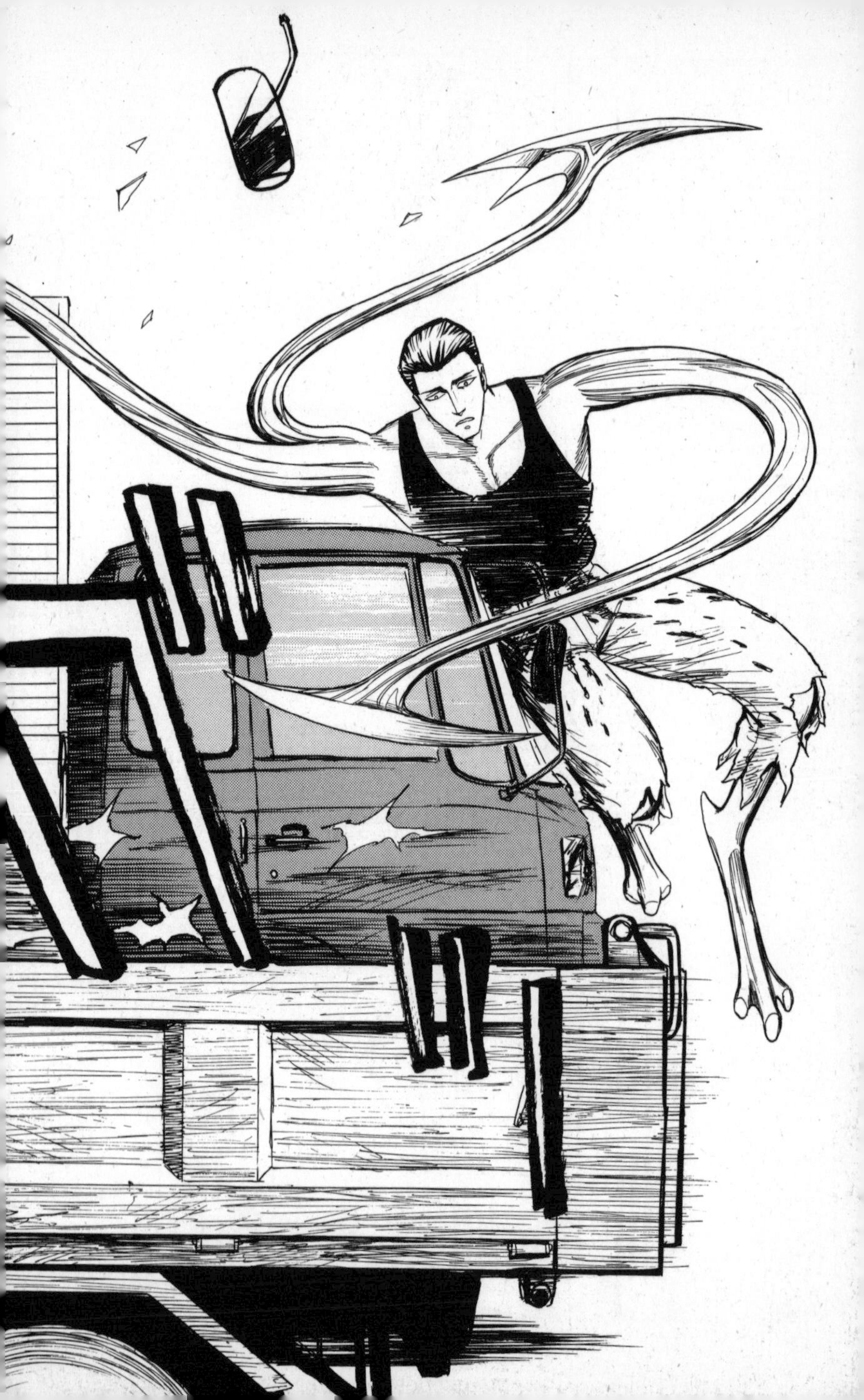

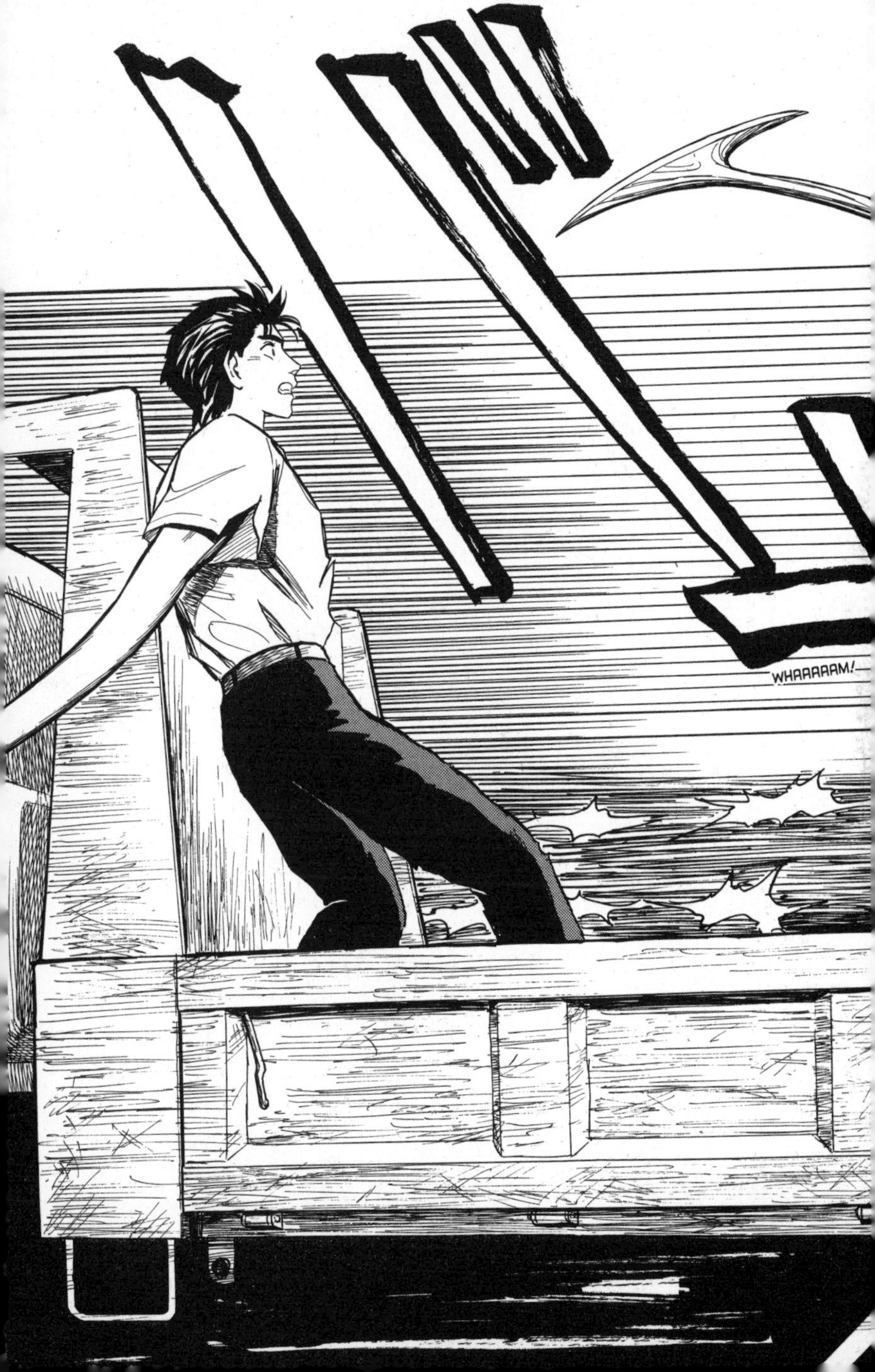
WHAAAAAAM!

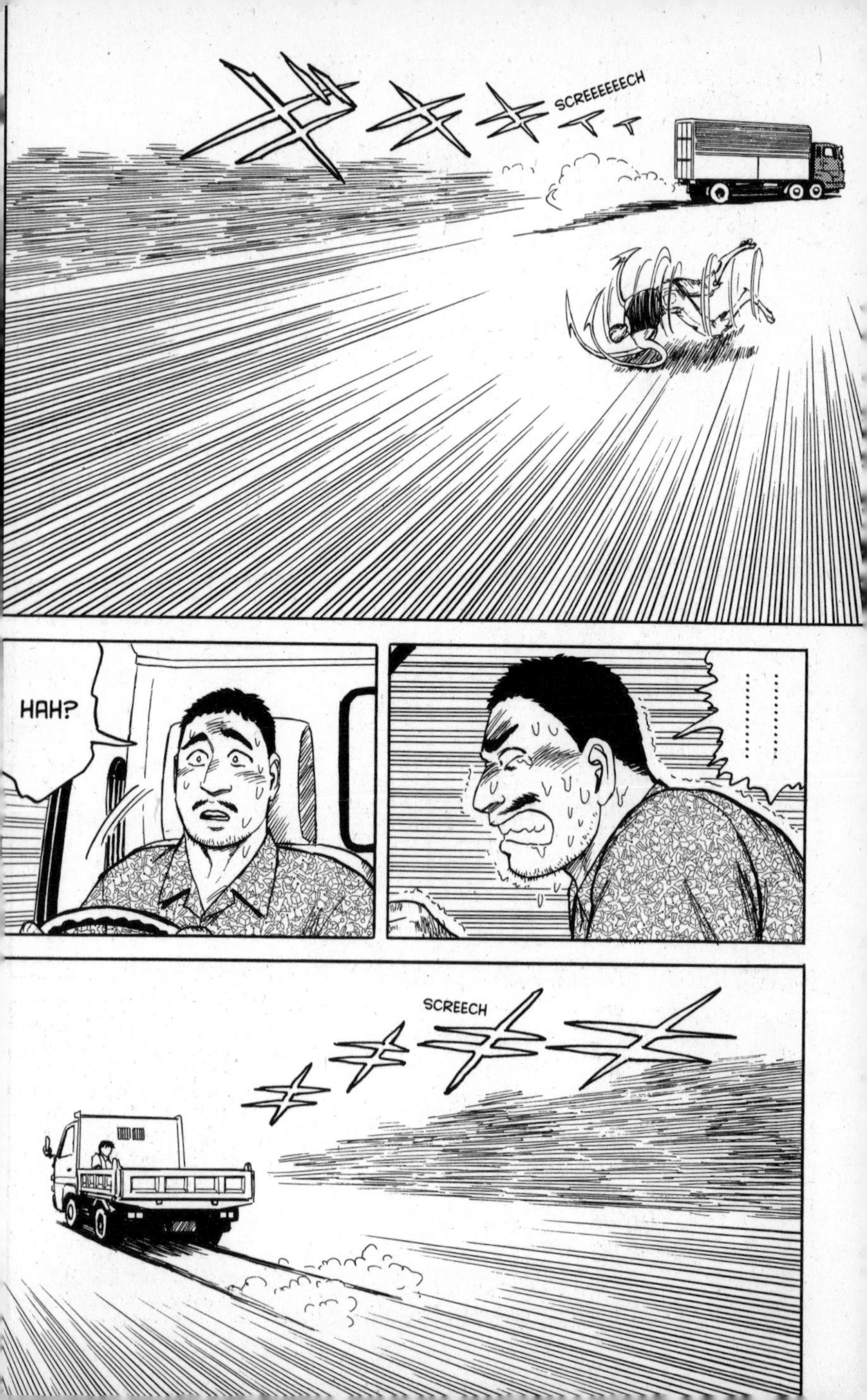
SCREEEEEECH
......
HAH?
SCREECH

THIS IMPOSSIBLE! THAT WASN'T HUMAN...NO WAY IT WAS HUMAN!

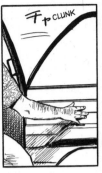

CLUNK

I'M GETTING THE HELL OUT OF HERE!

HEEEEY!

HEY! WAIT!

SLAM!

VROOM

DAMN IT! HE'S RUNNING AWAY!

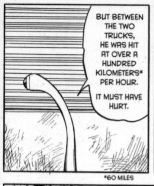

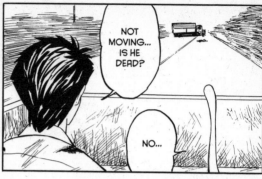

NOT MOVING... IS HE DEAD?
NO...
BUT BETWEEN THE TWO TRUCKS, HE WAS HIT AT OVER A HUNDRED KILOMETERS* PER HOUR.
IT MUST HAVE HURT.
*60 MILES
SWISH...
TWITCH
UNH...
ARE YOU OKAY?
EVERY-THING MOVING SLOWLY...
LOST TOO MUCH BLOOD. NEED BLOOD.
BLOOD?
HAVE TO EAT, THEN REST.
YOU'RE LUCKY, THEN! RIGHT?
WHAT'S WITH THOSE FEET?

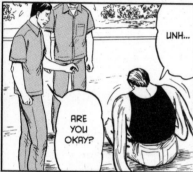

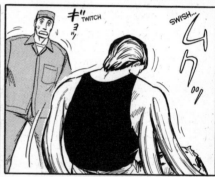

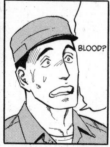

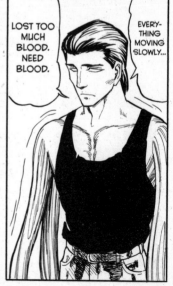

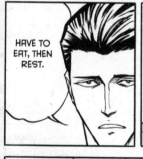

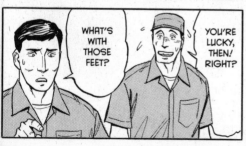

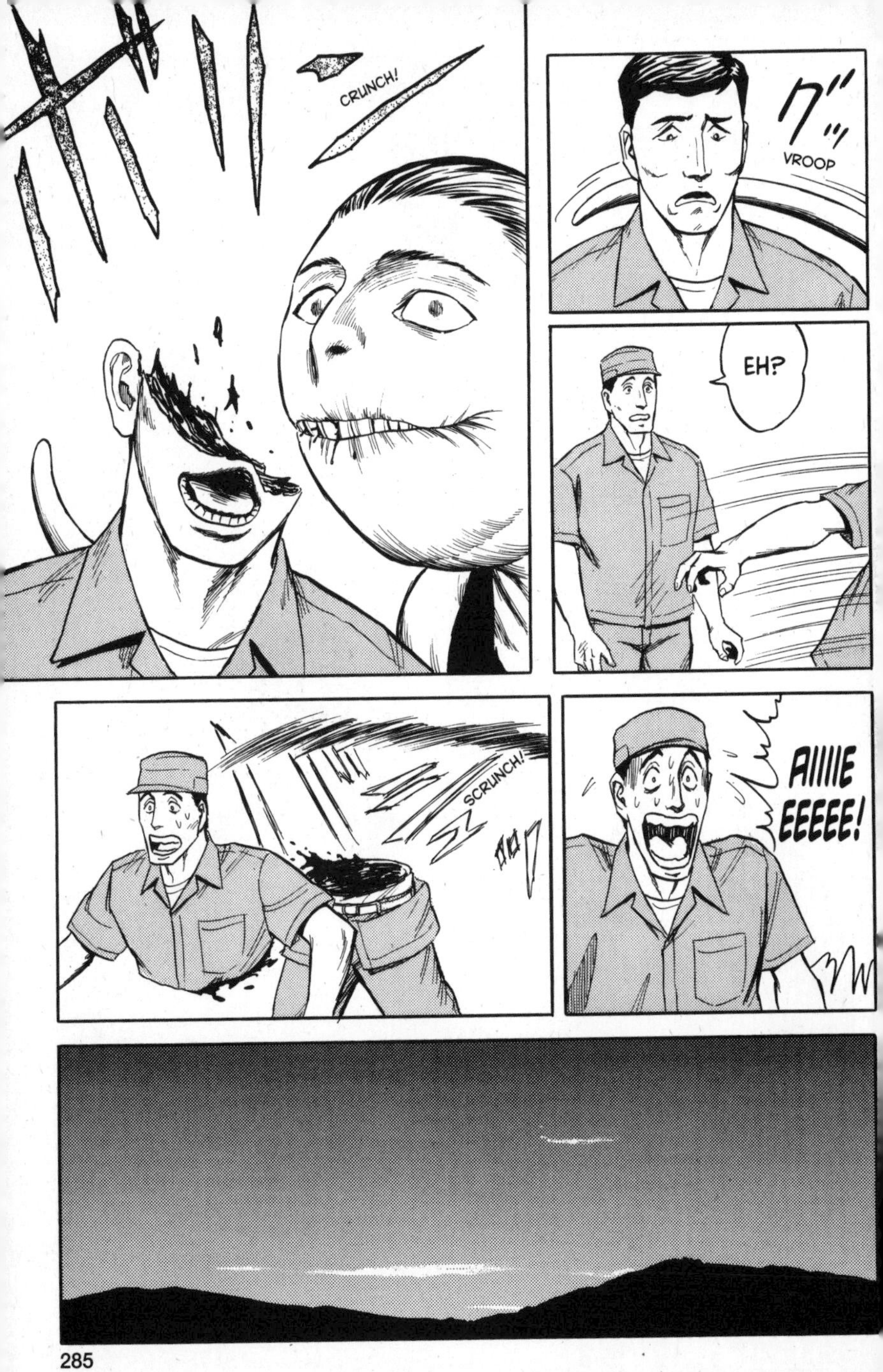
グッ
VROOP
EH?
CRUNCH!
AIIIIE
EEEEEE!
SCRUNCH!

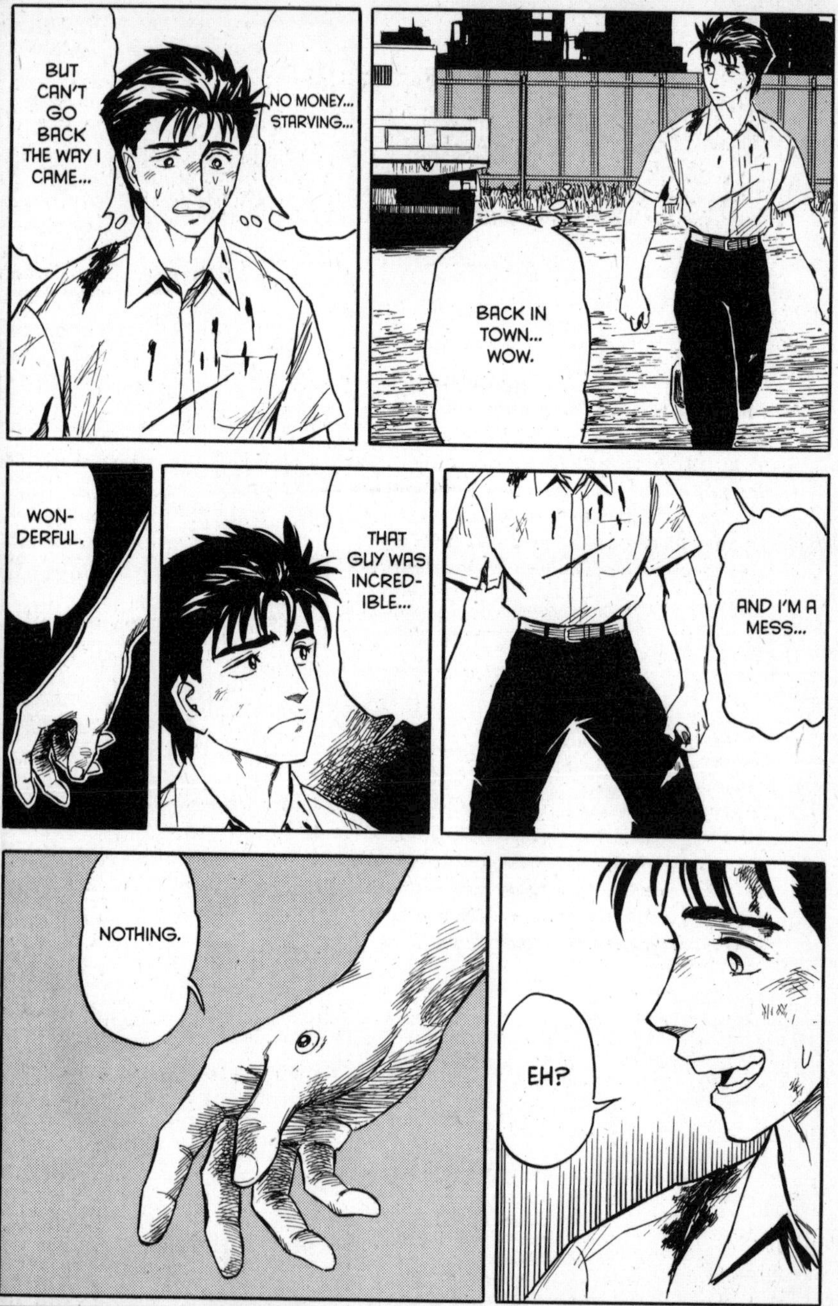
BACK IN TOWN... WOW.
NO MONEY... STARVING...
BUT CAN'T GO BACK THE WAY I CAME...
AND I'M A MESS...
THAT GUY WAS INCRED-IBLE...
WON-DERFUL.
EH?
NOTHING.

PARASYTE 5: THE END

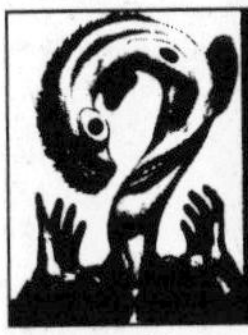

Interview with Hitoshi Iwaaki, recipient of the 17th Kodansha Manga Award

Q: There seem to be two basic patterns for the parasite's shape changes—some unravel in a spiral pattern, and some open outward from the mouth spherically.

Iwaaki: The spiral pattern is used for attacks, when they're in danger. When they have more time, and are eating people, we see the spherical pattern. When they're in a hurry, they need to make blades as fast as possible. Since the head is a sphere, that spiral pattern seemed the most logical choice.

Q: Recently in the story, we've seen the parasites disagree, and form groups.

Iwaaki: They're developing. Their mental powers are steadily maturing. They stand out on their own. Each of them is only thinking of his own interest, but to survive within human society, they need to form their own organizations. Parasites are, after all, a lot like humans. They are social animals. So this development seemed unavoidable.

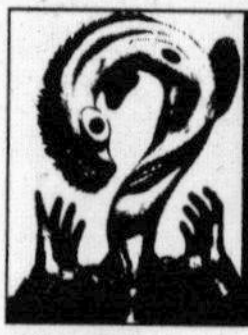

Interview with Hitoshi Iwaaki, recipient of the 17th Kodansha Manga Award

PARASYTE 5

Q: Is the choice of a high school as a primary setting of any significance?
Iwaaki: When I first started thinking about the series, I thought of the scene where Migi turns into a giant penis in front of the main character's girlfriend. When I thought of that scene, I realized that it would work best in a high school setting.

Q: Anything you'd like to try for your next series?
Iwaaki: Nothing in particular, but the fundamental idea that a book should never be boring stays true. It's not like I don't have ideas, but I won't know which I'm interested in until I play with them a little. I'm a long way from getting to that, basically.

(*Afternoon*, August 1993)

TRANSLATION NOTES

Japanese is a tricky language for most Westerners, and translation is often more an art than a science. For your edification and reading pleasure, here are notes on some of the places where we could have gone in a different direction or where a Japanese cultural reference is used.

Kishu, page 41

Kishu means jockey, and *gambare* is basically good luck, so this man is using his penname to cheer on his favorite jockey. Horse racing is quite popular in Japan, one of the two legal forms of gambling.

Hidari Tonpei and Hidari Bokuzen, page 42

Hidari Tonpei was a comedian popular in the sixties and seventies, and Hidari Bokuzen was an actor who appeared in both *Ikiru* and *The Seven Samurai*.

Tonan, page 81

Just means Southwest, meaning this school just has a generic name.

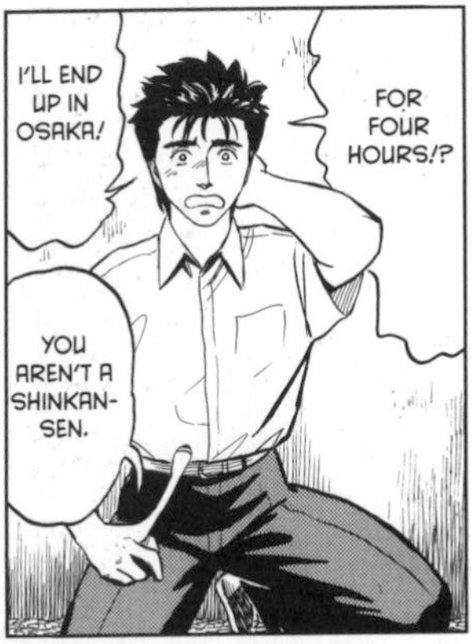
FOR FOUR HOURS!?
I'LL END UP IN OSAKA!
YOU AREN'T A SHINKAN-SEN.

Shinkansen, page 201

The *shinkansen* is the famous bullet train that goes from Tokyo to Osaka in two hours.

"Please do not run," page 203

Every train station in Japan plays this announcement, or has a sign posted to that effect. It actually refers specifically to running and jumping onto the train just before the doors close. Everyone does this anyway.

Miki's name, page 217

The kanji for Miki's name mean three and tree. This appears to be because he controls three parasites...

Final form, page 253

Kanzen tai could also be literally translated as "perfect body." But the connotations of the Japanese phrase are closer to "final" or "complete," while the English phrase "perfect body" usually implies something aesthetically pleasing.

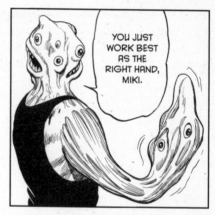

YOU JUST WORK BEST AS THE RIGHT HAND, MIKI.

Miki = right hand, page 258

Goto emphasizes the words Migi (or right) and Miki (three trees), pointing out the similarity in the sounds. (In Japanese, *gi* is written by adding two dots to the hiragana for *ki*, so to Japanese speakers, there's a similarity to these syllables.) In other words, the name Miki, like Migi, has a double meaning: Miki is normally the right hand but is also capable of controlling two other parasites.

"Five of them," page 259

This explains the origin of Goto's name: The first character in his name means "five."

Preview of Volume 6
of PARASYTE

We're pleased to present you with a preview from volume 6.
Please check our website (www.delreymanga.com) to
see when this volume will be available in English.
For now you'll have to make do with Japanese!

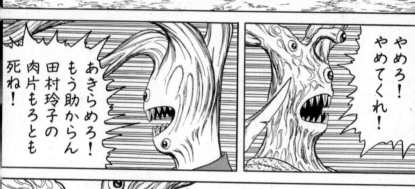

やめろ！
やめてくれ！

あきらめろ！
もう助からん
田村玲子の
肉片もろとも
死ね！

わたしは
味方なんだ
……！

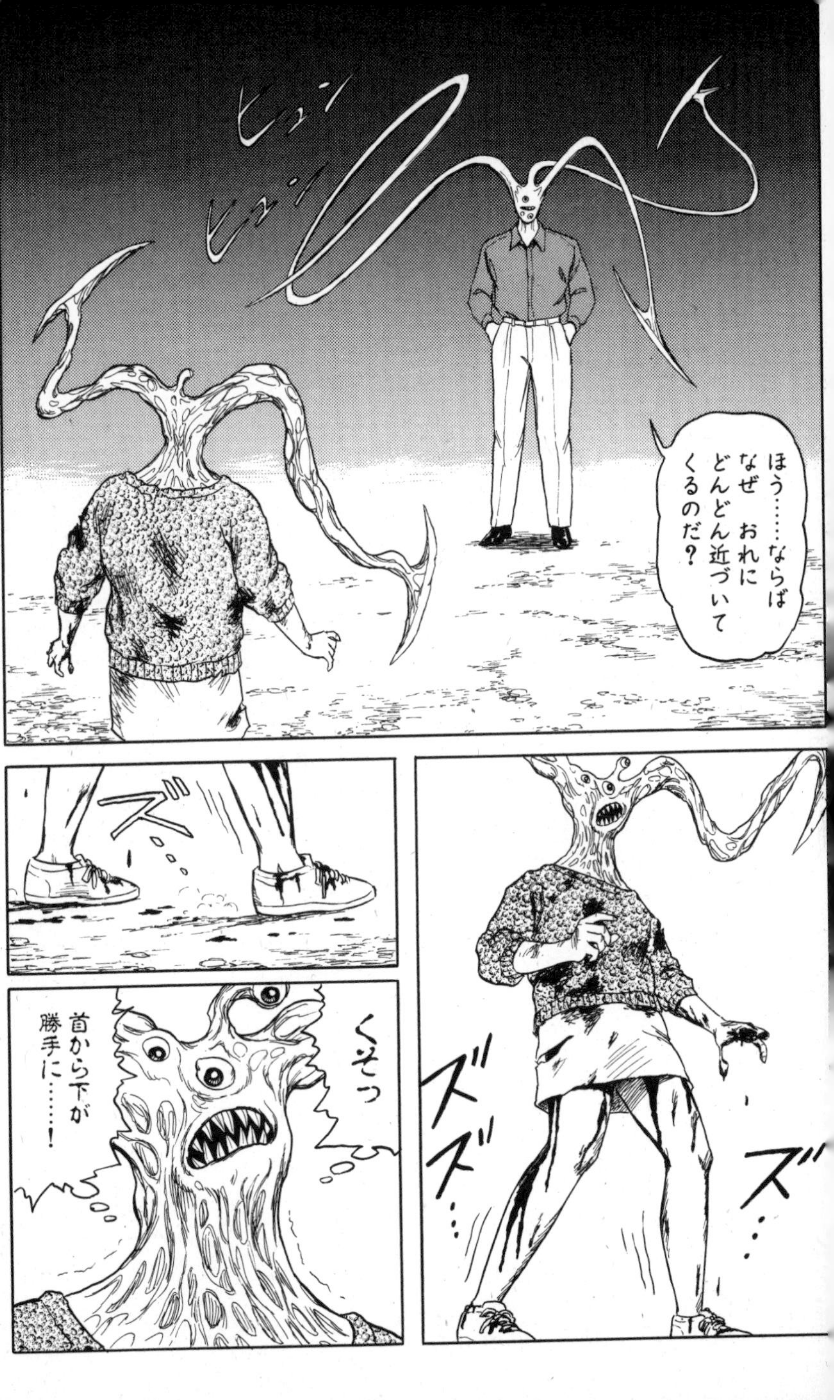
ヒュン ヒュン
ほう……ならば なぜ おれに どんどん近づいて くるのだ?
ズ…
ズズ…
ズ…
くそっ
首から下が勝手に……!

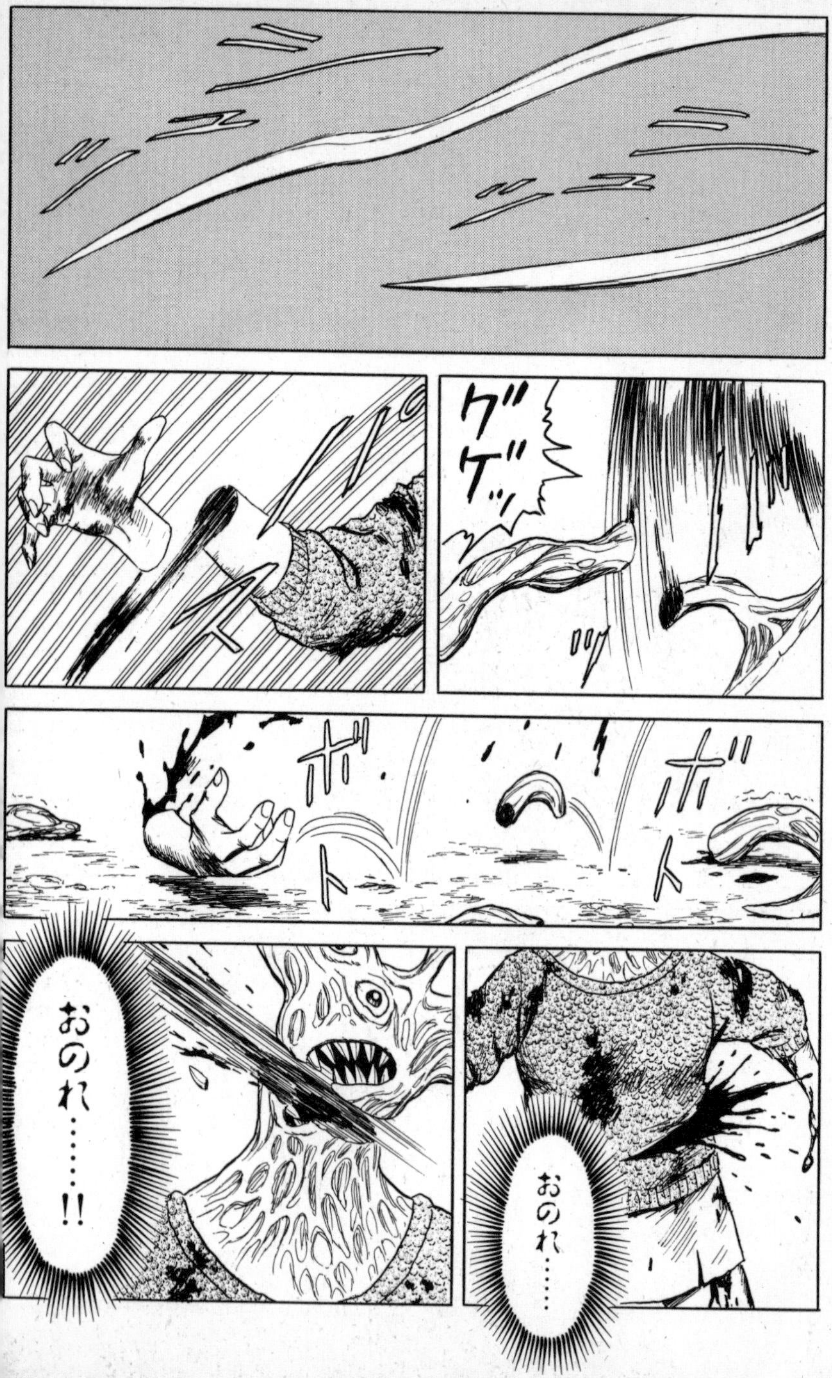

グゲッ
ボト
ボト
おのれ……
おのれ……!!

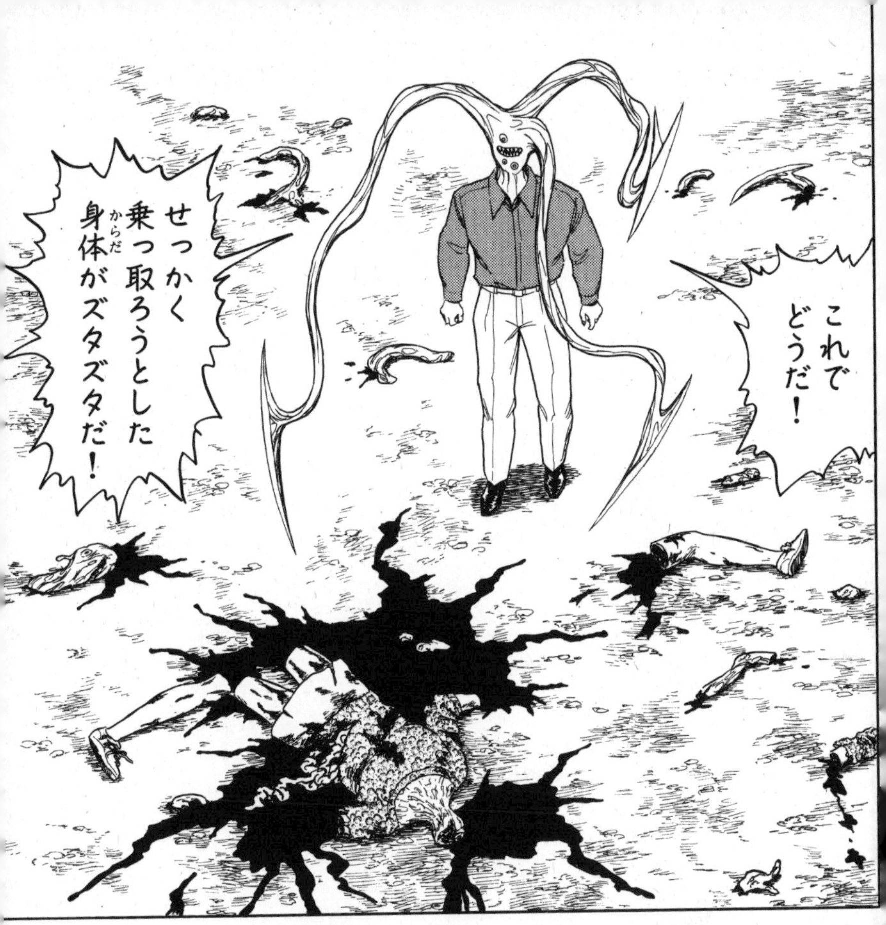
これでどうだ！
せっかく乗っ取ろうとした身体がズタズタだ！

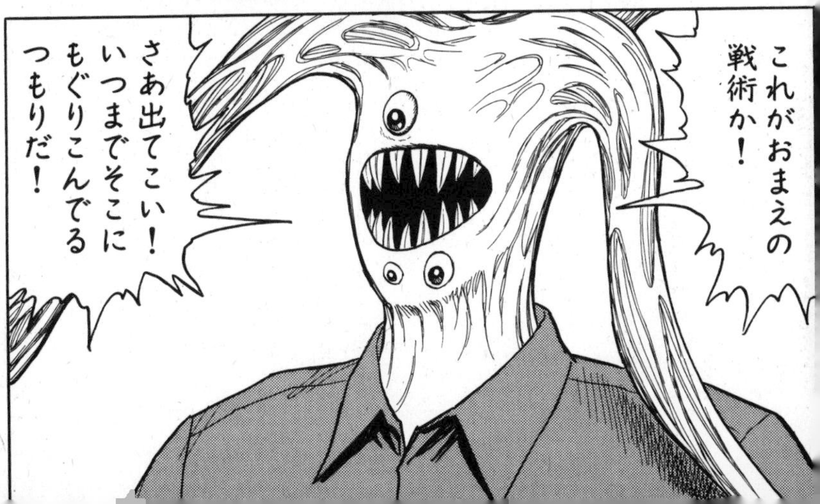
これがおまえの戦術か！
さあ出てこい！いつまでそこにもぐりこんでるつもりだ！

MUSHISHI

YUKI URUSHIBARA

THEY HAVE EXISTED SINCE THE DAWN OF TIME.

Some live in the deep darkness behind your eyelids. Some eat silence. Some thoughtlessly kill. Some simply drive men mad. Shortly after life emerged from the primordial ooze, these deadly creatures, mushi, came into terrifying being. And they still exist and wreak havoc in the world today. Ginko, a young man with a sardonic smile, has the knowledge and skill to save those plagued by mushi . . . perhaps.

WINNER OF THE KODANSHA MANGA OF THE YEAR AWARD!

Now a live-action movie from legendary director Katsuhiro Otomo (*Akira, Steamboy*)!

Special extras in each volume! Read them all!